Computer Communications and Networks

For other titles published in this series, go to
www.springer.com/series/4198

The **Computer Communications and Networks** series is a range of textbooks, monographs and handbooks. It sets out to provide students, researchers and non-specialists alike with a sure grounding in current knowledge, together with comprehensible access to the latest developments in computer communications and networking.

Emphasis is placed on clear and explanatory styles that support a tutorial approach, so that even the most complex of topics is presented in a lucid and intelligible manner.

Xiaoyu Yang • Lizhe Wang • Wei Jie
Editors

Guide to e-Science

Next Generation Scientific Research
and Discovery

 Springer

Editors
Dr. Xiaoyu Yang
Reading e-Science Centre
Harry Pitt Building
University of Reading
3 Earley Gate, Whiteknights
Reading, RG6 6AL
UK
kev.x.yang@gmail.com

Dr. Wei Jie
Fac. Professional Studies
Thames Valley University
School of Computing
St. Mary's Road TC372
Ealing, London W5 5RF
United Kingdom
wei.jie@tvu.ac.uk

Dr. Lizhe Wang
Pervasive Technology Institute
Indiana University
2719 East 10th Street
Bloomington, IN 47408
USA
lizhe.wang@gmail.com

Series Editor
Professor A.J. Sammes
Bsc, Mphil, PhD, FBCS, CEng
Centre for Forensic Computing
Cranfield University
DCMT, Shrivenham
Swindo SN6 8LA, UK

ISSN 1617-7975
ISBN 978-1-4471-2658-4   ISBN 978-0-85729-439-5 (eBook)
DOI 10.1007/978-0-85729-439-5
Springer London Dordrecht Heidelberg New York

British Library Cataloguing in Publication Data
A catalogue record for this book is available from the British Library

Cover design: deblik

Printed on acid-free paper

Springer is part of Springer Science+Business Media (www.springer.com)

Foreword

The way we carry out scientific research is undergoing a series of radical changes as a result of the digital revolution. Traditional scientific approaches are finding it increasingly difficult to solve complex problems and grand challenges without broadening horizons to exploit the use of new digital technologies that support collaborative working on one hand, and facilitate clever approaches to working with the huge quantities of data that can now be generated through modern experimental systems and computer simulations performed on supercomputers and grid computing facilities. We can throw into the mix of new emphasis on data sharing and open data, with access provided by web service technologies, new approaches to constructing and sharing workflow methods, and Web 2.0 technologies that enable communities, large and small, to document and share research outcomes and new knowledge. Simultaneously we are seeing greater emphasis on researchers sharing their primary data and analysis tools to accompany publication, enabling other researchers to reproduce and re-use their results. We are already past the point where researchers can analyse data by hand in the point-by-point that used to characterise research, which means that automated computational and data analysis systems need to be robust and flawlessly accurate. These requirements call for a comprehensive supporting cyberinfrastructure for modern scientific research, and e-Science will play an important role in addressing this challenge.

At the outset of the UK e-Science programme, the Director General of the Research Councils, John Taylor, wrote, "e-Science is about global collaboration in key areas of science and the next generation computing infrastructure that will enable it." This definition recognised that challenging scientific problems will increasingly be addressed by large teams working in different institutes – even in different countries – who will need access to a comprehensive cyberinfrastructure that should not only give access to massive computing capabilities, but also enable easy sharing of data and information in an era where huge quantities of data can be generated, and facilitate personal and team interactions required for genuine collaborative working.

This edited book comprises chapters authored by international e-Science experts and practitioners, presenting readers with e-Science practices and applications of how various technologies and tools can be employed to build essential infrastructures to support a new generation of scientific research. The book is organised by grouping the features of modern scientific research into five themes: (1) Sharing and Open Research; (2) Data-intensive e-Science; (3) Collaborative Research; (4) Automated Research, Reusability, Reproducibility and Repeatability; and (5) e-Science: easy Science. The different chapters within each topic provide introductions, descriptions and discussions of relevant e-Science methodologies, architectures, tools, systems, services and frameworks that are designed to address a range of different requirements. The expert authors also share their experiences and lessons learned in their e-Science work.

The book is a timely contribution to e-Science communities. I believe readers, especially researchers and developers of successive generations of e-infrastructure, will find this book useful.

Department of Earth Sciences   Professor Martin Dove
University of Cambridge
UK

Preface

Next generation scientific research has radically changed the way in which science is carried out. With the assistance of modern e-infrastructure as part of science, or experiments including high-performance computing capabilities, large-capacity data storage facilities and high-speed network infrastructure, the exploration of previously unknown problems can now be solved via simulation, generation and analysis of large amount of data, sharing of geographically distributed resources (e.g. computing facilities, data, script, experiment plan, workflow) and global research collaboration.

A term "science 2.0" or "research 2.0" is now emerging which has outlined the features of next generation scientific research: large-scale, team-based global research collaboration; open research and open data; collective intelligence; knowledge and resources sharing; etc. This needs an advanced environment and e-Science infrastructure which can meet the new features and requirements. For example, in collaborative research that involves diversity of participants, security, trust and privacy are becoming increasingly essential; faced with the deluge of scientific data, diverse data integration, heterogeneous data interoperability, domain information and knowledge representation and retrieval, linked data and structured data presents critical challenges; resource sharing involves the exchange, selection and aggregation of geographically distributed resources and the development of innovative and high-performance oriented applications; automatic, reproducible, reusable and repeatable research concerns the auto-coordination of various tasks involved in a research study, and provenance of the research result.

According to the features and requirements for next generation scientific research, this book is structured into five themes, which demonstrate how e-Science methods and techniques can be employed to facilitate next generation scientific research and discovery from the following aspects:

- Part I: Sharing and Open Research
- Part II: Data-Intensive e-Science
- Part III: Collaborative Research
- Part IV: Research Automation, Reusability, Reproducibility and Repeatability
- Part V: e-Science, Easy Science

Part I: Sharing and Open Research

"Science has always been a social process." Next generation scientific research promotes the open research and sharing of resources and knowledge. Grid computing technology is one of the key enabling technologies in resource sharing which aims at the synergy of the distributed high computing resources. Grid middleware, such as Globus Toolkit, gLite and UNICORE, provides an effective approach to share usually the high-performance computing resources (e.g. super computers, clusters). This formulates the mainstream of grid computing in e-Science. However, high-performance computing is not always available in many institutions; on the other hand, there exists much idle computing power. In order to address this need, we can also use peer-to-peer (P2P) grid computing technology to build a P2P Grid for the sharing of idle computing resources. For example, in the P2P Grid, labs can donate their idle computational resources in exchange for accessing other labs' idle resources when necessary. Part I contains four chapters which discuss the use of mainstream grid computing and the P2P Grid in e-Science.

Chapter 1 describes the development of an e-infrastructure which integrates the data grid and computing grid to facilitate the hydrology environmental science. It allows a wide range of hydrological problems to be investigated and is particularly suitable for either computationally intensive or multiple scenario applications. The chapter discusses the grid infrastructure system integration and development, visualisation of geographic information from grid outputs and implementation of hydrological simulations based on the infrastructure. Also, the chapter investigates the adaption of cloud computing into scientific research by extending the computing grid to utilise the Amazon EC2 cloud computing resources. Users can carry out a complete simulation job from job submission to data management and metadata management based on the tools available in the infrastructure.

Chapter 2 discusses the current state and future perspective of the German National Grid Initiative (NGI), namely, D-Grid. It describes the current D-Grid e-Infrastructure in detail, and provides a discussion on how D-Grid's future may look like with virtualisation and cloud computing striding ahead. Particularly, it discusses the incorporation of service level agreements (SLA) to allow D-Grid service providers to deliver the service level objectives (SLO) assured services to service customers.

In Chap. 3, the authors share their experience in developing a P2P grid middleware called OurGrid and deploying it to build the OurGrid Community. The chapter describes the mechanisms that effectively promote collaboration and allow the assemblage of large P2P Grids from the contributions of thousands of small sites. The authors present a successful case study of using OurGrid, and summarise their lessons learned and experience.

Chapter 4 introduces an approach to grid and overlay network research for the sharing of computing resources to enable the simulation of increased complexity and speed. It presents a Peer4Peer platform that provides the main infrastructure for efficient peer-to-peer simulation over the Internet.

Part II: Data-Intensive e-Science

Scientific research can be regarded in some sense as activities around a data lifecycle (i.e. acquisition, transfer, storage, analysis/data mining, visualisation). It is now increasingly facing the challenges of data explosion. For example, the high-energy physics experiment of the large hardon collider (LHC) at CERN in 2007 produced a stream of data at 300 MB/s, which is equivalent to a stack of CDs as high as the Eiffel Tower every week. Modern sciences have stronger demands for effective data curation and management than ever before. In Part II, we include three chapters, which present different methods for data management in e-Science.

Chapter 5 discussed how the NASA Jet Propulsion Laboratory in California, USA, developed successful science data systems for highly distributed communities in physical and life sciences that require extensive sharing of distributed services and common information models based on common architectures. It demonstrated that a well-defined architecture and set of accompanied software can vastly improve the ability to develop roadmaps for the construction of virtual science environments.

In Chap. 6, the authors develop a tool integration framework, namely, Galaxy, which enables advanced data analysis that requires no informatics expertise. The Galaxy tool has also been deployed as Amazon Web Service in the Amazon Cloud for open access.

Large-scale cross-disciplinary scientific collaborations usually involve diverse data integration, heterogeneous data interoperability and domain information and knowledge representation and retrieval. Chapter 7 proposes an integrated ontology management and data sharing framework which builds upon the advancements in object-oriented database design, semantic web and service-oriented architecture to form the key data-sharing backbone. The framework is implemented to cater data-sharing needs for large-scale sensor deployment from disparate scientific domains. This enables each participating scientific virtual organisation (VO) to publish, search and access data across the e-infrastructure in a service-oriented manner, accompanied by domain-specific knowledge.

Part III: Collaborative Research

Collaborative research is a distinct feature in modern scientific research. Interoperability, security, trust and privacy are key elements in collaborative research. Part III contains four chapters that discuss the aspect of collaborative environment, e-infrastructure interoperability and security, trust and privacy.

Chapter 8 proposes a collaborative environment to support the scientific processes of a solar-enabled water production and recycling application. This environment can perform complex tasks such as distributed instrument control, data collection from heterogeneous sources, data archival, data analysis and mining, data visualisation and decision support. It aims to address the issues of archival and management of multidimensional data from heterogeneous sensors and instruments, allowing efficient data sharing among different groups of scientists who are not computer experts, allowing different parties involved to publish and consume data and process, real-time decision support with control, etc.

Chapter 9 investigates challenges and provides proven solutions in the context of e-Science infrastructure interoperability. The chapter illustrates how an increasing amount of e-Scientists can take advantage of using different types of e-Science infrastructures jointly together for their e-research activities, and proposes seven steps towards interoperability for e-Science.

e-Infrastructure based on distributed computing could result in malicious intervention resulting in theft of the models and data that have significant commercial value. In order to tackle this problem, Chap. 10 proposes two distributed systems, one applicable for a computational system and the other for a distributed data system. A *configuration resolver* is used to maintain a list of trustworthy participants available in the virtual organisation. Users can then submit their jobs to the *configuration resolver*, knowing that their jobs will be dispatched to trustworthy participants and executed in protected environments. This security model was tested in the UK National Grid Service (NGS), and the performance overhead was measured.

Cloud computing has become a new computing paradigm as it can provide scalable IT infrastructures, QoS-assured services and customisable computing environments. As a new computing paradigm, cloud computing provides new methods and techniques for e-Science. However, cloud computing introduces new challenges with respect to security mainly caused by the unique characteristics inherited via virtual machine technology. Chapter 11 focuses on the challenges imposed on intrusion diagnosis for clouds. This chapter identifies the importance of intrusion diagnosis problem for clouds and the new challenges for this intrusion diagnosis. An appropriate solution is proposed to address these challenges and is demonstrated to be effective by empirical evaluation.

Part IV: Research Automation, Reusability, Reproducibility and Repeatability

A research study usually involves a series of tasks. For example, even a simple research study may involve three tasks which are data acquisition, data analysis and visualisation. In modern scientific research involving global collaboration, resource sharing and data deluge, a research study may include multiple complex tasks. For example, a computational experiment that spans multiple geographically distributed computation resources and analytical models involves sequences of tasks such as resource discovery, job submission, file staging, simulation, data harvesting and visualisation. Research process automation with less direct human control and research traceability are vital in scientific research. In order to address this need, workflow technology can be employed for the automation of a process where documents, information or tasks are passed from one participant to another to be processed, according to a set of procedural rules. A scientific workflow integrating all tasks required for a research study can be reusable, and the output from a scientific workflow can be reproducible and repeatable. This part includes four chapters discussing the scientific workflow, which will give you a guide of how workflow technologies are used in e-Science.

Chapter 12 discusses the requirements on scientific workflows, the state of the art of scientific workflow management systems as well as the ability of conventional workflow technology to fulfil requirements of scientists and scientific applications. In order to overcome the disadvantages of the conventional workflow, authors proposed a conceptual architecture for scientific workflow management systems based on the business workflow technology as well as extensions of existing workflow concepts. This can improve the ability of established workflow technology in scientific simulations.

Chapter 13 discusses the integration of *Kepler* workflow system into the *University of California Grid*. This architecture is being applied to a computational enzyme design process. The implementation and experiments validated how the Kepler workflow system can make the scientific computation process automated, pipelined, efficient, extensible, stable and easy to use.

Chapter 14 concerns the quality of a scientific workflow by service level agreement (SLA). This chapter describes related concepts and mapping algorithms to facilitate the resource reservation at each grid site and the user providing the estimated runtime of each sub-job correlated with a resource configuration. In particular, it describes several sub-optimisation algorithms to map sub-jobs of the workflow to the grid resources within an SLA context.

Considering the differences of using workflow in scientific research and the business world, where scientific workflows need to consider specific characteristics and make corresponding changes to accommodate those characteristics, Chap. 15 proposes a task-based scientific workflow modelling and performing approach for orchestrating e-Science with the workflow paradigm.

Part V: e-Science, Easy Science

This part mainly focuses on the application of e-Science in certain science domains.

Chapter 16 presents a robust face recognition technique based on the extraction of scale invariant feature transform (SIFT) features from the face areas. This technique has the potential to be employed in an e-infrastructure of a face recognition system with ATM cash machines.

Chapter 17 presents a framework for the metamodel-driven development of open grid services architecture (OGSA) based service-oriented architecture (SOA) for collaborative cancer research in the CancerGrid project. The authors extend the existing Z model and the generation technology to support OGSA in a distributed collaborative environment. They built a generic SOA model combining the semantics of the standard domain metamodel and metadata, and the Web services resource framework (WSRF) standard. This model can then employed to automate the generation of the trial management systems used in cancer clinical trials.

The last chapter, Chap. 18 the introduces e-Science practice and application in the Computer Network Information Centre (CNIC), Chinese Academy of Science (CAS). This chapter introduces the information infrastructures supporting scientific research from five aspects, which include digital network and communication infrastructure, high-performance computing environment, scientific data environment, digital library and virtual laboratory. CAS proposed an e-Science model, and stated that e-infrastructure should apply information infrastructure and digital technology in every aspect of research activity to enable better research and advanced research patterns. The chapter also presents a collaborative, environmental and biological e-Science application conducted in the Qinghai Lake region, Tibetan Plateau, to show how various information and communication technologies can be employed to facilitate scientific research, providing a cyberinfrastructure for protecting wildlife and ecological environment and decision making. CNIC realised that e-Science is the way leading to next generation scientific research, and has been promoting e-Science practice and application systematically: by e-Science, to easy Science.

Reading e-Science Centre   Dr. Xiaoyu Yang
University of Reading,
UK

Acknowledgements

We would like to thank the authors for their contributions, including those whose chapters are not included in this book.

We would like to express our gratitude to the Editorial Advisor Board members, Professor Martin Dove (University of Cambridge, UK), Dr. Andrew Martin (University of Oxford, UK) and Mr. Morris Riedl (Jülich Super Computing Centre, Germany), for their support and contributions to this book.

We also would like to acknowledge thoughtful work from many reviewers who provided valuable evaluations and recommendations.

Our special thanks go to Mr. Simon Rees and Mr. Wayne Wheeler from Springer for their assistance in the preparation of the book.

Contents

Part V e-Science, Easy Science

About the Editors

Xiaoyu Yang completed his postdoctoral research in e-Science at Earth Sciences Department of University of Cambridge, UK in 2008. He is currently working in Reading e-Science Centre, University of Reading, UK. Dr. Yang has research interests which include e-Science/e-Research, geoinformatics, Grid/Cloud computing, and distributed computing, etc. He worked in School of Electronics and Computer Sciences in University of Southampton, UK after his postdoctoral research at University of Cambridge. He earned MSc Degree in IT in 2001 and PhD degree in Systems Engineering in 2006 at De Montfort University, UK.

Lizhe Wang received his Doctor of Engineering from University Karlsruhe, Germany. He is currently a principal research engineer at Pervasive Technology Institute (PTI), Indiana University, USA. Dr. Wang's research interests include cluster and Grid computing, Cloud computing, multi-core system and energy-aware computing. He has published 3 books and more than 40 scientific papers. Dr. Lizhe Wang received his Bachelor of Engineering with honors and Master of Engineering both from Tsinghua University, China.

Wei Jie was awarded PhD in Computer Engineering from Nanyang Technological University (Singapore). He is currently a lecturer in computing at Thames Valley University (UK). Dr. Jie has been actively involved in the area of parallel and distributed computing for many years, and published about fifty papers in international journals and conferences. His current research interests include Grid computing and applications, security in distributed computing, parallel and distributed algorithms and languages, etc. He received his BEng and MEng in Beijing University of Aeronautics and Astronautics (China).

Contributors

Enis Afgan
Department of Biology and Department of Mathematics & Computer Science,
Emory University, Druid Hills, GA, USA
eafgan@emory.edu

Ilkay Altintas
San Diego Supercomputer Center, UCSD, 9500 Gilman Drive, MC 0505,
La Jolla, CA 92093, USA

Jörn Altmann
School of Information Technology, International University in Germany,
Campus 3, 76646 Bruchsal, Germany
jorn.altmann@acm.org

Nazareno Andrade
Departamento de Sistemas e Computação, Laboratório de Sistemas Distribuídos,
Universidade Federal de Campina Grande, Campina Grande, Paraíba, Brazil
nazareno@dsc.ufcg.edu.br

Junaid Arshad
School of Computing, University of Leeds, Leeds LS2 9JT, UK
sc06ja@leeds.ac.uk

Dannon Baker
Department of Biology and Department of Mathematics & Computer Science,
Emory University, Druid Hills, GA, USA

Hock Beng Lim
Intelligent Systems Center, School of Electrical and Electronics Engineering,
Nanyang Technological University, Singapore
limhb@ntu.edu.sg

C. Isabella Bovolo
School of Civil Engineering and Geosciences, University of Newcastle upon Tyne,
Newcastle upon Tyne NE7 7RU, UK

Francisco Brasileiro
Departamento de Sistemas e Computação, Laboratório de Sistemas Distribuídos,
Universidade Federal de Campina Grande, Campina Grande, Paraíba, Brazil
fubica@dsc.ufcg.edu.br

Radu Calinescu
Aston University, Birmingham B4 7ET, UK

Chee Keong Chan
Intelligent Systems Center, School of Electrical and Electronics Engineering,
Nanyang Technological University, Singapore
eckchan@ntu.edu.sg

Jinjun Chen
Faculty of Information and Communication Technology, Swinburne University
of Technology, Melbourne, Australia
jinjun.chen@gmail.com

Gen-Tao Chiang
Wellcome Trust Sanger Institute, Wellcome Trust Genome Campus, Hinxton,
Cambridge CB10 1SA, UK
gtc@sanger.ac.uk

Fook Hoong Choo
Intelligent Systems Center, School of Electrical and Electronics Engineering,
Nanyang Technological University, Singapore
efhchoo@ntu.edu.sg

Nate Coraor
Huck Institutes of the Life Sciences and Department of Biochemistry and
Molecular Biology, The Pennsylvania State University, University Park,
PA, USA

Daniel Crawl
San Diego Supercomputer Center, UCSD, 9500 Gilman Drive, MC 0505,
La Jolla, CA 92093, USA

Daniel J. Crichton
Jet Propulsion Laboratory, California Institute of Technology, Pasadena,
CA 91109, USA
daniel.j.crichton@jpl.nasa.gov

Wanchun Dou
State Key Laboratory for Novel Software Technology, Department of Computer
Science and Technology, Nanjing University, Nanjing 210009, China
douwc@nju.edu.cn

Martin T. Dove
Department of Earth Sciences, University of Cambridge,
Cambridge CB2 3EQ, UK

John Ewen
School of Civil Engineering and Geosciences, University of Newcastle upon Tyne, Newcastle upon Tyne NE7 7RU, UK

Stefan Freitag
Robotic Research Institute, TU Dortmund University, Otto-Hahn-Strasse 8, 44227 Dortmund, Germany
stefan.freitag@tu-dortmund.de

Cheng Fu
Intelligent Systems Center, School of Electrical and Electronics Engineering, Nanyang Technological University, Singapore
fucheng@ntu.edu.sg

João Coelho Garcia
INESC ID Lisboa/Technical University of Lisbon, Rua Alves Redol 9, 1000-029 Lisbon, Portugal

Jeremy Goecks
Department of Biology and Department of Mathematics & Computer Science, Emory University, Druid Hills, GA, USA

Katharina Görlach
Institute of Architecture of Application Systems, University of Stuttgart, Stuttgart, Germany
goerlach@iaas.uni-stuttgart.de

Wenzhuang Gui
Bureau of High-Tech Research and Development, Chinese Academy of Sciences, Beijing, China

Phalguni Gupta
Department of Computer Science and Engineering, Indian Institute of Technology Kanpur, Kanpur 208016, India
pg@iitk.ac.in

Andrew F. Hart
Jet Propulsion Laboratory, California Institute of Technology, Pasadena, CA 91109, USA

Kendall N. Houk
Department of Chemistry and Biochemistry, UCLA, Los Angeles, CA 90095, USA

John S. Hughes
Jet Propulsion Laboratory, California Institute of Technology, Pasadena, CA 91109, USA

Jun Ho Huh
Oxford University Computing Laboratory, Parks Road, Oxford OX1 3QD, UK
jun.huh@kellogg.ox.ac.uk

Mudasser Iqbal
Intelligent Systems Center, School of Electrical and Electronics Engineering,
Nanyang Technological University, Singapore
mmiqbal@ntu.edu.sg

Kejian Jin
Institute for Digital Research and Education, UCLA, 5308 Math Sciences,
Los Angeles, CA 90095, USA

Scott Johnson
Department of Chemistry and Biochemistry, UCLA, Los Angeles,
CA 90095, USA

Odej Kao
Electrical Engineering and Computer Science, Technical University Berlin,
Einsteinufer 17, 10587 Berlin, Germany
Odej.Kao@tu-berlin.de

Dimka Karastoyanova
Institute of Architecture of Application Systems, University of Stuttgart,
Stuttgart, Germany
karastoyanova@iaas.uni-stuttgart.de

Sean C. Kelly
Jet Propulsion Laboratory, California Institute of Technology, Pasadena,
CA 91109, USA

Seonah Kim
Department of Chemistry and Biochemistry, UCLA, Los Angeles, CA 90095, USA

Dakshina Ranjan Kisku
Department of Computer Science and Engineering, Dr. B. C. Roy Engineering
College, Durgapur 713206, India
drkisku@ieee.org

Prakashan Korambath
Institute for Digital Research and Education, UCLA, 5308 Math Sciences,
Los Angeles, CA 90095, USA

Marta Kwiatkowska
Computing Laboratory, Oxford University, Oxford, UK

Bill Labate
Institute for Digital Research and Education, UCLA, 5308 Math Sciences,
Los Angeles, CA 90095, USA

Frank Leymann
Institute of Architecture of Application Systems, University of Stuttgart,
Stuttgart, Germany
leymann@iaas.uni-stuttgart.de

Jian Li
Computer Network Information Center, Chinese Academy of Sciences,
Beijing, China

Xiping Liu
College of Computer, Institute of Computer Technology, Nanjing University
of Posts and Telecommunications, Nanjing 210003, China
liuxp@njupt.edu.cn

Raquel Lopes
Departamento de Sistemas e Computação, Laboratório de Sistemas
Distribuídos, Universidade Federal de Campina Grande, Campina Grande,
Paraíba, Brazil
raquel@dsc.ufcg.edu.br

Zhonghua Lu
Computer Network Information Center, Chinese Academy of Sciences,
Beijing, China

Ze Luo
Computer Network Information Center, Chinese Academy of Sciences,
Beijing, China
luoze@cnic.cn

Andrew Martin
Oxford University Computing Laboratory, Parks Road, Oxford OX1 3QD, UK
andrew.martin@kellogg.ox.ac.uk

Chris A. Mattmann
Computer Science Department, University of Southern California, Los Angeles,
CA 90089, USA
and
Jet Propulsion Laboratory, California Institute of Technology, Pasadena,
CA 91109, USA

Kai Nan
Computer Network Information Center, Chinese Academy of Sciences,
Beijing, China

Anton Nekrutenko
Huck Institutes of the Life Sciences and Department of Biochemistry and
Molecular Biology, The Pennsylvania State University, University Park,
PA, USA

Gang Qin
Computer Network Information Center, Chinese Academy of Sciences,
Beijing, China

Dang Minh Quan
School of Information Technology, International University in Germany,
Campus 3, 76646 Bruchsal, Germany
quandm@upb.de

Michael Reiter
Institute of Architecture of Application Systems, University of Stuttgart,
Stuttgart, Germany
reiter@iaas.uni-stuttgart.de

Morris Riedel
Juelich Supercomputing Centre (JSC), Juelich, Germany
m.riedel@fz-juelich.de

Lívia Sampaio
Departamento de Sistemas e Computação, Laboratório de Sistemas Distribuídos,
Universidade Federal de Campina Grande, Campina Grande, Paraíba, Brazil
livia@dsc.ufcg.edu.br

João Nuno Silva
INESC ID Lisboa/Technical University of Lisbon, Rua Alves Redol 9,
1000-029 Lisbon, Portugal

Jamuna Kanta Sing
Department of Computer Science and Engineering, Jadavpur University,
Kolkata 700032, India
jksing@ieee.org

Shava Smallen
San Diego Supercomputer Center, UCSD, 9500 Gilman Drive, MC 0505,
La Jolla, CA 92093, USA

Mirko Sonntag
Institute of Architecture of Application Systems, University of Stuttgart,
Stuttgart, Germany
sonntag@iaas.uni-stuttgart.de

James Taylor
Department of Biology and Department of Mathematics & Computer Science,
Emory University, Druid Hills, GA, USA
james.taylor@emory.edu

The Galaxy Team
Pennsylvania State University and Emory University
http://galaxyproject.org

Massimo Tistarelli
Computer Vision Lab, DAP, University of Sassari, Alghero, Sassari 07140, Italy
tista@uniss.it

Paul Townend
School of Computing, University of Leeds, Leeds LS2 9JT, UK

Luís Veiga
INESC ID Lisboa/Technical University of Lisbon, Rua Alves Redol 9,
1000-029 Lisbon, Portugal
luis.veiga@inesc-id.pt

Jianwu Wang
San Diego Supercomputer Center, UCSD, 9500 Gilman Drive, MC 0505,
La Jolla, CA 92093, USA
jianwu@sdsc.edu

Wenqiang Wang
Intelligent Systems Center, School of Electrical and Electronics Engineering,
Nanyang Technological University, Singapore
wqwang@ntu.edu.sg

Philipp Wieder
Service Computing Group, TU Dortmund University, August-Schmidt-Strasse 12,
44227 Dortmund, Germany
philipp.wieder@udo.edu

Jie Xu
School of Computing, University of Leeds, Leeds LS2 9JT, UK

Baoping Yan
Computer Network Information Center, Chinese Academy of Sciences,
Beijing, China

Yuxia Yao
Intelligent Systems Center, School of Electrical and Electronics Engineering,
Nanyang Technological University, Singapore
yxyao@ntu.edu.sg

Tianyi Zang
School of Computer Science and Technology, Harbin Institute of Technology,
Harbin 150001, China
tianyi.zang@gmail.com

Yuanchun Zhou
Computer Network Information Center, Chinese Academy of Sciences,
Beijing, China

Part I
Sharing and Open Research

Chapter 1
Implementing a Grid/Cloud eScience Infrastructure for Hydrological Sciences

Gen-Tao Chiang, Martin T. Dove, C. Isabella Bovolo, and John Ewen

Abstract The objective of this chapter is to describe building an eScience infrastructure suitable for use with environmental sciences and especially with hydrological science applications. The infrastructure allows a wide range of hydrological problems to be investigated and is particularly suitable for either computationally intensive or multiple scenario applications. To accomplish this objective, this research discovered the shortcomings of current grid infrastructures for hydrological science and developed missing components to fill this gap. In particular, there were three primary areas which needed work: first, integrating data and computing grids; second, visualization of geographic information from grid outputs; and third, implementing hydrological simulations based on this infrastructure. This chapter focuses on the first area, which is focusing on grid infrastructure system integration and development. A grid infrastructure, which consists of a computing and a data grid, has been built. In addition, the computing grid has been extended to utilize the Amazon EC2 cloud computing resources. Users can conduct a complete simulation job life cycle from job submission, and data management to metadata management based on the tools available in the infrastructure.

G.-T. Chiang (✉)
Wellcome Trust Sanger Institute, Wellcome Trust Genome Campus, Hinxton,
Cambridge CB10 1SA, UK
e-mail: gtc@sanger.ac.uk

M.T. Dove
Department of Earth Sciences, University of Cambridge, Cambridge CB2 3EQ, UK

C.I. Bovolo and J. Ewen
School of Civil Engineering and Geosciences, University of Newcastle upon Tyne,
Newcastle upon Tyne NE7 7RU, UK

Xiaoyu Yang et al. (eds.), *Guide to e-Science: Next Generation Scientific Research and Discovery*, Computer Communications and Networks, DOI 10.1007/978-0-85729-439-5_1, © Springer-Verlag London Limited 2011

1.1   Introduction: eScience, Grid, and Cloud Computing

A frequently used definition of eScience is that given by John Taylor, Former Director of the UK Government's Office of Science and Technology. His definition is: "eScience is about global collaboration in key areas of science, and the next generation of infrastructure that will enable it" [1]. Another definition sees eScience as a synthesis of information technology and science that enables challenges on previously unimaginable scales to be tackled [2].

Based on these definitions of eScience, there are two main core concepts. The first one is collaboration. eScience should bring researchers from the same or different fields together for collaborative work. A group of researchers could set up a virtual organization (VO) that shares the computer processing power, databases, data storage facilities, and scientific instruments of their institutions [3]. The eMinerals project is an example within which physicists, chemists, and computer scientists from different institutions are working together seamlessly.

The second concept is to develop and adopt new information technologies, which allow scientists to work on an infrastructure with a previously unimaginable scale. This concept brings in grid computing and cloud computing.

Many people use "grid computing" as an equivalent term to eScience. According to Ian Foster's definition, "grid computing is an infrastructure that enables flexible, secure, coordinated resource sharing among dynamic collections of individuals, institutions and resources" [4]. One can think that eScience as a conceptual term and grids/cloud as a technology term that implements the scope of eScience.

People use grid to mean different things. The most widely used "grid" refers to computing grid. These types of grids involve sharing the computing resources. The second usage of the grids refers to data grid. This type of the grids aims to allow easy data discovery and metadata management across the institutes. The third usage of the grid is collaboration grids. The type of the grid tries to improve the communication between collaborators. However, none of these single interpretations reflects the whole picture of the "grid." From the point of view of this project, the grid inhabits the intersection area of these three types of grid, as shown in Fig. 1.1.

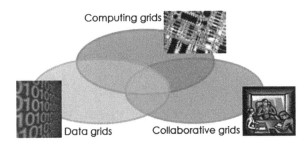

Fig. 1.1 From the point of view of this project, the grid infrastructure should consist of the most important parts from three types of grid: computing grids, data grids, and collaborative grids [5]

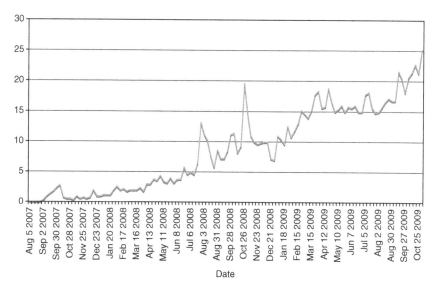

Fig. 1.2 The trend of "cloud computing" searches since 2007 [6]

The term "cloud computing" entered IT-speak at about the end of 2007 and has spread hugely. According to the Google Trends data shown in Fig. 1.2, the term "cloud computing" is now searched 25 times more compared to the time when the term was first launched (September 2007). It may, however, like many other fancy technological terms, fail to meet expectations and quickly cease to be fashionable. Interestingly, even if the term "cloud computing" does pass the hype peak, the cloud itself does now exist and is getting more attention and starting to change the ecology of the IT industry.

Just like "grids," there are many interpretations of "cloud." The most widely used definition, from Globus Alliance and presented in Supercomputing 2008, defines the cloud as a three layer service, as shown in Fig. 1.3.

The bottom layer is the Infrastructure as a Service (IaaS). IaaS integrates hardware resources such as computing, storage, and networks and delivers computer infrastructure as services. Amazon Web Services (AWS) is the most successful example. The second layer, Platform as a Service (PaaS), is the delivery of the computing platform. It reduces the complexity of managing underlying hardware and software layers. It provides the facilities to support the complete life cycle of a web application. Google App Engine is an example. Users can develop and host web applications on Google App Engine, which is hosted in the Google Data Center. The top layer is Software as a Service (SaaS). A simple definition of SaaS is an application hosted on a remote server and accessed through the Internet, for example, Gmail or Animoto, which produces video based on user-selected pictures and music. The entire process is carried out on the remote server.

The chapter only focuses on utilizing AWS, which is an IaaS service. Cloud services from PaaS and SaaS are beyond the scope of this chapter. The following

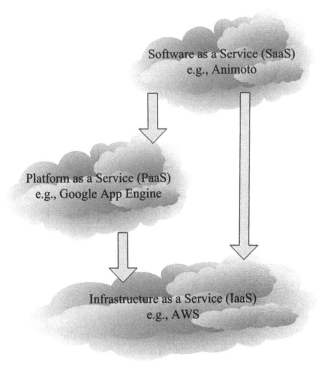

Fig. 1.3 The diagram of different cloud services. IT consists of Infrastructure as a Service (IaaS), Platform as a Service (PaaS), and Software as a Service (SaaS)

section will explain how a cloud computing or AWS resources be integrated as part of the computing grid and performing the simulations.

1.1.1   Grid Computing for Environmental Sciences

Grid computing has been widely used in high-energy physics, such as LHC Computing Grid (LCG) and biomedical research, such as Biomedical Informatics Research Network (BIRN). It is now being increasingly adopted by the earth and environmental science communities worldwide [7]. Several environmental eScience projects are briefly described below.

Climateprediction.net is running hundreds of thousands of different models using the same technology, called the Berkeley Open Infrastructure for Network Computing (BOINC) [8], SETI@home is the most well-known project using BOINC. BOINC allows people to join a project by contributing the idle computer power of their PC at home. The climateprediction.net project aims to gain a better understanding of how climate models are affected by small changes in the many parameters [9, 10].

The Grid ENabled Integrated Earth systems model (GENIE) aims to develop a computing framework, which will allow researchers to flexibly couple together components to form a unified Earth System Model.

The NERC DataGrid (NDG) aims to provide tools and information products that can be used to facilitate the processing chain that starts with raw data from a variety of sources and ends with graphical production [11].

The Geoscience Network (GEON) is a US collaborative project between several institutions, not only within the USA but also internationally, to develop a cyberinfrastructure for geoscientists. The vision of the GEON grid is to build a system in which geoscientists can sit in front of the terminal and easily access almost any kind of geoscience data, with easy means of visualizing, analyzing, and modeling those data [12].

The Dissemination and Exploitation of Grids in Earth Science (DEGREE) is an EU project aiming to find out the key requirements for deploying earth science applications in a grid environment. DEGREE uses EGEE grid middleware (gLite) and its infrastructure [7].

The eMinerals project has a primary focus on developing grid infrastructures to support computational scientists who perform simulations of the atomistic components of environmental processes. This project is largely based on technologies from eMinerals. eMinerals uses existing grid middleware tools such as Globus for integrating computing resources; Condor as a local batching system; and the Storage Resources Broker (SRB) for managing distributed data. In addition, it has developed several tools, such as Remote My Condor Submit (RMCS), to integrate the previous middleware from different grids [13].

Hydrology is the study of the movement, distribution, and quality of water and encompasses water in rivers, lakes, aquifers, and glaciers. Understanding the water cycle at a local and global scale can help to address issues such as the occurrence, distribution, and severity of hazards such as floods and droughts, erosion, shallow landslides, dam or embankment failures, debris flows, sediment transport, pollutant transport, and water quality failure.

Although there are many projects trying to adopt different grid technologies in the environmental sciences, grid computing for hydrological applications is still a relatively new field. Historically, HPC has been widely used in atmospheric science and oceanography because it can be used to overcome the spatial (gridded size) and temporal (time steps) resolution barriers and obtain better results [14].

The hydrological model scale was too small to be integrated as part of an earth system model. However, the situation is now changing. The earth system models, which integrate atmosphere, lithosphere, biosphere, and oceans as a whole system, are becoming important. People now realize that the environment is a complex system and each individual component of the earth system requires deeper study. In this situation, better understanding in hydrological science is required and thus the computational requirements for hydrological models are increasing as well. In addition to integrating hydrological models as part of the earth system model, the hydrological models are now also coupled with underground water models, ecosystem models, and land information systems.

Grid computing can be a valuable resource for computational hydrology, particularly since it is well-suited for computationally intensive applications such as large-scale parameter sweeps that run a number of jobs with different parameter settings, sensitivity analysis that tries to identify which source weigh more on studies' conclusions, and uncertainty analysis that studies the uncertainties in the conclusions of studies [15].

Grid computing can also be used for multiple scenario applications such as looking at the impacts of land use change or future climate change on the hydrology of a catchment. Such virtual experiments that run experiments in a virtual environment, by their very nature create a large number of simulations and hence vast amounts of data. These in turn require efficient data handling and metadata management tools, together with ways to visualize and capture relevant outputs. Simple visualization tools, such as Google Earth (GE), are particularly useful, as they allow geospatial, graphical, and animated outputs to be viewed in a freely available, easy to use, dynamic, interactive environment on the user's desktop.

CUAHSI[1] (Consortium of Universities for the Advancement of Hydrologic Science, Inc.) is the major largest organization dedicated on developing grid/cyber-infrastructure for hydrological applications. One of the projects under CUAHSI is called the Hydrologic Information System (HIS or CUAHSI-HIS). HIS is designed to provide several functions. It provides a uniform user access portal for comprehensive distributed water data from federal, state, and local agencies. It also allows users to publish their own datasets. One of the core services of HIS is called WaterOneFlow and is used for finding and retrieving hydrological observation data in the WaterML format. WaterML is an XML specification for describing and exchanging water observation data.

Most of the projects focus on solving either computing or data-oriented problems. For example, CUAHSI defines WaterML as the data exchange standard. The concept of using XML is the same as this project; however, WaterML mainly supports observation data and does not yet fully support with simulation outputs, which are mostly grid-based data. CUAHSI-HIS is evolving but at this moment it only focuses on data interoperability and is not integrating computing grid/data grid yet.

1.1.2   The Objective of This Chapter

The overall objective of this project is to describe how to build an eScience infrastructure suitable for use with hydrological applications. The infrastructure, which will be used in combination with System Hydrological European TRANsport model (SHETRAN), will allow a wide range of hydrological problems to be investigated and will be particularly suitable for either computationally intensive or

---

[1]CUAHSI, visited January 13, 2010 http://www.cuahsi.org/

multiple scenario applications. This eScience infrastructure will not only include traditional computing grid resources but can also be extended to utilize the cloud computing/AWS resources.

Since computing grid could generate a large amount of data, a data storage, retrieval, and management tools/data grid are required to be integrated in this infrastructure. SRB is the data management tool implemented in this project will also be discussed.

In order to deal with the visualization and metadata within the grid, XMLization is used in this project. Some tools have been developed to deal with XML files are discussed. Writing Keyhole Markup Language (WKML), which is a Fortran library allowing environmental scientists to visualize their model outputs in Google Earth. Writing Hydrological Markup Language (WHML) is used to describe the hydrological data. An XPath-based tool integrated with RMCS is developed to extract metadata and simulation outputs from XML files.

1.2 Building an eScience Infrastructure

1.2.1 Computing Grids

As described in Fig. 1.1, an ideal grid infrastructure should provide the functions of the intersecting parts of three types of grids: computing grids, data grids, and collaborative grids. The following section will focus on how to build computing grids and extending the computing grid to utilize cloud resources. It will also discuss the data grid, which is SRB in this project.

A computing grid may include high-performance computing (HPC), high-throughput computing (HTC), and desktop resources. The computing grid that has been built for this project is based on a Condor pool, which is part of University of Cambridge campus grid (CamGrid), NGS core resources (PBS clusters), and resources from a Wellcome Trust Sanger Institute (WTSI) sequencing farm (LSF clusters). Those are also called local batching systems. A computing gird is to provide an approach to integrate those resources across the network domain. This is usually done by implementing Globus gatekeeper that is an interface for allowing heterogeneous local computing resources to be integrated.

As shown in Fig. 1.4, one can submit jobs from anywhere across the Internet to this grid via the RMCS client, as long as one can authenticate with valid X509 certificates. The RMCS will then discover matching resources and allocate jobs to those resources, which may be physically located in different institutes.

1.2.1.1 Local Batching Systems

Local computing resources are managed by a batching or queuing system. When a computing job is submitted, the batching system applies a set of predefined rules to

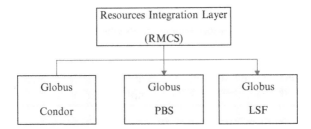

Fig. 1.4 Globus acts as an interface to different local batching or queuing systems such as Condor, Load Sharing Facility (LSF) and Portable Batch System (PBS). A Resources Integration Layer such as Remote My Condor Submit (RMCS) then integrates heterogeneous resources through Globus

the requested resources, defining the priority and execution order in relation to other requests. The jobs are allocated in the queue and executed whenever the resources are available [16]. The batching system can be seen as the bottom layer of a grid system. It allows a grid manager to enforce policies for the use of local cluster resources.

Condor is a workload management system developed at the University of Wisconsin. Condor provides a job queuing mechanism, scheduling policy, priority scheme, resource monitoring, and resource management. Users submit their serial or parallel jobs to Condor, Condor places them into a queue, chooses when and where to run the jobs based upon a policy, monitors their progress, and ultimately informs the user upon completion. Condor's architecture allows it to succeed in areas where traditional scheduling systems fail, such as managing heterogeneous computing resources [17].

The Condor pool used here has ten working nodes called the "badgers," plus a central manager called "cete." Each node has dual 3.12 GHz Xeon processors with 4 GB of memory. In addition, cete is part of the Cambridge and can access other computing resources located in different departments.

The Portable Batch System (PBS) was originally developed by NASA in the early- to mid-1990s. PBS is a job scheduler that allocates network resources to batch jobs. It can schedule jobs to execute in networked, multi-platform UNIX environments [16]. PBS is widely used in NGS resources (three core NGS sites, Oxford, Manchester, and Leeds, are using PBS).

Unlike Condor, PBS is traditionally used for managing homogeneous resources and it has better support for running parallel jobs using the Message Passing Interface (MPI) toolkit that allows many computers to communicate with each other.

The Load Sharing Facility (LSF) was developed by Platform Computing. LSF manages a group of computers and makes them work together as a single unit, combining computing power and sharing workload and resources. LSF is the major batching system used in STFC-RAL and WTSI.

LSF is a commercial product and provides some advanced features. For example, it is able to manage heterogeneous clusters using a multi-cluster feature.

This feature is similar to what a grid achieves. It can also manage both Linux and MS Windows machines together. One other feature is that the execution of binary files can be put in the LSF command line directly instead of using the wrapper scripts that other batching systems usually require.

The Sun Grid Engine (SGE) is an open source project aiming to facilitate the adoption of distributed computing solutions sponsored by Sun Microsystems. The original idea of the SGE project was trying to establish community-driven standards for distributed computing and enabling developers to develop applications across distributed heterogeneous compute environments. SGE is used in the AWS EC2 cloud resources and will be discussed later in this chapter.

1.2.1.2   Globus Toolkit

Globus is the most well-known grid middleware and was developed by the Globus Alliance, which consists of the Argonne National Laboratory and various research institutes. Globus provides a set of software tools to implement the basic grid services and capabilities required to construct a computational grid.

Globus consists of four major components, namely the security, data management, information services, and execution management components [18]. Different grid projects or infrastructures may choose different components to build their own grid. This project uses the security component, which is Grid Security Infrastructure (GSI) for privilege control and the execution management component or so-called Grid Resource Allocation and Management (GRAM) for integrating computing resources and scheduling computing jobs. Data management actually uses SRB instead of the Globus data management component.

The security component provides the Grid Security Infrastructure (GSI) for security checking. GSI uses the X.509 Public Key Infrastructure (PKI) and certificates for identity checking instead of a traditional username and password [19]. The certificate uses a digital signature to bind together a public key with identity information such as the name of a person, organization, e-mail, and so forth. The certificate can be used to verify that a public key belongs to an individual. At this moment, the grid resources used in this project uses certificates signed by the UK eScience Certificate Authority (CA), an entity which issues digital certificates for use by other parties in the grid community. However, for launching AWS cloud services, it requires certificates signed by AWS.

GRAM is the core product of Globus. GRAM allows users to submit, monitor, and cancel jobs in a computing grid environment without directly accessing the local batching system. However, GRAM itself is not a job scheduler. Instead it provides a protocol and single interface, which communicates to local batching systems. Users can submit jobs to GRAM without worrying about the back-end local batching system and GRAM can automatically generate job description files for local batching systems. GRAM thus greatly reduces the amount of work involved in using remote computing resources.

As shown in Fig. 1.4, Globus sits between local batching systems and the Resources Integration Layer. The "Globus" in Fig. 1.4 actually refers to GRAM rather than any other Globus components. GRAM, thus, can be seen as the core of the grid system.

1.2.1.3   Remote My_Condor_Submit (RMCS)

GRAM provides a single interface for different local computing resources. However, it requires an additional layer to query and manage the resources integrated by Globus. This layer may use different names, for example meta-scheduling, resources broker, and grid portal. I simply call them all the Resources Integration Layer (Fig. 1.4).

There are several tools that have been developed for this purpose, for example the Resources Broker (RB) or Workload Management Services (WMS) developed by EGEE; GridWay, now part of the Globus toolkit, and the RMCS developed by the *e*Minerals project. Each of them has their own strengths and weaknesses and is briefly discussed below.

The RB concept originally came from the LCG and is now widely used in EGEE, OSG, and NGS. RB queries the BDII, which contains the information collected by MDS and registered through the GLUE schema. RB is then able to help users to decide where the best resources are available and where the jobs are submitted to. It also provides functions for monitoring, canceling, retrieving outputs, and logging information.

GridWay was originally developed by the University of Madrid and now is part of the Globus meta-scheduler project. The aim of GridWay is to reduce the gap between grid middleware and applications. It provides users and application developers with a consistent and easier working environment for accessing grid resources [20]. Similarly to RB, GridWay collects resources information from MDS. Users can submit jobs based on this information or let GridWay decide where the jobs should go. Although GridWay is easier to deploy and use, it can only acquire basic resources information such as CPU, disk usage, and memory usage. On the other hand, RB can query resources based on more information from the applications layer, for example which software or libraries are provided by local resources.

Both RB and GridWay focus on providing an easier approach to integrating computing resources. However, RMCS (developed by *e*Minerals) was chosen in this project. RMCS does not use the MDS and cannot query/select resources based on information published in GLUE schema. The only chosen criterion for grid resources is availability via CPUs. From the perspective of resource brokering and meta-scheduling, RMCS is not as powerful as RB or GridWay. However, as mentioned above, the grid is not just about computing, it also involves data and metadata management. The power of RMCS is that it integrates computing, data and metadata management. Users can submit a single job that runs in the computing resources, sends outputs to the data grid, and extracts metadata information all at once.

RMCS is a tool developed by the *e*Minerals project to allow simplified job submission to remote grid resources with inbuilt meta-scheduling. It is a workload management system combining local batching systems into a single aggregated view and load balancing, data management, and metadata management functionality. The job submission is handled by Condor-G (a Condor component allowing submit jobs from Condor-G to Globus) and metadata capture and storage are handled by RCommands [21]. The RCommands framework consists of a back-end metadata database, a set of client tools, and an application server that maps Web services calls to SQL calls. Data management is handled using SRB Scommands, which are the SRB client command line tools for manipulating data managed by SRB.

The process of submitting a job is handled in three stages. First, data are downloaded to the computing resources from SRB. Second, the job is executed in the computing grids. Finally, data are uploaded back from the computing grids to the data grid, which is SRB. This workflow is managed using Condor DAGman, which is a simple workflow management system. Using DAGman means that MCS does not need to directly manage the workflow itself [22].

MCS uses a job description file, which is an extension of a standard Condor submission script. This job description file allows simple Condor job description in addition to directives controlling aspects of data and metadata storage using SRB and an XPath-based tool to extract information from XML files [23].

RMCS clients consist of a set of tools to submit, monitor, and manage jobs. The RMCS client can be installed on any desktop machine and uses port standard web port 80 to talk to the RMCS server.

1.2.2 Data Grids

Many different science fields today require the handling of large and geographically distributed data sets. The size of these data is now scaled up from terabytes to petabytes. For example, in high-energy physics LHC at CERN will produce several petabytes of data annually. In computational genomics, WTSI has generated 4 PB of data in 2009. In climate modeling, a large number of observed data such as satellite images and simulation results are generated regularly. However, this project focuses on hydrological applications and hydrologists are more interested in using the data grid to access geographically distributed data.

The combination of several issues such as large datasets, distributed data, and computationally intensive analysis makes data management in a grid environment much more complicated. Several tools have been developed to solve individual issues. However, a unified environment which allows users to deal with all these issues together is required. This environment is the so-called data grid [24].

The two fundamental services of a data grid are data access and metadata access. Data access services provide mechanisms to access, manage, and initiate third-party data transfer in distributed storage systems. Metadata access services provide mechanisms to access and manage information about the data stored in storage systems.

Several higher layer data grid services can be developed on top of those two core services, such as data replication management and data filtering. However, this project focuses on core data grid services. Thus, data replication and filtering are not considered in this project. I decided to use SRB as the data grid solution in this project for reasons that are explained in the following section.

1.2.2.1 Data Access: Storage Resources Broker (SRB)

In a grid environment, data may be stored in different locations with different storage devices. Applications should not need to be aware of those specific low-level data access mechanisms. Just as in a computing grid, users should not worry about all the different local batching systems. With a single command, a job can be submitted to the computing grid and allocated to local computing resources. Just as in a data grid, applications should be presented with a uniform mechanism for accessing data.

The SRB provides a uniform client interface to different storage or file systems. From the user's point of view, they can use the SRB to access distributed data from any network-accessible point. The SRB provides a virtual file system, with access to data being based on data attributes and logical names rather than on physical location or real names. The physical location is seen as a file characteristic only. One of the features of the SRB is that it allows users to easily replicate data across different physical file systems in order to provide an additional level of file protection [25].

The SRB also provides a metadata catalogue (MCAT) to describe and locate data within the storage systems. Files are actually stored in multiple "vaults." These vaults are repositories from which the MCAT server, which is used for mapping the location of logical and physical files [25], can extract files on demand.

There are several ways to access data within the SRB, such as web-based browser and search interface. However, Scommand is the major client tool used by RMCS as its components for data staging.

1.2.2.2 Metadata Access: Rcommands

The second core service of a data grid is metadata access. There are different types of metadata. *Application metadata* are used to describe the information in the scientific data set, the circumstances within which the data are obtained, or other information related to how the data have been processed. *Replica metadata* includes information for mapping file instances to physical storage locations. *System or environment metadata* are used to describe the fabric of the grid itself, for example, details of the storage system, where the computing jobs are running, the submit machines, CPU usage, and simulation time.

Although SRB provides MCAT, this project only uses MCAT for managing replica metadata that are used for mapping logical file names to physical locations.

The system and application metadata are handled by a more sophisticated metadata server, namely the Rcommands server.

The Rcommands framework was developed by STFC in collaboration with the *e*Minerals project. The framework provides a set of scriptable commands to associate metadata to files stored within distributed file system such as SRB, a set of FTP servers, or a set of files available over http. The Rcommands clients insert and modify metadata to a central metadata server, which is now a standard NGS service.

RMCS then parses the application metadata from XML files (CML, HML, or KML). The following chapter will describe more about how application metadata are extracted. In addition to application metadata, RMCS records some environmental variables and treats them as system metadata. Both application and some system metadata will be inserted to the metadata server (Rcommands server) using Rcommands clients, which are integrated as part of the RMCS.

The Rcommands framework uses a three-tier model to organize application metadata. The top level is the *study* level. This level is self-explanatory. It is possible to associate collaborators with this level. In this project, the study level is defined as the project level named SHETRAN. The next level is the *dataset* level, this is the most abstract level and users are free to interpret it in many ways. In this project, this level is used to define several simulation scenarios and each simulation scenario uses a dataset ID. The third level is the *data object* level and includes files generated by a single simulation run or the outputs from the subsequent analysis. An example of usage for this project is shown in Table 1.1.

1.2.3   Integrating EC2 to the Grids with RMCS

Amazon Web services (AWS) consists of several services, for example EC2, S3, the Elastic Blocking System (EBS), CloudFront, SimpleDB, and MapReduce. This pilot test uses only EC2, which is a Web service that provides resizable computing capacity in the cloud for integrating EC2 as part of the grid resources.

EC2 provides two groups of instance types: standard instances and high-CPU instances. Standard instances have memory to CPU ratios suitable for most general-purpose applications. High-CPU instances have higher CPU to memory ratios and suites for computer-intensive applications. Since SHETRAN is not a parallel job, a standard large instance (m1.large) would be good enough for this test.

Table 1.1   Three levels to represent metadata in Rcommands

Study	Project name: SHETRAN
Data set	Five data set, each dataset represent a simulation scenario
Data object	Each data object is a single simulation run

The most important benefit of cloud computing is its ability to customize the working environment. In the grid, users always require a system administrator's support to provide a suitable environment. The customization can be achieved and implemented by using Amazon Machine Image (AMI), which is a single file containing information on operating systems, memory, disk usage, and system configuration. Basically, AMI can be created with the following steps:

1. Create a directory in S3 that will be used for storing AMI.
2. Use AMI tools to create an AMI based on an existing machine.
3. Upload the AMI to the S3.
4. Register AMI.

Two images are created. One image is used for the head node of a cluster. The other one is used for computing nodes. The head node image consists of the software required by the Globus gatekeeper. These include the installations and configurations for grid middlewares such as Globus GRAM, Globus GSI, SRB Client (Scommands), Rcommands, the Local batching system (SGE), and Perl LibXML. For SHETRAN specific libraries, the Intel compiler and HDF5 and FoX libraries with WKML and WHML are required.

A common username (gridjobs) across the virtual EC2 cluster needs to be created and shares its home space via NFS. The local batching system, SGE, has to be configured to allow for dynamically adding and removing computing nodes. A UK eScience host certificate is also required for the head node. Lastly, the firewall has to be configured and security policies set up using the AWS management console.

The AMI for computing nodes is simpler. It does not need grid tools but just the Intel portable library and HDF5 library and the configuration of the/etc/fstab to mount the home directory when the instances are launched.

The environment has to be tested in two steps. The first step is to see if the SHETRAN simulation runs correctly. The second step is to see if staging outputs and metadata to SRB and Rcommands also work correctly. If the environment is proved to be working properly, AMI can be created using AMI tools. EC2 instances can be launched at any later time based on this AMI for SHETRAN simulations.

The EC2 instances and virtual cluster can be integrated with the grid using RMCS. The virtual cluster can be treated as a computing element in the RMCS database based on the Globus gatekeeper. If listing available sites using rmcs_status −l, one can see the EC2 virtual cluster is just like other clusters in the list.

The data grid uses the NGS SRB. All the simulation outputs will be staged back to the NGS SRB vaults. Metadata will be inserted into the Rcommand server. In principle, the output can be staged in S3 but it requires further software development for RMCS.

Up to this stage, we can only see available clusters and do not know the actual available EC2 resources. For testing purposes, five computing nodes and one head node were launched. The available EC2 resources can be seen from the AWS management console or from the EC2 command line tools.

```
[gtniees@iguana cloud]$ rmcs_status -l
The following machines are currently available to be submitted to  Clusters:
   - dl1.nw-grid.ac.uk-serial
   - ec2-79-125-12-242.eu-west-1.compute.amazonaws.com
   - gram.sanger.ac.uk-32
   - grid-compute.leeds.ac.uk
   - grid-compute.oesc.ox.ac.uk
   - grid-data.rl.ac.uk
   - ngs.leeds.ac.uk
   - ngs.oerc.ox.ac.uk
   - ngs.rl.ac.uk
   - ngs.rl.ac.uk-parallel
   - vidar.ngs.manchester.ac.uk
   - vidar.ngs.manchester.ac.uk-parallel
Condor pools:
   -     cete.niees.group.cam.ac.uk
```

Fig. 1.5 An example using the RMCS command to list the available clusters, which include the AWS EC2 virtual cluster

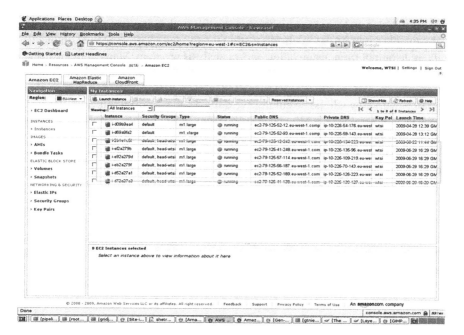

Fig. 1.6 Amazon Web Services (AWS) management console, which shows the available EC2 resources and their status

RMCS job description file (mcsfile) needs to be modified by changing/adding the hostname of the head node of the virtual cluster to the preferredMachineList. For example:

preferredMachineList= ec2-79-125-12-242.eu-west-1.compute.amazonaws.com

The jobs can be submitted using RMCS clients. The jobs will be executed on the EC2 virtual clusters. The outputs, including KML files, will be staged back to the NGS SRB as other RMCS grid jobs running on other grid sites (Figs. 1.5 and 1.6).

1.3   Geographic Information Visualization

The geobrowsers provide free and easy access to high-quality maps and high-resolution aerial photographs have revolutionized the way in which researchers can visualize geospatial data. Not only are researchers able to use these tools in their own data analysis tasks, but also they can create representations that allow them to present information to their collaborators or the wider public.

Many geobrowser tools (e.g., Google Earth, ArcGIS Explorer, NASA World Wind) accept geospatial data represented using the Keyhole Markup Language (KML), an XML-based language. KML can describe various primitive elements, such as points, lines, and polygons, with specific geographical information. For example, a point can be represented using the following relatively simple piece of code shown in Fig. 1.7.

Although this code looks straightforward, a file with many data points (and with more complex primitives) might normally be expected to be generated automatically as an output from a simulation or data analysis program. Many numerical and simulation computer programs used in several branches of science, such as climate, atmosphere, ocean, and hydrology, are written in Fortran, and there are a number of reasons why it would be useful to have a library to support writing.

XML in general, and KML specifically, from Fortran programs. Briefly, some of these reasons are:

First, to make it easy to write XML/KML documents from a Fortran program, reducing the burden on the programmer in terms of the amount of coding required

```
<?xml version="1.0" encoding="UTF-8"?>
<kml xmlns="http://earth.google.com/kml/2.2">
 <Placemark>
  <Point>
   <coordinates>-122.0822,37.4222</coordinates>
  </Point>
 </Placemark>
</kml>
```

Fig. 1.7 A simple example of Keyhole Markup Language (KML) file showing information about a single point

and also in terms of the prior familiarly with XML and KML required of the programmer. Second, to enable additional content, such as contour maps or charts, which are not included in KML, to be automatically generated from programs. Third, to be able to generate KML documents automatically from within a simulation program. For those reasons, a Fortran library called Writing KML (WKML), which is able to enable easy generation of KML files from the Fortran programs, has been developed and used for visualizing geographic information within grids.

The following is an example of how the WKML can be used, a fuller use case for hydrological science will be shown in the next section. This example shows some points: First, no part of the program needed an awareness of the syntax of KML. Second, the writing of the latitude and longitude points required one simple subroutine call kmlAddPoints, which clearly makes for condensed code when this process is repeated often in a program. Third, the subroutine calls kmlBeginFile and kmlFinishFile handle the correct beginning and ending of the KML file, again without requiring the programmer to know what XML/KML expects.

1.3.1 WKML Functions

WKML provides some higher-level functions, which allow user to generate KML files easily. Those functions provide single calls that output many KML elements so that the user does not need to worry about the details of individual elements. The following section will explore WKML functions in more detail.

The m_wkml_features module contains functions for creating vector data such as points, line, and polygons. These functions are probably the most-often used functions for environmental scientists.

The m_wkml_coverage module contains functions for displaying gridded data. Although representing raster or gridded data in KML may not be very efficient, it is still usable for some cases when using smaller datasets. For example, this module is very suitable for the hydrological virtual experiments in this project when the size of the visualization outputs can be configured.

The m_wkml_contours module provides functions to generate contour lines and polygons based upon a regularly distributed grid dataset. For example, users can use kmlCreateContours that is a generic interface from this module to plot contours in GE.

The m_wkml_vector module provides functions to plot vector fields (arrows) based on a regularly distributed grid dataset. This is the module requested by physical oceanography users, who usually use this module to plot the direction of the current of the ocean.

The m_wkml_chart module provides functions to plot charts using GNUPLOT or Google Chart API. This module provides functions to plot statistical charts and shown in GE. For example, in hydrology, the hydrograph can be plotted using the functions from this module (Fig. 1.8).

```
program write_kml_points
! Set up the XML file output channel
type(xmlf_t) :: xfile
real :: lat_long_positions(2,1)
! create the file
  call kmlBeginFile(xfile,"output.kml")
! Set up data
  lat_long_positions(1,1) = -122.0822
  lat_long_positions(2,1) = 37.4222
! Do the hard work with one subroutine call
  call kmlAddPoints(xfile,lat_long_positions)
! close the KML file neatly
  call kmlFinishFile(xfile)
end program write_kml_points
```

Fig. 1.8 A simple Fortran code to generate a KML file shown in Fig. 1.7

1.4 Case Study: Running a Hydrological Application SHETRAN

SHETRAN [26] is a three-dimensional (i.e., modeling the surface and subsurface structures) physically based hydrology modeling program which uses a spatially distributed rectangular finite difference grid to simulate coupled water flow, multi-fraction sediment transport, and multiple reactive solute transport in river basins. It is capable of modeling water flow on the ground surface and in stream channels; ground-water flow in saturated and unsaturated zones; river–aquifer interactions; rainfall interception by vegetation, evaporation, and transpiration; and snowpack formation and snowmelt and soil erosion and sediment yield arising from rain drop impact and overland flow based on time-and space-varying rainfall and other meteorological inputs (Fig. 1.9).

Within SHETRAN the spatial distribution of catchment properties, rainfall input, and hydrological response is achieved in the horizontal direction through the representation of the catchment by an orthogonal grid network and in the vertical direction by a column of horizontal layers at each grid square, thereby allowing a representation of the subsurface. Rivers, or links, are located along the edges of the grids and fluxes are calculated across all links and grid boundaries.

SHETRAN is a large and complex legacy model written in FORTRAN (primarily FORTRAN 77). Inputs are in the form of ASCII files and outputs have recently been modernized to give one HDF5 format file encompassing all the required simulation outputs. Free HDF5 data readers are available which allow the results to be visualized; however, substantial post-processing is usually required to produce good quality graphical outputs. It would be of great benefit to the hydrological modeler if

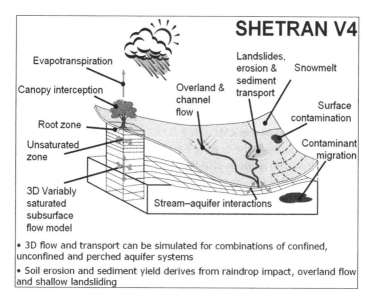

Fig. 1.9 Sketch of SHETRAN model

SHETRAN results could be analyzed and visualized in a more interactive way; however, at present SHETRAN is not compatible with standard visualization tools such as GIS and GE. The second aim of the project is therefore to develop and implement WKML to allow results from SHETRAN to be viewed using GE. This would also enable hydrologists to communicate and share results easily across the Internet.

1.4.1 Grid-Enabling SHETRAN

In order to run SHETRAN in the grid/cloud environment, the applications have to be grid enabled. Grid-enabling involves different stages. First, the data and application preparation involves the work needed to generate the data necessary for a parameter sweep. The second stage involves the use of XML for visualization and metadata management. The third stage is to configure the system and run the simulation jobs.

1.4.1.1 First Stage: Data Preparation

The first stage varies for applications. Different applications have their own file format and different requirement for parameter sweep. In this case, a Perl script called `SHETRAN-inp.pl` has been developed. `SHETRAN-input.pl` is designed to modify parameters in four major SHETRAN modules representing in different input files. `SHETRAN-inp.pl` will then generate the required input files for the simulation required and the `monty.dat` file, which maps RMCS Job ID and input files to a specific simulation job.

The main purpose of `SHETRAN-inp.pl` is to modify the value of a specific parameter when hydrologists want to carry out parameterization. Thus, most input files remain the same and only one parameter within a single input file is modified. This file is called the control file and the parameter is called the control parameter. `monty.dat` actually maps the RMCS Job ID to a single control filename.

In the *e*Minerals use case, the control file is a single plain text file that records key pair values. This control file is also the only configuration file for a simulation job. However, SHETRAN has several input files with different formats. Monty is not able to map a RMCS Job ID to multiple input files with different file names. `SHETRAN-inp.pl` thus archives the input files using tar and uses the filename of the tar file as a control file name.

`SHETRAN-inp.pl` creates a `$syear_$eyear.tar` file. The control file name uses the start year simulation (`$syear`) and the end year simulation (`$eyear`). The `$syear_$eyear.tar` file includes not only the SHETRAN input files but also other files, such as SHETRAN executable file, files for coordinate information, and files for GNUPLOT, required for running simulations in grid.

1.4.1.2   Second Stage: XMLization

As mentioned before, the grid infrastructure uses a standard XML parsing tool as part of the job life cycle. SHETRAN originally uses HDF5 for storing data and thus requires to develop an informatics layer using XML to replace or as an alternative of HDF5.

WKML is then used in SHETRAN main code to generate KML files. Two major WKML functions are used in this example. kmlCreateCells and kmlCreateContours can be used to generate simulation outputs and constants. Figures 1.10 and 1.11 are examples of ph_depth, the depth of water table generated by both functions.

Fig. 1.10 SHETRAN
simulation outputs using
`kmlCreateCells` [27, 28]

Fig. 1.11 SHETRAN
simulation outputs using
kml CreateContours
[27, 28]

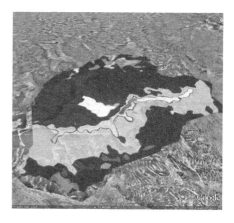

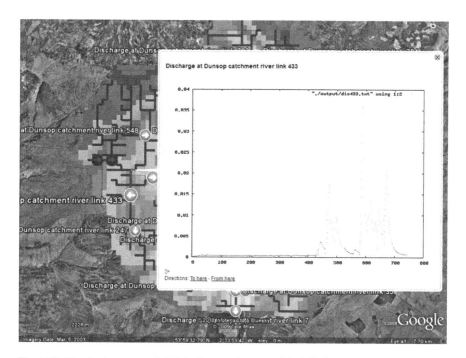

Fig. 1.12 The discharge at each link is shown using a graphical display

A value of 0 means that the water table is at ground level, and a value of 1 means the water table is 1 m below the ground.

In order to plot the hydrograph, which represent the discharge at the river links, another WKML function kmlAddChart_gnuplot can be used. The output is shown in Fig. 1.12.

```
Executable  = runSHETRAN-NGS.sh
PathToExe   = /ngs/home/gen-tao-chiang.ngs/SHETRAN/d639/
preferredMachineList = ngs.oerc.ox.ac.uk
jobType = performance

# Force overwriting when uploading / downloading files
SForce      = true
Sdir1       = /ngs/home/gen-tao-chiang.ngs/SHETRAN/d639/
Sget        = CONTROL.tar

# Specify where to store metadata
RDatasetID    = 639
#RDatasetName  = "dataset of SHETRAN test"

Sput     = hmltest.hml, vege.kml,config.hml, annualmax.hml
Rdesc    = "This is a test adding SRB instance as one of the metadata parameter"

GetEnvMetadata = true
XPathDefault  = hmltest.hml,config.hml
Xpath       = C_Discharge,
hmltest.hml:'//hml:DataElement/hml:Item[@Name="C_Discharge"]/@Value'
Xpath       = Can_Stor, hmltest.hml:'//hml:DataElement/hml:Item[@Name="Can_Stor"]/@Value'
Xpath       = C_Prec, hmltest.hml:'//hml:DataElement/hml:Item[@Name="C_Prec"]/@Value'
Xpath       = urban, config.hml:'//hml:ParameterElement/hml:Item[@Name="urban"]/@Value'
Xpath       = grass, config.hml:'//hml:ParameterElement/hml:Item[@Name="grass"]/@Value'

#run five years simulaton with 2 yrs overlap
Xpath       = Year1, annualmax.hml:'//hml:ParameterElement/hml:Item[1]/@Name'
Xpath       = Year2, annualmax.hml:'//hml:ParameterElement/hml:Item[2]/@Name'
Xpath       = Year3, annualmax.hml:'//hml:ParameterElement/hml:Item[3]/@Name'
Xpath       = Qmax1, annualmax.hml:'//hml:ParameterElement/hml:Item[1]/@Value'
Xpath       = Qmax2, annualmax.hml:'//hml:ParameterElement/hml:Item[2]/@Value'
Xpath       = Qmax3, annualmax.hml:'//hml:ParameterElement/hml:Item[3]/@Value'
```

Fig. 1.13 An example of mcsfile used in RMCS. The information provided by mcsfile includes the SRB collection of the data, preferred machine to run the simulation jobs, and metadata information

KML itself is not good enough for representing application level metadata. WHML is therefore used for inserting metadata in the SHETRAN simulation. A single simulation could generate more than one HML file. HML is another type of XML and more suitable for describing hydrological data. The HML files in which users are interested in extracting information can be defined in the mcsfile, as shown in Fig. 1.13.

XPathDefault specifies the list of HML files from which information is extracted. Xpath then specifies the variable name, HML file names, and the XPath to extract the information from. For example, Cumulative Discharge (C_Discharge), which is the total discharge at outlet, can be extracted from hmltest.hml. The percentage of different land uses, such as urban or grass, can be extracted from config.hml.

1.4.1.3   Third Stage: Run the Simulation Jobs in Grids

Running a number of simulations jobs is straightforward. Users need to configure a RMCS job description file as shown in Fig. 1.13. More detail about the flags used in job description file is described below.

PathToExe is the path to the SRB collection where the executable file is located. In this case, this will be the SRB collection for run-SHETRAN-NGS.sh.

RDatasetID is the Rcommand data set id that maps to a collection of simulation jobs. In this project, it is the ID for each simulation scenario. Sput indicates which files will be uploaded to SRB.

In mcsfile, there are some XPath tags relating to metadata extraction. The metadata can be extracted and saved in the Rcommands server. In addition to KML for visualization, HML is used for recording metadata. In HML, <DataElementArrayDefinition> defines the metadata variables which users are interested in. For example, C_Discharge is the cumulated discharge for the catchment. In DataElementArrayDefinition, the data types, units, and descriptions to explain the meaning of variables are defined. The actual data value will then be stored in <DataElement> tag.

HML is flexible and users can define their own data type. Even simple geographical information such as the boundary of a catchment can be defined in the tag <LocationDataArray>.

RMCS now uses an XPath-based syntax to extract the metadata. For example, in order to extract the value of C_Discharge from the HML file one can add the following line in the mcsfile:

Xpath=C_Discharge,   hmltest.hml:'//hml:DataElement/hml:Item[@Name="C_ Discharge"]/@Value'

where C_Discharge is the name of the parameter or the name of the key pair value. hmltest.hml is the name of the XML file or HML file which RMCS is going to extract the data from. The rest of the line is the XPath syntax used to extract the value of C_Discharge. It means to find out the <DataElement> within HML namespace, and extract data from element <Item> when the attribute Name is C_Discharge.

After creating a mcsfile and the monty.dat that is generated by SHETRAN-inp.pl, we can create the grid proxy and upload the proxy to the NGS proxy server and launch the job submission using this command: perlmonty.

1.4.1.4   Final Stage: Query/Filtering Outputs for Data Analysis

When the RMCS jobs are finished and the metadata are inserted into the Rcommands server, one of the Rcoomands called Rgem can be used to extract the information for data analysis. The syntax is shown below:

```
Rgem -d 617 -p 5 -o tt-1
-d 617: (dataset ID)
-p: (how many parameters)
-o: (output file name)
```

In this project, Rgem is used to extract the annual maximum discharge and their corresponding years. Table 1.1 is a subset of results showing discharge data at year 3001, 3006, 3011, 3016, etc. Year2 will then records discharge data in 3002, 3007, 3012, 3017, etc. This file generated by Rgem can be read in to Excel and plot a graph.

An example of annual maximum discharge data recorded in first file.

Year1	Qmax1
3001	27.1862
3006	23.3282
3011	41.4329
3016	34.1878
3021	30.3855
3026	20.9095
3031	37.0143
3036	28.0146

1.5 Discussions

This chapter shows how to build an eScience infrastructure consisting of the intersection of a computing grid, data grid, and collaboration grid. The computing grid includes resources from NIEeS, WTSI, and NGS. Moreover, the computing grid has been extended to utilize EC2, which is a commercial cloud computing service provided by Amazon.

This data grid uses NGS SRB as the production service. The main advantage is that it can be distributed and deployed on each NGS core site. Therefore, simulation outputs can be staged to nearby storage resources, reducing failures caused by network performance.

The RMCS server is the major component in integrating computing grids, cloud computing resources, and data grids. In addition, it manages the applications or user defined metadata. The hydrological virtual experiments undertaken in this project were submitted using RMCS.

RMCS was originally developed from the *e*Minerals project. RMCS is open source and can be obtained by contact authors. However, deploy RMCS is time consuming and not an easy task even for experienced system administrators. Deploying RMCS requires knowledge of Java, Web services, Globus, SRB, Condor, network, and database administration.

The technologies used in this project were largely based on tools developed by *e*Minerals project. The *e*Minerals project was found by NERC. It brings together simulation scientists, applications developers, and computer scientists to develop UK escience/grid capabilities for molecular simulations of environmental issues. This project proves that the eScience approach used in *e*Minerals and material simulations can be applied to wider and large-scale environmental science such as hydrology.

This infrastructure has been tested via undertaking SHETRAN simulations and has been proved to work and to be useful for hydrological applications. The jobs can be executed on the grid infrastructure and outputs staged back to the SRB. Users can also define their metadata and filtering their output data.

In terms of using the cloud resources, SHETRAN application is basically high-throughput computation and we found out there is no difference comparing to use local cluster or conventional grid resources running jobs on physical machines. It may not suitable for high-performance computing jobs, which requires sharing file system and large communication between processors. This part of the study beyond the scope of this project. At this moment, for high throughput computing, it works fine. The main issue is that staging input data into the cloud may cause problems depending on the network performance. For example, most SHETRAN input files are stored in the SRB resources at RAL but the cloud computing nodes are actually in Dublin. When running a single RMCS job, it occasionally fails at the first stage when RMCS tries to stage input files from SRB. This failure hardly occurs when using local resources.

References

1. Hey T, Trefethen A (2003) e-Science and its implications. Phil. Trans. Roy Soc (A) 361:1809–1825.
2. zalay A, Gray J (2006) 2020 Computing: Science in an exponential world. Nature 440:413–414.
3. Clery D (2006) Can Grid Computing Help Us Work Together. Science 303:433–434.
4. Foster I, Kesselman C, Tuecke S (2001) The Anatomy of the Grid: Enabling Scalable Virtual Organizations. The International Journal of Supercomputer Applications 15(3):200–222.
5. Dove, M., Walker, A., White, T., Bruin, R., Austen, K., Frame, I., Chiang, GT., Murray-Rust, P., Tyer, R., Couch, P., Kleese van Dam, K., Parker, SC., Marmier, C., Arrouvel, C. Usable grid infrastructures: practical experiences from the eMinerals project. in UK e-Science All Hands Meeting. 2007. Nottingham, UK. pp. 48–55.
6. Google Trend (2010) Available via Google. {http://www.google.co.uk/trends?q=cloud+computing. Cited 10 Feb 2010}.
7. Renard P, Badoux V (2009) Grid Computing for Earth Science. Eos Trans. AGU 90(14): 117–119.
8. Anderson D (2004) BOINC: A System for Public-Resource Computing and Storage, in 5th IEEE/ACM Inernational Workshop on Grid Computing. 2004: Pittsburgh, USA.
9. Allen M (1999) Do-it-yourself climate prediction. Nature 401:642.
10. Frame DJ, Aina T, Christensen CM, Faull NE, Knight, SHE, Piani, C, Rosier, SM, Yamazaki, K, Yamazaki, Y, Allen, M (2009) The climateprediction.net BBC climate change experimnet: dedsign of the coupled model ensemble. Phil. Trans. R.Soc. A 367(1890):855–870.
11. Lawrence, B.N., Cramer, R., Gutierrez, M., Kleese van Dam, K., Kondapalli, S., Latham, S., Lowry, R., O'Neill, K., and Woolf, A. The NERC DataGrid Prototype. in UK e-Science All Hands Meeting 2003. Notingham, UK. http://ndg.nerc.ac.uk/public_docs/AHM-2003-BNL.pdf.
12. Gahegana, M., Luob, J., Weaver, S.D., Pike, W., Banchuenb, T., (2009) *Connecting GEON: Making sense of the myriad resources, researchers and concepts that comprise a geoscience cyberinfrastructure.* Computers & Geosciences 35: pp. 836–854.
13. Dove M, De Leeuw NH (2005) Grid computing and molecular simulations: the vision of the eMinerals project. Molecular Simulation 31(5):297–301.

14. Mechoso C, Ma C-C, Farrara J, Spahr J, Moore R (1993) Parallization and distribution of a coupled atmosphere-ocean general circulation model. Monthly Weather Review 121:2062
15. Saltelli A, Ratoo M, Andres T, Campolongo F, Cariboni J, Gatelli D, Saisana M, Tarantola S (2008) Global Sensitivity Analysis. In: Saltelli A (ed) Global Sensitivity Analysis, John Willey & Sons, New York.
16. Papakhian, M., (1998) *Comparing Job-Management Systems: The User's Perspective.* IEEE Computational Science & Engineering 5(2): pp. 4–9.
17. Thain D, Tannenbaum T, Livny M (2005) Distributed Computing in Practice: The Condor Experience. Concurrency - Practice and Experience 17(2–4):323–356.
18. Foster I, Kesselman C (1997) Globus:A Metacomputing Infrastructure Tookit. International Journal of Supercomputer Applications 11(2):115–128.
19. Butler R, Engert D, Foster I, Kesselman I, Tuecke S (2000) A National-Scale Authentication Infrastructure. IEEE Computer 33(12):60–66.
20. Montero, R.S., Huedo, E., Llorente, I.M., (2006) *Grid Scheduling Infrastucture based on the GridWay Meta-scheduler.* IEEE Technical Committee on Scalable Computing (TCSC).
21. Bruin R, White TOH, Walker AM, Austen KF, Dove MT, Tyer RP, Couch PA, Todorov IT, Blanchard MO (2006) Job submission to grid computing environment. in UK e-Science All Hands Meeting 2006. Nottingham, UK. pp. 754–761.
22. Bruin R (2006) Development of a grid computing infrastructure to support combinatorial simulation studies of pollutant organic molecules on mineral surfaces, PhD Thesis, Department of Earth Sciences, University of Cambridge.
23. Couch, P., Sherwood, P., Sufi, S., Todorov, I., Allan, R., Knowles, P., Bruin, R., Dove, M., and Murray-rust, P. Towards data integration for computational chemistry. in UK e-Science All Hands Meeting 2005. Nottingham, UK pp. 19–22.
24. Chervenak A, Foster I, Kesselman C, Salisbury C, Tuecke S (2001) The Data Grid: Towards and Architecture for the Distributed Management and Analysis of Large Scientific Datasets. Journal of Network and Computer Applications 23:187–200.
25. Baru, C., Moore, R., Rajasekar, A., Wan, M. The SDSC Storage Resource Broker. in IBM Toronto Centre for Advanced Studies Conference (CASCON'98) 1998. Toronto, Canada pp. 1–12. https://www-927.ibm.com/ibm/cas/cascon/welcome.shtml
26. Ewen J, Parkin G, O'Connell PE (2000) SHETRAN: distributed river basin flow and transport modeling system. American Society of Civil Engineers Journal of Hydrologic Engineering 5(3):250–258.
27. Chiang G-T, White TO, Dove MT, Bovolo CI, Ewen J (2011) Geo-visualization Fortran Library. Computers & Geosciences, doi:10.1016/j.cageo.2010.04.012
28. Chiang G-T, White TO, Dove MT (2009) Geospatial visualization tool kit for scientists using Fortran. Eos Trans. AGU 90(29):249–250.

Chapter 2
The German Grid Initiative D-Grid: Current State and Future Perspectives

Stefan Freitag and Philipp Wieder

Abstract The D-Grid is a German national academic Grid initiative, which has been established in 2004. Since then, a variety of resource providers offer resources and services to a large and heterogeneous group of user communities. First, this chapter describes in detail the D-Grid e-Infrastructure as it is operated today. Apart from a brief historical digression, D-Grid's organizational structure and its infrastructure are introduced, complemented by the description of two example user communities. Based on the current state, this chapter then provides a discussion on how D-Grid's future may look like with virtualization and Cloud computing striding ahead. To this end, a prototype system with coexisting Grid and Cloud middleware is introduced, challenges at resource level are identified, and possible solutions are highlighted. Furthermore, the integration of state-of-the-art service level management, which enables D-Grid providers to guarantee distinct service levels, is discussed.

2.1 Introduction

Countries like the United Kingdom or the United States of America have started Grid initiatives in the late 1990s or early 2000s, as researchers as well as funding agencies were back then already aware of the need for large-scale distributed computing infrastructures. In 1999, for example, the Particle Physics Data Grid was

S. Freitag (✉)
Robotic Research Institute, TU Dortmund University, Otto-Hahn-Strasse 8,
44227 Dortmund, Germany
e-mail: stefan.freitag@tu-dortmund.de

P. Wieder
Service Computing Group, TU Dortmund University, August-Schmidt-Strasse 12,
44227 Dortmund, Germany
e-mail: philipp.wieder@udo.edu

Xiaoyu Yang et al. (eds.), *Guide to e-Science: Next Generation Scientific Research and Discovery*, Computer Communications and Networks, DOI 10.1007/978-0-85729-439-5_2, © Springer-Verlag London Limited 2011

brought into existence and still does exist as part of the Open Science Grid.[1] Four years later Germany was still missing an initiative focused on providing a uniform, national Grid infrastructure [1]. As a consequence, D-Grid was established in 2004. Now, in 2010, it is time to look back, analyze the overall development of D-Grid, and identify future challenges. This chapter addresses Cloud computing and quality-of-service (QoS) provisioning, two of the identified technical challenges. Another technical but also political challenge arose with the end of the phase 3 of the European Enabling Grids for e-Science[2] (EGEE) initiative and its transition toward the European Grid Initiative[3] (EGI). D-Grid with its services and infrastructure and the regional successor of EGI for Germany, the National Grid initiative Deutschland (NGI-DE), have to be consolidated into a single national Grid initiative. Problems of this consolidation are also outlined.

2.2   History of D-Grid

In 2004, a joint venture between German research and industry led to the establishment of the German Grid initiative called D-Grid.[4] One of D-Grid's major objectives is the creation and operation of an e-Science infrastructure in Germany. According to Hegering [1], D-Grid envisioned to change the paradigms for scientific work and collaboration. Apart from the availability of heterogeneous resources, remotely accessible independent of their geographic position and ownership, the plan has foreseen the creation of an organizational structure where virtual organizations span across multiple institutions and include researchers from various disciplines.

Prior to actually starting phase 1 of D-Grid, all academic stakeholders have been questioned and a thorough requirements analysis has been done. This is the reason why D-Grid supports a multitude of middlewares and services. The resulting environment has been complemented by an operational and administrative structure which later projects could build upon.

During D-Grid's phase 1, which last from 2005 to 2008 (as depicted in Fig. 2.1), it provided mainly IT services for academia, designed and developed by early adopters of the Grid communities. The focus in phase 2, however, was on the integration of additional IT services for a broader community including academia and industry.

In the current phase 3, the existing resource and service offerings serve as the foundation for the development of a management and operation layer that includes service level management, knowledge management, and virtual competence centers.

---

[1] http://www.opensciencegrid.org/

[2] http://public.eu-egee.org/

[3] http://www.egi.eu/

[4] http://www.d-grid.de/

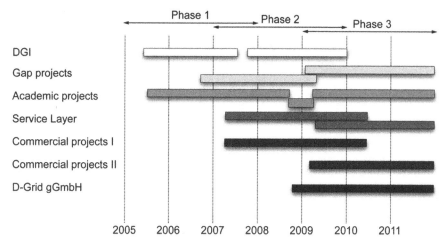

Fig. 2.1 Timeline of D-Grid and its projects

Academic and commercial projects continue operation and, in addition, so-called gap projects close open issues that were revealed in the first two phases of D-Grid. Figure 2.1 depicts the timeline for the phases 3 and the different types of started projects. An interesting point to be noted is the end of the D-Grid Integration Project (DGI), which is responsible for the integration of the projects' developments as well as overall operational issues, in 2010, while the projects of phase 3 continue until 2012.

2.3   Organizational Structure

The D-Grid landscape comprises several stakeholders. On the one hand, there are user communities organized in virtual organizations (we describe selected communities in Sect. 2.4) and on the other hand, resource centers build the resource foundation to support these virtual organizations (the D-Grid infrastructure is detailed in Sect. 2.5).

Before we approach the user communities, we introduce two outstanding stakeholders, namely the D-Grid gGmbH[5] and the D-Grid Integration Project. They both provide services for the various users, projects and resource providers, and they both act as interfaces to other national and international initiatives.

In addition to the two major groups of stakeholders, the D-Grid gGmbH and the DGI, several D-Grid boards and committees have been established over time. Within the phase 1 of D-Grid, a steering committee decided on the direction of

---

[5] A gGmbH is a nonprofit company with limited liability.

D-Grid. This committee consisted of representatives from each D-Grid project and members of the D-Grid Integration Project. At the end of D-Grid's phase 1, the steering committee became the D-Grid advisory board, which now counsels the D-Grid gGmbH in coordinating the different D-Grid activities.

2.3.1 The D-Grid gGmbH

In 2008, the D-Grid gGmbH was established. Its task is the coordination of the activities across the numerous D-Grid projects by identifying potential synergies and by initiating cooperation between the projects. A currently ongoing effort, for example, is the support of user communities in implementing business models and hence in creating sustainable infrastructures for the community-at-large. Moreover, the D-Grid gGmbH is responsible for public relations and for the international representation of D-Grid.

2.3.2 The D-Grid Integration Project

The D-Grid Integration Project focuses on the dissemination, integration, and bundling of the results acquired in the communities into a common and sustainable D-Grid platform.[6] The DGI is also responsible for generating quality-of-service (QoS) in terms of stability, reliability, and sustainability for this platform. In the long run, this will enable German e-Science communities to use D-Grid as a service. Additionally, DGI supports user communities with respect to platform-related issues and defines D-Grid's operational concept [2], that is, recommendations for the operation of compute and storage resources.

2.4 Selected User Communities

In the beginning of D-Grid, only a few communities, for example, from astrophysics, high-energy physics, and climate research communicated their demand for Grid technologies. Apart from these pure academic communities, others with strong industrial participation, like the financial business Grid or the media Grid, formed up in the second and phase 3 of D-Grid.

In the next section we describe the AstroGrid-D user community, a community characteristic for phase 1 of D-Grid, while Sect. 2.4.2 introduces one industrial use case that is in the focus of more recent D-Grid developments.

---

[6] A combination of compute, network, and storage resources including Grid middleware layers and value-added services.

2.4.1   AstroGrid-D

In AstroGrid-D, German astronomy institutes and supercomputing centers formed jointly an interdisciplinary partnership with the aim to create a Grid-based infrastructure for astronomical and astrophysical research. In case of AstroGrid-D not only geographically distributed compute and storage resources (e.g., distributed astronomical data archives) have to integrated into the Grid infrastructure, but also special hardware like remote-controlled radio telescopes, robotic telescopes, or gravitational wave detectors. Among the multitude of applications, we introduce here two specifically to show the spectrum covered by AstroGrid-D:

- GEO600[7] is a gravitational wave detector with an arm length of 600m contributing to the Laser Interferometer Gravitational Wave Observatory (LIGO). Since LIGO started its operation in 2005, it continuously measures data that is then filtered and analyze to search for potential signal patterns of gravitational wave sources.
- The Planck Process Coordinator (ProC) is a scientific workflow engine used within the Planck Surveyor project.[8] To utilize the D-Grid infrastructure, ProC interfaces with the Grid Application Toolkit (GAT[9]). GAT allows the submission of jobs to available resources, for example, via Globus Toolkit 2 (i.e., GRAM2), Globus Toolkit 4 (i.e., WS-GRAM), and gLite adapters as shown in Fig. 2.2, but also to plain cluster resources managed by batch systems like PBS or SGE.

The AstroGrid-D community also supports other research institutes newly entering the Grid to enable them to share their resources and make use of the compute and data resources already available in AstroGrid-D. This support activity forms a subtask for achieving the long-term goal of a framework for the collaborative management of astronomy-specific Grid resources within the D-Grid.

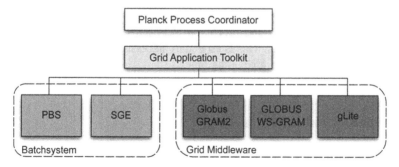

Fig. 2.2 ProC interface to job submission back-ends

---

[7] http://www.geo600.org/

[8] http://www.sciops.esa.int/index.php?project=PLANCK

[9] http://www.gridlab.org/WorkPackages/wp-1/

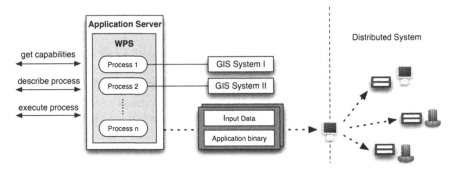

Fig. 2.3 An architectural overview of the Web Processing Service (WPS) and its integration [3]

2.4.2 Geospatial Data Processing

The D-Grid project SLA4D-Grid (Service Level Agreements for D-Grid[10]) features a multitude of geographical data processing use cases. Therefore, the Grid infrastructure provided by D-Grid is the basis for a set of specific services used inter alia for disaster prevention and recovery, or for planning purposes.

According to Fig. 2.3 a Web Processing Service (WPS), implemented following to the Open Geospatial Consortium's[11] WPS specification, offers a number of processes to end users while itself using other legacy Geo Information Systems (GISs) or third-party libraries. For executing a process, the respective input data together with the application binary is transferred via a gateway to the distributed system where the process is executed in parallel on a number of nodes. Once finished, the WPS fetches all results, concatenates them, and sends them to the end user.

Within the SLA4D-Grid project, the existing geographical data infrastructure will be extended with service level agreement (SLA) capabilities and integrated with the D-Grid service stack. Through this integration, it is possible for users and providers of geospatial data and processing services to negotiate and agree on quality-of-service parameters. This is especially necessary to offer customers reliable services and guaranteed processing times.

2.5 The D-Grid Infrastructure

The D-Grid infrastructure, as used by the various user communities, consists of heterogeneous resources distributed across the country and located mostly at research facilities and universities. In 2009, the total number of CPU cores available

---

[10] http://www.sla4d-grid.de/

[11] http://www.opengeospatial.org/

to D-Grid users exceeded 30,000 and the storage capacity reached approximately five PetaByte [4, 5]. In the beginning of D-Grid, the resources belonged either to the communities themselves or to the participating HPC centers. From 2006 to 2008, the Federal Ministry of Education and Research (BMBF) then funded additional compute, network, and storage hardware and thus supported the setup of the D-Grid core infrastructure. These special resources are subject to special requirements, as they have to:

- Support all D-Grid virtual organizations
- Support at least one Grid middleware out of gLite,[12] Globus,[13] and UNICORE[14]
- Prioritize D-Grid users, although resource usage by other users is allowed

Figure 2.4 shows the accumulated CPU hours (CPUh on the y-axis) consumed by D-Grid users on all compute resources during the time period from July 2008 to December 2009. The trend line shows the increasing accumulated usage of the Grid resources and with AstroGrid-D and bwGRID[15] the two major consumers of CPU hours are identified. For the first half of 2010, D-Grid estimates more than 75 million consumed CPU hours resulting in an overall utilization level of about 50%. An interesting fact is the absence of the high-energy physicists' community in the top ranks. Since years this community distinguishes itself by high resource demand, but until today this community was unable to or disinterested in utilizing D-Grid for their purposes.

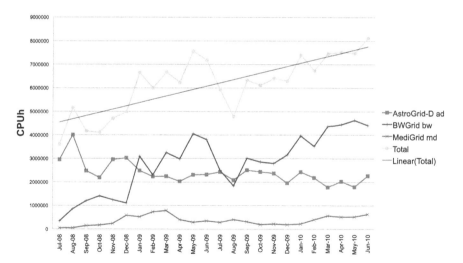

Fig. 2.4 Consumption of CPU hours by D-Grid virtual organizations (July 2008–June 2010)

---

[12] http://glite.web.cern.ch/glite/

[13] http://www.globus.org/toolkit/

[14] http://www.unicore.eu/

[15] http://www.bw-grid.de/, a regional Grid in Baden-Württemberg, Germany.

2.5.1   Central Services

The D-Grid service infrastructure is split up into central services, community services, and site-specific services. Most of the central services (see Table 2.1) are set up redundantly at two different physical locations and comprise all mandatory gLite, Globus Toolkit, and UNICORE services, including the gLite workload management system, the Globus MDS4 information system, and the UNICORE 6 registry.

In addition to these services, the DGI developed services for the resource and user registration. The resource registration in D-Grid is handled by the Grid Resource Registration Service (GRRS). Resources with interest to participate have to supply access information together with a host certificate for each Grid middleware offered. The GRRS also allows virtual organizations to modify the list of usable resources (e.g., to avoid using resources with inacceptable usage policies) and providers to ban virtual organizations from their resources.

A service strongly coupled with the GRRS is the so-called dgridmap service. For all resources, it provides information about the mapping from virtual organization members to local user accounts. Such a mechanism was required, since neither the Globus Toolkit nor the UNICORE middleware could interface directly with the virtual organizations' VOMRS[16] servers that are usually deployed to deliver this kind of information.

To summarize, community and D-Grid core resources have – depending on the supported Grid middleware – three options to retrieve authorization information for virtual organization members: (1) the VOMRS server, (2) the VOMS server,[17] or (3) the dgridmap service.

Apart from the central services denoted in Table 2.1, additional services are available in D-Grid. This includes the DGUS (D-Grid User Support) helpdesk that serves as a communication interface between resource providers and D-Grid users. If users experience problems in using a resource they create a trouble ticket that is assigned to and processed by the corresponding resource provider. At present, the

Table 2.1   D-Grid central services

Service	Location	Service	Location
GRRS	Juelich	DGUS helpdesk	Karlsruhe
VOMRS	Juelich, Karlsruhe	VOMS	Juelich, Karlsruhe
MDS4	Karlsruhe, Munich	WebMDS	Karlsruhe, Munich
gLite TopBDII	Juelich, Karlsruhe	gLite workload management	Juelich, Karlsruhe
UNICORE 6 CIS	Juelich	UNICORE registry	Juelich, Karlsruhe
Nagios	Karlsruhe	D-MON	Munich

---

[16] VO Membership Registration Service, see http://www.fnal.gov/docs/products/vomrs/.

[17] Required for gLite services and periodically synchronized with VOMRS.

DGUS portal is in the process of being replaced by the NGI-DE helpdesk portal that is the consolidation of the DECH Support portal of the former EGEE project and DGUS.

Furthermore, the D-Grid resources are monitored by a Nagios[18] service. Periodically the Nagios service probes, for example, the availability of a Grid middleware service endpoint, successful job execution, and data transfers. The results of the tests are available on a D-Grid Web site[19] and can be used for the automated creation of trouble tickets.

2.5.2   D-Grid Reference System

The plan to create a reference system for D-Grid resources came up in 2007, since a concise set of recommended middleware services, including up-to-date and verified installation and configuration instructions, which D-Grid resource users could rely on, was missing.

In close cooperation with the high-energy physicists' community, the DGI developed and implemented a prototype [6] being the predecessor of the reference system. This prototype supported the job submission to the middlewares gLite 3.0, Globus Toolkit 4.0.3, and UNICORE 5 with the same local resource management system on the back-end. The initial support for the three middlewares was mandatory, because most virtual organizations had not yet decided which of the middleware stacks to use and D-Grid wanted to enable all communities to access the compute resources. For the same reason, the reference system contains also three storage middlewares: dCache,[20] OGSA-DAI,[21] and the Storage Resource Broker.[22]

The integration of the three middlewares into a single cluster made the analysis of possible restrictions necessary. A popular example in this case is the strong dependency of the gLite on Scientific Linux as underlying operating system for the batch system worker nodes. Nevertheless, the first operating systems included in the reference system were Scientific Linux and SuSE Enterprise Linux, because D-Grid's Globus experts recommended a SuSE-based operating system to run the middleware on. In the latest release of the reference system,[23] Scientific Linux replaced SuSE Enterprise Linux completely, so that all nodes included in a reference system run the same operating system.

---

[18] http://www.nagios.org/

[19] https://sitemon.d-grid.de/nagios/

[20] http://www.dcache.org/

[21] http://www.ogsadai.org.uk/

[22] http://www.sdsc.edu/srb/index.php/Main_Page

[23] http://dgiref.d-grid.de

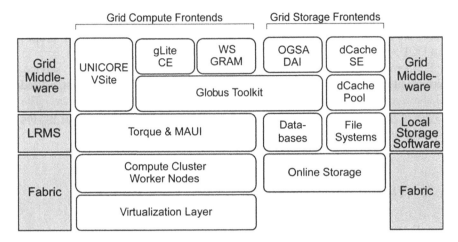

Fig. 2.5 Overview on the software layers of the D-Grid reference system

Table 2.2 Currently supported compute and storage middleware versions

Compute middleware	Version	Storage middleware	Version
gLite	3.1 and 3.2	dCache	1.9.5
Globus	4.0.8 and 4.2	OGSA-DAI	2.2
UNICORE	6.3		

The setup of the reference system is targeted at smaller and medium resource centers that have only limited expertise in Grid computing and commodity hardware.[24] An overview of the different layers of the software at the D-Grid reference system is given in Fig. 2.5. The virtualization layer underneath the batch system worker nodes is optional. Not shown in the figure is the interactive node that allows a login via gsiSSH.[25] The current release of the reference installation contains the Grid middleware version shown in Table 2.2.

On February 2009, the D-Grid advisory board decided to establish a new board responsible for the technical development and issues related to the reference system (and hence of D-Grid). The D-Grid Technical Advisory Board (TAB) consists of eight members: three resource providers, three D-Grid community representative, one member of the D-Grid Integration Project, and one WissGrid[26] member. One of the goals of TAB is the harmonization of the supported and installed middleware version at all D-Grid resources.

---

[24] Experiences at the TU Dortmund University have shown that of the proposed setup for reference systems scales up to 2,000 cores.

[25] Grid security infrastructure-enabled SSH.

[26] http://www.wissgrid.de/index_en.html

2.6   Challenges and Prospects of a Future D-Grid

The D-Grid environment as it is in operation today follows the original Grid paradigm as coined by Foster [7]: Resources are shared and de-centrally managed, standard and open protocols and interfaces are used, and the D-Grid delivers non-trivial services to its community. Although there is demand for these services and multiple applications are developed on their basis, the structure of the D-Grid is exposed to forces which make new concepts and the introduction of new technologies inevitable. Whether such changes are of benefit to the D-Grid community is difficult to judge and such a discussion is not the focus of this section. Though the focus of distributed system research and development undeniable points toward virtualized IT environments, Cloud-like service provisioning (often referred to XaaS – Everything as a Service), and novel business models. In the course of this development, guarantees regarding the quality of the services provided are becoming an ever-greater focus of attention. Therefore, it is now time for D-Grid to evaluate these new paradigms and concepts in order to plan the future of the German academic Grid environment. In the following sections, we provide this evaluation on a general not technically detailed level, focusing on Cloud-like resource usage and the introduction of quality-of-service guarantees within D-Grid.

2.6.1   Cloud Computing

Cloud computing emerged in 2007 as an enabling technology in the commercial sector. It utilizes virtualization and a pay-per-use business model to offer customers flexible ways for resource leasing. Since 2007 the concept got mature, a multitude of products appeared on the market with a significant amount of research projects paving the way for new methodologies and services. Nevertheless, Cloud computing still lacks a commonly accepted definition. Vaquero et al. compared in [8] various Cloud definitions to identify a least common denominator. This comparison provided no clear result, but many definitions mentioned three characteristics: scalability, virtualization, and a pay-per-use model.

Similar to the distinction in Grid computing, we distinguish between Compute and Storage Clouds. Additionally to this, Compute Clouds subdivide into three types:

- Software-as-a-Service (SaaS) Clouds

SaaS providers maintain software in a cloud infrastructure and make it available to customers via a network (usually the Internet). Hence, the customer no longer needs a local installation of the software, which most likely results in a reduction of the operational expenditure.

• Platform-as-a-Service (PaaS) Clouds

PaaS customers have access to software platforms and develop on top of them their own services. An advantage of PaaS usage is that customers can access provider tools (e.g., for billing) and do not need to develop them on their own.

• Infrastructure-as-a-Service (IaaS) Clouds

Customers request infrastructure (like compute, storage, or network) via interfaces like Amazon's Elastic Compute Cloud (EC2[27]) or the Open Cloud computing Interface (OCCI) [9]. To keep pace with changing customer demands, Cloud providers make use of virtualization technology for the dynamic reconfiguration of their unused capacities [10].

D-Grid has to identify effects of this new concept for resource and service provisioning in context of its major goal: building and offering a sustainable e-Science infrastructure for education and research. The access to this e-Science infrastructure and its use should be simple and transparent. Compared to Grid, Cloud computing seems a viable alternative for several reasons, two of which are of major importance for D-Grid:

• The interface to Compute and Storage Clouds is easy to understand and to use. Commercial providers like Amazon already offer plug-ins for web browsers (e.g., ElasticFox[28]) that allow the management of instances, mounting of Elastic Block Storage[29] volumes and the mapping of Elastic IP addresses.
• Compute Clouds often use platform, storage, and network virtualization to allow a fine-grained sharing of the physical resources. From the users' point of view, platform virtualization allows them to start their own virtual appliances, resulting in a uniform execution environment if applied across different resources. At present, Grid computing cannot supply this uniform environment as users must analyze the environment on each Grid resource and adapt their software to this environment.

To compare the benefits of a Cloud middleware to existing Grid middlewares and to evaluate ways for their coexistence on a single resource, the D-Grid Resource Centre Ruhr[30] (DGRZR) was modified to offer Grid as well as Cloud interfaces to its users. The Grid services provided by DGRZR include the recommended reference system middlewares as well as dCache and OGSA-DAI Grid storage middlewares, all running in virtual machines.

Parallel to these Grid middlewares and additional services required for user management and databases, the Compute Cloud middleware OpenNebula 1.4[31]

---

[27] http://aws.amazon.com/de/ec2/

[28] http://sourceforge.net/projects/elasticfox/

[29] http://aws.amazon.com/de/ebs/

[30] DGRZR commenced operations in April 2008 and currently offers ~2,000 compute cores and 125 Terabyte of mass storage to D-Grid users.

[31] http://opennebula.org/

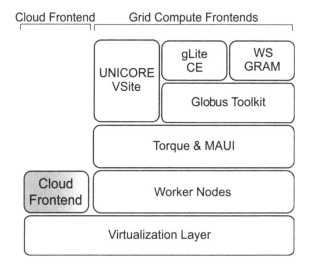

Fig. 2.6 Cloud-enabled software stack at D-Grid Resource Centre Ruhr (DGRZR)

(ONE) has been installed. ONE offers two interfaces for user interaction, one based on the Elastic Compute Cloud API and one based on the Open Cloud computing Interface specification.

Figure 2.6 shows the layered architecture of DGRZR after the installation of ONE. In contrast to the Grid middleware services, ONE (denominated "Cloud Frontend" in Fig. 2.6) is located directly on top of the virtualization layer.

The evaluation of ONE identified several open issues for the integration of a Compute Cloud middleware into the D-Grid software stack. These issues affect authentication, user management, the information system, and accounting.

2.6.1.1 Authentication

In terms of authentication ONE follows the key player in Cloud computing, Amazon. There, a user requires a valid combination of an access and a secret key before he or she can access the Cloud to upload his or her virtual appliances or execute remote commands via Cloud interfaces. In ONE, the access key corresponds to the users name in the ONE database[32] and the secret key is a password chosen by the user.

Users coming from the context of Grid computing are most likely not familiar with this access method. They are used to X.509 certificates, proxies, and proxy delegation. Those mechanisms were introduced in Grid computing to enable

---

[32] All information about users, execution hosts, and virtual machines is stored in a single database.

single-sign-on, since Grid users usually do not know at which resources their jobs are executed. This implies that for Grid users – organized in virtual organizations like in D-Grid – to use Cloud middleware, the most seamless mechanism would be support Grid-like authentication mechanisms, similar to the ones in Grid computing middlewares, via the Cloud API.

Although we consider further issues high on the agenda, like the attribute-based mapping of users as it is used in Grid computing, we see X.509-based authentication for Cloud resources as most important to ease the transition from Grid-based D-Grid to one operated in a Cloud-like fashion.

2.6.1.2   User Management

The way user information is stored in ONE and D-Grid differs substantially. ONE stores user information in a database that is held locally on the Compute Cloud resource. There, ONE classifies users in two categories: the super user called oneadmin and all others. Latter ones are created by oneadmin and are only allowed to manage resources belonging to or registered by themselves. In contrast to this, oneadmin is able to manage all objects (as there are virtual appliances, networks, hosts, and users) present in OpenNebula.

In D-Grid, all resources connect to a service central to the virtual organization, that is, a VOMRS server, and retrieve from there the list of VO members. Then, a service on the resource itself creates based on the list and local account information a file that contains the mapping from the Grid user X.509 certificate[33] to one or more local accounts.

2.6.1.3   Information System

The D-MON software collects and aggregates information from the D-Grid resources, thus serving as an information system. For this purpose, D-MON connects via adapters to the information systems CIS (UNICORE), MDS4 (Globus Toolkit), and BDII (gLite). Their output is filtered and presented to users in dynamic virtual organization specific views. Figure 2.7 shows the simplified layout of the software.

If Cloud resources become part of D-Grid, a new adapter is required. The information collected from a Compute Cloud resource may include the supported hard disk image formats (e.g., AMI or VMDK), available virtual appliances, pricing information, and hardware capabilities. In general, such an integration does not present a task related to the inclusion of Cloud middleware into a Grid environment, but it introduces the common problems when integrating different information representations (like already experienced in D-Grid through integrating three middlewares).

---

[33] The Distinguished Name (DN) of the X.509 certificate is used.

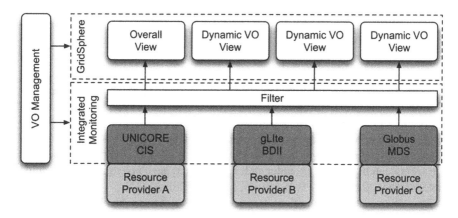

Fig. 2.7 Overview of the D-MON architecture

Table 2.3 Excerpt of the history table of one.db

vid	host name	stime	etime	pstime	petime
13	2313	1258384216	1258384219	1258384216	1258384219
12	1107	1258384210	1258384247	1258384210	1258384244

2.6.1.4   Accounting

Compute and storage accounting are important services in a Grid, not only for providers but also for virtual organizations. Accounting data is, for example, exploited to see what costs incur through the usage of resources. For the accounting of CPU hours, necessary information is attained from the log files of the batch system servers. This approach requires that all jobs are processed at batch system level. For the Cloud middleware this assumption is not valid, as jobs (i.e., virtual appliances) do not start at the level of the batch system, but at fabric level.

ONE lacks an accounting service, but with the information provided in the database one. db such a service can be realized. Combining the information from several database tables (e.g., from the history table as shown in Table 2.3, and the vm_attributes table) should be sufficient to generate the necessary accounting information. This includes inter alia information about the start time (stime), the termination time (etime) of the virtual appliances as well as the time for execution of the prolog (petime–pstime), all of which can be retrieved from the history table.

In D-Grid, accounting of compute resources is carried out by the Distributed Grid Accounting System (DGAS). To generate job-specific accounting data, a local DGAS service parses the batch system's accounting logs and publishes them in the Open Grid Forum Usage Record (OGF-UR) [11] format. For compatibility with D-Grid the accounting information generated from the ONE database must also be transformed to the UR format.

2.6.2   Quality-Of-Service Guarantees Through Service Level Agreements

The notion of an agreement on service quality was first developed by utility provides, like energy companies, and telecommunications providers. An agreement provides a contractual frame in which customer relationships are managed. According to [12], the TeleManagement Forum's SLA Handbook defines a service level agreement as "[a] formal negotiated agreement between two parties, sometimes called a service level guarantee. […], it is a contract (or part of one) that exists between the service provider and the customer, designed to create a common understanding about services, priorities, responsibilities, etc."

From there, a common notion of a service level agreement has been established throughout industry. SLAs are used to map business-level objectives to services and allow for proper monitoring and reporting. This is not limited to businesses, but to any consumer–provider relationship, for example in D-Grid between compute resource provider and application user, where automated management of SLAs is a key requirement for many application scenarios. This includes the initiation of an SLA between two parties, the provisioning of the service, and the monitoring of the SLA while a service is provided until the completion or termination of a service delivery.

The project responsible in D-Grid to develop solutions for quality-of-service provisioning is SLA4D-Grid. The primary objective of SLA4D-Grid is the design and realization of a service level agreement layer for the D-Grid infrastructure. This layer is situated between the D-Grid middleware and the D-Grid community layer and is integrated into the existing D-Grid infrastructure (as shown in Fig. 2.8). Communities may either use the SLA layer via SLA-enabled clients or through direct interfaces.

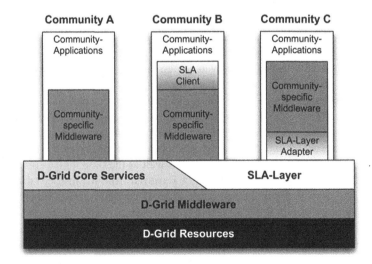

Fig. 2.8 Integration of the service level agreement (SLA) layer into D-Grid

The SLA layer is a value-added service and does not interfere with the present use of the D-Grid, nor does it require changes in communities that do not yet have a need for SLAs.

The service level agreement layer offers individual users, whole D-Grid communities, and the providers of D-Grid resources service usage under given guarantees, quality-of-service requirements, and predefined business conditions. For this purpose, service level requests and the corresponding offers are linked by service level agreements. By means of the SLA layer and with the assistance of other D-Grid services, such as monitoring and accounting, SLAs can be automatically created, negotiated, and their observance monitored, so that academic and industrial customers can use the D-Grid in an economically efficient manner and in accordance with their respective business models.

2.6.2.1 Requirements for Service Level Agreements in D-Grid

Based on the analysis of the D-Grid communities' applications and project use cases, requirements for the development, implementation, and deployment of a service level agreement framework have been gathered. The evaluation of these requirements revealed that in addition to generic requirements, which are more driven by the fact that QoS guarantees are needed than the actual use case-specific demands, the handling, incorporation, and adaptability of domain-specific requirements is of utmost importance.

The remainder of this section details a number of the most important requirements that are essential to integrate service level management capabilities into a large-scale national Grid environment.

Standard Protocols and Demand for (Negotiation)

A number of specifications, frameworks, and standards for defining, negotiating, executing, monitoring, and assessing service level agreements are available. This includes ITIL/ISO 20000 [13], the Web Service Level Agreement (WSLA) language [14], or Web Services Agreement (WSAG) [15]. To ensure interoperability with existing solutions, a standardized solution or de facto standard is required. The analysis of the applications scenarios also revealed that some require negotiation based on complex business objectives or the renegotiation of existing agreements.

Support for Different Application Domains with Individual Vocabularies

In addition to support common service level management functions like SLA template discovery or agreement negotiation, the SLA layer also has to support domain-specific vocabularies. Therefore, it is necessary to have an extensible specification for service level agreements, which allows the integration of domain-specific solutions without corrupting the generic interoperability. To achieve this, a set of service properties and quality-of-service parameters has to be defined to cover the majority of application scenarios. This set is then extended through communities or other D-Grid stakeholders that want to offer QoS qualities for their services.

Extensibility and Revision of SLA Templates

Experience from projects developing SLA-based solutions shows that it is not possible to automatically process "free-form" service level agreements which do not comply to certain formalisms known to both consumer and provider. Therefore, SLAs are in general based on templates, most often provided as XML Schema documents. These schemata have to be defined with adaptability and extensibility in mind, since templates change their characteristics in accordance with varying service offers or the assessment of the service and SLA life cycle. This leads to revisions of the templates over the history of a service offer.

Orchestration of Domain-Specific and Generic Services

Different application domains often share common requirements, such as the need to reserve resources or demand for long-term storage. Such requirements are best encapsulated into separate service offers which then are orchestrated to fulfill the quality-of-service negotiated between consumer and provider.

Scalability

Scalability in general and in a distributed Grid environment in particular is of utmost importance. Scalability requirements also have implications on service level management, assuming that at some point in the future every job submission in a distributed environment is governed by a service level agreement. Potential instruments to encounter these issues include massively parallel SLA negotiations and the negotiation of long-term framework contracts between consumers and providers to prevent large numbers of micro-negotiations.

Assessment of Agreements

Service level agreements can contain commission or penalties for SLA fulfillment or violation, respectively. Therefore, it is necessary to monitor service provision and to assess the monitoring data in accordance with the service level agreed.

Integration with D-Grid Central Services

The service level agreement layer has to realize the interfaces necessary to integrate with the central D-Grid services like monitoring, information provision, or VO management (see also Sect. 2.5.1). This task is complex, due to both the heterogeneous environment based on three middlewares, and the mere number of services, which have potentially overlapping functions and various underlying technologies.

2.6.2.2 Technological Foundations

The basic service stack D-Grid is based on the three different middleware products which are equally supported and are complemented by a number of central services required for most usage scenarios, including data management, monitoring, and VO management. The middleware is deployed on a large number of resources that are spread across Germany.

To enable this basic service stack with service level agreements, we rely on standards, existing results from European research projects such as BEinGRID, BREIN, and NextGRID, national German projects such as FinGrid and InGRID, and open source service implementations for SLA registries, SLA negotiation, and SLA-based resource planning. Those technologies are complemented by D-Grid specific extensions and service customizations to enable a maximum of business usage scenarios. The SLA stack is designed following service-oriented principles, realized through Web Services and implemented in Java.

The foundation of the SLA layer is a generic D-Grid service level agreement based on the WS-Agreement standard [15]. WS-Agreements have been chosen due to the interoperability requirement, its wide adoption within the Grid community [16], and the mature state of the specification within the standardization process. This generic SLA is specified taking the requirements from multiple heterogeneous user groups into account. Based on this generic SLA domain-specific ones are developed, for example, for the aforementioned business use case.

2.6.2.3 A Service Level Agreement Layer for D-Grid

The SLA management layer covers the complete SLA life cycle, including SLA design, contract establishment, SLA provisioning, and SLA monitoring [17]. As mentioned before, the SLA management layer is an add-on to the existing D-Grid infrastructure. It therefore has to interoperate seamlessly with the given infrastructure. Applications and users that want to make use of the new SLA features can use them in two ways. First, there will be a separate SLA client that allows the establishment of SLAs independent of the application that will later on make use of the negotiated SLAs. Second, applications can use a dedicated application programming interface (API) that allows easy use of the functions of the SLA management layer. Regarding, for example, the geospatial data processing infrastructure described in Sect. 2.4.2, the API will be exploited to achieve reliable and assessable quality-of-service guarantees such as maximum response time or potential indemnities for undelivered services.

The developments consist of two different kinds of artifacts. On the one hand, there are models and definitions for the actual service level agreements. On the other hand, there are components constituting the SLA layer.

The main output of the development of SLA models and definitions are term definitions and sample SLAs. Term definitions allow the unambiguous specification of particular quality-of-service aspects in SLAs. There will be generic terms that are to be used in various application domains, including terms about payments, penalties, etc. On the other hand, terms specific to the addressed application domains will be specified. Although these can be reused in other environments as well, their applicability is more restricted than that of the generic terms.

Sample SLAs will be developed in the form of SLA templates, which are used as the basis for negotiation and can be seen as proposals for actual SLAs. The open fields will be filled in during negotiation resulting in an actual SLA. SLA templates can also serve as best-practice examples for its intended as well as other domains.

The functions offered by the SLA management layer are as described in the following and pictured in Fig. 2.9. They are realized either as services accessible via Web Services interfaces or as components that are linked to applications locally.

The SLA negotiation components (Negotiation Service, SLA Template Factory, and SLA Template Storage) facilitate the negotiation and establishment of service level agreements for both the service customer and the service provider. They are guided by the requirements of their users and shield the applications from the peculiarities of the actual negotiation process used.

SLA4D-Grid will provide SLA Discovery functions to discover services based on QoS requirements and SLA templates. We expect these to be realized via registry services and components that facilitate interacting with registries, including simplified registration of services and SLA templates as well as facilitated query processing.

SLA Provisioning components automatically translate terms in SLAs to appropriate system and monitoring configurations and resource reservations. The translations will be implemented prototypically for the two selected use cases. Whether the quality provided actually matches the consumer's requirements is monitored by SLA-specific Monitoring services.

Except for trivial cases, workflows make use of multiple services, potentially provided by multiple providers. A workflow with overall QoS requirements therefore needs to have QoS guarantees for the individual steps of the workflow. Some of the steps might be executed most efficiently if allocated to the same service provider. An Orchestration Service will therefore be implemented which allows for the establishment of multiple SLAs and which can deal with co-allocation of tasks.

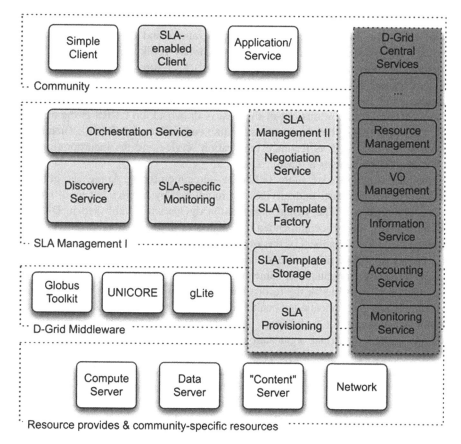

Fig. 2.9 The D-Grid SLA service stack

2.6.3   D-Grid and NGI-DE: Toward a Unified German Grid

One of the present challenges for D-Grid is the merger with the National Grid
Initiative Germany (NGI-DE), one of the regional successors of the EGEE project.
The aim of EGEE was the integration of national and regional compute and storage
resources into a European Grid infrastructure, thus providing distributed European
research communities non-intermittent access to resources. The EGEE project finished its phase 3 in 2010 and the transition toward the European Grid Initiative and
many national Grid initiatives is currently ongoing. The main task of EGI is the
coordination of the various NGIs, which themselves are responsible for providing
a reliable, secure, and sustainable e-Infrastructure build upon Grid and Cloud
resources. As D-Grid and NGI-DE have comparable objectives and provide similar
services, and two national Grid initiatives in Germany are not sensible, a merger of
the services and infrastructure has to be initiated.

D-Grid and NGI-DE use to a certain extent the same services, for example, the VOMRS for the management of virtual organizations and the gLite middleware services. Nevertheless, D-Grid supports with Globus Toolkit and UNICORE two Grid middlewares that are not part of NGI-DE. Therefore, the Grid Operations Center Database (GOC DB) used in NGI-DE supports only the registration of gLite services, while the D-Grid resource registration service (GRRS) supports all of the aforementioned middlewares out-of-the-box. A drawback on GRRS is the uncertainty about its further development, as funding ends in December 2010. Therefore selecting the GOC DB as resource registration service and the incorporation of potential enhancements is a sensible choice.

A similar situation exists in the field of resource monitoring. At present, in both Grid infrastructures hosts and services are monitored by Nagios, but by different virtual organizations. The virtual organization dgOps was established in D-Grid and the advisory board recommended the support of this virtual organization to all resource providers. Members of this organization submit from a central user interface probes to all D-Grid resources and evaluate the results. In NGI-DE the same is done by a virtual organization named ops. The consolidation into a single virtual organization responsible for the resource monitoring is desirable.

Not only has the duplication of central services to be tackled, but also the different operational concepts for both Grids. One long existing difference to serve as an example is the way virtual organization members are mapped to local users on a resource. In NGI-DE, so-called pool accounts are widely used and allow reusing local accounts after a certain time of inactivity, usually 2 weeks. After this period of time, an account is cleaned up and marked as available. The operational concept of D-Grid requires a strict one-to-one mapping from virtual organization member to local user accounts. Currently there is no concept for freeing and reusing local user account.

The consolidation of the NGI-DE and the D-Grid helpdesk a few months ago was the first successful step done on the road toward the merger of D-Grid and NGI-DE services.

2.7 Outlook

In this chapter, we have described the evolution and the current state of the German national Grid initiative D-Grid. To this end, we first provide an extensive overview of structural, technological, and administrative characteristics of this Grid environment. Then, the second part of the chapter is dedicated to an analysis of D-Grid in light of a changing distributed computing paradigm toward virtualized infrastructures, ubiquitous service offerings, and Cloud computing. We focus our evaluation on two central aspects: virtualized, Cloud-like service offers for an academic computational environment and, closely linked to the first aspect, the management of quality-of-service requirements by means of SLAs.

Although the current developments related to the two aspects are not explicitly synchronized, first steps have been made toward end-to-end service level management for an academic Cloud environment. Inter alia, requirements for offering additional commercial public Clouds to cover peak demands have been gathered and the respective SLA mechanisms have been researched. Furthermore, business-related requirements and legal prerequisites for such offers are currently evaluated and potentially incorporated into the solutions introduced in this chapter.

We envisage the different solutions to grow together in the process of time, providing virtualized solutions with strict and reliable guarantees for the services provided. This will be a first but essential step toward a dynamic academic computing environment. Moreover will these developments provide the basis for the implementation of more energy-efficient concepts, and offer the foundation for future-oriented distributed systems research, concise monitoring, accounting, and billing mechanisms. In case this is achieved without losing the diversity of service offerings for the large variety of D-Grid communities while unifying service level management environment, D-Grid is prepared for the future.

References

1. Hegering HG (2004) D-Grid: Schritte zu einer nationalen e-Science-Initiative. In: Von Knop J, Haverkamp W, Jessen E (eds) Proceedings of DFN-Arbeitstagung über Kommunikationsnetze, Gesellschaft fuer Informatik, Bonn, Germany, 285–292
2. Büchner O, Dohmen C, Eifert T, Enke H, Fieseler T, Frank A et al (2009) Betriebskonzept für die D-Grid Infrastruktur. http://www.d-grid.de/uploads/media/D-Grid-Betriebskonzept.pdf. Accessed 29 July 2010
3. Baranski B (2008) Grid Computing Enabled Web Processing Service. In: Proceedings of the GI-Days 2008. http://www.gi-tage.de/archive/2008/downloads/acceptedPapers/Papers/Baranski.pdf. Accessed 20 April 2010
4. Schwiegelshohn U, Brenner M, Bühler W, Carlson A, Fieseler T, Freitag S et al (2009) Statusbericht über die D-Grid Kern Infrastruktur. http://www.d-grid-ggmbh.de/fileadmin/downloads/Berichte/StatusberichtKern0109.pdf. Accessed 29 July 2010
5. Schwiegelshohn U, Brenner M, Bühler W, Carlson A, Fieseler T, Freitag S et al (2009) Statusbericht über die Kern-Grid-Infrastruktur. http://www.d-grid-ggmbh.de/fileadmin/downloads/Berichte/StatusberichtKern0208.pdf. Accessed 29 July 2010
6. Alef M, Fieseler T, Freitag S, Garcia A, Grimm C, Gürich W et al (2009). Integration of Multiple Middlewares on a Single Compute Resource. Future Gener Comp Sy 25(3): 268–274
7. Foster I (2002) What is the Grid? A Three Point Checklist. http://www-fp.mcs.anl.gov/~foster/Articles/WhatIsTheGrid.pdf. Accessed 20 April 2010
8. Vaquero LM, Rodero-Merino L, Caceres J, Lindner M (2009) A break in the clouds: towards a cloud definition. Comp Commun Rev 39(1):50–55
9. Edmonds A, Johnston S, Mazzaferro G, Metsch T, Merzky A (2009) Open Cloud Computing Interface Specification Version 5. Open Grid Forum, Lemont, Illinois, USA
10. Freitag S (2009) Virtualisierungstechnologien in Grid Rechenzentren. 2. DFN-Forum Kommunikationstechnologien, GI Proceedings 149:137–146
11. Mach R, Lepro-Metz R, Jackson S, McGinnis L, (2007) Usage Record Format. Open Grid Forum, Lemont, Illinois, USA
12. Lee JJ, Ben-Natan R (2002) What are Service Level Agreements? In: Integrating Service Level Agreements – Optimizing Your OSS for SLA Delivery, 1st edn. Wiley Publishing, Inc., Indianapolis, Indiana, USA

13. Addy R (2007) Effective IT Service Management – To ITIL and Beyond! 1st Ed. Springer-Verlag: Berlin / Heidelberg, Germany
14. Keller A, Ludwig H (2003) The WSLA Framework: Specifying and Monitoring Service Level Agreements for Web Services. J Network and Systems Management 11(1):57–81
15. Andrieux A, Czajkowski K, Dan A, Keahey K, Ludwig H, Nakata T, Pruyne J, Rofrano J, Tuecke S, Xu M (2007) Web Services Agreement Specification. Open Grid Forum, Lemont, Illinois, USA
16. Seidel J, Wäldrich O, Ziegler W, Wieder Ph, Yahyapour R (2007) Using SLA for Resource Management and Scheduling - A Survey. In: Talia D, Yahyapour R, Ziegler W (eds) Grid Middleware and Services - Challenges and Solutions, Springer, NY, USA, 335–347
17. The TeleManagement Forum (2005) SLA Management Handbook, Volume 2, Concepts and Principles, Release 2.5, The TeleManagement Forum, Morristown, New Jersey, USA

Chapter 3
Democratizing Resource-Intensive e-Science Through Peer-to-Peer Grid Computing

Francisco Brasileiro, Nazareno Andrade, Raquel Lopes, and Lívia Sampaio

Abstract The new ways of doing science rooted on the unprecedented processing, communication, and storage infrastructure that became available to scientists are collectively called *e-Science*. Due to their nature, most e-Science activities can only be successfully performed if researchers have access to high-performance computing facilities. Grid and voluntary computing are well-established solutions that cater to this need, but are not accessible to all labs and institutions. Peer-to-peer (P2P) grid computing has been proposed to address this very problem. In this chapter, we share our experience in developing a P2P grid middleware called OurGrid and deploying it to build the OurGrid Community. We describe the mechanisms that effectively promote collaboration and allow the assemblage of large P2P grids from the contributions of thousands of small sites. This includes a thorough review of the main mechanisms required to support the execution of bag-of-tasks applications on top of P2P grids: accounting, scheduling, security, and data caching. Besides, we discuss ways to allow P2P grids to interoperate with service grids. We also report a success case in the utilization of the OurGrid middleware in the context of e-Science. Finally, we summarize our experience in this area indicating the lessons we have learned, the present challenges, and future directions of research.

3.1 Introduction

Recent developments in information processing and communication technologies have substantially impacted the way scientific research is conducted. These technologies allow for not only an unprecedented level of interaction among researchers but also the federation of large quantities of resources distributed in different research facilities. It is currently possible, through the statistical multiplexing of

F. Brasileiro(✉), N. Andrade, R. Lopes, and L. Sampaio
Departamento de Sistemas e Computação, Laboratório de Sistemas Distribuídos, Universidade Federal de Campina Grande, Campina Grande, Paraíba, Brazil
e-mail: fubica@dsc.ufcg.edu.br; nazareno@dsc.ufcg.edu.br; raquel@dsc.ufcg.edu.br; livia@dsc.ufcg.edu.br

Xiaoyu Yang et al. (eds.), *Guide to e-Science: Next Generation Scientific Research and Discovery*, Computer Communications and Networks, DOI 10.1007/978-0-85729-439-5_3, © Springer-Verlag London Limited 2011

shared resources, to create high-performance infrastructures that enable the effective execution of resource-intensive research activities related to data analysis, simulations, visualization of results, etc.

The new ways of doing science, rooted on the unprecedented processing, communication, and storage infrastructure that became available to scientists, are collectively called *e-Science*. Indeed, e-Science activities play nowadays a fundamental role in the working methodology adopted by many research groups in the world. As a consequence, having access to high-performance computing facilities has become a must for many research areas.

Due to this demand, research in computer science has, for some time now, sought ways to expand the reach of high-performance computing infrastructures. This effort is particularly pronounced targeting the computing and storage demands of a subclass of parallel applications that can be decoupled in many independent tasks that do not need to communicate with each other. Because of this characteristic, these applications are frequently referred to as pleasantly or embarrassingly parallel, or still, bag-of-tasks (BoT) applications, since they can be trivially parallelized by simply simultaneously processing as many tasks as possible. This subclass of applications marries simplicity in requirements with a wide use in e-Science experiments. Examples of BoT applications abound in data mining, massive searches (such as key breaking), parameter sweeps, simulations, fractal calculations, computational biology, computer imaging, among others. High-performance computing infrastructures targeted to these applications are sometimes called high-throughput computing infrastructures [1].

One of the first initiatives in the sense of building high-throughput computing infrastructures provided a way to aggregate unused computing power in a local area network [2]. The next step was to increase the scale on the number of resources aggregated by harvesting the idle computing power in the Internet [3], what has been dubbed *public resource computing* or *voluntary computing*. Finally, *grid computing* has been proposed as a way to build virtual organizations (VO) aggregating computing resources that are under different administrative domains, and that are typically dedicated to the grid [4].

Despite being successful in providing nontrivial amounts of computing power, such shared infrastructures are not necessarily available for all. In the case of voluntary computing, it is necessary to set up a large control center that will be responsible for managing the potentially very large number of public resources that are contributed to the system. Moreover, a lot of marketing and dissemination effort needs to be placed in convincing resource owners to install the software that will allow them to contribute their resources to the system. Furthermore, usually, applications need to be modified to fit in the voluntary computing execution model. On the other hand, most grids in production (e.g., EGEE,[1] NGS,[2] D-GRID,[3] NorduGrid,[4]

---

[1] http://www.eu-egee.org/.

[2] http://www.ngs.ac.uk/.

[3] http://www.d-grid.de/.

[4] http://www.nordugrid.org/.

TeraGrid,[5] OSG,[6] NAREGI,[7] APAC,[8] and PRAGMA[9]) use complex grid middleware. Installing, configuring, and customizing these middleware is not a trivial task, and today requires a highly skilled support team. Substantial investment is also needed to keep the infrastructure operating with the required quality of service. Moreover, joining such grids involves a negotiation process that consumes time and may place players with smaller amounts of resources in a disadvantageous position in relation to larger players.

In summary, these mainstream technologies are not affordable to a considerable portion of the users with demands for high-performance computing. Therefore, if on the one side the massive use of computers by researchers fosters, at an ever faster pace, amazing developments for the society at large, on the other side it contributes to increase even more the gap between the research that can be conducted at the few large research labs that can afford the cost of implementing the above mentioned technologies and that conducted by the majority of small labs that cannot. Yet, the fact that a lab is not large has no relation with the importance of the research it develops. As a matter of fact, in countries with very few large labs, a substantial portion of all research developed is conducted by research groups organized around small- and medium-sized labs. Hence, it is of fundamental importance to envision alternative ways for making high-performance computing affordable to any user that requires it.

Peer-to-peer (P2P) grid computing has been proposed to address this very problem [5]. In a P2P grid, small- and medium-sized labs (and naturally large-sized labs as well) can donate their idle computational resources in exchange for accessing other labs' idle resources when needed. An incentive mechanism is implemented to promote the donation of resources. It must be such that peers that contribute to the system are rewarded in the proportion of their contributions.

In this chapter, we share our experience in developing a P2P grid middleware called OurGrid[10] and deploying it to build the OurGrid Community.[11] Before discussing P2P grids, we start Sect. 3.2 by presenting a more thorough overview on the alternative approaches for grid computing. Then, in Sect. 3.3, we focus our attention on P2P grids and present mechanisms to effectively promote collaboration and, hence, allow the assemblage of large P2P grids from the contributions of thousands of small sites. This is followed, in Sect. 3.4, by a thorough review of the main mechanisms required to support the execution of BoT applications on top of P2P grids. A discussion of ways to allow P2P grids to interoperate with other kinds of

---

[5] https://www.teragrid.org/.

[6] http://www.opensciencegrid.org/.

[7] http://www.naregi.org/.

[8] http://www.apac.edu.au/.

[9] http://www.pragma-grid.net/.

[10] http://www.ourgrid.org/.

[11] http://status.ourgrid.org/.

grid infrastructures is the subject of Sect. 3.5. We report a success case in the utilization of the OurGrid middleware in Sect. 3.6, and conclude the chapter in Sect. 3.7 indicating the lessons learned, the present challenges, and future directions of research in this area.

3.2   A Peer-to-Peer Approach for Grid Computing

The grid computing vision as popularized in the 1990s by Foster and colleagues and materialized mainly through the Globus Toolkit software focuses mainly in the establishment of virtual organizations (VO) [4]. Using the Globus Toolkit, a set of institutions can form unified virtual organizations that federate their infrastructures, enabling them to share resources such as computing power, scientific instruments, and data. One fundamental part of such configuration is the definition of resource access and sharing policies. Grids formed through the VO approach typically rely on existing social relations between the set of institutions to resolve the negotiations involved with this definition. For example, a usual procedure is for a set of institutions to rely on the hierarchy defined in a joint project and use project meetings to discuss and create a contractual agreement that participants must sign before joining the grid. This agreement defines resource provision requirements, access rights, and allocation policies. New participants typically negotiate their participation with a management entity and register their users and the applications these users intend to run on the grid.

A similar approach is taken by the high-throughput approach for federated institutions, best exemplified by the Condor software. Condor's initial goal was to scavenge the idle resources in one administrative domain [2]. Over the course of its existence, however, Condor tried a number of mechanisms to enable multisite resource sharing (see [1] for a chronicle of these methods). These mechanisms had in common among them and with the VO approach the necessity for negotiations among all partners interested in forming a grid.

A considerably different method for assembling a federated infrastructure and defining its policies is that of voluntary computing, popularized by the SETI@ home project. Voluntary computing relies on users trusting a central authority that manages the resulting virtual infrastructure and executes known applications on it. This model has produced a number of cases of success and certainly makes it easier for resource owners to provision the infrastructure. At the same time, however, it heavily relies on the role of the central authority and on how this authority and its cause motivate users to contribute resources. For this reason, the resulting infrastructure is typically also not a general-purpose one.

The P2P grid computing approach is motivated by the need for less costly mechanisms for infrastructure assembly than those required by virtual organizations and provided by voluntary computing.

In a P2P grid, participants are free to join and the assumptions about their behavior in the system are minimal [5]. A participant in the grid is typically a site that sometimes has demand for more service capacity than what it can provide with only its own resources and sometimes has idle capacity that can be made available to the other participants in the grid. Resource sharing is governed by minimal rules: The owner of a resource has priority in its use and applications from unknown parties can only use a resource if there is no threat it can pose using that resource.

The typical audience aimed at with this approach is that of small- and medium-sized research laboratories and companies that do not have access to initiatives that build contract-based grids. By enabling participants to provide only the idle capacity of their resources, P2P grids lower the cost of contribution; by allowing anyone to join the grid, P2P grids aim at democratizing access to computing power. The resulting infrastructure trades some of the more sophisticated resource uses that controlled user terms and agreements would enable for a much lower entrance barrier for participants and lower maintenance and governance costs.

In this chapter, we focus on OurGrid, the P2P grid middleware in whose development we have been involved. Other solutions have been put forward for P2P grid computing: Butt et al. [6] proposed organizing Condor pools in a P2P network with no central coordination, and XtremWeb [7], Triana [8], Cluster Computing on the Fly [9], and P3 [10] also envision a P2P network of shared resources. From an implementation perspective, OurGrid differs from these efforts mainly because it addresses the crucial issue of providing incentives for cooperation and caters for security for both resource providers and users.

3.3 Building a P2P Grid

The utility that users obtain from a grid is tied to the scale of the grid they can access. This makes assembling the grid and deciding its resource allocation policy crucial tasks.

In spite of lowering the costs of assembling the grid and facilitate access to its services, the P2P grid computing approach creates a challenging incentive problem to be solved. From the resource owner's perspective, providing service to the grid implies in some cost: Making resources available potentially increases energy and maintenance costs, as well as security risks. In some cases, the cost for providing service may be unimportant. For example, if the additional maintenance costs needed in a site are relatively small or if the benefit of contributing for research done by others in the grid is perceived as valuable. However, other users may perceive the costs of contributing to the grid as non-negligible. For users that perceive the costs as considerable, there is a social dilemma: Not contributing and still benefiting from the grid is the most profitable alternative, but if all users act like this, the social outcome is worse than that of prevalent contributions [11].

To avoid the situation where such incentive structure leads to low contributions and an overall suboptimal situation, resource allocation policy in OurGrid was designed so that it rewards peers that provide more resources to the system. This is done through an incentive mechanism called the Network of Favors [12].

This mechanism uses direct reciprocity to allocate contented resources to requesters based on their past contributions to the system, making it in the best interest of all peers to contribute. Any mechanism that rewards past behavior depends on an accounting of such behavior. In the setting of P2P grids formed by untrustworthy partners, such accounting is challenging.

The first part of this section discusses the design and properties of the Network of Favors. After that, we discuss the underlying accounting mechanism used by the Network of Favors that allows peers to autonomously estimate the work performed by the other peers in the grid. The section is completed with a discussion on how the Network of Favors can be extended to address the fact that in practical deployments more than one service can be traded in a P2P grid.

3.3.1 The Network of Favors

The Network of Favors (NoF, for short) is a decentralized resource allocation mechanism through which participants in a P2P grid collectively encourage service provision. A combination of a direct reciprocity mechanism and a prioritization policy form the NoF. Direct reciprocity is a simple mechanism that is robust to misinformation. Prioritization is a policy chosen to provide incentives in the case of resource contention while maximizing throughput in the system at all times.

Direct reciprocity means that each participant P_i reciprocates the behavior that each other participant P_j had toward it in the past according to a local record of their pair-wise interactions. Because P_i uses only local information it observed directly to decide whether to allocate a resource to P_j or not, a malicious peer cannot affect the decision by spreading misinformation. The allocation P_i will perform is as good as the evaluation it can make of its past interactions with its peers. We return to the matter of such precision in the next subsection. For the following discussion, assume P_i can account for the service it provides and receives from its peers.

From the perspective of the resource consumer P_j, a direct reciprocity mechanism only makes contributing to the grid the best strategy if interactions between P_j and P_i happen frequently enough, so that P_i's decision has an impact on the resources available to P_j [13]. In the particular setting of P2P systems, Feldman et al. and Lai et al. show that an incentive mechanism based on direct reciprocity is not effective for large populations in a file-sharing system due to high churn and to the fact that not all peers have content that interest all others [14].

However, different from a file-sharing system, in a P2P grid, interaction between any two peers is usually frequent. This is because both service requesters and providers interact with multiple and often many partners whenever they act in the system. Requesters typically participate in the system because they have demand for a large amount of service at once. This service is probably more than any participant in the grid can provide alone, what makes possible and likely that the consumer will interact with multiple providers. Furthermore, as we will discuss in Sect. 3.4, service consumers can increase the performance of their applications in a heterogeneous grid replicating tasks on different resources [15, 16]. Such replication potentially increases the number of providers a consumer interacts with. At the same time, a resource provider typically owns multiple resources, which can be split among multiple consumers at a given time. Finally, although multiple services may be provided in the grid, the number of services will be orders of magnitude smaller than the number of files in a file-sharing application. The reduction in the number of different services available again augments the chance of two peers interacting.

When effective, direct reciprocation has the advantage of simplicity over its alternatives in the design space. Two proposed alternatives to this approach that have received considerable attention from the community are reputation (sometimes termed indirect reciprocity) [14, 17, 18] and market-based mechanisms [19–21]. In the former, a peer allocates its resources to a requester according to the aggregate opinion of its peers about the requester; in the latter, participants use a currency and either bargaining or auctions to determine to which requester to allocate resources. Both of these alternatives demand the implementation of more sophisticated and less robust underlying mechanisms than direct reciprocity.

Given the mechanism for allocating resources, the grid still needs a policy that participants will follow. Using the NoF, each participant always provides its available resources and prioritizes peers that simultaneously request the same resource based on its local record of past interactions with the requesters. The local record of participant P_i of its interactions with P_j takes form of a balance, calculated as the value of service received minus the value of service provided, or zero if this value is negative. The balance is updated adding the value of service provided or subtracting the value of service received every time P_i interacts with P_j. The use of nonnegative quantification for past interactions aims at discouraging whitewashing attacks. A whitewashing attack is performed when the attacker leaves the system and returns as a newcomer, for instance, to get rid of a bad reputation. In the presence of cheap identities and both positive and negative records of interaction, a participant with negative balance in the system can always benefit from whitewashing. With nonnegative records, participants cannot increase their records in the eyes of other peers. This use of nonnegative balances was inspired on the work of Yamagishi and Matsuda [22].

The prioritization implemented in the NoF makes it so that whenever there is resource contention in the system, requesters that have contributed more in the past receive more service. This is less strict than other policies that could starve non-contributing participants. However, we chose to implement prioritization on the grounds that: (1) it eases bootstrapping the system, and (2) the absence of contention in the system can be taken as a sign of an acceptable level of service provision. Bootstrapping in face of allocation policies that deny service under certain conditions may lead to situations where all peers deny service to each other; this cannot happen through prioritization. The lack of rewards for cooperating participants only happens when the system is able to provide service to all requesters, in which situation it is possible to punish noncooperators only by decreasing the system's throughput, an alternative whose benefit is debatable.

When peers interact frequently, direct reciprocity and prioritization efficiently promote service provisioning in a P2P grid. For a detailed analysis of the conditions that affect the effectiveness of the NoF and other properties of this mechanism, we refer the reader to other publications [12, 23].

3.3.2   Accounting Computation Performed by Untrustworthy Parties

The local records of pair-wise interactions maintained by the participants in the NoF must be accurate if the system is to provide accurate prioritization. Performing such accounting robustly is not a trivial problem because there is uncertainty about resource consumption from the consumer's side and a potential benefit for the provider to misreport accounting information. This section presents a solution for this scenario based on exploring a typical usage pattern of grid participants to enable autonomous accounting of computation.

When providing a resource, providers benefit from forging the accounting of its service provision because this leads to an increased credit in the local records the other peers maintain for it. In the NoF, this translates into future prioritization in resource allocation. In such scenario, it is risky for a service consumer to trust accounting information from service providers.

An alternative to using information from the providers is to estimate the cost on the consumer side. The issue with this approach is that users typically do not know how many resources a typical task in their application consumes. Studies with users of supercomputers have exposed that users cannot predict accurately their applications' runtime even in a homogeneous platform [24]. To address this issue, we leverage the fact that participants in a P2P grid typically use the grid to augment a local infrastructure that cannot fully accommodate users' demand for computation. This implies that often each application submitted to the grid will run part on resources that are local to the peer to which the application user is associated and part on the resources of the other peers that compose the grid. The progress made by the part of the application that run on the local resources can then be used by a participant to estimate the relative computing power that the other peers are making available to run the application. The relative power can be continuously updated as users run more applications on the grid, moving toward more accurate estimates.

Santos et al. evaluate the efficiency of this autonomous accounting mechanism by comparing it against an optimal mechanism that is perfectly informed [25]. Their results show that even when there is high heterogeneity among the resources that comprise the grid, as well as among the processing demands of the individual tasks of the BoT applications, the accuracy of the autonomous accounting mechanism is only slightly worse than the perfect accounting, with a small bias toward peers with faster resources. In fact, this side effect may introduce an extra incentive for peers to provide their most powerful resources to the grid.

3.3.3   Reciprocity in Face of Multiple Services

The NoF was originally designed to share computation as the sole service in the grid. However, in practice, applications have requirements for multiple services. For example, some applications need as much data transfer, and thus network and storage services, as computation. Other applications need higher-level services such as datasets or software libraries besides raw computation.

Considering that multiple services are provided in the system complicates matters because participants may perceive differently the values and costs associated with different services. When choosing which peer contribution to reciprocate, a participant should then be interested not only in the probability that each peer will reciprocate, but also on how profitable a long-term relationship with that peer can be. This profitability, in turn, is a result of the services that a peer is likely to provide and request in the future.

The NoF has been enhanced to address this matter [23]. This extended mechanism, dubbed ExtNoF, performs nearly as well as utility-maximizing policies that have access to truthful information from other peers. It encourages the provision of multiple services by making it so that peers cluster with partners that lead to profitable relationships still using only their local information about past interactions.

If participants had access to the perceived values and costs of all their peers, the utility-maximizing strategy would be to combine a selection policy with a prioritization policy. The former determines which peers can submit requests for services, while the latter determines how to arbitrate between requesters. With the information about preferences of others, a participant is able to calculate whether it is possibly profitable to maintain a long-term relationship with each other peer and who are the peers that return most valuable services more often. However, because the information about the valuation of services may lead to prioritization if published, it becomes in the interest of participants to lie about this information. With this consideration, the NoF was extended without relying on such data. Instead, using the ExtNoF mechanisms, the participants recur to their own cost evaluations for evaluating the value of service provided by their peers. This valuation is then used for prioritization similar to the NoF, and peers use no selection policy.

Mowbray et al. have simulated the effects of the NoF for the allocation of resources in a grid where computation and storage services are provided and participants have different levels of service demand, different costs, and various service availability [23]. They found that in spite of not using the selection policy or the information about peers' preferences, the NoF performs similarly to the ideal policies, encouraging service provision in the grid even when the cost of providing service in the grid with idle resources approximates the benefit of receiving service from it when in high demand.

3.4 Supporting the Execution of Resource-Intensive Applications

Running applications on P2P grids presents several challenges. First of all, resources need to be appropriately exposed and discovered. Once resources are obtained, a suitable scheduling policy needs to be used to map the individual tasks of a parallel application to the appropriate resources, aiming at reducing as much as possible the time taken to execute the application as a whole. If the application manipulates large amounts of data, careful consideration should be made in order to reduce the impact that the delay associated to the data transmission through the wide area network that links the resources may have in the execution time of the application. Finally, security is a crucial aspect to be handled in an open system such as a P2P grid. This section discusses how the OurGrid middleware deals with each of these issues.

3.4.1 Exposing and Discovering Resources

A P2P grid build with the support of the OurGrid middleware has four main components: the OurGrid Peer, the OurGrid Worker, the OurGrid Broker, and the OurGrid Discovery Service. Figure 3.1 shows them all, depicting the architecture of an OurGrid system.

OurGrid is based on a P2P network, with each resource provider, or site (e.g., a research lab), corresponding to a Peer component in the system. Peers may enter and leave the system at any time without human interventions and without compromising the system operation.

Worker components run in the machines that will comprise the grid resources of a particular site. OurGrid strives to be nonintrusive, in the sense that, at any time, these resources can be claimed back by their owners. Resource owners are free to define the rules that specify when the resources of their site are available to the grid; for instance, the event that triggers the availability of a desktop to the grid can be specified as a number of minutes elapsed with inactivity in both the mouse and the keyboard. The worker is responsible for monitoring the resource availability, and, whenever it detects that the resource is available to be used by the grid, it informs the peer that manages its site. If the worker detects that the resource is no longer available, then, any grid jobs that may be running in the resource are immediately killed and the peer is informed about the new state of the worker.

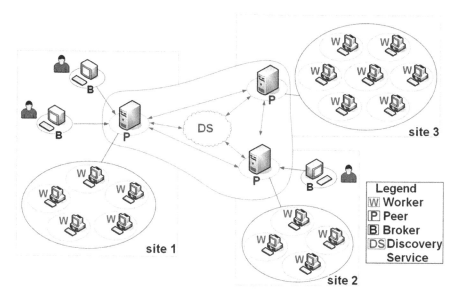

Fig. 3.1 OurGrid architecture

In order to avoid scalability limitations, OurGrid has no single "super-scheduler" that oversees all scheduling activities in the system. Each user runs a Broker component, which schedules the user's jobs and competes with other brokers for the system's resources. The broker also provides a user interface (UI) and implements a set of abstractions that hide the grid heterogeneity from the user [5].

Since the peer has information about the workers of its site, it is natural that brokers ask for resources to the peer. In OurGrid, a job is a collection of tasks that may run independently from each other. When the user submits a job, the broker analyzes the job and, depending on the scheduling strategy selected by the user, decides on the number of workers it needs to run the job. The broker then sends a request to the peer of its site asking for that number of workers. The peer immediately gives to the broker the local workers that are available and, if these are not enough to fulfill the broker's request, it contacts remote peers, to ask them for more resources.

Thus, requests for resources may arrive from brokers that are at the same site of the peer, in which case we say this is a local request, or they may arrive from peers at remote sites, which we call a remote request. A level of priority is defined between local and remote requests, with the former having priority over the latter. If required, local workers that were given to remote peers may be claimed back and used to fulfill local requests. Local resources are allocated in a balanced way among the several local brokers that may be requesting them. These resource allocation rules assure that OurGrid cannot worsen local performance, a property that has long been identified as key for the success of resource-harvesting systems [1]. The final level of priority is defined by the NoF mechanism, discussed in the previous section. When two remote requests are contending for the same worker, the peer allocates its worker taking into account the current balance that it maintains for the requesting peers. In summary, workers can be in one of the following states: (1) available, in which case they are ready to receive grid jobs to run; (2) donated, if they are processing remote jobs; (3) in use, when it is processing a local job; or (4) unavailable, in which case the owner of the resource is using it, and no grid jobs are allowed to run there.

Finally, the Discovery Service (DS) component implements a rendezvous service. The DS is a service that creates the notion of a single community of peers. The peers are configured to connect to the appropriate DS, which is responsible for connecting all the peers of a particular P2P grid. For fault tolerance reasons, the rendezvous service may be implemented by redundant DSs that keep their state synchronized in a lazy fashion. Each DS centralizes references for all the peers that make the community, allowing the peers to know each other on the fly. A peer that enters the community sends a message to one of the DS instances, informing about its entrance. The DS server includes the new peer into its list of active peers and sends this updated list to the peer in order to inform the new peer about the other active peers in the P2P grid. It also informs any other instances of the DS that may exist. From time to time, the DS sends heartbeats to all the known active peers to see if they are still alive. At these times, the DS may find out that some peer has left the grid. In this case, this peer is removed from the list of known active peers. Periodically, peers query one of the DS instances to update their membership vision.

3.4.2 Scheduling BoT Jobs in a P2P Grid

Despite the simplicity of BoT jobs, scheduling them on P2P grids is difficult due to two main issues. Firstly, efficient schedulers of BoT jobs depend on information about the individual tasks that comprise the job (e.g., estimated execution time in each different resource that may be available) and the resources that comprise the grid (e.g., processor speed, load, and network connection). However, this is difficult to be obtained accurately in a P2P grid. The main reasons for that are: (1) *wide distribution of resources*, which implies high network latency; (2) *heterogeneity of resources*, which complicates estimating execution time of tasks; (3) *sharing of resources*, which produces a wide resource load variation; and (4) *different administrative domains*, which means that resource owners are autonomous to define different local policies, and so, it may be impossible to get information from all grid resources. Secondly, since many BoT jobs manipulate large data sets, one must provide coordinated scheduling of data and computation to achieve good performance. Let us first describe how replication schedulers deal with the first issue. Then, we describe how data can be taken into account.

BoT jobs that do not manipulate large data sets can be efficiently scheduled in an OurGrid system by using the scheduling heuristic called Workqueue with

Replication (or simply WQR) [15]. WQR uses no information about tasks or resources. It randomly sends a task to a resource; when a resource finishes the execution of a task, another task is sent to it. This is akin to the well-known work-queue-scheduling algorithm. However, when there are no more tasks to send, a randomly chosen running task is replicated. Replication is the key to recovering from bad allocations of tasks to resources, since WQR uses no information. Paranhos et al. have shown that WQR performance is as good as traditional knowledge-based schedulers fed with perfect information [15].

However, WQR does not take data transfers into account. An alternative scheduling heuristic was proposed to take into account the demands of BoT data-intensive jobs [16]. This heuristic, called Storage Affinity, also uses replication to address the lack of information in the P2P grid environment. In addition, it exploits data reutilization to avoid unnecessary data transfers. The data reutilization appears in two basic categories: *inter-job* and *inter-task*. The former arises when a job uses the data already used by (or produced by) a job that executed previously, while the latter appears in jobs whose tasks share the same input data.

Data reutilization is gauged by the *storage affinity* metric. This metric determines *how close* to a site a given task is. The number of bytes of the task input dataset that are already stored at a specific site defines the notion of closeness between a task and a site. Tasks are allocated to resources that belong to the site that has the largest storage affinity, thus, minimizing the amount of data transfer required to execute data-intensive BoT jobs.

Information on data size and data location can be obtained a priori with less difficulty and loss of accuracy than, for example, information on CPU and network loads or the completion time of tasks. For instance, information on data size and location can be obtained from a disk cache service (such as the one that will be presented in the next subsection), which should be able to answer requests about which data elements it stores and how large each data element is. Alternatively, an implementation of a Storage Affinity heuristic can easily store a history of previous data transfer operations containing the required information.

A number of simulation experiments were conducted in a variety of scenarios to evaluate the performance of Storage Affinity [16]. The simulations compared the efficiency of Storage Affinity against XSufferage [26] and WQR. XSufferage is a well-known scheduler that takes data placement into account, but requires knowledge of the execution time of the tasks on each processor that composes the grid as well as information on the latencies and available bandwidth in the network that links the sites. WQR was considered for the opposite reason: It does not need information, but does not consider data placement either. On average, Storage Affinity and XSufferage achieve comparable performances. The results show that both data-aware heuristics attain much better performance than WQR. This is because data transfer delays dominate the execution time of data-intensive jobs, thus not taking them into account severely hurts the performance of the job execution. The results also confirm the power of replication to circumvent the unavailability of information. Storage Affinity is able to cope with the lack of dynamic information and yields a performance very similar to that of XSufferage.

Unfortunately, the performance of replication schedulers such as WQR and Storage Affinity does not come for free. These schedulers consume more cycles than those that do not use replication. There is thus a clear trade-off between the availability of information and the cost to efficiently compute a BoT job in a P2P grid. Nevertheless, the extra cost of replication was only noticeable when the number of tasks was of the same order of magnitude as the number of resources, or less. Also, by limiting replication, the cost can be substantially reduced without an important impact on the job execution performance [15, 16].

Nóbrega Jr et al. further investigated this trade-off by analyzing scheduling heuristics that use partial information to make decisions [27]. The motivation comes from the fact that although it is hard to obtain accurate information in grid environments, it is not impossible to have some of it. In practice, some information can be gathered using services that collect resources and network information [28, 29] and publish them in a grid information service (GIS) [30]. The results reported by Nóbrega Jr et al. show that the use of whatever information that is available reduces the cost of the scheduling maintaining the same execution efficiency.

3.4.3 Caching Data

The nodes that make up a P2P grid are commonly connected by wide area network channels of communication, characterized by relatively small bandwidth, when compared to the bandwidth available in the local area network. Thus, communication between sites in a P2P grid can be slow and the time needed to carry data between sites may be equivalent to a considerable amount of the time needed to process the task that consumes this data. Consequently, the gains obtained by parallelizing the applications can be neutralized by the time required to transfer the data to be consumed. Besides, if workers do not have enough space to store the data, the remote execution will be denied.

Fortunately, as we discussed before, several data-intensive applications have a high degree of data reuse, be it inter-job or intra-job. Thus, the limitations of bandwidth can be minimized by the persistence of data on the sites that have previously executed tasks that needed the data. This data can be used in future executions without the need to be transferred again. Of course, since the storage capacity in the sites that comprise the system is limited, old data may need to be removed to accommodate the new data required by the execution of other tasks. Thus, a disk cache system should be in place to manage the disk space that is offered to the P2P grid.

We consider that each peer manages a storage resource that is accessible to all the processing resources it manages (e.g., through a distributed file system). For each peer, the term local data refers to data that is consumed or produced by the tasks that are submitted locally to the peer, while remote data refers to data that is consumed or produced by the tasks that have been submitted from remote peers and execute in the local processing resources.

One challenge inherent in P2P caching is related to the way resources are shared among the peers. The problem is to fairly and efficiently allocate disk space among the peers: proportionally to the contribution of each peer and maximizing the usage of the shared resources. Another challenge to be overcome is to encourage peers to donate their storage resources. Without the spontaneous cooperation of peers it would not be possible to devise an efficient disk cache, hence the importance of this incentive. It is equally important to deal with free riders. Just as discussed in Sect. 3.3 in the context of processing, mechanisms to detect and marginalize free riders are also required in the context of a disk cache system.

The P2P disk cache management mechanism prioritizes storing the data of jobs that are submitted locally, giving the unused space for data that will be consumed by jobs submitted remotely. The disk cache never refuses to store local data, unless the data is larger than the whole disk space managed by the cache service. Local data stored in the disk cache is associated with a lifetime that, once expired, marks the data for removal, providing more space to store both local and remote data. The removal of cached data can follow any policy of data removal, such as LRU (Least Recently Used) or LFU (Least Frequently Used) [3, 31].

Remote data is stored in spare space not used by local data. When there is contention for resources, the allocation of space is based on a prioritization mechanism inspired by the NoF mechanism discussed in Sect. 3.3. A peer P_i establishes how much space is allocated to another peer (this peer's quota) considering the balance of storage favors that have been exchanged between P_i and the other peers in the P2P grid. A storage favor is defined as the action of providing a byte of data for the execution of a task submitted by one of the brokers connected to a given peer. This means that the act of storing the data is not accounted as a favor until the data is really consumed by an application. Each peer keeps track of favors received and delivered for each known peer, and a received favor counts as positive, while an offered favor is accounted for as negative. The reputation assigned to new nodes is zero. Again, disallowing the reputation of a peer to go negative prevents whitewash attacks.

The quota of a peer P_i on a peer P_j at time t is the reputation of P_i on P_j at time t times the total space available for storage of remote data on peer P_j at time t. A quota based on reputation ensures that the amount of space in the disk cache of a peer P_i provided to a peer P_j is directly proportional to the amount of favors offered by P_j to P_i in past interactions. Thus, the peers that make up the computational grid are encouraged to offer favors and to maintain remote data files on their disk caches. The more they contribute to the disk cache system the more their reputation increase, and this is the only way of increasing their quotas in other sites of the grid.

Besides encouraging collaboration, setting quotas based on reputation is a way of marginalizing free riders in favor of collaborators. It is important to note that in scenarios without resource contention, the quota is not included for space allocation. This decision was inspired by the work of Soares et al. [12, 32] and was taken to maximize the use of available space for disk cache, even if it means to benefit free riders on some occasions. Obviously, a peer that exceeds its quota may have data removed prematurely from the disk cache when space is requested by other peers with higher reputations.

Data removal may occur due to the arrival of storage requests from both local and remote jobs. The cache service never denies the storage requests that come from local jobs. On the contrary, it can deny service to a remote peer if there is not enough space to store the new data.

When data needs to be removed from a disk cache, some rules are followed to maintain as much data as possible and as longer as possible. First of all, expired local data is removed. If more data needs to be removed, the disk cache manager starts removing data from those remote peers which are exceeding their quotas. If the new data to be stored is local, and still there is not enough space available to store it, data of remote peers – from lower to higher reputations – starts to be deleted from the disk cache until there is enough space available to store the new data. If the new data comes from a remote node, the disk cache manager removes data from the requesting node and from nodes with lower reputations and stores the data if the quota of the remote node is not exceeded. It is possible that after all these removals, the manager finds out that it is not possible to store the new data because the cache does not have enough space even if remote and expired data are removed. In fact, before removing any data the disk cache manager analyzes the possibilities and discovers if it is possible or not to store the new data.

Simulation experiments were used to evaluate this disk cache system in two perspectives: The amount of data transfers saved due to the disk cache and the fairness and efficiency of the allocation of the shared disk space among the peers, marginalizing free riders during resource contention times. In all scenarios simulated, the marginalization of free riders occurred almost immediately in periods of resource contention, regardless of the number of nodes involved in the experiment. When there was no resource contention, the mechanism did not act, and the idle disk space was consumed by free riders. Thus, the efficiency of the cache was increased [33].

3.4.4 Security Issues

In a P2P grid, a peer will commonly run tasks from other unknown peers. This creates a very obvious security threat, especially in these days of so many software vulnerabilities. Therefore, a P2P grid must provide a way to protect local resources from remote, potentially malicious jobs. Also, since peers gain reputation for performing favors on behalf of other peers, one must also protect the execution of the jobs from malicious resource providers that instead of processing the tasks, simply output bogus data to increase their perceived performance and, as a consequence, the amount of credit they gain. Another security issue is related to the robustness of the peer's identity. A P2P grid middleware needs to guarantee that every interaction among peers has confirmed its origin and is associated with the unique identifier of the source peer, preventing the acceptance of forged, altered, or repeated messages. In the following, we discuss how these three issues were handled in the OurGrid middleware.

3.4.4.1 Protecting Workers from Malicious Jobs

OurGrid's mechanism for protecting workers leverages virtualization technologies and the fact that the tasks of BoT jobs do not need to communicate with each other.

Every time a worker is donated to a new broker, a fresh virtual machine is spawn by the worker to execute the tasks submitted by the broker. The virtual machine isolates the foreign code into a sandbox, where it can neither access local data nor use the network. This is implemented by a Virtualized Executor (VE) component.

From the task standpoint, the VE is totally transparent, that is, the task does not need to be modified in order to run on the VE. The VE uses a container of tasks without access to the network [34]. Thus, this approach offers a "double barrier" isolation to an attacker. Even when an attacker trespasses the first barrier (the native operating system security mechanism) and gains unauthorized access to resources, he or she is contained inside an offline virtual machine.

The OurGrid Worker supports different virtualization technologies. During the OurGrid installation process, the site administrator chooses which worker version is more appropriate for the site.

3.4.4.2 Protecting the Jobs from Malicious Workers

As mentioned before, the NoF creates an incentive for a resource to sabotage the tasks it runs, not executing them but, instead, returning back bogus results. There are two basic ways to deal with this problem. Tasks may introduce application-specific watermarks in the outputs that they produce that can later be checked by the broker. Alternatively, tasks are executed redundantly and have their outputs compared to detect wrong results produced by malicious workers.

Sarmenta [35] has proposed a mechanism called credibility-based sabotage detection that substantially reduces the amount of redundancy that is required to keep sabotage tolerance at very high levels. The reporting of sabotage incidents in the SETI@home system motivated this work. In the voluntary computing setting, there is only one application (or a limited number of them) that is executed. Thus, the use of the cheaper watermark mechanisms is not advisable, since it pays off for the attacker to reverse engineer the application to discover how the watermark is generated. After that, it can generate bogus outputs that will be accepted as correct, without the need of paying the cost of computing them.

On the other hand, in a P2P grid, many applications are executed. Therefore, a malicious peer has little information to decide for which applications a reverse engineering effort would pay off. Thus, in order to protect jobs from malicious workers, OurGrid applies a sabotage tolerance technique based on watermarks, analogous to the one proposed by Collberg and Thomborson [36].

3.4.4.3 Securing Peer Identities

OurGrid uses a simple authentication mechanism similar to the Simple Public Key Infrastructure (SPKI) [37], where the public key of the pair of asymmetric keys [38] is used as the peer unique identity. This is in conformance with OurGrid's characteristics of free entry and deployment simplicity. Note that each peer is free to generate its own identity. Since the OurGrid mechanism of incentive to collaborate ensures that changing the identity of a peer is not advantageous, the peers have interest in maintaining their identity.

Security mechanisms are implemented in the asynchronous communication layer of OurGrid. It uses asymmetric encryption keys to sign all messages sent and X.509 certificates that can be optionally validated by a Certification Authority [39].

Each OurGrid component that needs to communicate with another OurGrid component, within or across sites, has a pair of public/private asymmetric keys. The private key is secret and is used to sign each message sent by the component. The public key is attached to outgoing messages. The public key attached to the message can be used to validate the signature of the message just received, ensuring that the message was really sent by the component who has signed it. This solution prevents a malicious component from forging the address of the sender without being detected. Optionally, certificates can be used so that the receiving component can trust the true identity of the sender component. In this case, OurGrid can be configured with the group of Certification Authorities that are trusted. Thus, if the sending component has a certificate that is signed by any one of these authorities, then its identity is not only validated, but also trusted.

Finally, another issue regarding protecting an application from malicious resources is data privacy. Although this is an important concern, OurGrid does not provide any built-in mechanism to handle this potential problem. It assumes that applications are not very secretive, thus requiring no data security, which seems to be an appropriate assumption for many e-Science applications. Moreover, the application data is naturally scattered throughout the grid, making it much harder for a few malicious sites to obtain much of the application data. Naturally, the SPKI underlying infrastructure can be used at the application level to encrypt/decrypt data and provide the required privacy level.

3.5 Cooperating and Coexisting with Other Distributed Computing Infrastructures

With the emergence of many production grid infrastructures, sustainable operation of these infrastructures has become now the main issue to be addressed. In this sense, different grid systems are now seeking to interoperate, not only to increase their capacity, but also to make their operation more cost-effective. In particular, coupling grid infrastructures of different natures enhances the reach and usability of these infrastructures.

In the context of the European Commission co-funded EELA-2 project[12] research has been conducted to implement a solution for supporting the coexistence of a service grid and an opportunistic P2P grid on the same infrastructure. The advantages of this hybrid infrastructure are twofold: first, the coexistence allows idle resources belonging to the service grid to be used in an opportunistic way; second, the provision of an opportunistic grid allows shared resources to be added to the infrastructure, a feature that turns out to be very important for consortia in which many of the member institutions cannot afford the provision of dedicated resources.

In the EELA-2 hybrid grid, each part of the infrastructure runs its own grid middleware, with the service part running gLite,[13] while the opportunistic P2P part runs OurGrid. In order to interoperate these two parts of the infrastructure it was employed the gateway approach in which a gateway element is deployed to bridge the two systems [40]. In this case, jobs originated in one system run in the other in a completely transparent way, using the standard gLite user interface and the OurGrid broker.

A gLite-based service grid is composed by a set of resource centers running services to provide remote access to local dedicated computational resources and central services that form the backbone of the service grid. The gLite grid services can be thematically grouped into four groups: Access and Security Services, Information and Monitoring Services, Job Management Services, and Data Services. The prime aim of the Access and Security Services is to identify users, allowing or denying access to services, on the basis of agreed policies. The Information and Monitoring Services provide information about the gLite resources and their status. The published information is used to locate resources and for monitoring and accounting purposes. The Job Management Services are responsible for dealing with all aspects of the execution of a job on the grid. The Computing Element (CE) service represents a set of computing resources, individually referred to as Worker Nodes (WN), and normally aggregated in a cluster, localized at a resource center. A CE provides a generic interface to the cluster. Another important service in this group is the Workload Management System (WMS). The WMS is a Resource Broker responsible for the distribution and management of jobs across different resource centers. The Data Services are responsible for managing all aspects related to the location and movement of data among the resource centers of the grid. All the gLite Services can be accessed and used through the user interface (UI) service. The UI provides a set of command-line tools that allow users to authenticate themselves in the grid, submit jobs, retrieve their output, and transfer files to remote grid resource centers.

The life cycle of a typical gLite job can be summarized by the following steps: (1) the job is submitted via the user interface; (2) the WMS queues the job and

---

[12] E-science grid facility for Europe and Latin America, http://www.eu-eela.eu/.
[13] http://cern.ch/glite.

starts searching for a suitable CE to execute it; (3) the job is forwarded to the
chosen CE and is executed there; (4) after completion, the user can retrieve the job
output. At all times the job is tracked by logging services, which provide the user with
the view of the job state and further details of job processing. After the user
retrieves the job output, the middleware data on the job is passed to a job provenance service and purged from their original locations.

As described in Fig. 3.2, the Gateway implemented has five main components,
which are the Web Service Submitter, the Database, the Engine, the Plug-in
Manager, and the plug-in instances. The Web Service Submitter is the Gateway
job submission interface. One important feature of this component is to allow the job
sources to submit jobs to the gateway specifying in which destination grid they
want the job to be run, and also to cancel jobs already submitted. The submitter

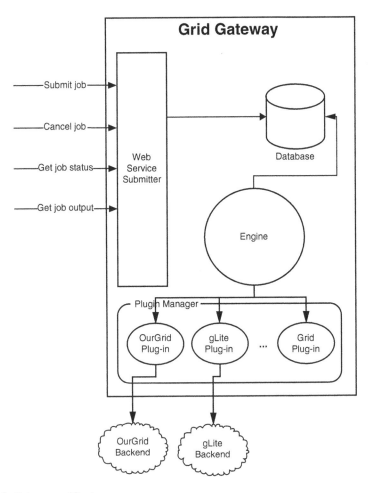

Fig. 3.2 Gateway architecture

communicates with the Database to insert and update jobs. The core of the gateway is the Engine. Its main function is to periodically retrieve new jobs from the Database and forward them to the plug-in that handles the job execution on the destination grid. One plug-in is an implementation of the GridHandler interface, which specifies the common operations of a grid plug-in. The basic operations defined by this interface are job submission and job status update. The Plug-in Manager is responsible for loading and storing the plug-ins deployed within the gateway. The Plug-in Manager reads the properties file of a plug-in and instantiates it accordingly.

Bridging from OurGrid to gLite and vice versa is then conducted by means of the Grid Gateway implementation mentioned above. The OurGrid to gLite bridging is achieved by deploying a modified version of the OurGrid Worker component, which manages the job execution in the gateway instead of executing the job itself. This modified worker represents all resources of the gLite grid, and it can be allocated for the OurGrid jobs as many times as requested. An OurGrid job is composed of a collection of tasks, where each task is submitted for execution on a Worker. When a new task arrives, the Worker invokes an instance of a component called Executor, which defines how a task will be executed. For the bridging purpose, the modified Worker has a new implementation of the Executor, the Gateway Executor that knows how to handle the task execution cycle using the gateway. The Gateway Executor converts the OurGrid task into the gateway canonical job format and submits it to the Gateway Web Service Submitter; after that, it monitors the job execution, doing periodical job status queries; once the job has finished with success, the Gateway Executor gathers the job outputs, otherwise it informs the Worker about the execution errors.

On the other way of the bridge, the transparency of job submission is obtained by modifying a gLite CE (Computing Element) that, instead of forwarding jobs to worker nodes, handles the job execution cycle on the gateway. Job submissions to this CE are converted into tasks executions over the OurGrid backend. This modification was achieved by creating a new JobExecutor in the CE, called *OGGEExecutor*. This executor handles the job register command, converting the job into the gateway job format and submitting it to the Gateway Web Service Submitter. It is also responsible for input/output files transfer and monitoring of the status changes of the submitted job.

3.6   A Success Story: The SegHidro Project

A great challenge for scientists and practitioners in the field of hydrology, hydrogeology, and water resources management is integration and effective collaboration in the process of generating knowledge and technology. Collaboration between all the participants in the process is mandatory to allow true integration of data, models, and knowledge. Moreover, a collaborative approach makes possible the aggregation of the computational resources required to address the highly demanding processing and data storage workloads involved.

Motivated by this challenge, the SegHidro project[14] has been developed since 2005 with the objective of producing an enhanced grid-computing platform that provides not only the capabilities for the integration of computing resources, but also an environment for the sharing and integration of data, models and, ultimately, knowledge. As a result, it promotes e-Science for hydro-informatics.

The SegHidro platform [47] provides a way of simulating hydrometeorological forecasting models – or cascade of models – specified by meteorologists, hydrologists, and engineers, in a wide variety of scenarios. These simulations require high-performance computing resources for their execution. These are provided through the OurGrid Community. The SegHidro Core Architecture (SHiCA) [41] is responsible for managing the submission of tasks to the grid following a prescribed workflow of models or any computer program. SHiCA enables the coupled models to consume their input data, which can be any input file, including the results of previous models in the workflow.

Note that, data produced and used in the context of SegHidro are essentially public and should be reused. In order to encourage data sharing among different users, we have used the OPeNDAP technology – Open-source Project for a Network Data Access Protocol [42], which is characterized by providing independence of data format and easiness for cutting data across geographical and temporal dimensions, according to the parameters of interest. Combined with OPeNDAP it is used a P2P grid information service, named NodeWiz [43], for discovering data distributed geographically and forming a catalog. Not only data, but also models and other software, are registered in the catalog and can be accessed and used by SegHidro users.

The primary targets of SegHidro are groups working collaboratively, including researchers and practitioners and their institutions. Coupling models developed by different groups and sharing data and simulations produced by them require the sharing of knowledge and expertise. SegHidro provides tools for enabling communication among its users, such as forums, mail lists, portals, and Wiki-based environments.

The SegHidro infrastructure is operational and several applications have already been developed by researchers and governmental water agencies in Brazil, including: (1) weather and seasonal climate forecasting using regional atmospheric models for downscaling; (2) reservoir planning and operation; (3) rainwater harvesting risk analysis; (4) integrated surface and groundwater management; (5) operation of water distribution networks; (6) agricultural planning; (7) flood forecasting; (8) soil conservation planning; (9) regional impact of climate change; and (10) regional collaborative studies on Prediction in Ungauged Basins (PUB).

One important aspect in all of these applications is the participation of interdisciplinary teams. An e-Science platform, such as SegHidro, provides a great opportunity and contribution for knowledge systematization and documentation by every group, so that their models and data can be appropriately handled by the system and effectively adopted by the partners and end-users.

---

[14] http://seghidro.lsd.ufcg.edu.br/.

Another remarkable aspect of the system is that most of the applications supported demand large amounts of processing power at particular times, when management decisions need to be taken. For instance, one of these applications is the management of reservoirs in the Northeastern region of Brazil. These reservoirs are abundant over the region and are the main source of water for municipal supply, agricultural and industrial production. Seasonal forecasts of rainfall are reliable and used operationally for supporting water management in the region [44]. The Water Agency of the State of Paraíba (AESA) applies this solution to 115 reservoirs in real time. AESA also uses SegHidro to assess the seasonal risks of the collapse of thousands of rainwater harvesting and storage systems, used in small rural settlements dispersed geographically over the State of Paraíba. In both cases, the availability of a high-throughput computing infrastructure is crucial to allow timely and appropriate management decisions to be taken. In the SegHidro project this is guaranteed through the federation of shared computing resources provided by the several organizations involved, through the OurGrid Community.

3.7 Conclusion

3.7.1 Lessons Learned

This chapter presented our experience with the development of the OurGrid middleware, and with the deployment and operation of the OurGrid Community. Overall, this experience points to the viability of the P2P approach to grid computing.

Technologies such as voluntary computing and P2P grids have shown the suitability of opportunistic infrastructures to support the efficient execution of BoT applications. Although we are not aware of any formal characterization of these applications, our intuition and experience with e-Science projects allow us to conjecture that the frequency distribution of the users of these applications is highly skewed, with a few applications serving a large community of users and a large number of applications serving few, if not a single user. Moreover, popular applications tend to have a much longer lifetime than the much less popular *ad hoc* applications, which are typically disposed after a relatively short-lived research project is over. Voluntary computing systems cover well the head of the distribution, since it is easier to attract donors for popular applications that usually have a higher impact. Moreover, since a large population of users is associated with these applications, the cost of adapting it to the voluntary computing master–slave programming model may be diluted. P2P grids, on the other hand, cater very well to the community of users in the long tail of the distribution.

By observing the evolution of the OurGrid Community during a certain period of time and analyzing the grid usage, it is possible to understand which benefits OurGrid users obtained. In particular, we have analyzed the system's logs for the time period spanning from March to November 2005. In the beginning of March, the OurGrid Community had about 5 active peers and about 60 machines. The community had been in production since December 2004. From April to October, the number of peers steadily grew to about 30 peers, comprising approximately 250 active machines. The major increases on the number of peers took place shortly after a new and more stable version of OurGrid had been released, namely the release of version 3.2, in July 2005.

The benefits obtained by OurGrid users in terms of available computing resources are apparent when we measure the percentage of the available machines that were donated by the peers during this period. If a peer is consuming a donated machine, it means that its local resources are, at this time, not enough to satisfy this peer's users. From March to May, about 40% of the grid machines were being donated. On the highest utilization levels, about 80% of the machines were donated. Note that the percentage of total used machines is typically higher, since it also includes the local resources owned by the peers.

Many users have reported the impact that the use of the OurGrid Community has on the turn-around time of applications. For instance, users of GerPavGrid, an application that performs planning of the investments in the maintenance of Porto Alegre's city road system, have reported that the response time when using the OurGrid Community was approximately 80 times faster than when the application was executed using only their locally available resources [45].

Despite its many success stories, the OurGrid Community is still a rather small system. In fact, due to administrative issues that caused the launching of version 4 of the middleware to be postponed for nearly 2 years, the OurGrid Community has shrunk and is currently mostly restricted to sites belonging to the Federal University of Campina Grande. Recent initiatives that promoted the use of the OurGrid middleware in projects co-funded by the European Commission have helped in publicizing the system and there is a high expectation that the OurGrid Community will soon start a new period of growth. The experience has shown is that it takes a lot of effort to promote a technology whose impact is directly proportional to the level of adoption that it experiences. Nevertheless, we are motivated to continue the promotion of P2P grid computing in general, and the OurGrid Community in particular.

3.7.2 Present Challenges and Future Directions

Our experience with the OurGrid Community has also served to identify a number of challenges ahead for advancing it even further. A present challenge is extending the OurGrid middleware to better suit contributors with diverse motivations. The development of the Network of Favors often has a positive reaction among grid participants that both provide and use grid resources. This mechanism, however, does not resonate with a second class of participants that turns out to be more common than originally thought: altruistic contributors.

Over time, a number of institutions have joined OurGrid with the sole purpose of contributing resources, and a brief experiment with combining voluntary computing with the OurGrid community suggests this approach is promising. Resource providers in these two use cases are not concerned with the return they can obtain through the Network of Favors, but with how their resources are used. For example, a domestic user contributing the idle time of his or her laptop may be more motivated to keep doing so depending on what applications run on his or her worker. Also, an institution that joined the grid to help a specific project may find it important that its resources are allocated to unknown peers only when this project does not need them.

We are currently researching how to incorporate mechanisms in the OurGrid middleware that leverage a wider range of motivations for resource contribution, in addition to the Network of Favors. Interdisciplinary research on cooperation points to a number of design levers that can be considered in this context [46].

A second major challenge identified in our experience is to align the use of idle computing resources with energy efficiency. The increasing awareness about the environmental implications of operating information technology infrastructures, together with the monetary aspect of energy consumption, demand solutions for opportunistic computing to be energy-efficient. Our efforts in this area include policies for establishing when worker nodes should be set to hibernate or operate in standby, or even be shut down. Also, smart scheduling may also be important for reducing energy consumption. Naturally, the challenge is to achieve energy efficiency without compromising too much the applications' execution time.

Finally, a continuing effort is the advancement of the OurGrid middleware to support more classes of applications. BoTs have proven to be a popular type of parallel application, but researchers often need to execute applications that demand communication with external servers or synchronization among tasks. Because of this, an active area of research has been the expansion of the gamma of applications that are suitable for P2P grid computing. Nevertheless, even though the number of applications supported has been increasing – for example, to comport data-intensive BoTs – further effort is still necessary to materialize the democratizing potential of P2P grid computing.

References

1. Thain, D., Tannenbaum, T. and Livny, M. (2005). Distributed Computing in Practice: The Condor Experience. In: Concurrency and Computation: Practice and Experience, 17(2–4), pp. 23–356.
2. Litzkow M., Livny M. and Mutka M. (1988) Condor - A Hunter of Idle Workstations. In Proc. of the 8th Intl. Conference of Distributed Computing Systems.
3. Anderson, D. P., Cobb, J., Korpela, E., Lebofsky, M. and Werthimer D. (2002) SETI@home: An experiment in Public-resource Computing. In: Communications of the ACM, 45(11), pp. 56–61.
4. Foster, I and Kesselman, C. (1998) The Grid: Blueprint for a New computing Infrastructure. Morgan Kaufmann.
5. Cirne, W., Brasileiro, F., Andrade, N., Costa, L., Andrade, A., Novaes, R. and Mowbray, M. (2006). Labs of the world, unite!!! In: Journal of Grid Computing, 4(3), pp. 225–246.

6. Butt, A., Zhang, R., Hu, Y.C. (2006) A self-organizing flock of condors, J. Parallel Distrib. Comput. 66 (1), pp. 145–161.
7. Fedak, G., Germain, C., Neri, V., Cappello, F. (2001). XtremWeb: A generic global computing system. In: Proc of the IEEE Int'l Symp. Cluster Computing and the Grid, pp. 582–587.
8. Taylor, I., Shields, M., Wang, I., Philp, R. (2003) Distributed P2P computing within triana: A galaxy visualization test case. In: IPDPS '03: Proceedings of the 17th International Symposium on Parallel and Distributed Processing.
9. Lo, V. M., Zappala, D., Zhou, D., Liu, Y., Zhao, S. (2004) Cluster computing on the fly: P2P scheduling of idle cycles in the internet. In: IPTPS' 04: Proc. of the 3rd International Workshop on Peer-to-Peer Systems, 2004, pp. 227–236.
10. Oliveira, L., Lopes, L., Silva, F., P3 (Parallel Peer to Peer): An Internet Parallel Programming Environment (2002). In: Web Engineering and Peer-to-Peer Computing Workshop, pp. 274–288.
11. Kollock, P. (1998). Social Dilemmas: The Anatomy of Cooperation. In: Annual Review of Sociology, 24, pp. 183–214.
12. Andrade, N., Brasileiro, F., Cirne, W. and Mowbray, M. (2007). Automatic grid assembly by promoting collaboration in peer-to-peer grids. In: Journal of Parallel and Distributed Computing, 67(8), pp. 957–966.
13. Nowark, M. A. (2006). Five Rules for the Evolution of Cooperation. In: Science, 314(5805), pp. 1560–1563.
14. Feldman M., Lai K., Stoica I. and Chuang J. (2004). Robust incentive techniques for peer-to-peer networks. In: Proc of the 5th ACM Conference on Electronic Commerce, pp. 102–111.
15. Paranhos, D., Cirne, W. and Brasileiro, F.V. (2003). Trading cycles for information: using replication to schedule bag-of-tasks applications on computational grids. In: Proc. of the 9th Intl. Conference on Parallel and Distributed Computing, pp. 169–180.
16. Santos-Neto, E., Cirne, W., Brasileiro, F.V. and Lima, A. (2004). Exploiting replication and data reuse to efficiently schedule data-intensive applications on grids. In: Proc. of the 10th Workshop on Job Scheduling Strategies for Parallel Processing.
17. Kamvar, S.D., Schlosser M.T. and Garcia-Molina, H. (2003). The EigenTrust algorithm for reputation management in P2P networks. In: Proc. of the 12th Intl. World Wide Web Conference, pp. 640–651.
18. Vishnumurthy, V., Chandrakumar, S., Sirer, E. (2003). KARMA: a secure economic framework for peer-to-peer resource sharing. In: Proc. of the 1st Workshop on Economics of Peer-to-Peer Systems.
19. Buyya, R. and Vazhkudai, S. (2001). Compute Power Market: towards a market-oriented grid. In: Proc. of the 1st IEEE/ACM International Symposium on Cluster Computing and the Grid, pp. 574.
20. Lai, K., Huberman, B.A. and Fine, L. (2004). Tycoon: A distributed market-based resource allocation system. HP Labs Technical Report cs.DC/0404013.
21. Schneidman, J., Chaki, Ng., Parkes, D., AuYoung, A., Snoeren, A.C., Vahdat, A. and Chun, B. (2005). Why markets could (but don't currently) solve resource allocation problems in systems. In: Proc. of the 10th USENIX Workshop on Hot Topics in Operating Systems, pp. 7.
22. Yamagishi, T. and Matsuda, M. (2003). The role of reputation in open and closed societies: an experimental study of online trading. Working paper 8, Center for the Study of Cultural and Ecological Foundations of the Mind, http://joi.ito.com/archives/papers/Yamagishi_ASQ1.pdf.
23. Mowbray, M., Brasileiro, F.V., Andrade, N., Santana, J. and Cirne, W. (2006). A reciprocation-based economy for multiple services in peer-to-peer grids. In: Proc. of the 6th IEEE Intl. Conference on Peer-to-Peer Computing, pp. 193–202.
24. Lee, C.B., Schwartzman, Y., Hardy, J. and Snavely, A. (2004). Are User Runtime Estimates Inherently Inaccurate? In: Proc. of the Workshop on Job Scheduling Strategies for Parallel Processing, pp. 253–263.

25. Santos, R., Andrade, A., Cirne, W., Brasileiro, F.V and Andrade, N. (2007). Relative Autonomous Accounting for Peer-to-Peer Grids. In: Concurrency and Computation: Practice and Experience, 19(14), pp. 1937–1954.
26. Casanova, H. et al. (2000). Heuristics for scheduling parameter sweep applications in grid environments. In: Proc. of 9th Heterogeneous Computing Workshop, pp. 349–363.
27. Nobrega, N., Assis, L. and Brasileiro, F. (2008). Scheduling CPU-Intensive Grid Applications Using Partial Information. In: 37th International Conference on Parallel Processing, pp. 262–269.
28. Massie, M., Chun, B. and Culler, D. (2004). The Ganglia Distributed Monitoring System: Design, Implementation, and Experience. In: Journal of Parallel Computing, 30(7), pp. 817–840.
29. Yalagandula, P., Sharma, P., Banerjee, S., Basu, S. and Lee, S.-J. (2006). S3: A scalable sensing service for monitoring large networked systems. In: Proc. of SIGCOMM'06 Workshops, pp. 71–76.
30. Brasileiro, F., Costa, L., Andrade, A., Cirne, W., Basu, S. and Banerjee, S. (2006). A large scale fault-tolerant grid information service. In: Proc. of 4th Intl. Workshop on Middleware for Grid Computing, pp. 14.
31. Podlipnig, S. and Böszörmenyi, L. (2003). A survey of web cache replacement strategies. ACM Computing Surveys, 35(4), pp. 374–398.
32. Soares, P., Oliveira, M., Guerrero, D. and Brasileiro, F. (2008). Solomon: Incentivando o Compartilhamento e Maior Disponibilidade em Sistemas de Armazenamento Entre-Pares. In: Anais do IV Workshop on Peer-to-Peer, pp. 1–12.
33. Silva, R., Brasileiro, F., and Lopes, R. Technical Report: Providing Efficiency and Fairness in a Disk Cache System for Computational Peer-to-Peer Grids. TR-1 (2010), available at http://www.lsd.ufcg.edu.br/~lsd/relatorios_tecnicos/TR-1.pdf.
34. Santhanam, S., Elango, P., Arpaci-Dusseau, A. and Livny, M. (2005). Deploying virtual machines as sandboxes for the grid. In: Proc. of the 2nd conference on Real, Large Distributed Systems, pp. 7–12.
35. Sarmenta, L. Sabotage-Tolerance Mechanisms for Volunteer Computing Systems (2002). In: Future Generation Computer Systems, 18 (4), pp. 561–572.
36. Collberg, C. S. and Thomborson, C. (2002). Watermarking, tamper-proofing, and obfuscation - tools for software protection. In: Software Engineering, IEEE Transactions on, 28(8), pp. 735–746.
37. Ellison, C., Frantz, B., Lampson, B., Rivest, R., Thomas, B., and Ylonen, T. (1999). RFC 2693: Spki certificate theory. Request for Comments (RFC) 2693, Network Working Group.
38. Kaliski, B. (1998). RFC 2315: Pkcs #7: Cryptographic message syntax. Request for Comments (RFC) 2315, Network Working Group.
39. Adams, C. and Farrell, S. (1999). RFC 2510: Internet X.509 public key infrastructure certificate management protocols. Request for Comments (RFC) 2510, Network Working Group.
40. Brasileiro, F., Duarte, A., Silva, R. and Gaudêncio, M. (2009). On the co-existence of service and opportunistic grids. In: Proc. of the First EELA-2 Conference, pp. 51–62.
41. Voorsluys, W., Araújo, E., Cirne, W., Galvão, C., Souza, E. and Cavalcanti, E. (2007). Fostering collaboration to better manage water resources. In: Concurrency and Computation. Practice and Experience, vol. 19, pp. 1609–1620.
42. Cornillon, P., Gallagher, J. and Sgouros, T. (2003). OPeNDAP: accessing data in a distributed, heterogeneous environment. In: Data Science Journal, vol. 2, pp. 164–174.
43. Basu, S., Banerjee, S., Sharma, P. and Lee, S. J. (2005). NodeWiz: peer-to-peer resource discovery for grids. In: Proc. 5th Intl. Workshop on Global and Peer-to-Peer Computing, pp. 213–220.
44. Galvão, C., Nobre, P., Braga, A. C. F. M. et al. (2005). Climatic predictability, hydrology and water resources over Nordeste Brazil. In: Regional Hydrological Impacts of Climatic Change – Impact Assessment and Decision Making (ed. By T. Wagener et al.), pp. 211–220. IAHS Publ. 295. IAHS Press, Wallingford, UK.

45. de Rose, C., Ferreto, T., Farias, M., Dias, V., Cirne, W., Oliveira, M., Saikoski, K., and Danieleski, M. (2006). Gerpavgrid: using the grid to maintain the city road system. In: Proceedings of the 18th International Symposium on Computer Architecture and High Performance Computing (SBAC-PAD'06), pp. 73–80.
46. Benkler, Y. (Forthcoming) Law, Policy, and Cooperation. In Balleisen, E. and Moss D., eds. Government and Markets: Toward a New Theory of Regulation. Cambridge University Press.
47. Galvão, C., Nóbrega, R., Brasileiro, F. and Araújo, E. (2009). An e-Science platform for collaborative generation of knowledge and technology in hydrology, hydrogeology and water resources. In: IAHS-AISH publication, vol. 331, pp. 500–504.

Chapter 4
Peer4Peer: e-Science Community for Network Overlay and Grid Computing Research

Luís Veiga, João Nuno Silva, and João Coelho Garcia

Abstract This chapter describes a novel approach to Grid and overlay network research that leverages distributed infrastructures and multi-core machines enabling increased simulation complexity and speed. We present its motivation, background, current shortcomings, and the core architectural concepts of the novel research proposed. This is an ongoing effort to further our peer-to-peer cycle-sharing platform by providing a scalable, efficient, and reliable simulation substrate for the Grid and overlay topologies developed by the research community. Thus, Grid and overlay simulations are improved due to (1) increased scalability of simulation tools with a novel parallel, distributed, and decentralized architecture; (2) harnessing the power of idle CPU cycles spread around the Internet as a desktop Grid (over a peer-to-peer overlay); and (3) a framework for topology definition, dissemination, evaluation, and reuse which eases Grid and overlay research. The infrastructure, simulation engine, topology modeling language (TML), management services, and portal comprise a cloud-like platform for overlay research.

4.1 Introduction

The last decade has witnessed the emergence of e-Science in some fields, where the leading scientific research can no longer be carried out resorting exclusively to laboratory equipment. Instead, e-Science research entails the acquisition, storage, and intensive processing of vast amount of data. This requires access to high-performance and/or large-scale computing infrastructures. Examples of e-Science research themes include not only simulations (social, particle physics, systems, and networks), but also drug research and molecular modeling, earth sciences, and bioinformatics.

L. Veiga (✉), J.N. Silva, and J.C. Garcia
INESC ID Lisboa/Technical University of Lisbon, Rua Alves Redol 9,
1000-029 Lisbon, Portugal
e-mail: luis.veiga@inesc-id.pt

Xiaoyu Yang et al. (eds.), *Guide to e-Science: Next Generation Scientific Research and Discovery*, Computer Communications and Networks,
DOI 10.1007/978-0-85729-439-5_4, © Springer-Verlag London Limited 2011

Researchers working in each specific e-Science field tend to aggregate around informal communities sharing tools, data sets, experiment results, data processing and/or simulation code, and sometimes, computing resources, in a distributed fashion being subjected to different levels of (de-)centralization. However, most e-Scientists have limited computing skills, as they are neither computer scientists, engineers, nor programmers, hence the paramount importance of increasing the simplicity and transparency of the tools, middleware, models, and algorithms that support e-Science activities.

More pointedly, in this chapter, peer-to-peer overlay networks and Grid infra-structures are discussed which are areas of very active research within the distributed systems, middleware, and network communities. The type of research we are addressing in this chapter is a part of computer science (developing protocols for overlay networks and Grid middleware is computer science). If this can be carried out with the very help of supporting infrastructures, middleware and applications deployed on a distributed system (reducing coding as much as possible), it is just another case of e-Science (even though it is not addressing fundamental sciences such as physics or chemistry; in fact, e-Science is also carried out on the other side of the sciences' *spectrum*, e.g., with statistical analysis employed in social sciences).

Given the large number of elements in such topologies (overlays and grids), an important fraction of the current research in this field is performed not on real systems but instead resorting to simulation tools (e.g., Simgrid [1], PeerSim [2], OverSim [3]), thereby reducing machine cost and administration issues.

Simulation of these topologies amounts to storing all the relevant information of the participating nodes in the simulated topology (either being simulated peers or simulated nodes integrated in a simulated Grid) and executing the protocol-described behavior of all participating nodes. This is very resource intensive as the data and behavior of a large number of nodes is being stored and simulated in a single machine.

Moreover, resorting to simulations enables researchers to carry out experiments with more elements (e.g., participating sites, applications) and more sophisticated behavior than would be possible by resorting exclusively to real, manually deployed, and user-driven applications. The results of these stress-test experiments enable researchers to argue and defend more realistic claims about their proposed overlay protocols, Grid middleware, and schedulers. In such competitive research areas, new ideas without strong results to back them up simply will not deserve full credit, regardless of their intrinsic value. As the Internet grows bigger, thus must simulations grow in size and, consequently, also in complexity. Often, simulation code and simulated results are the sole information sources available to perform repeated research, which is still infrequent in computer science but an adamant requirement in other fields, such as medical and biological sciences.

Currently, research in these fields is carried out using two alternatives which are sometimes combined. Protocols and algorithms are sketched and coded resorting to application programming interfaces provided by simulation tools (sometimes, protocol and algorithm code are directly inserted as extensions to the simulation tool source code). This allows the study of the algorithm and protocol properties, coordination, soundness, and behavior in very large-scale populations (usually, around thousands or millions of simulated computing nodes). The simulators (NS2 [4], GridSim [5], Simgrid [1], PeerSim [2], OverSim [3]) are programs that normally process an event queue serially, which contains protocol messages sent by nodes, and delivers them to addressed nodes by executing predefined methods on those objects. These tools are limited to the computing power and available memory of a single machine. Therefore, details of such simulations must be restricted to a minimum in order to simulate such vast populations within acceptable time frames. The simulations do not execute full application and operating system code, and do not monitor communication links with full accuracy.

Therefore, in order to demonstrate the feasibility of the actual deployment of a protocol and algorithm in a realistic test field, researchers must resort to an alternative approach. They make use of distributed test beds where a limited number (up to a few hundreds) of dedicated physical machines (or shared via virtualization technology) execute the actual complete code stacks (operating system, middleware, protocol, and application code), where the performance of the execution and communication is evaluated by employing real machines and real network links among the test-bed nodes.

Unfortunately, current overlay and Grid simulation are encumbered by architecture, scale, and performance limitations that cannot be solved simply by stacking more powerful computers. The performance of simulation tools is hindered because network and topology simulation code is mostly serial and manipulates a large global state, which is assumed to be consistent. Simulations are run in a centralized and sequential way therefore not drawing many of the advantages of increasingly prevalent multi-core machines or computing clusters. Thus, although the increased power of aggregated computers may be used to execute more Grid and overlay simulations simultaneously, it is not possible to run each individual simulation faster or to leverage more CPUs to run more complex simulations (larger number of elements) within a given time frame. Due to these limitations and memory demands, most simulations are today limited to just tens of thousand nodes which is not realistic given today's existing widespread usage of peer-to-peer systems.

Conversely, although existing utility and cloud computing infrastructures can manage large numbers of (virtual) machines, and can thus execute all the nodes of an experiment concurrently (or in parallel), it is currently unfeasible, both practically and financially, to allocate millions of machines in a dedicated test bed. An alternative source of computing power must be found and drawn from. Large-scale peer-to-peer infrastructures, usually dedicated to content sharing, may be leveraged as processor-sharing overlays (usually called cycle-sharing platforms).

In this chapter, we have described the motivation, vision, architecture, and current implementation and performance results of Peer4Peer, an ongoing project addressing the challenges described above. Peer4Peer prescribes the usage of a world-scale free and voluntary cycle-sharing peer-to-peer infrastructure to perform simulations of actual peer-to-peer protocols, algorithms, and Grid middleware, of virtually unbounded size and with increased performance, breaking the serial nature of current simulation tools. Furthermore, the peer-to-peer infrastructure can also be leveraged for content sharing and store programs, scripts, configuration of simulated network topologies, experimental results, and schedules for experiment/ simulation execution. This will facilitate the dissemination and reuse of research in areas of peer-to-peer protocols and Grid middleware. In summary, Peer4Peer is aiming at providing researchers with a platform to support e-Science, in the specific field of overlay and Grid simulation.

The remainder of this chapter is organized as follows. In the next section, we present a comprehensive portrait of how e-Science is carried out nowadays. In Sect. 4.2, we present the case for a novel approach to overlay and Grid simulation. Sections 4.3 and 4.4 present the main aspects of the broader long-term vision associated with the Peer4Peer project. In Sect. 4.5, we present the architecture of the current development efforts to deploy Peer4Peer, while Sect. 4.6 describes the main components and implementation details of the current deliverables. In Sect. 4.7, we offer evaluation and performance measurements of the implementation already carried out. Section 4.8 is dedicated to put into perspective the relevant related research in the main themes connected with our work, in a broader view. The chapter closes with some conclusions and future work.

4.2 Current Approaches to e-Science

The 1990s saw the birth of the cluster, a group of colocated general-purpose computers connected by a dedicated network, as a means to execute parallel scientific computations. PVM [6] provided a set of message-passing primitives, with implementations available on multiprocessors and LAN-connected workstations, while, from the distributed systems side, NOW (Network of Workstations) [7] provided an abstraction layer, allowing the transparent access to network scattered resources (storage and CPU). From that point on, the architecture of a typical parallel system has been moving away from massive multiprocessors (connected with a proprietary bus) to clusters of computer nodes (some of them multiprocessors themselves) connected with commodity network equipment (Gigabit Ethernet or Mirinet).

This evolution of execution environments affected the available programming systems as well as resource management and scheduling middleware. Although clusters allow avoiding the cost of acquiring a mainframe or supercomputer, they have some drawbacks: competition between local (usually interactive) applications and cluster-wide applications, configuration and performance difficulties when the cluster is heterogeneous, and, lastly, reduced bandwidth if the cluster network interconnect is used for multiple purposes.

At the same time, the development of the Internet allowed an easier access to remote resources. One of those resources was computing cycles. SETI@home [8] was one of the first systems to successfully use remote and scattered idle computer to process data and solve a scientific problem. Following these trends, today most parallel computations either run on clusters of computer nodes [9] or over the Internet [10, 11], and most fit in one of two categories: message passing or parameter sweep.

In message-passing applications, data is split and distributed among several nodes. Periodically messages are transmitted between nodes to transmit the relevant information, mostly changes on frontier data. To perform such communication, the most used API is MPI [12]. In parameter sweep application, a master process goes over a range of possible parameters by starting several concurrent slave processes which, while running the same program, are executed using different parameters. Once these slave processes conclude, results are transmitted to the master process and aggregated there.

In clusters of small dimension, the management of the nodes can be ad hoc and without the need of specialized software. For any medium-sized installation with several concurrent users, it is necessary to have a software layer that manages the available resources, the submitted jobs, and the authorized users. Resorting to nodes scattered over the Internet to create a sort of ad hoc cluster in order to perform a computation, amplifies both the benefits and problems of traditional clusters: Nodes are even more varied and unreliable, and networks have less bandwidth and are less secure.

Examples of cluster resource managers are Condor [13], Portable Batch System [14], or Sun Grid Engine [15]. Besides this software layer, clusters still need a distributed file system (such as AFS [16], CIFS [17], GPFS [18], or GlusterFS [19]) in order to guarantee a uniform file access on every node. These resource managers handle the submitted jobs queues and schedule those jobs to the available resources. This process takes into account the requirements (memory, and number of processors), the available resources, and other users' privileges, and uses different scheduling policies [20–23].

With Ian Foster's vision [24, 25] of a new computing infrastructure for research, the so-called Grid, the classical cluster disappeared from the center of the environment, becoming just a service for the creation of globally disperse communities. This vision encompasses two distinct development directions: the infrastructure to connect the various scattered resources (clusters) and the tools to ease the access to data, processing resources, and results.

One of the first initiatives for building a Grid infrastructure was Globus [26]. Besides the creation of an infrastructure to connect geographical disperse resources, Globus also helped define a series of standards related to authentication, resource accounting, and interfaces to access remote resources. This new vision of a global computing environment changed the way authentication should be performed. While on a local cluster system a simple user/password authentication scheme was simple enough, on a globally distributed environment it is not. As users from different organizations (with some local common interests but possibly with global conflicting ones) will interact and share resources, sophisticated authentication schemes and resource access policies are fundamental.

Classical parallel programming paradigms can also be deployed on the Grid: Users either develop a parallel application using a message-passing API or define a parameter sweep job. In addition to these models, grids frequently support the definition and execution of workflow patterns, where a set of resources are accessed and used according to a graph description where each node represents a job and each vertex represents a dependency and/or data transmission between jobs.

In order to allow the parallel execution of programs on grids, meta-schedulers (Globus GRAM [27], GridWay [28]) have been developed. This new software layer aggregates different clusters and provides a uniform view of the various resources available. As in a cluster, when submitting a job, the user defines how many processors are required and submits the execution code, the input files, and parameters. Based on this information, the meta-scheduler finds the best remote cluster to execute it.

Another vector of Grid research and development was centered on the creation of communities around research subjects. The fundamental aggregation software for such communities is research portals. Generic Grid portals (GridSphere [29], NINF [30], Nimrod/G [31]) allow for the interaction with the Grid using a simple user interface. With these portals, users can authenticate themselves on the Grid, and define parallel jobs without resorting to the command line or editing configuration files. Although Ganga [32] is a generic Grid framework for job definition and management that allows for the development of specific plug-in to be used by specific communities, at the moment, there are plug-ins to execute simulations in the context of CERN's LHCb and ATLAS experiments.

Other Grid portals are specific to a research community. Through a web-based graphical interface, users may access experimental and simulation data, reuse previously developed simulation code, and start jobs on computing clusters. NanoHub [33] is an example of such a portal. Besides the access to community web resources, it also allows for the execution of simulation codes using available Grid backends.

Another relevant Grid platform is LEAD [34], a project in which a service-oriented architecture (based on web services) is used to leverage and extend a weather simulation Grid. The high level of service composition in LEAD provides users with powerful tools for simulation data generation (Weather Research and Forecast model), storage (myLEAD), search (Algorithm Development and Mining, aDaM), and visualization (Integrated Data Viewer). This architecture not only provides resource discovery to leverage computing power (mostly from supercomputing centers, albeit these are not usually available in research developed in other fields), but also eases application development (resorting to a workflow system, analogous to DAGMan in Condor), and data management and search (by means of a metadata catalog).

Triana [35] is a Grid middleware framework that also aims at easing e-Science by, besides offering resource discovery and scheduling, providing an alternative application development model for Grid applications, coding-free for most researchers. This model is based on the graphical interactive composition of reusable components from an extendable component library (more than 500 developed covering, e.g., statistical analysis, signal, audio and video processing). Components are inserted into task-graphs akin to workflows and can be scheduled for execution in distributed manner. Although initially a stand-alone approach exclusively based on Java and RMI, Triana is now interoperable with Grid middleware, component frameworks, and web services. Thus, Triana becomes more of an application development architecture and model than strictly a Grid middleware.

While the fully institutional parallel computing has been growing with several Grid initiatives, a more lax approach to parallel computing has also grown. With the growth of the Internet, idle computing cycles on desktop computers became a resource to be used and aggregated. One of the first projects to successfully use this new resource was SETI@home [8]. Attaining a performance of about 27 TeraFLOPS it proved that embarrassingly parallel applications could be executed outside the classical computing centers. Several projects tried to develop efficient architectures for the execution of such problems on the Internet, but the only successful surviving system is BOINC [11, 36]. Although its architecture is simple, it is difficult to set up a BOINC server and gather donors, and this architecture is limited to the execution of parameter sweep simulations, not allowing the execution of regular message-passing parallel applications.

The cloud, in the form of utility computing infrastructures [37–39], is considered the next step in large-scale computing infrastructures allowing for the integration of grids (with computing clusters distributed across virtual organizations) and utility computing farms (Amazon Elastic Clouds [37]). Such infrastructures revolve around the instantiation of system-level virtual machines (e.g., Xen), of preset configurations, charged by the whole number of processing hours or calls to web applications. When applied to the parallel execution of simulations, these new infrastructures can be a viable and affordable source of computing power [40].

Although easily accessible, the resources provided by a computing cloud can only be used as a classical cluster, either to execute message-passing applications, web applications, or embarrassingly parallel problems.

The Archer platform [41] goes one step further from the classical Grid portal systems. It gathers around the same platform the users with similar computational requirements (simulation of computer architectures), but in the back end its approach diverges from the traditional Grid. Besides the usual Grid resources, Archer aggregates donated resources from the edge of the Internet (as any other distributed computing infrastructure) and uses cloud and utility computing infrastructures as a source of computing power.

We have seen that the actual source for computing cycles ranges from dedicated clusters to the edge of the Internet at users' homes. Utility computing infrastructures are also becoming a viable source of computing power to solve simulation problems. Existing software has also been adapting to the new requirements: It is possible to execute parallel MPI-based applications on clusters (dedicated or created on utility computing infrastructures), execute embarrassingly parallel application on the Internet (using distributed computing infrastructures), or execute workflows on the Grid (using for each step the best available resource).

To help use scattered and distributed resources, user communities have been gathering around Grid portals. These systems not only enable the sharing of knowledge (scientific results, educational material) but also allow an efficient access to distributed computing infrastructures. These portals only provide access to the Grid: set of institutional infrastructures where resources are lent or rented for a particular objective.

4.3 The Need for Next Generation Overlay and Grid Simulation

Clearly, the rich plethora of existing approaches to distributed computing and distributed resource and content sharing, described in the previous section, have enabled e-Science in various domains. Armed with such vast amounts of computing, storage, and communication resources, researchers in various fields (e.g., physics, chemistry, materials science, or biology) have achieved discoveries that could otherwise simply not have been possible in our lifetime due to limited computing power and resources.

Nevertheless, in several specific domains, simply amassing distributed resources is not enough. Simulation of distributed systems, namely peer-to-peer overlays and Grid middleware, is such a domain. Although the extra available resources can offer improved overall throughput (i.e., ability to perform more simulations simultaneously), by themselves they cannot guarantee improved speed (i.e., the elapsed time of each individual simulation).

In this chapter, we are addressing one of these specific domains where e-Science has offered only limited support for researcher interaction, content sharing, and some resource sharing but none for increasing the speed of experimentation. This is especially relevant in an era where multi-core and multi-CPU machines are becoming prevalent, and cloud computing is promising elastic allocation of cheaper computing resources. These aspects should be entirely leveraged and taken advantage of in order to improve the performance of the tasks comprising peer-to-peer and Grid simulation.

Currently, many researchers neither have access to clusters (nor grids), nor have an adequate budget for accessing commercial cloud computing platforms such as Amazon EC2. Furthermore, they face a conundrum when testing algorithms and middleware: They either use higher-level Grid/overlay simulators managing thousands of nodes but run serial, and not distributed or parallel simulations; or they use parallel and distributed lower-level system test beds but run complex OS/application code requiring computing power several orders of magnitude higher for experiments of comparable complexity.

Existing free large-scale distributed research test beds (e.g., PlanetLab [42], Emulab [43]) allow running experiments of complete distributed systems executing on real test-bed nodes or virtual machines, using complete system images (operating system, protocol/middleware, and application code) of each of the simulated participating sites in a distributed computation. However, the inherent overhead is prohibitive and simulating a small-to-medium size system (e.g., hundreds of nodes) would require roughly the same order of magnitude of test-bed nodes to be available simultaneously which is impracticable. Some interfaces for network (NS2) and overlay (OpenDHT) simulators are also offered but they only reduce the burden of having to ship entire virtual appliances to be executed at the test-bed nodes. They do not allow cooperation among several simulators to parallelize simulations or simulate larger, more complex topologies.

When simulations are designed, the models and representations used to describe topologies are often of low semantic level, ad hoc, and mostly programmatic. This forces researchers to actually write tedious code to instantiate nodes in the topology and intricate, tool-dependent code to implement basic data structures and behavior (routing, neighbor tables). Topology reuse, analysis, and both scholarly and teaching dissemination are greatly limited.

In summary, there are three important challenges that correspond to present shortcomings causing drag in these areas, regarding not only research but also even teaching:

- The serial nature of simulation tools, commonly involving centralized globally shared data and event queue manipulations, prevents the scale-up that could be provided by the increasing democratization of access to multi-core machines (e.g., dual-core laptops and quad-core desktops).
- The impossibility of executing simulations in distributed manner thereby preventing the scale-out that could be reached by engaging platforms for voluntary cycle-sharing, utility computing and Grid infrastructures (in test beds as PlanetLab full execution imposes an overhead that greatly limits simulation size).
- The dominance of programmatic descriptions of researched and tested topologies, locked in specific programming languages and simulator API idioms.

The aforementioned shortcomings cause a number of problems that hinder the expansion of current overlay and Grid research, in depth, breadth, and community impact. Examples of such restrictions include: limited simulation size and complexity; limited scope of results; inefficient employment of resources involved in experiments; lack of architecture/simulator-agnostic descriptions of protocols, middleware, and schedulers; very restricted ability to perform independent repeated research [44]; lack of a uniform repository for reusability of such research; global absence of accessible teaching platforms.

In the next sections, we describe in greater detail the ongoing work to achieve this with: (1) a global overview of the Peer4Peer proposal, (2) the architecture for its deployment, (3) details of the current implementation, and (4) some performance and scalability results.

4.4   The Peer4Peer Vision: Peer-to-Peer Cycle-Sharing, Parallelized Simulation, Data and Protocol Language

Peer4Peer's aim is to provide researchers with a cloud-like platform for network overlay research. This entails contributing to laying foundations that will contribute to step up research in peer-to-peer overlay and Grid topologies to a new level. In order to achieve this, we need to tackle existing limitations regarding scale, efficiency, and expressiveness by providing a new platform for overlay simulation research, as described in this section.

Therefore, in order to advance further, overlay and Grid simulation face new requirements:

- Increasing scalability of simulation tools with a novel parallel, distributed, and decentralized architecture.
- Harnessing the power of idle CPU cycles over the Internet by incorporating them in a desktop Grid or a public computing infrastructure (on a peer-to-peer overlay), avoiding the need for proprietary clusters, access to institutional grids or utility computing budgets.
- Further Grid and overlay research with a framework for integrated topology definition, dissemination, evaluation, and reuse.

To address the problems identified, the Peer4Peer approach is to attack them both in breadth and depth. This implies contributing with novel scientific solutions to specific problems (e.g., resource discovery on peer-to-peer systems), as well as providing the research community with a useful and usable simulation infrastructure integrated with a portal for easy access, configuration, and sharing.

The primary substrate for Peer4Peer is an extendable peer-to-peer overlay platform (the mesh) comprising possibly asymmetrical participant nodes, aggregating individual desktop peers as well as efficiently leveraging, if available, computing time on server clusters, Grid sites, and utility computing facilities.

Simulations of peer-to-peer overlay and Grid topologies are to be parallelized and distributed. What is now mostly a single main task in current simulation tools must be decoupled in order to allow concurrent progress of (partial) simulations of different regions of the simulated topologies. This results in higher speedups due to parallel execution and increases scalability by enabling the mesh to host simulations of potentially unbounded size and interaction complexity.

To overcome the lack of expressiveness of the simulation specification mechanisms in current tools, there is a need for a domain-specific language that allies greater expressiveness with the ability of reuse for teaching, study, and repeated research. Such topology modeling language (TML) will allow the specification of simulation requirements, flat, layered, multidimensional, hierarchical, and novel recursive topologies to simulate arbitrarily large systems. A TML must encompass, at least, rules to specify: entry, exit, routing and recovery protocols; neighbor tables; indexing and data stored at nodes and how/where to retrieve it.

Finally, available open-source groupware and content management systems may be extended to create a portal for groups and communities to interface with Peer4Peer and interactively share topologies, simulations, and results. An XML-RPC or REST-based interface enables automatic deployment and retrieval of results promoting embedding of Peer4Peer in web pages and mash-ups.

Simulated topologies need not be limited to content sharing. They could themselves be simulated cycle-sharing topologies as it is common in Grid infrastructures. Therefore, the use of a TML may allow the definition of policies regarding resource discovery, reservation, scheduling, accounting, recycling, redundancy, versioning, etc., to be enforced within each simulation.

Therefore, at its core, Peer4Peer is a recursive overlay topology comprising its substrate and all the simulated topologies. TML and its templates will be the empowering means to allow simulated topologies to define and explore new structures, behaviors, strategies, and their easy widespread sharing.

4.5   Current Peer4Peer Architecture

In this section, we describe the main aspects of the current Peer4Peer architecture, which is depicted in Fig. 4.1: the mesh of simulator nodes running the overlay simulator, the simulation calculating the evolution of the state of a simulated network overlay, the services supporting the establishment and management of the simulation network, the topology model that formally specifies the simulated overlay, and, finally, the portal providing access to the simulator and mechanisms for sharing all involved information (topologies, simulation scenarios, results, etc.).

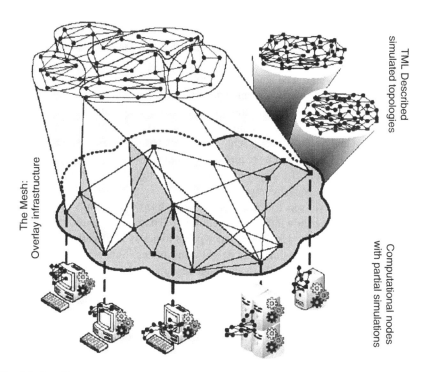

Fig. 4.1   Peer4Peer overall vision

4.5.1 Mesh: Cycle-Sharing Overlay

The mesh is a peer-to-peer overlay able to harness idle computing cycles from asymmetrical participant nodes. Thus, it incorporates specific mechanisms and interfaces to engage peers, individual desktop, server clusters, Grid sites, and utility computing time slices. Each type of peer has different capabilities and a dedicated module is able to access them (invoking corresponding middleware) and exploit them (representing them as higher capacity nodes) by giving them higher simulation loads.

The Peer4Peer mesh is extendable. It provides the fundamental support for simulation deployment, result caching, data storage, and resource discovery and management for cycle-sharing and distributed scheduling. On top of these fundamental mechanisms, more high-level services can be deployed such as retry-based fault-tolerance, replication for reliability, checkpointing and migration to ensure progress in long simulations, or more global evaluation aspects such as resource recycling, accounting, and quality-of-service. Though challenging, it must be noted that such high-level services can be implemented at the overlay/simulator-level. Therefore, the associated software development effort is much lower than implementing similar mechanisms within an operating system or virtual machine runtime.

The mesh follows a hybrid and hierarchical structure. In this sense, the mesh behaves as a recursive overlay topology. Regarding content and routing, the mesh is a structured overlay. Each top-level data item stored in the mesh is in itself either a topology description, a description of resource discovery and management policies, simulation setting, or results of simulation execution. Topology descriptions encompass node population, routing and communication protocol, and content placement rules. Resource and management policies to be enforced include: description of resource discovery, reservation, scheduling, accounting, recycling, redundancy, and versioning.

Simulation settings encapsulate topology, resource, and management policies. Simulation results include the outcome of simulations and aggregate properties such as average and total messages sent, etc. Simulated topologies are represented and managed across Peer4Peer as recursive topologies, that is, overlays where data items represent segments of the very Grid and overlay topologies whose simulation may span tens or hundreds of computers.

Regarding base-level services such as resource discovery (mainly with respect to CPU, memory, and bandwidth) and scheduling of (partial) simulations, the mesh will employ automatically designated super-peers to act as information hubs about resources of groups comprising their neighboring nodes. Super-peers will aggregate into a structured overlay only to exchange resources when there are not enough within each group.

4.5.2 Simulator: Parallel and Distributed Topology Simulation

At every node in the mesh, a number of concurrent simulator threads are executed. Each one is in charge of executing a number of simulation steps to simulate a specific region of the simulated topology, that is, it will perform a partial simulation.

This way, events localized in the vicinity of a simulated node cannot interfere with other simulated nodes at a distance preventing them from being influenced by it (i.e., out of the event – message – horizon for a given number of hops) until some time has passed. Partial simulations may run in the same or different nodes.

Each node of the mesh will execute a component of the distributed simulation engine. Communication among nodes running partial simulations of one topology simulation interact using a standard API that either manages shared memory or exchange messages via the mesh. The simulation engine component may have different versions in accordance to the type of underlying infrastructure providing computing cycles. All versions of the simulation component perform parallel (i.e., multi-threaded) execution targeting multi-core machines as even desktop computers can benefit from it. All versions can be deployable as virtual appliances.

Simulation components are to be executed primarily on common cycle-sharing desktop nodes. Nonetheless, executing simulations on server clusters, Grid sites, and utility computing infrastructures will leverage widespread middleware, libraries, and virtual machine support (e.g., shared memory, STM, Terracotta, MPI, Globus, and Xen).

Despite the simulations being distributed, consistency among simulation nodes must ultimately be enforced to ensure simulation accuracy and correctness, although a high degree of non-determinism is already present in this type of systems in real deployments. In order to achieve this, we partition the global simulation state and investigate the adaptation of optimistic consistency algorithms, such as divergence bounding and more recent vector-field consistency [45] employed. This leverages notions of locality-awareness employed in most massive multiplayer games that, while guaranteeing global consistency, employ region-based approaches to speed up most of the game interaction. The amount of time, or number of rounds, that mandate synchronization among regions, to ensure safety when interactions cross region boundaries, can be configured and tuned. Hard synchronization needs only to occur when events interfere with two or more of such simulated regions.

4.5.3 High-Level Services

Since the mesh is mostly comprised of voluntary desktop machines, node churn (entry, exit, or failure) will be high in most peer-to-peer overlays. Therefore, to ensure fairness and balance in resources used by running simulations and to prevent wasted efforts on node failure, a number of higher-level services need to be deployed on top of the basic mesh. These will be included in the basic client as plug-ins to the mesh protocol and simulator engine.

To ensure fairness, these modules will provide migration of partial simulations to perform load-balancing. Migration is also useful to attempt at colocating sibling partial simulations in the same mesh node or neighboring nodes. This will prevent network communication among simulation engines and increase speed.

To prevent wasted work, the simulation modules provide fundamental fault-tolerance and reliability support. Each partial simulation may be scheduled several times to different nodes in the mesh, its results gathered and compared in order to confirm their correctness. To ensure that very long running simulations make any progress, partial simulations will be checkpointed periodically and their state stored in the mesh as regular simulation result data.

Therefore, over time, execution of simulations over the mesh, together with the expectable fluctuations in the mesh membership, will trigger higher-level services such as migration in order to restore load-balancing, and to improve performance by aggregating simulated regions with more intensive intercommunication within neighboring mesh nodes, or even within same node if sufficient capability is available there.

As a bootstrapping configuration mechanism, to maintain proper balance with respect to scheduling across the mesh, in spite of the different capabilities of the nodes, we make use of special template simulations to benchmark average simulation performance on each platform.

4.5.4   Topology Modeling

A key aspect to performing network simulation is being able to formally describe the topology of the simulated network or overlay.

In order to allow faster and easier topology prototyping, development, deployment, testing, evaluation, and redistribution, we are designing a new domain-specific language (a topology modeling language – TML) to express everything in Peer4Peer: data, structure, behavior, and policies. TML prescribes a simple mostly declarative syntax, inspired in Java, allowing the definition of data structures, events, and rules (predicates) to trigger actions (e.g., sending messages).

TML syntax includes features for the overall simulation description and topology structure (e.g., flat, layered, multidimensional, hierarchical, and possible novel recursive topologies). This way, with reuse, TML allows easy definition of arbitrarily large systems in comparison with today's cumbersome programmatic approach. Regarding data structures inside simulated nodes, TML syntax encompasses rules to specify neighbor and routing tables. Concerning behavior, TML is used to express protocols (e.g., entry, exit, routing, and recovery). TML also allows the definition of preexisting data content placed at simulated nodes prior to simulation start.

TML consists actually as a front-end preprocessor that generates source code targeting simulators' APIs (currently, only PeerSim). Nonetheless, if allows independence of simulator API and details, and can be made to target other simulators. We also intend to explore approaches based on byte-codes to speed up simulation execution. Such an approach will ensure compatibility across platforms hosting the mesh and the topology simulator.

At a higher level, TML aims the enrichment of simulations by separating topology structure and routing from higher-level policies such as resource discovery, reservation, scheduling, accounting, recycling, redundancy, and versioning. Once defined, the description of a policy should be reusable in other simulations. This way, definitions of topology-related structure, data, behavior, and policy can be mixed-and-matched, resulting in increasing reusability, productivity, and observability of studied properties.

4.5.5   Integration and Portal Support

To ease the deployment of Peer4Peer, its clients are distributed by using a number of alternatives all of them incorporating the same message and simulation protocol to ensure portability and integration. However clients can be either stand-alone applications to be run on desktops, jobs on a Grid (for maximum performance), or several space-efficient virtual appliances; thereby easing deployment and taking advantage of concurrent execution of partial simulations that can take place in multi-core and cluster participating nodes.

A web portal supports content sharing of topologies, simulations, policies, and/or results among users, groups, and simulation-related communities. The main part of the development effort focus on allowing web interactive and automatic (scripted) interface with Peer4Peer. This is achieved by resorting to XML-RPC or REST-based interfaces. This also has the interesting outcome of allowing embedding of Peer4Peer in web pages and mash-ups, and automatic deployment and retrieval of results. This fosters the creation of a truly topology simulation community portal providing integrated and universal access to content and resources to perform simulations.

Finally, the portal, instead of a stand-alone infrastructure, can be integrated with available open-source groupware and content management systems to manage groups, communities, and social networks to interface with Peer4Peer and interactively share topologies, simulations, and results.

4.6   Implementation

The foundation of the current Peer4Peer's implementation is a platform aimed at the execution, with improved scalability and performance, of the peer-to-peer simulator, PeerSim, on top of a cycle-sharing infrastructure. This infrastructure is able to leverage the resources available at nodes included in local clusters or LANs, Grid infrastructures, and a custom peer-to-peer network of voluntary cycle-sharing nodes. PeerSim execution is parallelized and being made distributed.

The Peer4Peer platform implementation is depicted in Fig. 4.2 with its main software components and data flows. Peer4Peer implementation is based on the following components, following a top-down approach:

- Job management and portal services using nuBOINC [46], to store descriptions of job requests and primary replicas of topology descriptions, simulated protocols, experiment results, etc.

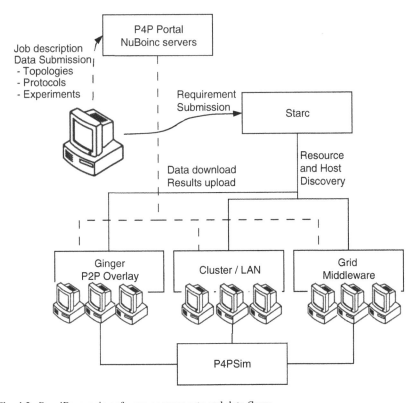

Fig. 4.2 Peer4Peer main software components and data flows

- Resource requirement description and resource discovery coordination using STARC [47].
- Peer-to-peer infrastructure enabled with cycle-sharing capabilities, called Ginger [48], with overlay membership management, decentralized resource discovery, distribution of computation, and decentralized data caching.
- Modified version of PeerSim (P4PSim) which runs protocol simulations in parallel, to take advantage of multi-core hosts for increased performance, and with support for distribution to allow for larger and more complex simulations.

Broadly, at the top, users submit job descriptions and data (topologies, protocols, experiment results, etc.) they want to make globally accessible to the Peer4Peer portal hosted by a number of nuBOINC servers. Job descriptions input data and simulation results may be cached elsewhere (namely, entirely on clusters or in chunks across a P2P overlay). At the bottom, every participating and donor node runs Ginger embedded with P4PSim to perform actual simulations.

Users may submit requirements (e.g., CPU cores and speed, memory, disk, network bandwidth) to STARC that will interface with three types of existing underlying network architectures: LAN and cluster managers, Grid middleware, and a P2P overlay (enhanced with cycle-sharing). This enables STARC to discover hosts able and willing to execute job tasks. Tasks are converted in gridlets (a work unit) that can be appended to resource requirement descriptions fed to STARC; they can be created either at the nuBOINC servers or previously by submitting nodes (by the Gridlet Manager in Ginger). The discovered hosts can retrieve job descriptions (optionally also embedded in gridlets) and data from nuBOINC servers or from the Ginger P2P overlay. When nodes do not belong to the Ginger overlay (relevant case but not the most interesting in the context of this work), the cluster coordinator or Grid middleware spawns a process with a Peer4Peer virtual appliance with P4PSim, Ginger middleware (for gridlet management and optional access to Ginger P2P overlay), and a nuBOINC client to access the portals.

4.6.1   Nuboinc: Peer4Peer Portal

nuBOINC [45], Peer4Peer's job management module, is an extended version of the Berkeley BOINC infrastructure. The main improvements provided by nuBOINC are the ability to submit jobs for legacy commodity applications or execution environments, PeerSim in our particular case, and the possibility to express a large set of jobs by a set of different input files or parameters for the same application, that is, different peer-to-peer simulations in PeerSim. Every participating (and donor) node runs a client-version of nuBOINC for information submission and retrieval from nuBOINC servers at Peer4Peer portal.

Regarding data submitted by users, topologies and protocols employ an early approach to TML (topology modeling language). Node topologies are represented as pairs of IDs of simulated nodes (representing links to neighbors, that can be reciprocal or not). Data structures can be represented by any self-contained Java class (i.e., containing as fields only primitive types and arrays of primitive types). Behavior is represented as individual methods that manipulate a set of macro-variables, replaced by the preprocessor. Method execution is triggered by condition rules (encoded as Java expressions). Although still in progress, this approach already offers relative independence of simulator API and details, and can be made to target any simulator (although the recommended simulator would be P4PSim for performance).

4.6.2   STARC: Resource Requirement Descriptions

The discovery of processing nodes for use in nuBOINC is based on STARC (see Fig. 4.3). STARC [47] is a middleware platform to make resource discovery more adaptive via extensibility (ability to incorporate new resources) and increased

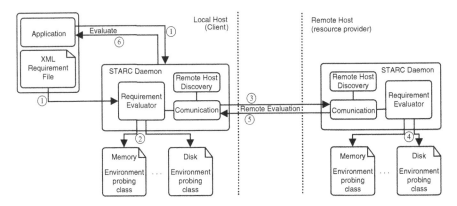

Fig. 4.3 STARC architecture

flexibility with better expressiveness in requirement description by employing XML files with a resource description algebra.

The STARC middleware is an assemblage of components, named STARC daemons that execute both in clients and in resource providers or donors. STARC uses XML requirement files stating application requirements. XML files state individual requirements (e.g., CPU), and allow for logical expressions combining requirements and their priority. Moreover, they described the assigned utility of resources and their depreciation on partial fulfillment, while employing fuzzy-logic to combine multiple requirements.

XML requirement files are fed to a locally running STARC daemon. This daemon is responsible for the discovery of remote hosts and the evaluation of the requirements on those computers. The requester will receive a list identifying the available hosts and indicating how capable they are of fulfilling the requirements. In general, these requirements can range from available memory or processor speed to certain libraries of helping applications.

In more detail, the local STARC daemon receives a XML requirement file that is interactively created when the user submits jobs to nuBOINC servers. From this file (Step 1 in Fig. 4.3) the STARC daemon reads the requirement and executes the relevant *Environment Probing Classes* (Step 2) in order to know how the resources fulfill the requirements. The requirements are evaluated using the values returned by the *Environment Probing Classes*. The evaluation of each resource is performed by a specific *Environment Probing Class*. The name of these classes is defined in the XML elements. This enables dynamic class loading. After local resource evaluation, if the request was originated from the local user, the STARC daemon contacts the remote daemons (Steps 3) by means of the *Communication* component. Each contacted Daemon evaluates the requirements (Step 4) and returns the resulting value (Step 5). The *Remote Host Discovery* module assembles and sorts the returned hosts, storing them in a list.

In cluster and LAN scenarios, the *Remote Host Discovery* module finds remote computers in the same subnetwork. Each host evaluates the requirements against its resources and returns the resulting utility values. These are combined with host identification in a bounded ordered list by the local STARC daemon. In most situations, STARC needs only pick the top result or iterate over the list for parallel scheduling. In Grid infrastructures, we are currently implementing a STARC module within the framework of MDS4 [49] with a set of resource providers (for monitoring node resources and availability).

In the case of peer-to-peer cycle-sharing, the set of hosts made available to STARC to evaluate must be reduced and not the entire overlay population as this hinders scalability. In this scenario, STARC operates exclusively on two sets of hosts returned by the resource discovery mechanism in Ginger (described next in the Section): direct neighbors in routing tables, and those returned by a lower-level resource discovery mechanism seeking CPU, memory, and bandwidth.

4.6.3 Ginger: Peer-to-Peer Discovery Cycle-Sharing, and Work Distribution

The Peer4Peer component that manages the distribution of computation is Ginger. Ginger is a middleware platform on a structured peer-to-peer overlay network (using the Pastry protocol [49]) that bases its operation around the concept of a gridlet (see Fig. 4.4). A gridlet is a fragment of data, capable of

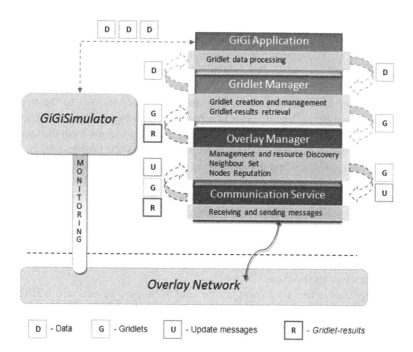

Fig. 4.4 Ginger architecture

describing all aspects of a work task, as well as the necessary changes for processing the data. When a job is submitted by an application for processing (e.g., to the Peer4Peer portal or directly to the overlay), it is partitioned into small tasks that are used to generate gridlets, which will be submitted to the overlay where they will be processed by other nodes. When the computation is complete, the results can be sent, in the form of gridlet-results directly to the sender node, becoming available in the overlay as cached results, or sent to nuBOINC servers.

The Ginger overlay, based on Pastry [50], is a structured overlay that offers scalable and efficient peer-to-peer overlay routing, and leverages peer-to-peer properties such as self-organization of nodes, complete decentralization, and fault-tolerance. The Pastry protocol provides Ginger with a neighbor set for each node created with a heuristic proximity that includes a limited number of the geographically nearest nodes. Ginger, itself, can be tested on a simulator that can also connect to and monitor, as a participant, an actual peer-to-peer overlay.

In the case of Peer4Peer, only a specific type of application is targeted: the actual simulation tools, in particular, P4PSim. Therefore, gridlets correspond to simulations included in the jobs submitted to nuBOINC. They carry the necessary information for donor nodes to retrieve topology, protocol, and experiment data (if they are smaller than 256 KB, they are embedded in the actual gridlet), as well as its estimated cost as requirements (expressed with STARC).

In the case of Peer4Peer, *Gridlet Management* amounts to create gridlets corresponding to the individual simulations requested in a job (e.g., by varying parameters given to the simulation, being topology, protocol, overlay size, etc.) and reassembling the results under the same job ID, confirming all gridlets have been executed (if not they can be retried/resubmitted), and storing all the results in a compressed folder. The results can be maintained cached in the overlay, as in PAST [51], fostering load-balancing, flexibility, and availability.

Besides basic routing and overlay maintenance, the *Overlay Manager* is responsible for making the resources shared by donor nodes connected to the overlay available and engaged efficiently. This is achieved by employing a tailored resource discovery mechanism. The importance of network topology stems from the fact that resource discovery mechanisms follow the links formed by the peer-to-peer overlay network topology. By sending update-type messages, each node will announce its resources, only to those nodes that belong to the node's neighbor set. When a request is submitted by a node, it checks the information provided by its neighbors and forwards the gridlet to the node that seems more capable of processing the gridlet. The main goals of Ginger are the correct routing of requests and accounting the associated computation cost and various performance criteria that define the best choice, as the memory available, or bandwidth of the connection, or other available resources in the node.

When a gridlet is received from the *Gridlet Manager*, a node with sufficient available resources to address this gridlet is selected as target for its routing. The statistics results of choosing that node for routing a request are stored in a table of reputation regarding that node. The *Overlay Manager* uses this table when, on the whole neighbor set, there is no availability that meets the cost of a gridlet. In this case, the selection of a node to route the gridlet is based on the reputation table that has information regarding previous statistics results, as cases of failure and who had less delay in processing the applications. Globally, the definition of a node with better availability is one that has higher availability according to a weighted measure of the defined metrics (proximity, CPU, memory, and bandwidth). Each metrics used to define the available resources contribute, in general, with similar weight in the weighted calculation of a node's availability.

4.6.4   P4PSim: Scalable and Efficient Peer-to-Peer Simulation

P4PSim is an extension (and partial reimplementation) of PeerSim, able to make use of multiple concurrent execution threads to perform topology simulations, instead of the serial version that is currently available. It partitions the topology in a configurable number of partitions, predefined with the number of available cores in a machine (an aggregate number of cores may be used across a group or cluster of machines). Each simulated node is assigned to a partition and marked with an immutable "color." Nodes can be randomly assigned to partitions or assigned taking the simulated topology connectivity in account, favoring the placement of neighboring nodes in the same partition. In the latter case, boundary nodes may have more than one color.

Each partition is assigned a thread or a core. All nodes belonging to the same partition are simulated by the same thread, avoiding the need for blocking synchronization. This way, all cores are most of the time fully used simulating the nodes in their partitions. When interactions among nodes in different partitions occur (i.e., sending a message), a synchronized queue for each partition is used.

P4PSim instances can be run in distributed manner in two ways: (1) in clusters, with Terracotta middleware [52] that provides mostly transparent distributed shared memory for Java applications, (2) over wide area by using Java RMI. In this latter approach, currently, each group of P4PSim instances synchronizes at the end of each simulated round. In this case, there is increased latency, but that is compensated for the higher available memory for much larger simulations and, because of their increased size, the multiple CPUs available for parallel simulation in each simulation round.

Regarding communication between simulated nodes, it is performed using two distinct communication mechanisms: (1) when nodes are simulated on the same P4PSim instance, or over Terracotta, a shared memory abstraction is used, while (2) if nodes are being handled by different P4PSim instances over wide area network (mostly for nodes on partition boundaries), simulated messages are batched in RMI invocations.

4.6.5   Other Issues: Security, Heterogeneity

The Peer4Peer platform aims at portability and leverages heterogeneous platforms by relying mostly on the Java and Python language, with users and donors being able to manage the privileges associated with the VMs running on their machines.

In the specific case of resource monitoring performed by STARC, it is also executed at host nodes within the boundaries of a virtual machine. This way, access to local resources (e.g., file system, communication, etc.) can be limited and con-figured. This extends to the vast majority of Environment Probing Classes. If one needs to access the native system directly, it can be subject to individual configura-tion and will not be executed without user's authorization. Finally, in the context of this work, STARC only schedules tasks associated with the execution of P4PSim instances that relies solely on Java.

4.7   Evaluation

The evaluation of the current Peer4Peer implementation is designed to show its feasibility regarding two main aspects: (1) ability to leverage available resources in donor nodes across peer-to-peer cycle-sharing overlays (the most decentralized and scalable scenario), and (2) the ability to perform simulations faster, by efficiently employing multi-core CPUs that are becoming prevalent in today's machines, even at laptop and desktop home machines.

4.7.1   Resource Discovery and Gridlet Routing in Ginger

To measure and evaluate the performance of resource discovery (i.e., gridlet routing to donor nodes) in the Ginger P2P cycle-sharing overlay, we resorted to tests con-sisting of simulating the flow of messages throughout the network on two distinct scenarios. For the purposes of these tests, simulation was performed resorting to unmodified serial simulation.

There are 1,000 nodes in the simulated system, divided into 2 groups of 500 nodes each: (1) a group of host nodes, which provides its processing cycles for performing work from others, and (2) another group of client nodes, who will sub-mit requests to take advantage of idle cycles available in the overlay. Two aspects that influence forwarding selection were tested: (a) measurement of the information about the neighbor's availability; (b) the ability that nodes have to learn about their neighbors by keeping historical records of statistics results (a simple measure of reputation).

In the first test (Test A), the information about the availability of a node is obtained from a weighted measure on the node's resources and its proximity to the local node. For effective measurements, tests should cover scenarios where there are enough resources, where the availability in the whole network meets the demand (point of saturation); and situations of excessive demand that the network cannot immediately overcome. Thus, the number of gridlets submitted to the overlay ranges over 300, 500 (1st point of saturation), 700, 900, 1,000 (2nd point of saturation), and 1,200 gridlets. The major goal of this test is to evaluate the performance and the efficiency of resource discovery approaches, namely regarding the number of messages needed to find a node able to execute a gridlet.

Three resource discovery variations were employed, regarding the metrics that decide routing: (1) CPU, memory, and bandwidth, (2) proximity in the node selection calculation, and (3) both combined. The first calculation only evaluates the availability in terms of resources, distributing the weight equally for the metrics: 33% for the CPU, 33% for memory, and 33% for bandwidth. The second calculation only evaluates the proximity of the node. And finally, a last calculation weights the two measures, favoring resources: 40% to proximity and 60% to resources shared equally for each metric in 20%.

From Fig. 4.5, it is possible to observe the resource discovery quality obtained by the three calculations. It shows that for a number of gridlets less than or equal to 500 the calculation based only in resources obtained the worst results, but above the 500 requests it has improved, compared with the performance of the other calculation variations. Note that until the point of saturation (500) there is no lack of resources in the network, but from that point on, the lack of resources is a constant. Therefore, we can infer that the calculation based on resources is favorable for situations of solicitation in scarcity in resources. The calculation based on the nodes proximity, has good quality efficiency as long as there are many resources available

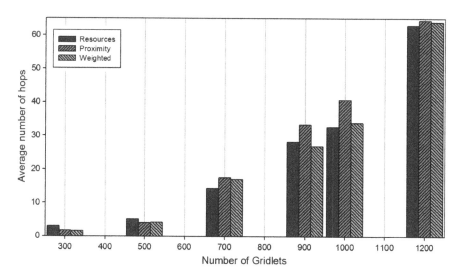

Fig. 4.5 Average number of hops to serve a gridlet in Test A

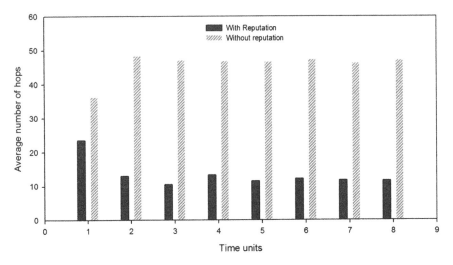

Fig. 4.6 Average number of hops to serve a gridlet in Test B

on the network and very low quality in situations of immediate lack of resources, since it is from 700 gridlets submitted on, that results start to decline.

The second test (Test B), addresses the reputation maintained in each node, where they acquire information about the statistics results of their neighbors in the past, and learn the best ways as they send more requests to the network. The gains of using this mechanism can be obtained from the difference between the performance of the system with and without the execution of the reputation mechanism. In this test, the simulation is executed always with the same overlay network nodes and the tasks are all submitted from the same node. The number of tasks is always the same, 700 gridlets in order to test the behavior of the system when there is a lack of resources on the network, and whether it can operate in a relevant scenario and influence the results.

According to Fig. 4.6, it is possible to observe the routing quality obtained using the reputation mechanism. The smallest difference occurs during the first iteration since the reputation system has not yet acquired the information about their neighbors. In the second iteration, a large reduction in the number of retransmissions made is already visible, remaining at that level from that point on. Therefore, we can say that this mechanism converges very quickly to best performance.

4.7.2 Parallel Simulation in P4PSim

P4PSim allows each execution thread to run the simulation of a subset of the simulated peer-to-peer network. The efficient parallelization of any application involves minimizing contention among concurrent tasks. In the case of P4PSim, it is essential to make sure that the simulated nodes assigned to an execution thread are as contiguous as possible so as to reduce locking and data transfer. As already mentioned, in order to minimize communication and contention between simulation threads (that may even run on different machines), the nodes of the simulated overlay can be assigned using an affinity metric, usually the number of hops between nodes, thereby resulting in the clustering of close simulated nodes in the same execution node.

We aimed to demonstrate the performance benefits when simulating the behavior of very large network overlays. Figure 4.7 depicts the evolution of execution times as the number of nodes increases for two different operating modes of P4PSim (excluding partitioning time). The partitioning process is the mechanism of assigning simulated nodes to execution nodes. In the random version, simulated nodes are randomly assigned to execution nodes, whereas in the partitioned version, the set of simulated nodes is partitioned based on proximity. The algorithm that is being simulated is the periodical exchange of a monotonically increasing value stored by the nodes of a Pastry [50] network.

The partitioning algorithms and simulation distribution are still being perfected but the benefits of executing the simulator concurrently are already amply apparent. As depicted in Fig. 4.7, for small simulations (5k nodes), the overhead of synchronizing the access to shared data erodes the benefits of parallelization

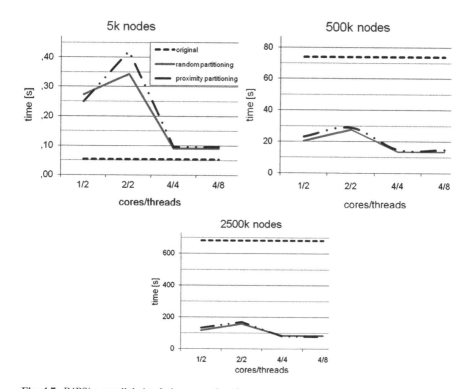

Fig. 4.7 P4PSim parallel simulation execution times

and therefore the execution times for parallel executions are between twice and eight times higher. However, as the number of simulated nodes grows, parallel execution becomes more efficient: for 2.5 million nodes, parallel execution is 4–8.6 times faster.

For the small number of threads and processors we experimented with, we observe that adding threads has a greater impact than adding cores. However, this effect will also be attenuated as the number of simulation execution threads increases.

4.8 Related Work

This section covers relevant work on the areas related with the scope of this work and its presiding vision: (A) Simulation tools/test beds, (B) Parallel/distributed computing, (C) Cycle-providing infrastructures, (D) Peer-to-peer overlays, and (E) Grid middleware.

4.8.1 Simulation Tools and Test Beds

Simulation facilitates design and improves productivity, reliability, avoiding costs in deployment. Tools offer different semantics/abstraction levels in simulation configuration and execution. Lower-level semantics is used in electronics design [53], computer architecture (Archer [41]), and network simulation (NS2 [4]). It allows fine-grained detail to define structure and behavior often with domain-specific languages. It provides precision in measurements and monitoring, with physical world phenomena (voltage, transmission delays).

Higher-level semantics offers lower overhead and addresses sophisticated behavior described with more abstract rules, yet defined programmatically, for example, neighbor-sets and routing of peer-to-peer overlay topologies (Peersim, Oversim [54]), distributed computing running Grid middleware (Simgrid [55], GridSim [5]), and general distributed systems over TCP [56]. Yet, they execute centrally managing event queues limiting simulation size and complexity. Test beds (PlanetLab [42], Emulab [43], SatteliteLab [57]) do allow parallel execution on geographically distributed nodes. Nonetheless, overhead is orders of magnitude higher (few rules vs. millions of instructions) in practice limiting simulation size and complexity [56].

Our project differs from these by combining higher-level semantics with parallel simulation distributed over actual cycle-sharing overlay infrastructures. More specifically, it tackles the apparent incompatible trade-off between the advantages of simulation tools and test beds (i.e., simulations size vs. parallelism). Although test beds (e.g., in the specific case of PlanetLab) can execute participating nodes in parallel and distributed fashion, their overhead is too great (usually requiring a complete virtual or real test-bed machine running OS, Java VM, and P2P protocol for each participating node). This clearly limits simulations to at most hundreds of simulated nodes. In Peer4Peer, simulation sizes can be much larger as each real machine may be simulating tens of thousands of participating nodes, also in parallel fashion.

In the case of overlay and Grid simulation tools, they are centralized, that is, for a given topology being simulated, the simulation tool can only leverage the available resources of a single machine. This clearly limits scalability as desktop/server computers' memory is bounded (even if larger than 8 or 16 MB), restricting the number of simulated nodes to tens of thousands (which is not realistic today as stated previously). Moreover, in the specific case of P2P simulations, usually larger sized, the simulation tools are actually of serial execution, which makes simulations of larger or more complex topologies very slow. In Peer4Peer, simulations are performed by P4PSim resorting to multiple threads (and processes), overcoming memory limitations and taking advantage of today's multi-core machines.

4.8.2   Parallel and Distributed Computing

Concurrent activities are implemented as processes/threads/tasks cooperating with data sharing and coordination. Coordination ranges from stricter shared memory (and DSM) and looser message-passing (MPI [12]) to rarefied Bags-of-Tasks (Ourgrid [58]). Activities may share data globally (DSM), partially in communication (MPI, MapReduce), or never in BoTs. Sharing eases programming avoiding explicit communication. Still, it requires consistency enforcement models.

Pessimistic approaches with locks/semaphores and DSM protocols [59] have poor performance and little scalability. Optimistic approaches allowing temporary inconsistencies are essential for performance in large scale. In Software Transactional Memory [60], consistency is enforced at commit. Eventual consistency [61] relies on ulterior reconciliation.

A number of recent middle-ground approaches do allow data divergence limited in time and scope [62], use locality-awareness [63], or both (vector-field consistency [45]). While cluster-based multiplayer gaming is a key current scenario, overlay simulation is still unaddressed.

4.8.3   Cycle-Providing Infrastructures

Early supercomputers linked CPUs by internal bus. Today, multi-cores equip cheaper, more compact multiprocessor computers. Previous increase of LAN speed fostered aggregating (even heterogeneous) computers into cluster systems (NOW [7], PVM [6]). Beyond access to remote clusters or supercomputers, users access computational grids [24] and shared/donated cycles (BOINC [36]).

Grid access implies belonging to virtual organizations of institutions exchanging computational resources. Underlying middleware (Globus [26]) handles all authentication, accounting, and resource allocation. In cycle-sharing, idle CPU time of PCs over the Internet is used for data processing, for example, biology, astronomy. Cycle-sharing is integrated with peer-to-peer techniques to federate clusters or build desktop grids (CCOF [64], Ourgrid, Ginger [48]).

Utility computing (Amazon EC2) employs virtualization techniques for on-demand execution of several VMs in a single real computer. Users launch VMs and create virtual clusters. Currently, however, no infrastructure enables simulation tools for faster or more complex simulations.

4.8.4 Peer-to-Peer Overlays

Peer-to-peer is effective in file-sharing, audio/video streaming, content/update dissemination, anonymity, and cycle-sharing [65]. Peer-to-peer overlays are split in two dimensions: structure and centralization, with hybrids in both. Structured (Chord,Pastry,CAN,Viceroy) map content to node identification with locality gains, load-balancing, ensured and range-based lookup queries.

Unstructured (Gnutella,FreeNet) allow unrestricted content placing and arguably tolerate node entry/exit churn (partially debunked in [66]). Most peer-to-peer are mostly or fully decentralized. Resource discovery [67] in peer-to-peer cycle-sharing finds computational resources: fixed (capabilities, applications) and transient (CPU/ memory availability).

Structured approaches adapt topologies to map resource descriptions/locations as searchable content either flat, layered, or N-dimensional [68]. Unstructured also centralize in super-peers, trees to speed search and minimize message flood, gossip.

Peer4Peer resorts to Ginger, an overlay hybrid of: structured for storage, result caching, capability matching; and unstructured for CPU availability, task forwarding in vicinities; super-peers for reputation and accounting. Cycle-sharing has not been harnessed before for larger-scale overlay and Grid simulation.

4.8.5 Grid Middleware

Grid initiatives not only mediate access to remote computing resources but also try to integrate into portals the tools needed by researchers. The LHC computing Grid allows access to scientific data, processing power, and also provides interfaces to simulation and analysis tools used by the physics community.

A relevant area is the development of user interfaces (Ganga [32]) to interact with the available tools. Other initiatives (Archer, NanoHub [33]) develop simulation tools and portals for easy access to them for configuration, execution results, and public data. Usefulness for the scientific community (integrated tools, data, common interfaces) fosters a large educational potential. A corresponding initiative will have similar impact in research reproducibility in overlay [44] and Grid communities.

4.9 Conclusion

This chapter presents the case for the use of a shared computing platform as the base for an e-Science community: the peer-to-peer overlay (P2P) and Grid middleware research community. The specific scientific problems tackled by this community, and how they are treated, are a great motivator for the establishment of an e-Science community: research work is based on simulation, most simulations are executed on a number of varied, yet well-established tools (e.g., PeerSim, Simgrid), the simulations test the performance of diverse network protocols in multiple scenarios, and results are usually compared with previous competitors. All these characteristics make this community fit well on mixed environment of grids, clusters, and cycle-sharing overlays.

Unfortunately, the current implementations of peer-to-peer simulators and the management of institutional clusters reduce the available computing resources (and their effective utilization) for research in this field. Furthermore, resources scattered on the Internet (accessed by means of a BOINC-like distributed computing infrastructure) allow the execution of more simulations, but without users being able to increase the complexity (number of nodes and their interactions) of the topology being simulated.

To tackle these architectural problems we presented a platform, Peer4Peer, that provides the main infrastructure for efficient peer-to-peer simulation on the Internet. This efficient simulation is addressed in three axes: (1) concurrent execution of independent simulations, (2) parallelization of single simulations, and (3) use of distributed computers (on the Internet, on clusters, or on utility computing infrastructures) to speed up simulations and to allow the simulation of more complex scenarios.

The architecture of Peer4Peer is composed by: (1) a job management and portal services using nuBOINC to submit job descriptions, data, and simulation topologies and protocols using a topology modeling language (TML), (2) expressive resource requirement description and resource discovery coordination using STARC, (3) peer-to-peer cycle-sharing infrastructure, Ginger, offering decentralized resource discovery, distribution of computation, and decentralized data caching; and (4) P4PSim to run protocol simulations parallelized, taking advantage of multi-core machines, with support for distribution to allow for larger and more complex simulations.

Current performance results are already very encouraging as we are able to achieve faster parallel simulations, and through the usage of cooperating P4PSim instances, Peer4Peer is able to handle larger simulations than on a single dedicated machine. Thus, we successfully speedup and scale overlay simulations with Peer4Peer.

Acknowledgments The authors wish to thank students Filipe Paredes and João Neto for their implementation efforts. This work was supported by FCT (INESC-ID multiannual funding) through the PIDDAC Program funds.

References

1. H. Casanova. Simgrid: A Toolkit for the Simulation of Application Scheduling. First IEEE/ ACM International Symposium on Cluster Computing and the Grid. 2001.
2. M. Jelasity, A. Montresor, Gian-Paolo Jesi, Spyros Voulgaris. The Peersim Simulator. http:// peersim.sf.net.
3. I. Baumgart, B. Heep, S. Krause. OverSim: A Flexible Overlay Network Simulation Framework. In Proc. Of the IEEE Global Internet Symposium, pp. 79–84. 2007.
4. T. Issariyakul, E. Hossain Introduction to Network Simulator NS2. ISBN: 978-0-387-71759-3 Springer Books 2009.
5. R. Buyya, M. Murshed. GridSim: A Toolkit for the Modeling and Simulation of Distributed Resource Management and Scheduling for Grid Computing. Concurrency and Computation: Practice and Experience (CCPE), Volume 14, Issue 13–15. Wiley Press 2002.
6. V. S. Sunderam. PVM: a Framework for Parallel Distributed Computing. Concurrency: Practice and Experience, Volume 2, Issue 4, pp. 315–339. 1990.
7. T. E. Anderson, D. E. Culler, D. A. Patterson A Case for Networks of Workstations: NOW. IEEE Micro vol. 15-1, pp. 54–64. 1995.
8. D. P. Anderson, J. Cobb, E. Korpela, M. Lebofsky, D. Werthimer. SETI@home: An Experiment in Public-resource Computing. Commun. ACM 45, 11. November 2002.
9. Top 500 Supercomputers. http://www.top500.org. 2010.
10. S. Choi, H. Kim, E. Byun, M. Baik, S. Kim, C. Park, C. Hwang. Characterizing and Classifying Desktop Grid. Proceedings of the Seventh IEEE international Symposium on Cluster Computing and the Grid (May 14–17, 2007). 2007.
11. B. Schmidt. A Survey of Desktop Grid Applications for E-science. Int. J. Web Grid Serv. 3, 3 (Aug. 2007), 354–368. 2007.
12. I. Foster. Designing and Building Parallel Programs (chapter 8 Message Passing Interface). ISBN 0201575949 Addison-Wesley. 1995.
13. M. Litzkow, M. Livny, M. Mutka, Condor: a Hunter of Idle Workstations. In Proceedings of the Eighth International Conference of Distributed Computing Systems, pp. 104–111. San Jose, CA, USA. 1988.
14. R. L. Henderson. Job Scheduling Under the Portable Batch System. In Proceedings of the Workshop on Job Scheduling Strategies For Parallel Processing. 1995.
15. W. Gentzsch. Sun Grid Engine: Towards Creating a Compute Power Grid. In Proceedings of the 1st international Symposium on Cluster Computing and the Grid. May 15–18. 2001.
16. Howard, J.H., Kazar, M.L., Nichols, S.G., Nichols, D.A., Satyanarayanan, M., Sidebotham, R.N., & West, M.J.. Scale and Performance in a Distributed File System. *ACM Transactions on Computer Systems* **6** (1): 51–81. February 1988.
17. Leach, P. and Perry, D.. Cifs: A common internet file system. Microsoft Interactive Developer. 1996.
18. F. Schmuck, R. Haskin. GPFS: A Shared-Disk File System for Large Computing Clusters. In Proceedings of the 1st USENIX Conference on File and Storage Technologies, January 28–30, 2002.
19. Gluster Inc. GlusterFS. http://www.gluster.org. 2010.
20. D. G. Feitelson, L. Rudolph. Gang Scheduling Performance Benefits for Fine-Grain Synchronization. Journal of Parallel and Distributed Computing, volume 16, pages 306–318. 1992.

21. J.P. Jones, B. Nitzberg. Scheduling for Parallel Supercomputing: A Historical Perspective of Achievable Utilization. Job Scheduling Strategies for Parallel Processing (JSSPP), pp. 1–16, 1999.
22. Y. K. Kwok and I. Ahmad. Static Scheduling Algorithms for Allocating Directed Task Graphs to Multiprocessors. ACM Comput. Surv., 31(4):406–471, 1999.
23. J. K. Ousterhout. Scheduling Techniques for Concurrent Systems. Proceedings of Third International Conference on Distributed Computing Systems, 22–30. 1982.
24. Foster; C. Kesselman. The Grid: Blueprint for a New Computing Infrastructure. Morgan-Kaufman. 1999.
25. I. Foster. The Grid: A New Infrastructure for 21st Century Science. Physics Today, 55(2): 42–47. 2002.
26. I. Foster. Globus Toolkit Version 4: Software for Service-Oriented Systems. IFIP International Conference on Network and Parallel Computing Springer-Verlag LNCS 3779, pp 2–13. 2006.
27. M. Feller, I. Foster, and S. Martin. GT4 GRAM: A Functionality and Performance Study. 2007.
28. Distributed Systems Architecture Group, Universidad Complutense de Madrid. GridWay Metascheduler http://www.gridway.org/. 2010.
29. J. Novotny, M. Russell, O. Wehrens, 2004. GridSphere: a Portal Framework for Building Collaborations: Research Articles. Concurr. Comput.: Pract. Exper. 16, 5: 503–513, Apr. 2004.
30. T. Suzumura, H. Nakada, M. Saito, S. Matsuoka, Y. Tanaka, S. Sekiguchi, The Ninf portal: an automatic generation tool for grid portals. In Proceedings of the 2002 Joint ACM-ISCOPE Conference on Java Grande (Seattle, Washington, USA, November 03–05, 2002). JGI '02. ACM, New York, NY, 2002.
31. D. Abramson, J. Giddy, L. Kotler. High Performance Parametric Modeling with Nimrod/G: Killer Application for the Global Grid?. Proceedings of the International Parallel and Distributed Processing Symposium (IPDPS 2000). USA. 2000.
32. K. Harrison, W. T. L. P. Lavrijsen, C. E. Tull, P. Mato, A. Soroko, C. L. Tan, N. Brook, R. W. L. Jones. GANGA: a User-Grid Interface for Atlas and LHCb in Proceedings of Computing in High Energy and Nuclear Physics. La Jolla, 2003.
33. G. Klimeck, M. McLennan, S. P. Brophy, G. B. Adams III, M. S. Lundstrom. nanoHUB.org: Advancing Education and Research in Nanotechnology. Computing Science and Engg. 10, 5 (Sep. 2008), 17–23. 2008.
34. Plale, B., D. Gannon, J. Brotzge, K. Droegemeier, J. Kurose, D. McLaughlin, R. Wilhelmson, S. Graves, M. Ramamurthy, R.D. Clark, S. Yalda, D.A. Reed, E. Joseph, V. Chandrasekar, CASA and LEAD: Adaptive Cyberinfrastructure for Real-Time Multiscale Weather Forecasting, Computer (Special issue on System-Level Science), IEEE Computer Science Press, Vol. 39, No. 11, pp. 56–63, Nov. 2006.
35. Ian J. Taylor, Ian Wang, Matthew S. Shields, Shalil Majithia: Distributed computing with Triana on the Grid. Concurrency and Computation: Practice and Experience 17(9): 1197–1214, 2005.
36. D. P. Anderson and G. Fedak. The computational and storage potential of volunteer computing. In IEEE/ACM Intl. Symposium on Cluster Computing and the Grid. May 2006.
37. Amazon.com, Inc.: Amazon elastic compute cloud, http://aws.amazon.com/ec2. 2010.
38. Enomaly Inc. Enomalism: Elastic computing platform - virtual server management. http://enomalism.com.
39. OpenNebula Project Leads. OpenNebula, The Open Source Toolkit for Cloud Computing, http://www.opennebula.org/start. 2010.
40. C. Evangelinos, C. N. Hill. Cloud Computing for Parallel Scientific HPC Applications: Feasibility of Running Coupled Atmosphere-Ocean Climate Models on Amazon's EC2. Proceedings of Cloud Computing and its Applications. http://www.cca08.org. 2008.
41. R. J. O. Figueiredo, P. O. Boykin, J. A. B. Fortes, T. Li, J. Peir, D. Wolinsky, L. K. John, D. R. Kaeli, D. J. Lilja, S. A. McKee, G. Memik, A. Roy, G. S. Tyson. Archer: A Community

Distributed Computing Infrastructure for Computer Architecture Research and Education. 2008.

42. Brent N. Chun, David E. Culler, Timothy Roscoe, Andy C. Bavier, Larry L. Peterson, Mike Wawrzoniak, Mic Bowman: PlanetLab: an overlay test-bed for broad-coverage services. Computer Communication Review 33(3): 3–12. 2003.

43. Brian White, Jay Lepreau, Leigh Stoller, Robert Ricci, Shashi Guruprasad, Mac Newbold, Mike Hibler, Chad Barb, Abhijeet Joglekar. An Integrated Experimental Environment for Distributed Systems and Networks. OSDI 2002.

44. S. Naicken, B. Livingston, A. Basu, S. Rodhetbhai, Ian Wakeman, Dan Chalmers. The State of Peer-to-Peer Simulators and Simulations. Computer Communication Review, 2007.

45. Luís Veiga, André Negrão, Nuno Santos, Paulo Ferreira: Unifying divergence bounding and locality awareness in replicated systems with vector-field consistency. Journal of Internet Services and Applications vol. 1(2), pp. 95–115, 2010.

46. J. Silva, L. Veiga, P. Ferreira. nuBOINC: BOINC Extensions for Community Cycle Sharing. Workshop on Decentralized Self Management for grids, P2P, and User Communities - SELFMAN (in conjunction with SASo 2008). Venice, Italy. October 20–24, 2008.

47. J. N. Silva, L. Veiga, P. Ferreira. Service and Resource Discovery in Cycle Sharing Environments with an Utility Algebra 24th IEEE International Parallel & Distributed Processing Symposium, Atlanta (Georgia) USA. April 19–23, 2010.

48. L. Veiga, R. Rodrigues, P. Ferreira. GiGi: An Ocean of Gridlets on a "Grid-for-the-Masses". Seventh IEEE International Symposium on Cluster Computing and the Grid, CCGRID 2007. Rio de Janeiro, Brazil. May 14–17, 2007.

49. J. Schopf, L. Pearlman, N. Miller, C. Kesselman, I. Foster, M. DArcy, and A. Chervenak, "Monitoring the grid with the Globus Toolkit MDS4," in Journal of Physics: Conference Series, vol. 46, no. 1. Institute of Physics Publishing, 2006, pp. 521–525.

50. A. Rowstron, P. Druschel. Pastry: Scalable, Distributed Object Location and Routing for Large-scale Peer-to-Peer Systems. IFIP/ACM International Conference on Distributed Systems Platforms (Middleware).Vol. 11, pp. 329–350. 2001.

51. A. Rowstron e P. Druschel, "Storage management and caching in PAST, a large-scale, persistent peer-to-peer storage utility," ACM SIGOPS Operating Systems Review, vol. 35, 2001, pp. 188–201.

52. Terracotta, http://www.terracotta.org/, 2010

53. J. A. B. Fortes, R. J. Figueiredo, M. S. Lundstrom. Virtual Computing Infrastructures for Nanoelectronics Simulation Proceedings of the IEEE. 2005.

54. Ingmar Baumgart, Bernhard Heep, Stephan Krause. OverSim: A Flexible Overlay Network Simulation Framework. Proceedings of 10th IEEE Global Internet Symposium (GI '07) in conjunction with IEEE INFOCOM 2007. 2007.

55. H. Casanova, A. Legrand, M. Quinson. Simgrid: a Generic Framework for Large-Scale Distributed Experiments. 10th IEEE International Conference on Computer Modeling and Simulation. 2008.

56. Chunqiang Tang. DSF: A Common Platform for Distributed Systems Research and Development. In Proc. of Middleware 2009, pp. 414–436. 2009.

57. Marcel Dischinger, Andreas Haeberlen, Ivan Beschastnikh, P. Krishna Gummadi, Stefan Saroiu. Satellitelab: Adding Heterogeneity to Planetary-scale Network Test-beds. SIGCOMM 2008: 315–326. 2008.

58. F. Brasileiro, E. Araujo, W. Voorsluys, M. Oliveira, F. Figueiredo. Bridging the High Performance Computing Gap: the Ourgrid Experience. CCGRID 2007 Seventh IEEE International Symposium on Cluster Computing and the Grid. Rio de Janeiro, Brazil. 2007.

59. Yuanyuan Zhou, Liviu Iftode, Jaswinder Pal Singh, Kai Li, Brian R. Toonen, Ioannis Schoinas, Mark D. Hill, David A. Wood. Relaxed Consistency and Coherence Granularity in DSM Systems: A Performance Evaluation. Sixth ACM SIGPLAN Symposium on Principles and Practice of Parallel Programming. 1997.

60. Maurice Herlihy, Victor Luchangco, Mark Moir, and William N. Scherer III. Software Transactional Memory for Dynamic-Sized Data Structures. Proceedings of the Twenty-Second Annual ACM SIGACT-SIGOPS Symposium on Principles of Distributed Computing 2003. 2003.
61. Terry, D.B., Theimer, M.M., Petersen, K., Demers, A.J., Spreitzer, M.J., Hauser, C.. Managing Update Conflicts in Bayou, a Weakly Connected Replicated Storage System. Proceedings of the fifteenth ACM Symposium on Operating Systems Principles. 1995.
62. H. Yu, A. Vahdat. The Costs and Limits of Availability for Replicated Services. ACM Transactions on Computer Systems. 2006.
63. J. Chen, B. Wu, M. Delap, B. Knutsson, H. Lu, C. Amza. Locality Aware Dynamic Load Management for Massively Multiplayer Games. Proceedings of the tenth ACM SIGPLAN Symposium on Principles and Practice of Parallel Programming. 2005.
64. V. Lo, D. Zappala, D. Zhou, Y. Liu, and S. Zhao. Cluster Computing on the Fly: P2P Scheduling of Idle Cycles in the Internet. In The 3rd International Workshop on Peer-to-Peer Systems (IPTPS'04) 2004.
65. S. Androutsellis-Theotokis, D. Spinellis A Survey of Peer-to-Peer Content Distribution Technologies. ACM Computing Surveys, vol. 36–4, p. 371. 2004.
66. M. Castro, M. Costa, A. Rowstron. Debunking some Myths about Structured and Unstructured Overlays. Symposium on Networked Systems Design & Implementation. Volume 2, p. 98. 2005.
67. P. Trunfio, D. Talia, H. Papadakis, P. Fragopoulou, M. Mordacchini, M. Pennanen, K. Popov, V. Vlassov, S. Haridi. Peer-to-Peer Resource Discovery in Grids: Models and Systems. Future Generation Computer Systems, archive Volume 23. 2007.
68. M. Cai, M. Frank, J. Chen, P. Szekely. MAAN: A Multi-attribute Addressable Network for Grid Information Services. Proc. 4th Int. Workshop on Grid Computing, GRID 2003. 2003.

Part II
Data-Intensive e-Science

Chapter 5
A Multidisciplinary, Model-Driven, Distributed Science Data System Architecture

Daniel J. Crichton, Chris A. Mattmann, John S. Hughes, Sean C. Kelly, and Andrew F. Hart

Abstract The twenty-first century has transformed the world of science by breaking the physical boundaries of distributed organizations and interconnecting them into virtual science environments, allowing for systems and systems of systems to seamlessly access and share information and resources across highly geographically distributed areas. This e-science transformation is enabling new scientific discoveries by allowing for greater collaboration as well as by enabling systems to combine and correlate disparate data sets. At the Jet Propulsion Laboratory in Pasadena, California, we have been developing science data systems for highly distributed communities in physical and life sciences that require extensive sharing of distributed services and common information models based on common architectures. The common architecture contributes a set of atomic functions, interfaces, and information models that support sharing and distributed processing. Additionally, the architecture provides a blueprint for a software product line known as the Object Oriented Data Technology (OODT) framework. OODT has enabled reuse of software for science data generation, capture and management, and delivery across highly distributed organizations for planetary science, earth science, and cancer research. Our experience to date shows that a well-defined architecture and set of accompanied software vastly improves our ability to develop road maps for and to construct virtual science environments.

5.1 Introduction

The NASA Jet Propulsion Laboratory (JPL) has researched and built data-intensive systems for highly distributed scientific environments for many years [1–5]. Due to the dynamic and changing mission environment for both solar system and earth

D.J. Crichton (✉), J.S. Hughes, S.C. Kelly, and A.F. Hart
Jet Propulsion Laboratory, California Institute of Technology, Pasadena, CA 91109, USA
e-mail: daniel.j.crichton@jpl.nasa.gov

C.A. Mattmann
Computer Science Department, University of Southern California, Los Angeles, CA 90089, USA
and
Jet Propulsion Laboratory, California Institute of Technology, Pasadena, CA 91109, USA

Xiaoyu Yang et al. (eds.), *Guide to e-Science: Next Generation Scientific Research and Discovery*, Computer Communications and Networks,
DOI 10.1007/978-0-85729-439-5_5, © Springer-Verlag London Limited 2011

robotic exploration, a number of critical architectural principles have emerged, helping us to define an architecture that can evolve with exploration and technological changes. Through our work at JPL, we have defined an architectural style for data and computational grids that is focused on the capture, processing, discovery, access, and transformation of digital data objects (and their rich metadata descriptions) across highly distributed environments. The framework, called the Object Oriented Data Technology (OODT) framework [1, 5] was selected as runner up for NASA Software of the Year in 2003 and has been extensively used not only within physical science environments such as planetary [4, 6], earth [3, 7], and astrophysics [8], but also in biomedical research [2, 9].

One of the central characteristics of the architecture is the application of architectural patterns [10] consistently across very different science environments. Up front, OODT stresses the aspects of the architecture that are common, leaving the domain-specific aspects (where/how to reuse existing modular OODT components, and nonfunctional parameters of the architecture like scalability, efficiency, etc.) to be ironed out and iterated upon during system development.

Over time, informed by our growing experience designing information systems to support scientific research, we observed common architectural patterns and canonical sets of services central to the successful development of systems within the different domains. The services include:

- Data capture deals with metadata extraction, content analysis, and detection (MIME-type and language detection) [11], along with validation against common metadata model, for example, ISO-11179 [12], and Dublin Core [13].
- Data discovery deals with the ability to describe resources (data, computation, identity, etc.) in a uniform fashion, and the methodologies for using those resource descriptions as a mechanism for discovery.
- Data access deals with the acquisition of data from heterogeneous stores (RDBMS'es, filesystems, etc.) using a uniform access method.
- Data processing deals with transformation (subsetting [14], interpolation, aggregation, summarization, etc.) of data once it has been accessed.
- Data distribution is the packaging of data and its metadata, and the plan for its eventual distribution to users downstream of the system.

These services allow for distributed, independent deployment, yet maintain the ability to work in concert with one another when needed. Building systems in this fashion allows construction of large-scale, virtual information systems that span organizational boundaries.

A second observation repeatedly impressed upon us through experience was the valuable contribution of a well-defined information architecture [15]. The information architecture formally characterizes the data that is manipulated by the system, and is critical to realizing the domain implementation. As part of designing the information architecture for any domain, we have been actively involved in developing a standard information model for the representation of information associated with data objects managed within different scientific domains. The data objects that are captured, managed, and exchanged by the system are described in the information architecture by a "metadata object" which provides a set of attributes for the data object, and relationships between objects, as described in the domain information model.

The OODT framework provides a set of core services and architectural patterns that simplify implementation of the above functions, which themselves are informed by the domain model (e.g., a cancer biomarker information model, a planetary science information model, etc). The loose coupling between each service and its associated domain model allows for the services to be easily developed to support multiple domains. Each of the OODT services can be deployed independently and then can be integrated using XML-based interfaces over a distributed, grid architecture. This service independence and insulation makes it possible to minimize the effects of organizational boundaries on accessing data repositories (either local or distributed) concurrently, compiling the results into a unified view, and making them available for analysis. The OODT framework is based on the software architectural notion of components [10]. Each component has well-known interfaces that enable them to be plugged together in a distributed, yet coordinated, manner. The components themselves sit on top of off-the-shelf middleware technologies so that they can be deployed easily into an enterprise topology.

Each of our domain implementations is working to build domain-specific applications on top of the common services framework provided by OODT. For example, the NASA Planetary Data System (PDS) used a Lucene-based search engine [16] that integrated with OODT to provide millisecond-speed searching across highly distributed databases using a text-based search interface. The benefit of the framework to these projects is that it has substantially helped in both building new data systems as well as integrating existing data systems, all while controlling software development costs through software reuse and standardized interfaces.

In this chapter, we will discuss the architectural patterns and experience in implementing an e-science [17] product line. The chapter will highlight the technical, scientific, management and policy challenges associated with building and deploying multi-organizational data systems. It will compare and contrast differences between planetary, earth and biomedical research environments and discuss the importance of a well-defined architecture and the need for domain information models. It will discuss key architectural principles in the design as well as the importance of having a well-defined operational model to ensure both reliability of the system as well as quality of the data and services.

5.2 Applying e-science Principles to Science

In this section, we will motivate some of the critical architectural principles derived from our experience in the e-science domain-constructing systems with OODT. Each principle that we detail below is summarized for the reader's convenience in Table 5.1.

Table 5.1 Architectural principles derived from our experience in the domain

Principle		Description
P1	Access and correlation	e-science software should providing uniform methods to bring together data in distributed environments to increase the chances of discovery
P2	Location independence	Users of e-science software should not concern themselves with the physical location of data or services
P3	Well-defined information architecture	Software changes rapidly in e-science systems. Data models and metadata attributes do not. Systems that can easily support this evolution are desired

Collaboration is a critical aspect of scientific research. Multicenter and multi-institutional collaborations are often critical to support and validate scientific hypothesis. Yet, far too often, systems are not architected to support construction of virtual scientific environments, particularly in support of performing analysis of distributed data. It is essential that the capture, management, and distribution of scientific data resulting from scientific studies and research be considered in terms of its value to sharing data. The *access and correlation of data* (P1) across distributed environments is critical to increasing the study power and validating the data from greater number of samples and contexts [9].

What we have found from our technology development of virtual scientific networks is that *location independence* (P2) has become a critical architectural tenant for the construction of modern e-science data systems. Location independence prescribes that the physical location of data and components should be transparent to those accessing them. In other words, whether data and software are local or are geographically distributed should not matter to human or application users. The implication is that the access and interpretation of the data objects should remain consistent despite multiple topologies for the system that may be in place.

As part of our work in the planetary science and cancer research communities (that we will elaborate on in Sect. 5.5 and again in Sect. 5.7 respectively) it has become apparent that a *well-defined information model* (P3) consisting of both rich data attributes implemented using well-known standards (such as ISO-11179 and Dublin Core) is also an important architectural principle. The planetary science data model [4, 6] consists of a set of over 1,200 data elements, including terminology such as *Target* to identify the celestial body targeted by the mission's instrument(s); *Instrument* to denote the name and type of the scientific instrument flown on the mission that records observations, and *Mission* to denote the unique name of the NASA mission for which data is being archived. On the cancer research side, we have developed a group of over 40 data elements [2, 9], including *Specimen Collected Code*, an integer value denoting the type of specimen, for example, blood sputum, etc., collected for a patient; *Study Site Id* which denotes a numeric identifier for a participate cancer research site; and *Study Protocol Id*, a numeric identifier denoting the protocol under which data has been collected, to name a few.

Though technology changes rapidly, the above work on data models does not. In the case of the planetary model, changes have been limited over the past 20 years;

an attribute was added here or there to account for some new mission, but those changes are few and far between – in all, tens of the 1,200 elements may have been modified, or added to. On the cancer research side, the same 40 data elements to describe cancer research data have been leveraged over the past 8 years in the context of the National Cancer Institute's (NCI) Early Detection Research Network (EDRN) project, again, with similar experiences – some new instrument technology, or new application drives the creation of a few attributes here and there; nothing more. These examples illustrate the importance of a *well-defined information model* (P3) as a means of allowing software technology and data modeling to evolve independently of one another.

In the next section, we describe our work on the Object Oriented Data Technology (OODT) framework, and its architecture, and demonstrate the relationship of the two of the aforementioned architecture principles summarized in Table 5.1.

5.3   The Architectural Model and Framework

"Expect the unexpected" has been the driving mantra behind OODT. Years of experience building implementations of this architecture for domains as diverse as planetary and earth science and cancer biomarker research have repeatedly impressed upon us the need for a flexible, architecturally principled core platform of software and services upon which to build domain-specific extensions. Our approach has favored using a core set of loosely connected, independent components [10] with well-defined interfaces over the more traditional monolithic system architecture. A number of observations culled from our experience have helped to influence this design decision. We can directly map these observations to the three architectural principles (recall P1-P3 from Table 5.1) described earlier.

The e-science domain [17] is focused on science, which in turn is focused on observation. Scientific instruments collect observations in the e-science world. For many decades, the resolution and frequency of the data returned from these instruments was minute, and disk space was expensive [18, 19]. In modern times, disk space is cheap, and instrument resolution and data capture ability are growing faster than the e-science systems that regularly must deal with the data. This situation has made it critical to develop e-science software based upon an overarching construct that was both open-ended and standards-based, to allow for necessary extension (principle P3 from Table 5.1). Furthermore, science is often subject to political considerations and policy factors that are subject to change. This oft-uncertain landscape amplifies the need for a system that can be quickly evolved to meet unexpected changes in the operational environment (principle P3 from Table 5.1).

Most data-intensive scientific information systems can be deconstructed into combinations of basic concepts of data *capture*, *discovery*, *access*, *processing*, and *distribution* (recall Sect. 5.1), as demonstrated in Fig. 5.1. The figure demonstrates the canonical science data pipeline in use by many e-science projects: In the upper left portion of the figure, a scientific instrument (in this case, represented by a remote sensing instrument, but the same would apply to any type of

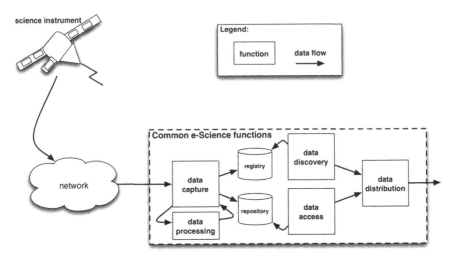

Fig. 5.1 Common e-science functions derived from architectural principles in Table 5.1. The relationship between the functions is demonstrated as data flow beginning with data capture, culminating with data distribution

observing sensor, e.g., a microscope, etc.) records data, and then sends it over a network to a data capture function. That data capture function then sends the recorded observations to a data processing function (either one time, or a series of times), which in turn may further process the provided data (and its descriptions, called *metadata*, or "data about data"), for example, if the data is an image, by down sampling the image, or resizing it. That processed data is then provided back to the data capture component, for persistence – the data is stored in a repository, and the metadata is stored in a registry. The data and metadata are then exposed downstream to users of the e-science system by a data discovery function (allowing search and discovery against the registry), and by a data access function (allowing the physical bits captured in the repository to be accessed). The combination of the retrieved data and metadata is then provided to a data distribution function for ultimate distribution to the community (occurring in the bottom right portion of Fig. 5.1).

By modeling these core concepts as a collection of loosely connected components, we have found that we can selectively utilize and rearrange them to create a variety of scientific environments uniquely suited to the needs of specific projects, independent of the project domain. In other words, some projects will have a strong focus on, for example, data ingestion and data distribution, but not so much on that of data processing (planetary science is an example, as well as cancer research). On the other hand, projects—including science domains—will focus entirely on that of data ingestion and data processing, omitting a strong focus on data distribution or on data discovery. With the base components in place, domain-specific intelligence can be layered on top to provide customization and tuning to the environment (principles P1 and P3 from Table 5.1).

Finally, the scope of the challenges being addressed across scientific disciplines today has driven a trend toward increased collaboration and partnership among researchers, often crossing organizational and institutional boundaries (principle P2 from Table 5.1). This new reality has placed a premium on the perception of location independence of data from the perspective of access and processing (principle P2 from Table 5.1). As will be evident from the following sections, we have found that the federated component model provides a powerful mechanism for connecting distributed data holdings into virtual scientific environments in which the physical location of data is largely transparent to system users.

Particularly for multi-institution implementations of large-scale data processing systems, the use of open, standards-based protocols for communication between distributed components of the system architecture is critical (principles P1, P2, and P3 from Table 5.1). Effective data capture, manipulation, storage, and dissemination are all predicated upon the existence of a shared protocol for communicating representations of data between components. Our approach has favored open standards like XML-RPC [20], Resource Description Framework (RDF) [21], and Representational Entity State Transfer (REST) [22] to improve its integration potential into as diverse an ecosystem as possible.

So far, we have restricted much of our focus to detailing the common software functions that are part of our reusable e-science architecture and framework. In the ensuing section, we will hone in on the information architecture, and discuss OODT's focus on reusable models and patterns for representing data in an e-science environment.

5.4   An Information-Centric Approach

Data-intensive systems in the e-science era must not only meet the expectations of a new generation of Internet savvy scientists but as distributed scientific data repositories, they will also be expected to support science in ways not conceived of when the system were originally designed. To meet these expectations there must be an unambiguous specification of the data objects the systems manage and the context within which they exist in the targeted domain. These specifications must contain a broad range of modeling information, from classical data models that define the structure of the data objects to descriptions of the science context in which the data objects exists. In addition, to enable the potentials of the semantic web [23], the specification must also define a rich set of relationships between the data objects in the domain to allow machine reasoning. Finally to support system interoperability at the data level, shared models must be developed by science domain experts to provide a common domain of discourse for both scientists and machines.

The information model is a key component of an e-science system. Lee [24] has defined an information model as a representation of concepts, relationships, constraints, rules, and operations to specify data semantics for a chosen domain of discourse.

In the Object Oriented Data Technology (OODT) reference architecture and framework, an information model is thought of as a network of data models where each data model deals with one or more aspects of the system. For example, the Planetary Data System (PDS) information model has data models for each of the four fundamental data structures used to store digital objects, such as images of the planet Mars. Other data models exist for the science interpretation of the images, the time and geometry data needed to register the image on the planet's surface, and the descriptive information about the planets including identification attributes and web-resource links for publications and authoritative information sources. Another data model prescribes a structure for packaging data objects into products that are registered, searched, located, and retrieved. Finally, the information model as a whole puts the products into their science context by defining the associations between products and adding taxonomical information such as asserting that Mars is a Terrestrial planet in the solar system.

Ontology-modeling tools, used to model the domain, are leveraged often in OODT. The tools help to explicitly record each "thing" in the domain as a class. For example, data product, target, and investigation are all modeled as classes in the PDS ontology as shown in Fig. 5.2. Figure 5.2 illustrates a few of the higher-level classes

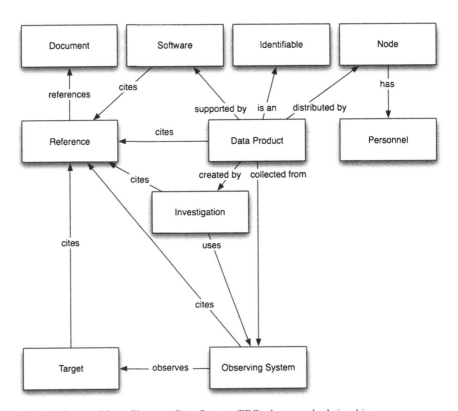

Fig. 5.2 Concept Map – Planetary Data System (PDS) classes and relationships

and their relationships that have been defined in the PDS information model. More specific things such as "planet" exist as subclasses. A preliminary list of things to be modeled can often be identified in the functional requirements of an information system. The resulting information classes are then operated on by the system's functions and services, aiding in addressing architectural principle P3 from Table 5.1.

Functional requirements for the e-science domain typically include those mentioned earlier in Sects. 5.1 and 5.3 (recall: data *capture, processing, discovery, access,* and *distribution*). These requirements suggest class attributes. For example, basic management of an object, such as object capture, suggests the need for a unique immutable identifier, a title for display purposes, a version identifier, and some type of description. An object status attribute is suggested by life cycle management functions.

The data processing requirement suggests the need for attributes that formally define the object's data structure. For example, the fundamental structure used for a grayscale image, an array, must have attributes that provide the dimension of the array, the number of elements in each dimension, and the array element data type.

The discovery and distribution functions both suggest a richer model, for example coordinate system attributes support common geographical information system queries on terrestrial planet surfaces. However, finding features in Saturn's rings or tracking a storm in Jupiter's atmosphere requires dynamic metadata from complex calculations in addition to that metadata that is statically generated. Finally, correlative information discovery and distribution require shared models with common taxonomies and associations across classes to meet requirements.

A vital concept within OODT and within the e-science domain as a whole is the *information object* [8]. Formally defined as the unique combination of a *data object* (the bits) and its descriptive metadata (or its *metadata object*), the concept is used to uniformly describe, to allow for comparison, and to identify all things in the e-science domain into a core component for the model. For example, a Mars image is a digital instance of a data object, a sequence of bits. Metadata is associated with the data object to define its structure and describe the object so that it can be processed and made useful to scientists. In a similar manner, conceptual things like investigations and physical things like instruments are modeled as information objects as well. This concept is illustrated in Fig. 5.3.

One of the canonical elements of an information model is its *data dictionary*. Whereas an ontology focuses on the definition of classes using attributes, a data dictionary focuses on the definition of the attributes. Intuitively a data dictionary defines an attribute as having a name, description, and a value. Our work within the context of e-science domains and OODT has led us to define attributes using a standard, more comprehensive data model. The model manages attributes separately from an attribute's permissible values and provides a range of specifications from effective dates, registration authority, submitter, steward, and classification schemes to the use of one or more natural languages for definitions. Data dictionaries also provide a means of defining the language of discourse for the e-science domain, namely the terms used by the scientists and the system to communicate. The importance of a standard model for the data dictionary is especially evident when considering

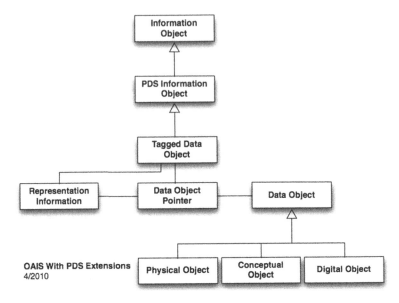

Fig. 5.3 UML class diagram of information object, adapted from [8]

system interoperability at the data level. System interoperability is best built by laying a common foundation for communicating the most basic components in the system, the attributes used to define e-science domain terminology.

Based on our experience in the context of OODT, a shared ontology is the single most important element for enabling system interoperability and science data correlation. Uschold [25] states that the process of assembling a single shared ontology automatically from separately developed ontologies is essentially cryptology. This is also true regarding the development of interoperable systems from disparate information models. The model-driven aspect of the OODT infrastructure focuses on the use of an ontology to generate almost all of the design, implementation, and operational artifacts, all the way from the information model specification and data dictionary to registry configuration files and XML schema (recall, this is a core architectural principle, P3, allowing for the separation of data and software models, as described in Table 5.1). We have summarized the OODT model–driven process in Fig. 5.4.

The system requirements and domain knowledge are captured in an ontology-modeling tool and exports from the ontology database are translated to various notations depending on the need (as shown in the upper left portion of Fig. 5.4). For example, an XML Metadata Interchange (XMI) file is generated for import into UML modeling tools for the creation of UML class diagrams and potentially software code. XML Schemas are generated for generating and validating XML documents used to capture metadata. RDFS/XML [21, 23] and OWL/XML [23] are supporting technologies used to implement search/browse functionality, and used traditionally in OODT-based project implement capture, discovery, and distribution of information in the OODT system.

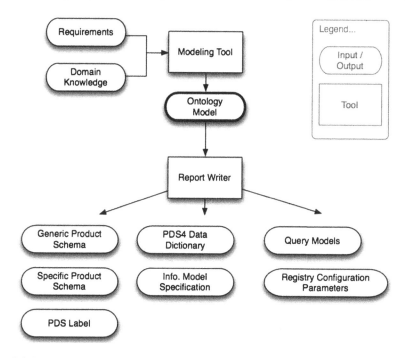

Fig. 5.4 The model-driven process of the (Object Oriented Data Technology) OODT architecture: separation of software and information model allows each to evolve independently. At the core of the process is the ontology, used to codify the requirements, flow through functionality to the actual components, and ultimately validate the implementation of OODT architectures

Armed with OODT's reference architecture, its core functions and principles, and its information architecture focus, the following sections illustrate real OODT deployments in the domains of planetary science, earth science, and cancer research. Along the way we will tie back the domain requirements, functionality, and ultimate architectural and implementation principles discussed, illustrating OODT's ability to effectively model and implement software in the e-science domain.

5.5 The Planetary Science Model

The planetary science discipline has engendered scientific achievements that are poised to stand the test of time. The robotic missions that have been flown to study the solar system represent some of mankind's greatest engineering achievement. Yet, the design, launch, and observations made by the spacecraft developed represent only part of the story. Capturing, processing, sharing, and analyzing the scientific results are critical stages in the overall mission necessary to increase the understanding of the universe in which we live. The planetary science data systems are invariably distributed and must be designed to support new science investigations with a variety of different types of data from images to complex data structures. Yet, there is a critical need to ensure that these systems can be interoperable to allow for interdisciplinary research as well as research multiple missions and studies.

In the early 1980s, the National Research Council formed the Committee on Data Management and Computation (CODMAC) [26]. CODOMAC focused on making a number of recommendations on the long-term management of planetary science data. The NRC report identified seven core principles (1) Scientific involvement; (2) Scientific oversight; (3) Data availability including usable formats, ancillary data, timely distributed, validated data, and documentation; (4) Proper facilities; (5) Structured, transportable, adequately documented software; (6) Data storage in permanent and retrievable form; and (7) Adequate data system funding.

In the late 1980s, the United States National Aeronautics and Space Administration (NASA) formed a facility known as the Planetary Data System (PDS) [4, 6] that is responsible for curation and management of all scientific data results from robotic exploration of the solar system. The structure of the PDS is based on the CODMAC report organized to provide scientific expertise on the use of the discipline-specific scientific data sets by the worldwide scientific community. Over the years, the PDS has become a national resource, housing well over 100 terabytes of data across eight nodes covering NASA missions starting in the 1960s. These nodes cover scientific discipline areas including planetary atmospheres, geosciences, imaging, magnetospheres, radio science, planetary rings, and small bodies. A node covering overall engineering of the system is based at the Jet Propulsion Laboratory. The overall structure of the PDS is depicted graphically in Fig. 5.5.

PDS has been a leader in defining data standards, working with missions and instrument teams, and developing data system technologies. It has also been instrumental in changing the scientific culture by working with the planetary science

Fig. 5.5 The geographic distribution of NASA's Planetary Data System. There are nine nodes geographically distributed across the USA, broken down by scientific expertise

community to publicly release and peer review the data it captures. It is often cited as a model by other domestic and international science data systems doing leading-edge scientific research [4, 6].

PDS has made several critical "architectural" [4, 6] decisions that have been paramount to its success. In the spirit of the OODT architectural principles (recall principle P3 from Table 5.1) PDS has defined a *Planetary Science Data Model* that all missions conform to when submitting data to the PDS. Having a common data model allows for searching across nodes, missions, instruments, and products in a uniform manner, which is important for turning the PDS federation into an integrated enterprise, as well as addressing a core e-science function of data discovery (recall Sect. 5.3). While many disciplines are addressing semantic interoperability after data has been archived, PDS is working, as early as possible, with the missions so they adopt the PDS data standards and use common terms for documenting science data. PDS's common data model, having transcended several technology upgrades and changes to the system, has remained critical to the entire project since its inception (in line with principle P3 from Table 5.1).

PDS continues to evolve toward a broader vision of an online, distributed system based on international standards. The focus of PDS, over the next 5 years, is to enable the PDS to move toward a fully online, distributed system that supports the evolving needs of both PDS data providers and users while improving the overall efficiency and reliability of the system. A further objective of PDS is to continue to architect tools that can be deployed in a variety of heterogeneous computing environments to allow for specific adaptation and use within different mission contexts as early as possible in the life of a mission, helping to address principles P1 and P2 from Table 5.1, and ultimately to realize the necessary e-science services such as data access, discovery, and distribution as shown in Fig. 5.1.

The PDS itself is a classic virtual organization where the organization represents a number of distributed elements, principally people, data, and systems. The purpose is to build a homogeneous federation of archives to promote greater interoperability and construction of the virtual science environment for planetary research. This leads to common governance challenges whereby policies for local versus federal control and standards must be well defined. The PDS allows a substantial amount of autonomy at each of the nodes, but requires that all data that is produced and captured within the PDS be compliant to a common set of data standards (addressing principle P3 from Table 5.1). This common model has helped to improve the ability to access and integrate data that is physically distributed across the PDS network. As PDS has evolved its technical implementation over the years, there has been continued migration toward creating a single, virtual system, where discovery and access to the data are transparent to the user. In other words, the physical topology of the system becomes less important as the maturity of the system and movement toward virtualization continues (in line with principle P2 from Table 5.1). This is illustrated in many ways by the recent work (2006 and beyond) helping to form the International Planetary Data Alliance (IPDA) [27]. The IPDA is an international standard organization, focused on the development of international standards for the purposes of enabling interoperability and data sharing of planetary science data archives across space agencies. In large part, many of the early work on IDPA has focused on implementing a common set of functions, defining the necessary information architecture, and realizing an implementation driven by the e-science aspects of OODT employed by PDS discussed thus far in this section. Beyond the location independence (principle P2 from Table 5.1), necessary access (principle P1 from Table 5.1) required for federating PDS within the USA, moving to an international virtual organization has only strengthened our belief in the small set of core principles upon which e-science systems can be based.

Besides the service-focused principles, even more so in PDS the information architecture (principle P3 from Table 5.1) emerges as a critical component of the system. PDS's information architecture largely employs the use of data dictionaries, core data elements, domain models, and other information-centric principles (recall Sect. 5.4) necessary in the e-science domain. Specifically, for our work on PDS and in planetary science as a whole, we have constructed an ontology that describes the planetary objects and their relationships within the domain. The ontology model allows capture of rich semantics within the model and mechanisms to export the model into both schemas and standard documentation for use by data producers within a mission (recall Fig. 5.4). The model contains the core elements of planetary science (missions, targets, spacecraft, data, etc) and is extended to engender domain-specific data services (subsetting, coordination transformation, mining, etc) beyond those core e-science services (recall Sect. 5.3) common to many e-science systems. Data that is captured and sent to the PDS is validated against the model to ensure semantic and syntactic compliance. The purpose is to build a homogeneous federation of archives.

Figure 5.6 shows the common information flow for data, whereby data providers (missions, instrument teams, and individual principal investigators) submit data to the PDS that is stored within the distributed system, and then distributed to the data consumers.

In summary, the planetary science community is benefiting from the e-science paradigm change through the ability to access, search, download and use scientific data results from missions. Without a well-defined data and software architecture, this would not be possible. The core data standards developed for the NASA Planetary Data System, for example, have been essential for representing metadata and data in a common way and ensuring that it can be located across highly distributed repositories and then loaded into common tools. The existence of such standards has helped to pave the way toward greater interoperability at an international scale.

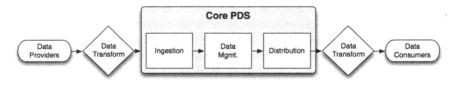

Fig. 5.6 Information flow within the Planetary Data System (PDS)

5.6   Earth Science Research

Earth science is another domain that has complex data sets that are captured across a variety of distributed data systems. These systems capture and process observational data acquired from satellites as well as other measurement instruments in a variety of data formats using different information models. In addition to capturing observational data, a significant amount of work occurs in the development of complex scientific models to analyze such challenges as climate change and weather prediction. As the computing capabilities have increased, there has been significant interest in sharing data across various communities and data systems. One such example is in the area of climate change to compare climate models to satellite observations.

Over the course of next few years, the Intergovernmental Panel on Climate Change (IPCC), the leading international organization studying global climate change, will undergo a battery of experiments whose results will be recorded in the 5th Assessment Report, or AR5 [28]. The experiments are geared toward simulating dozens of climate-related variables, from air pressure, to sea surface salinity, all the way to the world's temperature, which has been a huge subject of debate and interest (inter-)nationally, and of which major US and global funding initiatives have arisen from.

The UN Climate Change conference in Copenhagen meetings held during December 2009, which included participation from some of the most influential members of our global society, including US President Barack Obama, highlighted the importance of the upcoming IPCC AR5 activity. Decades-long climate model simulations over multiple variables and parameters require massive amounts of data and computation in order to provide meaningful results in a timely fashion. Further, these simulations require complex climate models, which themselves require tuning and observation by hundreds of scientists looking to identify the next important prediction that can be used to inform national policy and decision making based on the Earth's climate.

A recent IEEE workshop[1] brought together IT professionals and climate researchers with the goal of understanding how information technology, grid computing, data science, and computer science could be brought to bear to help climate scientists participating in AR5. One of the principal conclusions of this workshop (as well as that of a meeting[2] that preceded it) was identifying the role of technology in the AR5 was helping to shepherd in observational data as a means of climate model improvement and diagnostics. As it turns out, though the prior IPCC model runs (AR4) was deemed widely seminal, and produced over 2,000 peer-reviewed science publications, the organizers of AR5 believe that the reliability of projections (and also the number of publications resultant from this activity) could be improved if the models were validated and measured against remotely sensed observations.

---

[1] http://smc-it.org/workshops/crichton.html
[2] http://www.ipcc.ch/workshops-experts-meetings-ar5-scoping.htm

Within the last year, the Climate Data eXchange (CDX), an effort to improve use of NASA's earth observational data in the improvement and analysis of climate model outputs, was initiated under the supervision of NASA's JPL [29]. The major focus of CDX is directly *enabling* the aforementioned IPCC activity, and to provide NASA observational data products (both raw level 2 in the long-term and level 3 in the short-term) to the IPCC AR5 community. The data products vary broadly in their formats (e.g., HDF vs. netCDF), geographic coverage, access methods, and volume. Additionally, the science and observations within the data files are highly instrument specific, including temporal and spatial properties that must be harmonized in order for model comparison.

The crux of the problem is that global climate models provide measurements of parameters in all places at all times for which the model is run; observational data, on the other hand, does not. In turn, the CDX project's focus is that of obviating these heterogeneities and providing an open source software toolkit for use in the IPCC AR5, and to help its science users rapidly and programmatically improve and validate climate models.

A large effort has been made to deploy web-services and a client toolkit based on OODT [5]. Much of the focus on leveraging OODT for CDX to date has been to expose data access, discovery, and processing (subsetting) services (recall Fig. 5.1 and see Fig. 5.7) provided by NASA's mission science computing facilities,

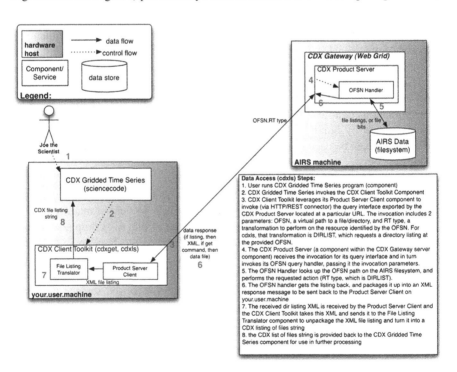

Fig. 5.7 The Anatomy of a (Climate Data eXchange) CDX operation. The client toolkit provides underlying data access services to the example application (CDX Gridded Time Series) by remotely contacting the CDX gateway service on the airscdx machine

specifically the Atmospheric Infrared Sounder (AIRS), the Microwave Limb Sounder (MLS), CloudSAT, and the Multi-angle Imaging SpectroRadiometer (MISR). OODT is focused on providing the substrate for unlocking data, metadata, and computations; the orchestration of those operations is provided by the CDX client toolkit as shown in Fig. 5.7.

The interactions illustrated in Fig. 5.7 demonstrate the manner in which CDX and the principles of OODT are changing the regular day-to-day activities of a climate researcher. We will use a use-case scenario to demonstrate. In our scenario, the climate researcher desires to build a time series comparison of a particular measurement (we will select water vapor for the purposes of discussion; many other measurements could be used) available from the AIRS data system. To begin, the researcher would select a series of observations for a time range, and then, for each day in that time range, download (recall data access from Sect. 5.3) around 240 Hierarchical Data Format (HDF) version 4 files [30] to his or her local drive, the sum of which would be used for a ground truth comparison against simulated NCAR Community Climate System Model (CCSM) version 3 data containing measurement predictions, for example, for water vapor. The model data, however, are stored in a separate archive, and in a different data format, NetCDF [31]. Once the data is downloaded (again, recall data access from Sect. 5.3, and Fig. 5.1), both sets (the HDF and netCDF) of data are loaded via an OPeNDAP interface [32] (recall principle P3 from Table 5.1) into a few Python scripts, responsible for: (1) averaging the observational data and ensuring it is on the same space/time continuum; (2) computing a statistic, for example, an average or a covariance needed to assess the observational data against its predicted values from the model (recall, data processing, and data access from Sect. 5.3 and Fig. 5.1).

As shown in Fig. 5.7, the CDX approach for addressing this use-case scenario involves pushing as much of the computation as close to the data as possible, insulating location of data and transference of service to the OODT middleware layer (steps 3, 4, 5, and 6 from Fig. 5.7) as possible, and ensuring the time series component is unaware of the actual remote data access and computation that is occurring (principles P1 and P2 from Table 5.1). The transformation of the water vapor observational measurements is removed from the actual Python program, and pushed to the remote OODT product service, colocated with the AIRS data as shown in the upper right portion of Fig. 5.7, addressing data processing, and solidifying its interface with data access, as demonstrated in Sect. 5.3 and Fig. 5.1.

To date, we have leveraged the CDX infrastructure and client toolkit to directly enable two critical use cases for climate change. The first example involves delivering NASA observational data to the Earth System Grid gateway at Lawrence Livermore National Laboratory (LLNL) with the direct intention of sharing the observational data for AR5 – to date, AIRS level 3 data, as well as MLS level 3 data has been delivered to the Earth System Grid, with the information being provided by the underlying CDX infrastructure. The second major use case involves performing model to observational data time series comparisons between AIRS level 3 data, and NCAR CCSM model output, available from LLNL, as described above.

Our experience has shown that a well-defined architecture and a set of common standards and software components are useful for deploying and building e-science architectures. Given the maturity of our work with the OODT software framework and the development of common information and software architectures, the Climate Data Exchange came together very quickly. While the common problems of heterogonous data systems existed, the experience and technologies available allowed us to deploy an infrastructure that could access climate observations and models, and bring them together into an environment that allowed for greater scientific discovery opportunities.

5.7 Cancer Research

The capture and sharing of scientific data to support advances in biomedical research is another domain that is benefiting from the e-science paradigm. As we have seen above in the planetary and Earth science disciplines, cancer research has experienced an explosive growth over the past decade in the amount of raw data produced by observational instruments. Furthermore, the inherent complexity of the challenges facing cancer researchers today has made the cooperative collaboration among geographically distributed researchers an attractive approach. As a direct result, the development and utilization of informatics tools capable of supporting these new "virtual organizations" has taken on a new importance in this domain as well – and so has the notion of e-science systems as the majority of this chapter has focused on.

In 2000, the Early Detection Research Network (EDRN) was formed as a collaborative research organization funded and led by the Cancer Biomarkers Research Group of the US National Cancer Institute [2]. The EDRN consists of scientists from more than 40 institutions around the USA who are focused on the discovery and validation of biomarkers for the early detection of cancer [2, 9]. The EDRN program has required an informatics infrastructure that is tightly integrated with its scientific program and supports the capture and sharing of biomarker data results.

As with other scientific domains, cancer biomarker research today involves the collection and processing of significant quantities of data (recall Fig. 5.1 from Sect. 5.3), as well as the assimilation of diverse information from many disparate sources for investigation and analysis (dealing with architectural principles P1–P3 from Table 5.1). What often distinguishes research in cancer biomarkers, however, is the heterogeneity of the information that its researchers must interact with (related to architectural principle P3 from Table 5.1). Everything from clinical studies, peer-reviewed publications, statistical data sets, imagery, and human and animal tissue samples can contribute something of value to the overall research picture. With so much technological progress having been made in recent years, however, investigators are increasingly finding themselves awash in data and faced with increasingly acute pressure to efficiently extract the signal from the noise. As a result, tools for managing and understanding this data have become critical to providing researchers with the ability to efficiently and reliably obtain, process, preserve, and publish research results.

Specimen tracking and query systems, relational models for biomarker data, literature search engines, and data warehousing technology for long-term secure storage and statistical analysis are concepts whose implementations have been around in one form or another for several years. The pressing challenge today is in the integration these tools and the data they contain into a seamlessly connected, multi-institution research platform to support the increasingly collaborative efforts of modern research scientists (dealing with location transparency as highlighted in architectural principle P2 from Table 5.1).

The EDRN is an excellent example of an e-science virtual organization. Its research is a coordinated effort by many distributed participants to join forces in attacking the complex and multifaceted problem of early detection of cancer. The viability of the EDRN model, where distributed participants collaborate and share data seamlessly, is predicated on the existence of a technology infrastructure capable of supporting domain-specific distributed research efforts. Such infrastructures are an example of science and technology working hand-in-hand to achieve results that would have been impossible to attain using a traditional, monolithic approach. e-science virtual organizations promote collaboration, and EDRN is no different. It was conceived with the understanding that none of its members had the requisite human, material, or financial resources to take on the challenge of finding new biological indicators for the early detection of cancer alone. Collaboration, however, provides an avenue for subdividing the problem, and targeting the resources and expertise of each individual institution for maximum effect (architectural principles P1 and P2 from Table 5.1).

Recognizing this, the EDRN has consistently placed a strong emphasis on the role of technology in helping to alleviate the technical, scientific, management, and policy challenges associated with conducting large-scale distributed scientific research. The development of an informatics infrastructure to promote the coordination of efforts and the sharing of research results has been a cornerstone of the organization's success.

Since the EDRN's inception, JPL has played a central role in the development of an enterprise-wide informatics infrastructure for the EDRN, focused on a number of concrete goals, and designed to provide a sturdy technological platform for the EDRN's distributed research efforts. Leveraging lessons learned from several of the planetary and earth science data systems discussed earlier, and taking into account the unique needs of researchers in the cancer biomarker domain, JPL leveraged the OODT software product line to develop a distributed research grid of tools and services that collectively came to be known as the EDRN Knowledge Environment, or EKE.

Utilizing OODT provided us with a strong base anchored in the principles of distributed information representation and sharing. The layered services approach used in the planetary and Earth domains was again leveraged here to develop domain-specific extensions to the core services as well as data-type specific tools for high-fidelity data analysis and interpretation (similar to the example in Sect. 5.5 from planetary where planetary specific data services were developed on top of those discussed in Sect. 5.3 and in Fig. 5.1).

The domain information model for EKE consisted of two key components: a semantic ontology, which described classes of information objects in the domain and explicitly mapped their relationships to one another; and a "data dictionary" consisting of terms whose definition had been agreed upon and that could be counted upon to have a shared interpretation across institutional boundaries (architectural principle P3 from Table 5.1).

Each component of EKE was designed to be in conformance with the EDRN domain information model. The fact that OODT was architected with an "Expect the Unexpected" mantra (as described in Sect. 5.3) was particularly valuable to us in this implementation as the domain information model expanded and evolved many times in a variety of directions that would have been very difficult to predict a priori.

Similar to planetary science, having a well-defined domain information model to guide development of the EKE infrastructure and tools was absolutely critical (as noted in architectural principle P3 from Table 5.1). Due to the open-ended design of the underlying OODT architecture, the natural evolution of the domain model did not pose a threat to the integrity of the infrastructure. On the contrary, the presence of a guiding model, even one in occasional flux, proved crucial to rationalizing implementation decisions in the context of the domain, and maintaining sanity in the face of integrating technologically and geographically diverse systems into a unified virtual scientific environment.

The EDRN Knowledge Environment was built around the now familiar principle of loosely connected components capable of communicating among one another by virtue of a shared information model. Rather than a traditional, monolithic stack of applications and services tied to a particular technology set physically installed into a single centralized location, this architecture permitted the development of an ecosystem of applications and service endpoints that were physically located near the data they manipulated, and yet transparently accessible from anywhere via the grid, dealing with architectural principles P1 and P2 from Table 5.1.

Although several of the component applications of OODT have been introduced earlier in the chapter (recall Sect. 5.3), a few merit more detailed discussion in the context of their ability to break down institutional barriers to data discovery and sharing and truly enable distributed scientific research.

The EDRN Resource Network Exchange, or ERNE, was one of the EDRN's early success stories. Designed as a distributed specimen query system, ERNE leveraged OODT's product and profile server architecture to provide unified query access to the numerous specimen repositories located at EDRN member sites (see Fig. 5.8 for a detailed view of this architecture). Prior to ERNE, a centralized query mechanism for specimens did not exist and there was no way for a researcher to reliably know with any certainty that he or she had a comprehensive understanding of specimen availability, short of actually contacting each site individually to inquire.

With the help of the Common Data Elements from the domain information model, it was possible to determine a set of data attributes that would be able to adequately describe specimen resources. However, because the specimen repository information systems at each of the sites were technologically heterogeneous, querying all of them in a unified manner meant the need for site-specific translations or

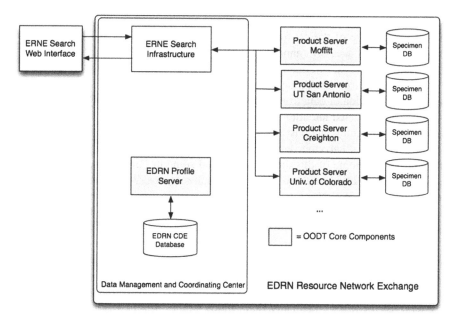

Fig. 5.8 The EDRN Resource Network Exchange (ERNE) deployment for EDRN. In the diagram, OODT services (product servers and profile servers) implement the functions of data discovery, access, and distribution

mappings between the ERNE query based on EDRN CDEs and the site-specific naming conventions in place at each repository.

By placing OODT product server software at each site and working with sites to develop the requisite mapping, it was possible to develop ERNE in a way that allowed for unified query access to the distributed specimen repositories without perturbing the host site's internal data model or operating procedures. As a result, ERNE queries run from the web-based query interface return a unified picture of the matching specimen resources available at each of the participating EDRN sites. As of this writing, ERNE had connected specimen resources at 13 different sites around the USA, totaling over a quarter million specimens.

The type of location-independent access (recall architectural principle P2 from Table 5.1) to data embodied by ERNE has been one of the overarching tenants of the EDRN's informatics infrastructure. Another way that EKE provides researchers with a truly virtual scientific environment is by seamlessly integrating with external (non-EDRN) data sources. The EDRN, while ambitious, is relatively small, and relatively young compared with similar organizations worldwide. EDRN recognized early on that collaboration, not only among its member sites, but also between itself and the myriad other international efforts at combating cancer through research, would be highly valuable to its research community. With that in mind, the EDRN has developed its Biomarker Database application [33] to flexibly integrate links to resources and content physically housed and cataloged in repositories external to the EDRN itself.

The Biomarker Database is an attempt to provide researchers with a unified picture of the state of the art for research on particular biomarkers. This curated resource provides access to annotated information from a wide variety of sources some within and some external to the EDRN itself. Because of the flexibility of the EDRN domain information model, and the architecturally supported abstraction of the physical location of data from an to end user perspective, the EDRN Biomarker Database has attracted attention for its ability to quickly provide researchers with context about ongoing and past research efforts related to a particular biomarker.

In the course of carrying out its research, the EDRN generates a considerable amount of data. Some of this data is "raw," and some has undergone various processing steps to transform it into an informational resource. While sharing information is central to EDRN's mission, it also aims to preserve its research assets, thereby organizing them into a long-term, national resource that can be leveraged to aid future research efforts.

The EDRN Catalog and Archive Service, or eCAS, provides a data warehousing capability that is central to providing long-term, secure storage of research datasets. The system enables data generated from across the EDRN enterprise to be added to the archive, while associated metadata is extracted, reviewed for quality, and indexed to provide a semantically rich catalog of the information assets stored in the repository.

The EDRN's data holdings are numerous, varied, and highly distributed as shown in Fig. 5.9. The EDRN recognized that providing centralized access to the accumulated knowledge would be key to promoting its efforts and increasing the value of the research results by facilitating the degree to which they could be discovered, understood, and utilized. JPL developed a dynamic portal interface to provide access to resources from across the EDRN enterprise from a single, centralized web interface. Because the EKE components and services each adhere to the EDRN domain information model (architectural principle P3 from Table 5.1), the relationships between EDRN data are consistent and predictable. Furthermore, EKE has centered on the use of Resource Description Format (RDF) [21] to provide text-based semantic representations of the data that can be passed between applications as necessary. By analyzing and aggregating RDF streams from each of the EKE components, the EDRN Public Portal is able to consistently provide up-to-date, richly annotated information that communicates the full extent of the resources available through the EDRN.

The EDRN Knowledge Environment provides a virtual scientific environment, a technology platform that supports the EDRN's core efforts to collect, organize, process, and share the vast amounts of critical research it conducts on a daily basis. The informatics infrastructure forms a comprehensive, architecturally principled, and pragmatic approach to supporting cancer biomarker research through tools and interfaces, which, though each may be distributed, are linked to one another through a common information model, and capable of bidirectional communication via the grid. JPL has leveraged the e-science reference architecture promoted via OODT, deconstructing the process of biomarker research into a set of functions, and providing a layered system with applications

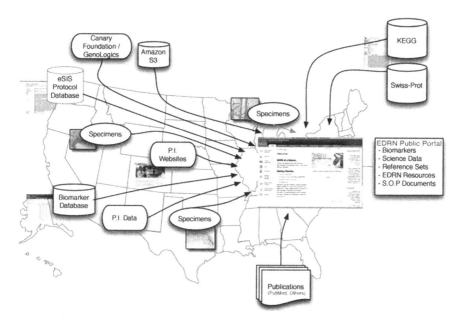

Fig. 5.9 The geographic distribution of the Early Detection Research Network (EDRN) and the variety of data managed in the e-science enterprise. The distributed data in the system is linked together via a semantic portal (in the center of the diagram), unifying the view of research and progress within the EDRN

on top of a core set of services to enable the logical integration of EDRN data. Furthermore, by integrating these domain-specific applications into an enterprise system, the informatics infrastructure enables EDRN as a national organization to provide the capability for managing the biomarker information assets at a national level.

The Early Detection Research Network (EDRN) is an excellent example of an e-science infrastructure for cancer research. The EDRN has been an important pathfinder to pioneer the use of informatics to deploy a distributed, model-driven architecture across geographically distributed cancer research laboratories. Our experience within EDRN confirmed our belief that a well-defined information model is critical to linking distributed, heterogeneous data systems together. The early work of developing a common information model that could be embedded within a distributed software service framework, such as OODT, quickly transformed the EDRN from a set of independent research laboratories into an integrated knowledge system where various data such as scientific datasets, biospecimens, study information, etc, could all be accessed and shared. Efforts to build and identify system architecture helped to provide a scalable and extensible architecture that has allowed for new services to be added. As a result, the EDRN has become a recognized e-science model for the cancer biomarker research community [2, 9].

5.8   Related Work

A considerable amount of work has been done in advancing the principles of e-science and applying them to the construction of systems across the full spectrum of scientific research. The fact that these principles are so broadly applicable speaks to the power of the approach. The contributions to the field are too numerous to cover in detail here, but we present a selection of e-science efforts that specifically relate to the development of virtual scientific environments for carrying out distributed research.

De Roure et al. [21] have addressed the issues related to applying a semantic layer to the traditional e-science grid concepts in an effort to add increased richness to the communication options available to e-scientists. De Roure shares in the vision of an infrastructure that achieves its goals through pragmatic decomposition of the problem into modular components that share a common communication methodology. In particular, he promulgates a scenario involving a *service-oriented* approach to building the e-science infrastructure, laying out in great detail both the advantages and the research challenges inherent to this approach. Emphasizing the importance of the "knowledge layer" in the construction of e-science infrastructures, De Roure further provides a road map of sorts, in the form of categorized research challenges, for moving from the present state of the art to a more comprehensive, semantically rich e-science environment.

Hey and Trefethen [34] describe large-scale efforts in the UK at building an e-science infrastructure, including an e-science grid test bed, to support research in multiple scientific domains. Motivated in part by the increasingly data-intensive work being carried out in European research facilities like the Large Hadron Collider (LHC), which is expected to generate on the order of petabytes of data annually, the program aims to leverage the power of the grid to support the access and analysis needs of scientists the world over. Hey references NASA's Information Power Grid (IPG) project as an "existence proof," and outlines the technical details of the UK's plan along with short- and long-term challenges, strongly emphasizing the need for international collaboration to ensure that the value of the effort is not constrained.

Yang et al. [35] provide a brief examination of e-science infrastructure interoperability, taking a key concept that initially fueled the rise of grid-based e-science systems and applying it to those systems themselves. Yang concludes that while the systems surveyed have each made significant strides in connecting their respective research cohorts, the middleware upon which these systems are built are for the most part not yet interoperable with one another. Yang argues that integrating these e-science initiatives will become increasingly important and should be the next step in the evolution of increasingly interconnected global scientific research.

5.9   Conclusion

The e-science paradigm is only increasing. The infrastructures that are being built around the world are changing the way in which science is performed. No longer is science constrained by the boundaries of a local laboratory. It is being conducted across geographical, organizational, and political boundaries allowing for worldwide collaboration among scientific researchers. As a result, a focused software architecture approach is critical to supporting the ambitious goals of building virtual science environments, by integrating distributed organizations.

In this chapter, we have described an architectural approach, a set of principles, an information model, and associated implementation framework that bridges the gap, allowing reuse of software and information architecture across scientific domains. Specifically, we have described the OODT architecture and implementation, used to build widely successful e-science applications in the areas of planetary science, earth science, and cancer research. We have addressed issues of data capture/curation, processing, dissemination, and preservation in each of these heterogeneous application domains using OODT as the linchpin upon which domain-specific information models and software are constructed.

While our work to date has been highly successful, a number of pertinent research questions remain. Our current work is focused on the areas of analysis of distributed data sets, large-scale, wide-area data movement, and cloud computing, each of which we believe fits within the architectural paradigms of e-science systems. We expect the focus on information and software architecture, OODT's principle foundations, to aid our efforts and help make a strong contribution to each of these emerging areas.

Acknowledgment The research was carried out at the Jet Propulsion Laboratory, California Institute of Technology, under a contract with the National Aeronautics and Space Administration.

References

1. D. Crichton, J.S. Hughes, S. Kelly and J. Hyon. "Science Search and Retrieval using XML". *In Proceedings of the 2nd National Conference on Scientific and Technical Data*, Washington D.C., National Academy of Sciences. March 2000. http://oodt.jpl.nasa.gov/doc/papers/codata/paper.pdf
2. D. Crichton, et al., "Creating a National Virtual Knowledge Environment for Proteomics and Information Management," in Informatics and Proteomics: Marcel Dekker Publishers, 2005.
3. D. Crichton, et al., "Facilitating Climate Modeling Research and Analysis via the Climate Data eXchange," In Proc. Workshop on Global Organization for Earth System Science Portals (GO-ESSP), Seattle, WA, 2008.
4. J. S. Hughes, et al., "The Semantic Planetary Data System," In Proc. 3rd Symposium on Ensuring Long-term Preservation and Adding Value to Scientific and Technical Data, The Royal Society, Edinburgh, UK, 2005.
5. C. Mattmann, D. Crichton, N. Medvidovic and S. Hughes. "A Software Architecture-Based Framework for Highly Distributed and Data Intensive Scientific Applications". In Proceedings of the *28th International Conference on Software Engineering (ICSE06)*, pp. 721–730, Shanghai, China, May 20th–28th, 2006.
6. J. S. Hughes, et al., "Intelligent Resource Discovery using Ontology-based Resource Profiles," Data Science Journal, 2005.
7. C. Mattmann, et al., "A Reusable Process Control System Framework for the Orbiting Carbon Observatory and NPP Sounder PEATE missions," in Submitted to 3rd IEEE Intl' Conference on Space Mission Challenges for Information Technology (SMC-IT 2009), 2009.

8. "Reference Model for an Open Archival Information System (OAIS)," CCSDS 650.0-B-1, 2002.
9. D. Crichton, S. Kelly, C. Mattmann, Q. Xiao, J. S. Hughes, J. Oh, M. Thornquist, D. Johnsey, S. Srivastava, L. Esserman, and B. Bigbee. "A Distributed Information Services Architecture to Support Biomarker Discovery in Early Detection of Cancer". Accepted for publication at the *2nd IEEE International Conference on e-Science and Grid Computing*, Amsterdam, the Netherlands, December 4th-6th, 2006.
10. R. N. Taylor, N. Medvidovic and E. Dashofy. *Software Architecture: Foundations, Theory and Practice*. Wiley Press, 2009.
11. Apache Tika. http://lucene.apache.org/tika/, 2010.
12. ISO/IEC CD 11179-3 Information Technology – Data Management and Interchange – Metadata Registries (MDR) – Part 3: Registry Metamodel (MDR3) (2002). http://www.jtc1sc32.org/sc32/jtc1sc32.nsf/Attachments/00DEC39D41D17B1288256A5300603FED
13. S. Weibel, J. Kunze, C. Lagoze, M. Wolf. Dublin Core Metadata for Resource Discovery. Internet Engineering Task Force RFC, 1998.
14. P. Cornillon, J. Gallagher, and T. Sgouros. Opendap: Accessing data in a distributed, heterogeneous environment. *Data Science Journal*, 2:164–174, 2003.
15. M. Cook. *Building Enterprise Information Architectures: Reengineering Information Systems*. Prentice-Hall, 1996.
16. Apache Lucene, http://lucene.apache.org/, 2010.
17. X. Yang, L. Wang, G. von Laszewski. Recent Research Advances in e-Science. *Cluster Computing*, vol. 12, pp. 353–356, 2009.
18. Gorton, P. Greenfield, A. Szalay and R. Williams. Data-Intensive Computing in the 21st Century. *IEEE Computer*, vol. 41, no. 4., p. 30, 2008.
19. R. T. Kouzes, G. A. Anderson, S. T. Elbert, I. Gorton, and D. K. Gracio. The changing paradigm of data-intensive computing. *IEEE Computer*, vol. 42, no. 1, pp. 26–34, 2009.
20. S. S. Laurent, J. Johnston and E. Dumbill. *Programming web services with XML-RPC*. O'Reilly Media, 2001.
21. O. Lassila and R. R. Swick. Resource description framework (RDF) model and syntax, *World Wide Web Consortium*, http://www. w3. org/TR/WD-rdf-syntax, 2010.
22. R. Fielding and R. N. Taylor. Principled Design of the Modern Web Architecture. *ACM Transactions on Internet Technology (TOIT)*, vol. 2., no. 2., pp. 115–150, 2002.
23. T. Berners-Lee and J. Hendler. Scientific publishing on the semantic web. *Nature*, vol. 410, pp. 1023–1024, 2001.
24. Y. Tina Lee (1999). "Information modeling from design to implementation" National Institute of Standards and Technology.
25. M. Uschold and G. M., "Ontologies and Semantics for Seamless Connectivity," SIGMOD Record, vol. 33, 2004.
26. CODMAC, Data Management and Computation, Vol. 1: Issues and Recommendations. Committee on Data Management and Computation, Space Sciences Board. Assembly of Mathematical and Physical Sciences, National Research Council, 1982.
27. D. Crichton. Core Standards and Implementation of the International Planetary Data Alliance. *37th COSPAR Scientific Assembly*. vol. 37, pp. 600, 2008.
28. IPCC Intergovernmental Panel on Climate Change, http://www.ipcc.ch/, 2010.
29. C. Mattmann, A. Braverman, D. Crichton. Understanding Architectural Tradeoffs Necessary to Increase Climate Model Intercomparison Efficiency. *ACM SIGSOFT Software Engineering Notes*, vol. 35, no. 3, July 2010.
30. B Fortner. Hdf: The hierarchical data format. *Dr Dobb's J. Software Tools and Professional Programming*, 1998.
31. R. K. Rew and G. P. Davis. Netcdf: An interface for scientific data access. *IEEE Computer Graphics and Applications*, 10(4):76–82, 1990.
32. P. Cornillon, J. Gallagher, and T. Sgouros. Opendap: Accessing data in a distributed, heterogeneous environment. *Data Science Journal*, 2:164–174, 2003.

33. Hart, C. Mattmann, J. Tran, D. Crichton, H. Kincaid, J. S. Hughes, S. Kelly, K. Anton, D. Johnsey, C. Patriotis. Enabling Effective Curation of Cancer Biomarker Research Data. In *Proceedings of the 22nd IEEE International Symposium on Computer-Based Medical Systems (CBMS)*, Albuquerque, NM, August 3rd-4th, 2009.
34. T. Hey and A. Trefethen. The UK e-Science Core Programme and the Grid. *Computational Science*, vol. 2329/2002, pp. 3-21, 2002.
35. X. Yang, et al. Recent Advances in e-Science. *Cluster Computing*, vol. 12, pp. 353–356, 2009.

Chapter 6
Galaxy: A Gateway to Tools in e-Science

Enis Afgan, Jeremy Goecks, Dannon Baker, Nate Coraor, The Galaxy Team, Anton Nekrutenko, and James Taylor

Abstract e-Science focuses on the use of computational tools and resources to analyze large scientific datasets. Performing these analyses often requires running a variety of computational tools specific to a given scientific domain. This places a significant burden on individual researchers for whom simply running these tools may be prohibitively difficult, let alone combining tools into a complete analysis, or acquiring data and appropriate computational resources. This limits the productivity of individual researchers and represents a significant barrier to potential scientific discovery. In order to alleviate researchers from such unnecessary complexities and promote more robust science, we have developed a tool integration framework called Galaxy; Galaxy abstracts individual tools behind a consistent and easy-to-use web interface to enable advanced data analysis that requires no informatics expertise. Furthermore, Galaxy facilitates easy addition of developed tools, thus supporting tool developers, as well as transparent and reproducible communication of computationally intensive analyses. Recently, we have enabled trivial deployment of complete a Galaxy solution on aggregated infrastructures, including cloud computing providers.

6.1 Introduction

Rapid growth in both the production and the availability of scientific data has revealed the inadequacy of existing data analysis approaches, technologies, and tools. This is particularly true in experimental biology, where the volume of data

E. Afgan, J. Goecks, D. Baker, and J. Taylor (✉)
Department of Biology and Department of Mathematics & Computer Science,
Emory University, Druid Hills, GA, USA
e-mail: eafgan@emory.edu; james.taylor@emory.edu

N. Coraor and A. Nekrutenko
Huck Institutes of the Life Sciences and Department of Biochemistry and Molecular Biology,
The Pennsylvania State University, University Park, PA, USA

The Galaxy Team
Pennsylvania State University and Emory University
http://galaxyproject.org

Xiaoyu Yang et al. (eds.), *Guide to e-Science: Next Generation Scientific Research and Discovery*, Computer Communications and Networks,
DOI 10.1007/978-0-85729-439-5_6, © Springer-Verlag London Limited 2011

produced by new technologies confounds the average experimentalist [1]. New tools and techniques are continually being developed to analyze this data. For the domain scientist, use of these newly available tools and technologies is often preceded by a steep or prolonged learning curve: discovering the most applicable tools, deploying them on appropriate computational resources, learning new user interfaces, etc. Also, arriving at the desired results often requires the domain scientist to become familiar with several tools and compose those into an appropriate workflow. Because of the differences in tools and tool interfaces, this task can easily result in additional complexities that need to be addressed by the scientist directly (e.g., developing wrappers to format tool input/output). Thus, in addition to the development of data analysis tools, there is a need for supporting tools and frameworks that make it possible to utilize otherwise available or upcoming cyberinfrastructure to process the data and deliver results directly to users [2, 3].

Users of such systems are often domain scientists focused on specific research problems that possess domain-specific knowledge but lack interest and knowledge to write computer programs. To support the scientific process, it must be possible for these scientists to share newly available scientific data and results with the remainder of the community. Critical to the scientific review process, these results should be easily verified and reproduced by others. When it comes to sharing results, thus far, scientists have primarily used the scholarly publishing process to announce their findings. However, the traditional publication process is not well suited for publishing the details of data-intensive computational analysis in a completely reproducible manner. In the e-Science context, and with the rapid advances in data discovery, scientists seek to publish their results quickly and continuously in a medium that allows analysis to be expressed more naturally, leading to a shift toward web-based, lightweight publication methods such as wikis and blogs.

Because of these changes in the scientific process, there is a significant need to provide research scientists with streamlined access to a variety of domain-specific tools that can be easily integrated and shared with others in the community. These are the aims of e-Science; they focus around delivery and sharing of highly focused solutions directly to domain scientists. Ideally, this enables a scientist to focus on his or her immediate work without requiring them to learn and understand how the underlying technology operates.

Here we describe an open-source software system, called Galaxy[1] [4, 5], that addresses many of the deficiencies associated with advancement of e-Science outlined above and facilitates scientists' focus on their domain. Galaxy provides an integrated analysis environment where domain scientists can interactively construct multistep analyses, with outputs from one-step feeding seamlessly to the next. The user interfaces are intuitive and consistent, requiring minimal user training and effort. Any software tool can easily be made available through Galaxy, and the underlying data management and computational details are completely hidden from the user, even when dealing with large-scale datasets and high-performance

---

[1] http://galaxyproject.org

computing resources. The environment transparently tracks every analysis detail to ensure reproducibility, and provides a workflow system for constructing reusable analysis, as well as an intuitive interface for constructing workflows from existing analysis. The Galaxy data library system provides secure data management and sharing, with fine-grained access controls and extensive metadata tracking. Thus, Galaxy provides an ideal solution for immediately delivering, integrating, and sharing e-Science tools directly to domain scientists, enabling scientists to focus on performing computational analyses rather than setting up and configuring computational tools.

The fundamental concept underlying Galaxy is a framework for tool integration. It focuses on accessibility, expandability, and result reproducibility. With that, it trades off some expressiveness in terms of user features for usability. Users may not possess the flexibility of complete programming language but they gain the ability to easily, rapidly, and consistently access a variety of domain-specific tools. Galaxy achieves this by conceptualizing domain-specific tools as an abstraction for doing data analysis. For domain scientists from historically non-computational fields (e.g., biology, psychology, sociology), this approach makes it possible to perform complex and reproducible analysis without programming or software engineering expertise.

With the continuous growth of the analysis data and thus increased computational requirements, alongside the usability features realized by Galaxy, there is a need to transparently provision necessary computational infrastructure. Galaxy supports this computational infrastructure demand at two levels: (1) by handling integration with an available workstation or a cluster and (2) by providing a ready solution to deploy Galaxy on aggregated computational infrastructures. This approach makes Galaxy extremely flexible and enables it to meet the needs of a spectrum of users, including tool developers, individual researchers, or entire labs.

This chapter describes the Galaxy framework in the context of a bioinformatics tool set and then generalizes the framework toward a tool execution and data analysis framework for any computational domain. Architecture, interface, and use cases are described, highlighting Galaxy's main features. Finally, current and future directions for Galaxy are described, focusing on job execution across distributed computing infrastructures. Leveraging distributed computing enables Galaxy to process increasingly large volumes of data using ever-larger resource pools.

6.2 Galaxy: A Tool Integration Framework

Galaxy is a software framework for making computational tools available to users without informatics expertise. It is available as a self-contained, portable, open-source software package, which can easily be deployed on existing computational resources. It provides a web-based interface for interactively performing analysis using computational tools. Galaxy provides abstractions to make it easy to integrate almost any computational tool: Any program that can be run from the command line can be integrated by providing an abstract description of how the program works (its parameters and the type of data it expects and generates). This serves both *researchers*, for whom a simple and intuitive user interface is automatically generated, and *tool developers*, who can now rapidly deploy their tools in a way that their experimental colleagues can actually use. Galaxy can also integrate other sorts of tools (e.g., external database interfaces or other web services).

Using the concept of tools as discrete units of analysis with well-defined parameterizations – the Galaxy framework provides a powerful web-based environment for performing complex analyses (Fig. 6.1). Analysis can be performed interactively, with Galaxy keeping a complete "history" that tracks every step of the analysis. Thus, unlike other approaches [6] that rely on careful engineering practices to

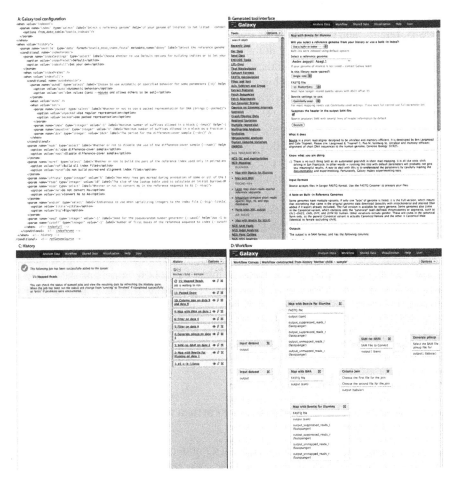

Fig. 6.1 An overview of analysis in Galaxy: (**a**) Tool developers describe their software using Galaxy tool configurations. (**b**) Galaxy generates a user interface for the tool. (**c**) Users provide parameters for the tool, Galaxy manages tool execution and stores all parameters and results in the history. (**d**) The workflow system allows multistep analysis to be reproduced, modified, or created from scratch

ensure transparency and reproducibility, in Galaxy the analysis framework automatically ensures that every detail of every step of an analysis is recorded and can be inspected later. Galaxy also includes a workflow system for constructing more complex analyses that execute multiple tools, using the output of one tool as the input of another tool. Workflows can be automatically extracted from histories, providing a way to rerun and verify the reproducibility of any existing analysis. Histories and workflows can be shared in a variety of ways, including as part of a publication.

6.2.1   Galaxy Goals

The aim of the Galaxy project is a simultaneous impact on individual researchers who want to simply use computational tools and on tool developers who want to publicize their tools while minimizing tedious overhead work associated with the necessary tasks (e.g., data source integration, UI development). Thus, the design of Galaxy relies on the following principles:

Accessibility: The most important feature of Galaxy is the ability for users to access and use a variety of domain-specific tools without a need to learn implementation or invocation details of any one tool or worry about underlying infrastructural details. Galaxy enables users to perform integrative analyses by providing a unified, web-based interface for obtaining genomic data and applying computational tools to analyze the data. Accessibility is further supported by enabling users to import datasets into their workspaces from many established data warehouses or upload their own datasets. Finally, full functionality of Galaxy is immediately accessible from a public web server,[2] available for download and simple local installation (see Sect. 6.3.1), or readily deployable on aggregated infrastructures thus sustaining any level of desired hardware support (see Sect. 6.3.4).

Simplicity of extension: A key feature of the Galaxy framework is the ease with which external tools can be integrated. Galaxy is completely agnostic to how tools are implemented – as long as there is a way to invoke a tool from a command line, a tool could be written in any language whether interpreted (e.g., Perl, Python, R) or compiled (e.g., C, Fortran). Galaxy requires only a high-level description of what parameters a user can provide for the tool, and how to construct a command line or configuration file based on those parameters. Note that when a user writes a tool configuration for Galaxy, they are not implementing a user interface; they are describing the abstract interface to that tool, which Galaxy can then use to adapt that tool to a specific user interface. As a result of such flexibility, functionality of Galaxy is not limited and can be expanded and adopted to not only a specific researcher or a lab but also a specific domain.

---

[2] http://usegalaxy.org/

Reproducibility of results: A key to good science is openness and thus the ability for others to repeat and validate derived results. Galaxy supports reproducibility by tracking derivation of users' analyses, by supporting the ability to repeat a given analysis (or part of thereof), as well as by effectively enabling tagging, annotation, and sharing of complete analyses. Such functionality enables a given analysis not only to be repeated but to also be given context and necessary description explaining underlying reasoning for a particular analysis step and to be easily shared with others.

6.2.2 Galaxy Components

As discussed in the previous section, Galaxy represents an integrated system that focuses on analysis accessibility, tool integration, and support for reproducibility of obtained results. To ensure flexibility and extensibility, Galaxy's architecture is highly modular, and is built for a set of distinct low-level components. These individual components operate at different levels and are not necessarily simultaneously utilized. Instead, when combined, they provide the integrated solution Galaxy has become known for. Figure 6.2 depicts these components.

6.2.2.1 Data Analysis

The primary interface to a Galaxy instance is through the web (although the Galaxy framework allows other interfaces to be implemented; see Sect. 6.2.3). The Galaxy *analysis workspace* contains four areas: the upper bar, tool frame (left column), detail

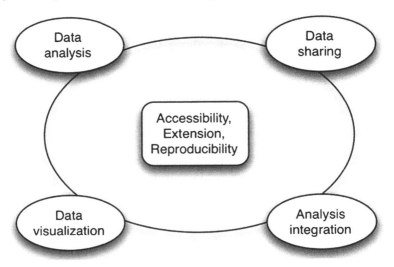

Fig. 6.2 Symbolical representation of components that together enable Galaxy aims

frame (middle column), and history frame (right column). The upper bar contains user account controls as well as help and contact links. The left frame lists the analysis tools and data sources available to the user. The middle frame displays interfaces for tools selected by the user. The right frame (the history frame) shows data and the results of analyses performed by the user. Pictured here are five history items representing one dataset and following analysis steps. Every action by the user generates a new history item, which can then be used in subsequent analyses, downloaded, or visualized. The Galaxy history page can display results from multiple genome builds, and a single user can have multiple histories. Figure 6.3 provides an overview of the analysis workspace.

The Galaxy *history* system stores all data uploaded by the user or generated by the analysis tools. Figure 6.4 illustrates how the history works. Each analysis step

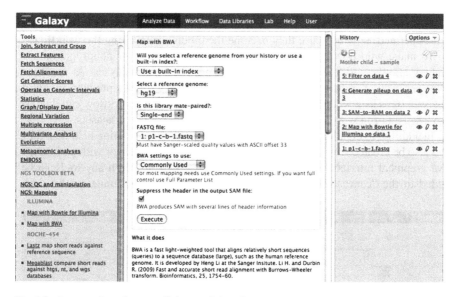

Fig. 6.3   A screenshot of current Galaxy web interface

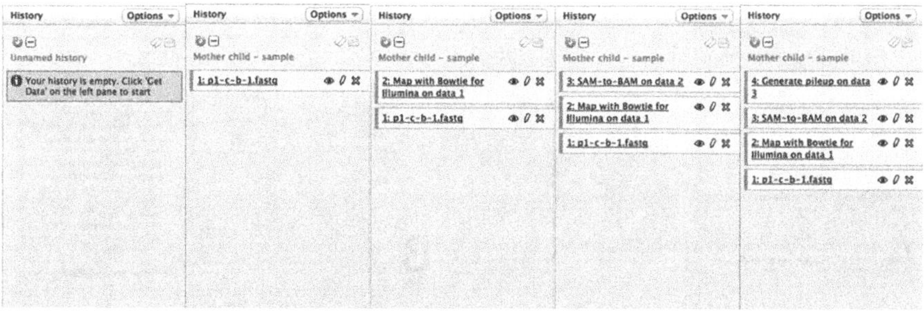

Fig. 6.4   Galaxy history stores uploaded data and analysis results. Original dataset is always preserved and every subsequent analysis adds a new entry into the history pane

(Bowtie mapping [7] and format conversion in this case) generates a new history item, leaving the original datasets intact. Thus if the user makes a mistake or wants to experiment with different parameter settings, they can always go back to the original data.

The ability to perform an analysis in a step-by-step fashion and then be able to simply repeat any part of it (using the same data and parameters or changing those) represents a significant step forward in terms of enabling analysis and realizing reproducibility. However, due to the nature of the research problem, it is often the case that the same analysis needs to be repeated using different data but with the same procedure (possibly using slightly different parameters). In order to enable effective realization of easy reuse, Galaxy supports the notion of *workflows*. The main feature of Galaxy that makes this possible is the structured abstract descriptions of tool interfaces. A Galaxy workflow consists of a specification of a series of tool invocations, where the input of a tool can be connected to the output of any previous tools. Input datasets and parameters are either specified in the workflow, or left undefined, in which case they become the inputs for invoking the workflow.

To make workflow construction as intuitive as possible for nonprogrammers, Galaxy allows workflows to be constructed from existing analyses. At any time after performing some analysis, a user will be able to extract a previous chain of analysis steps as a workflow (Fig. 6.5a). Once extracted, the workflow can then be modified and run with different parameters or different starting datasets.

In addition to creation of workflows with examples from existing histories, they can also be created from scratch using the Galaxy workflow editor with an interactive graphical interface. A graphical editor is provided in which any tool can be added to the "canvas" (Fig. 6.5b). A series of tools is then connected by links

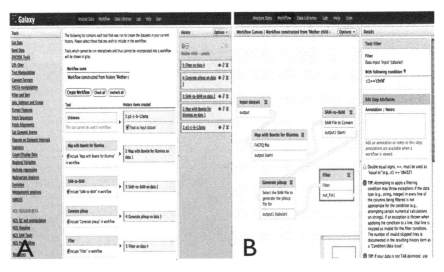

Fig. 6.5 Two ways to create workflows in Galaxy: (**a**) shows the interface for constructing a workflow from an existing history, (**b**) shows the workflow editor for explicit workflow construction and editing

representing the flow of data. The workflow editor is aware of which tools can be chained together: If the output of tool A is compatible with the input of tool B, these two can be chained together.

6.2.2.2 Data Sharing

At the core of accessibility and reproducibility is the ability to share one's findings in a way that is both useful and usable to others. Within Galaxy, sharing is supported from the ground up and is tightly integrated into user's experiences, facilitating the transition from solitary analysis to collaboration. Users can share their findings at multiple levels and with varying scopes: A user can share individual datasets, parts of an analysis, an entire analysis, as well as analysis conclusions. This wide range of sharing options is supported through the following set of components: history sharing, tagging, annotations, data libraries, and Galaxy Pages.

An individual can share his or her history with specific Galaxy users, make it available via a persistent web link (thus not requiring a Galaxy account), or publish it, enabling all users to access it via a web link and find it via search. A user viewing a history shared with them can simply inspect the history or choose to import it into his or her local workspace and manipulate it as desired. Internal to Galaxy, history sharing is enabled by associating a URL with each history element followed by implementation of a broad set of access policies.

Galaxy also supports *tagging* (or labeling) – applying words or phrases to describe an item. Tagging has proven very useful for categorizing and searching in many web applications. Galaxy uses tags to help users find items easily via search and to show users all items that have a particular tag. Tags support reproducibility because they help users find and reuse datasets, histories, and analysis steps; reuse is an activity that is often necessary for reproducibility. Along the ideas of sharing, Galaxy implements notion of community tags; a user can choose to tag a dataset with a set of tags that will be visible and searchable by anyone using Galaxy or simply use personal tags that are accessible only to the given user.

Along with tagging, Galaxy supports *user annotations* – descriptions or notes about an analysis step. Annotations are a critical component of reproducibility because they enable users to explain *why* a particular step is needed or important. Automatically tracked metadata (i.e., history elements) records what was done, and annotations indicate why it was done, facilitating reproducibility by recording both the details and the context of an analysis. Galaxy users can annotate a complete history or workflow and can annotate individual history or workflow steps. Annotations are visible when a user shares a dataset, workflow, or history, as well as within Galaxy Pages (see last paragraph in this section).

With the exponential increase in size and number of bioinformatics data [1], it is increasingly challenging to manage, organize, and make available datasets. As a step in alleviating this, Galaxy supports notion of *data libraries*. Data libraries represent Galaxy instance wide repository of input data sets that can be easily shared and incorporated into users' histories. Not only does the data available in data libraries not need to be uploaded by each user, but any data library element can be used any number of times by any number of users without duplicating the single disk file. Data libraries provide a hierarchical container for datasets, meaning that they can contain datasets, folders, and sub-folders. In addition, data versioning and sophisticated data access permission role system are implemented allowing role-based sharing of individual data library elements as well as making a data library public. Alongside data library sharing permissions, individual data library elements can enforce different actions based on selected user groups.

Galaxy *Pages* (Fig. 6.6) unify Galaxy's functionality to provide users with a medium to communicate and share a complete computational analysis. Pages are custom web-based documents that enable users to communicate about an entire computational experiment, and Pages represent a step toward the next generation of online publication or publication supplement. A Page, like a publication or supplement, includes a mix of text, figures, and graphs describing the experiment's analyses. In addition to standard content, a Page also includes embedded Galaxy items from the experiment: datasets, histories, and workflows. These embedded items provide an added layer of interactivity, providing additional details and links to use the items as well. Like histories, Pages can be shared at a range of levels. Importantly, pages can be published and serve as online supplementary materials for a journal paper; a recent paper describing a metagenomic study that surveyed eukaryotic diversity in organic matter collected off the windshield of a motor vehicle used a Page for its supplementary material[3] [8].

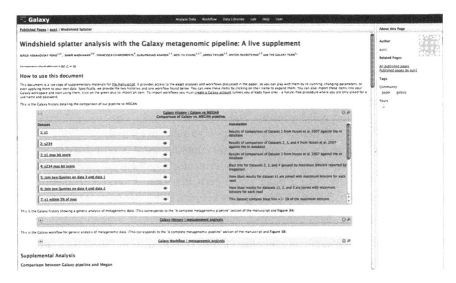

Fig. 6.6 A screenshot of a published Galaxy Page showing supplemental information for performed analysis and associated scholarly publication. Any part of information included on this Page can be easily copied into user's workspace thus supporting notions of accessibility and reproducibility. Shown page is available at http://main.g2.bx.psu.edu/u/aun1/p/windshield-splatter

---

[3] http://usegalaxy.org/u/aun1/p/windshield-splatter

6.2.2.3   Data Acquisition and Visualization

Modern biological analyses frequently involve both locally produced experimental data and community data available through a number of well-organized data warehouses including NCBI, UCSC, Ensembl, TIGR, GMOD, and others. These excellent resources provide users with the ability to query databases (e.g., with the UCSC Table Browser or the Mart system) and visualize features of the genomic landscape (e.g., with the UCSC Genome Browser, GBrowse, or Ensembl Browser). In other words, these resources represent two termini of a typical analysis: the beginning (obtain the data) and the end (visualize the results). Galaxy complements these resources, enabling data manipulation and aggregation of local data together with data acquired from these external sources. Results of analysis can then be sent back to these resources for visualization.

The Galaxy distribution includes tool configurations for integrating several important data sources, including UCSC Table Browser, BioMart, InterMine, GBrowse, directly into the data analysis interface native to Galaxy. Galaxy makes implementing connections to external data sources simple and straightforward. From Galaxy, any existing web-based resource can be integrated into Galaxy's web interface through its "proxy" functionality, requiring no changes to the existing resource. Because of that, any Galaxy instance can immediately use these data connections with no custom configuration.

Upon completion of an analysis, Galaxy users can easily visualize analysis results. Galaxy implements connections to external data visualization tools, including the UCSC Genome Browser (see Fig. 6.7), which can be accessed via web links within a dataset's history entry.

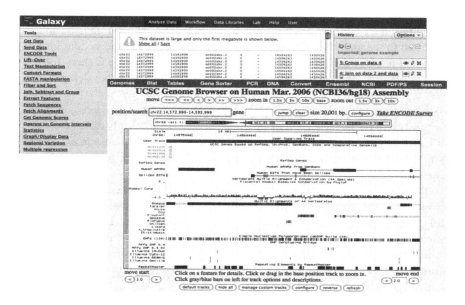

Fig. 6.7 Visualization example with Galaxy and UCSC Genome Browser

6.2.2.4 Access to Computational Resources

The Galaxy components discussed thus far focus on enabling and streamlining the process of analyzing data. However, increasing capabilities to produce large bioinformatics datasets also means an increasing need for computational resources. Thus, there is an obvious benefit – and, soon, a need – to enable the transparent acquisition of computing resources (e.g., computing power, storage space) to meet these demands. Galaxy makes it possible for users to acquire and utilize computational resources in two distinct ways. First, by providing an abstract interface to various compute clusters, allowing the use of existing resources users may have available. Second, by providing a self-contained solution for enabling Galaxy to be executed on distributed but aggregated infrastructures, for example, cloud computing [9] resources.

In the context of generating ever-growing data and the necessary transformation of this data into a biologically meaningful information, it is necessary to possess significant computational infrastructure and informatics support. In particular, meeting computational demands is especially difficult for individual researchers and small labs. For an experimental group with no computational expertise, simply running a data analysis program is a barrier, let alone building a compute and data storage infrastructure capable of dealing with DNA sequencing data. Galaxy as a whole represents the first step in hiding low-level details, such as running and assembling various tools, from users. Galaxy abstracts and automatically handles all aspects of interaction between users, tools, and the system. Through a job abstraction approach, Galaxy describes and encapsulates a job in an internal representation. This representation enables Galaxy to easily move across various systems as well as to support reproducibility. Once a job is described and is ready to be executed, depending on the configuration of Galaxy, an appropriate job runner is invoked and the job is submitted to the underlying resource(s). The job runner polls the system for job status and handles the produced output to integrate it back into Galaxy for the user. Availability and actions performed by job runners are further described in Sects. 6.3.2 and 6.3.3.

In addition to enabling streamlined execution of analysis jobs on local resources, provisions have been made to enable Galaxy to simply execute on virtualized compute infrastructures, including cloud computing resources. Cloud computing [10] has recently emerged and is ideally suited to the analysis of large-scale biological data. In this model, computation and storage exist as virtual resources, which can be dynamically allocated and released as needed. This model is well suited for many problems in bioinformatics data analysis, which intermittently require large amounts of compute power with fast access to enormous amounts of data. By coupling Galaxy and such environments, it is possible for anyone to acquire needed resources and perform desired analysis while not requiring informatics expertise. Section 6.4 discusses this functionality of Galaxy in great detail.

6.2.3   Galaxy Architecture

The Galaxy framework is a set of reusable software components that can be integrated into applications, encapsulating functionality for describing generic interfaces to computational tools, building concrete interfaces for users to interact with tools, invoking those tools in various execution environments, dealing with general and tool-specific dataset formats and conversions, and working with "metadata" describing datasets, tools, and their relationships. The Galaxy *application* is an application built using this framework that provides access to tools through an interface (e.g., a web-based interface). A Galaxy *instance* is a deployment of this application with a specific set of tools. The core components of the Galaxy framework are the *toolbox*, the *job manager*, the *model*, and the *web interface*, depicted in Fig. 6.8.

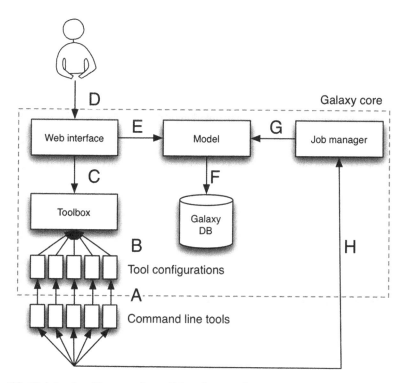

Fig. 6.8 High-level architecture of core Galaxy framework components. (**a**) Command-line tools are described within the tool configuration files and (**b**) validated within the toolbox. Available tools are made available through the web interface (**c**). As users submit jobs (**d**), web controllers interact with the model (**e**) to store the relevant information in Galaxy's database (**f**). As jobs become ready, the job manager polls the database (**g**), prepares the jobs, and submits them to the underlying resources (**h**). As jobs get complete, the job manager handles and imports them back into the Galaxy framework

The toolbox manages all of the details of working with command-line and web-based computational tools. It parses Galaxy tool configuration files (for an example of such a file see Sect. 6.3.2) that describe the interface to a tool – the parameters and input data it can take, their types and restrictions, and the outputs it produces – *in an abstract way that is not specific to any particular user interface.* This abstraction is critically important since it allows for changing how tools are displayed without needing to change their configuration (e.g., to leverage new accessibility features as web browsers improve, or to provide interfaces that are not web-based). The toolbox provides support for validating inputs to a tool, and for transforming a valid set of inputs into the commands necessary to invoke that tool. Additionally, the toolbox allows tool authors to provide tests for their tools (inputs and corresponding outputs) and provides support for running those tests in the context of a particular Galaxy instance.

The job manager deals with the details of executing tools. It manages dependencies between jobs (invocations of tools) to ensure that required datasets have been produced without errors before a job is run. It provides support for job queuing, to allow multiple users to each submit multiple jobs to a Galaxy instance and receive a fair execution order. The underlying method for execution is "pluggable." Currently jobs can be executed on the same machine where the Galaxy instance is running, or dispatched to a computational cluster using a standard queue manager (support for The Portable Batch System and Sun Grid Engine (SGE) systems is included, and other dispatch strategies can be implemented and plugged in easily).

The model provides an abstract interface for working with datasets. It provides an object-oriented interface for working with dataset content (stored as files on disk) and "metadata" (data about datasets, tools, and their relationships; stored in a relational database). Beyond providing access to the data, this component deals with support for different data types, data type specific metadata, and type conversions.

The web interface provides support for interacting with a Galaxy instance through a web browser. It generates web-based interfaces to the toolbox (for browsing and choosing tools), individual tools (building forms to accept and validate user input to a tool), and the model (allowing the user to work with all of the datasets they have produced). The web interface is currently the primary way to interact with a Galaxy instance, but the other underlying components do not need to know anything about the web, all web-specific aspects of Galaxy are encapsulated by the web interface. The web interface is the primary interface type for Galaxy and this was dictated by the fact that web browsers are present on every modern computer.

6.2.3.1   Implementation Details

The Galaxy framework is implemented in the Python programming language. Python has several advantages for our purposes. First, it is a lightweight dynamic language that allows us to rapidly implement new Galaxy features. While Python is concise and easy to write, it is also a highly structured language that is generally easy to read and understand. This is important since it makes customizing and extending the Galaxy framework much easier for users. Additionally, Python has a very powerful standard library, as well as an amazing variety of third-party open-source components; some of the best of which we have been able to take advantage of in building Galaxy. However, an important aspect of the Galaxy architecture is the abstraction between the framework and the underlying tools. Because the Galaxy toolbox interacts with tools through command-line and web-based interfaces, there is *no* requirement that a tool author use Python (e.g., the example in Sect. 6.3.2 uses a tool written in Perl). While Python is a powerful language for scientific computing, and many of the tools we provide for comparative genomic analysis are implemented in Python, frequently another language may suit a particular problem better, or simply be preferred by a tool author. We want Galaxy to be able to provide easy access to all useful computational tools – as long as a tool can be run through a command line or the web, Galaxy can incorporate it.

Galaxy includes its own web server and embedded relational database (SQLite), and a Galaxy download includes all dependencies: A user needs to just edit the configuration file and run one command to start interacting with and customizing their own Galaxy instance (see Sect. 6.3.1). However, if a particular Galaxy instance needs to support higher throughput, they can customize the web server, the underlying relational database, and the job execution mechanism. For example, the public Galaxy instance maintained by the Galaxy team at Penn State is integrated with Apache as the web server, uses the enterprise class relational database PostgreSQL, and executes jobs on a computational cluster with a queue managed by Torque PBS.

6.2.3.2 Software Engineering Details

Galaxy development follows a 2-week cycle, in which tasks are identified, integrated, and tested every 2 weeks. Between cycles the team meets to discuss errors that occurred during the past cycle, review changes that were made, and establish tasks for the next development cycle. By identifying projects that can be completed quickly, these short cycles allow students who are involved in the project for only a short time to still make a satisfying and useful contribution.

Regular code reviews are also a critical part of our process, whenever changes are checked into the Galaxy version control system, they are emailed to all members of the team for review. Thus we ensure that all code checked into Galaxy is seen by more than one person. Galaxy includes unit tests both for the framework, and for individual tools. These tests are run automatically whenever changes are made, and test failures are emailed to the team so that any regressions are identified immediately. In addition to e-mail, developers communicate through a software development–oriented wiki, that allows for writing documentation and feature specifications in a collaborative way, as well as tracking bugs, feature enhancements, and other issues.

6.3   Deploying and Customizing Galaxy

This section provides an overview of the steps required to deploy and customize an instance of Galaxy and establishes a need for tools such as Galaxy to transition toward a ubiquitous computing platform that is not dependent on any given infrastructure and/or tool set.

6.3.1   The Installation Process

The Galaxy framework can be freely downloaded by anyone from anywhere and used locally to perform data analyses or to support development of local tools. To make Galaxy attractive for developers, its installation process is very straightforward. Because Galaxy includes and manages all of its own dependencies, the only requirements for a Galaxy download is a local Python 2.4 or later interpreter and Mercurial[4] (an open-source version control system):

1. *Get the latest copy of Galaxy from the source repository.* We make the code available in several forms to ensure anyone can obtain it, but the easiest way to ensure you have a current copy of the Galaxy code is by using mercurial from the public repository available on bitbucket[5]: hg clone http://bitbucket.org/galaxy/galaxy-dist/
2. *Run Galaxy.* Execute command run.sh to start the application and the embedded web server. This command will download any required dependencies and perform the configuration process.

These three simple steps are all that is needed to have a running Galaxy instance, which can be immediately used to perform analyses using the default set of tools. This default configuration uses its own embedded web server and database, and executes analysis on the machine where it is installed. However, Galaxy can be easily configured to interface with an enterprise class database, high availability web server, or various computational clusters depending on the needs of a particular site (see Sect. 6.3.3). Additionally, users can customize many other aspects of a Galaxy instance, such as the appearance of the web interface, the data types the framework will recognize and understand, and the available computational tools. Ensuring a simple installation process allows anyone to utilize Galaxy without possible contention of public resources. In addition, developers can easily establish their personal environment for developing or customizing new tools.

---

[4] http://mercurial.selenic.com/

[5] http://bitbucket.org/

6.3.2   Adding Tools to Galaxy

In addition to simple installation procedure, another key requirement for winning developers is to make tool integration effortless. For example, consider integrating a simple PERL script which is run from the command line as "toolExample.pl FILE" which reads FASTA format sequence data from the file name FILE and prints the Galaxy Controller (GC) content – a statistical measure of the content for a DNA sequence – of all of the sequences. To integrate this tool into Galaxy, we create a "tool config" file like that shown in Fig. 6.9. This configuration file provides an abstract interface to the tool that can then be integrated into any Galaxy instance. To make a particular Galaxy instance aware of the tool, it simply needs to be added to "tool_conf.xml" configuration file in Galaxy's installation directory. Note that a tool can be written in any language or be a compiled executable – the Galaxy framework only needs to know how to run it and to pass it the necessary parameters.

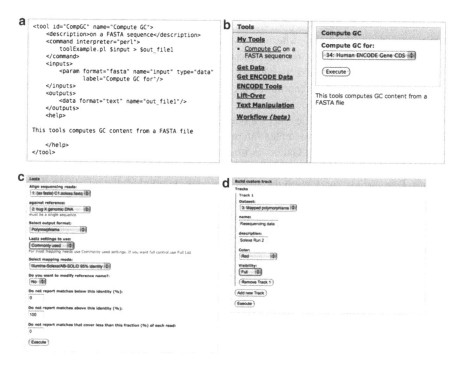

Fig. 6.9 (**a**) Tool configuration file for the example tool described in Sect. 6.3.2 and (**b**) the user interface to the tool as generated by Galaxy. Note the correspondence between elements of tool-Example.xml file and the user interface elements in the generated form. (**c**) An example of interface for lastZ short read wrapper. This interface uses a conditional construct allowing the user to switch between "Commonly used" parameters (shown) and "Full list" representing a multitude of options for this tool (**d**). An example of interface utilizing group repetitions. Here a user can build multiple custom tracks

For tools that require more complex interfaces, Galaxy provides additional constructs for describing tool input parameters. Galaxy allows groups of parameters to be repeated, and will automatically deal with the interface complexity of allowing the user to add and remove repetitions of the group (Fig. 6.9d). For example, in a plotting tool this could be used to allow the user to define an arbitrary number of plot series, each built from a different dataset with different parameters. It is also possible to define conditional groups of parameters, allowing the specific inputs that are available in a given section to depend on previous inputs (Fig. 6.9c). For example – again considering a plotting tool – it is possible to have different input parameters within a series, depending on whether the user has selected a line series or a point series. These grouping constructs can be nested to arbitrary depth, allowing input scenarios of substantial complexity to be specified simply and concisely.

6.3.3   Customizing Galaxy

In production environments where many users are intended to use Galaxy, the Galaxy instance should be customized to rely on high availability tools capable of handling user-generated load as well as to relegate job execution to a compute cluster, thus speeding up execution of jobs. The Galaxy framework supports such customizations via multiple abstraction levels implemented in the application. Specifically, all of database (i.e., model) interaction is handled through the SQLAlchemy[6] toolkit that mediates interactions between Galaxy and the underlying database server. In turn, Galaxy is implemented on top of an abstraction layer that does not change with the underlying database implementation. As a result, SQLite, PostgreSQL, and MySQL are immediately supported as underlying database servers. Customizing a given instance of Galaxy instance to use an alternative database server is done simply by changing a global configuration parameter. In addition, the implementation of Galaxy provides database migration scripts that ensure smooth transition from one Galaxy update to the next without compromising data stored in the database.

By default, Galaxy executes user-submitted jobs on the local system. Due to the computational demand such jobs impose on a given system, as the number of jobs grows, it is beneficial to farm those jobs out to a compute cluster and execute them in parallel. Comparable to the support for multiple database servers, Galaxy provides immediate support to execute jobs on the TORQUE PBS cluster manager and the Sun Grid Engine (SGE) cluster manager. Within Galaxy, support for multiple job managers is implemented at a conceptual level making it easy to add support for additional job management systems.

---

[6] http://www.sqlalchemy.org/

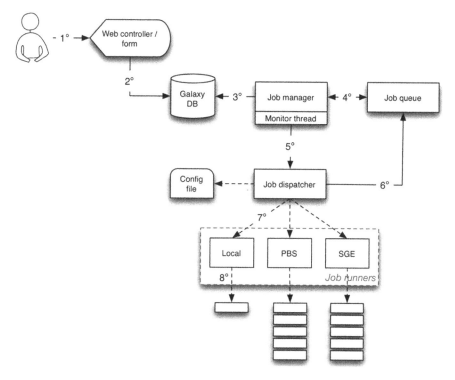

Fig. 6.10 Architecture of the job management component within Galaxy

Figure 6.10 shows the architecture of the job manager component within Galaxy. The Galaxy web controller receives a job and all data about the job is stored in the database (e.g., input data, user-selected parameters) (steps 1 and 2). The job monitor detects the change and proceeds to create a job wrapper – a Galaxy-specific representation of the job that contains all necessary components forming a job (e.g., input dataset, reference to external index files, full path for invoking a tool, complete set of job parameters) (step 3) and adds it to the end of a local queue (step 5). Relevant job data is also stored in the local database to enable job recovery in case a job or a machine was to fail. Next, depending on the configuration of Galaxy, the job is picked up from the job queue by a job runner (step 6). A job runner is a modular and pluggable component that implements necessary details for running a job on the underlying system. In case of the basic local job runner, this simply entails composing the complete tool invocation command and spawning a new thread (steps 7 and 8). In case of a cluster manager such as SGE, it entails creating a job wrapper script and submitting the job to an appropriate queue as well as monitoring the job.

6.3.4   Galaxy Accessibility

Anecdotal evidence suggests that Galaxy is usable for many biologists. Galaxy's public web server processes ~5,000 jobs per day. In addition to the public instance, there are a number of high-profile Galaxy servers in use, including ones at the Cold Spring Harbor Laboratory and the United States Department of Energy Joint Genome Institute. All of Galaxy's operations can be performed using nothing more than a web browser, and Galaxy's user interface follows standard web usability guidelines [11], such as consistency, visual feedback, and access to help and documentation. Hence, biologists familiar with genomic analysis tools and comfortable using a web browser should be able to learn to use Galaxy without difficulty.

Finally, Galaxy has been used in numerous life sciences publications by groups not affiliated with the Galaxy team, and its sharing features were recently used to make data available from a genome–environment interaction study published in *Science* [12].[7]

6.3.5   Galaxy Usage Example

To demonstrate the utility of Galaxy, here we show how it was used to perform and communicate a previously published metagenomic study that surveyed eukaryotic diversity in organic matter collected off the windshield of a motor vehicle [13]. The choice of a metagenomic experiment for highlighting the utility of Galaxy and Pages was not accidental. Among all applications of Next Generation Sequencing (NGS) technologies, metegenomic applications are arguably the least reproducible. This is primarily due to the lack of an integrated solution for performing metagenomic studies, forcing researchers to use various software packages patched together with a variety of "in-house" scripts. Because phylogenetic profiling is extremely parameter dependent – small changes in parameter settings lead to large discrepancies in phylogenetic profiles of metagenomic samples – knowing exact analysis settings are critical. With this in mind, we designed a complete metagenomic pipeline that accepts NGS reads as the input and generates phylogenetic profiles as the output.

The Galaxy Page for this study describes the analyses performed and includes the study's datasets, histories, and workflow so that the study can be rerun in its entirety: http://usegalaxy.org/u/aun1/p/windshield-splatter; to reproduce the analyses performed in the study, readers can copy the study's histories into their own workspace and rerun them. Readers can also copy the study's workflow into their workspace and apply it to other datasets without modification. Moreover, histories and workflows can be exported to other Galaxy instances, thus supporting additional means for result reproducibility.

Other recent examples of the use of Galaxy for analysis of genomic data include [14–16].

---

[7] http://main.g2.bx.psu.edu/u/fischerlab/h/sm1186088

6.4   Enabling the Next Step in e-Science

Overall, Galaxy provides an easy-to-deploy platform for data analysis, tool deployment, and analysis sharing and publication. An individual instance of Galaxy can easily be customized by adjusting its runtime environment (i.e., cluster support) to enable it to scale and meet the demand imposed by its users. However, this model of expansion does not fare well in several scenarios. For example, data analysis is often an intermittent activity: A research lab will often have periods when large amounts of data need to be analyzed followed by little or no data analysis needs. Alternatively, an individual researcher or a small lab may not have access to a large compute cluster needed to perform desired analysis; for such a scenario, it is often not worth purchasing and maintaining a compute system due to the associated cost, time, and knowledge required to maintain it, and then dealing with system aging. Also, in academic environments, a research lab's computing demands can grow or shrink based on current projects, interests, and funding levels. These needs translate directly into a dynamic demand for computational infrastructure support.

Because of the global trend toward resource aggregation [10], it is likely that, with time, organizations, labs, and universities will aggregate and virtualize many of the dispersed computational resources into a few dense datacenters that will be shared among all the users on as-needed basis [10]. Grid computing [17] represented a first step in this direction; cloud computing [9] represents the second step. Having all resources aggregated in a single location where sharing and access policies are defined opens opportunities for individual researchers, small labs, as well as large institutions to gain access to desired resources when needed. However, tools and applications need to be able to adjust to such environments and utilize them transparently, and, ideally, effectively. Figure 6.11 depicts this scenario.

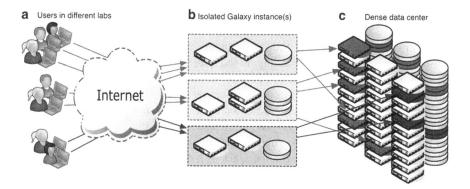

Fig. 6.11 Simplified overview of an aggregated distributed infrastructure and its perception by users: (**a**) Users in different labs access a dedicated application instance over the Internet with nothing more than a web browser, (**b**) these application instances appear to the users to be dedicated infrastructure with apparently infinite compute and storage resources, but are in fact virtual resources (**c**) which are allocated on demand from a large shared pool

In order to enable scientists to take advantage of these new models for computational resource allocation, we have focused on provisioning a general solution that can operate in the upcoming and developing infrastructures. One requirement that such a solution has is that it must not require or impose specific demands but, instead, must focus on utilizing the most general concepts that will persist beyond any single infrastructure configuration. In addition, like the Galaxy application itself, this solution should be easy to utilize and does not require informatics expertise.

6.4.1 Galaxy and IaaS

To meet the goals stated above, we have decided to implement a solution that targets the bottommost layer of an aggregated infrastructure – Infrastructure-as-a-Service (IaaS) level. Such solution relies only on the basic infrastructural components that can be expected to exist in a range of aggregated infrastructures (i.e., customizable operating system with access to persistent storage). Furthermore, our solution is implemented as a standalone application that does not require any external services (e.g., a broker service that coordinates user requests). This is an important design feature because users do not have to supply their credentials to anyone but the infrastructure providers. Overall, the described model minimizes dependencies and contributes to the robustness of the application (which is essential in self-managed, distributed systems).

To minimize user's exposure to the low-level infrastructure at which the system operates, there is a need to abstract user interaction so that only high-level operations are perceived by the user. Such solution effectively bridges the low-level IaaS design with the high-level, targeted Platform-as-a-Service (PaaS) solution. In return, the user is completely abstracted from the infrastructural details but the system design enjoys needed flexibility to be applicable in a range of custom environments.

Figure 6.12 depicts design of the derived solution. As shown in the figure, a user initiates interaction with the infrastructure through the local infrastructure console manager (step 1). Depending on the implementation of the infrastructure, the console manager may be a set of simple command-line tools or a web portal. Through the given interface, the user instantiates the Galaxy Controller (GC) machine image (step 2). GC is represented by a customized machine image that contains necessary tools to configure, start, and support the Galaxy application. For the case of virtualized infrastructures, GC image is an operating system image; for the case of dedicated infrastructures, GC is a physical machine where GC has been preconfigured. After a machine boots, GC starts automatically as a standalone process (step 3). The benefit of GC running as a standalone process is that it is independent of other processes running on the instance, including the Galaxy application, and can thus be used to control, manage, and react to the state of those processes. With that, GC coordinates all of the required services and components that are required to deliver a ready, on-demand instance of Galaxy.

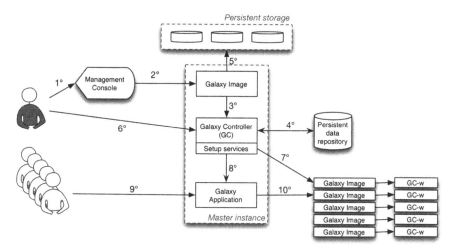

Fig. 6.12 Architectural view of the process and components required to enable scalable and user-specific deployment of (Galaxy) application in aggregated infrastructures

Because the GC image is common to all users of a given infrastructure and is thus a stateless instance, in order to personalize it to a given user and enable data persistence, GC needs to obtain user-specific data. This is realized by relying on the existence of an external data repository. After the GC image boots, it automatically retrieves GC-needed data from the repository (step 4). This data contains references to persistent storage volumes that are then attached by GC to the running instance as file systems and used by Galaxy application (step 5). If this data does not exist (as will be the case during first invocation of a given GC image by a user), data is obtained from a public data repository and then updated and stored in the user-specific repository for future invocations.

Once the GC has completed the initial system configuration, the user interacts with it directly (through a web interface) to request desired resource allocation (step 6). Requested resources are used by the Galaxy application associated with given GC to run user-submitted jobs. As requested resources are acquired, they are automatically configured as GC workers (GC-w) (step 7). Finally, the Galaxy application is started and made accessible for end users (step 8). At this point, from the end user's standpoint, given instance of Galaxy application is used like any other (steps 9 and 10). However, from the application administrator standpoint, the application instance has the potential of scaling with user demand as well as exhibiting portability across infrastructures.

The described architecture where a generic machine image is contextualized at runtime [18] by the GC (step 4 in Fig. 6.12) enables the same machine image to be used as a base for the master and worker instances. This allows more streamlined machine image administration (i.e., less maintenance overhead) and enables dynamic scaling of the size of a user's cluster. Once an instance boots, through the contextualization process, an instance is assigned a role of the master or worker.

Then, through cross-instance messaging, appropriate configuration can be completed allowing an instance to be added to an existing cluster at runtime.

The described architecture relies on only the basic services expected from any IaaS provider, namely existence of a general-purpose user data repository an attachable/mountable persistent storage. Any kind of a content delivery system can serve as the persistent data repository, even if it is external to the IaaS provider. Internal to GC, interaction with needed components can be implemented similar to the multiple job runners from the job manager component of the Galaxy application. As a result, it is easy to envision immediate availability of support for multiple IaaS providers.

In addition, the described approach allows a user to interact with the system through a web-based interface with all the necessary steps accomplished through a guided wizard. Low-level technical details are abstracted from a typical user and are automatically handled thus making the system easy to use. Finally, because of the distributed computing environment, the system was designed with an assumption that components will fail. By having GC run as a meta-application that manages lower-level components and functionality, it is possible for it to automatically address potential failures.

6.4.2 Galaxy and AWS

Recently, cloud computing [10] has emerged as a computational model that is rooted in the concepts of aggregated infrastructure ideas discussed throughout this section. In this model, computation and storage exist as virtual resources, which can be dynamically allocated and released as needed. With many providers of cloud computing services (e.g., Amazon Web Services (AWS), RackSpace, GoGrid, Mosso), this model presents an ideal scenario to verify the architecture described in Sect. 6.4.1. We have selected AWS as the service provider to verify our design because it represents a *de facto* standard in this area, showcased by proven availability and reliability of its services. Furthermore, by initially focusing on a well-accepted and readily available technology, benefits delivered by a given tool are immediately available for consumption by potential users. Also, the infrastructure architecture and the API set forth by Amazon and used by an implementation of GC have been accepted by other cloud infrastructure management projects (e.g., Eucalyputs [19], OpenNebula [20], Nimbus [21]) allowing for smoother transition as those services become more prominent or infrastructures based on those managers emerge.

6.4.2.1 GC Implementation

In order to implement the described design, within AWS, there was a need to create a customized Amazon Machine Image (AMI) packaged with necessary applications and services. Because it has to be possible for the same machine image to be instantiated by multiple, independent users, the image could not be fully preconfigured to contain all of the necessary user information (e.g., [22]). As a result, the image had to be configured to support boot time parameterization and contextualization [18]. In addition, because of the amount of time and effort required to update such image (e.g., each time an update to a tool is needed), we wanted to minimize the number of tools embedded into the image and rely on more flexible components that an instance could be associated with at runtime. As a result, generated AMI was preconfigured only with the basic components, including Python interpreter, message queuing system, and necessary user accounts (e.g., Galaxy, postgres). All of the domain-specific tools, Galaxy application, and the Galaxy Controller are obtained at instance boot time from attachable disk volumes that are easy to associate with individual users, perform tool updates, and persist beyond lifetime of any one instance.

Internally, GC was implemented as a web application within the Galaxy framework and enabled for standalone execution. At the implementation level, the GC is represented by two services, namely GC master and GC worker. The distinction among services is determined at runtime, based on the given instance's role, which is determined at instance boot time. All of the instance contextualization, master–worker communication, and status reporting is performed through a messaging system implemented using the AMQP standard [23] and using a RabbitMQ[8] server deployed on the master instance.

Following the general steps described in Sect. 6.4.1, we next provide more detailed actions performed after created machine image is instantiated:

1. User instantiates a master instance.
2. As part of startup process, start RabbitMQ server, download GC source code from either user's data repository or the public data repository and start the GC web application.
3. Within GC, create attachable storage resources (EBS volumes in case of AWS) from public snapshots for the Galaxy application and necessary index files (i.e., datasets) used by several Galaxy tools; attach them to the running instance, and import existing file systems.
4. Start NFS and enable sharing of relevant directories.
5. Unpack and configure SGE.
6. Allow a user to, through the GC web interface, configure their cluster: specify amount of persistent storage to be used for user data.
7. Create the user data external storage resource and appropriate file system.
8. Configure PostgreSQL database on the user storage resource to be used by the Galaxy application.
9. Start the Galaxy application.

   (a) Once Galaxy is ready, enable access to it from the web interface.

---

[8] http://www.rabbitmq.com/

10. The user can now start using the Galaxy application. As the need for cluster nodes increases (or decreases), through the web interface, the user may add (or remove) worker instances.

(a) As a worker instance boots, they mount NFS directories and notify master as being "alive."
(b) As instances report alive, authentication information to enable SGE to submit jobs is exchange with the master.

In order to support dynamic scaling of a user's cluster, the master repeats steps 9 and 10. Within the GC implementation, there is no distinction between the initial cluster startup and later cluster size scaling. Namely, after a user requests to add a number of worker instances, the master starts the instances specifying as part of the user data that these instances are workers. As instances boot, they start the worker configuration process and, through the messaging system, exchange needed information with the master (e.g., public ssh keys, NFS mount points). This allows the master to alter the configuration of the cluster and include those worker instances into the resource pool. The same process is followed when down scaling the size of the cluster.

Upon user-initiated termination of worker instances, GC stops all relevant services, terminates worker instances, exports file systems, and detaches external data volumes. Because data volumes used containing tools and index files are not modified during the life of a Galaxy instance, those disk volumes are deleted. The next time a given instance is instantiated, the volumes will be created just like the first time. User data volume is obviously left untouched. Information about given volume is stored in a user-specific persistent data repository (S3 bucket, in case of AWS).

6.4.2.2 Interacting with GC

GC, and thus the Galaxy application, is readily available for use by anyone.[9] A completely configured and functional cluster can be instantiated in as little as 5 min for a cost of less than $1. To instantiate an instance of Galaxy on the AWS cloud, and thus get access to the full spectrum of tools supported by Galaxy, the following steps are required:

1. Create an AWS account and sign up for Elastic Compute Cloud (EC2) and Simple Storage Service (S3) services.
2. Use AWS Management Console to start an EC2 instance.
3. Use GC web interface on started EC2 instance to start a desired number of compute instances.
4. Enjoy your personal instance of Galaxy on the cloud.

Because AWS services implement a pay-as-you-go access model for compute resources, it is necessary for every user of the service to register with the provider.

---

[9] http://usegalaxy.org/cloud

Once registered, the user is assigned an AWS access key and accompanying secret key. Note that step 1 is a one-time activity.

Step 2 is required every time a cloud instance of Galaxy is desired. As part of the instance startup process, the user interacts with the infrastructure provider management interface. In case of AWS, this can be either AWS Management Console or command-line tools. As part of this step, the user needs to choose appropriate machine image and provide account information. The provided account information is needed and used to acquire persistent storage for user-specific data. Provided account information is used locally only by the particular instance user is working with and is never shared or transmitted to another service or tool.

Once an instance boots and GC becomes available, through the web interface, the user finalizes the cluster creation by specifying the amount of persistent data storage they would like to associate with the given cluster. This is required because of the virtual and temporary structure of cloud instances: Once an instance is shut down, all modifications that were performed on the given system are lost. Therefore, in order to preserve the user data beyond the life of an instance, the external storage medium is required.

After the master instance completes the initial cluster setup and starts the Galaxy application, the user starts a desired number of worker instances. Moreover, the user can dynamically scale the number of worker instances over the course of life of the cluster. This is performed simply through the web interface while GC automatically handled all aspects of instance startup and cluster configuration (as described in Sects. 6.4.1 and 6.4.2.1). Figure 6.13 captures GC's current web interface.

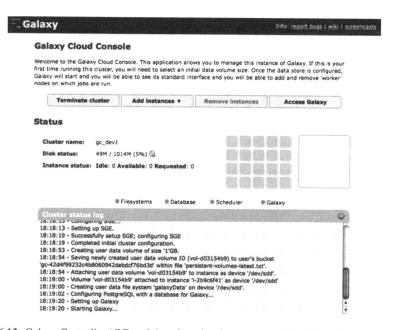

Fig. 6.13 Galaxy Controller (*GC*) web interface showing user controls and the cluster status

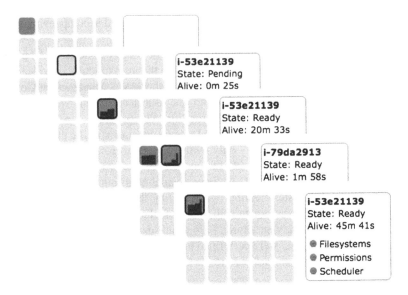

Fig. 6.14 The process of cluster size scaling from the user's standpoint as indicated in the Galaxy Cloud web interface

As can be seen in this figure, under cluster status, small icons represent individual worker instances. Furthermore, each icon graphically depicts the given instance's system load over the past 15 min (see Fig. 6.14). Such representation allows a user to immediately and quantitatively visualize the status and load of their cluster.

If the cluster becomes loaded and user decides more worker instances are needed, through the GC interface, the user can simply add additional worker instances. GC starts the requested number of instances and automatically configures those to be used by the cluster job manager, thus distributing the cluster's workload. Likewise, if a cluster is underutilized, the user may specify a number of worker instances to remove. Without disrupting currently running jobs or users accessing Galaxy, GC reconfigures the cluster to remove and terminate those instances. As part of future work, we will enable such cluster scaling to be done automatically by GC (within user-specified bounds). Figure 6.14 depicts the process of cluster scaling from the user's standpoint.

6.5 Related Work

Historically, several attempts have been made for the integration of biological analysis tools with the goal of making them available to bench biologists. These include ISYS [24], Biology Workbench [25], PLATCOM [26], and the Sequence Retrieval System [27]. ISYS is a downloadable platform, allowing software developers to add their own tools and databases. It includes a number of tools, such as a sequence and annotation viewer, a BLAST search launcher, and an Entrez sequence retrieval module. An important feature of ISYS is its DynamicDiscovery functionality, which suggests appropriate tools for a particular data type. However, ISYS requires programming experience and serves as a development platform rather than a ready-to-use tool. Biology Workbench is a comprehensive web-based collection of sequence analysis software. However, it is unsuitable for the analysis of large datasets, and cannot be used with genomic sequences and their associated annotations (these limitations are noted on the Biology Workbench Web site). PLATCOM provides a variety of utilities for comparative sequence analysis. However, this system lacks a history mechanism, and forces the user to choose a tool first and then the data, while Galaxy focuses on data and then provides the user with analysis choices. SRS has been successfully used for providing links to numerous databases and can, in principle, be used for tool integration using the complex "Icarus" language. Yet the existing public installations of SRS feature very few tools due to configuration difficulty (e.g., SRS at EBI only features EMBOSS, FASTA, BLAST, and HMMER) and cannot be scaled to analyze genomic datasets. Importantly, SRS is commercial software, which, even if obtained under an educational license, cannot be modified. On the other hand, Galaxy is absolutely free: The Galaxy source code is open to everyone and designed to make extension and customization easy. This openness is a core principle of our philosophy – drawing as many developers as possible into the software design process will ensure the high usability and applicability of our product.

Recently a series of new approaches for designing pipelines and tool integration have been proposed. These include Taverna [28, 29] and Gene Pattern [6]. Taverna provides language and software components to facilitate building of analysis workflows; it can be used to construct very complex distributed analyses, but requires the user to install local software and manage many of the details of invoking an analysis. As a result, it is most useful for computational users building workflows over distributed systems and not immediately beneficial for experimental biologists. On the other hand, using Galaxy requires only a web browser, and the user does not need to worry about the details of how complex analyses are allocated to computing resources. In fact, Taverna and Galaxy are complementary – Taverna workflows could be integrated into a Galaxy instance as tools. However, our goal is to make workflows so simple that experimentalists can use them without reading manuals. Galaxy workflows are based on the existing history system, which has been attractive for many users due to its simplicity.

Gene Pattern is an analysis environment supporting gene expression, proteomics, and association studies. It is distributed as a large, complex client/server application requiring substantial expertise for installation and configuration. All data in Gene Pattern come from the user – there is no notion of integrated data sources available in Galaxy, namely direct connection to commonly used databases such as UCSC Genome Browser, HapMap, or BioMart. Although integration of external tools is similar within Gene Pattern, the configuration files available within Galaxy offer more flexibility in terms of tool descriptions. In terms of end user usability features, Gene Pattern does not provide support for user tags while annotations are limited to workflows in form of an external document. Tagging and annotation are tightly integrated within Galaxy, ensuring reproducibility at all stages of an analysis. Gene Pattern supports sharing analyses and workflows with individuals or groups through external software tools. Sharing of items (datasets, histories, workflows) within Galaxy is supported at progressive levels and published to Galaxy's public repositories. Integration of sharing with Galaxy Pages thus supports embedding, publishing, and reuse of relevant analysis information. Finally, Galaxy can readily be instantiated on a cloud computing infrastructure thus eliminating immediate resource availability concerns.

6.6   Conclusions

e-Science came about in response to the growing need to streamline and merge computation and data analysis with scientific investigation. With the explosion of scientific data over the past decade, many sciences are becoming computationally driven. This is resulting in a shift in how science is done in those fields – a shift toward computationally intensive tasks. However, obtaining results from data analysis and computation does not come easy. Foremost, it requires development and availability of domain-specific tools. Next, it requires familiarity and ability to use those tools. Again, because computation has had a limited historical presence in many sciences, this step represents a barrier. The learning curve is difficult to be overcome because it requires scientists to step outside of their domain and become proficient in another science – computer science. Specifically, a scientist more often than not needs to learn how to write code and patch existing code. Not only is this often perceived as a significant burden by scientists but it leads to poor code design and likely poor tool development. Most importantly, because of the many *ad hoc* scripts or interactive methods used to perform an analysis, obtained results are rarely reproducible. Taken together, these issues leads to poor science.

To facilitate computational science, streamlined access to data analysis is needed. There is a need for access to domain-specific tools whose use does not mandate informatics expertise. Such an approach enables domain scientists to focus on their own research rather than being bogged down with low-level computational details. In response to this need, the Galaxy framework was developed.

Galaxy provides abstractions for tools that perform data analysis. Within Galaxy, seamless integration of one tool's output into another tool's input is supported from the ground up. Galaxy provides consistent and usable interfaces that shift the focus from running a tool to analyzing results. With a broad range of bioinformatics tools available by default within a Galaxy instance, Galaxy targets bioinformatics data analysis, with a specific focus on comparative and functional genomics, including the use of data generated with high-throughput DNA sequencing technologies [30, 31]. Furthermore, the Galaxy framework allows for easy addition of tools, thus enabling the framework to be extended to other domains (one known example includes the machine learning domain[10]). With continuous research and development, Galaxy offers a ready solution to many researchers in e-Science.

Nonetheless, Galaxy lacks the flexibility often encountered in research environments. Due to the continuous fluctuation of demand and supply for compute infrastructure, there is a need for Galaxy to be able to scale its computing usage accordingly. Furthermore, with the global increase in power and cooling demands of compute resources [32], coupled with the associated environmental impact, organizations are looking to reduce power usage and cut costs by aggregating all of the resources into dense data centers that can offer better economies of scale. As a result, there is a need for established tools to be able to utilize such infrastructures without being a major disruption to users. Galaxy Controller represents a step in that direction. Infrastructure-independent design enables it to utilize upcoming infrastructures while providing a ready solution for current needs. Coupled with the Galaxy application, presented method provides a complete solution for end users: Rooted in the basic requirements of IaaS while delivering SaaS functionality and avoiding exposure to the informatics details is a gateway to e-Science.

Acknowledgments Galaxy is developed by the Galaxy Team: Enis Afgan, Guruprasad Ananda, Dannon Baker, Dan Blankenberg, Ramkrishna Chakrabarty, Nate Coraor, Jeremy Goecks, Greg Von Kuster, Ross Lazarus, Kanwei Li, Anton Nekrutenko, James Taylor, and Kelly Vincent. We thank our many collaborators who support and maintain data warehouses and browsers accessible through Galaxy. Development of the Galaxy framework is supported by NIH grants HG004909 (A.N. and J.T), HG005133 (J.T. and A.N), and HG005542 (J.T. and A.N.), by NSF grant DBI-0850103 (A.N. and J.T) and by funds from the Huck Institutes for the Life Sciences and the Institute for CyberScience at Penn State. Additional funding is provided, in part, under a grant with the Pennsylvania Department of Health using Tobacco Settlement Funds. The Department specifically disclaims responsibility for any analyses, interpretations, or conclusions.

References

1. NCBI. (2009, February 3). *GenBank Statistics*. Available: http://www.ncbi.nlm.nih.gov/Genbank/genbankstats.html
2. E. Huedo, R. S. Montero, and I. M. Llorente, "A Framework for Adaptive Execution on Grids," Journal of Software - Practice and Experience, vol. 34, issue 7, pp. 631–651, June 2004.
3. E. Afgan and P. Bangalore, "Dynamic BLAST – a Grid Enabled BLAST," International Journal of Computer Science and Network Security (IJCSNS), vol. 9, issue 4, pp. 149–157, April 2009.
4. D. Blankenberg, J. Taylor, I. Schenck, J. He, Y. Zhang, M. Ghent, N. Veeraraghavan, I. Albert, W. Miller, K. Makova, R. Hardison, and A. Nekrutenko, "A framework for collaborative analysis of ENCODE data: making large-scale analyses biologist-friendly," Genome Research, vol. 17, issue 6, pp. 960–964, Jun 2007.
5. J. Taylor, I. Schenck, D. Blankenberg, and A. Nekrutenko, "Using Galaxy to perform large-scale interactive data analyses," Current Protocols in Bioinformatics, vol. 19, pp. 10.5.1–10.5.25, Sep 2007.

---

[10] http://galaxy.fml.tuebingen.mpg.de/

6. M. Reich, T. Liefeld, J. Gould, J. Lerner, P. Tamayo, and J. Mesirov, "GenePattern 2.0," Nature genetics, vol. 38, issue 5, pp. 500–501, 2006.

7. B. Langmead, C. Trapnell, M. Pop, and S. Salzberg, "Ultrafast and memory-efficient alignment of short DNA sequences to the human genome," Genome biology, vol. 10, issue 3, p. 25, Mar 4 2009.

8. P. Kosakovsky, S. Wadhawan, F. Chiaromonte, G. Ananda, W. Chung, J. Taylor, and A. Nekrutenko, "Windshield splatter analysis with the Galaxy metagenomic pipeline," Genome Research, vol. 19, issue 11, Oct 9 2009.

9. R. Buyya, C. S. Yeo, S. Venugopal, J. Broberg, and I. Brandic, "Cloud computing and emerging IT platforms: Vision, hype, and reality for delivering computing as the 5th utility," Future Generation Computer Systems, vol. 25, issue 6, pp. 599–616, June 2009.

10. M. Armbrust, A. Fox, R. Griffith, A. D. Joseph, R. Katz, A. Konwinski, G. Lee, D. Patterson, A. Rabkin, I. Stoica, and M. Zaharia, "Above the Clouds: A Berkeley View of Cloud Computing," University of California at Berkeley UCB/EECS-2009-28, February 10 2009.

11. J. Nielsen, *Designing web usability*, 1st ed.: Peachpit Press, 1999.

12. S. Peleg, F. Sananbenesi, A. Zovoilis, S. Burkhardt, S. Bahari-Javan, R. Agis-Balboa, P. Cota, J. Wittnam, A. Gogol-Doering, and L. Opitz, "Altered Histone Acetylation Is Associated with Age-Dependent Memory Impairment in Mice," Science, vol. 328, issue 5979, pp. 753–756, 2010.

13. S. Kosakovsky Pond, S. Wadhawan, F. Chiaromonte, G. Ananda, W. Chung, J. Taylor, and A. Nekrutenko, "Windshield splatter analysis with the Galaxy metagenomic pipeline," Genome Research, vol. 19, issue 11, pp. 2144–2153, 2009.

14. K. Gaulton, T. Nammo, L. Pasquali, J. Simon, P. Giresi, M. Fogarty, T. Panhuis, P. Mieczkowski, A. Secchi, and D. Bosco, "A map of open chromatin in human pancreatic islets," Nature genetics, vol. 42, issue 3, pp. 255–259, 2010.

15. R. Kikuchi, S. Yagi, H. Kusuhara, S. Imai, Y. Sugiyama, and K. Shiota, "Genome-wide analysis of epigenetic signatures for kidney-specific transporters," *Kidney International,* 2010.

16. J. Parkhill, E. Birney, and P. Kersey, "Genomic information infrastructure after the deluge," Genome biology, vol. 11, issue 7, p. 402, 2010.

17. *The Grid: Blueprint for a New Computing Infrastructure*, 1st ed.: Morgan Kaufmann Publishers, 1998.

18. K. Keahey and T. Freeman, "Contextualization: Providing one-click virtual clusters," in *IEEE International Conference on eScience*, Indianapolis, IN, 2008, pp. 301–308.

19. D. Nurmi, R. Wolski, C. Grzegorczyk, G. Obertelli, S. Soman, L. Youseff, and D. Zagorodnov, "The eucalyptus open-source cloud-computing system," in Cloud Computing and Its Applications, Shanghai, China, 2008, pp. 1–5.

20. I. M. Llorente, R. Moreno-Vozmediano, and R. S. Montero, "Cloud Computing for On-Demand Grid Resource Provisioning," Advances in Parallel Computing, vol. 18, pp. 177–191, 2009.

21. K. Keahey, I. Foster, T. Freeman, and X. Zhang, "Virtual Workspaces: Achieving Quality of Service and Quality of Life in the Grid," Scientific Programming Journal, Special Issue: Dynamic Grids and Worldwide Computing, vol. 13, issue 4, pp. 265–276, 2005.

22. H. Nishimura, N. Maruyama, and S. Matsuoka, "Virtual clusters on the fly-fast, scalable, and flexible installation," in *CCGrid* Rio de Janeiro, Brazil, 2007, pp. 549–556.

23. A. W. Group, "AMQP - A General-Purpose Middleware Standard," ed, p. 291.

24. A. Siepel, A. Farmer, A. Tolopko, M. Zhuang, P. Mendes, W. Beavis, and B. Sobral, "ISYS: a decentralized, component-based approach to the integration of heterogeneous bioinformatics resources," Bioinformatics, vol. 17, issue 1, pp. 83–94, Aug 14 2001.

25. S. Subramaniam, "The Biology Workbench--a seamless database and analysis environment for the biologist," Proteins, vol. 32, issue 1, pp. 1–2, Jul 1 1998.

26. K. Choi, Y. Ma, J.-H. Choi, and S. Kim, "PLATCOM: a Platform for Computational Comparative Genomics," Bioinformatics, vol. 21, issue 10, pp. 2514–2516, Feb 24 2005.

27. T. Etzold and P. Argos, "SRS--an indexing and retrieval tool for flat file data libraries," Bioinformatics, vol. 9, issue 1, pp. 49–57, 1993.

28. E. Kawas, M. Senger, and M. D. Wilkinson, "BioMoby extensions to the Taverna workflow management and enactment software," BMC Bioinformatics, vol. 7, p. 253, 2006.
29. D. Hull, K. Wolstencroft, R. Stevens, C. Goble, M. R. Pocock, P. Li, and T. Oinn, "Taverna: a tool for building and running workflows of services," Nucleic Acids Research, vol. 34, issue Web Server issue, pp. W729–32, 2006.
30. D. Hull, K. Wolstencroft, R. Stevens, C. Goble, M. R. Pocock, P. Li, and T. Oinn, "Taverna: a tool for building and running workflows of services," Nucleic Acids Research, vol. 34, issue Web Server issue, pp. W729–32, 2006.
31. S. Pepke, B. Wold, and A. Mortazavi, "Computation for ChIP-seq and RNA-seq studies," Nature methods, vol. 6, pp. S22–S32, 2009.
32. B. Moore, "Taking the data center: Power and cooling challenge," Energy User News, vol. 27, issue 9, p. 20, 2002.

Chapter 7
An Integrated Ontology Management and Data Sharing Framework for Large-Scale Cyberinfrastructure

Mudasser Iqbal, Wenqiang Wang, Cheng Fu, and Hock Beng Lim

Abstract Large-scale cross-disciplinary scientific collaborations require an overarching semantics-based and service-oriented cyberinfrastructure. However, the ad hoc and incoherent integration of computational and storage resources, data sources from sensor networks, as well as scientific data sharing and knowledge inference models cannot effectively support cross-domain and collaborative scientific research. Thus, we propose an integrated ontology management and data sharing framework which builds upon the advancements in object-oriented database design, semantic Web, and service-oriented architecture to form the key data sharing backbone. The framework has been implemented to cater for data sharing needs for large-scale sensor deployments from disparate scientific domains. This enables each participating scientific community to publish, search, and access the data across the cyberinfrastructure in a service-oriented manner, accompanied by the domain-specific knowledge.

7.1 Introduction

In modern scientific research, the scientific process, discovery, and exploration increasingly take place across the boundaries of various distinct fields. Although each scientific field specializes in a specific domain and aims at addressing the challenges encountered within the field, it has become more evident that seemingly distinct fields share a number of processes that require cross-disciplinary interaction. This interaction is manifested at two important levels. First, the data produced by a field is often used to calibrate or build the context of data in another field.

M. Iqbal (✉), W. Wang, C. Fu, and H.B. Lim
Intelligent Systems Center, School of Electrical and Electronics Engineering,
Nanyang Technological University, Singapore
e-mail: mmiqbal@ntu.edu.sg; wqwang@ntu.edu.sg; fucheng@ntu.edu.sg; limhb@ntu.edu.sg

Xiaoyu Yang et al. (eds.), *Guide to e-Science: Next Generation Scientific
Research and Discovery*, Computer Communications and Networks,
DOI 10.1007/978-0-85729-439-5_7, © Springer-Verlag London Limited 2011

Second, the scientific processes and methodologies established in one field provide guidelines in developing similar processes in a different field.

A good example is in the field of environmental science, which involves studying the interactions of the physical, chemical, and biological components of the environment, with particular emphasis on the impact of human activities on biodiversity and sustainability. Many scientific processes in environmental science require data and methodologies from the various participating fields. The challenge for such a process is that different data providers do not necessarily follow common standards and guidelines for managing their data sets. The same data element in different domains may be represented in different formats, under different units, and stored in different settings. Likewise, a certain data concept can have different meanings and require different interpretations under different domains. Thus, the users require efficient means to search and access geographically distributed leading-edge data sources so that they do not have to worry about how the data is being managed by the other party and how to access it. In addition, they should be provided with sufficient semantics of the data so that they can accurately interpret it to make good use f it. Thus, the key challenge of interoperability comprises two parts:

- Publish, discover, access, and extend semantics in noncoherent scientific efforts in order to allow creation of more sophisticated and complex processes.
- Build on top of the semantics management system to facilitate data discovery and access.

e-Science is a paradigm shift in scientific collaborative research that enables scientists to harness Web-based computing and data resources to execute their scientific processes faster, more efficiently, and on a large scale. Using remote software and experimental equipments, scientists cannot only access but also generate and process data from distributed sources, while making use of worldwide resources of computing, storage, and virtual laboratories. e-Science is thus vital to the successful exploitation of powerful next-generation scientific facilities. Although e-Science promises new vistas of scientific discovery by supporting collaborative scientific processes that span many disciplines, it poses new challenges to the technology backbone that is needed to support it. Existing modes of e-Science can only support collaborations at a very coarse level to deal with the heterogeneity of data accessibility standards that are used by each scientific community to manage its data. Such limitations hinder the pace of scientific discovery as it involves human intervention to resolve these issues that arise due to incoherent standards. There have been efforts to build semantics management systems and data exchange protocols to solve these problems. However, these efforts are isolated and inadequate for achieving different aspects of interoperability.

In this chapter, we propose a framework that integrates semantic Web, service-oriented architecture, and object-oriented ontology design in an innovative manner to create a smart e-Science cyberinfrastructure. The proposed framework builds a high-level ontology for this cyberinfrastructure that models data and its semantics as services that can be published and accessed. It models each participating scientific community as a virtual organization (VO) and allows its integration into the cyberinfrastructure through building and publishing its ontology in the object-oriented ontology schema. It provides tools for ontology creation based on the rich terminology and concepts in the cyberinfrastructure, adding new ontology concepts and their alignment with the overall cyberinfrastructure ontology. The object-oriented design allows efficient search and data querying that may involve complex reasoning on the ontologies from multiple VOs.

The framework also includes a universal data sharing component that hides the details of how different VOs have exposed their data (flat files, Web service based, etc.) and provides the data to the end users along with the data semantics so that the data can be correctly interpreted. We have performed actual case studies where the proposed framework has been implemented to accommodate large-scale scientific data sources from disparate domains. These participating communities are beginning to actively use the proposed framework for their day-to-day ontology management and data sharing tasks.

In the remainder of this chapter, we discuss the contemporary efforts in building collaborative scientific communities in Sect. 7.2; we present the design and implementation of the proposed framework in Sects. 7.3 and 7.4 respectively. Finally, Sect. 7.5 concludes this chapter.

7.2   Related Work

In the following sections, a survey on existing ontology management and data sharing efforts is presented.

7.2.1   Ontology Management Systems

Existing systems for managing ontologies focus on the following key areas: (a) loading ontologies from flat files, (b) importing ontologies from Internet sources, (c) graphically creating and modifying ontologies, (d) querying ontologies, and (e) storing ontologies. In this section, we will revisit the most notable of such systems and understand what they provide and where they lack.

International Business Machines' (IBM) Integrated Ontology Development Toolkit (IODT) [1] includes the Eclipse Modeling Framework (EMF) Ontology Definition Metamodel (EODM) and an Ontology Web Language (OWL) repository named Scalable Ontology Repository (SOR). EODM includes Resource Description Framework Schema (RDFS)/OWL parsing and serialization, reasoning, and transformation between RDFS/OWL and other data-modeling languages. These functions can be invoked and called by the applications that use ontologies. SOR is an OWL storage, inference, and query system based on Relational Database Management Systems.

The semantic Web portal project [2] aimed at developing a community portal for the semantic Web community. The purpose was to bring together research groups, research projects, software developers, and user communities from the semantic Web domain. Technologically, the mission was to create an ontology management environment needed for semantic Web–enabled community portals to make use of semantic Web technologies for enhanced information-processing facilities, to create means for the semantic interoperation between different communities.

The WebOnto's [3] ontology library is a client/server and graphically based system. It stores an ontology as a module with a unique name for identification. It supports asynchronous and synchronous ontology editing. Ontology searching is limited to ontology navigating or browsing (but graphical based). The ontology is represented by Operational Conceptual Modeling Language (OCML), which can support rule-based reasoning. It does not have any ontology versioning function or strong support in respect to ontology standardization issues.

Ontolingua's [4] ontology library is also a client/server-based system. It offers several options for reusing ontology: modular structure storage, lattice of ontology, naming policy, and a reference ontology (upper-level taxonomy). It supports collaborative ontology editing. Users can access the ontology library system via the Web. It also includes some relatively advanced searching features (wild-card and context-intensive searching). In addition, Ontolingua supports ontological language translating, ontology testing, and ontology integrating.

The DAML [5] ontology library system is part of the Defense Advanced Research Projects Agency (DARPA) Agent Markup Language (DAML) Program, which officially started in August 2000. The goal of DAML is to develop a language and tools to facilitate the concept of the semantic Web. The ontology library system contains a catalog of ontologies developed using DAML. This catalogue of DAML ontologies is available in Extensible Markup Language (XML), HyperText Markup Language (HTML), and DAML formats. People can submit new ontologies via the public DAML ontology library system.

The Simple HTML Ontology Extensions (SHOE) [6] ontology library system contains various ontologies (written in SHOE) with direct or indirect extensions of the upper-level ontology (Base ontology). SHOE flags itself with its versioning functions to solve inconsistencies caused by ontology evolution. SHOE itself is an extended HTML language with adding tags to represent ontologies and semantic data.

The Institute of Electrical and Electronics Engineers (IEEE) Standard Upper Ontology (SUO) Working Group [7] has invested tremendous effort, working with a large number of ontologists, to create a standard top-level ontology to enable various applications, such as data interoperability, information search and retrieval, automated inferencing, and natural language processing. Their ontology library system is very simple and is accessible in its preliminary form from their Web site. It contains a group of classified ontologies, such as ontologies in SUO-KIF (Knowledge Interchange Format), formal ontologies, and linguistic ontologies/lexicons. Only the very basic hyperlinks of the ontologies are provided to help users jump to the home pages hosted by the ontologies.

7.2.2   Data Sharing Systems

While the systems mentioned in the previous sections focused mainly on developing general-purpose ontology management and library systems, this section focuses on the attempts to address the collaborative science challenges. TeraGrid [8] is one of the foremost cyberinfrastructures used among the scientific community. It comprises geographically distributed immense amounts of computational and data resources that are accessible in a service-oriented manner. For job management (submission, workflow, etc.), it provides a set of software packages that can be used by the users to remotely administer their jobs on the resources that have been allocated to them. In spite of its large users-base, the TeraGrid does not provide a facility for seamless interoperation between the various scientific communities on-board the TeraGrid. Essentially, it only provides grid resources to the end users and a service-oriented means of managing them, while the operational and architectural challenges pertaining to the use of TeraGrid for cross-disciplinary science are left to the end users.

The Global Earth Observation (GEO) Grid [9] aims at providing an e-Science infrastructure specifically for earth science communities. It provides support for satellite imagery as well as geological and ground sensor data. Architecturally, GEO Grid provides different levels of interactions among its users depending upon the role that the user wishes to play. At the source sits a data publisher that can be of any earth science community, which provides data in a service-oriented manner. A VO manager forms a virtual portal where he can request services from different data publishers and provide to the end users. A VO manager may compose and provide complex services by using the basic services provided by data publishers. The key limitation of GEO Grid is that it mainly aims to serve the earth science data. In addition, although GEO Grid allows data publishers to specify meta-data, it requires them to implement data access services, which has a high risk of running into nonstandard data semantics and access methods.

An effort similar to GEO Grid is the London e-Science Center (LESC) [10], which also provides VO-based access to integrated services from multiple service providers. However, LESC's scope is far broader than that of GEO Grid in terms of supporting a variety of scientific facilities. Both GEO Grid and LESC are, however, limited in terms of not providing any tools or guidelines for standardizing data and resource ontologies to ensure precise interpretation of data. While the VOs may serve as a platform to access integrated data and services, the absence of standardized ontology definition and services definition framework makes the job of the VO manager, who is going to compose new services, very difficult.

OntoGrid [11] realizes this greatest challenge faced by grid computing regarding the ability to explicitly share and deploy knowledge to be used for the development of innovative grid infrastructure and for grid applications. To address this challenge the OntoGrid project aims to produce the technological infrastructure for the rapid prototyping and development of knowledge-intensive distributed open services for the semantic grid. However, the current test beds and implementations of OntoGrid do not demonstrate cross-disciplinary data exchange and interoperation.

MyGrid [12] aims to support the creation of e-laboratories to allow scientists to exchange valuable data and laboratory resources. Its current implementations are, however, limited to same-domain workflow service creations and cataloguing [13].

There have been attempts specifically to develop data sharing protocols for large-scale scientific collaborations. Scholl et al. [14] propose the locality-aware allocation of data objects onto a distributed network of interoperating databases. Baru [15] discusses technical, social, and regulatory challenges accompanying the collection, curation, and sharing of eScience data.

The above-mentioned frameworks provide reasonably sufficient and scalable grid resource provisioning infrastructures to the scientific communities to carry out compute/data-intensive tasks. However, none of them provides a scientific data sharing framework integrated with an ontology management system at the infrastructure level on top of which the participating scientific communities can securely expose, discover, and exchange their intellectual (data and methods) resources. In the absence of such a framework, these frameworks merely become passive resource providers. The framework proposed in this chapter fills this gap in the form of a semantic data sharing framework that can be readily adopted by the existing e-Science grids. In the following sections, the design and implementation details of the proposed framework have been discussed.

7.3 The Proposed Framework

This section first describes the architecture of the system for which the framework is being proposed. Then, the ontology management and data exchange components are described in detail.

7.3.1 System Architecture

Figure 7.1 shows the overall operational architecture of the proposed Smart e-Science data sharing framework. At one end, the architecture comprises of data sources from various participating scientific communities represented as VOs. As mentioned earlier, each VO may manage its data not only at different geographical locations but also in different formats (relational database, flat files, etc.) and may provide heterogeneous means to access the data (Web service, direct database access etc.). At the other end, applications as fundamental as a Web-based search and as complex as scientific data analysis reside, wanting to access the data from different VOs. In the middle sits the proposed framework that allows the VOs to publish their data and lets the applications discover the data from various VOs in a seamless fashion. The central middleware provides features for data access as it maintains the ontology from various VOs and hosts tools that allow user applications to post queries for accessing the data, for qualifying user queries for target databases, and for querying the databases.

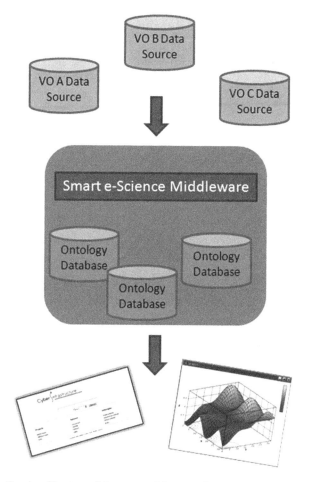

Fig. 7.1 Operational architecture of the proposed framework

Figure 7.2 shows the components of the proposed framework that allow seamless publishing and access to the data from heterogeneous sources. The framework comprises components responsible for ontology management (publishing, discovery, and search), data access, and the ontology database which may be managed in a localized or distributed fashion. The following sections elaborate on each of these components in detail.

7.3.2   Ontology Management

This section discusses the part of the framework that supports creation of a high-level ontology, integration of new existing ontologies into this hierarchy, and creation of new ontologies using the available conceptual base. We will also discuss

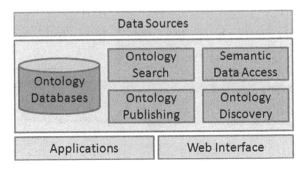

Fig. 7.2 Components of the data sharing framework

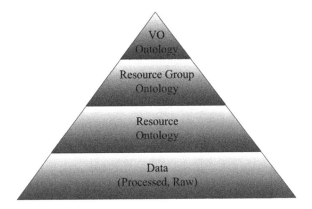

Fig. 7.3 The layered ontology design strategy

methodologies that have been developed for automated searching and querying ontology concepts that can be used by applications for interpreting data sets.

7.3.2.1 Conceptual Schema

Figure 7.3 shows the layered design of the proposed e-Science ontology. This design is motivated by the natural organization of data in a VO where a VO sits on top of the group of resources (ResourceGroup), which in turn defines each resource in the VO such as compute grid, sensor networks, data archives, etc. Each resource then produces its own data, which is exchanged between the participant VOs. Figure 7.4 shows the ontology framework that emerges out of the triangle design. The ontology considers that each VO is running some research and development (R&D) programs comprising some projects. In addition, each VO is assumed to consist of ResourceGroups, with the resource groups related to one or more projects. The resource group class is the highest-level class in the ontology hierarchy, with two immediate subclasses to categorize physical and nonphysical resources in the VO. The physical resources

a

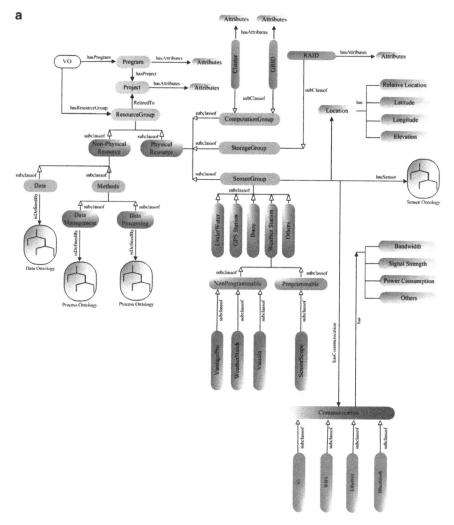

Fig. 7.4 (**a**) The cyberinfrastructure ontology; (**b**) the sensor ontology; (**c**) the data ontology; (**d**) the process ontology

superclass refers to all tangible resources such as computational, data, and networks of sensors. Each of these classes is then inherited by more specific physical resource types in order to explicitly elaborate the resource attributes.

On the other hand, the nonphysical resources superclass refers to data (raw as well as processed) and scientific methods that can be made available for reuse to client-VOs. The data and methods superclasses are then inherited by more specific data-related ontology hierarchy and methods-related process ontology hierarchy, which define characteristics such as type, nature, format, interpretation, input, output, and domain of data and scientific processes being expressed by the ontology.

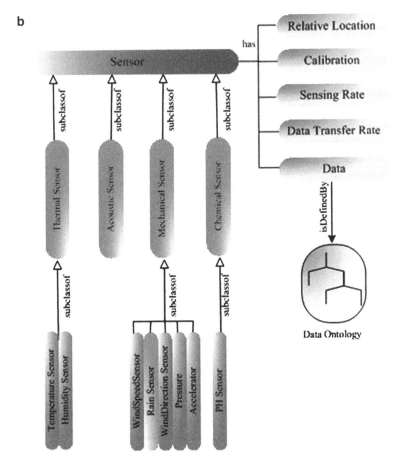

Fig. 7.4 (continued)

Since the purpose of defining an ontology here is to make the data resources sharable, it is the physical and nonphysical superclasses hierarchy that should be laid down with maximum details. Due to the lack of space in this chapter, the detailed ontologies for each of the subclasses in the ResourceGroup hierarchy cannot be provided. However, for the sake of completeness, we have shown a part of the expanded SensorGroup ontology section that specifies categorization of sensor groups into various domain-specific sensing units, such as weather stations, Global Positioning System (GPS) stations, buoys, and underwater stations. A SensorGroup has also been shown to have an associated geographical location identified by latitude, longitude, elevation, and, if needed, an x–y location relative to some reference.

Each SensorGroup may comprise multiple heterogeneous sensors and each sensor is identified by its attributes such as calibration coefficients, rate of sensing, data transfer rate, and the data itself. The ontology also caters for situations where a SensorGroup may have multiple instances of the same sensor which are differentiated by their relative location on the SensorGroup. This feature allows catering, for

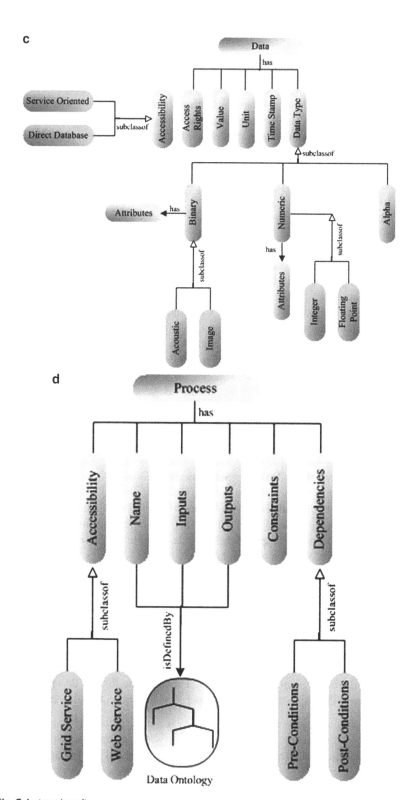

Fig. 7.4 (continued)

instance, to underwater sensors that may carry multiple temperature sensors, with each sensor responsible for reporting water temperature at a different depth. The data attribute under the sensor ontology is further expanded to represent different data types such as alpha (which includes alphanumeric), numeric, and binary data. The numeric data can be any whole or real number quantity such as water pressure, PH value, etc. The binary data represents sensors such as acoustics and imagery (such as satellite topographical images). In addition to the sensors, each SensorGroup may have other resources such as communication modules, battery power, and storage. Figure 7.4a shows the ontology schema that emerges out of the triangle design with Figs. 7.4b–d showing detailed ontologies of various components of the overall ontology in Fig. 7.4a.

In defining the ontology, our main sources for collecting commonly used terms in the sensor domain were the IEEE 1451.4 smart transducers template description language [16], Semantic Web for Earth and Environmental Terminology (SWEET) [17], Geography Markup Language (GML) [18], Sensor Web Enablement (SWE) [19], SensorML [20], Suggested Upper Merge Ontology (SUMO) [21] and OntoSensor [22], as well as domain-specific terminologies from environmental monitoring and seismic sciences. The ontology is implemented in Protégé with the data ontology expressed in OWL [23]. The reader may refer to the detailed OWL descriptions of the respective terms in the above-mentioned ontologies. Specifically, the SWEET ontology may be consulted for scientific sensor measurements such as water pressure, acoustic profile, underwater temperature, and relative humidity whereas geographical and topographical ontology elements should be searched in GML.

7.3.2.2 Object-Oriented Ontology Schema

With the overall ontology defined and represented in OWL, the next step is to decide how to store this ontology in order to support efficient semantics and data search. There are two possible approaches to store the ontology: as individual OWL files or as a database. While a repository consisting of OWL files is good for reasoning, this is far inefficient in data-related queries and searching concrete concepts. Databases have been found to have proven efficiencies for handling analytical as well as data transaction–related queries. Therefore, if the ontology has been defined carefully such that minimum reasoning is involved in searching and discovering concepts and relevant data, it makes more sense to translate the ontology into a database schema and then use this schema for semantic and data queries.

We have chosen an object-oriented database (OODB) as opposed to a relational database (RDB) in our proposed framework. The rationale for this design strategy is based on the following performance comparisons between OODB and RDB:

- The managing of objects used in sensor data is a clear factor for which OODB is chosen. The usage of a relational database will require object mapping to relational tables, which may grow to one third to one half of the application, thereby increasing development cost. Changes to the object structure will incur changes amplified by mapping code and make maintenance costly.

- To contain heterogeneous sensor data in a database, a complex relational structure relationship of up to three joints has to be formed. Multiple joints are slow in an RDB, which has a flat structure as compared to direct relationships in an OODB.
- Sensor networks are real-life data which comprise many relationships. These are too complex to be supported in an RDB while an OODB naturally and cleanly supports it.
- For an ontology-based structure that is inherently hierarchical, OODB performs exponentially faster than an RDB.
- Sensor data also vary in size. OODB directly supports such a character, making development and performance better.
- Sensor networks comprise nested complex objects which are easily handled in an OODB than in an RDB, which only supports simple, flat tables.
- An OODB allows the sharing of servers and databases on heterogeneous operating systems. This provides scalability for cyberinfrastructure for future developments as more sensor networks are included.
- Sensor data are flexible and extensible and an OODB accommodates such a characteristic. It allows any logical structures to be mapped to the desired physical structures. Inheritance, which occurs naturally in the context, allows reusing of old objects, which may change as sensors develop and improve over time, by specifying differences.
- An OODB allows seamless distributed deployment that makes it easy for the proposed framework to realize the ontology on even geographically distributed locations while providing seamless integrated search and discovery services.

Thus, each concept in the OWL is modeled as an object in the OODB. We have used DB4 [24] as the OODB management platform. DB4 is a programmatic toolkit that provides embedded database support for both traditional and client/server applications. It includes B+tree, Extended Linear Hashing, Fixed- and Variable-length record access methods, transactions, locking, logging, shared memory caching, and database recovery. We have created the ontology schema for the proposed framework using the Java Application Programming Interface (API) for DB4 on a hosted Linux machine. Figure 7.5 shows a typical hierarchy of classes in the object-oriented representation of OWL in DB4.

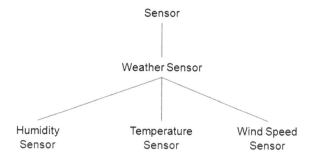

Fig. 7.5 Object-oriented representation of ontology

7.3.2.3 Ontology Creation and Publishing

Integration of a VO in the cyberinfrastructure begins with creating an instance of the ontology for the concepts in the VO and generating an OWL version of the ontology using a standard tool such as Protégé [25]. Figure 7.6 shows the entire flow of how the ontology of a new VO is published in the existing data sharing framework. Once the VO has been defined by the domain experts, an OWL parser extracts each OWL element and passes it on to an ontology objects identifier (OOI) component. OOI translates these OWL elements into DB4 schema objects with well-defined members and their semantics. An object-oriented ontology creator component resolves the relationships between the objects and generates a coherent ontology for the VO.

This ontology is then stored in the central or distributed ontology schema of the entire data sharing framework. Finally, an ontology validator component validates the stored ontology by cross-comparing the objects and their attributes defined in the ontology with the actual sample data from the VO. Upon successful validation, the ontology is considered published with its concepts readily discoverable by other participating VOs and the data accessible under user authentication policies.

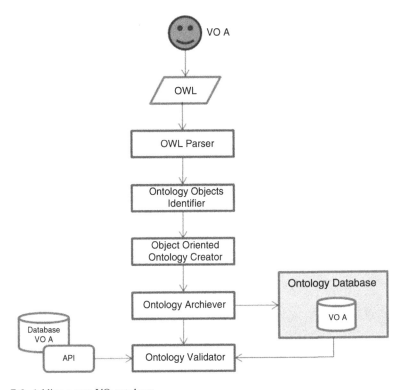

Fig. 7.6 Adding a new VO ontology

The ontology schema thus grows as the ontologies of increasing VOs are published in the schema and made accessible for concept search and data sharing. The following sections elaborate on these two critical aspects of the data sharing framework.

7.3.2.4   Ontology Search and Discovery

The ability to search concepts (objects) in the ontology database and discover relevant concepts and their semantics lies at the core of the data sharing framework. Figure 7.7 shows the layered workflow for a concept search activity. The user may send a concept query through a Web-based interface comprising one or more concepts to be searched for. A query-processing service parses the query using a natural language processor and extracts key words that may refer to concepts and/or their attributes in one or more VO ontologies. The key words are passed to an ontology query interface that queries and retrieves all objects that match the key words at various depths in the objects' hierarchy. Due to an object-oriented design, DB4 provides very efficient matching functions that allow matching key words at various depths of the ontology schema and retrieve the entire hierarchy involved in the search. It is important to note that in the case of DB4, no traditional ontology query language, such as SPARQL, is needed. DB4 provides its own set of libraries that allow creation of ontology concepts such as objects and specifications of various object parameters for the purpose of searching through the ontology database. The user is thus returned to the objects and their class members through the same Web

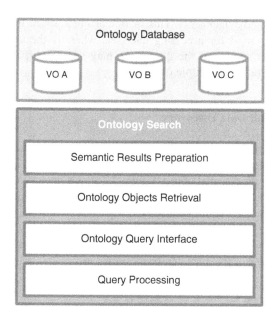

Fig. 7.7 Searching the ontology

interface, providing the semantics of the objects that matched the query. A typical query of this kind is:

Search: "Temperature Sensors in Singapore West"

This query involves three concepts and their corresponding objects which are related together through a spatial relationship. At this point the system allows discovering other objects related to the ones in the search result. Various relationships can be exploited in the discovery stage and in the recursive manner such as:

Discover: "is sibling, is super, is child"

The ontology search and discovery components allow users to locate the object of their interest in the participating VOs for which they would like to access the data and the semantics.

7.3.3 Semantic Data Access

The next critical part of the proposed framework is the tight integration of ontology management system with the data access component. In our proposed design, the ontology database carries the concepts and maintains their relationships. The actual sensor database is kept separate from this ontology and may be hosted as a huge central data archive, a distributed database with a unified schema, or kept with the data owners in various different formats such as a relational database, file system, etc. Thus, in addition to keeping the database concepts and their relationships, the ontology database also keeps record of the structures of the target databases so that queries can be formed dynamically. This section elaborates how the ontology management system is used for accessing data sets whereby the user has provided arbitrary semantics as part of the query that may span multiple ontologies and requires pulling data from multiple databases.

7.3.3.1 Query and Data Discovery

Once an object (or multiple objects) has been searched, the data access component comes into the picture that is responsible for providing seamless access to the data that are relevant to the selected object. Figure 7.8 shows the layered approach used by the data access component to ensure that only the authorized users get seamless access to the data along with its semantics, irrespective of how the data source manages the data.

The data query is first processed to find out various qualifiers specified by the user. A typical query of this type can be as simple as:

Query: "Get temperature data from Singapore west for the period from July 1, 2009 till August 1, 2009"

This query requires data to be accessed from a weather database and provides some spatial and temporal data query qualifiers. These qualifiers will assist the ontology

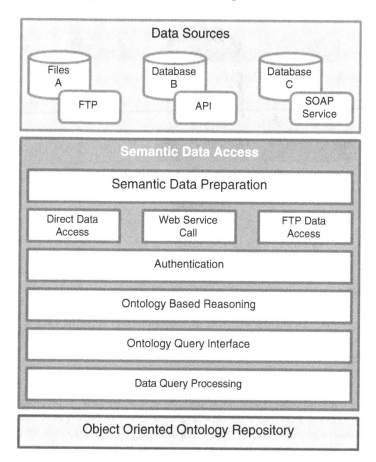

Fig. 7.8 Semantic data access

database to figure out which databases the data resides in and which objects to query in order to pull the correct data. This query is translated as:

Query: "Object: Sensor, Sub-Object: Temperature
Object: Location, value: Singapore west
Object Time Period: Range: July 1, 2009 – Aug 1, 2009"

The translated query is then used and analyzed by the ontology reasoning component that uses the ontology query interface to find out if any further reasoning is needed to arrive at specific instances of the objects from various VOs that satisfy the query criteria and provide interfaces to the data sources. While the above query is straightforward and translates simply to objects in the ontologies for VOs that have sensors residing in Singapore west, a query that will require reasoning will be of the following kind:

Query: "Get temperature data from the sensors that are deployed within 10 m from buildings in Singapore."

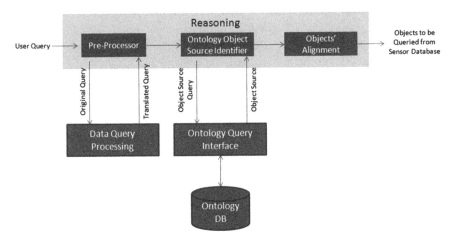

Fig. 7.9 The reasoning flow

In this case, none of the VOs provide such objects that can satisfy the query criteria. Thus, the reasoning component tries to resolve such a query by interrogating objects from geological map database of Singapore and superimposes their locations with those of temperature sensor objects. As a result, a set of sensor objects emerges whose locations are found to be within 10 m from the locations of building objects in the geological ontology.

Figure 7.9 shows the workflow of how the reasoning component operates and how it is linked with the ontology database and the sensor database. It preprocesses the user query to translate it into a list of relevant objects with their spatial and/or temporal features as requested in the query. For this purpose, it makes use of the *Data Query Processing* component that employs the natural language processing techniques for identifying dominant nouns in the query and their relationships. The set of objects identified in this step are handed over to the object source identifier that uses the *Ontology Query Interface* component to find out the semantics of the databases to which each of the query objects belong. These ontology objects are then aligned with respect to their scalar or vector features that have been requested in the query such as time period, proximity, etc. The output of the alignment step is the set of aligned objects for which the relevant sensor databases will be queried to fetch the data.

7.3.3.2 Ontology Mapped Data Access

Once the relevant objects have been discovered, their data access semantics are retrieved and user credentials are confirmed, if necessary. Then, respective data access components are invoked (direct database access, Web service call or FTP) depending upon the way the VO has exposed its data. A query may require multiple objects from different VOs, and thus multiple data access components may be invoked for data retrieval purposes. Upon retrieval, the semantics of the objects used to pull the data are included as the header along with the data result returned to the user so that the user can interpret the data easily regarding what the data represent and what are the units, format, sampling time, origin, and locale of the data. We have adopted XML as the format in which both the data semantics header and the data itself are bundled together before returning to the user. An example of an XML-based format of this returned data is as follows:

```
<query result>
        <data source> </data source>
        <result format>
                <column 1>
                        <data type> </data type>
                        <display format> </display format>
                        <precision> </precision>
                        <calibration formula> </calibration formula>
                </column 1>
                <column 2>
                        <...>
                </column 2>
                <column n>
                        <...>
                </column n>
                <column separator> comma </column separator>
        <result format>
        <data>
        column1,column2...column n
        column1,column2...column n
        </data>
</query result>
```

The first part of this XML describes the data (semantics) whereas the *data* tag comprises the actual data.

Relational database management systems (RDBMs) such as Oracle, MSSQL, MYSQL, etc. are widely used to manage raw sensor data. There are at least two basic modes of accessing the remote data: (a) using the Web service provided by the data provider to query the remote data base, and (b) directly querying the remote database if the database is accessible. The former scenario is only viable if such a Web service has been deployed. In this case, the client is usually limited by the set of queries supported by the Web service. The latter case, though flexible, brings a fundamental challenge of creating data access queries dynamically based on the use requests, given that the remote schemas will most likely be nonuniform with varying levels of complexity. That is, not only will the relational database schemas be most likely different from each other but also it is very likely that the data will not be managed in a relational database at all. In order to retrieve data from these heterogeneous data sources, the ontology database should also maintain the schema information of each database and use this information to dynamically generate data access queries such as SQL queries of file access logic. Here, we provide two solutions to address this challenge with relevant examples.

1. For each ontology object in the database that has corresponding data table(s) in the relational database, an SQL query template is generated and attached to the object's ontology. The object's ontology provides vital information to form the query template, such as projection columns, tables in the SQL *from* clause, and conditions in the SQL *where* clause. Certain parts in the template are left open according to the nature of the sensor data, such as time stamp restrictions, geographical location restrictions, etc. When a data query is issued through the ontology management system, the corresponding SQL template is first completed according to the actual conditions provided by the user before being sent to the RDBMs. Let us look at a simple example and analyze it with various data access flow steps as shown in Fig. 7.10.

A client VO issues the following query that is received by the ontology management system:

Query: retrieve temperature data for location A in time period T1 to T2

First, the query is parsed to find out the objects that the user is interested in. Then, the ontology database is queried to look for the relevant ontology objects, which are then aligned through reasoning. In this case, the identified ontology concepts are:

Ontology Object : Thermal Sensor, Time, Location

Then, the system tries to authenticate the user and qualify if the user is allowed to access the data he has requested. Once authenticated, the actual ontology objects relevant to the corresponding VO are retrieved from the ontology database and database queries are formed. The queries are formed based on the query template attached to the thermal sensor object. To do that, the *condition* in the template must be explicitly specified. There are two conditions in the query: SensorGroup must be A and sensing time ranges from T1 to T2. Both can be easily translated to SQL clauses as *SensorGroupId = A and Time stamp $\geq$ a and Time stamp $\leq$ b.*

RDBMS temperature table schema: *Temperature(SensorGroupId, Time stamp, Value)*
Mapping Query Template: Select *Value* from *Temperature* Where (*condition*)
Mapping Query Template Conditions: *SensorId = x, a $\leq$ Time stamp $\leq$ b.*
Query: get temperature information from thermal sensor in SensorGroup A from time T1 to time T2.

The final SQL is:

Select Value from Temperature where SensorGroupId = A and Time stamp $\geq$ T1 and Time stamp $\leq$ T2

Queries such as these are sent to the target VOs for data retrieval purposes. The corresponding ontology concepts are also retrieved from the ontology database that provides the meaning of the data sent by the target VOs. These data are converted to the format requested by the client VO, such as XML etc., and the data semantics are added as the header to the result set, which is then returned to the client VO.

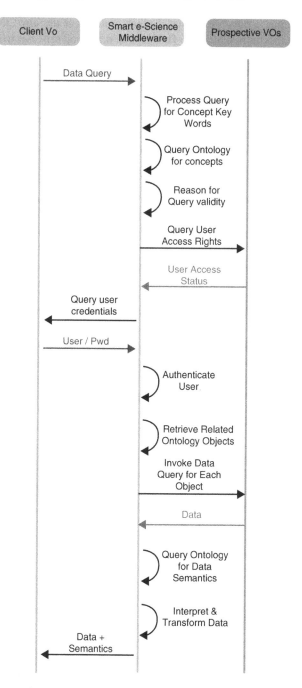

Fig. 7.10 Data access flow

2. In this scheme, a novel relational database schema is designed to store all the sensor data in a unified manner. The original relational schemas in different data provider VOs are mapped to this new unified schema and a set of data conversion modules continuously transform sensor data from their original databases to this new relation database. A unique set of SQL queries is defined to retrieve sensor data from the new database, and sensor objects in the ontology database can be easily mapped to this set of SQL queries should data queries be issued.

Let us look at the same query in the example in the first scheme. It can be translated into the following SQL queries based on this new unified schema:

Step 1: Find the sensor id of the thermal sensor in SensorGroup A

Select s.SENSOR_ID from SENSOR s, SENSOR_TYPE st, SENSORGROUP_SENSOR ss where s.SENSOR_ID = ss.SENSOR_ID and ss.SENSORGROUP_ID = A and s.SENSOR_TYPE_ID = st.SENSOR_TYPE_ID and st.SENSOR_TYPE_NAME = 'Thermal'

Step 2: Retrieve data (suppose sensor id retrieve from step 1 is k)

Select v.value from SENSOR_DISCRETE_DATA v, SENSOR where v.SENSOR_ID = s.SENSOR_ID and s.SENSOR_ID = k and v.TIME_SEC ≥ T1 and v.TIME_SEC ≤ T2

In this scheme, the SQL query structures are fixed and only those conditional variables (i.e., those with underlines in the above SQL statements) need to be substituted.

7.3.3.3 Data Conversion

Sensor data retrieved from RDBMs are usually in text or binary formats. XML is used to represented data in text format as XML is widely accepted by data analyzing applications and is the default format used in Web services. Object attributes in the ontology database can be used as XML tags and the conversion is rather straightforward. Techniques such as tag rewriting can be used to reduce the resulting XML file size for faster transmission in network environment. In case of binary data, a small catalog XML file is attached to each trunk of binary data which explains the format of the binary string so that it can be parsed correctly.

7.4 Implementation

7.4.1 Case Studies

The Cyberinfrastructure for the Center for Environmental Sensing and Monitoring (CI@CENSAM) [26] is an effort under the Singapore-MIT Alliance for Research and Technology (SMART) to integrate the data and services provided by various micro- to mesoscale sensor deployments for environmental monitoring in Singapore. These deployments include those for Continuous Monitoring of Water Distribution Systems (CMWDS), Ocean Modeling and Data Assimilation (OMDA), and Marine and Underwater Sensing (MUS). CI@CENSAM aims to develop a distributed data archive for multiple CENSAM research projects including both sensor- and model-generated data. The archive will associate data sets with appropriate geospatial, sensor, accuracy, and access control metadata to optimize the data's utility, security, and longevity for collaborative scientific efforts.

The CMWDS project will develop technologies to enable real-time monitoring of water distribution systems in Singapore. Its objectives include the demonstration of the application and control of a wireless sensor network-based cyber-physical infra-structure for high data rate, and real-time monitoring of hydraulic parameters within a large-scale urban water distribution system. Real-time pressure and flow measure-ments will be assimilated into hydraulic models to optimize the pump operations for the water distribution network. CMWDS also develops technologies to enable remote detection and prediction of pipe burst and leak events. We have developed statistical and wavelet-based algorithms to analyze high-frequency pressure mea-surements of hydraulic transient events to detect pipe bursts, as well as algorithms for localizing the bursts based on arrival times of the pressure fronts associated with the burst events. Finally, CMWDS also addresses the monitoring of water quality parameters. This task will involve a detailed evaluation of the long-term perfor-mance and robustness of water quality sensors (for measures such as pH, chlorine residue, turbidity, conductivity, and dissolved oxygen), the use/development of mul-tiparameter sensor technologies, and the application of cross-correlation techniques to interpret water quality signatures through in-network processing.

The OMDA project aims to achieve operational real-time assimilation and fore-casting capabilities for the Singapore region and surrounding seas. For this purpose, the Finite Volume Coastal Ocean Model (FVCOM) is used and is adapted for different configurations such as the coastal water around Singapore, the Singapore Straits and island, and the entire South China Sea (90E-140E; 20S-30N). The simulation of the ocean circulation and property distributions (temperature, salinity) will be carried out under lateral tidal forcing and surface forcing of wind stress, heat, and moisture fluxes, and will be validated with altimetric data as well as current velocity observations.

The MUS project's objectives include the development of sensors for environ-mental chemical monitoring that can be deployed on Automated Underwater Vehicles (AUVs). A major focus of MUS is a sensor based on mass spectrometry for monitoring of natural waters which measures low-molecular-weight hydrocar-bons, metabolic gases for geochemical studies, and volatile organic compounds for pollution monitoring. The other major focus is a sensor based on laser-induced fluorescence, capable of measuring higher-molecular-weight hydrocarbons, which are common components of oil leaks and spills, as well as biological entities such as chlorophyll, aquatic humic substances, and fluorescent tracers. An associated project under MUS will deploy inexpensive, low-power sensors for passively detecting dynamic and static pressure fields with sufficient resolution to detect near-field flow patterns and near- and far-body obstacles and vehicles, as well as mapping near-body objects. This will provide a unique capability for navigation in shallow-water and/or cluttered environments, for use with multiple AUVs, and for flow control in conventional and biomimetic vehicles.

The National Weather Study Project (NWSP) [27, 28] is a large-scale community-based environmental initiative in Singapore that aims to promote the awareness about weather patterns, climate change, global warming, and the environment. In this project, hundreds of mini weather stations are deployed in schools throughout Singapore. The data acquired by these weather stations include various weather parameters such as temperature, humidity, rain, wind speed and direction, barometric pressure, solar radiation, etc.

The Infrastructure for Mobile Data Management (IMDM) project processes the NWSP weather data to deliver weather information to mobile devices in real time for educational learning applications. This effort addresses several major challenges for mobile data delivery, such as unpredictable network bandwidth and quality of service. This infrastructure is based on sensor grid technologies to facilitate sensor data processing, data management, and data request handling. A mobile Web portal and applications are also being developed for users to easily access weather data via map-based interfaces. In addition, several services are also being developed for users to make use of the weather data on mobile clients. A set of APIs has been developed and published for developers who are interested in using the weather data. Besides managing weather data, the IMDM infrastructure is capable of handling other sensor data from heterogeneous data sources owing to its novel design and implementation.

7.4.2 Interoperability Challenges

Each of the deployments in CI@CENSAM, MUS, NWSP, and IMDM includes archived scientific data as well as real-time sensor resources with varied data sampling frequency and heterogeneous types of sensors pertaining to different vendors. In addition, the environmental, ocean, watershed, navigation, hydraulic, geospatial, solar, and seismic modeling applications running on these deployments require seamless sharing of scientific processes, data models, as well as raw data among them.

Based on our proposed infrastructure, we are building a large-scale Smart e-Science infrastructure to integrate hundreds of heterogeneous sensor resources distributed across a wide geographical area under the aforementioned projects into a single semantics-based service-oriented access model. This model has several important features. First, it connects heterogeneous sensor resources belonging to different scientific VOs via the Internet to automatically collect and aggregate sensor data in real time. Second, the varied types and formats of sensor data are linked to the ontology of the respective VO and the data are converted into a standard OWL format in order to bind data semantics with the data for ease of access and processing. Third, the sensor data are stored in a Central Data Depository (CDD) whose schema is also derived from the common concepts fund in the ontologies of three VOs. Fourth, the grid models of computational as well as storage resources are used as semantic services for the compute-intensive processing of sensor data. Fifth, the sensor data can be conveniently accessed and shared via the Web through mash-ups, blogs, and Web services. We are developing techniques and tools to efficiently publish, query, process, visualize, archive, and search the vast amount of sensor data in a unified manner.

7.4.3   Tools and Services

We have implemented the fundamental object-oriented ontology schema in DB4 from the concepts common to the aforementioned scientific installations. Java has

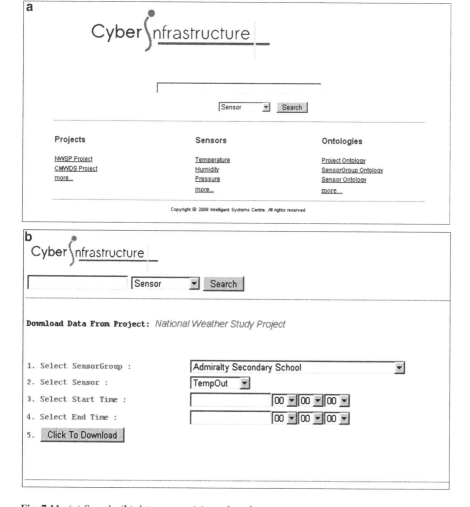

Fig. 7.11 (**a**) Search; (**b**) data access; (**c**) ontology browser

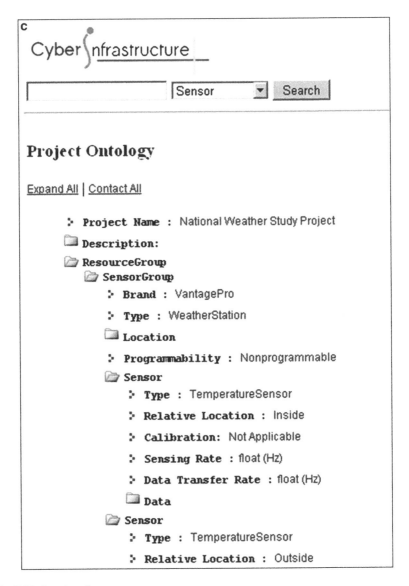

Fig. 7.11 (continued)

been used to implement various components of the data sharing framework such as ontology publishing, search, and data access.

A Web portal has also been developed that allows users to submit ontology search queries, as well as to browse through the ontology and submit basic data search queries. For data access, we have implemented direct database and Web service–based access to different data sources. The data access interface allows users to specify a deployment, a particular sensor, and the time period for which the data are needed. The ontology search and browsing interface allows users to search by project a group of sensors or a sensor. The results include the ontology objects displayed in a convenient tree-like format where users can browse the semantics of the various fields, data, sensor deployments, and the project itself. Figures 7.11a–c show the screen shots of various components in the Web portal.

7.5 Conclusions

In this chapter, we have proposed an integrated ontology management and data sharing framework that addresses the challenges of seamless data sharing in large-scale scientific collaborations by building on top of service-oriented architecture, semantic Web, and OODB design. The framework uses an overarching ontology that binds data resources in standard-based semantics and allows the participating communities to publish their data sources, search and browse ontologies from other data sources, and seamlessly access the data from the entire cyberinfrastructure using complex queries that may need reasoning. The use of OODBs to handle complex ontology representation, and search and reasoning tasks is a fundamental design aspect of the system that allows scalable and efficient integration of heterogeneous data sources. The proposed framework has been implemented to manage large-scale scientific data sources from disparate domains, thus providing real case studies of the communities that are actively using the proposed cyberinfrastructure.

Acknowledgments This work was supported by Microsoft Research, Intelligent Systems Center of Nanyang Technological University, Research Support Office of Nanyang Technological University, the Singapore National Research Foundation (NRF) under grant number NRF2008IDM-IDM001-005, and the Singapore NRF through the Singapore-MIT Alliance for Research and Technology (SMART) Center for Environmental Sensing and Modeling (CENSAM).

References

1. IBM Integrated Ontology Development Toolkit (IODT), http://www.alphaworks.ibm.com/tech/semanticstk
2. The Semantic Web Portal Project, http://sw-portal.deri.org
3. J. Domingue, "Tadzebao and Webonto: Discussing, browsing, and editing ontologies on the web", *Proc. of the 11th Knowledge Acquisition for Knowledge-Based Systems Workshop*, Apr 1998.
4. A. Farquhar, R. Fikes, and J. Rice, "The Ontolingua Server: A tool for collaborative ontology construction," *International Journal of Human-Computer Studies*, Vol. 46, Issue 6, pp. 707–727, Jun 1997.
5. The DARPA Agent Markup Language (DAML), http://www.daml.org
6. J. Heflin, J. Hendler, and S. Luke, "SHOE: A knowledge representation language for Internet applications," Technical Report CS-TR-4078 (UMIACS TR-99–71), Dept. of Computer Science, University of Maryland at College Park. 1999.

7. IEEE Standard Upper Ontology (SUO) Working Group, http://suo.ieee.org
8. TeraGrid, http://www.teragrid.org
9. N. Yamamoto, R. Nakamura, H. Yamamoto, S. Tsuchida, I. Kojima, Y. Tanaka, and S. Sekiguchi, "GEO Grid: Grid infrastructure for integration of huge satellite imagery and geoscience," *Proc. of the Sixth IEEE/ACM International Conference on Computer and Information Technology (CIT)*, pp. 75, 2006.
10. The London e-Science Center, http://www.lesc.ic.ac.uk
11. P. Alper, O. Corcho, I. Kotsiopoulos, P. Missier, S. Bechhofer, D. Kuo and C. Goble, "S-OGSA as a Reference Architecture for OntoGrid and for the Semantic Grid," *Proc. of the 16th Global Grid Forum (GGF16) Semantic Grid Workshop*, Feb 2006.
12. MyGrid, http://www.mygrid.org.uk
13. D. Hull, K. Wolstencroft, R. Stevens, C. Goble, M. Pocock, P. Li, and T. Oinn, "Taverna: A tool for building and running workflows of services," *Nucleic Acids Research*, Vol. 34, pp. 729–732, 2006.
14. T. Scholl, et al., "Scalable community-driven data sharing in e-science grids," *Future Generation Computer Systems*, Vol 25, Issue 3, pp. 290–300, Mar 2009
15. C. Baru, "Sharing and caring of eScience data," *International Journal on Digital Libraries*, Vol. 7, Issue 1, pp. 113–116, Oct 2007.
16. The Open Geospatial Consortium, http://www.opengeospatial.org
17. Semantic Web for Earth and Environmental Terminology (SWEET), http://sweet.jpl.nasa.gov/ontology
18. Geography Markup Language: http://www.opengeospatial.org/standards/gml
19. Sensor Web Enablement Working Group, http://www.opengeospatial.org/projects/groups/sensorweb
20. SensorML, http://www.opengeospatial.org/standards/sensorml
21. A. Pease, I. Niles, and J. Li, "The Suggested Upper Merged Ontology: A large ontology for the semantic web and its applications," *Working Notes of the AAAI-2002 Workshop on Ontologies and the Semantic Web*, Jul 2002.
22. D. J. Russomanno and J. C. Goodwin, "OntoSensor: An ontology for sensor network application development, deployment, and management," *Handbook of Wireless Mesh and Sensor Networking*, McGraw Hill, 2008.
23. OWL Web Ontology Language Reference, M. Dean and G. Schreiber (eds), W3C Recommendation, 10 Feb 2004. Latest version available at http://www.w3.org/TR/owl-ref/
24. H. Yadava, *The Berkeley DB Book*, Apress, Oct 2007.
25. Protégé, http://protege.stanford.edu
26. Cyberinfrastructure for the Center for Environmental Sensing and Modeling (CENSAM), http://censam.mit.edu/research/res5/index.html#sec4
27. National Weather Study Project, http://nwsp.ntu.edu.sg
28. H. B. Lim, M. Iqbal, W. Wang, and Y. Yao, "The National Weather Sensor Grid: A large-scale cyber-sensor infrastructure for environmental monitoring," *International Journal of Sensor Networks (IJSNet)*, Inderscience, Vol 7, No. 1/2, pp. 19–36, 2010.

Part III
Collaborative Research

Chapter 8
An e-Science Cyberinfrastructure for Solar-Enabled Water Production and Recycling

Yuxia Yao, Hock Beng Lim, Chee Keong Chan, and Fook Hoong Choo

Abstract We propose an e-Science cyberinfrastructure to support the scientific processes of a solar-enabled water production and recycling application. It forms the key resource sharing backbone that allows each participating scientific process to expose its sensor, instrument, data, and intellectual resources in a service-oriented manner, accompanied by domain-specific resource knowledge. The cyberinfrastructure integrates sensor grid, service-oriented architecture, and semantic Web in an innovative manner. We discuss the design of the ontology to describe the resources in the project, such as data, services, computational and storage resources. An object-oriented database is designed for flexible and scalable data storage. Data management issues are discussed within the context of the project requirements. Various data services are created to meet the needs of the users. In this manner, the cyberinfrastructure facilitates the resource sharing among the participants of the project. Complex workflows are also supported by the proposed cyberinfrastructure.

8.1 Introduction

e-Science usually involves multiple disciplines and applications. Many research efforts have focused on the development of cyberinfrastructures to support e-Science. However, most of these cyberinfrastructures tend to be generic and can only support simplistic applications. It is useful to start from the application point of view and design an e-Science cyberinfrastructure that can support a useful class of applications.

Y. Yao(✉), H.B. Lim, C.K. Chan, and F.H. Choo
Intelligent Systems Center, School of Electrical and Electronics Engineering,
Nanyang Technological University, Singapore
e-mail: yxyao@ntu.edu.sg; limhb@ntu.edu.sg; eckchan@ntu.edu.sg; efhchoo@ntu.edu.sg

Xiaoyu Yang et al. (eds.), *Guide to e-Science: Next Generation Scientific Research and Discovery*, Computer Communications and Networks,
DOI 10.1007/978-0-85729-439-5_8, © Springer-Verlag London Limited 2011

In this chapter, we discuss the infrastructure design for a self-sustained solar-enabled water production and recycling system, which is a very important and promising application that requires cross-domain collaboration. The objective of this system is to achieve waste water distillation using solar energy with close-to-zero energy support from the power grid. The components of this system include membrane water distillation reactor process system, thermal storage system, solar power harnessing system, solar energy storage system, weather monitoring system, and real-time instrument control system. In actual deployment, hundreds of instruments which are geographically distributed are deployed to carry out specific measuring and monitoring procedures, which generate large amounts of data. The system performs complex tasks such as distributed instrument control, data collection from heterogeneous sources, data archiving, data analysis and mining, data visualization, and decision support. Such a system is being developed in Nanyang Technological University under a major research program funded by the Singapore National Research Foundation. This research program involves a large interdisciplinary team of scientists and engineers.

There are several goals to achieve in this cross-domain project:

- It is necessary to efficiently archive and manage multidimensional data from heterogeneous sensors and instruments, with many real-time high-frequency data streams. The data are heterogeneous, that is, they are of different formats, different sampling frequency, and different data ownership.
- Efficient data sharing among different groups of scientists who are not computer experts should be allowed. Correct interpretation of data from different domains should be made possible. Data should be provided at various aggregation levels.
- Different parties involved in the project should be able to publish their own data and process, and also use the processes created in other scientific domains to allow the creation of more sophisticated and complex processes.
- Real-time decision support which involves scientific processes such as water distillation reactor process, solar power harnessing and storage, weather monitoring, etc. should be made available. This involves complex process management and instrument control across the entire system.

The complexity of the system has imposed great challenges in designing a cyberinfrastructure to support the above goals. First, the project requires a close collaboration between power engineers, water process engineers, control experts, computer scientists, and even weather experts. The system should be flexible to support the basic and ad hoc needs of these different groups of scientists. Second, the project requires resources such as weather information, geographic information, system information, etc. that are provided by other external parties. The system should support the seamless integration of data and services provided by the other resources. Third, the project requires an optimized amount of energy to produce purified water. As such, a complex process will be used to optimize the water processing. Computational, memory, sensor, and instrument resources are required to support smooth operation as well as real-time control.

To address these challenges, we propose an e-Science cyberinfrastructure to support the operations of the water production and recycling system. The cyberinfrastructure integrates sensor grid, service-oriented architecture (SOA), and semantic Web in an innovative manner. The proposed framework builds a high-level ontology for this cyberinfrastructure that models the resources used in this project such as sensors/actuators, computational resources, data resources, and process resources as services that can be published and accessed by various parties. The grid-enabled and service-oriented e-Science cyberinfrastructure provides support for dynamic selection of partners as well as abstractions through which the state of a scientific transaction can be captured and flexibly manipulated. Services provide higher-level abstractions for organizing applications in large-scale and open environments. They enable us to improve the productivity and quality of the development. Furthermore, if these abstractions are standardized, they enable the interoperability of services/resources produced by different parties. The proposed framework uses grid computing [1] to handle the management of diverse resources. Semantic and rule-based event-driven SOA [2] is used to demonstrate how semantics can be employed in SOA to share common vocabulary, knowledge, and services. The framework also uses SOA for the composition of services to support the development of scientific workflows for specific applications in water production and recycling.

In the remainder of this chapter, we discuss the system design in detail. Section 8.2 introduces the background on the solar-enabled water purification and recycling application and its system components. The motivation and concept of the smart e-Science cyberinfrastructure we proposed is also presented. Section 8.3 discusses the detailed cyberinfrastructure design, including the ontology design, the data management, and the workflow management of the system. Section 8.4 presents the detailed implementation of the cyberinfrastructure, including data acquisition and archiving, ontology implementation, and implementation of a sample workflow on visualization of solar radiation map. Section 8.5 concludes the chapter.

8.2   Background

8.2.1   Solar-Enabled Water Production and Recycling

8.2.1.1   System Overview

Global economic growth has caused excessive carbon emissions from burning fossil fuels and has been blamed for global warming and climate change. This, together with urban migration, has caused shortage of freshwater supplies in major cities around the world. Increasingly water is being provided from sources that require significant purification, such as seawater and wastewater. Seawater makes up 97% of the earth's water resource. The attraction of these sources is that they are essentially infinite supplies of water. However, the treatment processes for these sources require much more energy than for conventional water treatment of natural waters. This project aims to meet this challenge by developing and demonstrating self-sustaining water production and recycling technology based on solar energy. The technology would be suitable for Singapore and many other water-scarce regions of the world.

The global output of water from seawater desalination plants is still relatively minute – less than 0.1% of all drinking water. Each day about 25 Mm^3 of world water demand is produced in desalination plants. Membranes provide a practical means of water purification. For the production of high-purity water, it is a common practice to use reverse osmosis (RO) [3], which is a high-pressure membrane process. RO is used in seawater desalination and for purification of biologically treated "used water" to produce NEWater [4]. However, RO has a high demand for primary electrical energy. A far more efficient and economic approach to harvesting solar energy is to use solar thermal collection based on membrane distillation (MD) technology.

MD relies on hydrophobic microporous membranes with water transport as vapor through the pores. MD can achieve a very high-purity water product and does not require a pressurized system. In addition to MD desalination of salty water a novel application of MD is the membrane distillation bioreactor (MDBR) [5]. In the MDBR wastewater is converted to high-quality purified water by biological processing coupled to MD. The bioreactor is operated at raised temperature, using thermophilic bacteria, to provide the driving force for MD. Both MD desalination and MDBR convert impaired water to highly purified water at atmospheric pressure. The necessary driving force is thermal with feeds in the range of 50–75°C. A small amount of electrical energy is required for circulation and the major energy requirement is low-grade heat available from solar or waste heat. The novelty for this work is to integrate the MD-based processes with both solar collection and energy storage. The system achieves "multiple effects" energy usage through energy recovery.

8.2.1.2 System Architecture

The solar-enabled water production and recycling system comprises the following components:

1. Optimization of MD desalination and MDBR wastewater reclamation. The system aims to improve and to enhance the MD and MDBR processes so as to achieve a more productive water production and recycling process.
2. Solar thermal energy collection and storage system. The system aims to harness thermal energy through solar collectors, alignment, and solar troughs. The thermal energy will directly be applied to the MDBR and MD processes.
3. Solar photo-voltaic (PV) electric energy, storage and conversion system. The system aims to support the MD and MDBR systems' electrical energy needs. The objective is to maximize the efficiency of solar electric energy harnessing to achieve an energy self-sustaining operation of plants such as operating pumps, sensors, transmitters, and other equipment in the MD and MDBR distillation plants.

4. An overall close-loop control system to optimize the operation of the water production and energy consumption of the MD and MDBR systems using modern control techniques such as "model predictive control (MPC)" [6]. It requires a dynamic modeling of the MDBR and MD processes and takes into consideration the constraints of the system. Note that MPC relies on solving constrained optimization problems online. The computational load for such problems is much greater than for traditional control algorithms.
5. Data mining and decision support system. Experimental data and information generated from theoretical calculations and measured meteorological data will be used to study the proposed complex systems. It could lead to new knowledge about the influence of various parameters on the solar energy conversion efficiency and the recycling process. It could assist the theoretical calculations such as providing precise, long-term irradiance data for choosing plant locations and estimates of likely energy yield. Consequently, a new approach or a model could be developed for the analysis and prediction of the relationship between solar radiation and different meteorological variables.
6. A weather-monitoring network to collect solar irradiance statistics. The solar irradiance statistics is critical to the overall success of the system. As there is a weather-monitoring network established by the efforts of another group of scientists in Singapore, the system can directly tap on the existing resources through flexible integration.

Figure 8.1 shows the system components that cover the above subsystem. It is shown that each subsystem is a stand-alone system and yet they are interlocked

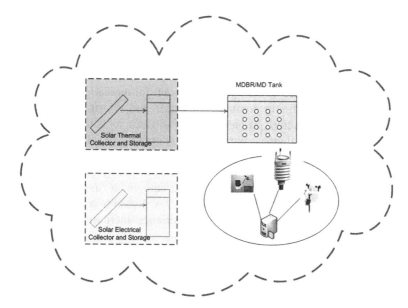

Fig. 8.1 System components

with each other and complement each other to become a complex cyber-physical system. It involves typical physical elements that form a scientific process such as solar thermal collector, solar thermal storage, and MDBR/MD processing tank. It also involves intensive computational cyber resources, e.g., process modeling, data mining, and prediction. The results from the cyber world will in turn affect the process of the physical elements. For example, the results from the solar prediction will affect the whole process to achieve optimized process. The whole system falls well into the kind of application that needs an e-Science approach to tackle the complex scientific processes.

8.2.2   e-Science Cyberinfrastructure

8.2.2.1   Motivation

The cyberinfrastructure makes applications dramatically easier to develop and deploy, thus expanding the feasible scope of applications possible within budget and organizational constraints, and shifting the scientist's and engineer's effort away from information technology development and concentrating it on scientific and engineering research. The cyberinfrastructure also increases efficiency, quality, and reliability by capturing commonalities among application needs, and facilitates the efficient sharing of equipment and services. Adopting the cyberinfrastructure will dramatically reduce the effort and expertise required to develop, deploy, and operate new distributed applications. Thus, it encourages more extensive development and use of such applications. It will provide facilities and supporting services that allow the community to do things that are not feasible otherwise. It also expands what can be accomplished for a fixed budget through sharing, reuse, and reduced duplication of both effort and facilities.

The cyberinfrastructure offers a reference point for mediating the interaction among applications, defining common interfaces and information representations. The cyberinfrastructure provides a set of software tools that make it easier to develop applications. It also provides, as an alternative to software that can be "designed into" an application, services that can be invoked over the network by applications. When this approach is adopted, responsibility for the installation and administration of software and supporting equipment (and more generally provisioning and operations, as described later) is shifted to a service provider, where an aggregation of expertise and experience increases efficiency and effectiveness.

Lastly, the cyberinfrastructure allows the sharing of common facilities and equipment and instrumentation. This can be more efficient, due to statistical multiplexing and as a way to reduce expensive duplication. Examples include sharing a high-performance supercomputer with massive memory and input–output performance.

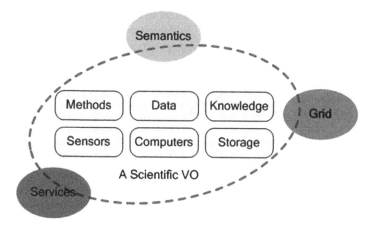

Fig. 8.2 The proposed service-oriented e-Science fabric

8.2.2.2   Smart e-Science Cyberinfrastructure

In our earlier work, we have proposed a proxy-based approach for smart e-Science cyberinfrastructure [7]. With this approach, the resources in a scientific facility (methods, data, storage, computers, etc.) are made available on grid-like conventional grid services. Figure 8.2 shows various components of the proposed grid infrastructure. The key entity in the infrastructure is a virtual organization (VO) that represents a resource-sharing facility in the grid. Each VO may provide one or more resources such as heterogeneous weather sensors, instrument monitoring sensors, actuators, computational and storage resources, scientific methods and knowledge, and grid-enabled service providers. Typical examples of VOs in our project include a weather network, a prototype for water recycling and production, scientific data centers, and supercomputing. The key idea is to enable each VO to access and share the resources of other VOs through distributed resource brokerage and user authentication. The proxy interface at each VO manages the VO-level ontology and exposes the resources in the VO as services, thus allowing for cross-domain interoperability.

The framework starts from an ontology design based on the common vocabulary set in the participating VOs. Each VO will then create an instance of this ontology in its domain and share it with the rest of the VOs on-board the grid.

The ontology considers that each VO runs some research and development (R&D) programs comprising some projects. In addition, each VO is assumed to consist of *ResourceGroups*, with the resource groups related to one or more projects. The ResourceGroup class is the highest-level class in the ontology hierarchy, with two immediate subclasses to categorize *physical* and *nonphysical* resources in the VO. The physical resources superclass refers to all tangible resources. In this project, it refers to the computational, storage resources and the sensors installed. Each of these classes is then inherited by more specific physical resource types in order to explicitly elaborate the resource attributes.

The nonphysical resources superclass refers to data (raw as well as processed) and scientific methods that can be made available for reuse to other parties. In this project, it refers to the raw data and the aggregated data as well as the methods and services provided by different parties. The data and methods superclasses are then inherited by more specific data-related ontology hierarchy and methods-related process ontology hierarchy that define characteristics such as the type, nature, format, interpretation, input, output, and domain of data and scientific processes being expressed by the ontology. The methods class hierarchy is of key importance in this e-Science ontology since it categorizes scientific methods into data management (acquisition, archiving, transfer) and data processing (any scientific processes that result in data transformation). The process ontology that defines these classes of methods thus forms the basis for providing service-oriented access to intellectual resources in the VO and allows for the creation of complex workflows. Another key advantage of binding methods in the same ontology hierarchy is that it allows operational standardization within the ontology, as each scientific method also becomes a subclass of a common ResourceGroup superclass. We will come back to this topic, commonly termed as *service composition*, in the next section.

The purpose of defining ontology here is to make the resources sharable. The physical and nonphysical superclasses hierarchy will be described with maximum detail. For example, each SensorGroup ontology can be categorized into various domain-specific sensing units, such as weather stations, membrane tank, solar thermal collection and storage system, solar PV energy collection and storage system, etc. A SensorGroup has also been shown to have an associated geographical location identified by latitude, longitude, elevation, and, if needed, an x–y location relative to some reference.

Each SensorGroup may comprise multiple heterogeneous sensors, with each sensor identified by its attributes such as calibration coefficients, rate of sensing, data transfer rate, and the data itself. The ontology also caters for situations where a SensorGroup may have multiple instances of the same sensor which are differentiated by their relative location on the sensor group. This feature allows catering, for instance, to MDBR tank; there are eight temperature sensors installed to measure different parts of the tank and can be further elaborated by providing the relative locations: right bottom, right cover, left bottom, left cover, etc. The data attribute under the sensor ontology is further expanded to represent different data types such as alpha (which includes alphanumeric), numeric, and binary data. The numeric data can be any whole or real number quantity such as temperature, voltage, or flow rate. In addition to the sensors, each SensorGroup may have other resources such as communication modules, battery power, and storage. Essentially, resource consumers in a scientific community need a service-oriented model to allow them to specify resource requirements and constraints. They need brokers that provide strategies for choosing appropriate resources and dynamically adapt to changes in resource availability at runtime to meet their requirements. In addition, in a service-oriented e-Science, there will be multiple, concurrent clients exercising different functionalities of the system for different scientific processes. Thus, the infrastructure must have a certain level of autonomy to decide on the best use of available resources to fulfill multiple users' concurrent uncoordinated requests.

The proposed cyberinfrastructure provides means to access the ontologies and sophisticated domain-specific knowledge and scientific methods can be encapsulated into computational components or services. Each service simply transforms input events into output events, adding new semantic information as necessary. This semantic-based approach helps in search, discovery, selection, composition, and integration of services and also in the automation of their invocation, composition, and execution. Our proposed framework uses semantic services as the basic programming model. We call these components semantic services since they provide access to various resource groups defined by the ontology of a VO. The infrastructure provides a backbone for water recycling and production application, which will be discussed in the next section.

8.3   Cyberinfrastructure Design for Water Production and Recycling

8.3.1   System Architecture and Components

The cyberinfrastructure design is targeted for the solar-enabled water production and recycling system. The system architecture, which is organized as a sensor grid, is shown in Fig. 8.3. The system consists of major components such as sensors and instruments, data acquisition devices, computational resources, data storage resources, and decision support system.

First, various sensors and instruments are deployed for the system. These include:

1. MD and MDBR experimental tanks on a building's rooftop at the Nanyang Technological University (a photograph of the setup is shown in Fig. 8.4). Sensors such as temperature sensors, voltage sensors, and flow rate sensors are deployed at relevant locations in the tank to monitor the environment. These parameters are critical to the wastewater purification process and require real-time monitoring.
2. A set of pyrometers, shadow rings, and sun trackers are deployed to measure the instant solar radiation value at different angles, e.g., horizontal, 15°, 20°, etc.
3. Eight solar PV panels are set up on the rooftop to harness the solar energy. The status readings such as voltage, current, and temperature of each solar PV panel are measured to study the performance of the PV panels. The amount of power generated from each panel is also recorded to determine the practical power generation using such PV panels.
4. Solar thermal harnessing and storage system.
5. Weather pattern study for energy prediction and control. Weather stations (mainly Vasaila, WeatherHawk, and VantagePro stations) are deployed across Singapore to measure weather parameters such as temperature, wind speed, and solar radiation [8]. The National Weather Sensor Grid (NWSG) [9] is designed to collect, archive, and process the weather data. These weather data are used to

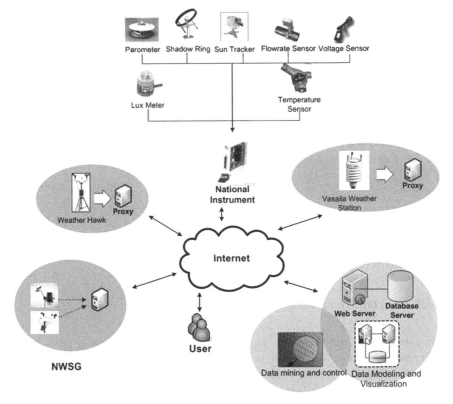

Fig. 8.3 System architecture

Fig. 8.4 Rooftop setup

determine the amount of energy that could be harnessed in real time and hence facilitate the decision on how to control the energy distribution in the water purification system.

The various sensor, computational, and storage resources in the system are located at different locations while connected to the sensor grid via proxies (PCs at schools, National Instruments data logger on the building rooftop, etc.). These proxies will upload the new sensor readings to the sensor grid backend server whenever there are new readings collected by the local logging system. The backend server would parse the data files it receives and store the individual readings into the database accordingly. The communication between the proxies and the backend server is done through the Internet. In case there is no Internet connection, other alternatives such as 3G can be used.

8.3.2   Ontology Design

Based on the physical components listed above, we have a table of physical concepts that should be included in the ontology (Table 8.1). Note that there are high-level concepts such as Sensor, Project, ResourceGroup, etc. They have been defined as root classes. Instances of each root class are also specified. For example, for Sensor class, instances are temperature sensor, flow rate sensor, voltage sensor, current sensor, wind speed, Lux sensor, etc. For each Project, instances include NWSG, pilot plant setup, rooftop setup, etc.

The third component includes the nonphysical elements such as data and process. Scientists involved in this project install the specific experimental instruments for their research purpose and, at the same time, reply on each other's research outputs. Hence, there is a high demand on data exchange mechanism to facilitate the collaboration process. On the other hand, the data process within each scientific domain is also desirable by the other domain. A typical example is the control component and the weather prediction model. The data mining process based on the weather data collected is an important input to the control component.

Table 8.1   Physical concepts in the ontology

Sensor	Sensor location	Average temperature
Weather station	VantagePro	Surface temperature
NWSG	Weather Hawk	Manufacturer
Singapore	Vaisala	MDBR tank
Station location	Temperature	MD tank
Project	Humidity	PV panels
Flow rate	Wind speed	Solar thermal collector
Voltage	Inside temperature	Solar storage tank
Current	Outside temperature	Shadow ring
Lux meter	School	Sun tracker
ResourceGroup	Rooftop setup	Pilot plant setup

Table 8.2 Nonphysical concepts in the ontology

Data rate
Data format
Data precision
Numbers
String
Audio
Process model
Data acquisition
Data pulling
getlatestData
gethistoricalData
getGooglemap
getAggregatedData

Hence, the infrastructure should be able to support such kind of process sharing. There is also resource sharing such as computational and storage resources.

Data are associated with physical concepts and are defined by data format, data precision, and data rate. Instances of data format include the necessary instances that should cover the requirements of the data generated from the system. Process ontology is defined to fulfill the requirements from the point of view of specific applications. For example, one of the root classes is data pulling while there are instances such as getlatestdata, gethistoricalData, and getAggregatedData (Table 8.2). They are designed to support specific applications, which we will discuss later.

8.3.3 Data Management

There are mainly two challenges for the database design in this project. First of all, the database should be flexible for various setups at different locations or from different organizations. As shown earlier, in this project, we have three data sources involved. One is a small-scale experimental setup at the rooftop of a building S2.2 for water processing. The second one is a large-scale pilot plant setup near Changi airport. The third one is the weather station network spreading over Singapore. It is challenging to store the data collected from different parties with different formats, sampling frequency, etc, in one uniform database. Secondly, the system is very dynamic in the sense that the type of sensors varies from temperature sensor, flow rate sensor, voltage sensor, and sensors which are related to weather stations. There could be new sensors added at a later stage of the project. Hence, the database should be open to such dynamics and handle new sensors or even new organizations seamlessly.

To this end, we have designed an object-oriented database system (Fig. 8.5). Each object in the project is described as an entity. For example, we have VO representing

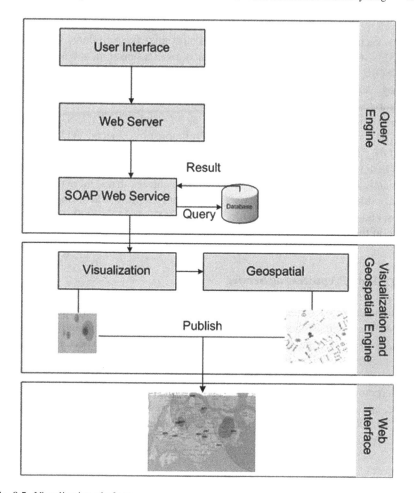

Fig. 8.5 Visualization platform

various system setups, e.g., rooftop, pilot plant, or weather station network. At VO level, each individual station is attached with a VO_DETAIL table to describe the attributes of a station, e.g., its location and name. The attributes are listed in a table called VO_ATTRIBUTE whereby each attributed is given an attribute id. In this way, we can add in new attributes to each VO flexibly.

Level STATION represents each subcomponent in each organization. The division of subcomponents depends on the functionality each organization would like to have. For example, level STATION in the weather station network represents each individual weather station. In rooftop experiment, STATION represents the subsystems involved, e.g., MDBR tank, PV system, Apricus system, or other measurement instruments (MIs). Similarly to VO object, each STATION is associated with a STATION_DETAIL table to describe the details of each station.

A STATION_ATTRIBUTE table is used to list down the attributes describing the stations, such as station name, location, and customized descriptions.

At SENSOR level, each individual sensor is given a sensor id, and attached with a SENSOR_DETAIL table which describes a specific sensor, e.g., sensor type, accuracy, vendor, location, and respective data table. A SENSOR_ATTRIBUTE table is used to show necessary sensor attributes.

The relationship between objects, such as VO and STATION, STATION and SENSOR, are described by respective relationship objects: VO_STATION, STATION_SENSOR. Data can be stored either at VO level, STATION level, or SENSOR level, depending on the requirement. Such a database design is flexible for dynamic system design and development. We can see that if there is a new VO, coupled with new stations and sensors, it is convenient to add in the new VOs, stations, and sensors each object table VO, STATION, and SENSOR. Similarly, we can add in the details of each component in respective detail tables.

8.3.3.1 Data Preprocessing Service

Data streamed into the database are usually raw data, which are noisy and incomplete in nature. Data with such anomalies are meaningless for scientific applications and are unable to provide the desired information that the scientists expect. For example, in this project, the scientists require a visual solar radiation map in Singapore that can provide richer details of solar radiation's intensity and variation over a large spatiotemporal domain. Thus, the raw data should be first cleaned, aligned, interpolated, and aggregated before they can be used to generate a visual solar radiation map. The following sections detail the issues and techniques related to each of these data processing steps.

8.3.3.2 Data Cleaning Service

Sensor data are sometimes noisy due to environmental disturbances or due to faults in the sensor hardware. There may even be incomplete, missing, or inaccurate data [10]. Thus, data cleaning is an important step for improving the quality of data. We consider both offline cleaning of the historical data and online cleaning of the real-time streaming data. Based on signal processing and statistical techniques [11], we have developed data cleaning services to clean the data obtained from a single weather station. Besides the time series data from a single weather station, the data from a group of weather stations in close geographic vicinity can be used to improve the accuracy of data cleaning.

Specifically, we have implemented a k-distances algorithm to remove the outliers/spikes from the solar readings in a single weather station. For this purpose, a sliding window-based approach is used to obtain a set of readings and identify the outliers in the set. For each reading in the window, its Euclidian distance from the rest of the readings in the window is calculated. The average distance is then compared with a threshold which is determined based on the correlation between the data. If the average distance is larger than the threshold, the reading is classified as an outlier and is removed from the data set. A new reading averaged from the remaining samples in the sliding window is used to replace the outlier. The efficiency of this algorithm is affected by the size of the sliding window and the threshold. The limited space in this chapter does not allow us to provide extensive details of the algorithm.

8.3.3.3   Data Alignment and Interpolation Service

Data alignment issue arises due to the different sampling rates configured for various sensors. Thus, given a specific point in time, the availability of the data from each sensor cannot be guaranteed. To address this issue, it is required to align the data over a time dimension. We have implemented data aggregation algorithms that aggregate data from each sensor in a certain time window, e.g., within 30 min.

In sensor networks deployed over a wide area, sensor nodes (weather stations) are deployed at discrete sites. In this case, it is not possible to obtain sensor data from each geographical point in the area. This requires interpolating sensor data over the entire geographical space. The quality of the interpolation results highly depends on the data that are involved in the interpolation. In addition to employing existing interpolation methods such as inverse distance interpolation and kriging algorithms, our system offers other characteristics that can be exploited to improve the accuracy of interpolated data. The rationale behind employing system characteristics is to find the spatial dependence between the locations void of a real sensor and the locations that are involved in the interpolation process with real sensor data. In the current implementation, the data are aligned by aggregating data every 30 min. For interpolation, the inverse distance algorithm is employed.

8.3.4   Workflow Management

For workflow-based jobs [12], we have designed a Workflow Management middleware service that handles execution of the user's job, which may include executing multiple services on the grid and responding to the user with the results. The workflow management service makes use of the Resource Discovery and Brokerage service to discover the data as well as services that the user requires, and then executes the job based on the execution policy defined by the user.

8.3.4.1   Workflow Tools and Services for Solar Radiation Map

One of the complex workflows we have handled is the solar map visualization process. The workflow is started by the user request submitted via the Web interface.

Users can specify the detail level of the solar map such as daily, weekly, monthly, or yearly. A real-time solar map is also provided upon request. The Middleware service handles the workflow by dividing the work into multiple services: data request service at a specific aggregation level; googlemap service; image processing service; data interpolation service; computational resource request, etc. These services are provided at atom level and can be discovered by Resource Discovery. The implementation of such a process will be shown in detail in Sect. 8.4.

8.3.4.2 Workflow for Data Mining and Control

One of the prominent innovations in this research project is the "close-to-zero energy" concept, which means the entire production process will solely rely on solar energy, either from directly harnessed solar energy or from that stored in batteries. Hence, the process is largely determined by the weather condition and has to fine-tune the operations accordingly. Therefore, a short-term prediction of the weather condition, especially the solar energy harnessed a few hours later, is critical to the operation of the system and has to be taken into account for control purposes. In this section, we present the workflow management for weather data mining and the distributed control system to optimize the operation.

There are three main objectives for the control system. First of all, it is crucial to maintain a minimum requirement for temperature in the MD process tank. This is because the system is error prone to the number of bacteria existing in the tank which can only remain alive above a certain degree of temperature. In case of low power supply due to extreme weather conditions, the limited resources should be used to maintain the temperature instead of production. The second purpose of the control system is to optimize the output of the process: the ratio of the amount of clean water derived to the amount of energy spent. Actuators at different levels are fine-tuned to control the flow rate, temperature in the tank, the distribution of solar energy for direct use and storage, etc. The parameters are determined by experts in optimized control. The last purpose is to ensure a fault-tolerant system. Hence, frequent reports of the critical control points are needed.

To achieve the above objectives, the control system is designed as three tiers: (1) Daily control. An optimization model takes daily solar energy harnessed as the input from a daily weather prediction model (DWPM) and decides the distribution of the solar energy harnessed. Part of the energy will be stored in batteries to maintain the operation under extreme weather conditions. Part of the energy will be directly applied to the operation; (2) Short-term control according to the variation of solar radiation during the day. In the first tier, daily control is based on the solar energy harnessed within the whole day. However, the weather condition varies from time to time. Hence, a short-term weather prediction model (SWPM) is used to predict the trend of the solar radiation in the next few hours, e.g., the solar energy will be less in the next 2 h. Then a control module will evaluate based on the prediction and switch to battery power if there is not enough solar energy derived. On the other hand, if the solar energy is excessive, more energy will be stored into the batteries; (3) High-frequency control for fault-tolerant and safety checks. There are monitoring points in the system which are critical to the lifetime of the system. Hence, the low-level control is to guarantee smooth operation by checking the values reported from these monitoring points. Either a threshold-based or model-based method can be adopted to check against the reported values and decide if the system is running safely. The threshold or model is determined by the domain experts.

As we can see, the control system involves a complex combination of software, hardware, and decision-making system, which forms a typical close-loop cyber-physical infrastructure. Under the umbrella of our proposed semantic e-Science cyberinfrastructure, we handle the smooth execution of each component involved. The first tier control process is auto-initiated each day. A grid-user authentication model is used to check the user privilege. After that, workflow management service will identify sub-jobs: DWPM model for that particular day. The result will be fed back to the control module to pursue the next step. According to the predicted value of the solar energy that will be harnessed on that day, distribution of the solar energy for direct usage and for storage is calculated by the "solar distribution model." Commands are sent to the solar harnessing system to control the energy converting rate. The second tier control is auto-initiated every few hours to check the real-time solar energy pursued. Sub-jobs are identified by the SWPM model to predict the variation of solar radiation. If extreme weather is encountered (low solar energy), commands are sent to the solar storage system to release solar energy to maintain the system operation. Actuators in the MDBR/MD are tuned to undergo the extreme weather, e.g., slowing down the flow rate, shutting down certain valves, etc.

8.4 Implementation

8.4.1 Data Acquisition and Archiving

In this real-life deployment, we address the challenges of seamless data acquisition from heterogeneous weather sensors which are deployed throughout the schools in Singapore as well as the sensors and actuators located on the rooftop. We have established an extensive and growing cyberinfrastructure. The hardware setup includes Linux servers and PCs (for compute and data grid resources), weather stations such as Davis Vantage Pro 2 (http://www.davisnet.com) and WeatherHawk (http://www.weatherhawk.com), rooftop equipments and sensors (such as flow rate sensor, voltage sensor, and temperature sensor), National Instruments data acquisition units, etc. The software environment includes Apache Web server (for the Web portal), MySQL server (for the weather database), Globus Toolkit 4.0 (for the grid middleware), Labview (http://www.ni.com/labview/), and our cyberinfrastructure middleware and software stack.

The sensors used for this implementation have basic capabilities. They are able to provide data based upon a data acquisition policy determined by the proxy. Thus, the proxy in this case serves as the key entity to resolve issues such as connectivity and data acquisition. However, as more powerful sensor nodes are available, more sophisticated tasks can be executed on the nodes themselves. For each type of equipment, a data connector has been developed to convert the binary readings to text files. Equipments were studied and calibrated to perform accurate readings.

For weather stations, we have basically three types: VantagePro, WeatherHawk, and Vasaila. Each has its own configuration and data format. We have developed three data connectors and installed them on each proxy to convert to standard data format. For rooftop equipments, national instrument has provided connectors to convert the voltage reading from each sensor to a meaningful calibrated reading and stored them on a PC where the proxy was located. The standard format of each data file acquainted at the proxy includes a station_id that has been assigned to this particular equipment when they joined the infrastructure, and a list of sensor names associated to this station. This information will be used as meta information of the data and facilitates data archiving and data exchange processes. Since each VO, station, and sensor has respective meta information in the database, through a meta scheduler, we can parse the data file and insert each data tuple into the database automatically.

8.4.2   Ontology Implementation

Ontology Web Language (OWL) was selected to implement data and process ontologies in this project. OWL facilitates greater machine interpretability of Web content than that supported by XML, RDF, and RDF Schema (RDF-S) by providing additional vocabulary along with formal semantics. OWL can be used to describe the classes and relations between them that are inherent in Web documents and applications. OWL may include descriptions of classes, properties, and their instances. Given such an ontology, the OWL Formal Semantics specifies how to derive its logical consequences, i.e., facts not literally present in the ontology, but entailed by the semantics. The advantage of OWL over standard XML schema is that OWL is a knowledge representation and helps accurate interpretation through rich semantics.

We made use of the Protégé OWL for implementing the guidelines for building ontologies for our case study domains. The steps to define this ontology are as follows:

1. All elements from the rooftop equipments, pilot plant setup, and weather stations were identified and conceptualized as classes.
2. Various high-level concepts such as NWSP project, solar project, ResourceGroup, Data and Sensor were identified as root classes.
3. A scientific VO was considered as the origin of the ontology. In our case, VO is the solar project and NWSP project.
4. Relationships such as *has*, *subClassOf*, *isDefinedBy* between the root classes with the VO were identified. The solar project has two setups, one at the rooftop and the other at pilot plant.

5. Subclasses for each of the root classes were identified with their attributes and placed in the ontology hierarchy.
6. Specific instances of various classes, such as WeatherStations, ThermalSensors, VoltageSensors, Computer, and RAID, were created.
7. The Data and Process ontologies were defined for each VO.

Each VO will provide access to their resources via server-side services whereas other VOs will utilize those services by deploying client-side services. We have implemented a number of services to expose both physical and nonphysical resources. The server-side services have been implemented in Java and deployed in Apache Axis to produce server- and client-side SOAP wrappers. We provide implementation details of a sensor data retrieval service GetSensorData.

Each service comprises methods that can be categorized based on the type of information they provide in two parts: (a) meta data–related methods and (b) data-related methods. The meta data–related methods deal with obtaining meta information about the service itself, such as the list of methods that the service provides and the signatures of those methods so that they can be accessed. Table 8.3 lists the meta data–related methods of the GetSensorData service. The data-related methods provide the actual sensor data. These data come from sensor deployments, with each deployment having a specific number and type of sensors; the data-related methods also include those methods that provide such information. This is critical for cross-disciplinary data sharing since a client VO that wishes to access the data from a particular server VO should first know *what* to ask for so that the server VO can provide the relevant data. Thus, methods such as listDeploymentSites provide a list of all sensor deployment sites that the server VO wishes to expose to others. Having obtained the list of sites, the client VO can then choose one or more of the sites from where it wishes to retrieve real-time or archived data. Once the client VO has selected the deployment sites, the next step is to know what sensors have been deployed at that particular site, what the attributes of each sensor are, and how to interpret and translate the data, if needed. For this purpose, the GetSensorData service provides a method, getSiteOntology, that encapsulates this information as ontology in OWL format. The client can then process the OWL document to retrieve the details of sensors and their data. Finally, the getData method can be invoked by the client with the specification of deployment sites, sensors, and period of data to be retrieved (if accessing archived data). The client can also choose from a number of formats in which the data should be provided, such as OWL, XML, and ASCII. We treat the solar project as a client VO and the NWSP project as a server VO. The solar project can also provide services as a server VO to share its resources. The NWSP data are exposed through the methods shown in Table 8.3.

Table 8.3 Meta data–related methods of the GetSensorData service

Method	Description
listDeploymentSites	Return a list of all sensor groups available
getSiteOntology	Return all attributes of the sensor group specified
getData	Return the data for the specified sensor group of the specified start

8.4.3 Implementation of a Visualization Engine for Solar Radiation Map

A visualization engine is composed of three components: a backend query engine, a visualization and geospatial engine, and a Web interface, as shown in Fig. 8.5.

8.4.3.1 Query Engine

Users issue queries via a Web interface by specifying the time duration of data that must be used to generate the solar radiation contour map. This user request is passed over to the server-side query engine by the Web server. First, raw solar radiation data from all the weather stations are obtained in the XML format by using the data download Web service provided by the sensor grid. After parsing the XML data, the data cleaning procedure is carried out that removes the abnormal spikes from the data using the k-distance technique. Missing values are then filled up by calculating a moving average of adjacent readings along the time dimension. To interpolate the data points for locations void of real sensors, we have divided Singapore's geographical map into a set of grid cells with a size of 0.01° by 0.01°. The solar reading at each grid location was estimated by using the inverse distance interpolation method.

8.4.3.2 Visualization and Geospatial Engine

In this work, we use MapleSoft [13] and Google Maps [14] to develop an integrated visualization and geospatial platform. The visualization engine is implemented using Maple, which is a tool many scientists often use for scientific computing purposes and is powerful in optimized computations and visualization. Maple is split into two parts, the kernel and the "front end." The kernel interprets expressions and returns result expressions. The Maple front end provides a graphical user interface (GUI), which allows the creation and editing of Notebook documents which can contain a program code with pretty printing, formatted text together with results including typeset mathematics, graphics, GUI components, tables, and sounds. In this work, we have only used the kernel component. Maple provides numerous plotting functions such as line plots, contour plots, and 2D and 3D plots. It satisfies the requirements for most of the scientific applications.

The geospatial engine is implemented by using Google Maps, a powerful open source geospatial visualization service. It provides various Application Programming Interfaces (APIs) for the users to add overlays over the geographical map of the region. In our application, weather stations at different schools are displayed on the map. This is implemented by overlaying a "kml" document provided by Google Maps. The real-time data generated from the weather stations are displayed as an html document and refreshed regularly. Google Maps also provides services to

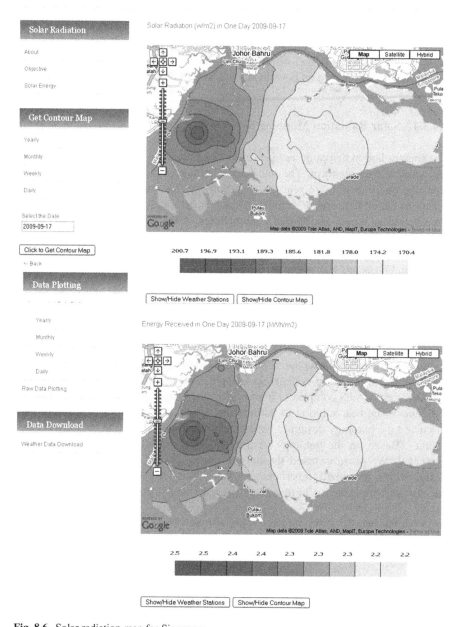

Fig. 8.6 Solar radiation map for Singapore

overlay images, such as the images generated by Maple plotting services. By specifying the boundaries of the images (in the format of longitude and latitude), Google Maps can overlay the images onto exact locations on the map. In addition, AJAX/JQuery data request calls are used to obtain most updated data from the server side.

8.4.3.3   Web Interface

We have developed a Web portal to showcase the platform. It enables the users to input their requirements and displays the visualization results. Moreover, other related services such as data download are also provided on the portal.

8.4.3.4   Solar Radiation Mapping Services

The solar radiation mapping service is developed based on the integrated geospatial and visualization platform. The interpolated data points at each grid cells passed from the query engine are sent to MapleSoft. We use one of the Maple plotting functions called ListcontourPlot. The average solar radiation value of the selected time period is shown at different contour lines. After the map is generated, it is embedded within Google Maps and published on the portal. Currently, preliminary results including the solar radiation statistics and maps on daily, weekly, monthly, and annual basis are searchable on the portal (Fig. 8.6).

8.5   Conclusion

In this chapter, we presented a smart e-Science cyberinfrastructure for water production and recycling system. Such applications involve cross-domain knowledge and can be very complex in terms of system design. The e-science cyberinfrastructure is the best solution to address the issues in such complex systems. We discussed the ontology design to handle heterogeneous sensor and instrument data sources. Based on the ontology design, an object-oriented database design was presented. We also discussed the data management and workflow management design within the cyberinfrastructure. A solar radiation map application has been successfully implemented to illustrate the capabilities of the cyberinfrastructure.

Acknowledgments This work was supported by Microsoft Research, Intelligent Systems Center of Nanyang Technological University, Research Support Office of Nanyang Technological University, and the Singapore National Research Foundation (NRF) under grant number NRF-G-CRP-2007-02.

References

1. J. Joseph, C. Fellenstein, *Grid Computing*, IBM Press, 2004.
2. T. Erl, *Service Oriented Architecture: Concepts, Technology, and Design*, Prentice-Hall, 2005.
3. J. Zibrida, R. Zuhl, J. Lewis and Z. Amjad, "Advances in reverse osmosis application in water reuse," Corrosion 2000, Mar 2000.

4. http://www.pub.gov.sg/NEWater/Pages/default.aspx
5. J. Phattaranawik, A. Fane, A. Pasquier and W. Bing, "A novel membrane bioreactor based on membrane distillation", Desalination, Vol. 223, No. 1–3, pp. 386–395, Mar 2008.
6. K. Ling, J. Maciejowski and B. Wu, "Multiplexed Model Predictive Control," 16th IFAC World Congress, Prague, Jul 2005.
7. H. B. Lim, M. Iqbal, Y. Yao, and W. Wang, "A smart e-Science cyberinfrastructure for cross-disciplinary scientific collaborations," To appear in *Semantic e-Science*, Springer Annals of Information Systems (AoIS), Springer-Verlag, 2010.
8. National Weather Study Project, http://nwsp.ntu.edu.sg
9. H. B. Lim, M. Iqbal, W. Wang, and Y. Yao, "The National Weather Sensor Grid: A large-scale cyber-sensor infrastructure for environmental monitoring," International Journal of Sensor Networks (IJSNet), Inderscience, Vol 7, No. 1/2, pp. 19–36, 2010.
10. K. Ni, et. al., "Sensor network data fault types", ACM Trans. Sensor Networks, Vol. 5, No. 3, pp. 1–29, May 2009.
11. F. Koushanfar, M. Potkonjak, A. Sangiovanni-Vincentelli, "Error models for light sensors by statistical analysis of raw sensor measurement," Proc. of the IEEE Sensors, pp. 1472–1475, Oct 2004.
12. X. Yang, R. Bruin, M. Dove, "Developing an end-to-end scientific workflow," Computing in Science and Engineering, vol. 12, no. 3, pp 52–61, May/Jun 2010. http://www.computer.org/portal/web/csdl/doi/10.1109/MCSE.2010.61
13. MapleSoft, http://www.maplesoft.com/
14. Google Maps, http://code.google.com/apis/maps/

Chapter 9
e-Science Infrastructure Interoperability Guide: The Seven Steps Toward Interoperability for e-Science

Morris Riedel

Abstract This chapter investigates challenges and provides proven solutions in the context of e-science infrastructure interoperability, because we want to guide worldwide infrastructure interoperability efforts. This chapter illustrates how an increasing number of e-scientists can take advantage of using different types of e-science infrastructures jointly for their e-research activities. The goal is to give readers who are working in computationally driven research infrastructures (e.g., as within European Strategy Forum on Research Infrastructures (ESFRIs) scientific user community projects) the opportunity to transfer processes to their particular situations. Hence, although the examples and processes of this chapter are closely aligned with specific setups in Europe, many lessons learned can be actually used in similar environments potentially arising from ESFRI projects that seek to use the computational resources within EGI and PRACE via their own research infrastructure, techniques, and tools. Furthermore, we emphasize that readers should get a sense of the concept and benefits of interoperability, especially by using sustainable standard-based approaches.

Since several decades, traditional scientific computing has been seen as a third pillar alongside theory and experiment and since 10 years the grid community has provided a solid e-science infrastructure base for these pillars to achieve e-science. e-Science is known for new kinds of collaboration in key areas of science through resource sharing using that infrastructure. But a closer look reveals that this base is realized by a wide variety of e-science infrastructures today while we observe an increasing demand by e-scientists for the use of more than one infrastructure to achieve e-science. One of the relatively new "e-science design pattern" in this context is the use of algorithms through scientific workflows that use concepts of both high-throughput computing (HTC) and high performance computing (HPC) with production applications of e-science infrastructures today.

This chapter illustrates ways and examples of realizing this infrastructure interoperability e-science design pattern and will therefore review existing refer-

M. Riedel (✉)
Juelich Supercomputing Centre (JSC), Juelich, Germany
e-mail: m.riedel@fz-juelich.de

Xiaoyu Yang et al. (eds.), *Guide to e-Science: Next Generation Scientific Research and Discovery*, Computer Communications and Networks, DOI 10.1007/978-0-85729-439-5_9, © Springer-Verlag London Limited 2011

ence models and architectures that are known to promote interoperability, such as the open grid forum (OGF) open grid services architecture (OGSA), the common component architecture (CCA), and the Organization for the Advancement of Structured Information Standards (OASIS) service component architecture (SCA). The review of these reference models and architectures provides insights into numerous limitations that arise due to not having suitable reference models in the community or because of following numerous proprietary approaches in case-by-case interoperability efforts without using any standards at all.

As its main contribution, this chapter therefore reveals a concrete seven-step plan to guide infrastructure interoperability processes. So far, reference models in grids have only addressed component-level interoperability aspects such as concrete functionality and semantics. In contrast, we change the whole process of production e-science infrastructure interoperability into a concrete seven step–based plan to achieve it while ensuring a concrete production grid impact. This impact is in turn another important contribution of this chapter, which we can see in the light of separating the "e-science hype" from "e-science production infrastructure reality." Hence, this chapter not only presents how technical interoperability can be achieved with current production infrastructures, but also gives insights on operational, policy, and sustainability aspects, thus giving a complementary guidance for worldwide grids and emerging research infrastructures (i.e., ESFRIs or other virtual science communities), as well as their technology providers and e-scientists.

This chapter illustrates how the aforementioned steps can significantly support the process of establishing grid interoperability and, furthermore, gives concrete examples for each step in the context of real e-research problems and activities. The chapter also puts the processes into the context of interoperability field studies and uses cases in the field of fusion science (EUFORIA) and bioinformatics (WISDOM and Virtual Physiological Human).

9.1 Introduction and Overview

Many e-science infrastructures provide a wide variety of services to end users on a daily basis today. This wide variety of services leads to the fact that the infrastructures are complex and that their interoperability is not as straightforward as was foreseen since the beginning of e-science and grid computing. This non-interoperability can be partly explained by the infrastructure complexity since it is far more difficult than the interoperability of power grids that have been used for comparison with computational grids and e-science infrastructures earlier.

We motivate the content of this chapter by its relevance to existing and emerging e-science communities and organize this contribution in two major parts. In the first part, we seek to understand why interoperability in general and the contribution of this chapter in particular are so important to e-science communities. In the second part, we aim to provide a process that guides the work of e-science communities when the need for interoperable e-science infrastructures is identified. This includes a profound understanding of how many e-scientists actually work. By understanding and actually working with several of these communities via case studies, we identified one major "toolset" that many e-scientists would like to use. This toolset can be essentially described as the use of different types of computing for one larger scientific purpose within their given frame of reference – in other words, their e-science environments. As this toolset is essentially independent of any particular e-science topic and is applicable to a wide variety of e-science endeavors, we called it an "e-science design pattern." We define it as one algorithm that uses both fundamental computing paradigms, (a) HTC and (b) HPC, using the same client technology.

With the help of many computer scientists, e-science environments are continuously augmented with functionalities that enable the use of these different computing paradigms and as such the use of the aforementioned toolset. In this context, the design pattern has been implemented in many e-science communities (e.g., e-Health [1], Fusion [2], etc.) and one of its goals is to help new e-science communities to better identify whether their need of computing is similar. This guides the process of identifying whether their particular e-science community really requires interoperable infrastructures and the usage of different computational models. Many discussions revealed that the usage of these computational paradigms on e-science infrastructures is not only less understood but also significantly categorized as being rather trivial. In the motivational section of this chapter, we explore the fact that the interoperability problem is indeed quite the opposite of trivial.

In order to achieve an implementation of this design pattern, e-scientists and dedicated computer scientists that are also part of many e-science communities work hard to meet the short-term expectations of e-scientists. With respect to interoperable infrastructure usage, this often leads to interoperation instead of standard-based interoperability. To better understand the drawbacks of these short-term activities, we provide a short background study in the existing reference models that promote interoperability and in various different approaches that tackle interoperability problems on a case-by-case basis. Our studies revealed that only open standards have the true potential to provide sustainable interoperable solutions.

This is nothing new and one might wonder why all the different e-science infrastructures are still not fully interoperable? Another question might be how the problem of non-interoperability relates to the aforementioned relevant e-science communities. We provide answers to these questions in the form of a guide, briefly introducing the aforementioned design pattern and a process that provides solutions. This process is organized into seven steps toward interoperable e-science infrastructures, which significantly promote and increase the chance of interoperability while at the same time do not fully solve the interoperability problem. Throughout the chapter, we provide case studies in context and in relation to real existing interoperability challenges in production e-science infrastructures such as the European Grid Initiative (EGI) as well as the Distributed European Infrastructure for Supercomputing Applications (DEISA) and the Partnership for Advanced Computing in Europe (PRACE).

Here we would like to take the opportunity to point out one important aspect of this guide that is related to the topic of discussion. The title of this chapter is not *"seven steps toward commercially driven business infrastructure interoperability"* which will realize interoperability among enterprise-driven technologies. The main issue in this book in general and of this chapter in particular is clearly academically driven e-science infrastructures. We thus focus on their corresponding production environments that are used on a daily basis to perform e-science. We sometimes only point to interesting commercial aspects (e.g., time-to-market) and leave the question of whether these steps can be used in e-business infrastructures open to further research. One further important aspect worth mentioning is that we did not invent the seven steps and only put them in a sequential order in order to better understand them and thus be able to distinguish them from each other. We will experience throughout the descriptions of the steps that many of them are closely linked and require nontechnical skills (e.g., collaboration) while at the same time the majority of the steps have overlaps in certain specific aspects (e.g., open standards). Although we believe that we have covered the process of approaching interoperability as best as possible, we are open to additional aspects that might lead to the definition of other meaningful steps (e.g., step number eight or nine).

This book chapter is structured as follows. After the introduction in Sect. 9.1, we discuss motivational thoughts on interoperability relevance in Sect. 9.2. We illustrate a new design pattern in e-science that takes advantage of the interoperability between different e-science infrastructures in Sect. 9.3. Section 9.4 describes the seven steps and Sect. 9.5 offers a summary to the reader. References and Glossary are provided at the end.

9.2 Motivation and Relevance

Let us begin with one important recent project in the e-healthcare domain in the United States that directly points to the problem although on a perhaps slightly bigger scale. It is a perfect example of where the grid and e-science community is currently heading and why interoperability is so urgently important. Philip J. Scott writes in an interesting article [3] that President Barack Obama kicked off the so-called HITECH Act with $19.2 billion that in its true outcome aims to have electronic health records for the whole US population by 2014. It refocuses the attention of health-care interoperability and budgets $20 million specifically for "advancing health-care information enterprise integration through activities such as technical standards analysis and establishment of conformance testing infrastructure." Since major scientists, vendors, and stakeholders have been working in isolation for many years, the United States requires a costly project that enables interoperability in this context.

This is directly comparable to our more computationally driven e-science environment where grid middleware vendors (e.g., Globus, UNICORE, gLite, ARC, etc.) kept working in isolation for many years in order to meet short-term needs of certain e-science communities and computing infrastructures. Although specific projects (GRIP, UNIGRIDS, OMII-EUROPE, EMI, etc.), with a scope similar to the one mentioned earlier, have been started in order to get technologies to be able to work together, again? and again, we have seen how the lack of cooperation and the lack of standards have created what we now call "e-science infrastructure islands" (i.e., DEISA/PRACE, EGI, NAREGI, etc.). This term thus refers to different types of infrastructures that use different (middleware) technologies which essentially cannot work together, because they are incompatible.

While the EU Grid Interoperability Project (GRIP) focused on enabling the interoperation between Globus and UNICORE through hacks (i.e., security) and work-arounds (adapters), the follow-on EU project Uniform Interface to Grid Service (UniGrids) focused on achieving the interoperability between UNICORE and Globus through open standards in the early days of the OGF. Both UNICORE and Globus did not cooperate substantially over the years, leading to a lot of boundary conditions in interoperability and thus another project where standard-based interoperability was a key goal: the Open Middleware Infrastructure Institute (OMII) – Europe. In contrast to UniGrids, the OMII–Europe project included the gLite middleware, which in parallel to UNICORE and Globus evolved over time to satisfy the demands of users from the high-energy physics (HEP) community around the Large Hadron Collider (LHC). More recently, the European Middleware Initiative (EMI) was set up to harmonize (also through interoperability) the middleware development within Europe, adding to the UNICORE and gLite interoperability activities the Nordic middleware advanced resource connector (ARC). The complementary initiative for Globus in Europe (IGE) project was formed to align Globus with such activities.

The large-scale funding example in the e-healthcare interoperability domain mentioned earlier and the aforementioned series of funded EU projects concerning middleware interoperability lead us to the very essence of the motivation of this chapter. If we describe this motivation in two words it would be essentially "reduce costs." These projects have been funded and provided with money from numerous sources to overcome the limitations of working together – that is what interoperability simply means [3]. The reason why this money is necessary is the crucial point we seek to address in this contribution by providing means to not only understand but also pursue through a guiding process a different path, most likely not leading to such projects.

This chapter is thus particularly useful for e-science communities that are just about to start getting into contact with the computationally driven e-science infrastructure domain. Apart from many independent e-research endeavors, we would like to point to the numerous ESFRI projects [4] in particular. Many of these projects plan to use the e-science infrastructures EGI and PRACE as part of their own e-science environments, thus creating their science-specific research infrastructures. Such a creation process should not be isolated from other similar e-science communities and should continuously build on technology for vendor and infrastructure cooperation. With this continuation process, this chapter also becomes relevant to existing e-science communities that would like to improve their capability in terms of interoperable technologies through open standards.

In this context, it is important to understand the following particularly delicate issue with these e-science communities, which also employ computer scientists who in turn bridge the traditional e-science environments to the more recent computationally driven e-science infrastructures. While being at the same time major emerging end users of the aforementioned infrastructures, many e-scientists and computer scientists of these communities have not been involved in standard definition processes or technology requirement definitions in the past. We can thus envisage a new wave of e-science application enabling work and software reengineering, which is becoming relevant not only to the e-science communities but also to the e-science infrastructure communities and middleware vendors.

When there is no cooperation and no process, we will again have a landscape with numerous e-science technologies sticking to proprietary interfaces that are essentially non-interoperable, requiring, once again, projects such as the one mentioned earlier. It is the aim of this chapter to provide guiding principles for both understanding why and whether interoperability could be relevant to a specific e-science community and providing a solution based on a process. But in order to provide a solution, we first seek to understand how many e-scientists work with the identification of a specific "design pattern" often used within e-science communities. After that, we can put our solution in the context of e-science applications that implement this design pattern and can thus give guidance to many other communities.

9.3   An Emerging Design Pattern in e-Science

This section provides the necessary background for the state-of-the-art e-science infrastructures and several of their interoperability problems existing today. It classifies existing production e-science infrastructures and introduces one new emerging design pattern in e-science that requires the use of multiple different interoperable e-science infrastructures. It briefly surveys existing approaches to tackle the purely technology-based interoperability problems, lists known evaluation approaches, and thus provides a reasonable foundation for the understanding of the more concrete seven steps toward interoperability in the next section.

The fundamental goal of this section is to provide pieces of information that enable readers to fully understand whether their scientific endeavor really requires interoperability of e-science infrastructures. We have seen many scientific workflows that can be essentially modeled as a greater algorithm using (a) HTC and (b) HPC with a client on e-science infrastructures. In this section, we therefore propose a so-called design pattern in e-science alongside several others [5]. It can be considered as a toolset of e-scientists who use different types of computing for one larger scientific purpose within their specific e-science environments. It helps to get readers on the same page when talking about general grid interoperability but focusing on the specific interoperability of production e-science infrastructures as addressed in this chapter.

Hence, this toolset is essentially independent from any particular e-science topic and applicable to a wide variety of e-science endeavors. This once more leads to the meaning of "e-science design pattern." It is just one way of providing an abstract notion that is not too specific but gives a reasonable frame of reference in the context of the two basic computational paradigms as well as the e-science infrastructure providing resources for them. It enables easier comparison regardless of whether the readers' e-science research environment actually requires interoperable e-science infrastructures or not. This section emphasizes on the differences in the computing paradigms and, more notably, on the different infrastructures that offer resources for these kinds of computational models.

Implementations of these design patterns have been demonstrated in various scientific endeavors. Throughout this chapter we will use two major case studies in order to understand how implementation of the design pattern can actually benefit from the process given in Sect. 9.4. The first e-science case study within the e-Health domain is the WISDOM workflow [1], which implements the design pattern. The second case study is from the fusion domain majorly driven by the EUFORIA project and its multi-grid workflows [2]. Both workflows are used in production and lead to profound knowledge about where interoperability must be improved and how it can be sustainably achieved using our proposed process.

9.3.1 State-of-the-Art e-Science Infrastructures

Since the beginning of the grid computing research over a decade ago and after the formulation of the e-science definition by John Taylor [6], many different e-science infrastructures have emerged that offer production services to scientifically driven end users (i.e., e-scientists). Hence, a closer look reveals that the definition of Taylor about *"the next infrastructure that will enable it"* or Fosters' vision of *"one worldwide Grid like the power Grid"* [7] is not a reality today. In general, we can consider that such aforementioned next-generation e-science infrastructures, or computational grids, represent a solid base for the three pillars of science: (1) theory models, (2) experiments in laboratories, and (3) computational techniques (simulation and data analysis). Today, we already have numerous outcomes and results of e-science that may be considered a roof on top of these pillars and which therefore enable collaboration in key areas of science via infrastructures.

In more detail, we observe that these pillars are based on one foundation, which in turn consists of a plethora of different e-science infrastructures that are not fully interoperable today and thus lead to limitations when using more than one. In principle, this plethora can be partly explained by the underlying motivation of mainly satisfying end users with different computational paradigms. These paradigms are (1) HTC used by farming applications and (2) HPC that makes intensive use of computational core interconnections with massively parallel applications.

The e-science applications that take advantage of these computational paradigms are significantly different. Applications that use the HTC paradigm are typically called farming applications and often use one program to modify multiple datasets. These applications execute their program on a single core/CPU and this can be done in parallel with many other cores/CPU available. Hence, these applications do not interact with each other although they might run at the same time, and are therefore independent of each other. This allows for the distribution of HTC application elements within a grid without requiring that all these elements reside on one specific computational resource inside a specific e-science infrastructure.

In contrast, applications that use the HPC paradigm are typically called massively parallel applications using many cores/CPUs for one particular program. Parts of the program communicate with other parts using parallel programming and communication models (e.g., message passing interface (MPI)). Hence, the cores frequently interact with each other and thus the grid resource interconnection typically provides a low-latency connection via dedicated technologies (e.g., InfiniBand). Only large clusters or supercomputers offer these physical capabilities while all parts of the HPC application must be computed on one particular resource within one given grid infrastructure.

As a consequence, we can classify numerous existing e-science infrastructures using these computational paradigms as shown by Riedel et al. [8]. Well-known e-science infrastructures such as DEISA and TeraGrid are driven by HPC needs and large-scale parallel computing. More recently, PRACE evolved as an infrastructure dedicated to serve the needs of extraordinary large-scale parallel applications that are capable of scaling up toward the usage of peta-scale systems (e.g., BG/P system JUGENE of the Juelich Supercomputing Centre).

A well-known HTC-driven e-science infrastructure in the United States is the Open Science Grid (OSG). In Europe, the initial infrastructures oriented toward the use of HTC and large-scale data analyses are the Nordic DataGrid Facility (NDGF) and the Enabling Grid for e-Science (EGEE) infrastructure. More recently, Europe is about to provide a pan-European e-science infrastructure by interconnecting National Grid Initiative (NGI) grids, which will be known as the European Grid Initiative (EGI). NGIs are typically represented as regional grids within Europe such as the NDGF in the north and the National Grid Service (NGS) in the United Kingdom. Furthermore, NGIs can represent national infrastructures provided by member countries of the larger EGI.eu collaboration. In other words, the EGI infrastructure is created from numerous smaller NGI infrastructures where interoperability is a key issue. This is even more interesting as an increasing number of small-scale HPC systems become a part of the larger EGI infrastructure through NGIs. Riedel et al. [8] classify these particular NGIs as smaller hybrid infrastructures (e.g., UK NGS, and German D-Grid) offering not only HTC but also small-scale HPC resources.

Looking at the deployed technologies of these aforementioned infrastructures, we understand why interoperability is necessary. HPC-driven grids deploy UNICORE in Europe (i.e., DEISA, PRACE) and Globus in the United States (i.e., TeraGrid). EGEE and EGI are still largely based on gLite and ARC although there is a plan that the EGI Universal Middleware Distribution (UMD) gives NGIs the freedom to choose the particular technologies they want to deploy. Technologies in question for the UMD from the computational domain would be gLite, ARC, UNICORE, and Globus components while at the same time it is also clear that not every site within the NGIs can actually deploy all of the provided stacks or UMD components. This is another motivation why this chapter is not only relevant for the interoperability between e-science infrastructures such as DEISA and EGI, but also provides solutions to improve the interoperability within the larger EGI infrastructure, which is essentially one big umbrella of NGI-based infrastructures.

The two case studies that we use repeatedly throughout this chapter use several of the aforementioned different e-science production infrastructures to achieve one high-level scientific goal. The WISDOM workflow and the EUFORIA workflow require HPC and HTC resources. Therefore, these workflows take advantage of DEISA for HPC workflow elements and EGI (initially EGEE) for computations that embrace the HTC model in the workflow. As such both cases implement design patterns that we need to define more precisely.

9.3.2 Algorithm Using Different Computational Paradigms

While many end users are satisfied using one dedicated infrastructure to perform their science procedure, we observe an increasing demand by end users for using multiple infrastructures jointly for one larger scientific approach. Often, they employ one particular client technology that is commonly used in the corresponding field of e-science, but which was augmented with client libraries to access the middleware of the e-science infrastructures. In practice, this approach follows a multi-infrastructure workflow that we can further precisely define with the help of an algorithm as follows:

```
Begin

   Begin GridInformationProvisioning
      Grid Information Providers (GIPs) publish pieces of
      information about infrastructures (HPC and HTC resources)
   End

   scienceworkflowfinished = false

   WHILE (scienceworkflowfinished)
      Begin Brokering
         End-user uses client technology (CT) and performs application setup
            and defines HPC or HTC requirements for next scientific workflow step
         Compute resource (CR) of corresponding HPC and HTC infrastructure is
            found based on the information exposed by GIPs
      End

      Begin JobSubmitToResource
         If CR.type is HTC then
            End-user of CT submits HTC job to a HTC resource
            using middleware MA of the corresponding infrastructure IA
         End If
         If CR.type is HPC then
            End-user of CT submits HPC job to a HPC resource
            using middleware MB of the corresponding infrastructure IB
         End If
      End

      Begin AnalysisScienceComplete
         If end-user need no further computing then
            scienceworkflowfinished = true
      End

   End While

End
```

This pseudo-code defines more clearly our so-called emerging design patterns used by e-scientists more recently in science workflows that cross the boundaries of e-science infrastructures. As stated earlier, this interoperability is not really present and thus many of these workflows are based on hacks and workarounds, and made possible via tweaks of extensive development to support different technologies (e.g., integration of several client libraries in parallel). Several of these hacks and workarounds can be found in Riedel et al. [9], written by the author on behalf of the work undertaken in the OGF Grid Interoperation Now (GIN) community group. These solutions are neither sustainable nor do they use the underlying infrastructure resources in the most efficient manner. Nevertheless, the workflow can be implemented.

While the pseudo-code is very general we map it to one of our specific case studies in the context of the ITER fusion e-science community [2]. This community seeks to use the HTC-driven infrastructure EGEE/EGI (i.e., IA in the algorithm) together with the HPC-driven infrastructure DEISA (i.e., IB in the algorithm). We call this the EUFORIA workflow since the EUFORIA project made this workflow possible. The particular challenge here is that the middleware technologies gLite (i.e., MA in the algorithm) of EGEE/EGI and UNICORE (i.e., MB in the algorithm) are not interoperable and thus use different interfaces and protocols for job submission and management as well as different data transfer and storage methods. The execution of this algorithm leads to several open challenges when non-interoperable infrastructures must be used with one client technology.

At the time of writing, production runs have been based on supporting these different technologies in the dedicated client technology leading to high efforts in supporting two proprietary interfaces (UNICORE and gLite) at the same time. More recently, the use of open standards has been tested for production runs that in turn would enable this community to support only this particular standard in the client technology instead of different proprietary interfaces. Nevertheless, this case study leads to numerous lessons learned that have been fed back to the standardization organization in order to improve the open standards used for this case study.

Another case study that implements this algorithm is the multigrid WISDOM workflow [1], which also seeks to use the HTC-driven infrastructure EGEE/EGI in conjunction with the HPC-driven infrastructure DEISA. This case study is thus very similar to the previous one since both adopt the larger design pattern while implementing the aforementioned algorithm. Although the application challenges are different the non-interoperability between UNICORE and gLite is also here the major showstopper of efficiency. In fact, it prevents this particular e-science community from offering one particular portal solution that can efficiently be coded (e.g., with one client technology) still supporting both middleware systems.

In earlier days, the WISDOM workflow used only HTC resources within EGEE in production, but by implementing the design pattern and thus gaining access to HPC resources as well, the execution of the WISDOM workflow is significantly faster today. In more detail, molecular docking was performed on EGEE and computationally intensive molecular dynamic (MD) simulations have initially used EGEE as well. But using the parallel computing paradigm in particular for the MD workflow step on HPC resources has led to a significant speed-up since those MD simulations could leverage the power of parallel computing techniques with dedicated application packages (i.e., AMBER, more recently NAMD). This e-science community has already explored the usage of open standards since the OMII-Europe project and is continuously improving their framework toward the use of open standards. With standards, WISDOM e-scientists would only require to support one set of interfaces in their client frameworks. Moreover, this case study has enormously contributed to lessons learned of open standards within the OGF.

9.3.3 e-Science Infrastructure Interoperability Approaches

The work on interoperability in e-science infrastructures has a long history. We organized workshops such as the International Grid Interoperability and Interoperation Workshops (IGIIW) 2007 and 2008 [10]. We had special issues on interoperability within the *Grid Computing Journal* in 2009 [11]. In 2010, we organized a mini-symposium at the PARA2010 conference on distributed computing infrastructure interoperability. We thus studied elaborate literature work that all significantly contributed to the findings given in this chapter. Complementary to the academic approach, we also performed many field interoperability tests and research to understand and overcome challenges, such as the work within the GIN working group [9], within OGF, or, more recently, the OGF HPC-BP profile interoperability tests. In addition, we worked over years in the plethora of grid and e-science interoperability projects ranging from GRIP and UniGrids to OMII-Europe and the EMI.

Given all this experience and the lessons learned in the particular topic of e-science infrastructure interoperability, we are able to essentially describe in one sentence the approach of the next chapter which follows an important quote by Albert Einstein: *"The significant problems we have cannot be solved at the same level of thinking with which we created them."* That is the major conclusion we already provide before going into technical details. The aim is to raise awareness and point exactly to where the problems are when we review the existing reference models and component-based approaches. To solve the interoperability dilemma in a really sustainable way we need another approach of thinking. In other words, we need a new "mindset" for e-scientists in order to effectively take advantage of the aforementioned "toolset" (i.e., design pattern implementation) and with this the efficient use of resources in more than one e-science infrastructure. It also requires a whole new "skillset" (i.e., not only one middleware, but standards and collaborative methods as well) including a whole process covering cooperation, continuous improvements, and even long-term sustainability and policies.

Hence, one particular approach typically cannot satisfy the whole production even when based on pure open standards, and one reference model is good, but surely not enough. In the last analysis, standards give e-scientists the power to choose the technologies they want and the freedom to select the infrastructure that might be best to tackle a certain scientific problem. However, there are a wide variety of other factors that prevent e-scientists from the effective use of multiple e-science infrastructures ranging from usage rights to standards that are not strong enough to bring out the best of computing resources (e.g., missing capabilities that make a difference in performance). We encourage the reader to take these mentioned issues into account when reviewing the following survey about reference models and approaches. Note the difference between problems existing on the same level and possible solutions arising from other levels of thinking.

9.3.3.1 Reference Models That Promote Interoperability

By starting with the high-level approaches, the interoperability between different technologies can be significantly supported by reference models and its related elements as defined in [12]. Such models are defined via their entities and their corresponding relationships or generally provide an overall reference architecture to a whole problem domain. The first kind of reference model that is relevant for the e-science community is the Open Grid Services Architecture (OGSA) and its roadmap [13]. Since its initial definition, only rare adoption is observed within grid production technologies, and fully OGSA-conforming systems that provide all the services required by this architecture still do not exist. We thus argue that OGSA is too complex to be a realistic reference model for e-science infrastructures and their corresponding technologies in order to promote interoperability in the near future. Other critiques of OGSA include its very high-level description and the lack of important interactions between underlying specifications of different areas (i.e., compute, data, security, information).

Another reference model in the field of grid computing is the Enterprise Grid Alliance (EGA) reference model, which defines a collection of interconnected (i.e., relationships) grid components (i.e., entities) under the control of a grid management entity. It thus defines entities and relationships, but on a very high level, which is not specific enough to really enable interoperability between different production e-science technologies or products from different vendors. Its focused problem areas are enterprise grids, and therefore the whole reference model has only very minor (specific) overlaps with entities and relationships of technologies typically found in production e-science infrastructures today. Hence, the design of this reference model is optimized for business infrastructures rather than for e-science purposes.

There are further reference models or larger architectures that exist in the greater field of distributed systems or that touch the field of services oriented architectures (SOAs), but all of them are not particularly useful to enable e-science infrastructure interoperability. The Common Component Architecture (CAA) forum defines a minimal set of standard interfaces that a HPC-oriented component framework has to provide [14]. It is thus very specifically tuned for HPC, including even low-level functions and required services (e.g., memory management) in the same specification. It is therefore not realistically applicable to enable the interoperability between both HPC- and HTC-driven e-science infrastructures.

Another approach that is worth analyzing is the OASIS Service Component Architecture (CSA) [15], which is a set of specifications that describe a reference model that is based on the concepts of SOAs. It builds on open standards using existing technologies like Web services for building applications and systems that are driven by business demands. Since the SOA-based approach is very close to our commonly used communication pattern in e-science infrastructures with grid services that are also based on SOAs, the use of this approach seems to be promising. But a closer look reveals that this model provides (similar to OGSA) a huge model with a lot of entities and furthermore is driven by commercial needs (similar to EGA). We can conclude that this model too is not really suitable to promote interoperability among production e-science infrastructures today.

Another relevant grid reference model that is worth analyzing is described by Bratosin et al. [16]. This contribution argues that a good theoretical conceptual model of the grid is missing. Therefore, the authors provide a very formal description of a grid reference model in terms of so-called colored Petri Nets (CPNs). Although it clarifies perhaps basic grid concepts at a conceptual level it has no practical relevance at all for the interoperability between production e-science infrastructures. It enables a full formal evaluation, but lacks significant important factors such as being services-based, standard-based, and realistically implementable in production grids today.

In summary, Table 9.1 highlights interesting insights and enables us to conclude that there is still no reference model available that covers all of the relevant factors. CAA seems to be most suitable for the aforementioned interoperability, but at the same time is very detailed and optimized for one specific purpose, which is applications in HPC. But although they are standard-based these standards are relatively out of the domain of grids and need to be significantly adjusted to be of relevance to HTC-based infrastructures.

As a conclusion, we argue that the lack of a reference model is actually a hindrance while performing e-science procedures using more than one production e-science infrastructure. Experience in the field shows that many projects have therefore started to follow their own approach instead of referring to model-based proprietary approaches.

Table 9.1 Existing reference models at a glance and their comparison using relevant factors

Relevant factors	OGSA	EGA	CAA	CSA	CPN
Service-based	Yes	Yes	Yes	Yes	No
e-Science context	Yes	No	Yes	No	Yes
Detailed enough	No	No	Yes	Yes	No
Realistically implementable	No	No	Yes	No	No
Standard-based	Yes	Yes	Yes	Yes	No
Adoption in e-science production technologies	No	No	No	No	No
Relationships between functional areas	No	Yes	No	Yes	No

9.3.3.2 Component-Based Approaches to Enable Interoperability

In order to tackle the challenge of non-interoperable e-science infrastructures, many proprietary and case-by-case approaches have been performed in the past, so here we briefly survey them as a solid basis for the understanding of later sections. A full survey is out of the scope of this chapter since it has been already published in earlier work [8], but we still provide a glimpse here that will significantly help to understand the different steps offered in Sect. 9.4. Hence, complementary to the high-level approaches (i.e., reference models) in the previous paragraph, this paragraph surveys rather low-level approaches (i.e., based on components).

The low-level approaches are all named after components, because they refer to concepts that are particularly bound to certain components that can be found in a dedicated grid technology deployed on a specific infrastructure. Hence, these approaches cannot help solve interoperability in general, but represent a good source to learn about issues and challenges that are relevant to understand the problem of interoperability existing today. Many of these approaches represent only short-term solutions that have been created via workarounds, hacks, or non-maintainable component modifications. A plethora of component-based approaches exist that tackle the interoperability problem of technologies and thus their infrastructures. We only list these approaches in Table 9.2 and refer to Riedel et al. [8] for more descriptions and examples of these approaches.

To sum up, what all approaches have in common is that they require "transformation logic," which transforms one protocol or schema into another. Transformation logic is time-consuming and difficult to maintain since any new version of technologies (e.g., interface or protocol change) affects the transformation logic and it must be kept up to date in order to maintain the interoperability of infrastructures (e.g., different versions of transformation logic). We thus conclude that transformation logic should be avoided when enabling a sustainable interoperable solution as this can only be established when *open standards* are used. Such standards are difficult to define and to agree on, but without requiring any form of transformation logic they are the only path to reach sustainable interoperable solutions.

Table 9.2 List of component-based approaches and their transformation logic descriptions

Approach	Transformation logic
Additional layer	Located in client layer on top of middleware
Neutral bridge	Located in neutral bridge to contact all middleware systems and being contacted with one dedicated neutral protocol
Mediator	Located in a mediator component that is able to contact a few middleware systems and being contacted with one dedicated protocol
Gateway	Located in the central gateway that can be contacted with every protocol and can contact any middleware system
Adapter	Located in one middleware to contact another specific middleware

9.3.4   Evaluation of Interoperability Benefits as a Key Challenge

One of the major challenges in the context of e-science infrastructure interoperability is the precise evaluation of the benefits that can be achieved when actually using more than one e-science infrastructure. Several approaches exist and are listed in this section since we can partly explain the lack of infrastructure interoperability because evaluations that demonstrate positive aspects are nontrivial. The reason they are complex and nontrivial lies in the fact that interoperability provides benefits on higher levels and thus depends on the many important features that are part of the lower level within known grid technologies (e.g., resource management system in terms of scheduling) or the avoidance of transformations.

The benefit of (a) *"aggregated resource usage"* can be, in principle, evaluated by indicating the number of sites that are available before being interoperable and after interoperability has been established among different infrastructures. A greater number of systems may prove that they might lead to a better aggregated resource usage. In this context, another suitable evaluation metric is the result of having (b) *"more variety of resources."* That means we can measure how many different system architectures are available before interoperability is established and how many different kinds of resources are available to e-scientists afterwards.

Some evaluations can be made using principles of performance analysis starting with the (c) *"decrease of the turnaround time of jobs."* For example, using open standard interfaces can be evaluated against using proprietary interfaces of grid technologies. Here the measurements on getting rid of the transformation logic in general might lead to a decrease of the turnaround time. Also, depending on the application and its use on specific architecture features (e.g., task/core mappings), the greater variety of available resources might again decrease the turnaround time by better exploiting a computational resource that was not available before infrastructure interoperability was established. Of course, in this context we can even reuse metrics as the (d) *"typical speed-up measurements"* that are already in use in HPC. This is useful when an HTC-driven infrastructure is connected to an HPC-driven infrastructure, thus allowing access to a whole different computational paradigm. It also seems feasible to show the benefits of using HTC and HPC resources together in order to achieve a (e) *"lower time-to-solution."*

Further evaluations are possible in terms of maintenance of the different versions of transformation logic that limits interoperability and its sustainability. The (f) *"cost of maintenance of different versions"* might be difficult to define but surely points to the several issues that are related to it. In production setups we have to support $n * n$ version of the transformation logic. This is because protocol A might have n versions deployed in one infrastructure while protocol B might have n versions deployed in another infrastructure. As each technology might interact with each other, the transformation logic overhead becomes $n * n$.

9.4 The Seven Steps Toward Interoperable e-Science Infrastructures

The initial sections of this chapter described the state of the art in e-science infrastructures and also explained the open issues and challenges in having a reference model that is based on open standards in order to prevent any form of transformation logic. These elements are clearly fundamental views today, and in addition we observe that increasing number of technologies that are relevant for e-science infrastructures have started adopting several open standards. At the same time we can also observe that the rate of interoperability has not really significantly increased. We believe that the reason for this lies in the complexity of e-science infrastructure interoperability, which consists of many more challenges than those that we can easily overcome by adopting common open standards in technologies. No doubt, standards are a good step toward the right direction, but it must be complemented with a whole process that takes the dynamics of change of the infrastructure environments into account that are governed by policies.

The particular focus of this chapter is therefore the provisioning of some elements of such a process that is necessary to promote and to achieve interoperability between production e-science infrastructures such as EGI or PRACE. The seven steps give technology developers as well as infrastructure providers a guide as to how interoperability problems can be tackled. They are all only steps toward interoperability and thus do not intend to provide full solutions that are particularly optimized for specific components. Another view would be to see them as different "access points" regarding how to reach more interoperable solutions in a technology- and infrastructure-agnostic way. Figure 9.1 illustrates an overview of these seven steps that have the potentiality to increase the chance for interoperability between e-science infrastructures.

9.4.1 Step 1: Open Standard-Based Reference Model

The first step toward interoperability is to define a standard-based reference model, which embodies the basic goal of an interoperable network of grid services to achieve production e-science infrastructure interoperability. The goal is that this model can be looked up for various purposes and consists of a number of entities, relationships, and concepts that all roll up in a reference model that is realistical to implement and to be deployed in production infrastructures.

In comparison with other software engineering approaches in our context, the reference model is more abstract than a framework since it also deals with non-middleware-specific aspects and infrastructure deployment issues and guidance. We thus have a broader scope in comparison to other approaches surveyed in the previous chapter in order to address the great complexity of infrastructure interoperability problems. We further argue that true interoperability cannot be established by just focusing on middleware interoperability approaches or frameworks.

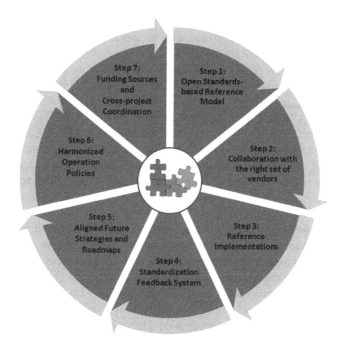

Fig. 9.1 Overview of the seven steps toward e-science infrastructure interoperability

9.4.1.1   Guiding Principles of Reference Models

The architectural blueprint of such a reference model must be defined by typical principles for software-engineering reference models that we also find in [12]. First and foremost, it should be "abstract" in the sense that the elements and concepts defined by the model are an abstract representation of these elements. Therefore, when describing the reference model architecture, an actual grid service deployed on one particular production infrastructure may have certain performance characteristics, but the concept of a grid service itself is rather part of the reference model.

Another applied principle must be that such an infrastructure reference model defines entities (e.g., reference model core building blocks) and relationships that describe how those entities interact with one another or use each other. Here, a pure list of entities (e.g., a set of standard-based grid services) alone is not sufficient to describe a suitable reference model. Therefore, one should particularly emphasize on their relationships using layered stack definitions and/or encapsulation methods in an analogy to the ISO/OSI reference model.

The third important principle that governs the reference model architectural design is that it does not attempt to describe "the whole grid" or solve "all Grid problems" that exist. Although it seems to be difficult to reach an agreement on the scope of a reference model between various adopters, the focused problem space is important. Such a reference model is thus used to clarify "*a network of interoperable services within production e-science infrastructure environments with HPC and*

HTC resources" as the specific problem area and thus only provides a collection of entities, relationships, and concepts to tackle certain known "*interoperability problems*" within those particular environments.

Fourth, but most importantly, the aforementioned reference model must be "grid technology agnostic." That means that it would not be useful if it made assumptions about specific grid technologies such as the grid middleware systems (e.g., gLite, UNICORE, and ARC) that are often in place in our particular "production e-science infrastructure environments" today (i.e., EGEE/EGI, DEISA/PRACE, NDGF, etc.). Hence, the reference model is a mechanism for understanding the interoperability problems faced, not the particular grid middleware solutions involved. As a consequence, such a reference model describes the reference model independent of real-world grid technologies or infrastructures in order to provide value to reference model adopters today as well as in the future.

Finally, it is worth mentioning that a basic reference model is not just an architectural model that can be applied to infrastructure interoperability setups but one that also represents a basis platform for further innovative concepts. In other words, the reference model must cover basic grid functionality areas (i.e., computation, data, information, security) but it can in turn be the basis for more advanced grid functionality areas (e.g., grid workflows and meta-scheduling, SLA methods, and collaborative grid visualization frameworks). Hence, in the sense of service-based e-science infrastructures, the reference model should describe basic services that can be reused by a wide variety of higher-level grid services.

9.4.1.2 Follow an Open Standard-Driven Design Approach

The first key element of the aforementioned reference model design approach is to use open standards for both the entities that are part of the reference model and their relationships to one another wherever possible. With this approach aspect the work of developers who create objects, which behave precisely according to the reference model standard elements, is made easier. In this sense, the core building blocks of the reference model architecture use open standards, and thus developers can copy their implementations to use them again and end users can switch technologies more easily. Furthermore, it satisfies the earlier stated requirement of keeping the "transformation logic" as zero in order to avoid any adoption risk in terms of maintainability.

Even more important is the standard-based approach to achieve our major goal, which is an interoperable network of service-based grid technologies, which implement the reference model design. Hence, it is expected that the majority of grid technology providers in general and grid middleware vendors in particular will adopt the standards of the reference model to reach interoperability between their services. Having these standard-based service implementations from different vendors and providers in turn deployed on the wide variety of production e-science infrastructures brings the vision of an interoperable network of grid services closer to the end users. This vision should significantly drive the design approach and one example is illustrated in Fig. 9.2, offering more concrete details in using the open

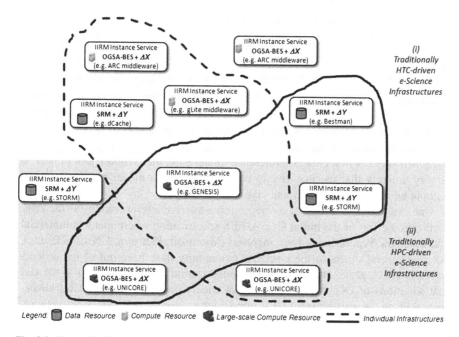

Fig. 9.2 Network of interoperable grid services that realize the vision of individual infrastructures providing access to individual functions (e.g., data and computation). ΔX and ΔY indicate the refinements of the open standards and links of different specifications

standards SRM (i.e., standard in data area) and OGSA-BES (i.e., standard in compute area), with their refinements (ΔX and ΔY) as a high-level example.

At first glance, this network of interoperable grid services seems to be realizable by purely using Web service standards that are already adopted in many production grid middleware systems today. Known examples are Web service standards that deal with the basic communication aspects such as SOAP over HTTP or WS-Addressing of W3C. Hence, it means that a reference model must ensure that the basic communication aspects are clarified as well. At the time of writing, a valuable approach for a reference model might be to follow "the fundamental grid design approach" of using SOAs and related technology aspects of Web services as well as their established commonly used open standards. Hence, the interactions between the example of services shown in Fig. 9.2 are based on this aforementioned fundamental grid communication pattern and are kept out of the figure for simplicity.

9.4.2   Step 2: Collaboration with the Right Set of Vendors

The second step toward the interoperability of technologies and thus toward the interoperability of a significant fraction of the landscape of e-science infrastructures is the closest possible collaboration among the vendors interested in adopting such an aforementioned reference model. Hence, this step brings us close to areas other than computer science such as sociology and communication among individuals who represent vendors with different, but often also overlapping, interests. Although this step somehow seems pretty obvious it is often neglected and its true power in achieving agreements is usually far underestimated.

Given that, one key aspect is that the collaboration is established as early as possible. In more detail, when a group of vendors in a specific field aims to create and adopt a specific reference model that promotes interoperability, it is wise to get as many of the vendors in the field on board as early as possible. When a sub-fraction of known vendors first creates a reference model and other vendors join in later, it is very unlikely that the majority of concepts of such a model will be accepted without numerous discussions and clarifications.

One example in the field of e-science infrastructure interoperability is the standardization effort of the initial OGSA-BES specification where many commercial and academic vendors have been involved (Microsoft, Platform, UNICORE, etc.), but also several others in the e-science community have been out of the process (initially ARC, gLite, etc.) during its standardization process. That led to the fact that adoptions of OGSA-BES are still not widely deployed in several infrastructures such as the well-known EGEE infrastructure since several necessary requirements from the gLite and EGEE community are not satisfied.

One example that looks promising is standardization efforts of the OGF PGI working group wherein the majority of vendors from the e-science infrastructure community are involved as shown in Table 9.3. We assume that cloud and virtualization technologies are important but are one level lower than grid technologies and thus they do not directly affect their standardization process.

9.4.2.1 Seek First to Understand Than to Be Understood

Involving all the grid technology providers of the e-science infrastructures into the process is not enough. Equally important and challenging is the mutual understanding of the vendors during the process. Initially, the different backgrounds and unique

Table 9.3 Grid technology vendors (and projects) and their related production e-science infrastructures that participate in the OGF Production Grid Infrastructure (PGI) working group

Grid technology vendor/project	Production e-science infrastructure
ARC	NDGF
gLite	EGEE/EGI/OSG (as part of VDT)
UNICORE	DEISA/PRACE
Globus (IGE project)	TeraGrid
OMII-UK software stacks	NGS
NAREGI	NAREGI infrastructure
EDGES/EDGI	BOINC-based infrastructures (i.e., Desktop Grids)

motivations of the vendors in general and their corresponding e-science infrastructures in particular lead to a huge requirement collection. To provide one example, as part of the PGI process, all the different vendors came up with more than 200 requirements for a secure job management interface including data-staging and data management.

A closer look reveals, however, that many of these requirements in the example of PGI are duplicated since the mutual understanding about the different terms and their semantics is a true challenge in the standardization process. This is one example where communication aspects among individuals come into play in this interoperability step. In many cases, the missing common semantics about terms (e.g., sandbox, workspace, and job-space) and concepts (e.g., data-pull and client-initiated data-staging) lead to situations where long, often annoying discussions take place which end in the conclusion that all talked about "*different things*" but finally meant the "*same things.*" Here a very important guideline is to first seek to understand the other grid technology vendor before wanting to be understood.

One important aspect that can be supported by getting all the vendors on board early is the agreement process within standardization. Of course, this chapter cannot provide concrete solutions in order to reach agreements among the different grid technology vendors. Here, we refer to valuable methods known in the literature such as the so-called "*principled negotiation concept*" from R. Fisher and W.L. Ury published in their book *Getting to Yes* [17]. But a general guideline is surely to seek WIN/WIN situations where it seems to be better to adopt two concepts as part of the same standard (if possible) in parallel rather than not agreeing, leading to a specification that misses valuable concepts altogether. And if the agreement process is really about to fail, there might be some situations where voting is a meaningful option. Although not completely fair, the voting mechanism can lead to majority decisions that represent better value than leaving important crucial standardization aspects out of specifications making them potentially worthless.

Finally, there might be vendors who are invited to a standardization process (e.g., within a respective working group), but hesitate to join the efforts. In this case, we can state that one should not underestimate an agreement among the majority of vendors in one specific field such as within e-science infrastructures. Such agreement and standards that will later be used in production therefore still have a high potential to influence certain vendors to adopt the standard even after its specification process. The pressure of the community needs and the desire of the end users to choose the technologies they want can finally make a difference as well.

9.4.3   Step 3: Reference Implementations

The third step toward interoperability augments the theoretical consideration of a reference model with practical expertise of its adoption within technologies. We can thus consider this step as a complementary effort to the rather theoretical reference model design in general and the use of open standards in particular. Thus the reference implementation of the reference model and other adoptions reveals more important practical aspects than what usual theoretical architectural setups provide. We thus argue that it makes sense to develop a reference implementation during the standardization process. Although it is more cumbersome and changes often might be applied to it, the reference implementation provides clarity to theoretical thoughts and thus brings focus to the standardization process avoiding drifts into too academic and theoretical approaches.

In many cases, a reference implementation of the aforementioned reference model and its standard-based entities leads to insights where open standards can be improved for practical use. In other words, the entities and relationships in our reference model are based on open standards but in several cases these standards also need refinements. Such refinements should be based on an analysis process, which takes many different existing approaches as well as lessons learned from experimental field experience within the production grid interoperability applications as input. Expected outputs of this analysis are typically a couple of nonsupported, but required, concepts, which have the potential to significantly improve the efficiency of interoperability applications on production e-science infrastructures. In order to support these concepts within the reference model and its continuous evolution, its entities that are based on specific grid community standards should be improved by the experience that only a real implementation provides.

9.4.3.1 Include Relationships and Identify Missing Links

Since a reference model does not only emphasizes its entities (i.e., refined open grid standards in our example), the design approach should also carefully investigate the relationships between different standardization specifications. This is one of the aspects that a reference implementation of the design approach can provide. In this context, a greater reference model must be distinguished from the profiling approach, which often takes a collection of available emerging standards and defines it as a profile of these standards while often the very important relationships between them are neglected and only rarely profiled in standards. This in turn leads to so-called *missing links between standard specifications* and furthermore to a wide collection of rather small profiles that in fact are partly profiles of profiles. As a consequence, we argue that as the number of specific problem area–oriented profiles rises, the probability of having different vendors adopting the same collection of profiles significantly decreases. Although our initial experience in interoperability setups based on such profiles may be good (e.g., HPC-BP interoperability), we argue that it is still not good enough to match production infrastructure requirements.

In contrast, a production reference model design approach not only defines the relationships between its entities, but also investigates thoroughly the "*missing links between specifications."* Here the reference implementation again is a valuable step since it points in many cases to such missing links that particularly arise from different functionality areas such as data, computation, information, and most notably security. As a consequence, the core building blocks (i.e., refined standard service entities) and their links (i.e., relationships) create a reference model that defines the basic functionality required in production e-science infrastructures through a set of *"basic well-defined standard interfaces."* The reference model design approach and its reference implementation should follow the idea of *"keep it simple and standardize the essential services"* since the more complex a reference model is (e.g., OGSA), the more manifold the standard adoption will be (e.g., profiles of profiles). As a consequence, the derived reference architecture defines all the basic functionality that is required in e-science production infrastructures as *"a set of well-defined standardized service interfaces"* that must be commonly adopted by grid technology providers covering the areas of computation, data, information, and security.

To sum up, a thorough investigation of lessons learned from experimental work with early reference implementations can lead to improvements of the reference model design. As a consequence, these reference models have the potential to realize a network of interoperable grid services, which in turn realize individually formed infrastructures that are practically validated, cover essential areas (e.g., computation and data issues), and suit end users needs as shown in Fig. 9.3.

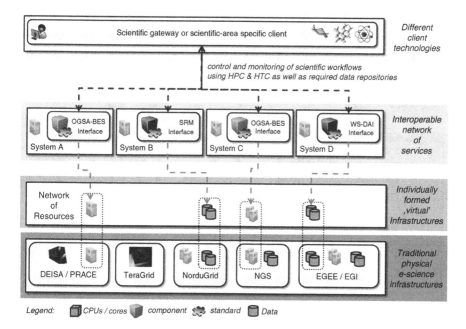

Fig. 9.3 Individually formed "virtual infrastructures" realized via the design approach of a reference model based on common open standards validated by reference implementations

9.4.4 Step 4: Standardization Feedback Ecosystem

After the rather short-term and initial steps toward interoperability in the earlier sections, this section addresses aspects from a medium-term perspective. In our specific context, this step is about working with lessons learned from adoptions of open standards that have been already partly deployed on production e-science infrastructures leading to an emerging interoperability setup among them. One example is that some middleware vendors have already deployed OGSA-BES on production e-science infrastructures like UNICORE in DEISA. In turn, this has enabled the use of these interfaces in production use cases by end users (e.g., Virtual Physiological Human (VPH) e-Health community), leading to numerous important lessons learned on how these standards can be improved.

Thus the fundamental guideline of this step is to ensure that there is a channel feeding back to the standardization activities which is not easy to establish in a meaningful way. The fundamental challenge of providing this feedback channel is that the use of standards in production e-science infrastructures is very complex and thus often covers the joint use of multiple standards at the same time. This in turn makes it difficult to channel all the different lessons learned about technology interoperability and end user experience into one working group focused on one dedicated issue (e.g., job management without security). In this sense, we argue that it makes sense to create a standardization feedback ecosystem as shown in Fig. 9.4.

Figure 9.4 illustrates one example of the aforementioned standardization feedback ecosystem in the context of OGF standards. Early adopters of open standards

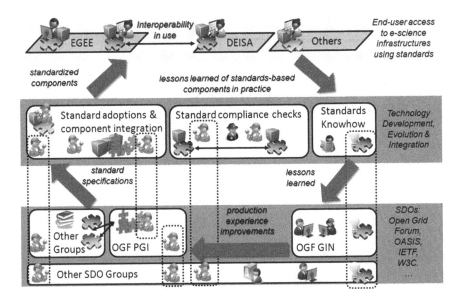

Fig. 9.4 Example of one standardization feedback system within OGF using the GIN community group and PGI working group to channel lessons learned back to standardization

work together under the umbrella of the GIN group in order to enable cross-grid applications on the production e-science infrastructures. This is thus a key element of the fourth step toward interoperability in general and the ecosystem in particular. This important element ensures that the early open standard adoptions are already used with real e-science applications from production grids and thus lead to invaluable lessons learned from the real end user perspective.

However, in terms of technical feasibility the use of early adoptions of the open standards with e-science applications goes far beyond the effectiveness that pure standard compliance checks or numerous interoperability demonstrations with *"/bin/date-based applications"* can provide. One example in this context is the standard-based demonstrations that many grid technology providers have shown in the past at the supercomputing conference series, which in the majority of cases have been only prototype-based demonstrations that do not really reflect the full use of the potential of e-science infrastructures available today.

But the guidelines within this fourth step go much further, since the aforementioned aspect is just one direction of the channel between standardization and the production e-science infrastructures. Another important direction must ensure that all the lessons learned about standard-based components in practice can lead to valuable feedback for the next iteration of specifications. This is illustrated in the second part of the red cycle on the right part of Fig. 9.4, where the know-how of using early versions of standards in practice is used by the PGI working group. The aim of such an important element of the feedback cycle (e.g., PGI) is to differentiate the concerns in terms of lessons learned from different technical areas and thus channel relevant feedback from production usage back to the corresponding working groups of the different single technical areas (e.g., computation, security, data, and information). Such a process is far underestimated in complexity.

In both the aforementioned elements it is again important that members of production grids and relevant technology vendors are part of such groups. This is very helpful because they act as mediators between complex multi-technical-area production requirements and multiple corresponding single-technical-area–focused standardization groups. We observed in the past that in several cases the latter groups are driven by academic concerns (e.g., PHD studies not related to production grids) rather than real production e-science infrastructure needs.

Finally, it is also important to have regular interactions between the channeling group (e.g., PGI) and the other corresponding standardization groups. In an ideal situation, we argue that members of the channeling group should be actively participating in the other groups and vice versa so that a fruitful collaboration can be established. Furthermore, new aspects within standardization groups can be directly addressed with individuals that have production grid experience.

In the context of our field studies WISDOM and EUFORIA, this particular step leads to numerous lessons learned of how the specific standards in context can be improved. Therefore we provide the following specific list that gives an example of how powerful this step four can be and how this is significantly increasing the suitability of open standards in real production environments.

The following table essentially lists the concepts that are relevant and thus represent a high priority arising from these specific use cases. It also briefly mentions to what extent existing standards are currently satisfactory and unsatisfactory. We therefore list concepts that need to be supported in tuned standards that are expected to be delivered by PGI and briefly explain their possible "tuning" aspects. This is one concrete outcome of the standardization feedback ecosystem (Table 9.4).

Table 9.4 List of specific standard improvements as an example when taking step four into account

Concept name	Description
Production grid-driven realistic reference model based on open standard	Although we used several standards in this drug discovery use case (OGSA-BES, JSDL, GLUE2, GridFTP, security profiles, etc.) their usage in conjunction as a whole ecosystem so to say was rather unclear. This mainly includes computing, data, security standards, as well as information flow aspects and standards. A reference model or a greater realistic reference architecture would be important.
Grid application improvements	Grid application job descriptions satisfied basic needs in this use case but were not satisfactory enough to describe an application in this multigrid setup. Some improvements covering but not limited to application-type classification (e.g., parallel), application-type refinements (e.g., pre-installed, submitted), revised application executable definition, application software statements, application family extension (e.g., LIBRARY), application software requirements, application output joins, etc.
Application execution adjacencies	In this workflow, we had several challenges in the execution environment itself. Thus we need better support of scientific application executions with standard-based information aspects on the lowest possible level (i.e., resource management system level) covering but not limited to common environment variables, common execution modules, execution module characteristics.
High performance computing extensions to open standards	While executions using CREAM-BES on EGEE had been relatively acceptable, submission with UNICORE-BES to DEISA lacked important HPC specific information. Therefore, we seek to submit and execute applications more efficiently than currently possible with GLUE2, JSDL, or OGSA-BES covering aspects but not limited to network topology (torus, global tree, Ethernet, etc.), shape reservation (x X y X z), network information enhancements, available shape characteristics, high message support, task/core mapping definition, available task/core mappings, etc.

(continued)

Table 9.4 (continued)

Concept name	Description
Sequence support for computational jobs	An analysis of lessons learned obtained from the WISDOM use case leads to specific missing features encountered during production grid interoperability with respect to the support of automatically started pre- and post-processing functionalities within JSDL using different application execution modes. AMBER, for instance, consists of a set of applications (~80 executables) and some of them are used to transform input data in a suitable format for production runs and/or transform outputs in several other formats necessary for further analysis. Of course, these transformation and short running pre-processing steps should be executed in a serial mode, while the actual corresponding molecular dynamic simulation is executed in a parallel mode. Pre-job sequences (pre-processing, compilation), post-job sequences (post-processing).
Manual data-staging support	Use cases revealed that in many cases the scientists require a more flexible mechanism during data-staging processes in order to better coordinate distributed data and computation. This is true, irrespective of whether data are transported to where the computational resource resides, or if computation is decomposed and job submissions are performed toward the location of data or even a hybrid of both methods is adopted. One example is the careful manual data input selection (aka manual data-staging) from the outcome of the EGEE workflow step in order to use only good results for the time-constrained workflow step in DEISA.

9.4.5   Step 5: Aligned Future Strategies and Roadmaps

The fifth step toward interoperability is about the alignment of future strategies among different grid technology providers. In many cases we observe that interoperability could have been reached by design if the corresponding technology providers would have worked together on a roadmap. In this sense, this step goes one level further than the fourth step about standardization in terms of an even closer collaboration between technology providers. While in academically driven e-science this is straightforward with regard to collaboration among scientists we acknowledge that such collaboration might be problematic in the field of business where exposing future designs might lead to risks in terms of time-to-market.

In step five, we clearly state the demand to align whole technology roadmaps about planned components or future strategies on developments. This is different from working together in standardization groups to define a couple of interfaces or protocols for components that are already designed or already in production and are subject to being re-factored toward the support of open standards. The benefit of this step toward interoperability lies in taking advantage of the different experiences of the technology providers as well as their special dedicated focus within technologies. The alignment of future strategies enables better harmonization among the components deployed and used on e-science infrastructures. In other words, aligned roadmaps enable the use of components from one technology provider by different components of another technology provider and vice versa.

One example of this step can be currently observed in the transition period of EGEE toward EGI and one of its major technology providers, EMI. EMI in turn is an umbrella of three distinct grid middleware technologies used on various e-science infrastructures and these are gLite (used in EGEE), ARC (used by NDGF), and UNICORE (used by DEISA). Within EMI these middleware providers collaborate in terms of aligning future strategies and technology roadmaps and thus jointly define the design of the next generation of grid technologies used in e-science for the next decade in Europe. This was different in the past where UNICORE was particularly focused on a design that satisfied HPC end users in DEISA and where gLite was focused on satisfying the needs of HTC-driven and data-oriented end users within EGEE.

But the aforementioned difference in focus and uniqueness in supporting different technological aspects or computational paradigms is one of the major benefits of the alignment process within EMI. UNICORE has been used for 10 years in HPC while gLite requires HPC support at the present, and thus would it not be wise to cooperate when 10 years of experience are available? The support for large-scale distributed data management in UNICORE can be improved while gLite has experience with this for over 10 years now. In addition, new technologies can be made interoperable by designs such as a common grid registry or support for messaging.

9.4.6   Step 6: Harmonized Operation Policies

So far untouched is another very important factor regarding policies in moving toward full interoperability between e-science infrastructures. In this context, it is important to understand the difference between what is possible in terms of technology interoperability and what is possible in terms of interoperability governed by policies of production e-science infrastructures. Full operational interoperability can only be achieved when the technology-based interoperability is present but harmonized operation policies also exist. The latter is a difficult topic where a concrete solution cannot be given here, but some elaboration of the problem might lead to aspects in policy definition and change that promote interoperability.

The guidance of this step is thus oriented toward the creation of dedicated groups that work on the harmonization of operational policies. To provide one example, the field of security is always an important challenge, not only on the technological side but also on the level of policies. Therefore, the Joint Security Policy Group (JSPG) comprises members of many difficult e-science infrastructures such as EGEE, DEISA, NDGF, OSG, and others. The outcome of this group complements the activities of the Middleware Security Group (MWSG), which is more focused on technology interoperability but has members of the same production infrastructures. But *"who is really allowed"* remains a policy decision.

Nevertheless, apart from building such groups a concrete guidance cannot be given here and thus we can only point to certain known methods that leave the field of e-science such as the known Harvard Concept (i.e., *"getting to yes"* [17]) by Fisher. We can only emphasize on the importance of harmonized operation policies and necessary agreements among the production e-science infrastructures in various fields like security, resource usage, and information, to list a few. Agreements can often be reached by the openness of decision-makers and in some cases agreements can be significantly supported by technology improvements.

One example of the aforementioned aspects is the EUFORIA project that represents one large fraction of the ITER fusion community. E-Scientists of this community would like to use EGEE for HTC-based computations while they prefer DEISA for large-scale HPC application runs. The EUFORIA framework to access different e-science infrastructures is largely based on proxies that have been in the past neither supported by UNICORE nor accepted by the DEISA infrastructure. But more recently, EUFORIA has used EGEE and DEISA resources jointly with their EUFORIA framework. In this case, the agreement in terms of DEISA security policies was supported by technology improvements. UNICORE was enhanced with optional proxy support and UNICORE significantly increased its possibility to express more detailed policies (with XACML [18]). Given that, policies can be defined in such a way that only end users from EUFORIA are allowed to use proxies while all others have to use their full certificates.

9.4.7 Step 7: Funding Sources and Cross-Project Coordination

The final step toward a sustained interoperability of worldwide production e-science infrastructures is clearly in the synergy of funding sources and cross-project coordination, which are tightly linked in many ways. In fact, we can observe that the reason for many non-interoperable technologies deployed on production e-science infrastructures either lies in different funding sources or that it is developed in different funded projects. The ideal situation would be clearly to have a joint source of funding and not project-based (i.e., time-limited) funding, which in turn would lead to more sustainable planning. Nevertheless, we respect the reality of the given funding models and just point to known issues to raise the awareness that fully sustained interoperability of academically driven e-science infrastructures goes partly beyond the control areas of project-based infrastructure and technology providers.

A first example addressing the different funding sources can be found in taking a closer look at the technologies of UNICORE and Globus. In many technological aspects UNICORE and Globus are quite similar or could at least benefit from a very close collaboration, but they have been developed over a decade by different funding sources, which are NSF for Globus in the United States and EC for UNICORE in

Europe. This has led to non-interoperable solutions in the past, which can be at least partly explained by the different funding sources. Both will collaborate more closely as a result of the EU project collaboration of EMI and the IGE project, which represents Globus in Europe. Hence, the collaboration is supported by one dedicated European project that bridges the NSF-funded Globus projects in the United States.

In order to sustain the efforts of the previous six steps, it is therefore necessary that decision-makers in different funding sources collaborate (i.e., NSF and EC) or dedicated projects should be in place that enable the coordination to reach out to projects that are funded by different sources (e.g., IGE and Globus). In our particular example, this means an exchange of ideas and the funding roadmap on the one hand and the prioritization of the use and adoption of common open standards on the other hand. This collaboration ensures interoperability among different funding sources in general and a way of promoting interoperability using open standards in the grid technologies in particular. The latter method concerning standardization is at the time of writing the most promising way since the different funding sources and models are not likely to change in the next few years.

The second example addresses the requirement to collaborate across projects since the current funding models lead to numerous different projects. The example of step five with EMI was project-internal and promotes collaboration across different technology providers in only one project. In contrast, step seven emphasizes the demand of collaborating across project borders using clear project-delivery roadmaps that puts the project in the larger landscape of the community. The EU SIENA project is one example that takes this role of coordination.

9.5 Conclusions and Summary

This chapter introduced an important new key design pattern used by several applications of production e-science infrastructures such as EGI and DEISA/PRACE. This design pattern is an algorithm that jointly uses the computational paradigms HTC and HPC and their corresponding different infrastructures. We learned that the non-interoperable e-science infrastructures can be classified using the computational paradigms HTC and HPC. The lack of interoperability of these infrastructures in turn leads to several limitations in jointly using infrastructures that the aforementioned algorithm requires and thus decreases the applicability of performing new forms of science with e-science infrastructures.

Interoperability of technologies has been a problem area since many decades in general and since the beginning of grids in particular. Overcoming the interoperability problem means tackling several challenges on different levels (technological and policy-wide) and often relates to the problem of getting to an agreement among different technology or infrastructure providers. In the beginning, we briefly surveyed many approaches to solve this problem and we can conclude that open standards are the key in combination with an effective process that has the potential to create sustainable solutions for this problem for decades to come.

The seven steps toward interoperability for e-science that have been described in this chapter aim to provide such an aforementioned process in order to give technology developers and research infrastructures (e.g., ESFRI) guidance on how interoperability problems can be tackled. They are all only steps toward interoperability and do not intend to provide full solutions. Another view would be to see them as different "access points" on how to reach interoperability solutions or how to increase the chances of interoperability between e-science infrastructures.

Although one might argue that the seven steps toward the interoperability of grid technologies are obsolete by the new cloud paradigm, we rather believe they are still relevant even when certain technologies/infrastructures are exchanged with, and influenced by, emerging cloud-based technologies. All in all, this chapter is about the process as a guide toward technology interoperability making only very specific examples in the context of grids as these have been the source of experience as a new form of distributed systems in the last decade.

Whatever will appear in the near future with academically driven grids and enterprise-oriented clouds as infrastructures, the majority – if not all – steps will also play a significant role in achieving interoperability between upcoming new designs in distributed systems. We thus strongly encourage developers as well as decision-makers to take the seven steps of this chapter into account and adopt them to their corresponding field of research infrastructures, technology environment, or market situation.

References

1. M. Riedel, A.S. Memon, M.S. Memon, D. Mallmann, A. Streit, F.Wolf, Th. Lippert, V. Venturi, P. Andreetto, M. Marzolla, A. Ferraro, A. Ghiselli, F. Hedman, Zeeshan A. Shah, J. Salzemann, A. Da Costa, V. Breton, V. Kasam, M. Hofmann-Apitius, D. Snelling, S. van de Berghe, V. Li, S. Brewer, A. Dunlop, N. De Silva; Improving e-Science with Interoperability of the e-Infrastructures EGEE and DEISA; Proceedings of the 31st International Convention MIPRO, Conference on Grid and Visualization Systems (GVS), May 2008, Opatija, Croatia, Croatian Society for Information and Communication Technology, Electronics and Microelectronics, ISBN 978-953-233-036-6, pages 225–231
2. M. S. Memon, M. Riedel, A. S. Memon, F. Wolf, A. Streit, Th. Lippert, Marcin Plociennik, Michal Owsiak, David Tskhakaya, Christian Konz, Lessons learned from jointly using HTC- and HPC-driven e-science infrastructures in Fusion Science, proceedings of the IEEE ICIET 2010 Conference, Pakistan
3. Scott, Philip J: Meeting the challenges of healthcare interoperability, in Healthcare IT Management, Vol. 4, Issue 3, 2009, ISSN: 1782–8406
4. ESFRI Roadmap, ISBN 978-92-79-10117-5, European Communities, 2008
5. Gardner, Henry; Manduchi, Gabriele; Design Patterns for e-science, Springer 2007, ISBN: 978-3-540-68088-8
6. Taylor, J.: enhanced-Science (e-Science) Definition, http://www.e-science.clrc.ac.uk
7. Foster, I: The Grid 2 – Blueprint for a New Computing Infrastructure, Elsevier, ISBN: 1-55860-933-4
8. M. Riedel, F. Wolf, D. Kranzlmüller, A. Streit, T. Lippert, Research Advances by using Interoperable e-Science Infrastructures – The Infrastructure Interoperability Reference Model applied in e-Science, Journal of Cluster Computing, Special Issue Recent Advances in e-Science, Cluster Computing (2009) Vol. 12, No. 4, pp. 357–372, DOI 10.1007/s10586-009-0102-2

9. M. Riedel, E. Laure, Th. Soddemann, L. Field, JP Navarro, J. Casey, M. Litmaath, J.Ph.Baud, B. Koblitz, C. Catlett, D. Skow, C. Zheng, P.M. Papadopoulos, M. Katz, N. Sharma, O. Smirnova, B. Kónya, P. Arzberger, F. Würthwein, A.S. Rana, T. Martin, M. Wan, V. Welch, T. Rimovsky, S. Newhouse, A. Vanni, Y. Tanaka, Y. Tanimura, T. Ikegami, D. Abramson, C. Enticott, G. Jenkins, R. Pordes, N. Sharma, S. Timm, N. Sharma, G. Moont, M. Aggarwal, D. Colling, O. van der Aa, A. Sim, V. Natarajan, A. Shoshani, J. Gu, S. Chen, G. Galang, R. Zappi, L. Magnoni, V.Ciaschini, M. Pace, V. Venturi, M. Marzolla, P. Andreetto, B. Cowles, S. Wang, Y. Saeki, H. Sato, S. Matsuoka, P. Uthayopas, S. Sriprayoonsakul, O. Koeroo, M. Viljoen, L. Pearlman, S. Pickles, David Wallom, G. Moloney, J. Lauret, J. Marsteller, P. Sheldon, S. Pathak, S. De Witt, J. Mencák, J. Jensen, M.. Hodges, D. Ross, S. Phatanapherom, G. Netzer, A.R. Gregersen, M.Jones, S. Chen, P. Kacsuk, A. Streit, D. Mallmann, F. Wolf, Th. Lippert, Th. Delaitre, E. Huedo, N. Geddes, Interoperation of World-Wide Production e-Science Infrastructures, Concurrency and Computation: Practice and Experience, 21 (2009) 8, 961–990

10. International Grid Interoperability and Interoperation Workshop (IGIIW) 2007, 2008, Online:http://www.fz-juelich.de/jsc/igiiw

11. M. Riedel and G. Terstyanszky, Grid Interoperability for e-Researc, Journal of Grid Computing Vol. 7, No. 3, September 2009, pp. 285–286, DOI 10.1007/s10723-009-9138-z

12. OASIS Reference Model for Service Oriented Architecture 1.0, Official OASIS Standard, 2006

13. Jordan, C., et al.: Defining the Grid: A Roadmap for OGSA Standards v.1.1. OGF Grid Final Document Nr. 123 (2008)

14. Armstrong, R., Toward a Common Component Architecture for High-Performance Scientific Computing, 1999

15. OASIS TC OpenSCA, http://www.oasis-opencsa.org/sca

16. C. Bratosin, W. v.d. Aalst, N. Sidorova, N. Trcka, A Reference Model for Grid Architectures and its Analysis, LNCS, Vol. 5331/2008, pp. 898–913

17. Fisher, Roger, & Ury, William. 1981 Getting to yes: negotiating agreement without giving in / Roger Fisher and William Ury; with Bruce Patton, editor Houghton Mifflin, Boston

18. Moses, T., et al.: eXtensible Access Control Markup Language. OASIS Standard (2005)

Chapter 10
Trustworthy Distributed Systems Through Integrity-Reporting

Jun Ho Huh and Andrew Martin

Abstract With the growing influence of e-Science, substantial quantities of research are being facilitated, recorded, and reported by means of distributed computing. As a result, the scope for malicious intervention continues to grow and so do the rewards available to those able to steal the models and data that have significant commercial value. Researchers are often reluctant to exploit the full benefits of distributed computing because they fear the compromise of their sensitive data or the uncertainty of the returned results. In this chapter, we propose two types of trustworthy distributed systems – one suitable for a computational system and the other for a distributed data system. Central to these systems is the novel idea of *configuration resolver*, which, in both designs, is responsible for filtering trustworthy hosts and ensuring that jobs are dispatched to those considered trustworthy. Furthermore, the *blind analysis server* enables statistical analyses to be performed on sensitive raw data – collected from multiple sites – without disclosing it to anyone.

10.1 Introduction

In recent years, distributed systems have enjoyed a huge burst of popularity, most chiefly in the commodity computing model described as 'Cloud Computing'. The term applies to a broad range of systems architectures, often categorised under the headings of Software/Platform/Infrastructure as a Service – and perhaps also subsumes one of its progenitors 'Grid computing'.

A clear driver for such adoption is the benefit of using shared resources: Load can be balanced across large numbers of hosts, peaks easily accommodated, and massive initiatives run as background tasks on systems which would otherwise be idle. To these is now added a 'green' agenda – that by taking advantage of economies of scale

J.H. Huh (✉) and A. Martin
Oxford University Computing Laboratory, Parks Road, Oxford OX1 3QD, UK
e-mail: jun.huh@kellogg.ox.ac.uk; andrew.martin@kellogg.ox.ac.uk

Xiaoyu Yang et al. (eds.), *Guide to e-Science: Next Generation Scientific Research and Discovery*, Computer Communications and Networks,
DOI 10.1007/978-0-85729-439-5_10, © Springer-Verlag London Limited 2011

and careful location of data centres, the 'carbon footprint' of any given computational task can be minimised.

Demand for such models of computing also arises from unprecedented volumes of data for processing. Evidence-based science, and basic observations 'born digital' are driving this, as is closer scrutiny of results, giving rise to strong requirements on provenance, accurate data acquisition and integrity in processing. This pattern is repeated across government, business, social networking and more. Some applications give rise to more esoteric requirements, such as 'digital rights management' for all kinds of data, and elaborate rules for combining policies where several such managed data sources are merged – perhaps within a 'blind analysis' combination where neither data owner is permitted to see the other's raw data, but both are interested in the results.

All of this takes place against a background of everincreasing sophistication in attacks. Precisely because there are so many high-value digital assets being brought into existence, there are also many attackers seeking to subvert them. There is much money to be made from subverting online business and much political capital to be gained from manipulating certain scientific results. Even as processes are more transparent, there is ever more motivation to 'tweak' results just slightly in order to achieve a better result.

Our focus in this chapter is to explore how technologies allied to *Trusted Computing* can help to address these challenges, through the use of soundly based practically feasible architectures and designs. In the following section, we survey some motivating examples, and describe our perspective on the special challenges they represent: These requirements are summarised in Sect. 10.3. In Sect. 10.4, we present a sketch of the existing technologies for trust and virtualization which will form the basis of our architectures. This puts us in a position to discuss in Sect. 10.5 the ways that other authors have proposed for using those technologies in a grid context – and the measure of consensus achieved in such accounts so far. Section 10.6 surveys the remaining gaps.

In Sect. 10.7, we present our own substantive contribution: designs for trustworthy distributed systems, using in particular our concept of a *configuration resolver* to broker data about acceptable trustworthy system configurations. After this, we evaluate those designs against the requirements from Sect. 10.3. Section 10.9 is a different form of evaluation: a consideration of how these technologies could be deployed within the UK's *National Grid Service*. Our conclusions and discussion of future work are at Sect. 10.10.

10.2 Motivating Examples

The domains of *e-Science* and *e-Health* provide us with good examples for motivation: They are somewhat more accessible than many other domains where confidentiality (of designs) is of greater concern. The following examples serve to illustrate the common security problems of sharing computational resources or aggregating distributed data within a virtual organisation.

10.2.1 *climateprediction.net and Condor Grids*

The first example application arises with the climate*prediction*.net project [1], which functions by distributing a high-quality climate model to thousands of participants around the world. It stands (or falls) on its ability to ensure the accuracy of the climate prediction methods and collected data. As a politically charged field, it could become a target for moderately sophisticated attackers to subvert the results.

This project highlights a common dual pair of problems:

1. From the participant's (resource provider) perspective, the untrusted code runs on their trusted system; they need to be convinced that the code is not malicious, and the middleware used by the code (if any) is trustworthy.
2. From the scientist's perspective, their trusted job is executed in an untrusted host without any assurance of the running environment; this host might return arbitrary or fabricated results never having run the original code, or steal their sensitive models and data.

Such *volunteer computing* models represent one of the most challenging possible environments for computational integrity – but also one of the greatest possible assets for their task. At its peak, for example, climate*prediction*.net was by some measure the largest computational climate model in the world. Some tasks are amenable to duplication – so that if participants return fake results, these are discovered by comparison with those from elsewhere – but this is plainly a waste of computational resources.

Similar threats undermine the security of a Condor system [2] which allows relatively smaller jobs to be distributed in a Campus Grid setting [3]. To mitigate the second problem, it provides a digital certificate infrastructure for the scientist to identify resource/service providers and vice versa. Without robust mechanisms to safeguard the keys from theft, however, this solution offers only a modest improvement over legacy architectures. Moreover, rogue administrators might replace the compute nodes with malicious ones, tamper with them, or subvert their security configurations to steal sensitive data and/or return fabricated results.

Even grids or clouds constructed from nodes within a managed data-centre are subject to the same concerns: The system manager may be subverted by a competitor (through straightforward bribery, or through some sophisticated Trojan).

10.2.2 *Healthcare Grids*

In 'e-Health', it is not hard to imagine instances where the clinical data is highly sensitive, and only the processed subsets may be released; nor is it hard to imagine scenarios where reconciliation of data from different sources is needed, but neither clinic trusts the other to see the raw data. Such data cannot normally be made available outside the healthcare trust where it is collected, except under strict ethics committee guidance, generally involving *anonymisation* of records before release [4].

Nevertheless, anonymisation reduces the amount of information available, precision of estimates and flexibility of analysis; and as a result, bias can be introduced [5]. For example,[1] a researcher might be looking at association between age, diet and progression of colon cancer, and is aware that the risk immensely increases when one reaches the age of 50. Patient records for the first two attributes would be accessed through a GP practice and the third through a specialist clinic. The National Health Service (NHS) number [7] uniquely identifies a patient across the grid to enable the linking of data. In this scenario, a graph plotted with anonymised age – '30–35', '35–40' ... '65–70' – is likely to miss out the important micro-trends all together; in fact, these would be better observed with datasets closer to age 50. A supporting graph plotted with the *actual age*, say, between 45 and 55, would show these trends more clearly and improve the quality of the results.

Moreover, this distributed query would require a concrete identifier, such as the NHS number, to join patient records collected from the GP and specialist clinic. In reality, however, it is unlikely that either would give out such potential identifiable information without the necessary confidentiality guarantees. Hashing NHS number can provide some assurance, but it would still be vulnerable to brute force attacks. These problems require a trustworthy application to perform *blind* reconciliation and analysis of the data from mutually untrusting security domains: The researcher would only see this application running and the end results; the raw data should never be accessible to the researcher.

10.3 Security Requirements

The motivational examples have in common a likely reliance upon technical measures of security aimed at substantially enhancing protection for job/result integrity and confidentiality. Mindful of the security challenges discussed from these examples, this section identifies a set of security requirements for designing trustworthy distributed systems.

1. *Secure job submission*: Both the integrity and confidentiality of the job secrets should be protected upon job submission. Attackers should not be able to steal or tamper with the job secrets that are being transferred via untrusted midddleware services.
2. *Authorisation policy management*: When the job arrives at the participant system, the job owner's rights should be evaluated against the authorisation policies. The job should only be processed further if the job owner is authorised to run their queries or codes on the participant system.
3. *Trustworthy execution environment*: A trustworthy job execution environment should be provided – the jobs should be executed free from any unauthorised interference (e.g. attempts to modify data access query or model code), and the

---

[1] This example has been developed with help from David Power and Mark Slaymaker who are involved in the GIMI project [6], and Peter Lee who is an intern at the Auckland Hospital.

confidentiality of the job secrets should be protected from processes running outside this environment. The user, before submitting the job, should be able to verify that this trustworthy execution environment is guaranteed at the participant system. Similarly, the participant should be ensured that only a verified, integrity-protected environment is used in their system for executing the jobs.

4. *Job isolation*: The jobs should be isolated from each other and from the host. This is to prevent rogue jobs from compromising the host, or stealing the secrets and results of other jobs running in the same host. Job isolation should also prevent a malicious host from compromising the job integrity, confidentiality and availability.

5. *Protecting the results*: The integrity and confidentiality of the results should be protected from adversaries, malicious hosts and jobs trying to corrupt/read the results.

6. *Digital rights management*: In distributed data systems, unauthorised access or modification of sensitive data should be prohibited, wherever they may be processed.

7. *Blind analysis of data*: The raw data should not be disclosed to the end user. Only the processed, anonymised results should be made accessible for analysis.

10.4   Trusted Computing and Virtualization

The security requirements strongly indicate the need for the user to verify integrity of remote job execution environments, and the data owner to retain control over their data regardless of the system to which it migrates.

Faced with the prospect of modern PCs (and other devices) having so much software that their behaviour is unpredictable and easily subverted, the Trusted Computing Group [8] has developed a series of technologies based around a Trusted Platform Module (TPM) – a hardware chip embedded in the motherboard – which helps to provide two novel capabilities [9]: a cryptographically strong identity and reporting mechanism for the platform, and a means to *measure* the software loaded during the platform's boot process. These include, for example, the BIOS, bootloader, operating system and applications (see Fig. 10.1). Further details of the TPM's functionality are defined in the TPM Main Specification [10] published by the Trusted Computing Group.

Measurements are taken by calculating a cryptographic hash of binaries before they are executed. Hashes are stored in Platform Configuration Registers (PCRs) in the TPM. They can only be modified through special TPM ordinals, and the PCRs are never directly written to; rather, measurements can only be *extended* by an entity. This is to ensure that no other entity can just modify or overwrite the measured value. A 20-byte hash of the new measurement is generated based on the PCR's current value concatenated with the new input, and a SHA-1 performed on this concatenated value.

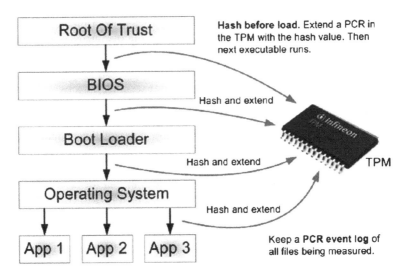

Fig. 10.1 Authenticated boot

A PCR can be either static or dynamic. A static PCR can reset only when the TPM itself resets – the PCR cannot be reset independently. Static PCRs are normally used to store the measurements. The chapter refers to a static PCR whenever a PCR is mentioned. A dynamic PCR, on the other hand, can be reset independently from the TPM, so long as the process resetting the PCR is under sufficient protection. We refer to such dynamic PCRs as 'resettable PCRs'.

In a trustworthy system, every executable piece of code in the *authenticated boot* process will be measured and PCRs extended sequentially (*transitive trust*). The notion of transitive trust provides a way for a relying party to trust a large group of entities from a single root of trust: The trust is extended by measuring the next entity before it is loaded, storing the measurement in the TPM, and passing the control to the measured entity (see Fig. 10.1).

Hence, any malicious piece of code (e.g. a rootkit) executed during the boot process will also be recorded and identified. A 'PCR event log' is created during boot process and stores all of the measured values (and a description for each) externally to the TPM. These values can be extended in software to validate the contents of the event log. The resulting hash can be compared against the reported, signed PCR value to see if the event log is correct.

10.4.1 Sealed Storage

Trusted computing provides the means to *seal* (encrypt) data so that it will only successfully decrypt when the platform measurements are in a particular state [9]. The seal process takes external data (information the TPM is going to protect) and a specified PCR value, encrypts the data internally to the TPM using a *storage key* and creates a sealed data package.

An application – responsible for keeping track of this package – sends the package back to the TPM to recover the data. A nonce, known only to an individual TPM, is also included in the package to ensure that only the TPM responsible for creating the package can unseal it.

The whole purpose of sealing is to prevent any unauthorised attempt to unseal the package. The TPM enforces two restrictions upon decrypting the sealed package:

- It ensures that the package is only available on the TPM that created it – the TPM checks whether the nonce included in the package matches the one held internally.
- It compares the current PCR value to the specified PCR value stored in the sealed package – the operation aborts if these values do not match.

The implication is that the external data only becomes available to an application when the correct value (an acceptable platform configuration) is in the specified PCR. Section 10.7 discusses the use of sealing to protect sensitive data from a malicious/compromised host.

10.4.2   Remote Attestation

Sealed storage provides a high degree of assurance that the data is only available if the acceptable configuration is present. But how does an external application – that has not performed the seal operation – know that such a configuration is present in a remote platform? Trusted computing provides the means to undertake *remote attestation* [9]: proving to a third party that (in the absence of hardware tampering) a remote platform is in a particular software state.

Remote attestation involves the TPM reporting PCR value(s) that are digitally signed with TPM-generated 'Attestation Identity Keys' (AIKs), and allowing others to validate the signature and the PCR contents. The application wanting to attest its current platform configuration would call the TPM_Quote command specifying a set of PCR values to quote, an AIK to digitally sign the quote, and a nonce to ensure its freshness. The TPM validates the authorisation secret of the AIK, signs the specified PCRs internally with the private half of the AIK and returns the digitally signed quote.

The external application validates the signature by using the public half of the AIK, and validates the AIK with the AIK credential – a certificate issued by a trusted Certificate Authority (a 'Privacy CA') which states the platform has a valid TPM. The PCR log entries are then compared against a list of 'known-good' values to check if the reported PCRs represent an acceptable configuration. This list is often referred to as an 'application whitelist'.

Attestation can be used on a platform that supports authenticated boot (see Fig. 10.1) to verify that only known pieces of software are running on it.

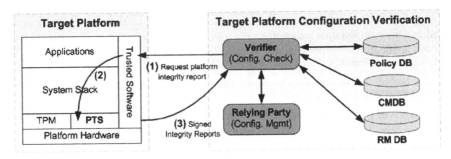

Fig. 10.2 TCG's runtime attestation model

Additions or modifications to any executable will be recorded during the boot process, and noticed when log entries and PCR values are checked. With such mechanisms in place, the external application can, in theory, identify whether a remote platform has been compromised by a malware or not.

10.4.3 Runtime Attestation Model

Figure 10.2 gives an overview of the Trusted Computing Group's runtime attestation model [11]. In a trusted platform, the Platform Trust Services (PTS) provide the capability to select hardware and software components to be measured during the authenticated boot process. They are also responsible for computing the measurements of the selected components and the creation of an integrity-report containing these measurements. The Verifier checks the incoming integrity-reports using the Policy Database, Configuration Management Database (CMDB), and Reference Manifest (RM) Database. These databases hold known-good configurations for platforms. If an attesting platform has an unknown or unexpected configuration, the Verifier informs the Relying Parties not to trust this platform.

The proposed systems in Sect. 10.7 are inspired by this runtime attestation model. Each administrative domain is managed by a central Verifier – which we have called the 'configuration resolver' – that checks the configurations of the participant platforms when they first register with the Verifier. Only those verified to be trustworthy become available to the Relying Party (the end users).

10.4.4 Virtualization

Virtualization is a key technology used in many trusted computing solutions to provide strong isolation for the trusted (TPM-measured) applications – this combination is referred to as 'trusted virtualization'. Virtualization allows a single physical host to share the computing resources between multiple operating systems [12, 13].

Each operating system runs in a Virtual Machine (VM) of its own, where it is made to believe that it has dedicated access to the hardware. A virtual machine is also referred to as a 'compartment'.

A thin layer of software called a Virtual Machine Monitor (VMM) operates on top of the hardware to isolate virtual machines and mediate all access to the physical hardware and peripherals. A virtual machine runs on a set of virtual devices that are accessed through virtual device drivers. Typically, a highly privileged 'monitor virtual machine' is created at boot time and serves to manage other virtual machines.

Numerous design efforts have been made to remove avoidable inter-virtual-machine communication mechanisms such as might be exploited to undermine the isolation guarantees. The aim is to make a virtual machine behave in the same way (and have the same properties) as a physically isolated machine. In such designs, the virtual machine monitor ensures that all memory is cleared before being real-located and each virtual machine has its own dedicated memory and disc space. Both Intel and AMD processors now provide hardware support for full, efficient virtualization [14, 15]. With the help from these processors, the virtual machine monitor can simulate a complete hardware environment for an unmodified operating system to run and use identical sets of instructions as the host. Hardware virtualization can also speed up the execution of virtual machines by minimising the virtualization overhead.

The majority of current grid middleware solutions, including the Globus Toolkit [16], rely on operating systems' access control mechanisms to manage isolation between user accounts. For example, operating system–enforced access control policies prevent malicious software (installed by a third party unknown to the host) from gaining unauthorised access to the jobs running under different user accounts. However, millions of lines of code contained in a mainstream operating system must be trusted to enforce these policies correctly [17]. A single security bug in any one of the privileged components might be enough for an attacker to hijack it, elevate its privileges and take control of the host and the jobs running inside.

Virtualization, on the other hand, is capable of providing much stronger isolation through the relatively smaller virtual machine monitor and monitor virtual machine [18]. A malware (through privilege escalation) would have to compromise both components – which are designed to resist such attacks – in order to break the isolation [19]. In a trustworthy, virtualized system, these two components (as well as other trusted software) would be measured during authenticated boot and their integrity would be reported through attestation.

A few authors [20, 21] have discussed the benefits of isolating the jobs and trusted applications in their own virtual machines:

- Job isolation prevents a rogue job from compromising the host or other jobs running in the same host.
- In-memory attacks aimed at modifying the behaviour of the trusted applications are made more difficult.
- Privilege-escalation attacks are limited to the isolation boundaries of a virtual machine.

10.5   An Emergent Consensus View

Great strides have been made in using trusted virtualization to design security architectures that aim to satisfy the requirements identified in Sect. 10.3. This section
identifies similarities between these trusted virtualization approaches, establishes an
'emergent consensus view' (see Fig. 10.3) and demonstrates its shortcomings in the
areas of platform configuration discovery/verification and provision of trustworthy
execution environment.

10.5.1   Attestation Tokens and Sealed Key Approach

The term 'attestation token' is commonly used to describe a participant's credentials
[22, 23]. Typically, it contains the participant's platform configurations and the
public half of a non-migratable TPM-key. The private half is bound to the platform's
TPM and PCR values corresponding to its trusted computing base. Information
contained in an attestation token should be sufficient for a user to verify the identity
and trustworthiness of the platform.

   Löhr et al. [22] combine the Perseus virtualization framework and remote attestation to propose a Trusted Grid Architecture. In the Trusted Grid Architecture,
users collect attestation tokens of service providers, and verify their platform
configurations using a locally managed whitelist (see Fig. 10.3). Upon job submission, the job secret is encrypted with a service provider's public key (obtained from
their attestation token), guaranteeing that only a securely configured platform will
be able to access the private key and decrypt it. If the service provider's trusted
computing base has changed, the private key will no longer be accessible to process
the job further.

   The virtualization layer is extended to include services that support secure job transfer and execution. Grid jobs are transferred across an encrypted, integrity-protected

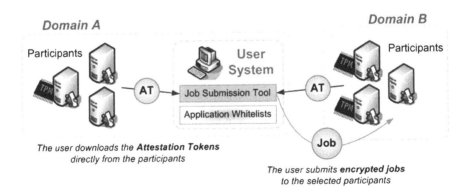

Fig. 10.3 A consensus view

communication channel established with trusted middleware components, and their data is written to disc using a secure storage service. The attestation service uses the attestation token to verify the state of the trusted software layer prior to submitting the job data. The job data is encrypted using the public key (obtained from the token) so that only a securely configured software layer can decrypt it and execute the job.

The Trusted Grid Architecture, however, provides no mechanism for verifying integrity of the job execution virtual machine and the returned results. It also fails to isolate amply the trusted components. Most of its security controls are enforced in a virtual machine that also contains a large amount of untrusted software. For example, the grid management service runs in the same compartment as the storage encryption service. This extra complexity increases the likelihood of vulnerabilities and makes attestation less meaningful. Moreover, the chapter does not discuss how the users collect the attestation tokens and how the application whitelists are managed in a distributed environment.

Due to the lack of useful semantic (including security) information that can be conveyed through the standard binary attestation, many [24, 25] have suggested the use of 'property-based attestation' [26] to report more security-relevant information. Security-relevant properties of the platform are attested rather than the binary measurements of the software. In consequence, trust decisions made based on integrity-reports are simplified.

10.5.2   Grid Middleware Isolation

Cooper and Martin [27] make a strong argument that the complex grid middleware services, which usually have a high likelihood of vulnerabilities, cannot be trusted to secure the users' data and credentials. For example, at least five different vulnerabilities had been found in the Globus Toolkit [16] that allow unauthorised users to compromise the middleware [27].

In the architecture proposed by Cooper and Martin, the middleware stack is isolated in an untrusted compartment of its own and is not relied upon to perform trusted operations. As a result, even if an attacker manages to compromise the middleware, they would not have gained sufficient privileges to undermine the security of a distributed system.

10.5.3   Job Isolation

The use of virtual machine isolation has been discussed many times as a solution to the 'malicious host problem' [24, 27, 28]. Typically, a job runs on a separate, dedicated virtual machine, where its code is executed free from unauthorised interference. The job secrets are decrypted inside the virtual machine and protected from rogue virtual machines or host. From a participant's perspective, job isolation could also protect their host from rogue jobs [29].

Terra [30] is a virtualization architecture developed on the VMware virtualization platform [12]. VMware is modified to support encrypted and integrity-protected discs. Using their trusted virtual machine monitor, existing applications can either run in a standard virtual machine, or in a 'closed-box' virtual machine that provides the functionality of running on a dedicated closed platform. The trusted virtual machine monitor protects confidentiality and integrity of the contents of the closed-box by intercepting the disc I/O requests and encrypting the disc sectors. The closed-box is strongly isolated from the rest of the platform. Hardware memory protection and secure storage mechanisms intend to protect the contents from rogue administrators.

The authors suggest that Terra could be used to enable a secure grid platform. A closed-box would isolate the job and protect its contents from a malicious host. This closed-box would access its own integrity measurement by performing a system call through the trusted virtual machine monitor. The job owner would use this measurement to verify the integrity of the job execution environment.

10.5.4 Trusted Execution Environment

Cooper and Martin's architecture [27] aims to provide a 'trusted execution environment'. A grid job is encrypted and runs on an integrity-protected virtual machine where it cannot be accessed from the host platform; the data is safely decrypted inside this virtual machine during execution. Remote attestation is used to verify this environment before dispatching the job.

Their solution works by distributing a job composed of two virtual machines: The first virtual machine runs the job, and the second enforces the trusted execution environment. This second virtual machine, referred to as the 'job security manager', isolates the security layer from the job, and allows the solution to work seamlessly with all legacy virtualization and middleware software.

One potential loophole comes from the fact that they are less concerned about the 'malicious code' problem – untrusted code running on a participant's platform. The job owner specifies the virtual machine instance, and its security configurations are not checked before being used. The system relies on virtualization alone to isolate rogue jobs from the host.

The type of attacks a malicious virtual machine can perform would be restricted if virtualization offers complete isolation, but no existing solution guarantees this property right now (although, it is the objective of many). For example, in Xen, each virtual machine has two rings: one for sending requests and one for receiving responses; these form the inter-virtual-machine communication mechanism [31]. A rogue job could potentially hijack a privileged process and manipulate this communication channel to perform buffer overflow attacks on the privileged virtual machine.

10.6   Missing Pieces and Potential Solutions

Having described the consensus view, this section identifies the missing components and suggests potential solutions.

The first missing piece is a platform configuration discovery service. In the Trusted Grid Architecture [22], the users are expected to collect the attestation tokens directly from the participants. How the users would actually manage this process, however, is not considered in depth. Generally, it is assumed that a central service is already available for the users to discover participants' platform configurations. In consequence, various security and management issues associated with developing a 'match-making service' as such are often overlooked.

In the consensus view, the burden of performing attestation and managing the application whitelists rests with the users. This seems unrealistic in large-scale distributed systems, however, since the whitelist entries will be modified and updated constantly. An average user will not have sufficient resources to cope with these changes. Referring back to the Trusted Computing Group's runtime attestation model (see Sect. 10.4.3), the 'Configuration Verifier' is missing in the consensus view. Some suggest passing on the problem to a trusted third party [24, 32], but further elaboration is needed.

Something like the Configuration Verifier could be configured to centrally manage the application whitelists and perform configuration verification (attestation) on behalf of the users. It would be responsible for keeping up-to-date whitelists through various vulnerability tests and data collected. This type of service is described by the Trusted Computing Group as an aggregation service and has been suggested in a number of projects [23, 28]. For instance, Sailer et al. [33] encourage the remote users to keep their systems at an acceptable patch level using a package management database. This database gets updated whenever a new patch is released so that the new versions are added to the whitelist and the old versions are removed.

From the participants' perspective, an 'integrity-report-based job verification' mechanism is also missing. Only the users (job owners) are capable of verifying the participants' platform configurations, and not vice versa. The participant usually relies on a basic digital certificate to identify the users and authenticate the job virtual machines. This provides no assurance for the security state of the job virtual machines.

In the context of data grids – where the jobs might try to access sensitive data – the data owner should have full control over the software used for executing the query and protecting the accessed data. Virtual machine isolation can only prevent other rogue virtual machines from stealing the accessed data. If the job virtual machine itself is malicious and tries to run malicious queries on the database, then isolation will not be sufficient.

Basic PKI-based encryption and digital signatures are often used to protect the data once they leave the data owner's platform [34]. However, considering the number of connected nodes and the security threats associated with each, these security measures alone cannot provide the necessary confidentiality, privacy and integrity guarantees. A more reliable Digital Rights Management system is needed to allow the data owner to maintain full control over their data. The data access policies and privacy policies need to be consistently enforced throughout the distributed system. The end user should only be able to access the processed, anonymised results which are just sufficient to perform the requested analysis.

Meanwhile, Australia's Commonwealth Scientific and Industrial Research Organisation (CSIRO) has developed the Privacy-Preserving Analytics (PPA) software for analysing sensitive healthcare data without compromising its privacy [35]. Privacy-Preserving Analytics allows analysis of original raw data but modifies output delivered to the researcher to ensure that no individual unit record is disclosed, or can be deduced from the output. This is achieved by shielding any directly identifying information and deductive values that can be matched to an external database. Duncan and Pearson [5] discuss the benefits of being able to access the raw data:

- No information is lost through anonymising data prior to release and there is no need for special techniques to analyse perturbed data.
- It is relatively easier to anonymise the output than modifying a dataset when it is not known which analyses will be performed.
- Clinical decisions will be based on more reliable information and treatments can be more tailored to individuals with the likelihood of problems.

Privacy-Preserving Analytics (or any other secure analysis tools available), combined with remote attestation, could provide the necessary confidentiality and privacy guarantees for the data owner to freely share their raw data in the virtual organisation. For instance, attestation could verify that a trustworthy Privacy-Preserving Analytics server is responsible for performing data reconciliation and anonymising the output before releasing the results to the researcher.

10.7 Trustworthy Distributed Systems

We propose two types of distributed systems that aim to satisfy the security requirements (see Sect. 10.3), and bridge the gaps identified in the consensus view (see above). A configuration management server called the 'configuration resolver' plays a central role in both systems, maintaining an up-to-date directory of trustworthy participants and handling the job distribution process.

Section 10.7.1 describes how the configuration resolver manages configuration verification and job distribution processes. Based on the new security primitives that make use of the resolver, Sects. 10.7.2 and 10.7.3 describe a computational system and a distributed data system that are trustworthy.

10.7.1 The Configuration Resolver

Building on the consensus view of the trusted distributed systems, a central configuration management server is added to each administrative domain to manage the trustworthy participants' platform configurations and a whitelist of locally acceptable platform configurations (see Fig. 10.4). This configuration management server is referred to as the 'configuration resolver'. To become part of the trusted domain, a participant registers with the local configuration resolver by submitting its Configuration Token (CT). The token content is shown below.

$$CT = \left(PCR\ Log, AIK, \{cred(AIK)\}_{CA}, P_K, \{cred(P_K)\}_{AIK}, \{Description\}_{SK} \right)$$

This token includes the Attestation Identity Key (AIK) and an AIK credential issued by the Certificate Authority ($\{cred(AIK)\}_{CA}$). A public key credential, signed by this AIK, is also included to state that the private half has been sealed to *two* PCR values which correspond to (1) a trustworthy authenticated boot process, and (2) per-job virtual machine image files (see Fig. 10.5). The PCR Log contains the full description of the authenticated boot process and the virtual machine image files. In addition,

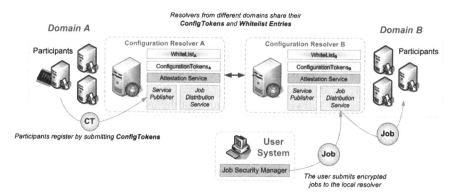

Fig. 10.4 Consensus view with the configuration resolver

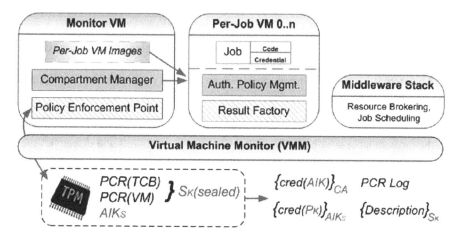

Fig. 10.5 Participants' trusted computing base

a service Description is included, signed by the private half of the sealed public key, demonstrating that the users should use this public key when submitting jobs to this participant.

The resolver verifies the trustworthiness of the platform by comparing the PCR Log with the whitelist. If the platform is trustworthy, its configuration token is added to the resolver's token repository, ensuring that only the trustworthy participants are ever advertised through the resolver. There, the burden of verifying the integrity-reports rests on the resolver.

As a minimum, the authenticated boot process will measure the BIOS, bootloader, virtual machine monitor and privileged monitor virtual machine. Therefore, the first PCR value is sufficient to state that the platform is running in a virtualized environment and its monitor virtual machine is securely managing the per-job virtual machines (see Fig. 10.5). Additionally, the second PCR value guarantees the exact software and security configurations of a per-job virtual machine (job execution environment). This second value is stored in a *resettable* PCR (see Sect. 10.4) since the virtual machine image files are re-measured and verified at runtime. These security properties allow the user to have strong confidence in the correctness of the data or computational results returned from this platform.

Note, in contrast to the reviewed approaches (see Sect. 10.6), the participant controls the virtual machine instances that are allowed to be used in their platform. This is responsible for meeting Requirement 3 (see Sect. 10.3). However, this also restricts the number of software environments that the user can choose from, and will affect the overall usability of job submission.

To improve usability and flexibility, the resolver allows a participant to submit multiple configuration tokens (for a same platform), all representing the same authenticated boot process but each sealed to a different per-job virtual machine image. Such tokens could be used to offer multiple services by configuring each software environment to provide a different service, or to offer multiple software environments for a single service, providing the user with more options.

The configuration resolver performs a range of security and platform configuration management functions through the following services (see Fig. 10.4):

- An internal 'attestation service' is responsible for performing all attestation-related functions to ensure that only trustworthy participants register with the resolver.
- An external 'service publisher' provides the necessary APIs for the participants to register and advertise their services through the resolver. It makes use of the attestation service.
- The users submit jobs through an external 'job distribution service', which selects the most suitable sites by looking up the service Descriptions and dispatches the jobs to them.
- An external 'whitelist manager' allows the domain administrators to efficiently update the whitelist entries.

Each participant becomes a member of the resolver's WS-ServiceGroup [36] and has a ServiceGroupEntry that is associated with them. An entry contains service information by which the participant's registration with the resolver is advertised.

The configuration tokens are categorised and selected according to the type of services they advertise. It is assumed that there is a public key infrastructure available to verify the participant's identity.

10.7.2   Computational Distributed System

In an idealised computational distributed system, the user would not care about where their job travels to as long as their sensitive data and results are protected. It would therefore make sense for the resolver to perform trusted operations such as selecting suitable sites and dispatching jobs on behalf of the Job Owner (JO). The resolver's TPM is used to measure the configurations of its external and internal services, and generate an attestation token (AT(CR)) to attest its security state to the users:

$$\text{AT}(\text{CR}) = \left(\text{PCR Log}, \text{AIK}(\text{CR}), \{\text{cred}(\text{AIK})\}_{\text{CA}}, P_{\text{K}}(\text{CR}), \{\text{cred}(P_{\text{K}})\}_{\text{AIK}} \right)$$

Much like the configuration token described previously, the resolver's public key credential ($\{\text{cred}(P_{\text{K}})\}_{\text{AIK}}$) identifies the corresponding private key as being sealed to its trustworthy state. The PCR Log describes the fundamental software stack and the services that have been measured during the resolver's authenticated boot process.

In the user system, all the job security functions are enforced by the 'job security manager' virtual machine (see Fig. 10.6): It is designed to perform a

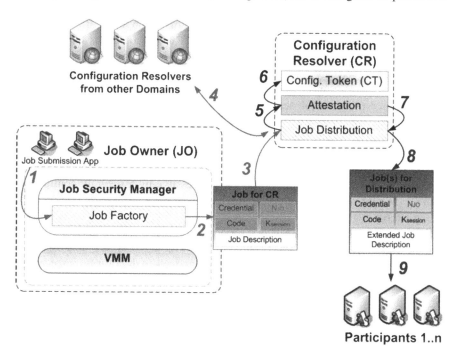

Fig. 10.6 Creation and distribution of an encrypted job

small number of simple security operations to minimise the attack surface. Attestation of the job security manager, monitor virtual machine and virtual machine monitor is sufficient to be assured that the job security functions have not been compromised – these components form the trusted computing base of the user system. Upon installation of this architecture, the user system will be capable of securely submitting jobs to the resolver and verifying the returned results.

10.7.2.1 Creation and Distribution of an Encrypted Job

All end user interactions are made via the external 'job factory'. It provides the minimal interface (APIs) necessary for development of a job submission application. Such an application should be designed to allow the user to specify the job description (requirements), the credentials and the code to be executed.

Imagine that a scientist (the job owner in this scenario) is carrying out an experiment that aims to predict the future climate state. The scientist submits the prediction model code through their job submission application and specifies the job description (**1**, Fig. 10.6). The job factory creates a secure job containing the following attributes (**2**, Fig. 10.6):

$$\text{Job} = \left(\{\text{Credential}, \text{Code}, \text{K}_{\text{session}}, \text{N}_{\text{JO}} \}_{\text{PK(CR)}}, \text{Job Description} \right)$$

A symmetric session key ($\text{K}_{\text{session}}$) is included as part of the job secret; it will be used by the participant to encrypt the generated results. This session key is sealed to the PCR corresponding to the user system's trusted computing base; this prevents a compromised job security manager from decrypting the returned results. N_{JO} represents the job owner's nonce.

Before encrypting the job secret, the trustworthiness of the resolver is verified by comparing the PCR Log (obtained from the resolver's attestation token, AT(CR)) against the locally managed whitelist of known-good resolver configurations. If the resolver is trustworthy, the job secret – containing the user Credential, Code, session key and nonce – is encrypted with the resolver's public key. This sealed key approach ensures that the secret is only accessible by a securely configured resolver. The job is then submitted to the local resolver's job distribution service (**3**, Fig. 10.6).

When the job arrives, the distribution service first attempts to decrypt the job secret with the sealed private key. Then it communicates with the local Resource broker – that is linked to the VO-level central information service – to discover resource availability. It requests configuration tokens – for those with available resources – from the resolvers managing other administrative domains (**4**, Fig. 10.6). This request contains the job requirements, specifying the required software and hardware capabilities. Such information is obtained from the Job Description.

The resolvers from other domains select the tokens that match the job requirements and return them to the local resolver. The local resolver uses its internal attestation service to iterate through each token and verifies the integrity-report by comparing the PCR values against the local whitelist (**5, 6, 7**, Fig. 10.6). Only those with acceptable configurations (for running the climate prediction model code) are selected and merged with the locally filtered tokens. Finally, the most suitable participant is selected from this merged list to run the job.

The job is recreated for the selected participant: During this process, the job secret is encrypted using the target participant's public key, and the Job Description is extended with the host address (**8**, Fig. 10.6). These jobs are dispatched to the job-manager of the selected participant who reads the unencrypted Job Description and schedules the job. On its turn, the job is forwarded to the participant's policy enforcement point (**9**, Fig. 10.6). Note that middleware services such as the job-manager can only read the extended Job Description for scheduling the jobs.

10.7.2.2   Operations of the Trustworthy Execution Environment

Figure 10.7 demonstrates how the job gets processed at the participant system. Any security processing required before becoming ready to be deployed in a per-job virtual machine is done through the policy enforcement point. It first measures the selected per-job virtual machine image (and the configuration files), and resets the resettable PCR with the new value. Typically, this image consists of a security patched operating system and trustworthy middleware stack – the 'authorisation policy management service' and the 'result factory' (see Fig. 10.7).

In order to decrypt the job secret, the policy enforcement point attempts to unseal the private key sealed to the participant's trusted computing base and the

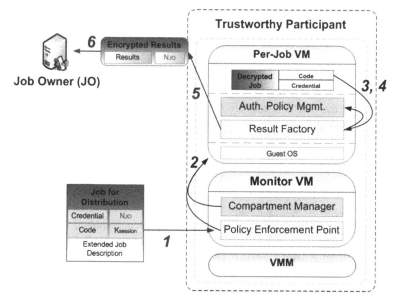

Fig. 10.7 Operations of a per-job virtual machine

virtual machine image. The private key will only be accessible if the platform is still running with trustworthy configurations *and* the image files have not been modified. This is intended to guarantee that only an integrity-protected virtual machine has access to the job secret.

If these security checks are passed, the 'compartment manager' allocates the requested size of memory, CPU time and speed (specified in the Job Description); and launches a virtual machine from the verified image and deploys the decrypted job (**2**, Fig. 10.7). Inside this virtual machine, the policy management service decides whether the scientist is authorised to run their prediction model in the participant platform. If the conditions are satisfied, the model is executed to simulate a probabilistic climate forecast (**3**, **4**, Fig. 10.7). The result factory generates a secure message containing the simulation Results (**5**, Fig. 10.7):

$$R = \left\{ \text{Results}, N_{JO} \right\}_{K_{session}}$$

The job owner's nonce (N_{JO}) is sufficient to verify that the results have been generated from an integrity-protected virtual machine and unmodified code has been executed. The entire message is encrypted with the job owner's symmetric session key ($K_{session}$), which is protected by the job owner's TPM. This prevents attackers from stealing or tampering with the Results.

10.7.2.3 Verification of the Results

At the job owner's system, the job factory receives the message R and decrypts it using the sealed session key (**6**, Fig. 10.7). Note that if the job factory has been modified during the job execution period, the session key will no longer be accessible as the PCR value (corresponding to the trusted computing base) would have changed. Hence, a compromised job factory can neither read the Results nor return fabricated Results to the original application.

The decrypted message is forwarded to the job factory which compares the returned nonce (N_{JO}) with the original. A matching value verifies the accuracy and the integrity of the results. These are then delivered to the scientist's application.

10.7.3 Distributed Data System

One of the pieces missing from the consensus view is a trustworthy, Privacy-Preserving analysis tool. As a potential solution, some combination of the 'Privacy-Preserving Analytics' software and attestation has been discussed in Sect. 10.6 to enable blind analysis of distributed data. This section expands on the idea and describes a 'Blind Analysis Server' (BAS) that allows analyses to be carried out securely via a remote server (see Fig. 10.8): The user submits statistical queries by means of a job; analyses are carried out on the raw data collected from trustworthy sites, and only the processed results are delivered to the user.

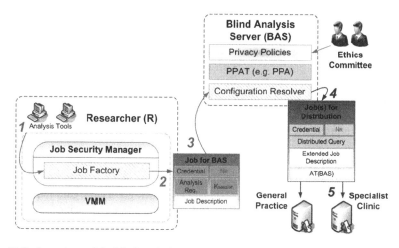

Fig. 10.8 Operations of the blind analysis server

The blind analysis server consists of the following components:

- The configuration resolver (see above).
- 'Privacy-Preserving Analysis Tool' (PPAT) – this can be any software designed to reconcile distributed raw data and run analyses on the reconciled information; the tool enforces privacy policies on the processed results to protect the privacy of the sensitive data.
- 'Privacy Policies' – specify privacy rules governing the release of processed information; these are defined under strict ethics committee guidance to comply with legal and ethical undertakings made.

We imagine that an ethics committee would define the privacy policies for different types of analyses supported by the blind analysis server. This would be more practical than relying on the data owners to figure out their own sticky policies when it is not known which analyses might be performed. Moreover, it would be difficult to reconcile and make sense of such policies collected from different data sources.

The three components mentioned above form the trusted computing base of the blind analysis server. The server attests its security state through an attestation token (AT(BAS)):

$$AT(BAS) = \left(PCR\ Log, AIK(BAS), \{cred(AIK)\}_{CA}, P_K(BAS), \{cred(P_K)\}_{AIK} \right)$$

This attestation token contains a public key credential signed by the AIK(BAS) which identifies the private key as being sealed to the PCR value corresponding to its trusted computing base.

The rest of the section uses the healthcare grid example (see Sect. 10.2.2) to explain how the security operations have changed from the computational architecture with the blind analysis server in place.

10.7.3.1   Distribution of Job(s) Through the Blind Analysis Server

A researcher is carrying out a study that looks at association between age (data available from a GP practice) and progression of colon cancer (data available from a specialist clinic). The researcher specifies the analysis requirements via an external analysis tool to observe how the cancer status has changed for patients aged between 45 and 55 (**1**, Fig. 10.8). The analysis tool should provide an appropriate interface for capturing the information required to run the analysis queries.

The job factory, after receiving the analysis requirements, verifies the security state of the blind analysis server by comparing the PCR Log (obtained from the server's attestation token, AT(BAS)) against the known-good configurations. It then creates a data access job (**2**, Fig. 10.8) and encrypts the secret using the server's public key (P_K(BAS)). The analysis requirements are encrypted as part of the job secret. This job is then submitted to the configuration resolver running inside the analysis server (**3**, Fig. 10.8).

The resolver is configured to manage the metadata of the participants' databases. Hence, by looking at the researcher's analysis requirements, the resolver is capable of selecting relevant sites and constructing distributed data access queries. The resolver selects trustworthy GP and specialist clinic systems to collect the data from and constructs a distributed query. The analysis server's sealed private key is used to sign the distributed query inside the TPM – it will only be accessible for signing if the trusted computing base has not been modified. This query as well as its signature is included in the job secret. The resolver dispatches a series of encrypted jobs to the policy enforcement points of the selected GP and specialist clinic systems (**4, 5**, Fig. 10.8).

The unencrypted part of the job now includes the analysis server's attestation token (AT(BAS)) which can be used by the job recipients (data owners) to verify the trustworthiness of the server before processing the jobs. The researcher's session key is omitted from the job secret since this key will only be used when the analysis server returns the final results to the researcher.

10.7.3.2   Operations of a Trustworthy Data Access Virtual Machine

Once the job arrives at the clinic, the policy enforcement point checks the security state of the analysis server using its attestation token (AT(BAS)) – this is how the job is authenticated at the clinic (**1**, Fig. 10.9). It would detect a job dispatched from a compromised analysis server and prevent, for example, the server sending a malicious query. To simplify Fig. 10.9, the policy enforcement point (which should be part of the monitor virtual machine) is drawn inside the virtual machine monitor.

After job authentication, the per-job virtual machine image files are checked for integrity. The middleware stack installed on this virtual machine provides a common interface for the job to access the patient data. For instance, if implemented in Java, such services would include the Java Database Connectivity, connection

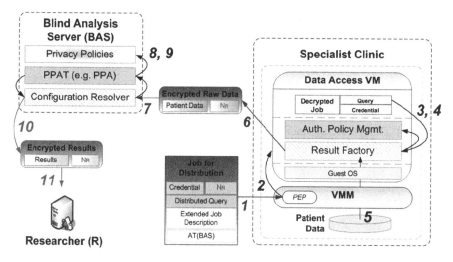

Fig. 10.9 Operations of a data access virtual machine

string and Java virtual machine. Again, the sealed private key – bound to the PCR values corresponding to both the trusted computing base and virtual machine files – is intended to guarantee that only a trustworthy virtual machine has access to the decrypted job secret to execute the query (**2**, Fig. 10.8). The signature of the query is verified using the analysis server's public key (obtained from AT(BAS)): A valid signature proves that the query originates from a trustworthy analysis server and the encrypted secret correlates with the attestation token. The result factory checks the query for any attempt to exploit vulnerabilities in the database layer (e.g. SQL injection) before executing it (**3**, **4**, **5**, Fig. 10.8).

A secure message containing the accessed data and the researcher's nonce (N_R) is encrypted with the data owner's symmetric session key (**6**, Fig. 10.9). This session key, in turn, is encrypted using the analysis server's public key (obtained from the server's attestation token). Note, in contrast to the computational architecture, this result message is sent back to the analysis server and not to the researcher (**7**, Fig. 10.9). The session key can only be decrypted if the analysis server's trusted computing base has not changed. Hence, a compromised server will not be able to steal the patient data.

10.7.3.3   Reconciliation of Collected Data

This result message and the encrypted session key arrive at the job distribution service of the resolver. First, the session key is decrypted using the sealed private key; the session key is then used to decrypt the result message. The returned nonce (N_R) is compared with the original to verify that the job has been processed (and the data has been accessed) through an integrity-protected virtual machine.

The internal analysis tool (PPAT) reconciles the collected data and generates association between the patients' age and colon cancer progression (**8, 9**, Fig. 10.9). During this process, the privacy policies are enforced to protect privacy of the patient data. Attestation of the analysis server is sufficient to establish that these policies will be enforced correctly.

The final results are encrypted with the researcher's session key (obtained from the original job secret) and sent back to their job security manager (**10, 11**, Fig. 10.9). The researcher studies these anonymised results via the external analysis tool, knowing that the results are accurate and their integrity has been protected.

10.8 Observations

This section explains how the proposed distributed systems are responsible for meeting the security requirements identified in Sect. 10.3, and bridging the gaps identified in Sect. 10.6. Remaining performance, whitelist management, and job delegation issues are also discussed.

10.8.1 Satisfying the Requirements

Job submission is a two-step process. First, a job is submitted to the local configuration resolver; the job secret is encrypted using the resolver's public key. The sealed key approach ensures that only a securely configured resolver can decrypt the job secret. Second, the resolver selects a trustworthy participant suitable for running the job; the job secret is encrypted using the public key of this selected participant and dispatched through an untrusted public network. The private half is strongly protected by the participant's TPM. These features are responsible for meeting the 'secure job submission' requirement (see Requirement 1).

A combination of the sealed key mechanism and attestation is responsible for meeting the 'trustworthy execution environment', 'authorisation policy management', and 'job isolation' requirements (see Requirements 2–4). The trustworthiness of the trusted computing base and per-job virtual machine images of the participant are verified when they register with the local resolver. In this way, the resolver maintains a list of trustworthy participants.

The job is dispatched with its secret encrypted using the selected participant's public key. The private half is only accessible if neither the trusted computing base nor the virtual machine image has changed. The integrity of the virtual machine image is verified with runtime measurement of the files. These features are intended to guarantee a trustworthy execution environment that contains a securely configured authorisation policy management service. Moreover, the verification of the trusted computing base is sufficient to know that the virtual machine monitor is securely configured to provide strong isolation between the job virtual machines.

Virtual machine isolation ensures that the code is executed free from any unauthorised interference, including threats from rogue administrators to subvert the results. These results, before being sent back, are encrypted using the job owner's symmetric key that is strongly protected by the job owner's TPM. These features satisfy the 'protecting the results' requirement (see Requirement 5).

Finally, the provision of the blind analysis server aims to satisfy the 'digital rights management' and 'blind data analysis' requirements (see Requirements 6, 7). The data owners verify the security state of the blind analysis server before allowing the query to run. Two properties checked are: (1) the state of the 'Privacy-Preserving Analysis Tool' installed and (2) the integrity of the data privacy policies. The accessed data is encrypted in a way that only a securely configured server can decrypt the data. These properties provide assurance that the integrity-protected policies will be enforced correctly upon data processing, and only the anonymised results will be released to the user.

10.8.2 Filling in the Missing Pieces

In Sect. 10.6, we identified the missing components from existing trusted virtualization approaches. This section explains how these missing components are dealt with in the proposed systems.

Many of the existing work on trusted distributed systems – likes of the Trusted Grid Architecture [22], trusted delegation for grid [27] and Terra [30] – expect the end user to collect the attestation tokens (or PCR quotes) from participant machines and make trust decisions. Typically, this requires the user to (1) manage an application whitelist of trustworthy system configurations, (2) discover available participant machines and download their attestation tokens, and (3) verify their security configurations and make trust decisions. We argue that this requirement is unrealistic given the dynamic nature of large-scale distributed systems.

In the proposed systems, the configuration resolver manages all of the above operations on the user's behalf, taking away the burden of performing attestation and managing application whitelists from the user. The participants' security configurations are verified when they first register with the resolver, and only those considered trustworthy are listed and used.

After identifying the local resolver, the user can submit their jobs without worrying about attestation or what the security configurations mean to them. All the user has to do is specify the job description and their security preferences, and submit their jobs to the correct resolver. The resolver will find trustworthy participants that satisfy the user's preferences and dispatch the jobs on the user's behalf. This shift in responsibility (of performing attestation) should also improve overall *usability*.

Another missing piece is the integrity-report-based job verification mechanism for the participant. In most of the existing work, the participant relies on basic PKI to identify users and authenticate job virtual machines; however, this provides no information about the security state of the job virtual machines.

In the proposed systems, the participant creates baseline virtual machine images which are allowed to be deployed on their machine, and seals the private half of the TPM-key to the image files. This sealed key approach, together with runtime verification of the image files, guarantees the integrity of the job virtual machines. With these mechanisms in place, the participant can be assured that only those securely configured are ever used on their machine as baseline images for executing the jobs.

10.8.3 Performance Degradation

One of the key drivers behind the development of computational distributed systems is high performance [37]. However, the suggested use of virtualization and various cryptographic operations necessarily incur a performance penalty [29].

Running a job inside a virtual machine requires extra information flow upon accessing the hardware. Each I/O request would go through a number of virtual device drivers before reaching the physical hardware; the same applies when receiving an I/O response. A recent study [38] suggests that a typical virtualized, distributed system incurs 20% performance penalty over native execution. With the introduction of native hardware support in all recent CPU architectures [14, 15], however, this overhead can be minimised with time to come.

Moreover, attestation involves expensive public key operations for signing the PCR values and validating the signatures. It also involves comparing the reported PCR event log against the whitelist entries and verifying the trustworthiness of a platform.

To improve performance, the attestation service (of the configuration resolver) could be configured to minimise the use of attestation. Since the trusted computing base of the participant platform is designed to be relatively static, the previous attestation results could be used again and again up to a given expiry date. A fresh attestation would be performed when the previous results expire, avoiding the need to attest every time a job is submitted. If the trusted computing base changes at a time before the expiry date, the sealed key mechanism would detect it and inform the resolver. The resolver would then request for the latest configuration token to perform a fresh attestation.

10.8.4 Whitelist Management

In systems spanning multiple administrative domains, different domains will likely have different software requirements and whitelist of acceptable configurations. While the administrators for one domain will be competent with the required list of software and their acceptable configurations for the local users, they will not know about all the software requirements in other domains. In consequence, multiple configuration resolvers could introduce availability issues depending on the level of inconsistency between their whitelists.

For example, if configuration resolver A is more active in inspecting software vulnerabilities and updating the whitelist entries than other domains, configuration tokens collected from configuration resolvers B, C, and D are likely to be classified as untrustworthy by resolver A, and their services will not be advertised to the users in Domain A. In order to minimise the level of inconsistency, the whitelist manager (in the resolver) needs to support functions that would enable efficient discovery and sharing of whitelist updates. The authors participated in research [39] that explores these issues in detail and suggests what the content of whitelist entries should be and how entry update messages should be shared.

10.8.5 Job Delegation

In practice, the job recipient might delegate some parts of the job on to other participants – this is known as *job delegation*. In the Trusted Grid Architecture [22], the user is capable of verifying the service providers' platform configurations against a set of known-good values ($good_U$). Using its job submission protocol, the user may also check to see if the service provider's list of known-good values ($good_P$) – which specifies all the acceptable configurations of possible job delegatees – satisfies the condition $good_P$ $good_U$. If this condition is satisfied, the user submits the job to the provider knowing that the job will only be delegated to other service providers whose platform configurations also satisfy $good_U$. However, the main concern with this type of approach is that the burden of managing the whitelists ($good_U$, $good_P$) rests on the users and the service providers.

Although job delegation has not been considered in the proposed systems, the configuration resolver could be configured to verify the configurations of possible job delegatees before dispatching the job. Since the resolver already has access to all the trustworthy participants' platform configurations (configuration tokens), it could exchange several messages with the potential job recipient to determine whether all the possible job delegatees are also trustworthy. This would involve the job recipient sending a list of identities of the possible delegatees to the resolver, and the resolver checking to see if all of the possible delegatees are registered. The job would only be dispatched if all of the delegatees are also trustworthy.

The advantage of this approach is that the users and service providers would not have to worry about maintaining up-to-date whitelists, or attesting and verifying the trustworthiness of the possible job delegatees.

10.9 Example Integration with the UK National Grid Service

This section demonstrates how the proposed security components 'could' be integrated with the UK National Grid Service [40]. Some of the important practicality and interoperability issues are also uncovered.

10.9.1 The National Grid Service Overview

The National Grid Service is a UK academic research grid, intended for production use of computational and data grid resources spanning multiple institutions across the country. The aim of the National Grid Service is to provide a reliable and trusted service using open, standards-based access to the distributed resources.

The grid consists of four core sites at Oxford, Manchester, Leeds and STFC-AL, as well as five partner sites at Cardiff, Bristol, Lancaster, Westminster and Queens. Each site contributes to the provision of computational or data nodes. The nodes sitting on the core sites provide transparent access to the resources by using an identical middleware stack and similar filesystems, whereas the partner sites provide a more heterogeneous environment.

Each site consists of several Computing Elements (CEs) which are the front ends to a number of worker nodes (resource providers). The CEs provide gatekeeper and job-manager functionality. A gatekeeper receives a job from a Resource broker and calls a job-manager to submit the job to a worker node through the Portable Batch System. Each CE uses its own information service, known as the Grid Resource Information Service (GRIS), to publish static and dynamic information about the resource availability. The GLUE Information Schema [41] is used for publishing such information. At each site, a LDAP directory called the Grid Index Information Service (GIIS) is used to collate information from many GRISs. Information from all the sites is collected and aggregated by the Berkeley Database Information Index system [42] (a central information repository), which holds information about all services and resources available in the grid. It queries the GIIS at each site to collect this information. The LDAP is used for making the aggregated information available to the users.

10.9.2 Integration

As the first step of integration, the configuration resolver would be deployed at each site to publish a filtered list of configuration tokens (representing trustworthy participants) through the GIIS (see Fig. 10.10). These tokens would have to be signed

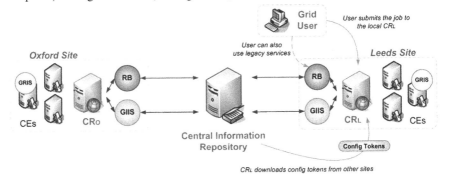

Fig. 10.10 Example int egration with the UK national grid service

by the configuration resolver for authenticity and to indicate that these represent trustworthy participants.

The central information repository would then query the GIIS at each site to collect these tokens and make them available to all the configuration resolvers. In this scenario, the GIIS would merely act as a proxy between the resolver and the central information repository. The signatures of the tokens would be validated by the central information repository before aggregating them. The resolvers would have to be authenticated at the central information repository before being granted access to the aggregated tokens; verification of the resolvers' digital certificates and attestation tokens would be sufficient for this purpose. This integration would allow each site, through their own configuration resolver, to discover all the trustworthy nodes available across the entire grid.

Consider a job submission scenario. A researcher, who wishes to run their job in the National Grid Service, submits a job to the local configuration resolver. First, the resolver communicates with the local Resource broker to discover resource availability through the central information repository. Note, this is a 'push architecture' where the Resource broker polls all CEs (through the central information repository) to find out about the availability of the worker nodes. The resolver, using the LDAP, downloads the configuration tokens for those with available resources from the central information repository. Tokens that match the job requirements are returned, representing trustworthy, relevant participants available in other sites. The resolver then iterates through each token and verifies the trustworthiness of the reported configurations by comparing the PCR values against the local whitelist. Only those with acceptable configurations will be selected and merged with the tokens from the local site. Finally, the resolver selects the most suitable participant, encrypts the job secret with the selected participant's public key and dispatches it.

The encrypted job secret and session key as well as the extended job requirements are sent to the CE to which the selected worker node is connected. The job-manager of this CE reads the unencrypted job requirements and schedules the job to the selected worker node. The middleware services as such will not be able to read the encrypted job secret and session key.

When these arrive at the worker node, its policy enforcement point first attempts to decrypt the job secret. The sealed key approach ensures that the private key is only accessible if the node is still running with trustworthy configurations. Then an integrity-protected virtual machine is launched to provide an isolated, protected job execution environment. The sensitive models run within this virtual machine, and the generated results are encrypted using the session key and returned to the researcher.

10.9.3 Observations

There would be a significant overhead involved in upgrading the participant systems to support trusted computing and virtualization. Various security virtual machines will have to be installed, and the virtual machine monitor will have to be configured to manage these securely. Although this is a large change, the advantage of the discussed approach is that legacy components such as the GIIS and the central information repository can be used with only small modification.

Moreover, many existing cloud systems [43–45] already support virtualization and submission of job virtual machines. With the recent introduction of hardware support for virtual machine execution (see Sect. 10.4.4), it seems likely that future developments will also make use of virtualization. The administrative tasks involved in upgrading such systems would be much smaller.

Despite the security enhancements, the use of the configuration resolver will increase the number of messages being exchanged upon job submission. The user submits a job to the local configuration resolver rather than to the Resource broker. The resolver requests configuration tokens from the central information repository and filters the trustworthy participants. Once these checks are done, it encrypts the job with the selected participant's public key and submits the job on the user's behalf.

These extra messages and cryptographic operations will affect the overall performance of job submission. However, for those wanting to submit performance critical jobs, the legacy services are still available for use. Such jobs can be submitted directly to the local Resource broker and skip all the trusted computing operations (see Fig. 10.10). Usability will not be affected as much since the user relies on the resolver to carry out attestation and job submission.

10.10   Conclusion

A wide range of research is conducted, archived and reported in the digital economy. Different types of distributed systems have been deployed over the years to facilitate the collection and modelling of the dispersed data, or the sharing of the computational resources. A problem arises, however, when the models or data have commercial value. They then become lucrative targets for attack, and may be copied or modified by adversaries. Despite ongoing research in the area of distributed system security, there remains a 'trust gap' between the users' requirements and current technological capabilities.

To bridge this 'trust gap', we proposed two different types of distributed systems: one applicable for a computational system and the other for a distributed data system. Central to these systems is the *configuration resolver*, which maintains a list of trustworthy participants available in the virtual organisation. Users submit their jobs to the configuration resolver, knowing that their jobs will be dispatched to trustworthy participants and executed in protected environments. As a form of evaluation, we suggested how these ideas could be integrated with the UK National Grid Service, and highlighted the potential security enhancements.

As high performance is one of the key drivers behind the development of computational distributed systems, the proposed security mechanisms sit uneasily with these aspirations. Despite several suggestions for improving performance (see Sect. 10.8.2), a more accurate assessment would be necessary to analyse the performance implications and devise enhancement strategies. Hence, future work should consider constructing a prototype implementation of the proposed components, integrating them with existing systems such as the National Grid Service, and measuring the performance overhead. This work will also help uncover other interoperability and usability issues.

Acknowledgments The work described is supported by a studentship from QinetiQ. David Power, Mark Slaymaker, and Peter Lee provided help with the healthcare grid example. David Wallom, Steven Young, and Matteo Turilli provided insights on the National Grid Service.

References

1. 2009.http://www.climateprediction.net/ (accessed February 08, 2010).
2. Thain, D, T Tannenbaum, and M Linvy. "Distributed computing in practice: the Condor experience." *Concurrency - Practice and Experience*, 2005: 17(2–4):323–356.
3. Wallom, D C, and A E Trefethen. "OxGrid, a campus grid for the University of Oxford." *UK e-Science All Hands Meeting*. 2006.
4. Power, D J, E A Politou, M A Slaymaker, and A C Simpson. "Towards secure grid-enabled healthcare." *Software Practice and Experience*, 2002.
5. Duncan, G T, and R W Pearson. "Enhancing Access to Microdata While Protecting Confidentiality." *Statistical Science*, 1991: 6(3):219–232.
6. Simpson, A C, D J Power, M A Slaymaker, and E A Politou. "GIMI: Generic Infrastructure for Medical Informatics." *Proceedings of the 18th IEEE Symposium on Computer-Based Medical Systems*. 2005. 564–566.
7. Freeman, R. "Medical records and public policy: the discursive (re)construction of the patient in Europe." *Workshop 9: 'Policy, Discourse and Institutional Reform*. ECPR Joint Sessions of Workshops, 2001.
8. *Trusted Computing Group Backgrounder*. 2006. https://www.trustedcomputinggroup.org (accessed February 09, 2010).
9. Grawrock, D. "The Intel Safer Computing Initiative." 119–142. Intel Press, 2006.
10. "TPM Main Specification Version 1.2." *TCG Workgroup*. 2003. http://www.trustedcomputinggroup. org/resources/tpm_main_specification.
11. TCG. "TCG Infrastructure Working Group Architecture Part II - Integrity Management." November 2006. http://www.trustedcomputinggroup.org/resources/infrastructure_work_ group_architecture_part_ii__integrity_management_version_10.
12. Sugerman, J, G Venkitachalam, and B Lim. "Virtualizing I/O Devices on VMware Workstation's Hosted Virtual Machine Monitor." Proceedings of the General Track: 2002 USENIX Annual Technical Conference. USENIX, 2001. 1–14.
13. Xen. "Xen: Enterprise Grade Open Source Virtualization A XenSource White Paper." 2005. http://xen.xensource.com/files/xensource_wp2.pdf.
14. Adams, K, and O Agesen. "A comparison of software and hardware techniques for x86 virtualization." *Proceedings of the 12th international conference on Architectural support for programming languages and operating systems*. ACM, 2006. 2–13.
15. Strongin, G. "Trusted computing using AMD "Pacifica" and "Presidio" secure virtual machine technology." Information Security Technical Report, 2005: 10(2):120–132.
16. Foster, I, C Kesselman, G Tsudik, and S Tuecke. "A security architecture for computational grids." *Proceedings of the 5th ACM conference on computer and communications security*. ACM, 1998. 83–92.

17. Sadeghi, A R, and C Stüble. "Taming "Trusted Platforms" by Operating System Design." *Information Security Applications.* Lecture Notes in Computer Science, 2004. 2908: 1787–1801.
18. Hohmuth, M, M Peter, H Hartig, and J S Shapiro. "Reducing TCB size by using untrusted components: small kernels versus virtual-machine monitors." *EW11: Proceedings of the 11th workshop on ACM SIGOPS European workshop.* ACM, 2004. 22.
19. Stumpf, F, M Benz, M Hermanowski, and C Eckert. "An Approach to a Trustworthy System Architecture Using Virtualization." *Autonomic and Trusted Computing.* Lecture Notes in Computer Science, 2007. 191–202.
20. Figueiredo, R J, P A Dinda, and J A Fortes. "A case for grid computing on virtual machines." *23rd IEEE International Conference on Distributed Computing Systems (ICDCS'03).* IEEE Computer Society, 2003.
21. Keahey, K, K Doering, and I Foster. "From sandbox to playground: Dynamic virtual environments in the grid." *5th International Conference on Grid Computing (Grid 2004).* IEEE Computer Society, 2004.
22. Löhr, H, HV Ramasamy, and A R Sadeghi. "Enhancing Grid Security Using Trusted Virtualization." *Autonomic and Trusted Computing.* 372-384: Lecture Notes in Computer Science, 2007. 372–384.
23. Yau, P W, A Tomlinson, S Balfe, and E Gallery. "Securing Grid Workflows with Trusted Computing." *ECCS (3).* Lecture Notes in Computer Science, 2008. 510–519.
24. Vejda, T, R Toegl, M Pirker, and T Winkler. "Towards Trust Services for Language-Based Virtual Machines for Grid Computing." *TRUST.* Lecture Notes in Computer Science, 2008. 48–59.
25. Mao, W, F Yan, and C Chen. "Daonity: grid security with behaviour conformity from trusted computing." *STC.* ACM, 2006. 43–46.
26. Sadeghi, A R, and C Stuble. "Property-based Attestation for Computing Platforms." NSPW '04: Proceedings of the 2004 workshop on New security paradigms. ACM, 2004. 67–77.
27. Cooper, A, and A Martin. "Trusted Delegation for Grid Computing." *The Second Workshop on Advances in Trusted Computing.* 2006.
28. Wang, D, and A Wang. "Trust Maintenance Toward Virtual Computing Environment in the Grid Service." *APWeb.* Lecture Notes in Computer Science, 2008. 166–177.
29. Pradheep, S S, S Santhanam, P Elango, A Arpaci-dusseau, and M Livny. "Deploying Virtual Machines as Sandboxes for the Grid." *In Second Workshop on Real, Large Distributed Systems (WORLDS 2005).* 2005. 712.
30. Garfinkel, T, B Pfaff, M Rosenblum, and D Boneh. "Terra: A Virtual Machine-Based Platform for Trusted Computing." *Proceedings of the 19th ACM Symposium on Operating Systems Principles (SOSP '03).* ACM, 2003. 193–206.
31. Barham, P, et al. "Xen and the art of virtualization." *SOSP '03: Proceedings of the nineteenth ACM symposium on Operating systems principles.* ACM, 2003. 164–177.
32. Nagarajan, A, V Varadharajan, and M Hitchens. "Trust management for trusted computing platforms in web services." STC '07: Proceedings of the 2007 ACM workshop on Scalable trusted computing. ACM, 2007. 58–62.
33. Sailer, R, T Jaeger, X Zhang, and LV Doorn. "Attestation-based policy enforcement for remote access." *CCS '04: Proceedings of the 11th ACM Conference on Computer and Communications Security.* ACM, 2004. 308–317.
34. Luna, J, M D Dikaiakos, T Kyprianou, A Bilas, and M Marazakis. "Data Privacy considerations in Intensive Care Grids." *Global Healthgrid: e-Science Meets Biomedical Informatics.* IOS press, 2008. 178–187.
35. O'Keefe, CM. "Privacy and the Use of Health Data - Reducing Disclosure Risk." *Health Informatics,* 2008: 3(1).
36. Maguire, T, and D Snelling. "Web Services Service Group 1.2 (WS-ServiceGroup)." OASIS Open, 2004.
37. Foster, I, and C Kesselman. "The Grid: Blueprint for a New Computing Infrastructure." Chapter 2: Computational Grids. Morgan-Kaufman, 1999.

38. Ruth, P, x Jiang, D Xu, and S Goasguen. "Virtual Distributed Environments in a Shared Infrastructure." *Computer*, 2005: 38(5):63–69.

39. Huh, JH, J Lyle, C Namiluko, and A Martin. "Application Whitelists in Virtual Organisations." *Future Generation Computer Systems*, 2009: (Under Revision).

40. Geddes, N. "The National Grid Service of the UK." *e-Science and Grid Computing, International Conference on*, 2006: 94.

41. Andreozzi, S, et al. "GLUE Specification v. 2.0." February 2009. http://forge.gridforum.org/sf/docman/do/downloadDocument/projects.glue-wg/docman.root.drafts.archive/doc15023.

42. "Berkeley database information index v5." *EGEE Web*. November 2009. https://twiki.cern.ch/twiki//bin/view/EGEE/BDII.

43. "Amazon Elastic Compute Cloud (Amazon EC2)." *Amazon Web Services*. http://aws.amazon.com/ec2/ (accessed February 17, 2010).

44. "Enomaly - Product Overview." *Enomaly*. http://www.enomaly.com/Product-Overview.419.0.html (accessed February 17, 2010).

45. Nurmi, D, et al. "The Eucalyptus Open-Source Cloud-Computing System." CCGRID '09: Proceedings of the 2009 9th IEEE/ACM International Symposium on Cluster Computing and the Grid. IEEE Computer Society, 2009. 124–131.

Chapter 11
An Intrusion Diagnosis Perspective on Cloud Computing

Junaid Arshad, Paul Townend, and Jie Xu

Abstract Cloud computing is an emerging paradigm with virtual machine as its enabling technology. As with any other Internet-based technology, security underpins widespread success of Cloud computing. However, Cloud computing introduces new challenges with respect to security mainly due to the unique characteristics inherited via virtual machine technology. In this chapter, we focus on the challenges imposed on intrusion diagnosis for Clouds due to these characteristics. In particular, we identify the importance of intrusion diagnosis problem for Clouds and the novel challenges for intrusion diagnosis for Clouds. Also, we propose a solution to address these challenges and demonstrate the effectiveness of the proposed solution with empirical evaluation.

11.1 Cloud Computing

The advent of Internet technologies has directed the revival of e-Science. It has significantly changed the methods used in e-Science along with the emergence of new computing paradigms to facilitate e-Science research. Cloud computing is one of such emerging paradigms which makes use of the contemporary virtual machine technology. The consonance between Internet and virtual machine technologies enables Cloud computing to emerge as a paradigm with promising prospects to facilitate the development of large-scale, flexible computing infrastructures, available on-demand to meet the computational requirements of e-Science applications. Cloud computing has witnessed widespread acceptance mainly due to compelling characteristics, such as Live Migration, Isolation, Customization, and Portability, thereby increasing the value attached with such infrastructures. The virtual machine technology has profound role in it. Amazon [1], Google [2], and GoGrid [3]

J. Arshad (✉), P. Townend, and J. Xu
School of Computing, University of Leeds, Leeds LS2 9JT, UK
e-mail: sc06ja@leeds.ac.uk

Xiaoyu Yang et al. (eds.), *Guide to e-Science: Next Generation Scientific Research and Discovery*, Computer Communications and Networks, DOI 10.1007/978-0-85729-439-5_11, © Springer-Verlag London Limited 2011

represent some of commercial Cloud computing initiatives whereas Nimbus [4] and OpenNebula [5] represent academic efforts to establish a Cloud.

Cloud Computing has been defined in different ways by different sources; however, for the purpose of our research, we define Clouds as *a high-performance computing infrastructure based on system virtual machines to provide on-demand resource provision according to the service level agreements established between a consumer and a resource provider.*

A system virtual machine, as described in this definition, serves as the fundamental unit for the realization of a Cloud infrastructure and emulates a complete and independent operating environment. Within the scope of this chapter, we define the Cloud platforms focused at satisfying computation requirements of compute-intensive workloads as *Compute Clouds* whereas those facilitating large-scale data storage as *Storage or Data Clouds.* For the rest of this chapter, we use terms *Cloud computing* and *Clouds* interchangeably to refer to our definition of compute Clouds. As described in the above definition, Cloud computing involves on-demand provision of virtualized resources based on Service Level Agreements (SLA) [6], thereby facilitating the user to acquire resources at runtime by defining the specifications of the resource required. The user and the resource provider are expected to negotiate the terms and conditions of the resource usage through SLAs so as to protect the quality of service being committed at resource acquisition stage.

11.2   Intrusion Diagnosis for Clouds

In order to stimulate extensive adoption of Clouds, there is need to develop mechanisms focused at improving the security of such infrastructures. This is aggravated by the adoption of *pay-per-use* model by Cloud providers whereby customers usually pay for the resources they use. Related to this, Clouds inherit unique characteristics such as diversity, mobility, and flexibility from virtual machines, which present novel security challenges and, therefore, require dedicated efforts to address them [7]. In this chapter, we focus on the challenges due to one of these characteristics, i.e., diversity. As described in Fig. 11.1, virtual machines provide the ability to host multiple different execution environments on a single physical machine, which enables a Cloud provider to be able to address diverse user requirements with same physical resources. However, it also poses a number of novel security challenges, such as evaluating the impact of an intrusion on the guest virtual machines [8]. From Fig. 11.1, a security module residing in the domain 0 of a virtualized resource has to evaluate the impact of an intrusion on the guest virtual machines. This process becomes nontrivial given the potentially different security requirements of the guest virtual machines. We define the impact of an intrusion on a virtual machine as the *Level of Severity* (LoS) of the intrusion. Also, intrusion diagnosis is traditionally defined as the process to discover the cause of an intrusion [9]. For the purpose of our research, we define intrusion diagnosis to be *the process to evaluate the level of severity of an intrusion for a virtual machine.* For the rest of this chapter, we use the terms intrusion diagnosis and intrusion severity analysis interchangeably to refer to the process defined above.

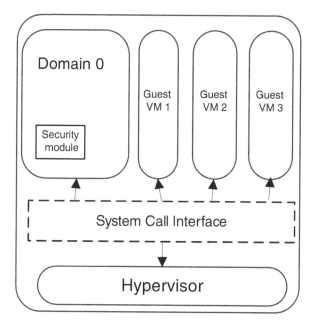

Fig. 11.1 A virtualized resource

Intrusion diagnosis, as defined above, has a significant impact on the overall security of a system, such as selecting appropriate response mechanism, depending on the mechanisms used to achieve this evaluation. This will enable provision of an intelligent response selection mechanism, which facilitates triggering response mechanisms based on the severity of an intrusion for the victim application. Furthermore, a customized severity analysis also facilitates delivery of virtual machine–specific quality of service with respect to security, which is vital for a user-oriented environment of Clouds computing. This is envisioned to enable the Cloud providers to devise Quality of Service (QoS)–based pricing strategies, taking into account the quality of security service delivered in relation with the security requirements of virtual machines. To the best of our knowledge, we are the first to identify the intrusion diagnosis problem, highlight its importance, and propose a solution to address it for virtual machine–based systems in general and Clouds in particular [8].

11.2.1   Requirements of Clouds for Intrusion Diagnosis

As described earlier in this chapter, Cloud computing inherits unique characteristics from virtual machines, which present novel challenges for security in general and intrusion diagnosis in particular. In relation to this, we describe the requirements of Clouds with respect to intrusion diagnosis and their comparison with contemporary efforts.

- Comprehensive Severity Evaluation

  One of the defining characteristics of virtual machines is their ability to facilitate hosting multiple execution environments on a single physical machine. This governs diversity in the infrastructure, which demands a comprehensive severity evaluation. Furthermore, diversity also requires comprehensive representation of security characteristics of the guest virtual machines whereas contemporary efforts lack this comprehensiveness as described in the previous section.

- Real-time Operation

  Clouds support flexible infrastructure where guest virtual machines can be created, migrated, and deleted at runtime. This requires a security module to be considerate of the dynamic nature of the infrastructure. Traditional severity evaluation methods are static by nature mainly due to the static nature of the infrastructures. Furthermore, addition, deletion, and migration of nodes in traditional infrastructures are not particularly frequent. Therefore, traditional methods do not meet this requirement of Clouds.

- Automatic Approach

  With regards to flexibility and dynamic nature of Clouds, an automated approach is mandatory. However, the existing approaches are largely manual due to their dependence on a human administrator. As described earlier in this chapter, the automatic existing approaches lack mechanisms to automate the severity evaluation, which hampers their ability to match this requirement of Clouds.

- Customization

  As described earlier, Cloud inherit diversity from virtual machines. Now, each guest virtual machine can potentially have different security characteristics. For example, a physics workload can have different priorities for security attributes as compared to a social science workload. Furthermore, we hold that security characteristics of an application dictate the severity of an intrusion on that application [10]. Therefore, it is necessary for a severity evaluation approach for Clouds to enhance customization to a virtual machine level. On the contrary, existing methods for severity evaluation lack customization as policy definition is mostly done at group or domain level comprising a number of nodes.

- Minimized Response Time

  Due to the runtime behavior of a Cloud computing infrastructure, intrusion response time becomes critical. It is, therefore, required for a severity evaluation method to be integrated with other security modules such as intrusion detection and response systems. Traditional methods do not fulfill this requirement as most of the security modules are considered to be isolated.

As explained by the comparison above, we conclude that existing efforts to evaluate intrusion severity do not fulfill the requirements of Clouds. Therefore, an intrusion severity analysis method is required which meets the requirements described above. In [8], we have proposed such a method and we intend to explain it in detail in the following sections of this chapter.

11.2.2 Contemporary Efforts for Intrusion Diagnosis

With respect to traditional distributed systems such as Grids, the intrusion diagnosis problem is not relevant at host level. This is because Grids allocate a complete physical node to a particular workload. Therefore, the security module in this case can be implemented as traditional host or network-based system. However, as described in the previous section, both these approaches introduce a trade-off between visibility and isolation.

Related to this, intrusion severity analysis has been studied in contemporary literature particularly in network-based systems where a security module is usually installed at the border node and is responsible for the whole network. The state of the art in this regard can be divided into two types, i.e., administrator dependent and intrusion response systems (IRS). With respect to intrusion response systems, most of the existing systems are based on the alerts from an intrusion detection system (IDS) or other information about an attack. There are some IRSs which do take into account the level of severity when selecting a response mechanism; however, this metric is again supposed to be decided by an administrator at an initial stage of site policy definition. Therefore, both types of contemporary systems involve a decisive human factor, which can prove to be the weak link in the severity evaluation process.

With respect to severity evaluation, few mechanisms have been proposed to facilitate a human administrator. In this regard, [11] and [12] present more formal methods to evaluate the severity or impact of intrusions for different applications. In [11], the severity evaluation is proposed to be a function of *Criticality*, *Lethality*, *Countermeasures*, and *Net Countermeasures*. As can be inferred from their names, the subjective nature of these terms hampers their applicability in a flexible, diverse, and user-driven system such as Clouds. Furthermore, the analysis is assumed to be performed by a human administrator, which leads to manifold problems. First, metrics such as Criticality and lethality are relative rather than absolute. Therefore, these require an in-depth knowledge of the system under attack, the attack itself, and also parameters defining the current status of the victim. Second, the metrics such as Countermeasures and Net Countermeasures are only applicable for well-known intrusions. Finally, the manual analysis also deteriorates the response time for an intrusion.

Common Vulnerability Scoring System (CVSS) [12] defines three metric groups and formula to calculate the impact of a vulnerability. The objective of this method is to facilitate a system administrator to perform the manual analysis so as to designate impact factor of a vulnerability before it is exploited. It does take into account custom security requirements by the notion of *Environmental Metrics*, but these are optional and do not affect the score unless explicitly included by the user. This approach has several limitations. First, it assumes manual execution of the whole process, i.e., a representative of user has to decide on the values of different metrics such as the Availability, Confidentiality, and Integrity Impacts. These metrics then contribute to the resultant impact metric. Second, the metrics are overly abstract which impede a human's ability to clearly specify the application-specific metrics. For instance, availability, integrity, and confidentiality are proposed to have three levels of impact, i.e., *none, partial,* or *complete.* These terms are too vague to accurately express the impact of a vulnerability on a particular attribute of security.

From the above discussion, we conclude that none of the contemporary mechanisms address the requirements of Clouds with respect to intrusion diagnosis as established in the previous section. Therefore, we hold that a more fine-grained analysis is required, facilitated by comprehensive representation of user requirements.

11.3   An Automatic Intrusion Diagnosis Approach for Clouds

As highlighted in the previous section, there is a need to establish a dedicated intrusion diagnosis mechanism for Clouds. We address the requirements described in previous section as follows: First, we achieve comprehensive and virtual machine–specific severity evaluation by quantifying security at the virtual machine level, thereby improving the representation of virtual machine security characteristics in our evaluation. With respect to real-time behavior, we incorporate SLA state and attack frequency in our analysis that makes it state- or time-aware. Also, we propose to establish our system in the hypervisor of a virtualized resource, which enables our approach to be considerate of the creation, migration, or deletion of guest virtual machines efficiently. In order to facilitate automation, we minimize the human factor by incorporating security requirements with SLA, thereby allowing applications to interact with virtualized resources without any human intervention. Furthermore, the severity evaluation process is triggered automatically without any human input, again eliminating the human factor. Finally, we have proposed an abstract model for integrated intrusion detection and diagnosis system in [8]. By integrating the severity evaluation with intrusion detection system, we envisage to reduce the intrusion response system and eliminate the human factor as well.

We establish our solution on the assumption that the severity of an intrusion for a particular virtual machine depends on a number of factors including security requirements of the application hosted by the virtual machine, the state of any Service Level Agreement (SLA) negotiated beforehand, and the frequency of attack on a security requirement. There can be other parameters; however, we hold that these are the most important of the factors and therefore restrict our research to these factors. We also believe that the severity problem can be treated as a special case of traditional classification problem as it essentially involves segregating intrusion trails into different categories. Finally, we use both supervised and unsupervised learning algorithms to implement our proposed solution.

With respect to virtual machine–specific security requirements, one option can be to render the security policy definition and management a responsibility of the virtual machine itself. This can be achieved by instrumenting a policy engine within each virtual machine, which will coordinate with detection and diagnosis modules in the privileged virtual machine. This approach is attractive due to the ease of implementation and simplicity of the resultant system. However, it breaks the isolation property as, in the event of a successful attack, an attacker can modify the security policies to facilitate its malicious objectives. Furthermore, a guest virtual machine needs to be trustworthy to be delegated such responsibility which is contradictory to our assumption that all guest virtual machines are treated as compromised. Due to these limitations of this approach, we adopt an approach that guarantees isolation while ensuring customization with respect to security policies. We propose using service level agreements to negotiate security requirements for a virtual machine. Following this approach, a customer is envisaged to specify the security requirements as part of the service level agreement at the resource acquisition phase. It requires quantification of security as explained in [10] and summarized in the following section.

With respect to SLA state, we designate the time remaining for completion of job as the SLA state. This is because of our understanding that severity of an intrusion is also affected by the time available for response. Ideally, the SLA state would be calculated by using different parameters such as quality of service metrics and available resources, etc. This requires establishment of complete monitoring infrastructure because of which we render this as out of the scope of our research. However, we assume that SLA state is available to us as an aggregate metric that can be used for formal analysis such as the one described in this document. Finally, the frequency of attack attempts on a particular security requirement depicts either the value of the target or likelihood of success of attack attempt against the security requirement under attack. This therefore requires relatively immediate and more effective response mechanism to avoid recurrence of such attack attempts. For this reason, we designate the frequency of attacks on a security requirement as an important factor to dictate the severity of an intrusion.

As stated earlier, we propose to solve the severity problem by treating it as a classification problem. Related to this, a characteristic of supervised learning techniques is that they involve an initial training or leaning phase to serve as a basis for online classification. However, with the problem focused in our research, no previous knowledge of severity of intrusions for applications is maintained which makes it difficult to use supervised learning techniques. Furthermore, most of the unsupervised learning techniques are more suitable for offline analysis as the classifications tend to change over the length of analysis datasets. This characteristic makes them inappropriate for systems that require real-time classification such as the one under consideration in our research. We, therefore, decided to use both supervised and unsupervised classification techniques to achieve our objectives. We use an unsupervised classification technique, i.e., K-means, to prepare the training datasets for further analysis and use supervised classification technique, i.e., Decision Trees, for real-time severity analysis. The motivation of our choice for these techniques is explained in a later section. We describe both these learning techniques along with a formal description of our solution in the following sections.

11.3.1   Fault Model

The system proposed for our research resides in a system-level virtual machine (VM) under a Type1 Hypervisor [13]. The VM is a part of a platform virtualization–based high-performance computing infrastructure called a Cloud as defined earlier in this document. As the VM is a system-level virtual machine, it is envisaged to emulate an independent node in traditional high-performance computing infrastructures such as Compute Grids. The applications running on the VM and the processing being performed at the VM are assumed to be a part of a compute-intensive job and will consequently have limited, presumably predefined, interactions with resources outside the VM such as interaction with a remote data sources. As Cloud computing promotes the idea of on-demand computing whereby a customized VM is created for each resource request, a VM will generally have very limited number of users, for instance, members of a particular research project or even a single user for whom the VM has been created. The proposed system is envisaged to be a part of the local administrative components of a hypervisor in the domain 0 to achieve isolation from the host VMs. However, this limits the visibility of the system to the system calls executed by the VM being monitored. Due to this fact, we assume the hypervisor to be trustworthy whereas the virtual machines hosted by a hypervisor are assumed to be compromised.

The fault model for the proposed system consists of arbitrary intrusions that can occur in an intermittent fashion and can be categorized as external malicious interaction software faults, which can be subdivided into content or timing faults as described by [14]. Figure 11.2 describes the fault model proposed for our research categorized into timing and content faults. The faults listed in the diagram have been identified as important from the perspective of a compute-intensive workload being executed in a Cloud resource. Additionally, we only take into account the faults that can be mitigated at the system call level. As is evident from Fig. 11.2, the fault model excludes the faults that can occur at "site level," i.e., the Hypervisor or the Dom 0 being compromised is not included in the fault model for this research. The source of faults for our research is considered to be application-specific vulnerabilities that allow an intruder to compromise the VM and possibly use the resources allocated to the VM to accomplish malicious motives, and operational mistakes, i.e., mistakes in configuration of VMs which can be exploited to enable a VM to infect a neighbor VM.

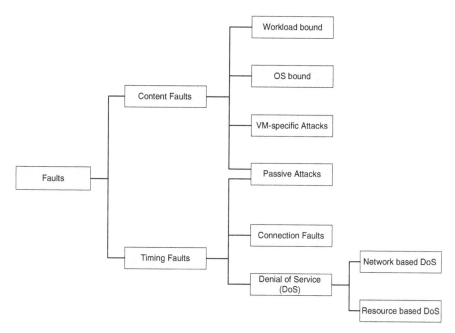

Fig. 11.2 The proposed fault model

11.3.2   System Definition and Architecture

As described earlier, we use security requirements, service level agreement state and frequency of attack on a security requirement, as parameters to evaluate the severity of an intrusion. The resultant metric of severity or impact factor is envisioned to be used by an intrusion response system to trigger appropriate response mechanism toward achieving end-to-end operation. We present the formal description of our system below followed by the architecture representation.

Let $C = \{s1, s2, s3, \ldots, sm\}$ be a set of system calls where $m = |C|$ is the number of system calls. Data set D can be defined as a set of labeled sequences $\{< Z_i, R_i > | Z_i \in C^*, R_i \in \{1,2,3,4,5\}\}$ where Z_i is an input sequence and R_i is a corresponding class label denoting one of the five possible severity levels, i.e., "Minimal," "Medium," "Serious," "Critical," and "Urgent." Given the data set D, the goal of the learning algorithm is to find a classifier h: $C^* \rightarrow \{1,2,3,4,5\}$ that maximizes given criteria.

As part of the resource acquisition phase, security requirements are collected from the user along with other resource requirements. These security requirements are then used to formulate the diagnosis policy which lists the priorities of the different security requirements for a particular virtual machine. Let P_{ds} be such a diagnosis policy for a VM. It can be described as $P_{ds} = \{P_{ds^i}, P_{ds^{i+1}}, \ldots, P_{ds^n}\}$ where P_{ds^i} represents a particular policy statement in the diagnosis policy.

Also, each system call SC_i can be mapped to one of the three attributes of security, i.e., if A_{type} is a set of the three security attributes, i.e., $A_{type} = \{$Availability, Confidentiality, Integrity$\}$, then $SC_{i(type)} \in A_{type}$ where $SC_{i(type)}$ represents the type of attack attempted by the system call SC_i with respect to the three attributes of security. Furthermore, given the granularity of our data to be system calls, a system call can be mapped to one or more security requirements and vice versa. This requires mapping to be performed between the system calls and the security requirements. Let a security requirement be represented by set R described as $R = \{R_i \cdot R_{i+1,\dots, Rn}\}$, and let $R_{i\,type}$ denote the type of security attribute represented by R_i. Now, if DnS_i represents a diagnosis signature with respective diagnosis policy P_{dsi} and the attack type attempted by current system call is denoted by $SC_{i\,(type)}$, then we can say that

$$SC_{i(type)} \subset R_{type}$$

Therefore, if R_i denotes the requirement affected by SC_i, we can write the mapping function as below. We also describe the results of this mapping in a later section.

$$R_i = f(R_{type}, SC_i, P_{dsi})$$

Finally, if S_t denotes the SLA state, *freq* represents the frequency of the attack on the security requirement, and Pr_i denotes the priority of the affected security requirement for the VM, then we can write the impact factor or the level of severity as:

Level of Severity $= f(R_i, Pr_i, S_t, freq, DnS_i)$ where DnS_i is the diagnosis signature and is defined as $DnS_i = \{DS_i, D_i, TIMESTAMP\}$ where DS_i represents the detection signature, i.e., the information passed on from the detection engine to the diagnosis module. This information is implementation dependent and is envisaged to vary across different implementations; however, we assume that it includes at least SC_i, VMID and Detection decision.

As described earlier, the result of this activity is an aggregate metric, which is envisioned to be used in cooperation with an intrusion response system to select an appropriate response to the intrusion under consideration.

We present the architectural representation of our system in Fig. 11.3. In this representation, we focus on *dom0*, the most privileged domain of a virtualized resource. As described in the diagram, we envisage our system to be established in *dom0* to achieve maximum isolation from the monitored hosts. The system is also envisaged to interact with other components, both within the virtualized resource and also with the global administrative components such as a resource manager. We have performed rigorous evaluation of the presented architecture using Architectural Trade-off Analysis Method (ATAM) [15], the details of this evaluation are not presented here to preserve the focus of this chapter.

11.3.3 Quantification of Security

We hold that the severity of a security attack for a particular virtual machine depends upon different attributes including the security characteristics of the virtual machine. One approach to capture security characteristics of virtual machines can be heuristic

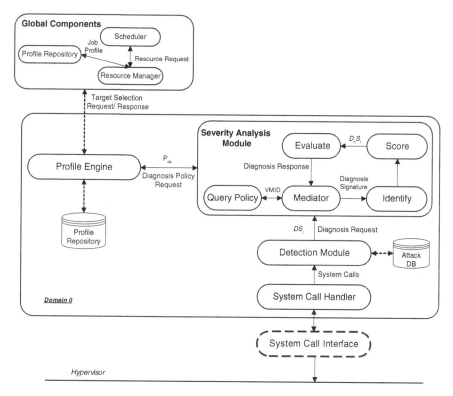

Fig. 11.3 Architectural representation of the system

method whereby applications hosted in virtual machines can be assumed to have certain security attributes. These assumptions are usually based on the experience of security expert with applications under consideration. However, this approach is limited with respect to identifying security attributes for the substantially diverse nature of candidate applications for virtual machine–based systems in general and Clouds in particular. An alternate approach is to encourage the users of virtual machines to explicitly specify the corresponding security attributes. A feasible implementation of this approach is to enable the user to choose/prioritize security attributes from a set of given attributes. This enables both the user of the virtual machine and the governor of the Cloud system to be synchronized regarding the security requirements of the virtual machine. We adopt this approach due to the degree of customization offered and the potentially comprehensive representation of a virtual machine's security characteristics. In order to ensure minimal human intervention and seamless end-to-end operation, we envisage gathering security characteristics of a virtual machine during the resource acquisition phase, as part of the service level agreement, in the form of security requirements. However, incorporation of security as part of a service level agreement requires its quantification so as to achieve an appropriate level of granularity to facilitate comprehensive representation of the security characteristics of a virtual machine. In this section, we summarize our efforts to quantify security into seven security requirements whereas detailed explanation and evaluation is described elsewhere [8, 10].

The security requirements are described from the perspective of a workload running in a virtual machine. As a virtual machine can act as an independent node on the network, the hypervisor is not concerned about the message level security parameters such as key size, encryption algorithm, etc. Therefore, we limit our research to the metrics which can be monitored by a hypervisor using system calls. This has advantage of being agnostic of the applications running in a virtual machine. Furthermore, the security requirements described here can be defined as high-level primarily because each of the requirements can be further divided into more fine-grained metrics. However, it is intentional to group similar metrics under a common classification so as to minimize the complexity governed by the proposed approach. Having said that, the security requirements described here are not mean to be exhaustive and only represent an effort as a proof of concept.

We have used the fault model described in the previous section as the basis for our study and have formulated seven security requirements. The preferences for these can be specified as "High," "Medium," and "Low" by the user of a service as part of the resource request. A "low" preference for a certain security requirement, therefore, means that the impact of a successful attack breaching that security requirement is assumed to have low impact on the expected behavior of the particular workload. For example, e-social science applications usually deal with confidential data processing where the confidentiality of data is rendered more important than on-time delivery of results [16]. In this case, the owner of an e-social science application may wish to designate a "low" or "medium" preference for denial of service attacks and a "high" preference for backdoor protection. In relation with our overall research objectives, we envisage to use these preferences to evaluate the level of severity of an intrusion for a particular workload.

We also assume a resource provider to use these security requirements to possibly group its resources based on their capabilities to fulfill these requirements to a certain level. This can be achieved by the resource provider by using appropriate infrastructures or technologies to guarantee the committed security attributes. For example, if a resource provider has committed to provide assurance for protection against denial of service attacks, it is expected that appropriate mechanisms have been installed to protect against such attacks.

The security requirements described above are listed in Table 11.1 in accordance with the three attributes of security, i.e., Integrity, Availability, and Confidentiality as described by [14]. These are meant to be a subset of the faults covered by the

Table 11.1 Proposed security requirements

Security attributes	Requirements
Integrity	Workload state integrity
	Guest OS integrity
Availability	Zombie protection
	Denial of service attacks
	Malicious resource exhaustion
	Platform attacks
Confidentiality	Backdoor protection

fault model described in an earlier section and are envisaged to be specified as part of a resource request along with their priorities by the consumer of the service.

11.3.4   Classification

Classification is a popular machine learning technique regarded as the process of segregating different items of a dataset into multiple groups or classes based on their characteristics or traits. Given a particular dataset, the goal of a classifier is to build a model of class distribution in terms of the quantified characteristics of the constituent objects of the dataset. In more formal terms, let $Z = \{(d_1, c_1), (d_2, c_2), \ldots, (d_n, c_n)\}$ be a dataset where $d_i \in D$ which represents the individual data items, and $c_i \in C$ which represents the class to which the particular data item belongs. In this case, a classifier h is a function such that $h: D \rightarrow Y$, i.e., it defines a mapping between a data item and its class based on some attributes.

In relation to this, the severity of a security attack on a system is also dependent upon certain attributes including the security requirements of the processes affected by the attack, the frequency of attack, and the time available for reaction. Also, the severity of a security attack is usually described in terms of different levels such as *"High," "Medium," and "Low"* which can also be treated as different classes of the potential effects of a security attack. We use these generalizations as our motivation to use classification techniques to solve the problem of severity analysis for virtual machine–based systems in general and Clouds in particular.

With respect to learning and classification, there are two major categories of techniques, i.e., supervised and unsupervised. As suggested by their names, supervised techniques require an initial training phase where the algorithm is trained using existing dataset with appropriate classification. The algorithm then uses this knowledge to perform real-time classification on test data. Conversely, unsupervised techniques do not require any existing classification examples and usually use multiple runs to fine-tune the classification patterns. K-means, Expected Maximization (EM), Gaussian Mixture, and Self-Organization Map (SOM) are some examples of unsupervised learning techniques whereas Decision Trees, Support Vector Machines, and Regression Analysis are some example of supervised learning techniques. We now describe our selected unsupervised and supervised techniques, i.e., K Means and Decision Trees, respectively.

11.3.4.1   K Means Clustering

K-means clustering [17] is an algorithm to classify objects based on attributes/features into K number of classes. The classification is done by minimizing the sum of squares of distances between data and the corresponding cluster centroid. Formally, for a given dataset $S = \{s_1, s_2, s_3, \ldots, s_n\}$, K-means classifies data items into k classes based on the attributes of data items, where $n < k > 1$. The objective of

K-means is to minimize the distance between the items surrounding each centroid which is formally represented as:

$$J = \sum_{j-1}^{k} \sum_{i-1}^{n} \left\| X_i^{(j)} - c_j \right\|^2$$

where $\left\| X_i^{(j)} - c_j \right\|^2$ is a chosen distance measure between a data point $X_i^{(j)}$ and the cluster center. c_j is an indicator of the distance of the n data points from their respective cluster centers. Our selection of K-means for our research was motivated by the simplicity of the technique and its ability to support more than two classes for classification purpose.

11.3.4.2 Decision Trees

Decision trees are a popular supervised classification technique that uses a series of questions or rules about the attributes of the class to classify datasets into classes. As characterized by their supervised nature, they require training datasets to establish a classifier which is then used for test data. Decision tree algorithms are based on the concept of *measures of impurity* or heterogeneity of the data, i.e., the metrics which demonstrate the presence of heterogeneous groups or classes of data in a given dataset. These metrics can be one of *Entropy, Gini Index,* or *Classification Error.* There are a number of different algorithms to implement decision trees; however, C4.5 [18] and its improved version C5.0 are the most popular ones. In both C4.5 and C5.0, *Information Gain* is used to decide the class of each data item which can be describe as under:Given a set R of objects, and an attribute A,

$$Gain(R,A) = Entropy(R) - \sum \left((R_v / R) Entropy(R_v) \right)$$

where R_v is the subset of R that has the attribute value v, the sum $\sum$ is over each attribute value of A, and $|R_v|$ is the number of elements in the set R_v.

Another important supervised classification technique is neural networks. We have selected decision trees for our research because of the following reasons:

1. Decision trees are simplistic as compared to neural networks and hence easier to manipulate.
2. Neural networks historically require more training data as compared to decision trees.
3. A critical phase in constructing neural networks is to choose the number of neurons and layers. This process is complex and skewed toward the experience of the designer. Also, the construction is based on trial and error method rather than any formula.
4. Historically, decision trees are proven to be better classifiers of unknown data as compared to neural networks.
5. An added benefit of using decision trees is the rule generation which can be used for subsequent rule-based modeling.

11.4   Evaluation

In order to evaluate our approach to predict severity of an attack for a particular virtual machine, we conducted several experiments based on experimental datasets. As we use both unsupervised and supervised learning techniques, we present our experiences with both preparing training datasets using K-means and building and testing classifier using decision trees. Furthermore, we assume a user of virtual machine to have maximum privileges for the virtual machine. Therefore, exploits targeted at exceeding privileges are out of scope of our research. For now, each system call is treated as a separate event and is classified independent of preceding or following system calls. Considering chains of system calls to detect attacks has been proposed by [15]; however, we render it as an opportunity for future work. Furthermore, as there will be a single diagnosis system per virtualized resource, we assume that all the system calls being analyzed are executed by the same virtual machine.

11.4.1   Datasets

For experiments, we choose publicly available system call sequences from the University of New Mexico. Our choice of system call dataset is motivated by the fact that our proposed system is envisaged to be instrumented in the dom0 and the granularity of data available to our system is assumed to be system calls. The University of New Mexico (UNM) provides a number of system call data sets. Each data set corresponds to a specific attack or exploit. However, given the age of these datasets and the system used for their generation, they do not contain virtual machine–specific exploits. This limits the coverage of our evaluation to the remaining six security requirements; however, as all of the traditional exploits still apply to virtual machine–based systems, we do not envisage any major deviations in the results. Furthermore, the datasets are also limited in the sense that they only list the names of the system calls executed by a process without its parameters. This can have an effect on the mappings between the system calls and the security requirements. Finally, one of the assumptions of our research is that the diagnosis module only deals with system calls identified as malicious by an intrusion detection system. However, the datasets do not acknowledge this assumption and consequently this limits the effectiveness of our results. We envisage rectifying these problems with more rigorous experiments and evaluations with real datasets facilitated by implementation of our proposed solution with one of the existing hypervisors.

As we assume a user of virtual machine to have maximum privileges for the virtual machine, exploits targeted at exceeding privileges are out of scope of our research. Also, security attacks which exploit network vulnerabilities to take control of the victim are not applicable because proposed system is not assumed to monitor network traffic. Consequently, the datasets we have used are synthetic FTP and INETD data. We divide our test dataset into two sub datasets without compromising the integrity. This is because our proposed system is meant to deal with individual system calls and does not take into account the contextual information contained in these datasets. Therefore, each system call is treated as a separate event and is classified independent of preceding or following system calls. Furthermore, as there will be a single diagnosis system per virtualized resource, we assume that all the system calls being analyzed are executed by the same virtual machine.

11.4.2 Data Cleansing and Harmonization

In order to perform experiments to evaluate our approach, the datasets needed to be cleansed to rectify the discrepancies described in the earlier section and mold them to match our requirements. The first step toward this process was the mapping between system calls and the security requirements with the objective to know which security requirements are affected by a particular system call. We used the classification of system calls proposed by REMUS [19] facilitating grouping of system calls based on threat levels. We only focus on system calls which pose threat levels 2 and 3 because threat level 1 is defined as full access to system which is one of the assumptions of our research, whereas threat level 4 is harmless. The mapping has been performed by manual analysis of each system call description, and results are presented in Table 11.2. As is described by the table, there are system calls which can potentially affect more than one security requirements and therefore have been mapped against multiple system calls. Also, for Platform Attacks, i.e., attacks which exploit characteristics of virtual machines, mapping is performed based on existing literature.

Table 11.2 Mappings between system calls and security requirements

Workload state integrity	*Truncate, ftruncate, dup2, flock, ioctl, write, close, lseek, fcntl, umask, select, _llseek, _newselect, writev, poll, pwrite, mprotect, msync, mmap, munmap, mremap, signal, setpgid, uselib, sigreturn*
Guest OS integrity	*rmdir,ioctl,truncate,ftruncate,brk,delete_module,write,close,umask,setpgid, uselib,capset*
Zombie Protection	*nfsservctl,ioperm,iopl,socketcall*
DoS	*Umount,mkdir,rmdir,umount2,ioctl,nfsservctl, truncate, ftruncate, quotactl, dup, dup2, flock,fork,kill,iopl,reboot,ioperm,clone,modify_ldt, adjtimex,vhangup, vm86, delete_module, stime, settimeoday, socketcall, sethostname, syslog, setdomainname, _sysctl,exit,ptrace*
Malicious resource exhaustion	*creat,fork,flock,setrlimit,setpriority,clone,sched_setparam,vfork,sched_sets chedular,swapon,swapoff,mlock,mlockall,nice,ipc,mlock,mlockall,sigsus pend,pause,waitpid,wait4,sched_yield*
Platform attacks	*Ptrace*
Backdoor protection	*Nfsservctl,dup,dup2,flock,ioperm,iopl,socketcall,read,readv,fcntl,select, fsync,poll,pread,sendfile*

The second step in data preparation stage is to harmonize the frequencies of system calls. As described earlier, the available datasets contain both malicious and non-malicious system calls. The effect of this problem with data is aggravated by the fact that frequency of an attack on a security requirement is an important parameter in our analysis. Therefore, the initial experiments performed revealed the results being skewed toward patterns with higher frequency. We address this problem by normalizing the frequency attribute of data based on the standard score method with custom parameters as given below.

$$\gamma = 3 * \omega - 0.060 * \frac{\mu(\omega)}{3.77 * \sigma(\omega)}$$

where

γ = normalized frequency
ω = original frequency
$\mu(\omega)$ = mean of original frequency and,
$\sigma(\omega)$ = standard deviation of original frequency

This normalization process limits the value of frequency in the range of zero to three which is synchronous to the priorities of each security requirement. With regards to the service level agreement state, we envisage this to be an aggregate metric generated as a function of multiple attributes including quality of service attributes, resource availability, and performance. However, this detailed analysis is out of scope of our research and therefore, we generate service level agreement state using the rand()function in MATLAB [20] to represent an aggregate metric.

The final step toward data preparation is to use unsupervised learning technique, i.e., K-means [17] to predict the severity of each system call event. This is to facilitate the training phase of our supervised classification technique, i.e., decision trees. We have used MATLAB to perform this step. As with any unsupervised learning technique, K-means requires multiple runs to achieve a mature classification. For our experiments, we performed various runs with different parameters and a stable classification is determined by manually verifying the classes assigned to randomly chosen events. The final configuration used to achieve a stable output is given below:

$$(\delta, \alpha) = \text{kmeans}\,(\rho, k, \theta)$$

where δ represents the predicted severity for a particular system call event, α represents the centroids calculated for the given data, ρ represents the dataset being analyzed which in our case is a matrix prepared using the steps described earlier, k represents the number of classes or clusters to be generated which in our case is five, and θ represents the number of replications performed to get the output which in our case was 100. As k-means uses distance to segregate different classes, the distance used in our case is the Euclidean Distance. We should emphasize here that the data prepared as a result of this process is not envisaged to be 100% error free both because of the crudeness of the data and the simplicity of the approach.

11.4.3   Evaluation and Discussion

In order to evaluate our proposed approach, we used decision trees as a supervised classification technique for experiments on the data prepared as a result of the process described in the previous section. There are a number of algorithms to perform decision tree analysis; however, we have used C5.0 [21] because of its proven efficiency in different applications. We use See5 software [21] to perform our experiments with the C5.0 algorithm. Given the training data, we first constructed different classifiers, i.e., decision trees by using different permutations of the attributes involved and compared the predicted classes against the classes assigned during the data preparation stage. This process reveals different error rates for different classifiers. It also generates a tree classifier and a set of rules for each classifier. The rules generated as a result of this analysis can be used to model rule-based systems. Figure 11.4 presents an example of such rules whereas Fig. 11.5 presents an example of a decision tree generated by C5.0. As shown in the decision tree, the decision nodes represent the attributes, i.e., security requirements whereas the boxes present the predicted severity classes. As described earlier, we use five classes or levels of severity proposed by [22], i.e., *Urgent, Critical, Serious, Medium, and Minimal.*

We use these classifiers on our tests datasets to evaluate accuracy of each classifier against unseen data. We have compiled the results of this evaluation in Table 11.3. As part of the prediction of class for unseen or test data, C.50 also generates a confidence

```
Rule 1: (53, lift 7.4)
     req1 <= 0
     req4 <= 0
     -> class1 [0.982]
Rule 2: (88, lift 4.5)
     req1 < 0
     req4 <= 0
     -> class2 [0.989]
Rule 3: (159, lift 2.5)
     req1 <= 0
     req4 > 0
     req5 <=0
     -> class3 [0.994]
Rule 4: (81, lift 4.9)
     req4 > 0
     req5 > 0
     -> class4 [0.988]
Rule 5: (19, lift 20.1)
     req1 > 0
     req4 > 0
     -> class5 [0.952]
```

Fig. 11.4 An example decision tree by C5.0

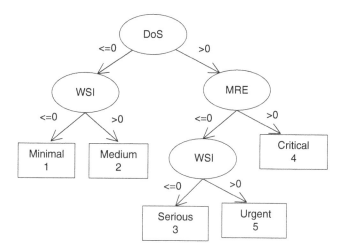

Fig. 11.5 Rules generated for decision tree

Table 11.3 Evaluation of classifiers with training and test data

		Test Data 1		Test Data 2	
Classifier	Training Data	Without confidence	With confidence	Without confidence	With confidence
1	0.0%	77.1%	77.1%	79.8%	79.8%
2	0.2%	77.1%	52.5%	79.8%	73.6%
3	4.2%	90.9%	38.7%	87.9%	39.14%
4	13.4%	56.2%	31.6%	57.8%	6.2%
5	25.6%	97.9%	24.5%	98.5%	6.2%
6	27.7%	77.1%	77.1%	79.8%	79.8%

metric called Confidence, with a value of between 0 and 1, which facilitates rigorous analysis by revealing the assurance of the predicted value. Analysis of predicted values revealed that there are predictions with low confidence value which should be adjusted. In accordance with this, we consider a prediction to replace the original value if the confidence is more than 80%. This helps us remove inconsistencies where the confidence value is low. As shown in the table, error rate for classifiers differs with and without considering confidence metric which helps us improve our understanding of the classifiers.

An interesting observation from our experiments is the unexpected behavior of classifiers to test data. Table 11.3 presents the results of our experiments with the training and the two test datasets. It lists the error rates for each classifier when evaluated against test datasets both with and without consideration of the confidence value of the prediction. As can be seen in the table, the most consistent classifier of all is the one which gives maximum error rate for the training data, i.e., 25.6%. The decision tree for this classifier has not been presented here because of limited space. However, the classifier with 0% error rate for the training data presents a high error rate of 77.1% for both analyses, with and without confidence metric. As can be seen, the results of the best performing classifier are not ideal and, to our best understanding, this is largely due to the quality of data we used for our experiments. As explained in the earlier sections, we have made efforts to normalize and clean data using different techniques; however, discrepancies are still assumed to be present in the data. This limits our ability to perform a rigorous evaluation of our approach. Given this unsatisfactory quality of data, we are motivated to render these results as encouraging to carry out further research with better data. As stated earlier in this text, efforts are underway to implement the proposed system with one of the existing hypervisors. This will enable us to address the problem of data quality and cleansing and facilitate a more rigorous evaluation of our approach.

On the contrary, based on our experience with the use of machine learning techniques to problems such as intrusion diagnosis, we hold that machine learning techniques have promising prospects in this respect. Although our experiments involved rather simple machine learning algorithms, however, the results produced demonstrate the effectiveness of the approach even with imperfect data. Furthermore, the results also highlight the need to address the Data Problem for computer security research such as the one described in this chapter.

11.5   Conclusions and Future Work

We hold that security underpins extensive adoption of Cloud computing. However, there are novel challenges which need to be addressed in order to improve the security of such infrastructures. The focus of our research is to investigate issues introduced by the unique characteristics of virtual machine. In this chapter, we have presented our efforts to identify and address one such problem – evaluating the level of attack severity for virtual machines on a same physical machine. To the best of our knowledge, we are the first to identify and propose a solution to this problem for Clouds. As described in the chapter, we propose using machine learning technologies facilitated by service level agreements to achieve our objectives. The evaluation conducted as part of our research reveals challenges and opportunities for further research in this domain. In particular, we highlight the *Data Problem*, i.e., the unavailability of appropriate datasets to conduct effective research. Although the results of our research were marred by lack of appropriate data, we render them encouraging. Our efforts also demonstrate the challenges involved in optimizing machine learning techniques and highlight opportunities for their use in related research.

We intend to extend our research to implementation with real Cloud environments. In particular, we plan to contribute our research to improve the dependability of iVIC Cloud infrastructure [23]. In relation to this, efforts are underway to implement our system with Xen [24] hypervisor. Furthermore, as has been identified during evaluation, we intend to consider chains of system calls for our analysis as well. This will improve the application of our proposed solution to a wider domain.

References

1. *Amazon Elastic Computing Cloud* Available at: aws.amazon.com/ec2
2. Google Cloud. Available at: www.googlecloud.com
3. GoGrid: *Scalable Load-Balanced Windows and Linux Cloud-Server Hosting.* Available at: http://www.gogrid.com/
4. Nimbus. Available at: www.workspace.globus.org
5. OpenNebula Project. http://www.opennebula.org
6. Burchard, L., M. Hovestadt, O. Kao, A. Keller, and B. Linnert: *The Virtual Resource Manager: An Architecture for SLA-aware Resource Management,* in the IEEE International Symposium on Cluster Computing and the Grid. 2004. p. 126–133.
7. Tal Garfinkel, Mendel Rosenblum: *When Virtual is Harder than Real: Security Challenges in Virtual Machine Based Computing Environments.* In the Proceedings of 10th Workshop on Hot Topics in Operating Systems, 2005 – usenix.org
8. Junaid Arshad, *Integrated Intrusion Detection and Diagnosis for Clouds.* In the proceedings of Dependable Systems and Networks (DSN), Student Forum 2009.
9. John D. Strunk, Garth R. Goodson, Adam G. Pennington, Craig A. N. Soules, Gregory R. Ganger. Intrusion detection, diagnosis, and recovery with self-securing storage. Technical report CMU-CS-02-140. May 2002.
10. Junaid Arshad, Paul Townend, *Quantification of Security for Compute Intensive workloads in Clouds.* Submitted to International Conference on Parallel and Distributed Systems (ICPADS) 2009.
11. Stephen Northcutt and Judy Novak; Network Intrusion Detection: An Analyst's Handbook, 3 rd edition New Riders Publishing Thousand Oaks, CA, USA ISBN:0735712654
12. Peter Mell and Karen Scarfone *A Complete Guide to the Common Vulnerability Scoring System* Version 2.0 www.first.org/cvss/cvss-guide.html
13. IBM Systems, Virtualization version 2, release 1 available at: publib.boulder.ibm.com/ infocenter/eserver/v1r2/topic/eicay/eicay.pdf
14. Algirdas Avi zienis, Jean-Claude Laprie, Brian Randell and Carl Landwehr: *Basic Concepts and Taxonomy of Dependable and Secure Computing,* IEEE Transaction on Dependable And Secure Computing, Vol. 1, No. 1, January-March 2004.
15. Rick Kazman, Mark Klein, Mario Barbacci, Tom Longstaff, Howard Lipson and Jeromy Carriere *The Architecture Tradeoff Analysis Method* Technical Report, CMU/SEI-98-TR-008 ESC-TR-98-008 available at http://www.pst.ifi.lmu.de/lehre/WS0102/architektur/VL9/ ATAM.pdf
16. Wei Jie, Junaid Arshad, Richard Sinnott and Paul Townend; Towards Shibboleth based Security for Grids – A State-of-art Review on Grid Authentication and Authorization Technology. Accepted for ACM Computing Surveys. Association for Computing Machinery 2009.
17. J. MacQueen. Some methods for classification and analysis of multivariate observations, volume 1 of *Proceedings of the Fifth Berkeley Symposium on Mathematical statistics and probability,* pages 281–297, Berkeley, 1967. University of California Press.
18. Quinlan, J. R. C4.5: Programs for Machine Learning. Morgan Kaufmann Publishers, 1993
19. Massimo Bernaschi, Emnuele Gabrieli, Luigi V. Mancini; Remus: a security-enhanced operating system in the proceedings of ACM Transactions on Information and System Security 2002.
20. The MathWorks – MATLAB and Simulink for Technical Computing. http://www.mathworks.com
21. Information on See5/C5.0 www.rulequest.com/see5-info.html
22. Severity Levels: http://www.internetbankingaudits.com/severity_levels.htm
23. Jinpeng Huai, Qin Li, Chunming Hu; *CIVIC: A Hypervisor based Computing Environment* in the Proceedings of the 2007 International Conference on Parallel Processing Workshops.
24. Paul Barham_, Boris Dragovic, Keir Fraser, Steven Hand, Tim Harris, Alex Ho, Rolf Neugebauery, Ian Pratt, Andrew Warfield; *Xen and the Art of Virtualization* in the Proceedings of *SOSP'03,* October 19.22, 2003.

Part IV
Research Automation, Reusability, Reproducibility and Repeatability

Chapter 12
Conventional Workflow Technology for Scientific Simulation

Katharina Görlach, Mirko Sonntag, Dimka Karastoyanova,
Frank Leymann, and Michael Reiter

Abstract Workflow technology is established in the business domain for several years. This fact suggests the need for detailed investigations in the qualification of conventional workflow technology for the evolving application domain of e-Science. This chapter discusses the requirements on scientific workflows, the state of the art of scientific workflow management systems as well as the ability of conventional workflow technology to fulfill requirements of scientists and scientific applications. It becomes clear that the features of conventional workflows can be advantageous for scientists but also that thorough enhancements are needed. We therefore propose a conceptual architecture for scientific workflow management systems based on the business workflow technology as well as extensions of existing workflow concepts in order to improve the ability of established workflow technology to be applied in the scientific domain with focus on scientific simulations.

12.1 Introduction

Originally, workflows have been created to meet the IT support needs of the business world. In short, they are compositions of tasks (also referred to as activities) by means of causal or data dependencies that are carried out on a computer. They are executed on a workflow management system (WfMS) [1]. A workflow that utilizes Web services (WSs) as implementations of tasks is usually called *service composition*. Web services are the most prominent implementation of the service-oriented architecture (SOA). The Web Service technology is an approach to provide and request services in distributed environments independent of programming

K. Görlach (✉), M. Sonntag, D. Karastoyanova, F. Leymann, and M. Reiter
Institute of Architecture of Application Systems, University of Stuttgart, Stuttgart, Germany
e-mail: goerlach@iaas.uni-stuttgart.de; sonntag@iaas.uni-stuttgart.de;
karastoyanova@iaas.uni-stuttgart.de; leymann@iaas.uni-stuttgart.de;
reiter@iaas.uni-stuttgart.de

Xiaoyu Yang et al. (eds.), *Guide to e-Science: Next Generation Scientific Research and Discovery*, Computer Communications and Networks,
DOI 10.1007/978-0-85729-439-5_12, © Springer-Verlag London Limited 2011

languages, platforms, and operating systems. It is applied in a very wide range of applications where integration of heterogeneous systems is a must.

In recent years, the workflow technology has gained more and more attention in the scientific area [2] and the term *scientific workflows* has been coined. Workflows in science provide multiple benefits: (1) They contribute to sharing knowledge by being available as services for collaborating scientists. (2) With the help of workflows, a community-based analysis of results is supported. (3) Workflows are able to deal with huge amounts of data, e.g., collected by sensors or calculated by scientific algorithms. (4) Workflows are capable of running in distributed and highly heterogeneous environments—a common scenario in scientific computations where a great variety of platforms and programming languages are usually employed. (5) The automation of steps during workflow design and execution allows scientists to concentrate on solving their main scientific problems. (6) Workflows can be utilized to conduct scientific simulations in a parallel and automated manner.

Since the WS and workflow technologies are established in the business area, it is reasonable to use them in the scientific domain, too, especially because the two areas exhibit many similar requirements on the IT support. For example, WSDL (Web Services Description Language) [3] can be used for the specification of service interfaces and BPEL (Web Services Business Process Execution Language) [4] for the specification of scientific workflows. As there are much more WS standards and a lot of additional requirements imposed by the scientific domain, there is a need for an advanced analysis of usability of the WS and Workflow technology in the field of scientific applications. This chapter discusses the requirements on workflows in the scientific domain, and the ability of conventional workflow technology regarding these requirements. Furthermore, we propose extensions of conventional workflow technology that significantly improve the ability to apply established workflow technology in the scientific domain.

A special kind of scientific workflows that we focus on are simulation workflows. Simulations are typically *complex calculations* which predestinate them for a realization with workflow technology. Examples are partial differential equations (PDE) that must be solved to determine temporal or spatial changes of simulated objects. *Remote access* to data outside the actual scientific workflow management system (sWfMS) is another characteristic of simulation workflows.

In this chapter, after introduction, we discuss the application of conventional workflow technology in the scientific domain in detail. Therefore, in Sect. 12.3, we point out the most important requirements on scientific workflows and compare them with requirements on conventional, i.e., business workflows. Furthermore, we present a workflow system architecture meeting the requirements on scientific workflows and a prototype implementing this architecture. In Sect. 12.4, we show an example scenario for the simulation of "ink diffusion in water" implemented with the help of our prototype. Afterward in Sect. 12.5, we present extensions of conventional workflow technology in order to bridge the gap between conventional workflow technology and unfulfilled requirements arising by the new application domain e-Science. Finally, in Sect. 12.6, we conclude and look out on future work.

12.2 Background and Related Work

Several approaches were already created for using workflows in scientific applications to meet some of the requirements imposed by that domain. Existing scientific WfMSs are usually built from scratch and do not rely on the workflow technology as it is established in the business area. Here we give a short overview of the systems Triana, Taverna, Kepler, and Pegasus that focus on a specific scientific domain and/or on supporting specific functionality. Additionally, we briefly introduce Trident which is one of the very few systems that applies conventional workflow technology for scientific applications.

Triana [5] focuses on supporting services and workflow execution in distributed environments. It provides predefined services, e.g., signal or image processing, static analysis, and visualization, useful in diverse domains. Such local or remote services as well as local applications can be composed in workflows. Triana workflows are data-driven and specified with a WSFL[1]-like notation. For workflow and service execution, Triana basically supports peer-to-peer systems and Grid environments that enable dynamic resource allocation. Recently, efforts are made toward supporting WSs and integrating Web Services Resource Framework (WSRF) [6].

Taverna [7] is a workbench for biologists that allows a data-centric specification and execution of workflows. In contrast to Triana, it supports only services with known locations. Taverna aims at supporting long-running, data-intensive workflows and the interaction with users. It provides semantic service discovery, fault handling mechanisms, and provenance information.

Similar to Taverna, *Kepler* [8] is mainly used in the bioinformatics domain. It allows the integration of different types of resources (e.g., databases or Grid resources) and of different tools (e.g., MatLab[2]). Kepler provides a service library that includes services with capabilities for advanced data exchange, e.g., mediation or data hub functionality. These services can be used to build compositions. So-called directors enable flexible control strategies for service compositions. For execution, a Kepler workflow is translated into a Java program and the utilized services are mostly local Java applications, too.

Pegasus [9] is rather a workflow compiler than a WfMS. It cooperates with Condor DAGMan[3] and supports input of DAGMan workflows. Such workflows represent a template without resource bindings. These templates are the basis for Pegasus users to describe their demands for the resource mapping. Based on this template, Pegasus determines an execution strategy. For optimized strategies, intelligent planning algorithms are used to cope with data movements and application runs on heterogeneous and dynamic execution environments. Additionally, Pegasus aims at reducing the accumulated amount of data during workflow execution.

---

[1] Web Services Flow Language: http://www.ibm.com/developerworks/library/ws-ref4/

[2] MathWorks Website: http://www.mathworks.com/

[3] http://www.cs.wisc.edu/condor/dagman/

More precisely, it identifies existing data that does not need to be produced once more and it performs garbage collection.

In contrast to previous approaches, *Microsoft Trident* [10] applies conventional workflow technology. It uses the Microsoft Workflow Foundation as technology platform and a control flow-oriented modeling language based on the Extensible Orchestration Markup Language (XOML). Trident also supports some modeling extensions such as data flow edges. The Microsoft system consists of independent components for workflow modeling and execution. For some components, multiple implementations exist. For example, scientists can choose between different workflow composers (i.e., a modeling tool) such as a text editor or a graphical modeler. A workflow composer offers basic and composite activities that can be chosen from a workflow catalog. Additional activities can be created by scientists using Visual Studio. Furthermore, the user can customize the workflow composer by including domain-specific workflow packages that exist for astronomy, biology, meteorology, or oceanography. For the execution of workflows, two different ways are provided. First, it is possible to execute the workflow in the Trident WfMS. Second, a workflow can be executed by compiling it into a usual application and run it on Microsoft .Net platforms.

In the remainder of this chapter, we will use the terms process model, workflow model, process (instance), and workflow (instance) in the following meaning: In conventional workflow technology, a *process model* depicts the structure of a process in the reality. A real word process model describes in many cases human interactions. A part of a process model that is executed on a computer is called a *workflow model* [1]. A workflow model specifies actions that need to be performed and control or data flow dependencies between these actions. This workflow model can be seen as a template from which each *workflow* is instantiated, i.e., a *workflow instance* created from a workflow model. After all, an individual workflow instance can be executed by a workflow engine.

12.3 Applying Conventional Workflows for Scientific Computations

As shown in the previous section, only few approaches rely on the conventional workflow technology as described in [1] or in the Workflow Reference Model.[4] Since it is an established technology, there already exist standards and tools that can be used as basis for further development. Therefore, we make efforts to use the conventional workflow technology for scientific computations.

At first, life cycles of conventional and scientific workflows are presented and compared. The outlined differences in these life cycles reveal the need for extensions of the conventional workflow technology when being applied for scientific

---

[4] http://www.wfmc.org/reference-model.html

simulations. Afterward main requirements on WfMSs in the scientific domain are discussed and a conceptual architecture for sWfMSs is proposed that fulfills these demands. Finally, a prototypical implementation of this architecture is presented.

12.3.1   Life Cycle of Workflows

The workflow life cycle, is important to understand the actions needed to set up and run workflows as well as the user roles that carry out these actions. In conventional workflow technology, the life cycle is well-known and accepted by the community [1]. It consists of different repeatable management phases that are dealt with by different user groups or roles (see Fig. 12.1a).

A workflow is modeled by business specialists that know the concrete steps that are performed to achieve a certain business goal. A specialist with IT knowledge explicitly deploys the workflow on an engine, i.e., makes it executable. Execution of a workflow is triggered by a client or employee, often late after deployment. A workflow model can be instantiated multiple times. Workflow monitoring can deal with individual running workflow instances or aggregated information over several instances. It can also present statistics on the overall state of a system including running and completed workflow instances. Hence, monitoring can be valuable for both administrators/IT specialists and business analysts. Finally, a business analyst analyzes one or more workflow executions and may deduce a need for business process reengineering.

The life cycle for scientific workflows heavily distinguishes from its business counterpart (see Fig. 12.1b). We inferred the life cycle from observations about the way scientists create and conduct experiments and from known properties of scientific simulations and computations [11]. Typically, there is only one user group, the scientists, playing the roles of a modeler, user, administrator, and analyst. The focus of their work is usually on single workflow instances. To be precise, scientists do not distinguish between workflow models and instances or are not aware of a difference

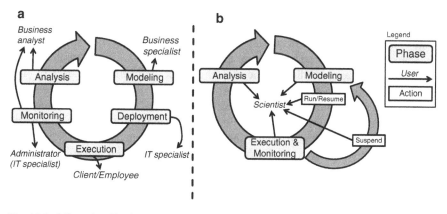

Fig. 12.1 Life cycle of business (**a**) and scientific workflows (**b**)

between models and instances, respectively. They set up a simulation and execute it once at a time. Because scientists typically develop their workflow in a trial-and-error manner, modeling and execution phases are not arranged in a strict sequence. In fact, they can be carried out alternatively. An additional cycle therefore leads from execution back to modeling phase with the help of a "suspend" operation on the workflow instance, which remains hidden from the scientists. Technical details are transparent for scientists altogether. For instance, conventional workflow adaptation is experienced as scientific workflow modeling; the deployment (of parts of a workflow) is part of the "run/resume" operation [12], which is also hidden for the scientist. Workflow execution starts immediately after modeling. The traditional execution and monitoring phases are merged into a single phase in the scientific workflow life cycle because from a scientist's point of view, monitoring only visualizes a running workflow (instance). After execution, a scientist can analyze the computed results and may re-model and re-execute the workflow possibly with different parameters.

12.3.2   Main Requirements on Scientific Workflow Management Systems

Workflows in the scientific area make use of a data-centric approach. Typically, huge amounts of data have to be processed, e.g., 5 GB data per day is transmitted by the Hubble telescope, and probably need to be processed by a workflow. The modeling language for scientific workflows is primarily *data-driven*, sometimes with support of a few control structures (e.g., in Taverna, Triana). That means, for accommodating the scientists' needs, the main focus of the modeling language should be on data flow while the control flow is considered secondary. Additionally, the language has to provide modeling constructs for *advanced data handling*, e.g., data references, and pipeline mechanisms since typically huge amounts of data are processed [13].

One of the most important requirements on sWfMSs is *usability* since the majority of users of sWfMSs are not computer scientists. A scientist needs the support of easy-to-use tools, automation as far as possible, and maximal flexibility in the usage of the sWfMS. First, this means that scientists want to model their workflows in a convenient way. Second, they want to run their workflows and store their data on resources that are specified by the user himself or automatically chosen by the sWfMS. Scientists need the same support for services used in traditional workflows, i.e., scientists should be able to specify the services to be used in a scientific workflow themselves, or to delegate the service discovery to the sWfMS. The need for automation in sWfMSs basically includes the deployment of workflows, the provisioning of workflows, services and data, the instantiation and execution of workflows, and the service discovery. Additionally, the automation of data transformation is desirable as well as support of data vs. function shipping decisions.

A sWfMS should be *flexible*. With flexibility, we denote the ability of a system to react to changes in its environment. Approaches to flexibility of workflows can be divided into two groups. First, a workflow can be modified – be it automatically or manually – according to the changed situation (known as *adaptation*). Such modifications can address different workflow dimensions (logical, functional, organizational dimension [1]) and may be applied to workflow models or single workflow instances. Second, a workflow can be modeled in a way that avoids its modification even in the presence of a changing environment (known as *avoid change*). Avoid change can be achieved by different mechanisms (e.g., role-oriented staff queries on organizational databases, alternative paths in the workflow model, automatic re-execution of a task).

The need for flexibility mechanisms in scientific applications and simulations is manifold. Setting up a scientific experiment is often not a chain of actions that lead to the expected result right from the beginning, but rather a trial-and-error process (cf. Sect. 12.3.1) [14]. That means a scientist examines an experiment while conducting it. If it deviates from the expectations, the scientist modifies the workflow to get the desired course. These modifications comprise changing the workflow structure, adding or removing activities, correcting erroneous data, and others. A sWfMS is therefore required to support these kinds of process logic adaptation, ideally especially for running workflows.

Usually, scientific computations are dealing with huge amounts of data or allocate enormous computing resources. Thus, they are typically long-running although often being conducted in powerful computer clusters or Grid environments. The reliability of the underlying infrastructure cannot be guaranteed: Networks may fail; servers may be temporarily unavailable due to administration; servers may move to another location. Hence, failures during execution cannot be avoided especially in scenarios with long-running computations. If an application is not explicitly programmed to cope with such unforeseen failures, its unsuccessful termination would mean a loss of data, time, and money. Avoid change mechanisms are required: If an activity implementation (i.e., a computation) is not available, e.g., because of a server crash, another implementation with identical semantics may be invoked at run time without interrupting the workflow execution.

During workflow execution, scientists want to *monitor* the process run. Therefore, a sWfMS should support the ability to monitor the status of the workflow execution. For example, the scientist is interested in knowledge about running, finished or faulted activities, allocated resources, and the dynamical choice of a service implementation. Inspecting the produced data is also a need.

After carrying out a scientific experiment, its *reproducibility* is of utmost importance for different reasons. Scientists who are not involved in the execution of the workflow need to be able to retrace the simulation, have to review the findings, or need to use the results. The operating scientist may want to repeat a workflow or parts of it to draw conclusions, and to prove statements and assumptions. Additionally, the scientist may share the results with people he collaborates with. While following and reproducing workflow runs and their (intermediate) results, scientists use provenance information [15]. Data provenance enables scientists to study new results and determine data derivation paths. Workflow provenance enables scientists to study process execution and covers the flow of a workflow instance including the nature and the course of decisions in the execution path, used resources and services, metadata (e.g., timestamps) for service invocation, and error logs.

All relevant data has to be stored by a sWfMS. Finally, provenance information should be displayed in a way that (non-computer) scientists understand the execution of workflows including the derivation of data.

The *robustness* of scientific workflows is an important issue since scientific workflows are long-running. The term robustness denotes the ability of being error-resistant. The needed flexibility mechanisms mentioned above are a way to improve the robustness of a system. But additional approaches are needed to protect the execution progress from being lost in case of unforeseeable failures, to reach a consistent system state even in the presence of failures, and to proceed a simulation/experiment after a failure.

Scalability of sWfMSs enables acceptable performance for workflow execution. Scientific workflows should scale with the number of users, number of utilized services, data or calculation resources, and involved participants. Today, typical scientific workflows are mostly executed in a central manner on a single machine. A decentralized workflow enactment can help to scale via distributed process execution. It can be achieved, e.g., by parallel execution in distributed and heterogeneous execution environments using provisioning techniques.

The requirements presented above are valid for the entire scientific domain. Certainly, there are *specific requirements* for each specific scientific domain, e.g., life science, medical science, chemistry, or mechanical engineering. Specific domain-related requirements and the fact that it is hard to cover all scientific domains in one WfMS create the need to extend sWfMSs and the workflow models and possibly adapt these models and their instances. This includes, e.g., domain-specific services, result displays, or meta-models for semantic annotations.

The special type of scientific workflows we focus on, the simulation workflows, imposes additional requirements on sWfMSs. Like scientific workflows, simulations are characterized by data-intensive and compute-intensive load. Naturally, simulations represent long-running calculations since scientists frequently study complex systems. Therefore, simulation workflows require the support of long-running workflow instances. Additionally, simulation workflows demand the possibility to integrate different tools in one simulation workflow as well as a heterogeneous execution environment with integration of databases, computation nodes, and sensor nets. Finally, simulations represent a special domain that requires domain-specific modeling language constructs. For example, complex simulations can consist of multiple cohering workflows. Therefore, there is the need to share context data between these workflows in a simulation. Furthermore, the user should be supported in typical simulation tasks such as parameter searching, for example.

12.3.3   Comparing Conventional and Scientific Workflow Technology

The main intention of (conventional) workflows is the *automation* of processes. In conventional workflow technology, this comprises the instantiation and execution of workflows. Additionally, humans have to be integrated in the course of actions which results in an automated "invocation" of human beings during execution of workflows. This requirement is not among the most important requirements for scientific workflows. Nevertheless, scientific workflows can benefit in this field since setting up and conducting scientific experiments and simulations often includes manual tasks that are currently not part of scientific workflows. However, in general, scientists make higher demands on automation while using workflow technology. As non-computer scientists, they want to use the whole power of work-flow technology without the need for further education, i.e., they require an auto-mated (i.e., hidden) deployment of workflows and services since the location of execution is not predefined in all cases in e-Science. Rather in the workflow, scientists want to specify the location where services have to be automatically deployed and executed. Supplementary, this creates the need of automated ser-vice and workflow provisioning. Finally, an automated data transformation as well as an automated service discovery is desirable for scientific users. Triana [5] provides the specification of the location for service execution. With the help of these mechanisms, it even allows to specify the way sub-workflows have to be executed, i.e., how many instances of a sub-workflow have to be created and the distribution of these instances in the execution environment. A special control unit is responsible for data transfer realizing data dependencies between the instances. For the distribution of sub-workflow instances, Triana also provides an automatic specification.

Almost all sWfMSs provide a *service catalog* with predefined services. When starting the particular sWfMS, it automatically searches for these predefined ser-vices and if they are still available, the user can choose them in the service catalog for integration into workflow models. Although these service catalogs are extend-able, an automatic service discovery based on semantic data is not sufficiently considered by sWfMSs in most cases until now. The sWfMS Triana provides advanced mechanisms for workflow deployment and execution since it is special-ized on distributed execution of workflows. However, most sWfMSs are specialized by provided services in the service catalog. For example, Taverna [7] and Kepler [8] provide mainly services needed for biological algorithms or services providing access to biological databases. Moreover, a service catalog is an important factor of the usability of a sWfMS.

Next to the service catalog, the *usability* of a sWfMS strongly depends on sup-ported tools needed for the realization of the whole workflow lifecycle. Hence, Taverna, Triana, and Kepler provide the modeling of workflows (including the sup-port of a service catalog), starting workflow runs "by mouse click," integrated *monitoring* and result visualization tools. In summary, easy-to-use tools in combi-nation with wide-ranging automation are key factors of usability. In conventional workflow technology, required tools often exist but their usability leaves a lot to be desired for scientific users. Additionally, service registries allowing service cata-logs in WfMS are not sufficiently supported. As suggested before, the scope of automation in conventional workflow technology needs to be extended in order to meet requirements on usability for scientific workflows.

Most conventional *modeling languages* for business workflows are control flow–driven since they are designed for the implementation of control flow–oriented processes. However, scientists think data-oriented which creates the need for new modeling constructs in order to allow, e.g., an explicit specification of data flow in scientific workflows. The modeling languages of sWfMSs (e.g., in Taverna and Triana) are mostly hybrid languages that are mainly data-driven with support of a few control structures. Intentionally, the additional control structures allow an enhanced support of controlling mechanisms for the data flow.

Furthermore, modeling languages for scientific workflows have to support advanced data handling mechanisms. In conventional workflow technology, the handling of huge amounts of data is not a primary requirement. Therefore, new mechanisms should upgrade the workflow technology. For example, Pegasus [9] optimizes the execution of scientific workflows by reusing data that was already generated and is still up to date. Hence, the workflows' execution time can be reduced because the data does not have to be generated again.

In conventional workflow technology, the *reproducibility* of workflow runs particularly comprises executed activities, invoked services, and corresponding resources during workflow execution. For scientists, research results are only accepted and usable if they are repeatable which constitutes the need for the collection of huge information sets in order to enable the reproducibility of almost the whole workflow run. Especially, existing monitoring and auditing mechanisms of conventional workflow technology are not sufficient. Origin of the data and their manipulation is not tracked, but this type of information is of high importance for scientists. Therefore, in sWfMSs, a special provenance component should support the traceability and reproducibility of workflow runs. That component combines information about a workflow instance including the nature and the course of decisions determining the path through the workflow with information about the origin and the manipulation of data.

Requirements on *robustness* are quite similar for conventional and scientific workflows. Recoverability of faulty workflow runs is an important issue already considered by conventional workflow technology. Therefore, scientific computations seriously benefit from conventional workflow technology. However, an increased flexibility of workflows would further improve their robustness [16]. Imagine a workflow that automatically reacts to a changed environment: If a server becomes unavailable, an alternative server can be chosen at runtime; if a network connection error occurred, a simple retry operation could solve the problem. Although flexibility is a key point in scientific workflow management, it is insufficiently unaddressed in currently existing scientific workflow systems. For example, Triana and Kepler just allow the modification of simulation/experiment parameters during workflow execution as adaptation mechanism; Pegasus and Taverna implement avoid change concepts such as retry of service invocation [14]. In conventional workflow technology, there are already many approaches addressing the mentioned kinds of flexibility. We believe that it is of high value to harness the results of existing concepts.

Scalability is already addressed by conventional workflow technology regarding tasks in workflows, workflows themselves, and humans integrated in workflow execution. Since scientific workflows require a dynamic infrastructure for workflow and service execution, scalability regarding resources strongly suggests the execution of scientific workflows in Grid or Cloud environments. Of course, the execution of conventional workflows in Grids and Clouds is already an ongoing issue since it seems natural to use workflow and service-based execution mechanisms in such kind of distributed execution environments. In the scientific domain, Pegasus is especially designed for the execution of workflows in Grid environments. It plans the execution of scientific workflows in Grids, i.e., Pegasus maps Grid resources to workflow tasks. Triana also enables the execution of workflows in Grids and additionally introduces an abstraction level (in the form of an API) that allows scientific users to integrate different types of infrastructures in the same way.

For scientific or simulation workflows conventional workflow technology can deal with the demand on heterogeneous execution environments and their long-running character. The mechanism for the integration of hardware such as databases in conventional workflow technology constitutes a beginning for the integration of sensor nets as well. Nevertheless, further studies are needed in order to efficiently integrate sensor nets to exploit the valuable characteristics of sensor nets. Conventional workflow technology also easily enables the integration of different tools in a workflow implementing one simulation. Nevertheless, the data exchange between different tools is still difficult since they rarely share the same data format.

The interaction between workflow models assembled in one simulation is modeled in a so-called choreography [17] in conventional workflow technology. However, in order to assemble simulation workflows, the support of shared context data is missing. In the scientific domain, only a small number of WfMS especially promote the application for simulations. All together do not consider choreographies of workflows. Among other things, Kepler is used for the implementation of simulations (cf. [18]). The support of tools such as MatLab emphasizes the competence of Kepler for the modeling and execution of simulation workflows. A language that specifically addresses requirements of scientists on a workflow language for simulations is GriCoL [19]. For example, it supports special mechanisms for parameter searching. In order to prove the concepts a use case "molecular dynamics simulation of proteins" was successfully implemented by biology scientists using GriCoL [19].

Finally, it has to be noticed that discussed sWfMSs except Trident [10] do not follow the architecture given by conventional management systems. Nevertheless, they are representatives of sWfMSs established in e-Science. Typically, early sWfMSs set a high value on frameworks integrating tools for the support of the whole life cycle and emphasize less on a sophisticated runtime environment for workflows. Upcoming sWfMSs, e.g., Trident or Sedna [20], confirm the approach to use conventional workflow technology in e-Science since they successfully integrate its mechanisms and benefit from its attributes.

12.3.4 Architecture for Scientific Workflow Management Systems

In order to meet the requirements on WfMSs in the scientific domain, we propose a conceptual architecture for sWfMSs that is shown in Fig. 12.2. Individual components in this architecture are discussed in the following.

Since the user interface offers the functionality provided by the sWfMS to a (non-computer) scientist, the usability is the main requirement to be met by the user interface. We propose a *Graphical User Interface (GUI)* with four main components: a service catalog, a workflow modeler, a monitor, and a result display. The GUI is connected to the runtime environment to realize workflow deployment, execution, monitoring, and other functionalities.

The *service catalog* provides the user with a list of available services that can be used in the workflow modeler. The discovery of such services includes among other things the search for new services in the user domain and the identification of services that are no longer available. The underlying mechanisms should be initiated either explicitly by the user or automatically by the sWfMS.

The *workflow modeler* supports the scientific user during workflow specification/modeling. Graphical modeling as well as program like "modeling" has to be provided since many scientists prefer to code their workflows. The modeling language is mainly data-driven with support of control structures. Additionally, the language has to provide mechanisms for the handling huge amounts of data.

The GUI enables the user to select his favored services from the service catalog and compose them using the workflow modeler. The deployment information of such services can be specified by the service provider itself, by the workflow modeler, or automatically by the sWFMS. For example, lots of parallelism in scientific workflows is achieved by parallel workflow instances. The number of these instances

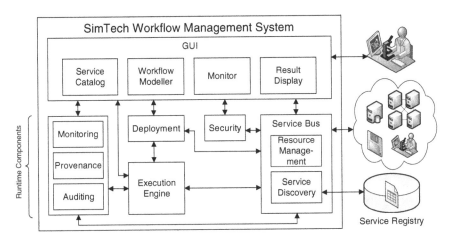

Fig. 12.2 Architecture of a simulation workflow management system

can be huge if multi-scale simulations or for parameter search in simulations are conducted (where one instance for each element in the parameter range is created). In such cases, it is reasonable to distribute the execution of instances which in turn only can be decided in the workflow context. These and other scenarios impose the necessity for specification of service deployment information by the workflow modeler. Since only advanced modelers use this feature, default deployment information is needed for the cases where this information is specified neither in the service catalog nor by the user.

Scientists should be able to execute workflows using the GUI. In order to improve the usability of the GUI workflow and data provisioning, workflow and service deployment as well as workflow instantiation and execution should be automated and thus rendered transparent to the user.

The *monitor* is the third main part of the GUI. It allows the user to inspect the workflow execution and to identify unexpected occurrences or faults in the workflow execution. In order to afford a user reaction, the user should have interactive control on workflow execution and possibility to adapt particular workflows.

Using the *result display*, the final outcome as well as intermediate results of a workflow is presented in an appropriate way. The kind of presentation depends very much on the domain and on the particular data with its specific structure. Support of simulations additionally requires the availability of result visualization. For a customized result visualization adapted to the particular simulation, it is possible to compose special services in a visualization workflow that is part of the simulation workflow. Overall, the result display has to be adaptable/configurable in order to meet the different user requirements.

The main purpose of the *runtime environment* is to carry out the workflows. This comprises navigation through a workflow, maintaining its state, and invoking service implementations, storing workflow-specific run time data, and dealing with experiment dates and simulation results. The architecture's run time components (see Fig. 12.2) are similar to those of existing conventional WfMSs but extended by additional functionality to meet the requirements related to the scientific area, e.g., provenance tracking or scientific data handling. The runtime components for the simulation WfMS are the execution engine, the service bus, the security and deployment components as well as monitoring, auditing, and provenance. All mentioned modules may have access to persistent storage mechanisms to durably save process data. These process storage components differ from the scientific data handling components and are not shown in Fig. 12.2 for better readability.

The *execution engine* runs the scientific workflow instances, which means that it instantiates workflow models with provided input data, navigates through the graphs of activities, and triggers the execution of activity implementations and handles faults and events from the outside. The engine thereby maintains instance data such as the state of a workflow instance and its activities and variables. Furthermore, the execution engine should support transaction concepts in order to support fault handling, e.g., by compensation of completed work. The engine should provide mechanisms to cope with workflow model and instance adaptations at run time.

The *service bus* primarily deals with the task of invoking services that implement workflow activities. Therefore, it discovers and selects services, routes messages, and transforms data. Two major components can be distinguished: the resource management and the service discovery.

Since resources have different properties, the *resource management component* is used, e.g., to identify servers or Grids that have enough storage capacity and calculation power to carry out a computationally intensive task. Furthermore, the resource management is responsible for data vs. code shipping decisions at run time.

The *service discovery* queries service registries (such as UDDI) to find services by means of descriptive information (e.g., interfaces, and semantic annotations). The service discovery component delivers a list of candidate services. On the one hand, this capability is used by the service catalog component of the GUI. On the other hand, it is the basis for flexibility mechanisms regarding activity implementations, i.e., late binding [21] and rebinding of failing activities. The late binding strategy denotes the process of selecting a concrete service as late as possible, i.e., during workflow execution at the latest.

The *deployment component* transforms workflow models into an engine-internal representation, installs them on the engine, and publishes the workflows as services. A so-called deployment descriptor prescribes how to make the workflow runnable on a specific engine. The deployment descriptor may, for instance, statically bind services, specify selection rules, or influence resource management decisions. Although the deployment is triggered by the GUI, its complexity should be hidden especially to scientific users.

The *security component* has two main functions, namely, to ensure both local and remote security policies. The local security protects the GUI from unauthorized access. The remote security protects services provided by the sWfMS from remote access. Furthermore, it enables the service bus to access secured resources such as scientific databases that request a user login.

Finally, there is a group of components that are rather passive with respect to workflow execution: the auditing, provenance and monitoring component. The *auditing* component is responsible for recording workflow or activity related events, e.g., the start time of a workflow or the duration of an activity execution. The *monitoring* component uses the events related to a single workflow run and indicates the status of this workflow run. The *provenance* component records data that goes beyond simple auditing information. All together these components enable the examination of workflow runs and their reproducibility.

12.3.5 Prototype

In the context of the DFG Cluster of Excellence Simulation Technology (SimTech),[5] we developed a first prototype that implements the conceptual architecture for sWfMSs mentioned above. SimTech concentrates on simulation technology,

---

[5] http://www.simtech.uni-stuttgart.de/

ranging from molecular dynamics and modern mechanics over numerical mathematics and systems analysis to data management and interactive visualization as well as high-performance computing. In our field, we make efforts in creating a sWfMS especially tailored to requirements for simulation workflows. The underlying technical complexity ought to be hidden for scientists to enable them to concentrate on their core competencies. The prototype presented in this chapter focuses on the modeling of scientific and simulation workflows. We decided to rely on BPEL [4] as workflow language for various reasons. It is widely accepted in industry and research, supports integration of legacy applications by using WSs as activity implementations, and there are a number of open source BPEL tools that can be used as basis for a sWfMS. However, in order to satisfy requirements of scientists and simulation workflows, extensions to standard BPEL are needed.

We use the Eclipse BPEL Designer[6] as starting point for a tool to model simulation workflows but the tool needs extensions in order to support newly introduced modeling constructs. On the basis of Eclipse, we implemented different perspectives corresponding to the different phases in the lifecycle of simulation process management. A "SimTech modeling perspective" (see Fig. 12.3) provides for the

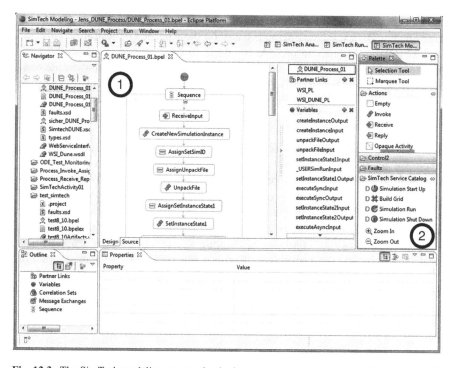

Fig. 12.3 The SimTech modeling perspective in the prototype including a workflow modeler (**1**) and the service catalog (**2**)

---

[6] http://www.eclipse.org/bpel/

design of workflows with the help of the modeler and the service catalog. The "SimTech runtime perspective" supports the user during workflow execution to follow the simulation progress. The result display shows intermediate results in this perspective. At last, the "SimTech analysis perspective" allows analyzing the outcome of workflow runs and therefore contains the result display and the monitoring component. In contrast to the runtime perspective, the result display is highlighted here.

The service catalog was recently implemented and allows the use of services as building blocks in DUNE[7] (Distributed and Unified Numerics Environment) simulations represented as BPEL workflows. Currently, efforts are being made to support other simulation frameworks and visualization services. With the visualization services, users are able to specify result visualization in a way similar to the actual simulation. The monitor is a proprietary implementation which is fitted for the special needs in simulations. This means that, e.g., in DUNE simulations, special DUNE events can be monitored instead of ordinary BPEL events. In our further work, we will improve the monitor component with additional features. The implementation of the result display is currently in progress. It will enable a user-defined result display. Calculation steps needed to display data will be provided as services and workflows, respectively.

The runtime environment of our prototype uses open source software for all components. The execution engine is based on the Apache Orchestration Director Engine[8] (ODE). In order to provide the basic functionality of a service bus, we use Apache Axis2.[9] In our prototype, Axis2 invokes services that implement workflow activities but extensions are needed for two main objectives: service discovery and resource management. Currently, we provide a service registry for data services based on Apache jUDDI[10] that can be used to choose data sources at runtime.

In order to support resource management functionalities in the service bus, we developed a set of generic Web Service interfaces to deal with external data sources, scientific applications, or computing environments. The WS interface to invoke scientific applications consists of a generic adapter that provides fundamental functionality: The adapter manages all instances of the simulation applications and assists basic operations like generate directories, files access, execute supporting services like configuring, compile source code, or start a scientific application without user interaction. To run applications with user interaction or in an asynchronous manner, a plug-in that fulfills the special needs of the application is necessary.

---

[7] DUNE, a C++ template library for solving partial differential equations with grid-based methods: http://www.dune-project.org/

[8] http://ode.apache.org/

[9] http://ws.apache.org/axis2/

[10] http://ws.apache.org/juddi/

The ingredients of the generic adapter are a basic WS, an instance pool, a program manager, and a callback WS. The basic WS is the main interface for a client to communicate with the generic Web Service interface. It offers basic operations to interact with the instances of simulation applications synchronously or asynchronously. The instance pool manages every instance of simulation applications individually. The program manager implements all operations needed to execute simulation applications like create directory structures, install compiler, compile source code, or start executable programs. It provides functionality for applications with or without user interaction. Beyond that, the program manager supports an interface that can handle the program output, e.g., for troubleshooting. The callback WS serves the notification by an asynchronously running simulation application. For example, an application can notify its state (e.g., runnable, busy) to the generic WS interface. To do this, the simulation application must be enriched with a platform-specific callback stub.

The WS interface for data sources provides a framework for data access from a BPEL workflow to handle huge amounts of data stored in different sources. The database domain has inspired generic activities like Select, Update, Insert, and Delete. Our prototype currently supports comma-separated value files (CSV) and relational databases (SQL).

For the auditing, monitoring, and provenance components, we developed an integrated database environment. To store the audit information, the environment can use different database systems. The ODE execution engine uses an Apache Derby[11] database management system (DBMS) to store all audit information. As a result of an evaluation, we have replaced Derby with the more suitable open source DBMS PostgreSQL.[12] It is also feasible to utilize the commercial IBM DB2[13] DBMS. Using the audit information and based on the management tools of the DBMSs or an external tool such as SQuirreL,[14] it is possible to extract monitoring information like the status of a workflow or the number of running instances.

12.4 A DUNE-Based Simulation: An Example Distributed and Unified Numerics Environment (DUNE)

We implemented several workflows that perform simulations with different complexity to prove the viability of the architecture and prototype of the SimTech WfMS. For complexity reason, we demonstrate a simple example: a fluid dynamics problem that simulates the diffusion of an ink drop into a box of water with the help of the finite elements method (FEM). In the scientific experiment, the ink diffusion

---

[11] http://db.apache.org/derby/

[12] http://www.postgresql.org/

[13] http://www-01.ibm.com/software/data/db2/

[14] http://squirrel-sql.sourceforge.net/

in water can be expressed as partial differential equation (PDE) in three spaces and one time dimension with particular conditions:

$$\frac{\partial c}{\partial t} + \nabla \cdot (uc) = 0 \quad in \, \Omega \times T$$

$$\Omega \subset \mathbb{R}^3 \text{ is a domain}$$

$$T = (0, t_{end}) \text{ is a time interval}$$

$$c: \Omega \times T \rightarrow \mathbb{R} \text{ is the unknown concentration}$$

$$u: \Omega \times T \rightarrow \mathbb{R}^3 \text{ is a given velocity field}$$

$$\text{intitial condition: } c(x, 0) = c_0(x), \qquad x \in \Omega$$

$$\text{boundary condition: } c(x, t) = b(x, t), \qquad t > 0, \qquad x \in \Gamma_{in}(t) = \{ y \in \partial\Omega \mid u(y, t) \cdot v(y) < 0 \}$$

Here $v(x)$ is the unit outer normal at a point y $\partial\Omega$
and $\Gamma_{in}(t)$ is the inflow boundary at time t

To solve this PDE, we used the FEM framework of DUNE (Distributed and Unified Numerics Environment). DUNE fits a wide range of simulation problems and is therefore frequently used SimTech. For example, it contains software libraries that provide modules for solving PDEs. These C++ source code libraries include, e.g., implementations of grid-based techniques such as finite elements. Furthermore, DUNE contains different solver libraries, e.g., for linear equations, for vector and matrix calculations, or iterative solvers. Other libraries support data import and export for various file formats.

In order for the scientists to execute a DUNE-based simulation, first the source code for the simulation program must be created for the target runtime platform (e.g., operating system, multi-core support). After compilation, the source code of the executable simulation application must be copied into a specific directory structure. In detail, the creation of a typical DUNE-based simulation consists of the following 12 steps:

1. Create a new DUNE module.
2. Define dependencies to other existing DUNE modules.
3. Implement custom modules if needed.
4. Construct the main routine which uses the modules. (Simulation parameters like space dimension must be defined in the main routine or in the modules.)
5. Integrate file importers and exporters for the data.
6. Generate a configuration file specifying the build sequence.
7. Compile required modules and the main routine using the GNU build system.[15]

---

[15] http://www.gnu.org/software/libtool/manual/automake/

8. Create files with input data for the simulation, e.g., initial grid description.
9. Copy the executable code and all needed files in a suitable directory structure.
10. Run the simulation.
11. Store the results.
12. Delete outdated data, e.g., compiler output.

A DUNE-based application created this way is monolithic and cannot be executed stepwise or with user interaction. To achieve this, we enrich the DUNE library at step four. Hence, step ten can be divided in subtasks:

(a) Initialize MPIHelper[16] if multi-core support is needed.
(b) Create a basic FEM grid.
(c) Calculate the FEM grid refinement steps with respect to the boundary values.
(d) Refine the FEM grid.
(e) Set initial values and the FEM grid.
(f) Solve the simulation for one time step.
(g) Write the (intermediate) result data.
(h) Repeat subtask f. and g. for all required time steps.

Until now, a C++ program is created in order to execute this simulation. Since we want to use workflow technology for the execution of this simulation, we modeled two different BPEL processes for two use cases. The first use case executes the DUNE-based application without user interaction. The second use case supports user interaction and therefore requires the integration of a gSOAP[17] server.

In Fig. 12.4, a workflow model for the second use case is represented. It uses a so-called WS DUNE plug-in that is an extension of the generic WS interface presented in Sect. 12.3.5. At the beginning of the workflow, the activity

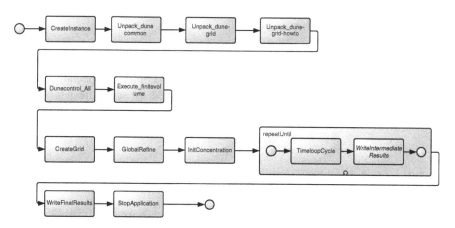

Fig. 12.4 Workflow to simulate the ink concentration in water

---

[16] http://www.mpi-forum.org/

[17] http://www.cs.fsu.edu/~engelen/soap.html

CreateInstance invokes the WS DUNE plug-in to initialize a unique Instance-ID and some metadata like timestamps managed by the instance pool.

The activity *Unpack_dune-common* creates all required directories and copy software artifacts like the GNU build system into these directories. Afterward, *Unpack_dune-grid* inserts the source code of the DUNE C++ framework into the created directories. *Unpack_dune-grid-howto* provides the source code for the concrete simulation to a specified directory. After these preparatory operations, *Dunecontrol_All* builds the executable simulation application. This activity combines the generation of modules, code fragments, and files concerning steps one – nine. *Execute_finitevolume* starts the interactive simulation application. Thus, we can control the substeps 10a to 10g with BPEL activities to calculate the ink diffusion simulation.

To simplify the execution of the use case, we use a single core machine without the need for the MPIHelper (substep 10a). Therefore, *CreateGrid* and *GlobalRefine* initialize the simulation at substep 10b or 10c and 10d, respectively. Afterward, *InitConcentration* (substep 10e) reads initial values from a database and integrates these values in the FEM grid. *TimeloopCycle* represents substep 10f, and together with the enclosing *repeatUntil* activity, it iteratively calculates single time steps in the simulation. For each time step, *WriteIntermediateResults* writes intermediate result data in a database (substep 10g). Activity *WriteFinalResults* that is also part of substep 10g stores the final result data in a database, and *StopApplication* finally cleans the workspace of all data fragments that are no longer needed, e.g., intermediate results or compiler output.

12.5 Scientific Domain Intended Extensions for Conventional Workflow Technology

In this section, we present extensions of conventional workflow technology intended for the use of workflows in the scientific domain. Especially, these adaptations meet unfulfilled requirements established by scientific simulation workflows.

12.5.1 Modeling Language

As starting point for the modeling of scientific workflows, we use BPEL [4] since it is the de facto standard for modeling business workflows. In [22], the ability of BPEL to be used as modeling language for scientific workflows is already documented. It should be especially noted that BPEL and its support of transaction models upgrades the robustness of scientific workflows which is one of the goals in our work.

Applying conventional workflow technology for scientific simulations imposes the need for the introduction of new language constructs in order to achieve the required expressiveness of workflow modeling languages. Existing simulation modeling languages are various since simulations are applied in various fields. Often the languages are close to mathematical representations, e.g., in MatLab. Higher modeling languages are mainly given by simulation libraries written in C++, e.g., DUNE, ODEMx.[18] As mentioned before, usability is an important issue in the scientific domain. Therefore, some efforts were made in graphical modeling of simulations, e.g., Simulink.[19]

In this section, we present some modeling concepts specifically designed for scientific simulation workflows in general and for an increased expressiveness of BPEL for simulations in particular. In [13], the gentle reader can get further information about modeling language constructs for simulation workflows based on BPEL. In comparison to GriCoL, a graphical language for simulation workflows in Grids, we identified data handling and pipelining mechanisms on workflow level as well as different layers of abstraction, explicit data flow, and shared data as core concepts for simulation workflows that are currently not supported by BPEL.

12.5.1.1   Data-Centric Workflow Models

The data-centric character of scientific workflows demands adaptation of the language. Since BPEL is a control-driven language, control structures that scientists want to use in their workflows are already supported by BPEL. The specification of data-driven workflows is not completely addressed by BPEL until now. An extension, namely BPEL-D [23], exists that allows the modeling of *data dependencies* between activities in the BPEL process. In a pre-deployment step, BPEL-D processes are translated into standard BPEL and hence, the data dependencies are not used during execution. Since data dependencies in data-driven workflows require a delivery of control as well, BPEL-D is not adequate for the use in scientific workflows. However, it can be used as a starting point. Enabling the modeling of "real" data-driven workflows with BPEL is one future work issue.

The handling of huge amounts of data has impact on the performance during scientific workflow execution. For the most part, this challenge must be met by the workflow runtime environment. However, there are possibilities in the modeling language to improve the handling of huge amounts of data. In [24], we presented an improvement of data handling by the introduction of data references that is recently implemented in the SimTech prototype (cf. Sect. 12.3.5). Dealing with huge amounts of data in BPEL processes results in lots of transmissions of large data sets which make the usage of BPEL very costly for scientific workflows. The majority of scientific data is of no importance for the process logic itself and thus

---

[18] http://odemx.sourceforge.net/

[19] http://www.mathworks.com/products/simulink/?BB=1

Fig. 12.5 A visualization
workflow using data
references

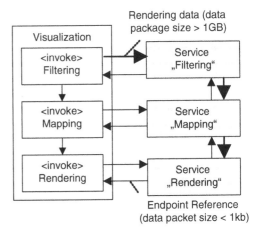

can be ignored by the WfMS. By using data references, the transfer of huge amounts of data through the engine can be minimized or even avoided without losing relevant information. Figure 12.5 illustrates the idea to use data references.

The scientific workflow in Fig. 12.5 represents a general visualization process. It successively invokes a filtering service, a mapping service, and a rendering service. A workflow engine in the WfMS is responsible for the execution of the visualization workflow and for the invocation of services. A visualization workflow receives a lot of data during the simulation. Consequently, the execution of the visualization workflow in Fig. 12.5 demands multiple exchanges of huge data sets through the engine. Usage of pointers in the visualization workflow shifts the responsibility for data transport to participating services and therefore scales down the amount of data that has to be transferred through the workflow engine.

12.5.1.2 Simulation Workflow Container

Typically, simulations have complex character and often more than one workflow model is assembled in a so-called choreography. Hence, the simulation represents a context for assembled workflows. Since in workflows there are variables that represent the state of the simulated system, we need to support shared context data in simulation workflows. Therefore, we propose the introduction of *simulation workflow containers* that hold assembled workflows in choreographies together with shared data structures. Data structures are held in variables typed with XML schema. Different types of values result in different types of variables that hold data structures. State variables and simulation parameters represent shared context data and therefore embodied by reference variables that allow the storage of data values outside of the simulation model. Reference variables are visible for all workflows that are enclosed in the simulation workflow container.

For an enhanced context, it should generally be possible to use data references in simulation workflows.

When the simulation model is executed by a centralized workflow engine, the data value is held in the local storage of the engine. For distributed engines, there is the need for an optimized distribution of such shared data. At first, the data value can be held on any node X and the other nodes send requests for the data whenever it is required. When choosing the node that stores the value, the number of data transfers for reference resolution should be considered for an optimized performance in simulation execution. In general, the node with the minimal number of data transfers between all nodes should store the data value.

Some kinds of simulations additionally require synchronization of workflows assembled in a simulation workflow container. This means especially synchronization regarding a model property. A possible use case is the intention to model a time scale whose value and variation is equal in each workflow. Another possible use case is the parallel processing of one data item by multiple workflows or workflow instances.

Simulation workflow containers as stated above can be used as well for multi-scale and multi-physics simulations. In multi-scale simulations, one model of one system is simulated on different scales. The simulation on different scales means different modifications of one system property, e.g., the variation of time or a length quantity. The execution of multi-scale simulations depends on the use case. Scientists want to run multi-scale simulations sequentially as well as in parallel. In contrast to multi-scale simulations, multi-physics simulations demand multiple models of one system. Each model represents another point of view on the system with another physical theory as basis. These different models are possibly coupled and executed sequentially or in parallel.

Multi-scale simulations can be realized by one simulation workflow container that holds the system model. The container is parameterized with the scale, i.e., the modification of the particular system property. With that it is possible to simulate multiple scales by running multiple instances of the container. These instances can be executed sequentially or in parallel.

Multi-physics simulation can be realized with workflows by nesting simulation workflow containers. The overall container involves one simulation workflow container for each simulation model. In that case, the overall container assembles no simulation workflows while the child containers hold workflow choreographies. The support of coupling mechanisms between simulation models can be realized by message exchanges between simulation workflow containers.

12.5.2 Runtime Environment

The runtime environment offers means to execute workflows. This section discusses workflow execution on distributed and centralized workflow engines and shows how convenient data handling in workflows can be achieved.

12.5.2.1 Distributed vs. Central Execution

The architecture in Fig. 12.2 and our current prototype rely on a centralized workflow engine while the used WSs can be distributed among different machines hosted by different organizations. This is the common approach in both conventional and scientific workflow management. It is a known fact that scientific workflows are often long-running and that they usually process large data sets that have to be transmitted between services and workflow engine [11]. When a centralized workflow engine runs many workflow instances in parallel that deal with huge amounts of data (e.g., in a parameter sweep), it can become a bottleneck for the whole system even if the used services are distributed. Additionally, a malfunction of the workflow server means a breakdown of all running simulations until the server restarts. The employment of a decentralized workflow engine can address these and other problems. In our former work, we investigated whether a workflow engine that is distributed with the help of a process space-based middleware is beneficial to the scientific domain [25]. The "engine" is a set of activity clients that can be installed on several machines (even at process runtime). They communicate via tokens that are written to and read from process spaces. That way control and data are exchanged. The process spaces themselves can also be installed on several machines. In such an infrastructure, the processes can be executed even in the presence of server failures if redundant functionality (i.e., services) and data replication mechanisms are employed. The engine is no single bottleneck anymore. Intelligent distribution of activity clients on machines that host the used services can minimize the network load and hence speedup workflow execution. Of course, a distributed workflow enactment has also downsides. Previously unconnected components have to be wired which results in an increased coordination and configuration effort. Furthermore, new sources of failures are introduced such as the unavailability of process spaces or tokens that are written but never read because of faulted activity clients. In summary, decentralized workflow systems have many properties that can be advantageous for scientific applications. But it needs to be decided on a case basis if these advantages outbalance the described effort.

12.5.2.2 Interaction with Data Stores and Huge Data Sets in Workflows

In the context of scientific and especially simulation workflows, the management of data sets is a fundamental issue [26]. Typical challenges are to integrate heterogeneous data sources and to cope with huge amounts of data [18]. As mentioned earlier, we propose to rely on BPEL as starting point for a simulation workflow language. In BPEL, data is loaded into processes with WS invocations. The access to data therefore must be wrapped by WSs. While this functionality is desired in business scenarios, it provides a serious drawback for a practical use in the scientific domain. Scientists want to access data directly from within their workflows [13]. We therefore extended BPEL by special data management activities that can be used to directly access several kinds of external data sources, e.g., data stored in databases or CSV files. No WS wrappers are needed anymore. These activities are geared toward established data management patterns such as query, insert, update, or delete. It is possible to reference queried data with special Set Reference variables and hence leave this data in a data source (i.e., outside of the workflow engine). Parts of that data can be loaded explicitly into processes if needed for process execution by a retrieve data activity. This avoids stuffing huge amounts of data not needed by a workflow into the BPEL engine. Another aspect of our approach is late binding of data sources. Data sources can be registered with non-functional properties in an extended UDDI registry. Data management activities can then be bound to concrete data sources at process runtime by matching specified requirements on data sources and provided features of registered data sources. This enables an increased robustness of the overall workflow execution in case data sources fail and alternative data sources with similar properties are available.

12.5.3 Flexibility Mechanisms

Quite a lot of research is already done in the field of flexibility of business workflows and conventional workflow technology. Following approaches are especially interesting for scientific workflows. Note that we do not claim the list to be complete. (1) Late binding of services increases flexibility of workflows because concrete services are selected at execution time [21]. (2) The approach of parameterized processes [27] is a BPEL extension to release interacting activities from the specification of service interfaces (port type and operation pairs). That way, services can be late-bound independent of their interfaces. (3) BPEL'n'Aspects [28] is a nonintrusive mechanism to adapt the logic dimension of BPEL process models or instances with the help of the AOP (aspect-oriented programming) techniques [29]. It is possible to extend workflows with additional behavior, to replace or delete elements (activities, transition conditions). Cumbersome instance migration operations [30] are not be needed. (4) The process space-based workflow enactment [31] (see Sect. 12.5.2) opens new possibilities for workflow logic adaptations during execution. Workflows can be modified by installing/uninstalling as well as and configuring/reconfiguring activity clients.

Scientific workflows in general and simulation workflows in particular impose novel requirements on the workflow meta-model and execution environment. Such requirements are not yet accounted for in the discussed flexibility mechanisms. In the following, we sketch considerations about needed extensions in the meta-model and execution environment for simulation workflows.

12.5.3.1 Modeling Language Extensions

The integration of sensors and hence streaming data into workflow imposes the need for a new connector, namely, a data pipeline. In contrast to data or control connectors, pipeline edges can be evaluated several times and hence activity instances that are the source or target of a pipeline connection may be executed several times. This imposes new use cases for adaptation of workflows. For example, a concept is needed to exchange sensors or insert/delete sensor activities at runtime. Such a concept will differ very much from exchanging, inserting, or deleting activities that invoke services because sensors continuously deliver streams of data whereas the communication with services is based on sending and receiving messages.

12.5.3.2 Execution Environment Extensions

Due to the need of enormous computing and storage capacities, simulations are often conducted in Grids. With the introduction of the Web Services Resource Framework (WSRF) [6], Grid resources can be provided as stateful Web Services and can thus be orchestrated in service compositions (e.g., in a BPEL process). Such a stateful environment imposes new requirements on flexibility mechanisms. For example, when changing a running workflow by choosing another service that is to be invoked, it may happen that the service resides on another resource than the data it relies on. This implies that the data needs to be shipped between the resources. This data shipment can be implemented by the Enterprise Service Bus (ESB) transparently for the scientist. Currently, ESBs do not provide data shipping functionality because services used in business scenarios are self-containing logic. However, the specification of a data dependency between resources/services/tools would simplify the solution of this problem. Late binding and function shipping mechanisms could render the situation even more complex.

An important requirement of scientists on an execution environment for simulations is the reproducibility of results. A sWfMS with advanced flexibility capabilities therefore needs a mechanism to track (automatic or manual) changes that were made during execution of workflows. Tracking changes are currently not implemented by the presented approaches to flexibility. Another reason for the need of advanced flexibility features in scientific workflow management is the way scientists create and execute their experiments and simulations. They usually do not distinguish between models and instances of workflows. That means the focus of their work is on single workflow instances. Scientists often unconsciously switch between phases of modeling, execution, and monitoring of workflows. They are unaware of the technical realization of their actions and in fact do not want to cope with such details. However, from a software engineering point of view, it is desirable to consider these technical aspects. We therefore extended and modified the business workflow life cycle to reflect the needs of scientists (Fig. 12.6) [14]. This enhanced life cycle reveals that scientists transparently make use of two categories of adaptation operations when manually modifying their simulation workflows. First, adapting the structure of workflows (i.e., the logic dimension) entails a redeployment of the workflow or parts of it. Of course, deployment should be transparent for the scientists. It is nevertheless mentioned here because of its importance from a technical point of view [12]. Second, modifications on the functions dimension (e.g., changing criteria for selection of a service) can be conducted without a need

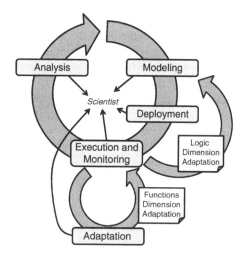

Fig. 12.6 Life cycle of scientific workflows geared toward the technical realization with the help of conventional workflow technology

for redeployment. In order to support scientists in developing simulations and experiments in the described trial-and-error manner, a tool is needed that combines the capabilities of a workflow modeling tool and a progress monitor. That means it allows modeling a workflow, executing it, and modifying it at runtime. Such a tool implements the proposed blending of modeling, execution, adaptation, and monitoring phases of the life cycle of scientific workflows. A major part of the solution is to execute incomplete workflows (or workflow fragments) in a straightforward manner. A finished workflow fragment execution must not be considered completed. It must be possible to continue modeling of the workflow and to resume its execution. In conventional workflow technology, deploying and executing workflow fragments is currently an unsolved issue.

12.6   Conclusion

In this chapter, we discussed the qualification of established workflow technology for the evolving application domain of e-Science as well as the state of the art of scientific workflow management systems. We discussed in detail the qualification of conventional workflow technology for e-Science based on the most important requirements of scientific workflows and simulations workflows in particular. We outlined benefits as well as arising technical problems and gave recommendations as of how to solve these problems. Furthermore, by means of the life cycles for business and scientific workflows, we explained that conventional workflow technology needs thorough extensions in order to be suitable for application in scientific experiments, computations, and simulations. We presented a workflow system architecture that is based on conventional workflow technology and tailored to the needs of scientists and explained how the foreseen system meets general requirements of scientists and scientific workflows. Further, a prototype that implements the architecture and is especially designed to support the modeling and execution of simulation workflows was introduced. An example scenario of "ink diffusion in water" that runs on the prototype demonstrates the feasibility of the approach.

Because of the data-centric character of scientific workflows, conventional workflow modeling languages (e.g., BPEL) need adaptations when being applied in the scientific domain. In order to efficiently handle huge amounts of data in scientific workflows, we introduced data references in BPEL and conventional workflow technology in general. Furthermore, we draw on an existing approach to integrate explicit data flow in BPEL since modeling languages for scientific workflows have to support explicit data flow modeling constructs. Prospectively, conventional workflow languages need to be adapted in order to handle data streams. Scientists want to divide large data sets in components and process a stream of these components in a scientific workflow. Furthermore, scientists want to integrate sensor data in scientific workflows which also establishes the need for stream data in the modeling language for scientific workflows. Especially for simulations, we introduced the modeling concept of simulation workflow containers holding an assembly of simulation workflows and shared context data. In future, this concept will be implemented and integrated in the presented prototype. Nevertheless, for simulation, conventional workflow languages need further extensions, e.g., in order to efficiently handle parameter searches. In addition, we will pay special attention on further development of choreographies for simulation since they represent eligible matches (cf. for example [32]).

In the runtime environment, we primarily intend to extend our approach to integrate data and process provenance for scientific workflows. The starting point is the presented integrated database environment for workflow and simulation data based on a special Web Services interface. Furthermore, we plan to develop methods for performance optimization especially by optimizing the global resource utilization in scientific workflows.

Furthermore, special attention will be paid on flexibility aspects. This promises both an improved robustness of the system as well as an explorative workflow modeling for scientists (i.e., trial-and-error modeling). Mechanisms to flexibility have impact on modeling and execution of workflows. Since we want to pursue an engineering solution, we want to make use of existing flexibility approaches. We therefore sketched existing candidates and argued that these need extensions in order to satisfy requirements of scientific and simulation workflows. Currently, we are working on the blending of modeling, execution, and monitoring phases of workflows to support the trial-and-error approach of workflow development of scientists. The first prototype will allow changing of parameters at runtime. As next step, we want to integrate the BPEL'n'Aspects approach into the prototype in order to provide more complex change operations. A challenge will be the development of a generic format for tracking changes, obtaining information about automatic and manual modifications in order to allow reproducibility and confidence in simulation results, and a method to visualize changes in a practical way.

References

1. F. Leymann, D. Roller: *Production Workflow: Concepts and Techniques*. Prentice Hall, Englewood Cliffs, NJ, 1999.
2. I.J. Taylor, E. Deelman, E.B. Gannon, M. Shields (ed.): *Workflows for e-Science – Scientific Workflows for Grids*. Springer, 2007.
3. R. Chinnici, J.-J. Moreau, A. Ryman, S. Weerawarana: *Web Services Description Language (WSDL) Version 2.0 Part 1: Core Language*. 2007.
4. A. Alves, A. Arkin, S. Askary, C. Barreto, B. Bloch, F. Curbera, M. Ford, Y. Goland, A. Guízar, N. Kartha, C. K. Liu, R. Khalaf, D. König, M. Marin, V. Mehta, S. Thatte, D. van der Rijn, P. Yendluri, A. Yiu: *Web Services Business Process Execution Language Version 2.0*. 2007.
5. D. Churches, G. Gombas, A. Harrison, J. Maassen, C. Robinson, M. Shields, I. Taylor, I. Wang: *Programming Scientific and Distributed Workflow with Triana Services*. Concurrency and Computation: Practice and Experience. Special Issue on Scientific Workflows, 2005.
6. S. Graham, A. Karmarkar, J. Mischkinsky, I. Robinson, I. Sedukhin: *Web Services Resource (WS-Resource) V1.2*. OASIS, 9 December 2004.
7. T. Oinn, M. Greenwood, M. Addis, M. Nedim Alpdemir, J. Ferris, K. Glover, C. Goble, A. Goderis, D. Hull, D. Marvin, P. Li, P. Lord, M.R. Pocock, M. Senger, R. Stevens, A. Wipat, C. Wroe: *Taverna: Lessons in Creating a Workflow Environment for the Life Sciences*. Concurrency and Computation: Practice and Experience 2006, 18(10):1067–110.
8. I. Altintas, C. Berkley, E. Jaeger, M. Jones, B. Ludascher, S. Mock: *Kepler: An Extensible System for Design and Execution of Scientific Workflows*. SSDBM, 2004.
9. E. Deelman, J. Blythe, Y. Gil, C. Kesselman, G. Mehta, S. Patil, M.-H. Su, K. Vahi, M. Livny: *Pegasus: Mapping Scientific Workflows onto the Grid*. Lecture Notes in Computer Science, Volume 3165/2004, Second European AcrossGrids Conference, Springer, 2004, pp. 11–20.
10. R. Barga, J. Jackson, N. Araujo, D. Guo, N. Gautam, Y. Simmhan: *The Trident Scientific Workflow Workbench*. In: IEEE eScience Conference, 2008.
11. R. Barga, D. Gannon: *Scientific versus Business Workflows*. In: [2], 2007.
12. M. Sonntag, D. Karastoyanova, F. Leymann: *The Missing Features of Workflow Systems for Scientific Computations*. In: Proceedings of the 3 rd Grid Workflow Workshop (GWW) (to appear), 2010.
13. M. Sonntag, K. Görlach, D. Karastoyanova: *Towards Simulation Workflows With BPEL: Deriving Missing Features From GriCoL*. In: Proceedings of the 21st IASTED International Conference Modelling and Simulation (MS 2010), 2010
14. M. Sonntag, D. Karastoyanova: *Next Generation Interactive Scientific Experimenting Based on the Workflow Technology*. In: Proceedings of the 21st IASTED International Conference Modelling and Simulation (MS 2010), 2010.
15. L. Moreau, B. Clifford, J. Freire, Y. Gil, P. Groth, J. Futrelle, N. Kwasnikowska, S. Miles, P. Missier, J. Myers, *The Open Provenance Model Core Specification (V1. 1)*. Future Generation Computer Systems, 2009.
16. D. Karastoyanova, F. Leymann: *Making scientific applications on the Grid reliable through flexibility approaches borrowed from service compositions*. In: N. Antonopoulos, G. Exarchakos, A. Liotta (Eds.), Handbook of research on P2P and Grid systems for service-oriented computing: Models, methodologies and applications (Information Science Publishing, 2010).
17. G. Decker, O. Kopp, F. Leymann, M. Weske: Interacting services: from specification to execution. In: Data & Knowledge Engineering. Vol. 68(10), Elsevier Science Publishers, 2009.
18. D. Pennington, D. Higgins, A.T. Peterson, M.B. Jones, B. Ludäscher, S. Bowers: Ecological niche modeling using the Kepler workflow system. In: [2], 2007.
19. N. Currle-Linde, P. Adamidis, M. Resch, F. Bös, J. Pleiss: *GriCoL: A language for scientific grids*. In: Proceedings of the 2nd IEEE International Conf. on e-Science and Grid Computing, 2006.

20. B. Wassermann, W. Emmerich, B. Butchart, N.Cameron, L. Chen, J. Patel: *Sedna: A BPEL-Based Environment for Visual Scientific Workflow Modeling*. In: [2], 2007.
21. S. Weerawarana, F. Curbera, F. Leymann, D.F. Ferguson, T. Storey: *Web Services Platform Architecture: Soap, WSDL, WS-Policy, WS-Addressing, WS-Bpel, WS-Reliable Messaging and More*. Prentice Hall, 2005
22. A. Akram, D. Meredith, R. Allan: *Evaluation of BPEL to Scientific Workflows*. In Cluster Computing and the Grid (CCGrid), pages 269–274. IEEE Computer Society, 2006.
23. R. Khalaf: *Supporting business process fragmentation while maintaining operational semantics: a BPEL perspective*. PhD thesis, University of Stuttgart. 2008.
24. M. Wieland, K. Görlach, D. Schumm, F. Leymann: *Towards Reference Passing in Web Service and Workflow-based Applications*. Proceedings of the 13th IEEE Enterprise Distributed Object Conference (EDOC 2009). 109–118 (2009).
25. M. Sonntag, K. Görlach, D. Karastoyanova, F. Leymann, M. Reiter: *Process Space-based Scientific Workflow Enactment*. In: International Journal of Business Process Integration and Management (IJBPIM) Special Issue on Scientific Workflows (to appear), Inderscience Publishers, 2010.
26. E. Deelman, A. Chervenak: *Data Management Challenges of Data Intensive Scientific Workflows*. Proc. IEEE Int'l Symp. Cluster Computing and the Grid (CCGRID '08), pp. 687–692, 2008.
27. D. Karastoyanova: *Enhancing flexibility and reusability of web service flows through parameterization*. PhD thesis, TU Darmstadt and University of Stuttgart, 2006.
28. D. Karastoyanova, F. Leymann: *BPEL'n'Aspects: Adapting Service Orchestration Logic*. In: Proceedings of the 7th International Conference on Web Services (ICWS 2009)
29. G. Kiczales: *Aspect-Oriented Programming*. In: Proceedings of ECOOP'97, Finland, 1997.
30. B. Weber, S. Rinderle, M. Reichert: *Change Patterns and Change Support Features in Process-Aware Information Systems*. In: Proceedings of Conference on Advanced Information Systems Engineering (CAiSE), 2007.
31. D. Martin, D. Wutke, F. Leymann: *A Novel Approach to Decentralized Workflow Enactment*. In: Proceedings of the 12th International IEEE Enterprise Distributed Object Computing Conference (EDOC 2008), 2008.
32. A. Barker, P. Besana, D. Robertson, J. Weissman: *The Benefits Of Service Choreography For Data-Intensive Computing*. In: Proceedings of the 7th International Workshop on Challenges of Large Applications in Distributed Environments (CLADE'09), in conjunction with HPDC'09: The 18th International Symposium on High Performance Distributed Computing, pages 1–10. ACM, 2009.

Chapter 13
Facilitating e-Science Discovery Using Scientific Workflows on the Grid

Jianwu Wang, Prakashan Korambath, Seonah Kim, Scott Johnson,
Kejian Jin, Daniel Crawl, Ilkay Altintas, Shava Smallen, Bill Labate,
and Kendall N. Houk

Abstract e-Science has been greatly enhanced from the developing capability and usability of cyberinfrastructure. This chapter explains how scientific workflow systems can facilitate e-Science discovery in Grid environments by providing features including scientific process automation, resource consolidation, parallelism, provenance tracking, fault tolerance, and workflow reuse. We first overview the core services to support e-Science discovery. To demonstrate how these services can be seamlessly assembled, an open source scientific workflow system, called *Kepler*, is integrated into the *University of California Grid*. This architecture is being applied to a computational enzyme design process, which is a formidable and collaborative problem in computational chemistry that challenges our knowledge of protein chemistry. Our implementation and experiments validate how the Kepler workflow system can make the scientific computation process automated, pipe-lined, efficient, extensible, stable, and easy-to-use.

13.1 Introduction

"e-Science is about global collaboration in key areas of science and the next genera-tion of infrastructure that will enable it."[1] Grid computing "coordinates resources that are not subject to centralized control by using standard, open, general-purpose

---

[1] John Taylor, Director General of Research Councils, Office of Science and Technology, UK.

J. Wang (✉), D. Crawl, I. Altintas, and S. Smallen
San Diego Supercomputer Center, UCSD, 9500 Gilman Drive, MC 0505, La Jolla,
CA 92093, USA
e-mail: jianwu@sdsc.edu

P. Korambath, K. Jin, and B. Labate
Institute for Digital Research and Education, UCLA, 5308 Math Sciences, Los Angeles,
CA 90095, USA

S. Kim, S. Johnson, and K.N. Houk
Department of Chemistry and Biochemistry, UCLA, Los Angeles, CA 90095, USA

Xiaoyu Yang et al. (eds.), *Guide to e-Science: Next Generation Scientific Research and Discovery*, Computer Communications and Networks,
DOI 10.1007/978-0-85729-439-5_13, © Springer-Verlag London Limited 2011

protocols and interfaces, and deliver nontrivial qualities of service" [1]. For over a decade, Grid techniques have been successfully used to enable or facilitate domain scientists on their scientific computational problems by providing federated resources and services. Yet the software that creates and manages Grid environments, such as the Globus toolkit,[2] gLite,[3] and Unicore,[4] alone is not sufficient to manage the complex job control and data dependencies for many domain-specific problems. Such problems require combining more than one complex computational code into flexible and reusable computational scientific processes [2–4]. Scientific workflow systems [5, 6] enable researchers to design computational experiments that span multiple distributed computational and analytical models, and in the process, store, access, transfer, and query information. This requires the integration of a variety of computational tools, including the domain-specific software, database programs as well as preparation, visualization, and analysis toolkits [2, 3].

In this chapter, we explain how scientific workflow systems can facilitate the e-Science discovery in Grid environments by providing features such as scientific process automation, resource consolidation, parallelism, provenance tracking, fault tolerance, and workflow reuse. The chapter is organized as follows. In Sect. 13.2, we summarize the core services needed for e-Science discovery. Section 13.3 demonstrates an assembly of these services by integrating the Kepler workflow system[5] into the University of California Grid (UC Grid).[6] In Sect. 13.4, an application for a theoretical enzyme design computation process is explained using the integrated architecture. We concluded the chapter in Sect. 13.5.

13.2   The Core Services to Support e-Science Discovery

Nowadays, various services have been provided by the infrastructure to support e-Science discovery. e-Science problems build upon increasingly growing scientific data and require large-scale computational resources. Commonly, data and computation resources are distributed in geographically sparse locations and have a variety of usage modes. A typical computational experiment involves various tasks. By providing pipeline tools to connect the tasks and automate their execution, scientific process automation is becoming increasingly important to help scientists easily and efficiently utilize the data and computation resources to solve their domain-specific scientific problems. The infrastructure for e-Science should also enable scientists to interact with during the whole experiment lifecycle, such

---

[2] http://www.globus.org/toolkit/

[3] http://glite.web.cern.ch/glite/

[4] http://www.unicore.eu/

[5] http://kepler-project.org

[6] http://www.ucgrid.org/

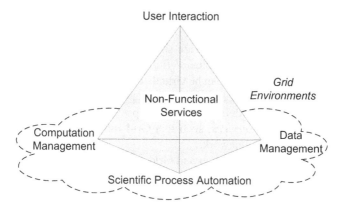

Fig. 13.1 A core service classification to support e-Science discovery

as triggering and adjusting the processes, monitoring their execution, and viewing the resulting data. Furthermore, nonfunctional services, such as security and failure recovery, are also important to ensure the whole process to be secure and fault tolerant. As shown in Fig. 13.1, computation management, data management, scientific process automation, user interaction, and nonfunctional services are the core service categories to support e-Science discovery. Also these services are complementary to each other, and are often integrated in many e-Science projects.

In this section, we describe the main services in each category, discussing their purposes, challenges along with the approaches and tools to enable them.

13.2.1 Computation Management

Over the past decade, Grid computation techniques have been successfully used to assist domain scientists with their scientific computational problems. Widely used Grid software includes the Globus toolkit, gLite, Unicore, Nimrod/G,[7] and Condor-G.[8] More details on Grid computation management can be found in [7, 8].

13.2.1.1 Service-Oriented Computation

A Web service is "a software system designed to support interoperable machine-to-machine interaction over a network".[9] Original Web services, also called big Web

---

[7] http://messagelab.monash.edu.au/NimrodG

[8] http://www.cs.wisc.edu/condor/condorg/

[9] http://www.w3.org/TR/ws-gloss/#webservice

services, are based on standards including XML, Web Service Definition Language (WSDL), and Simple Object Access Protocol (SOAP). Another set of Web services, called RESTful Web services, are simple Web services implemented based on HTTP protocol and the principles of Representational State Transfer (REST) [9]. Heterogeneous applications can be virtualized and easily interoperate with each other at Web service level by following the standards and protocols. The Open Grid Services Architecture [10] defines uniform exposed service semantics for Grid components, called *Grid services*, such that Grid functionalities can be incorporated into a Web service framework.

Through the introduction of Web and Grid services, a large number of computational resources in different scientific domains, e.g., bioinformatics, are becoming easily usable, and in turn introducing new challenges including service semantics, discovery, composition, and orchestration [11].

13.2.1.2 Local Resource Management

A compute cluster resource is a collection of compute nodes connected through a private fast interconnect fabric, e.g., Infiniband, Myrinet, or even local area network (LAN), and operated by an organization such as a university. A *local resource manager* is an application that is aware of the resources in a cluster and provides an interface for users to access them. The job submission and execution on a cluster is usually managed through resource manager software, such as the Torque,[10] Sun Grid Engine (SGE, renamed as Oracle Grid Engine recently),[11] or Load Sharing Facility (LSF).[12] A *resource scheduler,* on the other hand, can simply allocate jobs in a first in first out (FIFO) basis, or follow some complex scheduling algorithms (e.g., preemption, backfilling, etc.) such as the Maui,[13] Moab,[14] or SGE scheduler. A resource manager can use multiple schedulers. For example, Torque can be integrated with either the Maui or Moab.

The cluster owner sets policies on resource consumption such as which groups have access to it, how many resources can be allocated, whether they can run parallel jobs or only serial jobs, etc. This information is fed into the resource manager and is used when the scheduler executes jobs. A scheduler constantly monitors the cluster status and recalculates job priorities according to changes in the cluster environment.

Detailed techniques on local resource management can be found in [12, 13].

---

[10] http://www.clusterresources.com/products/torque-resource-manager.php

[11] http://www.sun.com/software/sge/

[12] http://www.platform.com/workload-management

[13] http://www.clusterresources.com/products/maui-cluster-scheduler.php

[14] http://www.clusterresources.com/products/moab-cluster-suite.php

13.2.1.3 Resource Allocation

Resource allocation is the process of assigning resources associated with a Grid for a user application. It is a key service since there are usually many available local resources and many user applications to be executed within one *Virtual Organization* (VO), where many different groups share resources through a collaborative effort.

One challenge here, called *resource scheduling*, is how to get a resource allocation result that satisfies user requirements, since resources in the Grid are not exclusive and may meet competing user requirements. It is already proved that the complexity of a general scheduling problem is NP-Complete [14]. So many approximation and heuristic algorithms are proposed to achieve suboptimal scheduling on the Grid [15]. Scheduling objectives are usually classified into *application centric* and *resource centric* [15]. The former one targets the performance of each individual application, such as makespan, economic cost, and quality of service (QoS). The latter one targets the performance of the resource, such as resource utilization and economic profit. Although it is an active research area, the proposed solutions are not ready to be widely deployed in production environments and it is still common that users or communities provide their own simple resource allocation strategies using Grid interfaces to contact each local resource.

13.2.2 Data Management

Data management on the Grid, sometimes called Data Grid, can be seen as a specialization and extension of the Grid as an integrating infrastructure for distributed data management [16]. This includes data acquisition, storage, sharing, transfer, archiving, etc. Representative Data Grid software includes the Globus toolkit, OGSA-DAI,[15] Storage Resource Broker (SRB),[16] and its recent successor called integrated Rule Oriented Data System (iRODS).[17] More comprehensive scientific data management and Data Grid surveys can be found in [16–20].

13.2.2.1 Data Acquisition

In general, scientific data may be created either from computations such as scientific calculations and image processing, or through data collection instruments such as an astronomy telescope, earthquake-monitoring devices, meteorology sensors, etc.

---

[15] http://www.ogsadai.org.uk/

[16] http://www.sdsc.edu/srb/index.php

[17] https://www.irods.org/

Once the experimental data is collected, it needs to be stored and transferred to the location where computing models can be run using that data to interpret the relationship or predict future events. The data often need to be shared among many researchers.

Data acquisition in large-scale observing systems, such as the National Ecological Observatory Network (NEON),[18] is an emerging application area. These systems accommodate a broad spectrum of distributed sensors and continuously generate very large amount of data in real-time. Heterogeneous sensor integration [21] and data stream processing [22, 23] are two main challenges [24]. The details of these two problems are not in the scope of this chapter.

13.2.2.2 Data Storage

Reliability, failover, and input/output (I/O) throughput are critical factors for large datasets storage. Typical solutions include storing the data through RAID[19] to achieve storage reliability by providing redundancy, and employing distributed parallel file systems using metadata tables, such as Lustre[20] and Parallel Virtual File System (PVFS)[21] to get higher I/O throughput.

One challenge on the Grid is how to provide a logical and simple view for researchers to access various types of geographically distributed data storage across a Grid environment. This is commonly handled by data storage abstraction techniques. For example, a logical data identifier, rather than its physical location, is provided to users to realize uniformed and easy data access. One tool that provides data abstractions is the SRB, which is a client-server middleware that provides a uniform interface for connecting to heterogeneous federated data resources over a network. The Replica Location Service (RLS)[22] in the Globus toolkit also support data abstraction. Additionally, both SRB and RLS support data replica functionality to manage the multiple copies of the same data, which will get better response time for user applications by accessing data from locally "cached" data stores.

13.2.2.3 Data Transfer

A data transfer moves data between two physical locations. It is necessary to share data within the VO or realize better computation balance and performance. Challenges here include performance, security, and fault tolerance.

---

[18] http://www.neoninc.org/

[19] http://en.wikipedia.org/wiki/RAID

[20] http://www.lustre.org/

[21] http://www.pvfs.org/

[22] http://www.globus.org/toolkit/data/rls/

There are many data transfer tools, e.g., FTP (File Transfer Protocol), scp (secure copy), GridFTP, SRB, and others. FTP [25] is one of the universally available file transfer application, which functions over a network using TCP/IP-based communication protocol such as the current Internet. scp [26] is a simple shell command that allows users to copy files between systems quickly and securely. Using the above two tools does not need the expertise in Grid systems. GridFTP is built on top of FTP for usage in Grid computing with the data encryption through the Globus Grid Security Infrastructure (GSI).[23] Additionally, GridFTP can provide third party transfer, parallel streams, and fault tolerance. The SRB also provides strong security mechanisms supported by fine-grained access controls on data, and parallel data transfer operations.

13.2.2.4 Metadata

Metadata is usually defined as "data about data," which is regarded as "structured data about an object that supports functions associated with the designated object" [27]. Metadata is useful to understand, access, and query the designated object. The metadata structures vary for different targets and usages [28]. Commonly used metadata categories in e-Science projects consist of dataset metadata (size, creator, format, access method, etc.), application metadata (applicable operation system information, license, etc.), resource metadata (node number, CPU speed, memory size, disk capacity, etc.), and workflow metadata (creator, language, etc.).

Semantics and ontology are more sophisticate techniques to describe and process metadata [29]. A domain ontology represents the particular meanings of terms as they apply to that domain. For example, the myGrid ontology helps the service discovery and composition in bioinformatics domain [30].

13.2.3   Scientific Process Automation

Scientific workflows are a common solution to realize scientific process automation [31, 32]. Workflow is a higher-level "language" in comparison to classic programming languages, such as scripting and object-oriented languages. The advantages of using workflow languages for scientific process include: (1) Many workflow systems support intuitive process construction by "dragging and dropping" via a graphical user interface (GUI). (2) The components or sub-workflows in workflow are easy to share and reuse. (3) Many workflow languages support task parallelism intuitively (see Sect. 13.2.3.2). (4) Workflow systems usually have built-in provenance support (see Sect. 13.2.3.4). (5) Some workflow systems are able to dynamically optimize process execution in Grid or other distributed execution environments.

---

[23] http://www.globus.org/security/overview.html

Widely used scientific workflow systems include Kepler, Pegasus,[24] Taverna,[25] Triana,[26] ASKALON,[27] and Swift.[28] More detailed scientific workflow surveys can be found in [5, 6, 31, 32].

13.2.3.1 Workflow Model

Although there are different languages for representing scientific workflows [33–35], workflows commonly include three types of components: tasks, control dependencies, and data dependencies [36]. For example, in Fig. 13.2, the tasks T2 and T3 will be executed under different conditions. Additionally, T4 needs to get data from either T2 or T3 to start its execution.

The tasks in the scientific computation process need to follow certain dependency logic to be executed. Usually the dependency logic can be described using *control flow*, *data flow*, or a *hybrid* of both. In control flows, or control-driven workflows, explicit control structures (including sequence, loop, condition, and parallel) describe the dependency. In data flows, or data-driven workflows, data dependencies describe the relationships among tasks. Two tasks are only linked if the downstream task needs to consume data from the output of the upstream task. The hybrid method uses both control and data dependencies to enable powerful and easy logic description. Many scientific workflow systems, e.g., Kepler, Triana and Taverna, use hybrid methods.

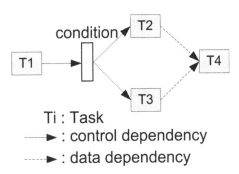

Fig. 13.2 An example workflow composed of tasks and dependencies

---

[24] http://pegasus.isi.edu/

[25] http://www.taverna.org.uk

[26] http://www.trianacode.org

[27] http://www.dps.uibk.ac.at/projects/askalon/

[28] http://www.ci.uchicago.edu/swift/

13.2.3.2   Task Parallelism

Task parallelism occurs when the tasks in one workflow can execute in parallel, providing a good execution performance. The task parallelism patterns can be classified into three basic categories: *simple parallelism, data parallelism,* and *pipeline parallelism* [37]. Simple parallelism happens when the tasks do not have data dependency in a data-driven workflow, or are in the same parallel control structure in a control-driven workflow. Data parallelism describes parallel execution of multiple tasks while different tasks processing independently on different parts of the same dataset. This employs the same principle as single instruction multiple data (SIMD) parallelism [38] in computer architecture. Pipeline parallelism describes a set of data that are processed simultaneously among a group of sequential tasks, each task processing one or more data elements of the set.

The difference between data parallelism and pipeline parallelism is illustrated in Fig. 13.3. In Fig. 13.3a, multiple instances of *Task 1* can be executing in parallel, each task consuming one-third of input data set, meanwhile other tasks have to wait for their input data. In Fig. 13.3b, *Task 1* can only consume one portion of all the input data for each execution. After *Task 1* finishes its processing on the initiate input data, the output data of *Task 1* will trigger the execution of its downstream tasks and meanwhile *Task 1* will continue to process its next input data. So all the tasks in the Fig. 13.3 can be executing simultaneously, each processing its own data.

13.2.3.3   Workflow Scheduling

Workflow scheduling maps the tasks of a process and its data to proper computational resources, in order to meet expected performance, such as minimal execution

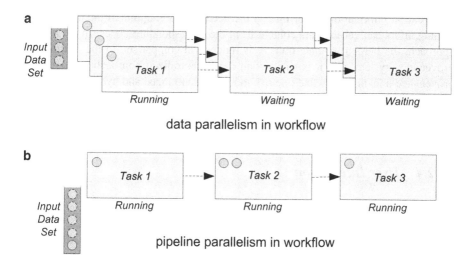

Fig. 13.3 Data and pipeline parallelism in workflow

time. After scheduling, tasks in one workflow might be executed on many local resources in parallel on the Grid.

Workflow scheduling belongs to the application-centric scheduling category of resource allocation (see Sect. 13.2.1.3), and focuses on the scheduling of process-based applications. Scheduling can be done either statically or dynamically based on whether it is flexible to diverse resource environments. Many heuristic scheduling approaches, such as genetic algorithm, are used to achieve suboptimal solutions [39, 40]. The local computation resource capacity, its advanced reservation capability, and real-time status are usually needed to make decisions during the scheduling.

13.2.3.4 Provenance Management

Provenance plays a critical role in scientific workflows, since it allows or helps "determine the derivation history of a data product, starting from its original sources" [41]. Comprehensive surveys on provenance management can be found in [41, 42].

A major challenge of provenance management in Grid environments is how to efficiently store provenance information and easily query it in the future. There are three typical approaches to collect the execution information for data provenance: *centralized*, *decentralized*, and *hybrid* [43]. Centralized approach stores all data generated during a workflow's distributed execution in one centralized center. However, storing the data content of all distributed nodes in a single, centralized center is inefficient, especially when the dataset size is large. In a decentralized approach, provenance data is stored on the local node when it is generated (i.e., no data needs to move to a centralized center). While it is efficient to separate data storage to each distributed node locally, it becomes difficult to query and integrate this data in the future. In the hybrid approach, provenance data are stored locally in distributed nodes, and a centralized provenance catalog is employed to maintain the metadata and location information. After finding the needed data endpoint at the provenance catalog, users can get the data content from the corresponding nodes. In the hybrid approach, the burden for data transfer is reduced in comparison to the centralized provenance system, and it is easier than the decentralized approach to do future provenance tracking. Note that one risk in both decentralized and hybrid approaches is that users may not be able to access the distributed nodes after the workflow execution, which is true when a resource is only open to some users for a limited time.

13.2.4 User Interaction

13.2.4.1 User Authentication

Grid credentials are commonly used to identify users to Grid resources. All certificate signing authorities (called CAs) need to have a policy to authenticate users before they issue user credentials. A user requests a Grid certificate only once to be authorized to use Grid resources. In some organizations such as UC Grid, all users can be positively identified as members of an organization using a Security Assertion Markup Language (SAML)[29] assertion from a Shibboleth Identity Provider (IdP).[30] Typically, IdPs will provide sufficient information to issue a Grid credential such as first name, last name, unique identifier, e-mail address, etc.

Some CAs let users keep credentials in their custody whereas other organizations maintain them in a credential management server such as MyProxy.[31] In the latter case, the credentials never leave the signing machine and only the short-lived credentials (called delegated proxy credentials) are provided to users. Users can always check out credentials from those servers. The delegated proxy credentials usually have a short lifetime of less than 8 h and will be destroyed when they expire. Many CAs additionally have an annual renewal policy for their certificate, so when users are no longer associated with the original project, their certificates can be revoked. Their identities are published in a certificate revocation list, which is then distributed to all organizations where their certificates are trusted.

13.2.4.2 Portal

A Grid portal is a web server that provides web interfaces to Grid services such as job submission, file transfer, job status check, and resource information monitoring. Some Grid portals provide generic capabilities that can be used by many types of users whereas others, such as Science Gateways,[32] typically target a specific community of users. A Grid portal stores user information such as login identifier, the Grid resources the user is entitled to, the status of their submitted jobs, etc. When users login to a portal, they are redirected to a credential management server, which allows the portal to authenticate Grid services on behalf of the user through a delegated proxy credential. Since a Grid portal holds some information about the role of the user, it can also authorize some Grid services such as job submission.

One challenge here is to allow users to access multiple distributed resources and applications without separate authentications, which are usually supported by single sign-on techniques. GridShib[33] allows a portal to sign proxy certificates for the uniquely identifying subject assertion from a federated single sign-on service such as Shibboleth.[34] Shibboleth implements a federated identity standard based on SAML to provide identification and attributes of members in a federation. The primary purpose of Shibboleth is to avoid multiple passwords for multiple applications, interoperability within and across organizational boundaries, and enabling service providers to control access to their resources.

---

[29] http://saml.xml.org/

[30] http://shibboleth.internet2.edu/about.html

[31] http://grid.ncsa.illinois.edu/myproxy/

[32] https://www.teragrid.org/web/science-gateways/

[33] http://gridshib.globus.org/

[34] http://shibboleth.internet2.edu/

13.2.4.3 Job Monitoring

Users often like to know the overall load status and availability of resources. They also want to know the current execution status, e.g., which tasks are executing on which computers with which data. Therefore, job monitoring services are also important for user interaction.

Some general job status information can be retrieved when the job is submitted to a Grid resource. For example, the Scheduler Event Generator (SEG) service in the Globus toolkit gets the status of jobs such as pending, active, or done. The SEG service queries local cluster resource managers such as SGE or PBS, and the job status information can be retrieved through the command-line or optionally pulled into a Grid portal or other GUI interfaces to display to users using a subscription application programming interface (API).

To view overall job statistics, typically cluster monitoring systems such as Ganglia[35] or Nagios[36] are deployed and display queue information, node information, and the load on the cluster. A Grid monitoring service is also deployed to collect information from each resource's cluster monitoring tool, summarize it, and display it. This provides overall Grid job statistics that can be used by managers to ensure users' needs are being met. Such services are typically modeled after the Grid Monitoring Architecture [44], which was defined by Global Grid Forum. It includes three main parts: (1) a *producer*, a process that produces events and implements at least one producer API; (2) a *consumer*, a process that receives events and implements at least one consumer API; and (3) a *registry*, a lookup service that allows producers to publish the event types and consumers to search them. Examples of Grid monitoring tools include the Globus Monitoring and Discovery Service (MDS).[37]

13.2.4.4 Data Visualization

Data visualization is the creation of a visual representation of data, meaning "information which has been abstracted in some schematic form, including attributes or variables for the units of information" [45]. Through the presentation of visualized data, it is easy for scientists to study, analyze, and communicate with one another. The primary reference model is called the filter-map-render pipeline [46]. The filter stage includes data selection, extraction, and enrichment; the map stage applies a visualization algorithm to generate a viewable scene; and finally the render stage generates a series of images from the logical scene. To optimize the performance of data visualization, especially for large data set, many parallel visualization algorithms have been developed [47–49].

---

[35] http://ganglia.sourceforge.net/

[36] http://www.nagios.org/

[37] http://www.globus.org/toolkit/mds/

13.2.5 Nonfunctional Services

We categorize a service to be *"nonfunctional"* if it is not usually explicitly used by users, but useful to ensure a certain property of the e-Science discovery, such as security. These services are often transparently provided in the whole lifecycle of user usage. These services are also orthogonal to other services in that they can be integrated with each of them.

13.2.5.1 Security

Several security concerns in specific services have been discussed in Sects. 13.2.2.3 and 13.2.4.1. A key challenge of security management in Grid environments is that there is no centrally managed security system [50]. The GSI provides secure communication through authenticated services among resources and is widely used in many Grid systems and projects. It operates on the single sign-on concept; that is, a single user credential will be valid among multiple organizations that trust the certificate authority (CA) of that credential. In GSI, every user needs to have a pair of X509 certificates. One is the private key that is used to encrypt the data, and the other is public key that is used to decrypt the data once it reaches the target resource. This kind of process is called asymmetric encryption because the keys that encrypts and decrypts are not the same. In practice, all Grid communications including GridFTP use short-lived proxy certificates that allow the process to act on behalf of the user. The bearer of this proxy certificate has exactly the same capabilities as the original X-509 certificate holder until the proxy certificate expires. In a Grid infrastructure, these proxy certificates are often leased from a certificate management server, such as MyProxy. The advantage of having proxy certificates is that a Grid user can securely store the long-lived private key in a secure machine and release only short-lived proxy credentials on a publically accessible certificate management server during Grid computing.

13.2.5.2 Failure Recovery

Due to the large number of resources in a Grid, there is a high probability of a single resource component failure during an application execution. Further, providing fault tolerance in a Grid environment can be difficult since resources are often distributed and under different administrative domains. Failures may occur in every level in the Grid architecture [51], which includes: (1) computational platforms, e.g., selected nodes for a job may run out of memory or disk space while the job is still running; (2) network, e.g., a local resource is temporarily unreachable during job execution; (3) middleware, e.g., a Grid service fails to start the job; (4) application services, e.g., domain-specific application gets an execution exception due to unexpected input; (5) workflow system, e.g., infinite loops during workflow execution; or (6) user, e.g., a user credential expires during workflow execution.

Many of these issues fall into the domain of system and network administrators, who must design infrastructure to provide redundant components. Here, we address only parts at the workflow level, where *redundancy*, *retry*, and *migration* are the main fault tolerance policies. Using simultaneous execution on redundant resources, workflow execution will have a lower chance to fail. The workflow system can also retry a failed resource or service after a certain amount of time. In migration, a workflow system will restart on a different resource. For the latter two cases, checkpoint and intermediate data usually need to be recorded so that only a sub-workflow rather than the whole workflow will be re-executed.

13.3 Integrating the Kepler Workflow System in the University of California Grid

To demonstrate how the services in Sect. 13.2 can be seamlessly assembled, Kepler scientific workflow system is integrated into the UC Grid. The interoperation of these services and the characteristics of our integration will be discussed. We will also demonstrate how the capabilities of Kepler, including resource consolidation, task parallelism, provenance tracking, fault tolerance, and workflow reuse, can facilitate UC Grid on scientific process automation. Almost all the implementations in this architecture are open source or follow open standards.

13.3.1 University of California Grid

The UC Grid is a federation of all participating compute resources among UC campuses. Any organization that is willing to accept or follow the established policies and trust relations of UC the Grid policy management authority can also be an autonomous member of UC Grid. Typically, the UC Grid resources are open to all faculty, staff, and students who are members of any UC campus. The owners of the resources determine when and how much of those resources are allocated to the UC Grid resource pool.

As shown in Fig. 13.4, the UC Grid architecture mainly consists of four parts.

The UC Grid campus portal. This is the web interface, front-end to the UC Grid in a single campus. It provides the user interface and serves as a single point of access for users to all campus computing resources. It communicates with the Grid appliances in a single campus. Because the users are known only at the campus level, all applications for a Grid account starts at the campus portal. The campus portal takes the request from the users and authenticates them through a Shibboleth-based campus service, and if the authentication process is successful, it sends a request to the UC Grid portal to sign an X-509 certificate for the user.

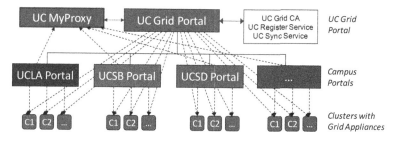

Fig. 13.4 The architecture of University of California Grid

The UC Grid portal. This is the web interface where users can login to access all the clusters in all ten campuses of the University of California. This is the super portal of all campus Grid portals and issues certificates for the entire UC Grid through the UC Grid CA. Once issued to a user, a certificate is pushed to the UC Grid MyProxy server that leases a corresponding short-lived credential every time the user logs in to the Grid portal. Any resource updates on campus portal will be updated on the UC Grid portal immediately through a Web service.

The UC MyProxy server. The primary purpose of this server is to store user credentials and release them to the UC Grid portal when users login to the portal.

Grid appliance nodes. These nodes are functionally equivalent to head nodes of a compute cluster where the UC Grid portal software is deployed. These nodes need to be open only to the Grid portals and compute nodes inside the cluster. Additionally, these nodes need to be a job submission host to the local scheduler such as Torque, LSF, or SGE.

The UC Grid is based on Globus toolkit 4.0.7, using its GridFTP, GRAM, MyProxy, and MDS services. We have also implemented several services to meet our own requirements. Two important ones are the UC Sync Service and the UC Register Service. The UC Sync Service makes sure all database on both the campus portal and UC wide portal are synchronized so that they have updated user, cluster, and application information. The UC Register Service is an automated process to authenticate, authorize, and issue credentials for new users on the UC Grid portal. For authentication purpose, it relies either on a Shibboleth-based service or, in the absence of such services, make use of a secure shell (SSH) based authentication mechanism. During the authorization process, a cluster administrator has to verify the Unix user identifier of new user on a cluster.

The UC Grid portal consists of application software that runs a portlet that is pluggable user-interface components in a portal to provide services such as Grid services. We employ Gridsphere[38] as our portlets container, which guarantees interoperability among portlets and portals through standard APIs.

---

[38] http://www.gridsphere.org

The usage modes are quite different for users who already have access to some compute clusters and users who do not have access to any clusters. So users are classified into different user categories in the UC Grid: *cluster user* and *pool user*. Cluster users are those users with a Unix user identifier on one of the clusters who can access their resources directly without the Grid portal web interface. Pool users on the other hand are those users who do not have an account on any of the clusters or on the cluster where they want to run an application. The jobs submitted by pool users are run through guest accounts on all participating clusters when unused cycles are available on that cluster. Pool users can access the resources only by authorizing through their Grid credentials. Currently, pool users can only submit precompiled application jobs that are deployed in advance by the cluster administrator, as the Grid portal does not have a mechanism to allow the pool users to upload their own binary files and guarantee the right run time architecture for that job. Some of the applications that pool users regularly use are Mathematica, Matlab, Q-Chem, NWChem, Amber, CPMD, etc. Typically, pool users need not worry about the target cluster as it is determined by the Grid portal depending on the dynamic resource availability, and also the application availability on any of the clusters.

13.3.2 Kepler Scientific Workflow System

The Kepler project aims to produce an open source scientific workflow system that allows scientists to easily design and efficiently execute scientific workflows. Inherited from Ptolemy II,[39] Kepler adopts the *actor-oriented modeling* [52] paradigm for scientific workflow design and execution. Each actor is designed to perform a specific independent task that can be implemented as *atomic* or *composite*. Composite actors, or sub-workflows, are composed of atomic actors bundled together to perform complex operations. Actors in a workflow can contain *ports* to consume or produce data, called *tokens*, and communicate with other actors in the workflow through communication channels via *links*.

Another unique property inherited from Ptolemy II is that the order of execution of actors in the workflow is specified by an independent entity called *director*. The director defines how actors are executed and how they communicate with each other. Since the director is decoupled from the workflow structure, a user can easily change the computational model by replacing the director using the Kepler graphical user interface. As a consequence, a workflow can execute sequentially, e.g., using the Synchronous Data Flow (SDF) director, or in parallel, e.g., using the Process Network (PN) director [53].

Kepler provides an intuitive graphical user interface and an execution engine to help scientists to edit and manage scientific workflows and their execution. In the Kepler GUI, actors are dragged and dropped onto the canvas, where they can be

---

[39] http://ptolemy.eecs.berkeley.edu/ptolemyII

customized, linked, and executed. Further, the Kepler execution engine can be separated from the user interface, thereby enabling the batch mode execution.

Currently, there are over 200 actors available in Kepler, which largely simplify the workflow composition. We will briefly describe the main distinctive actors that are used in this chapter.

Local execution actor. The *External Execution* actor in Kepler is the wrapper for executing commands that run legacy codes in a workflow. Its purpose is to call the diverse employed external programs or shell-script wrappers.

Job submission actors. Kepler provides two sets of actors that can submit jobs to two typical distributed resources: Cluster and Grid. Each set has actors to be used for different job operations, e.g., create, submit, and status check.

Data transfer actors. There are multiple sets of data transfer actors in Kepler to support moving data from one location to another by different ways, e.g., FTP, GridFTP, SRB, scp, and others.

Fault tolerance actor. An actor, called *contingency* actor, is provided in Kepler to support fault tolerance for workflow execution [54]. This actor is a composite actor that contains multiple sub-workflows, and supports automatic exception catching and handling by re-trying the default sub-workflow or executing the alternative sub-workflows.

Besides the above actors, Kepler also provides the following characteristic capabilities.

Inherent and implicit parallelism. Kepler supports inherent and implicit parallelism since it adopts a dataflow modeling approach [55]. Actors in Kepler are independent from each other, and will be triggered once their input data are available. Kepler workflow execution engine will parallelize actor execution automatically at runtime according to their input data availability. In addition, workflow composition in Kepler can be greatly simplified, since explicit parallel primitives, such as parallel-for, are not needed.

Pipeline parallelism. The execution of the tokens in the token set can be independent and parallel. Kepler supports pipeline parallelism by token streaming, blocking, and buffering techniques [37].

Provenance tracking. Kepler provenance framework [56] supports collection and query on workflow structure and execution information in both local and distributed environments [57].

13.3.3   Integrated Architecture

By integrating Kepler into UC Grid, an overall architecture is presented in Fig. 13.5. Most of the services described in Sect. 13.2 are supported here.

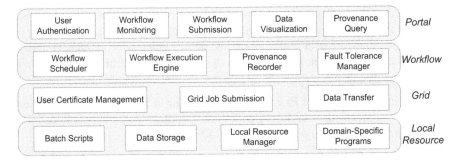

Fig. 13.5 A layered architecture to facilitate e-Science discovery

13.3.3.1 Portal Layer

The portal layer mainly provides the user interaction services described in Sect. 13.2.4 to enable users to interact with cyberinfrastructure and accomplish their e-Science discoveries.

User authentication. In order for the Grid portal to execute Grid services on behalf of users, it must be provided with a delegated credential from a credential management server (MyProxy server is used here). When users login to the portal, they enter their username and corresponding MyProxy password. The portal will retrieve and store the short-lived delegation credentials so that users can interact with Grid services. When the users log out, the delegated credentials are destroyed.

Workflow submission. Users select a workflow by browsing the workflow repository in the Grid portal. The Grid portal then presents a web interface for users to configure the workflow parameters and upload the required input files that need to be staged on the target computing resources. Users are also allowed to upload their own workflows to the portal, but require authorization to avoid intentional or unintentional security problems. For example, malicious code might be inserted into a workflow by executing file delete commands in the Kepler External Execution actor. Once approved, the workflow is uploaded to the workflow repository and made available to other users through the Grid portal.

Workflow monitoring. After a workflow is submitted through the Globus GRAM service for execution, the portal will monitor the progress and completion of the workflow execution by querying the Globus SEG service running on the target resource. Users can log in anytime to check the status, or the portal will send a notification e-mail when the execution is done.

Data visualization. Users can either download the output data to their local computer to visualize the data locally or choose one of the deployed application visualization services, e.g., Jmol,[40] to visualize the data through the portal itself.

---

[40] http://jmol.sourceforge.net/

Provenance query. During and after workflow execution, users can check provenance information via the query user interface in the portal. The query can utilize the provenance information from all previous workflow runs. For example, a user may want to understand how a parameter change influenced the results of one workflow, or how workflows are connected by a certain dataset.

13.3.3.2   Workflow Layer

The workflow layer provides the scientific process automation services described in Sect. 13.2.3.

Workflow scheduler. Currently, static workflow scheduling is supported by explicitly describing the scheduling policy in a separate workflow. Globus GRAM jobs are submitted through the workflow to initiate workflow task execution on resources. For workflow task execution on remote resources, data needs to be staged in before execution and staged out after execution. The capabilities of the resources must be known to achieve better overall load balancing. Sophisticated dynamic workflow scheduling capability is being studied as future work, such as optimal input data distribution on multiple resources based on the resources' capability and real-time load status.

Workflow execution engine. Once an invocation request is received from the workflow scheduler along with the corresponding workflow specifications, the workflow execution engine will parse the specification, and execute the actors based on their dependencies and director configuration.

Provenance recorder. During workflow execution, the provenance recorder listens to the execution messages and saves corresponding information generated by the workflow execution engine, such as an actor execution time and its input/output contents. It also saves a copy of the workflow for future verification and re-submission. The provenance will be stored locally and optionally merged into a centralized provenance database upon the workflow execution completion.

Fault tolerance manager. The fault tolerance manager will be triggered by exception messages generated from workflow execution engine, and will check whether the source of the exception is contained within a Contingency actor. If so, the alternative sub-workflows defined in the Contingency actor will be invoked with the corresponding configuration policy. Otherwise, the exception will be passed to the next higher-level Contingency actor, until the top level of the workflow is reached, where the workflow execution failure message will be reported and workflow execution will stop.

13.3.3.3   Grid Layer

The Grid layer consolidates multiple resources and manages their computation and data resources, providing unified services for the portal and workflow layer.

This layer is where the Globus toolkit software, such as GRAM, GridFTP, and MyProxy Server, is located.

User certificate management. There should be at least one CA, which stores the long-lived credentials for users. The short-lived credentials are then pushed into a MyProxy server. The portal gets the delegated credential when users login to the portal. A workflow can also get the delegated credential through a MyProxy actor.

Grid job submission. A GRAM service will enable job submission on any accessible resources. A workflow execution can invoke multiple GRAM services on different resources to realize parallel computation.

Data transfer. GridFTP permits direct transfer of files between the portal and the cluster resources or vice versa. Third party transfers can also be made between two local resources. A GridFTP actor is used to transfer data during workflow execution.

13.3.3.4 Local Resource Layer

The services provided by each compute cluster resource are located in the local resource layer. The compute nodes are not accessible directly from a portal. UC Grid communicates with the cluster through its Grid Appliance Node (see its details at Sect. 13.3.1) with both public and private interfaces.

Batch scripts. The batch job script syntax and terminologies vary according to the type of scheduler. The Globus GRAM service executes a job manager service at the target to create the job submission script using information such as executable name, number of processors, memory requirement, etc. It is also useful to create "shims" in the workflow [58], such as creating job scripts in accordance with the scheduler configuration of the host cluster.

Data storage. Each cluster provides data storage service for their users up to a certain size limitation. Cluster users can store their data permanently on the clusters they can access, whereas pool users must save their data in portal provided storage servers. The data generated on the cluster by pool users must be downloaded; otherwise, the data gets cleaned up periodically to make room for other pool users.

Local resource manager. A local resource manager is used to manage the job submission in a cluster. Several local resource managers are supported by the GRAM, such as SGE and PBS, which schedule jobs to the nodes in the cluster.

Domain-specific programs. Domain-specific programs are deployed to clusters to accomplish certain domain-specific computation problems. The applications widely used in UC Grid include Mathematica, Matlab, Q-Chem, NWChem, Amber, CPMD, etc.

13.4   Application in Computational Chemistry

In this section, we demonstrate how the services and integrated architecture described in Sects. 13.2 and 13.3 can facilitate e-Science discovery by applying them to a challenging application in computational chemistry. The detailed information about the application can be found at [59].

13.4.1   Theoretical Enzyme Design Process

Enzymes are nature's protein catalysts that accelerate and regulate all metabolic reactions. To design new catalysts computationally and then to make them with molecular biological techniques will be a breakthrough in technology. An inside-out design approach has been developed [60]. In the process, quantum mechanical calculations give a *theozyme* [61], or *theoretical enzyme*, which is theoretical optimum catalyst. Numerous protein scaffolds are then screened to determine which can be used to display the side chains to mimic the geometry of the theozyme; this procedure generates a large library of potential catalysts that are evaluated for fidelity to the theozyme. The best of these are subjected to mutations to obtain a design that will both fold and catalyze the reaction. Typically, a theozyme with active sites is matched at least once per scaffold (226 protein scaffolds so far) to potentially accommodate the orientation of the model functional groups. The computation process needs to be repeated for many times with different theozymes and calculation options. The goal of this application is to accelerate and facilitate this important computation- and data-intensive process for chemists.

13.4.2   Conceptual Enzyme Design Workflow

As shown in Fig. 13.6, the conceptual enzyme design workflow takes quantum mechanical theozymes as inputs, and goes through three discrete steps before validation by experiments. The goal of this workflow is to standardize the enzyme design process through automation, and eliminate the need for unnecessary human interaction. Sequences of tasks in the enzyme design process are repeated using the same series of programs, which must be executed to design and evaluate an enzyme

Fig. 13.6 Conceptual workflow of enzyme design process

for a new chemical reaction. For example, a theozyme with active sites is matched at least once per scaffold to potentially accommodate the orientation of the model functional groups.

Computational methodology for enzyme design has been developing using quantum mechanics and molecular dynamics. We locate structures of catalytic sites (theozyme) for the aromatic Claisen rearrangement of an allyl coumarin ether using density functional theory. The resultant theozymes are incorporated into existing stable protein scaffolds using the Rosetta programs of Zanghellini et al. [60]. The residues in the vicinity of active site are then optimized with RosettaDesign [62, 63]. The designs are further evaluated using molecular dynamics.

The entire enzyme design process can be performed independently for different scaffolds, and the total computation time for each scaffold can vary. The number of matches per theozyme is about 100–4,000, and computation time for a single scaffold on one CPU core is usually 1–3 h. The number of enzyme designs generated by RosettaDesign per match is about 100–15,000, and computational time on one CPU core is usually 0.5–2 h. One whole computation time required for all 226 scaffolds could take months on one single CPU core and the total number of generated enzyme designs is about seven million.

13.4.3   Enzyme Design Workflow in Kepler

The conceptual enzyme design workflow in Sect. 13.4.2 is composed in Kepler to make it executable. We will explain the details of the composition in this section.

13.4.3.1   Workflow for Execution on Local Cluster Resources

As shown in Fig. 13.7, a workflow is implemented to utilize the tens to hundreds of computing CPU cores in one cluster. The top-level workflow structure is the same as the conceptual workflow in Sect. 13.4.2. The connection links between the actors describe their dependencies, which determine that each input data, namely each scaffold, has to go through the three processing tasks sequentially. Once the output data of one actor is generated, it will trigger the execution of downstream actors. For instance, the RemoveBChain actor will start processing once it gets output data from the RosettaMatch actor.

Inside a composite actor, such as RosettaMatch, the sub-workflow dynamically creates job scripts according to a user's inputs and submits them to a job scheduler such as SGE on the cluster using Kepler job actors. By distributing the jobs for all scaffolds through the job scheduler on the cluster, the jobs can be concurrently executed on many nodes on the cluster and the concurrency capability is limited only by the node capacity of the cluster.

One computational characteristic in the enzyme design process is that the execution time for different scaffolds varies greatly, which could be minutes or hours.

Therefore, we adopt a set as the input of the workflow and elements of the input sets will be processed independently. With pipeline parallel support in Kepler, one scaffold does not need to wait for the completion of the other scaffolds before being processed by the downstream tasks.

13.4.3.2   Workflow for Execution on UC Grid

By adopting Globus as the Grid security and service infrastructure, the workflow shown in Fig. 13.8 is used to scheduling application execution among two cluster resources in UC Grid. For a local cluster, we execute the Kepler workflow shown in Fig. 13.7 through the Globus GRAM service deployed on the cluster.

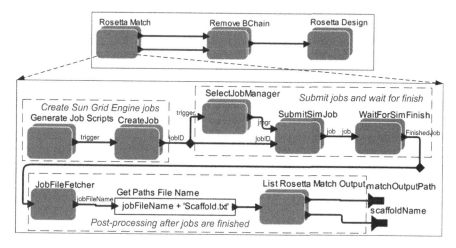

Fig. 13.7   Kepler workflow for enzyme design processes on one cluster

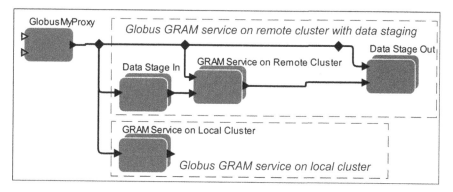

Fig. 13.8   Kepler workflow for enzyme design processes on UC Grid. The GRAM service actor will invoke the workflow shown in Fig. 13.7 on the target cluster

For the remote cluster, besides the workflow execution, two extra tasks need to be added: (1) Input data needs to be staged in to the remote clusters in advance of the workflow execution. (2) Output data needs to be staged out from remote cluster back to the local cluster. We employ the GridFTP to do the data stage in and out. The computations on the two clusters are independent of each other, so there is no control or data flow connections among the actors for these executions in the workflow, and the Kepler engine will run them in parallel. The workflows in Sect. 13.4.3.1 are easily reused in the two-level workflow structure. One challenge for this workflow is how to optimize the load balance on multiple clusters and the data stage in/out overhead.

13.4.3.3 Provenance and Fault Tolerance Support in the Workflow

While using more clusters increases computational capacity, it also increases the probability of failure. Although these exceptions happen only occasionally, the whole execution of the enzyme design workflow will crash without fault tolerance support.

To support fault tolerance at the workflow level, we adopt the Contingency actor for some sub-workflows. A simplified example is shown in Fig. 13.9, where the JobExecutionWithFT actor is a customized Contingency actor. There are two sub-workflows (shown in the bottom part of Fig. 13.9) in the actor, namely *default* and *clean-and-quit*, which will be invoked according to the configurations of the JobExecutionWithFT actor. The default sub-workflow submits a job, checks the job status, and throws an exception if the job fails. As specified in its configuration

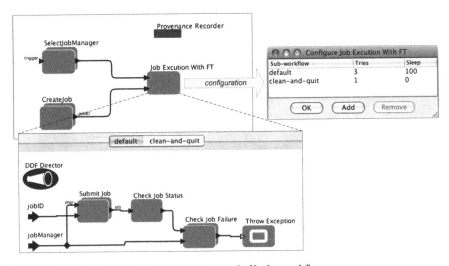

Fig. 13.9 Fault tolerance and provenance support in Kepler workflow

(shown in the right part of Fig. 13.9), after catching the exception, the JobExecutionWithFT actor will re-execute the default sub-workflow after sleeping for 100 s. If the default sub-workflow still gets exceptions after three retries, the clean-and-quit sub-workflow, which cleans intermediate data and stops the whole execution, will be executed with the same input tokens.

The exception handling logic can be easily expressed with the Contingency actor; no explicit loop and conditional switch is needed in the workflow. Further, the input data for sub-workflow retry does not need to be explicitly saved since they are automatically recorded by the provenance recorder and will be fetched for re-execution.

Besides fault tolerance, Kepler provenance also supports collection and query on workflow structure and execution information in both local and distributed environments. Each enzyme design workflow execution will generate millions of designs, and chemists may need the workflow to be executed many times with different input models. Kepler provenance can help chemists to track the data efficiently in the future, such as querying which input model was used to generate one particular design.

13.4.4 Experiment

To measure the speedup capabilities of the workflows, we chose two clusters in UC Grid as test bed where Globus toolkit 4.0.7 and Sun Grid Engine job scheduler are deployed. Cluster 1 has 8 nodes, each with 24 GB of memory and two 2.6 GHz quad-core CPUs. Cluster 2 has 30 nodes, each with 4 GB of memory and two 2.2 GHz single-core CPUs.

Our first experiment executed the enzyme design workflow described in Sect. 13.4.3.1 on cluster 2 with different usable CPU core configurations. We also executed another workflow that only had the RosettaMatch part of the enzyme design workflow in order to determine the speedup difference. We ran the workflows with different inputs. As shown in Table 13.1, all these tests, no matter the differences of workflow structures and inputs, have good scalability and speedup when the usable core number grows.

Table 13.1 Workflow execution on one local resource with different CPU cores

Workflow	Workflow input	Output data	Total job number	Workflow execution time (unit: hour)		
				1 core	25 core	60 core
RosettaMatch	10 scaffold	0.29 GB	10	3.38	0.69	0.63
RosettaMatch	226 scaffold	27.96 GB	226	128.61	5.52	3.06
RosettaMatch + RemoveBChain + RosettaDesign	10 scaffold	10.92 GB	296	533.61	29.32	11.24

Table 13.2 Workflow execution on UC Grid with different local resources

Workflow	Workflow input	Total job number	Workflow execution time (unit: hour)		
			Cluster 1 (64 core)	Cluster 2 (60 core)	Cluster 1 and 2
RosettaMatch	10 scaffold	10	0.33	0.63	0.36
RosettaMatch	226 scaffold	226	1.52	3.06	1.33
RosettaMatch + RemoveBChain + RosettaDesign	10 scaffold	296	6.17	11.24	4.21

We also tested the workflows in Sects. 13.4.3.1 and 13.4.3.2 to know the concurrence performance on the Grid which is shown in Table 13.2. From the experiment data of the workflow execution only on cluster 1 and 2 (listed at the fourth and fifth column of Table 13.2), we know cluster 1 is about twice as fast. So approximately twice as many inputs are distributed to cluster 1 and cluster 1 is set as the local cluster when the workflows are executed on the two clusters, and its experiment results are listed at the sixth column. The experiment data demonstrates the good concurrence performance in the second and third tests. The poor performance in the first test is because there are too few jobs in comparison to the number of CPU cores. We can also see the speedup ratios are not as good as those in the first experiment. The reasons are twofold: (1) It is hard to realize good load balance on multiple clusters since the execution time for different scaffold varies. (2) The data stage in and out phases for remote cluster may cause a big overhead if the size of transferred data is very large.

13.5 Conclusions

Increasingly e-Science discoveries are being made based on the enhanced capability and usability of cyberinfrastructure. In this chapter, we have summarized the core services to support e-Science discovery in Grid environments. The five service dimensions, namely computation management, data management, scientific process automation, user interaction, and nonfunctional services, are all important constituents and complementary to each other. To demonstrate how these services can be seamlessly assembled, we explained an integration of the Kepler workflow system with the UC Grid, and its application in computational chemistry. The implementation and experiments validate the capability of this integrated architecture to make a scientific computation process automated, pipelined, efficient, extensible, stable, and easy-to-use. We believe that, as the complexity and size of scientific problems grow larger, it is increasingly critical to leverage workflow logic and task distribution across federated computing resources to solve e-Science problems efficiently.

Acknowledgments The authors would like to thank the rest of the Kepler and UC Grid community for their collaboration. We also like to explicitly acknowledge the contribution of Tajendra Vir Singh, Shao-Ching Huang, Sveta Mazurkova, and Paul Weakliem during the UC Grid architecture design phase. This work was supported by NSF SDCI Award OCI-0722079 for Kepler/CORE, NSF CEO:P Award No. DBI 0619060 for REAP, DOE SciDac Award No. DE-FC02-07ER25811 for SDM Center, and UCGRID Project. We also thank the support to the Houk group from NIH-NIGMS and DARPA.

References

1. Foster I (2002) What is the Grid? – a three point checklist. GRIDtoday, Vol. 1, No. 6. http://www-fp.mcs.anl.gov/~foster/Articles/WhatIsTheGrid.pdf
2. Sudholt W, Altintas I, Baldridge K (2006) Scientific workflow infrastructure for computational chemistry on the Grid. In: Proc. of the 1st Computational Chemistry and Its Applications Workshop at the 6th International Conference on Computational Science (ICCS 2006):69–76, LNCS 3993
3. Tiwari A, Sekhar AKT (2007) Workflow based framework for life science informatics. Computational Biology and Chemistry 31(5–6):305–319
4. Yang X, Bruin RP, Dove MT (2010) Developing an End-to-End Scientific Workflow: a Case Study of Using a Reliable, Lightweight, and Comprehensive Workflow Platform in e-Science. Computing in Science and Engineering, 12(3):52–61, May/June 2010, doi:10.1109/MCSE.2010.61
5. Taylor I, Deelman E, Gannon D, Shields M (eds) (2007), Workflows for e-Science. Springer, New York, Secaucus, NJ, USA, ISBN: 978-1-84628-519-6
6. Yu Y, Buyya R (2006) A Taxonomy of Workflow Management Systems for Grid Computing. J. Grid Computing, 2006 (3):171–200
7. Foster I, Kesselman C (eds) (2003) The Grid: Blueprint for a New Computing Infrastructure. Morgan Kaufmann Publishers, The Elsevier Series in Grid Computing, ISBN 1558609334, 2nd edition
8. Berman F, Fox GC, Hey AJG (eds) (2003) Grid Computing: Making The Global Infrastructure a Reality. Wiley. ISBN 0-470-85319-0
9. Richardson L, Ruby S (2007) RESTful Web Services. O'Reilly Media, Inc., ISBN: 978-0-596-52926-0
10. Foster I, Kesselman C, Nick J, Tuecke S (2002) The Physiology of the Grid: An Open Grid Services Architecture for Distributed Systems Integration. www.globus.org/research/papers/ogsa.pdf
11. Singh MP, Huhns MN (2005) Service-Oriented Computing: Semantics, Processes, Agents. John Wiley & Sons
12. Buyya R (ed.) (1999) High Performance Cluster Computing: Architectures and Systems. Volume 1, ISBN 0-13-013784-7, Prentice Hall, NJ, USA
13. Buyya R (ed.) (1999) High Performance Cluster Computing: Programming and Applications. Volume 2, ISBN 0-13-013785-5, Prentice Hall, NJ, USA
14. El-Rewini H, Lewis TG, Ali HH (1994) Task Scheduling in Parallel and Distributed Systems, ISBN: 0130992356, PTR Prentice Hall
15. Dong F, Akl SG (2006) Scheduling Algorithms for Grid Computing: State of the Art and Open Problems. Technical Report No. 2006-504, Queen's University, Canada, http://www.cs.queensu.ca/TechReports/Reports/2006-504.pdf
16. Chervenak A, Foster I, Kesselman C, Salisbury C, Tuecke S (2000) The data Grid: Towards an architecture for the distributed management and analysis of large scientific datasets. Journal of Network and Computer Applications. 23(3): 187–200. July 2000, doi:10.1006/jnca.2000.0110

17. Gray J, Liu DT, Nieto-Santisteban M, Szalay A, DeWitt DJ, Heber G (2005) Scientific data management in the coming decade, ACM SIGMOD Record, 34(4):34–41, doi://10.1145/1107499.1107503
18. Shoshani A, Rotem D (eds) (2009) Scientific Data Management: Challenges, Existing Technology, and Deployment, Computational Science Series. Chapman & Hall/CRC
19. Moore RW, Jagatheesan A, Rajasekar A, Wan M, Schroeder W (2004) Data Grid Management Systems. In Proc. of the 21st IEEE/NASA Conference on Mass Storage Systems and Technologies (MSST)
20. Venugopal S, Buyya R, Ramamohanarao K (2006) A taxonomy of Data Grids for distributed data sharing, management, and processing. ACM Comput. Surv. 38(1)
21. Yick J, Mukherjee B, Ghosal D (2008) Wireless sensor network survey. Computer Networks, 52(12): 2292–2330, DOI: 10.1016/j.comnet.2008.04.002.
22. Fox G, Gadgil H, Pallickara S, Pierce M, Grossman RL, Gu Y, Hanley D, Hong X (2004) High Performance Data Streaming in Service Architecture. Technical Report. http://www.hpsearch.org/documents/HighPerfDataStreaming.pdf
23. Rajasekar A, Lu S, Moore R, Vernon F, Orcutt J, Lindquist K (2005) Accessing sensor data using meta data: a virtual object ring buffer framework. In: Proc. of the 2nd Workshop on Data Management for Sensor Networks (DMSN 2005): 35–42
24. Tilak S, Hubbard P, Miller M, Fountain T (2007) The Ring Buffer Network Bus (RBNB) Data Turbine Streaming Data Middleware for Environmental Observing Systems. eScience 2007: 125–133
25. J. Postel and J. Reynolds, File Transfer Protocol (FTP), Internet RFC-959 1985
26. secure copy, http://linux.die.net/man/1/scp
27. Greenberg J (2002) Metadata and the World Wide Web. The Encyclopedia of Library and Information Science, Vol.72: 224–261, Marcel Dekker, New York
28. Wittenburg P, Broeder D (2002) Metadata Overview and the Semantic Web. In Proc. of the International Workshop on Resources and Tools in Field Linguistics
29. Davies J, Fensel D, van Harmelen F. (eds.) (2002) Towards the Semantic Web: Ontology-driven Knowledge Management. Wiley
30. Wolstencroft K, Alper P, Hull D, Wroe C, Lord PW, Stevens RD, Goble C (2007) The myGrid Ontology: Bioinformatics Service Discovery. International Journal of Bioinformatics Research and Applications, 3(3):326–340
31. Ludäscher B, Altintas I, Bowers S, Cummings J, Critchlow T, Deelman E, Roure DD, Freire J, Goble C, Jones M, Klasky S, McPhillips T, Podhorszki N, Silva C, Taylor I, Vouk M (2009) Scientific Process Automation and Workflow Management. In Shoshani A, Rotem D (eds) Scientific Data Management: Challenges, Existing Technology, and Deployment, Computational Science Series. 476–508. Chapman & Hall/CRC
32. Deelman E, Gannon D, Shields MS, Taylor I (2009) Workflows and e-Science: An overview of workflow system features and capabilities. Future Generation Comp. Syst. 25(5): 528–540
33. Brooks C, Lee EA, Liu X, Neuendorffer S, Zhao Y, Zheng H (2007), Chapter 7: MoML, Heterogeneous Concurrent Modeling and Design in Java (Volume 1: Introduction to Ptolemy II), EECS Department, University of California, Berkeley, UCB/EECS-2007-7, http://www.eecs.berkeley.edu/Pubs/TechRpts/2007/EECS-2007-7.html
34. Scufl Language, Taverna 1.7.1 Manual, http://www.myGrid.org.uk/usermanual1.7/
35. SwiftScript Language Reference Manual. http://www.ci.uchicago.edu/swift/guides/historical/languagespec.php
36. Wang J, Altintas I, Berkley C, Gilbert L, Jones MB (2008) A High-Level Distributed Execution Framework for Scientific Workflows. In: Proc. of workshop SWBES08: Challenging Issues in Workflow Applications, 4th IEEE International Conference on e-Science (e-Science 2008):634–639
37. Pautasso C, Alonso G (2006) Parallel Computing Patterns for Grid Workflows, In: Proc. of Workshop on Workflows in Support of Large-Scale Science (WORKS06) http://www.iks.ethz.ch/publications/jop_grid_workflow_patterns

38. Flynn MJ (1972) Some Computer Organizations and Their Effectiveness. IEEE Trans. on Computers, C–21(9):948-960
39. Wieczorek M, Prodan R, Fahringer T (2005) Scheduling of scientific workflows in the ASKALON grid environment. SIGMOD Record 34(3): 56–62
40. Singh G, Kesselman C, Deelman E (2005) Optimizing Grid-Based Workflow Execution. J. Grid Comput. 3(3–4):201–219
41. Simmhan YL, Plale B, Gannon D (2005). A survey of data provenance in e-science. SIGMOD Record, 34(3):31–36
42. Davidson SB, Freire J (2008) Provenance and scientific workflows: challenges and opportunities. In: Proc. of SIGMOD Conference 2008:1345–1350
43. Wang J, Altintas I, Berkley C, Gilbert L, Jones MB (2008) A High-Level Distributed Execution Framework for Scientific Workflows. In: Proc. of the 2008 Fourth IEEE International Conference on e-Science (e-Science 2008):634–639
44. Tierney B, Aydt R, Gunter D, Smith W, Swany M, Taylor V, Wolski R (2002) A Grid Monitoring Architecture. GWDPerf-16-3, Global Grid Forum http://wwwdidc.lbl.gov/GGF-PERF/GMA-WG/papers/GWD-GP-16-3.pdf
45. Friendly M (2009) Milestones in the history of thematic cartography, statistical graphics, and data visualization. Toronto, York University, http://www.math.yorku.ca/SCS/Gallery/milestone/milestone.pdf
46. Haber RB, McNabb DA (1990) Visualization Idioms: A Conceptual Model for Scientific Visualization Systems. IEEE Visualization in Scientific Computing:74–93
47. Singh JP, Gupta A, Levoy M (1994) Parallel Visualization Algorithms: Performance and Architectural Implications, Computer, 27(7):45–55 doi:10.1109/2.299410
48. Ahrens J, Brislawn K, Martin K, Geveci B, Law CC, Papka M (2001) Large-scale data visualization using parallel data streaming. IEEE Comput. Graph. Appl., 21(4):34–41
49. Strengert M, Magallón M, Weiskopf D, Guthe S, Ertl T (2004) Hierarchical visualization and compression of large volume datasets using GPU clusters. In: Proc. Eurographics symposium on parallel graphics and visualization (EGPGV04), Eurographics Association: 41–48
50. Welch V, Siebenlist F, Foster I, Bresnahan J, Czajkowski K, Gawor J, Kesselman C, Meder S, Pearlman L, Tuecke S (2003) Security for grid services. In: Proc. of the Twelfth International Symposium on High Performance Distributed Computing (HPDC-12). IEEE Press
51. Plankensteiner K, Prodan R, Fahringer T, Kertesz A, Kacsuk PK (2007). Fault-tolerant behavior in state-of-the-art grid workflow management systems. Technical Report. CoreGRID, http://www.coregrid.net/mambo/images/stories/TechnicalReports/tr-0091.pdf
52. Ludäscher B, Altintas I, Berkley C, Higgins D, Jaeger E, Jones M, Lee E, Tao J, Zhao Y (2005) Scientific workflow management and the Kepler system. Concurrency and Computation: Practice and Experience, 18 (10):1039–1065
53. Brooks C, Lee EA, Liu X, Neuendorffer S, Zhao Y, Zheng H (2007) Heterogeneous Concurrent Modeling and Design in Java (Volume 3: Ptolemy II Domains), EECS Department, University of California, Berkeley, UCB/EECS-2007-9, http://www.eecs.berkeley.edu/Pubs/TechRpts/2007/EECS-2007-9.html
54. Mouallem P, Crawl D, Altintas I, Vouk M, Yildiz U (2010). A Fault-Tolerance Architecture for Kepler-based Distributed Scientific Workflows. In: Proc. of 22nd International Conference on Scientific and Statistical Database Management (SSDBM 2010):452–460
55. Lee EA, Parks T (1995) Dataflow Process Networks. In: Proc. of the IEEE, 83(5):773–799
56. Altintas I, Barney O, Jaeger-Frank E (2006) Provenance Collection Support in the Kepler Scientific Workflow System. In: Proc. of International Provenance and Annotation Workshop (IPAW2006):118–132
57. Wang J, Altintas I, Hosseini PR, Barseghian D, Crawl D, Berkley C, Jones MB (2009) Accelerating Parameter Sweep Workflows by Utilizing Ad-hoc Network Computing Resources: an Ecological Example. In: Proc. of IEEE 2009 Third International Workshop on Scientific Workflows (SWF 2009) at Congress on Services (Services 2009):267–274

58. Radetzki U, Leser U, Schulze-Rauschenbach SC, Zimmermann J, Lussem J, Bode T, Cremers AB (2006) Adapters, shims, and glue-service interoperability for in silico experiments. Bioinformatics, 22(9):1137–1143
59. Wang J, Korambath P, Kim S, Johnson S, Jin K, Crawl D, Altintas I, Smallen S, Labate B, Houk KN (2010) Theoretical Enzyme Design Using the Kepler Scientific Workflows on the Grid, In: Proc. of 5th Workshop on Computational Chemistry and Its Applications (5th CCA) at International Conference on Computational Science (ICCS 2010):1169–1178
60. Zanghellini A, Jiang L, Wollacott AM, Cheng G, Meiler J, Althoff EA, Röthlisberger D, Baker D (2006) New algorithms and an in silico benchmark for computational enzyme design. Protein Sci. 15(12):2785–2794
61. Tantillo DJ, Chen J, Houk KN (1998) Theozymes and compuzymes: theoretical models for biological catalysis. Curr Opin Chem Biol. 2(6):743–50
62. Dantas G, Kuhlman B, Callender D, Wong M, Baker D (2003) A Large scale test of computational protein desing: Folding and stability of nine completely redesigned globular proteins. J. Mol. Biol. 332(2):449–460
63. Meiler J, Baker D (2006) ROSETTALIGAND: Protein-small molecule docking with full side-chain flexibility. Proteins 65:538–548

Chapter 14
Concepts and Algorithms of Mapping Grid-Based Workflow to Resources Within an SLA Context

Dang Minh Quan, Odej Kao, and Jörn Altmann

Abstract With the popularity of Grid-based workflow, ensuring the Quality of Service (QoS) for workflow by Service Level Agreements (SLAs) is an emerging trend in the business grid. Among many system components for supporting SLA-aware Grid-based workflow, the SLA mapping mechanism is allotted an important position as it is responsible for assigning sub-jobs of the workflow to Grid resources in a way that meets the user's deadline and minimizes costs. To meet those requirements, the resource in each Grid site must be reserved and the user must provide the estimated runtime of each sub-job correlated with a resource configuration. With many different kinds of sub-jobs and resources, the process of mapping a Grid-based workflow within an SLA context defines an unfamiliar and difficult problem. To solve this problem, this chapter describes related concepts and mapping algorithms. In particular, several suboptimization algorithms to map sub-jobs of the workflow to the Grid resources within an SLA context are described. The simulation results show the efficiency of those mapping algorithms.

14.1 Introduction

Grid computing is viewed as the next phase of distributed computing. Built on Internet standards, it enables organizations to share computing and information resources across departments and organizational boundaries in a secure and highly efficient manner.

D.M. Quan (✉) and J. Altmann
School of Information Technology, International University in Germany,
Campus 3, 76646 Bruchsal, Germany
e-mail: quandm@upb.de; jorn.altmann@acm.org

O. Kao
Electrical Engineering and Computer Science, Technical University Berlin,
Einsteinufer 17, 10587 Berlin, Germany
e-mail: Odej.Kao@tu-berlin.de

Xiaoyu Yang et al. (eds.), *Guide to e-Science: Next Generation Scientific Research and Discovery*, Computer Communications and Networks,
DOI 10.1007/978-0-85729-439-5_14, © Springer-Verlag London Limited 2011

Many Grid users have a high demand of computing power to solve large-scale problems such as material structure simulation, weather forecasting, fluid dynamic simulation, etc. Alongside a vast number of single-program applications, which has only one sequential or parallel program, there exist many applications requiring the co-process of many programs following a strict processing order. Since those applications are executed on the Grid, they are called Grid-based workflows.

Traditionally, to run the application, scientific users submit it to a Grid system and the system tries to execute it as soon as possible [1]. However, that best-effort mechanism is not suitable when users are industry corporations which want to run dynamic fluid simulation to help produce cars. These users need a continually concurrent result at a specific time, hence requiring that the application must be run during a specific period. Because they are commercial users, they are willing to pay for the results to be on time. This requirement must be agreed on by both users and the Grid system before the application is executed and can be done legally by a Service Level Agreement (SLA) because its purpose is to identify the shared goals and objectives of the concerned parties.

A good SLA is important as it sets boundaries and expectations for the subsequent aspects of a service provision. An SLA clearly defines what the user wants and what the provider promises to supply, helping to reduce the chances of disappointing the customer. The provider's promises also help the system stay focused on customer requirements and assure that the internal processes move in the proper direction. As an SLA describes a clear, measurable standard of performance, internal objectives become clear, measurable, and quantifiable. An SLA also defines penalties, thereby allowing the customer to understand that the service provider truly believes in its ability to achieve the performance levels set. It makes the relationship clear and positive, establishes the expectations between the consumer and the provider, and defines their relationship.

One of the core problems in running a Grid-based workflow within an SLA context is how to map sub-jobs of the workflow to Grid resources. An automated mapping is necessary as it frees users from the tedious job of assigning sub-jobs to resources under many constraints such as workflow integrity, on time conditions, optimal conditions, and so on. Additionally, a good mapping mechanism will help users save money and increase the efficiency of using Grid resources. In particular, the SLA context requires that the mapping mechanism must satisfy two main criteria:

- The algorithm must ensure finishing the workflow execution on time. This criterion is quite clear because it is the main reason for an SLA system to exist. The criterion imposes that the underlying Grid infrastructure must be High-Performance Computing Centers and the resources must be reserved.
- The algorithm must optimize the running cost. This criterion is derived from the business aspect of an SLA. If a customer wants to use a service, he must pay for it and therefore has the right to an appropriate quality.

The workflow, the resource configurations, and the goal influenced by the SLA context define a complicated mapping problem. This chapter will present related concepts and a mechanism, which includes several suboptimization algorithms, to map sub-jobs of the workflow to the Grid resources within an SLA context, thus satisfying the specific user's runtime requirement and optimizing the cost. At present, the size of the Grid is still small. For example, the Distributed European Infrastructure for Supercomputing Applications (DEISA) includes only 11 sites. Based on that, a distributed mapping model for very large size Grid is not an urgent requirement at present and thus not focused on. The goal of this work is to provide a fast and effective response solution while ensuring the QoS for customers, reducing the overhead of the workflow execution time, and encouraging the utilization of the services.

The chapter is organized as follows. Section 14.2 describes the related concepts. Section 14.3 presents the problem statement and Sect. 14 4 describes the algorithm. Section 14.5 describes the performance evaluation and Sect. 14.6 concludes with a short summary.

14.2 Basic Concepts

14.2.1 Service Level Agreement

The main purpose of an Information Technology organization is to provide a computing service which satisfies the customers' business requirements. To achieve this, the organization needs to understand those requirements and to evaluate its own capability of providing the service and of measuring the service delivered. To realize this process, the service and level of delivery required must be identified and agreed between the organization and its users. This is usually done by Service Level Agreements (SLAs), which are contracts developed jointly by the organization and the customers.

An SLA identifies the agreed-upon services to be provided to a customer so as to ensure that they meet the customer's requirements. It identifies customers' expectations and defines the boundaries of the service, stating agreed-upon service level goals, operating practices, and reporting policies. Webopedia defines an SLA as *"a contract between an ASP (Application Service Provider) and the end user which stipulates and commits the ASP to a required level of service. An SLA should contain a specified level of service, support options, enforcement or penalty provisions for services not provided, a guaranteed level of system performance as relates to downtime or uptime, a specified level of customer support and what software or hardware will be provided and for what fee."*

A common SLA contains the following components:

- Parties joining the agreement which is made between the service provider and the service user: The two participants should exist as individuals, either by name or by title and both sides must sign the document.
- Type and the time window of the service to be provided: The SLA must state clearly which service will be provided and the time window during which the

service is provided to the user. In fact, there are a lot of system components contributing to the type of definition of the service. They can be the number of processors, processor speed, amount of memory, communication library, and so forth.

- The guaranty of the provider to provide the appropriate service and performance: The SLA must state clearly how well the service will be provided to the user as Quality of Service. Penalties must also be figured out if a certain QoS cannot be satisfied.
- The cost of the service: Business users wishing to use any service have to pay for it with the cost depending on the quantity of service usage and how long the user uses it.
- The measurement method and reporting mechanism: The SLA defines which parameters will be measured and the method of measuring. Data collected from the monitoring procedure are important as they help both the user and provider check the validity of the SLA.

14.2.2 Grid-Based Workflow

Workflows received enormous attention in the databases and information systems research and development community [2]. According to the definition from the Workflow Management Coalition (WfMC) [3], a workflow is *"The automation of a business process, in whole or parts, where documents, information or tasks are passed from one participant to another to be processed, according to a set of procedural rules."* Although business workflows have great influence on research and development, another class of workflows emerges naturally in sophisticated scientific problem-solving environments called Grid-based workflow. A Grid-based workflow differs slightly from the WfMC definition as it concentrates on intensive computation and data analyzing but not on the business process. A Grid-based workflow is characterized by the following features [4]:

- A Grid-based workflow usually includes many applications which perform data analysis tasks. However, those applications, which are also called sub-jobs, are not executed freely but in a strict sequence.
- A sub-job in the Grid-based workflow depends tightly on the output data from the previous sub-job. With incorrect input data, the sub-job will produce a wrong result and damage the result of the whole workflow.
- Sub-jobs in the Grid-based workflow are usually computationally intensive tasks, which can be sequential or parallel programs and require long runtime.
- Grid-based workflows usually require powerful computing facilities such as supercomputers or cluster on which to run.

Obviously, that the Grid-based workflow and the business workflow have the same primary characteristic as they both have a procedure that applies a specific computation into selected data based on certain rules. Each Grid-based workflow is defined by three main factors:

- *Tasks*: A task in the Grid-based workflow is a sub-job, i.e., a specific program doing a specific function. Within a Grid-based workflow, a sub-job can be a sequential program or a parallel program and usually has a long running period and needs powerful computing resources. Each sub-job requires specific resources for the running process such as operating system (OS), amount of storage, CPU, memory, etc.
- *Control aspect*: The control aspect describes the structure and the sequence in processing of sub-jobs in the workflow.
- *Information aspect*: The information aspect of the Grid-based workflow is presented by data transmissions. The dependency among sub-jobs can also be identified by the data transmission task. A sub-job is executed to produce a number of output data, which become the input data for the next sub-job in the sequence. These data must be transferred to the place where the next sub-job is executed. Within a Grid-based workflow, the quantity of data to be transferred between two sub-jobs varies from several KB to a 100 GB depending on the type of application and its scope.

Most of existing Grid-based workflows [5–7] can be presented under Directed Acyclic Graph (DAG) form; so, only the DAG workflow is considered in this chapter. Figure 14.1 presents a sample of a workflow as a material for presentation.

The user specifies the required resources needed to run each sub-job, the data transfer between sub-jobs, the estimated runtime of sub-jobs, and the expected runtime of the entire workflow. In more detail, we will look at a concrete example, a simple Grid workflow as presented in Fig. 14.1. The main requirement of this workflow is described as follows:

- Each sub-job having different resource requirements of hardware and software configurations. Important parameters such as the number of CPUs, the size of

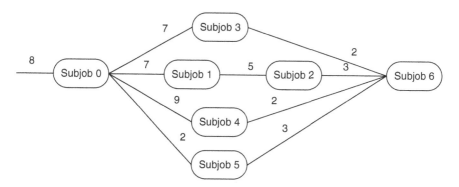

Fig. 14.1 A sample Grid-based workflow

Table 14.1 Sub-jobs' resource
requirements of the workflow
in Fig. 14.1

Sj_ID	CPU	Storage	Exp	Runtime
0	51	59	1	21
1	62	130	3	45
2	78	142	4	13
3	128	113	4	34
4	125	174	2	21
5	104	97	3	42
6	45	118	1	55

storage, the number of experts (some applications need special expert support from the HPC center in order to run successfully), and the estimated runtime for each sub-job in the workflow are described in Table 14.1. The data in Table 14.1 is specially selected for the presentation purpose.

- The number above each edge describes the number of data to be transferred between sub-jobs.

There are two types of resources in the resource requirements of a sub-job: adjustable and nonadjustable. The nonadjustable resources are the type of RMS, OS, and communication library. If a sub-job requires a supercomputer, it cannot run on a cluster. If a sub-job requires Linux OS, it cannot run on Windows OS. Other types of resources are adjustable. For example, a sub-job which requires a system with CPU 1 GHz can run on the system with CPU 2 GHz; a sub-job requiring a system with 2 GB RAM can run on the system with 4 GB RAM. Commonly, all sub-jobs in a workflow have the same nonadjustable resources and different adjustable resources.

The distinguishing characteristic of the workflow description within an SLA context lies in the time factor. Each sub-job must have its estimated runtime correlative with the specific resource configuration on which to run. Thus, the sub-job can be run on dedicated resources within a reserved time frame to ensure the QoS (this is the runtime period). The practical Grid workload usually has a fixed input data pattern. For example, the weather forecasting workflow is executed day by day and finishes within a constant period of time since all data has been collected [7]. This characteristic is the basis for estimating the Grid workload's runtime [8], and the runtime period of a sub-job can be estimated from statistical data. The user usually runs a sub-job many times with different resource configurations and different amount of input data before integrating it to the workflow. The data from these running is a dependable source for estimating future runtimes. If these parameters exceed the pre-determined limitation, the SLA will be violated. Within the SLA context, the resources are reserved over time. If a sub-job runs out of an estimated time period, it will occupy the resource of another reserved sub-job, a situation which is not permitted in an SLA system.

The time is computed in slots with each slot equaling a specific period of real time, from 3 to 5 min. We use the slot concept because we do not want to have arbitrary start and stop time of a sub-job. Moreover, a delay of 3 min also has little significance for the customer. It is noted that a sub-job of the workflow can be either a sequential program or a parallel program and that the data to be transferred among sub-jobs can be very large.

14.2.3 Grid Resource

The computational Grid includes many High-Performance Computing Centers (HPCCs). Sub-jobs of the workflow will be executed in HPCCs as it brings many important advantages:

- Only these HPCCs can handle the high computing demand of scientific applications.
- The cluster or super computer in an HPCC is relatively stable and well maintained. This is an important feature so as to ensure finishing the sub-job within a specific period of time.
- The HPCCs usually connect to the worldwide network by high-speed links, whose broad bandwidth makes the data transfer among sub-jobs easier and faster.

The resources of each HPCC are managed by a software called local Resource Management System (RMS). In this chapter, RMS is used to represent the cluster/supercomputer as well as the Grid services provided by the HPCC. Each RMS has its own unique resource configuration, with difference including the number of CPUs, amount of memory, storage capacity, software, expert, and service price. To ensure that the sub-job can be executed within a dedicated time period, the RMS must support advance resource reservation such as Computer Center System (CCS) [9]. Figure 14.2 depicts a sample CPU reservation profile in such an RMS. In our system, we reserve three main types of resource: CPUs, storages, and experts. An extension to other resources is straightforward.

For present purposes, suppose that we have three involved RMSs executing the sub-jobs of the workflow. The reservation information of the resources is presented in Table 14.2. Each RMS represented by an ID_hpc value has a different number of free CPUs, storage, and expert during a specified period of time. The sample resource reservation profiles of the RMSs are empty.

If two output-input-dependent sub-jobs are executed under the same RMS, it is assumed that the time used for the data transfer equals zero, and assumption can be made since all compute nodes in a cluster usually use a shared storage system such as NFS or DFS. In all other cases, it is assumed that a specific amount of data will be transferred within a specific period of time, thus requiring the reservation of bandwidth.

The link capacity between two local RMSs is determined as the average capacity between two sites in the network, which has a different value with each different RMS couple. Whenever a data transfer task is on a link, the available period on the

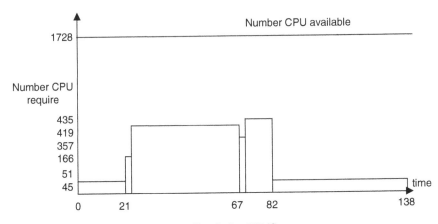

Fig. 14.2 A sample CPU reservation profile of a local RMS

Table 14.2 RMSs resource reservation

ID	ID_hpc	CPUs	Storage	Exp	Start	End
31	2	128	256,000	8	0	1,000,000
23	0	128	256,000	9	0	1,000,000
30	1	128	256,000	6	0	1,000,000

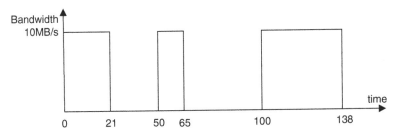

Fig. 14.3 A sample bandwidth reservation profile of a link between two local RMSs

link will be determined. During that specified period, the task can use the whole bandwidth, and other tasks must wait. Using this principle, the bandwidth reservation profile of a link will look similar to the one depicted in Fig. 14.3. A more precise model with bandwidth estimation [10] can be used to determine the bandwidth within a specific time period instead of the average value. In both cases, the main mechanism remains unchanged.

14.3   Formal Problems Statement and State of the Art

14.3.1   Formal Problem Statement

We have many RMSs joining the Grid. We have a workflow including a set of dependency sub-jobs. We have to distribute those sub-jobs of the workflow over different RMSs in a way that ensure the dependency, deadline, and minimal cost. The formal specification of the described problem includes the following elements:

- Let R be the set of Grid RMSs. This set includes a finite number of RMSs, which provide static information about controlled resources and the current reservations/assignments.
- Let S be the set of sub-jobs in a given workflow including all sub-jobs with the current resource and deadline requirements.
- Let E be the set of edges in the workflow, which express the dependency between the sub-jobs and the necessity for data transfers between the sub-jobs.
- Let K_i be the set of resource candidates of sub-job s_i. This set includes all RMSs, which can run sub-job s_i, $K_i \subset R$.

Based on the given input, a feasible and possibly optimal solution is sought, allowing the most efficient mapping of the workflow in a Grid environment with respect to the given global deadline. The required solution is a set defined in Formula 14.1.

$$M = \left\{ \left(s_i, r_j, start\_slot\right) \mid \left(s_i \in S, r_j \in K_i\right) \right\}$$ (14.1)

If the solution does not have *start_slot* for each s_i, it becomes a configuration as defined in Formula 14.2.

$$a = \left\{ \left(s_i, r_j\right) \mid s_i \in S, r_j \in K_i \right\}$$ (14.2)

A feasible solution must satisfy following conditions:

- *Criterion 1*: The finished time of the workflow must be smaller or equal to the expected deadline of the user.
- *Criterion 2*: All $K_i \neq \varnothing$. There is at least one RMS in the candidate set of each sub-job.
- *Criterion 3*: The dependencies of the sub-jobs are resolved and the execution order remains unchanged.
- *Criterion 4*: The capacity of an RMS must equal or be greater than the requirement at any time slot. Each RMS provides a profile of currently available resources and can run many sub-jobs of a single flow both sequentially and in parallel. Those sub-jobs which run on the same RMS form a profile of resource

requirement. With each RMS r_j running sub-jobs of the Grid workflow, and with each time slot in the profile of available resources and profile of resource requirements, the number of available resources must be larger than the resource requirement.

- *Criterion 5*: The data transmission task e_{ki} from sub-job s_k to sub-job s_i must take place in dedicated time slots on the link between the RMS running sub-job s_k to the RMS running sub-job $s_i . e_{ki} \in \cdot E$.

In the next phase, the feasible solution with the lowest cost is sought. The cost C of running a Grid workflow is defined in Formula 14.3. It is the sum of four factors: the cost of using the CPU, the cost of using the storage, the cost of using the experts' knowledge, and finally the expense for transferring data between the resources involved.

$$C = \sum_{i=1}^{n} s_i \cdot r_t * \left(s_i \cdot n_c * r_j \cdot p_c + s_i \cdot n_s * r_j \cdot p_s + s_i \cdot n_e * r_j \cdot p_e \right) + \sum e_{ki} \cdot n_d * r_j \cdot p_d \quad (14.3)$$

with $s_i \cdot r_t$, $s_i \cdot n_c$, $s_i \cdot n_s$, $s_i \cdot n_e$ being the runtime, the number of CPUs, the number of storage, and the number of expert of sub-job s_i respectively. $r_j \cdot p_c$, $r_j \cdot p_s$, $r_j \cdot p_e$, $r_j \cdot p_d$ are the price of using the CPU, the storage, the expert, and the data transmission of RMS r_j respectively. $e_{ki} \cdot n_d$ is the number of data to be transferred from sub-job s_k to sub-job s_i. If two dependent sub-jobs run on the same RMS, the cost of transferring data from the previous sub-job to the later sub-job is neglected.

The ability to find a good solution depends mainly on the resource state at the expected period when the workflow runs. During that period, if the number of free resources in the profile is large, there are a lot of feasible solutions and we can choose the cheapest one. But if the number of free resources in the profile is small, simply finding out a feasible solution is difficult. Thus, a good mapping mechanism should be able to find out an inexpensive solution when there is a wealth of free resources and to be able to uncover a feasible solution when there are few free resources in the Grid.

Supposing the Grid system has m RMSs, which can satisfy the requirement of n sub-jobs in a workflow. As an RMS can run several sub-jobs at a time, finding out the optimal solution needs m^n loops. It can easily be shown that the optimal mapping of the workflow to the Grid RMS as described above is an NP-hard problem.

14.3.2 State of the Art

From the description in Sect. 14.3.1, though, we can see that this is a scheduling problem and that it has many distinguished characteristics.

- An RMS can handle many sub-jobs of the workflow simultaneously. The RMS supports resource reservation.

- A sub-job is a parallel application.
- The destination of the problem is optimizing the cost. The user imposes some strict requirements on the Grid system and pays for the appropriately received service. It is obvious that the user prefers top service at the lowest possible cost. The expense of running a workflow includes the cost of using computation resources and the cost of transferring data among sub-jobs.

Many other previous works [1, 7] have the same Grid-based workflow model as we have. But there are no resource reservations and the goal is to optimize the runtime. Some works about supporting QoS for the Grid-based workflows such as [11–13] use resource reservation infrastructure and have the goal of optimizing the cost. However, they assume a workflow with many sub-jobs, which are sequential programs, and a Grid resource service handling one sub-job at a time. Other related works such as the job shop scheduling problem (JSSP), and the multiprocessor scheduling precedence-constrained task graph problem have similar context with [11–13] but without resource reservation. Moreover, they aim at optimizing the runtime. All above works depend tightly on the characteristics of workload, resource, and goal. Thus, adapting them to our problem faces many difficulties concerning poor quality, long runtime, or inapplicableness [14].

As no previous work has a similar context, we describe here a strategy to handle the requirements. In particular, our strategy focuses on techniques to limit the search space to the high probability area basing on specific characteristics of resource and workload. This brings better results than just plainly apply proposed algorithms, as they do not recognize those specific features.

14.4 Algorithms

The mapping mechanism includes three sub-algorithms. The L-Map algorithm finds the cost-optimal mapping solution for a light workflow in which the amount of data to be transferred among sub-jobs is not much (L stands for light). The H-Map algorithm finds the cost-optimal mapping solution for heavy workflows in which the amount of data to be transferred among sub-jobs is large (H stands for heavy). The w-Tabu algorithm finds the runtime optimal solution for both cases of workflows (w stands for workflow).

Figure 14.4 presents the basic principle of the proposed mapping mechanism. Each sub-job has different resource requirements regarding the type of RMS, the type of CPU, and so on. There are many RMSs with different resource configurations. The initial action is finding among those heterogeneous RMSs the suitable RMSs, which can meet the requirements of the sub-job. The matching between the sub-job's resource requirement and the RMS's resource configuration is done by several logic checking conditions in the WHERE clause of the SQL SELECT command. This work will satisfy Criterion 1. Suppose that each sub-job has m RMSs in the candidate list, we could have m^n configurations.

```
1. Determine candidate RMSs for each sub-job.
   If resource in the Grid free {
2.          if workflow has little data transfer
                 Call L-Map algorithm
3.          if workflow has a lot of data transfer
                 Call H-Map algorithm
   }else {
4.          Call w-Tabu algorithm
            then call L-Tabu or H-Map
   }
```

Fig. 14.4 Mapping mechanism overview

If there are a lot of Grid resources free at a specific time period, the L-Map or the H-Map algorithm is called to find the cost-optimal solution. If there are few Grid resources free, the w-Tabu is called to find a feasible solution. Starting from this feasible solution, the L-Map or H-Map will find the optimal solution. In fact, the signature of having many or few Grid resources free and the method to call on the w-Tabu algorithm are integrated in the L-Map and H-Map algorithms. All of those algorithms have a relatively short runtime and can uncover good quality mapping solutions as in [14, 15]. The following sections will describe each algorithm in detail.

14.4.1 w-Tabu Algorithm

The main purpose of the w-Tabu algorithm is to find out a feasible solution when there are few free Grid resources. This destination is equal to finding a solution with the minimal finished time. Within the SLA context as defined in Sect. 14.2, the finished time of the workflow depends on the reservation state of the resources in the RMSs, the bandwidth among RMSs, and the bandwidth reservation state. It is easy to show that this task is a nondeterministic polynomial time (NP) hard problem. Although the problem has the same destination as most of the existing algorithm mapping a DAG to resources [1], the defined context is different from all other contexts appearing in the literature. Thus, a dedicated algorithm is necessary. We proposed a mapping strategy as depicted in Fig. 14.5. This algorithm has proven to be better than the application of Min-min, Max-min, Suffer, GRASP, w-DCP to the problem as described in Quan [14].

The main idea of the w-Tabu algorithm is that we define a set of starting points in the search space and then perform searching using a special Tabu procedure from those starting points. A set of referent configurations C_o is created as starting points.

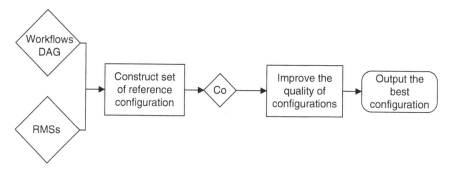

Fig. 14.5 w-Tabu algorithm overview

After that, we use a specific module to improve the quality of each configuration as much as possible with the best configuration being selected. This strategy looks similar to an abstract of a long-term local search such as Tabu search, Grasp, SA, and so on. However, a detailed description makes our algorithm distinguishable from them.

14.4.1.1   Generating Reference Solution Set

Each configuration from the reference configurations set can be thought of as the starting point for a local search, so it should be spread as widely as possible throughout the searching space. To satisfy the space spreading requirement, the number of the same map sub-job:RMS between two configurations must be as small as possible. The number of the member in the reference set depends on the number of available RMSs and the number of sub-jobs. During the process of generating a reference solution set, each candidate RMS of a sub-job has a co-relative *assign_number* to count the times that RMS is assigned to the sub-job. During the process of building a reference configuration, we use a similar set to store all defined configurations having at least a map sub-job:RMS similar to one in the creating configuration. The algorithm is defined in Fig. 14.6.

While building a configuration with each sub-job in the workflow, we select the RMS in the set of candidate RMSs, which create a minimal number of similar sub-job:RMS with other configurations in the similar set. After that, we increase the *assign_number* of the selected RMS. If this value is larger than 1, meaning that the RMS were assigned to the sub-job more than one time, there must exist configurations that contain the same sub-job:RMS and thus satisfy the similar condition. We search these configurations in the reference set which have not been in the similar set, and then add them to the similar set. When finished, the configuration is put to the reference set. After all reference configurations have been defined, we use a specific procedure to refine each of the configuration as much as possible.

```
assign_number of each candidate RMS =0
While m_size < max_size {
 Clear similar set
 For each sub-job in the workflow {
   For each RMS in the candidate list {
     For each solution in similar set {
           If solution contains sub-job:RMS
              num_sim++
           Store tuple (sub-job, RMS, num_sim) in
           a list }}
   Sort the list
   Pick the best result
   assign_number++
   If assign_number > 1
      Find defined solution having the same
      sub-job:RMS and put to similar set
}}
```

Fig. 14.6 Generating reference set algorithm

14.4.1.2 Solution Improvement Algorithm

To improve the quality of a configuration, for this problem, we use a specific procedure based on short-term Tabu search. We use Tabu Search because it can also play the role of a local search but with a wider search area. Besides the standard components of Tabu Search, there are some components specific to the workflow problems.

The Neighborhood Set Structure

One of the most important concepts of Tabu Search as well as local search is the neighborhood set structure. A configuration can also be presented as a vector. The index of the vector represents the sub-job, and the value of the element represents the RMS. With a configuration a, $a=a_1a_2...a_n$ | with all $a_i \subset K_i$, we generate $n*(m-1)$ configurations a' as in Figure \ref{fig436}. We change the value of x_i to each and every value in the candidate list which is different from the present value. Each change results in a new configuration. After that we have set A, $|A|=n*(m-1)$. A is the set of neighborhoods of a configuration. A detailed neighborhood set for the case of our example is presented in Figs. 14.7 and 14.8.

The Assigning Sequence of the Workflow

When the RMS executed each sub-job, the bandwidth among sub-jobs was determined, the next task is to locate a time slot to run sub-job in the specified RMS. At this point, the assigning sequence of the workflow becomes important. The sequence of

Fig. 14.7 Neighborhood structure of a configuration

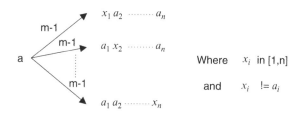

Fig. 14.8 Sample neighborhood structure of a configuration

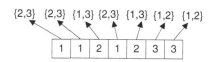

Table 14.3 Valid start time for sub-jobs of workflow in Fig. 14.1

Sub-job	Earliest start	Latest start
0	0	0
1	28	28
2	78	78
3	28	58
4	30	71
5	23	49
6	94	94

determining runtime for sub-jobs of the workflow in an RMS can also affect the final finished time of the workflow, especially when there are many sub-jobs in the same RMS.

In general, to ensure the integrity of the workflow, sub-jobs in the workflow are assigned based on the sequence of the data processing. However, that principle does not cover the case of a set of sub-jobs, which have the same priority in data sequence and do not depend on each other. To examine the problem, we determine the earliest and latest start times of each sub-jobs of the workflow under an ideal condition. The time period for data transfer among sub-jobs is computed by dividing the amount of data to a fixed bandwidth. The earliest and latest start and stop times for each sub-job and data transfer depend only on the workflow topology and the runtime of sub-jobs but not the resources context. These parameters can be determined using conventional graph algorithms. A sample of these data for the workflow in Fig. 14.1, in which the number above each link represents the number of time slots for data transfer, is presented in Table 14.3.

The ability of finding a suitable resource slot to run a sub-job depends on the number of resources free during the valid running period. From the graph, we can see sub-job 1 and sub-job 3 as having the same priority in the data sequence. However, sub-job 1 can start at max time slot 28 while sub-job 3 can start at max time slot 58 without affecting the finished time of workflow. Suppose that two sub-jobs are mapped to run in the same RMS and the RMS can run one sub-job at a time.

If sub-job 3 is assigned first and in the worst case at time slot 58, sub-job 1 will be run from time slot 92; thus, the workflow will be late by a minimum of 64 time slots. If sub-job 1 is assigned first at time slot 28, sub-job 3 can be run at time slot 73 and the workflow will be late by 15 time slots. Here, we can see the latest time factor is the main parameter for evaluating the full effect of the sequential assigning decision. It can be seen through the affection, mapping sub-job having the smaller latest start time first will make the lateness less. Thus, the latest start time value determined as above can be used to determine the assigning sequence. The sub-job having the smaller latest start time will be assigned earlier. This procedure will satisfy Criterion 3.

Computing the Timetable Procedure

The algorithm to compute the timetable is presented in Fig. 14.9. As the w-Tabu algorithm applies both for light workflow and heavy workflow, determining the parameter for each case cannot be the same. With light workflow, the end time of the data transfer equals the time slot after the end of the correlative source sub-job. With a heavy workflow, the end time of data transfer is determined by searching the bandwidth reservation profile. This procedure will satisfy Criteria 4 and 5.

The Modified Tabu Search Procedure

In the normal Tabu search, in each move iteration, we will try assigning each sub-job $s_i \subset S$ with each RMS r_j in the candidate set K_i and use the procedure in Fig. 14.9

```
With each sub-job k following the assign sequence {
    Determine set of assigned sub-jobs Q, which having output
    data transfer to the sub-job k
    With each sub-job i in Q {
        min_st_tran=end_time of sub-job i +1
        If heavy weight workflow {
        Search in reservation profile of link between RMS running
        sub-job k and RMS running sub-job i to determine start and
        end time of data transfer task with the start time >
        min_st_tran } else {
            end time data transfer = min_st_tran }
    }
    min_st_sj=max end time of all above data transfer +1
    Search in reservation profile of RMS running
    sub-job k to determine its start and end time with
    the start time > min_st_sj
}
```

Fig. 14.9 Determining timetable algorithm for workflow in w-Tabu

to compute the runtime and then check for overall improvement and select the best one. This method is not efficient as it requires a lot of time for computing the runtime of the workflow which is not a simple procedure. We will improve the method by proposing a new neighborhood with two comments.

Comment 1: The runtime of the workflow depends mainly on the execution time of the critical path. In one iteration, we can move only one sub-job to one RMS. If the sub-job does not belong to the critical path, after the movement, the old critical path will have a very low probability of being shortened and the finished time of the workflow will have a low probability of improvement. Thus, we concentrate only on sub-jobs in the critical path. With a defined solution and runtime table, the critical path of a workflow is defined with the algorithm in Fig. 14.10. We start with the last sub-job determined. The next sub-job of the critical path will have the latest finish data transferred to the previously determined sub-job. The process continues until the next sub-job is equal to first sub-job. Figure 14.11 depicts a sample critical path of the workflow in Fig. 14.1.

Comment 2: In one move iteration, with only one change of one sub-job to one RMS, if the finish time of the data transfer from this sub-job to the next sub-job in the critical path is not decreased, the critical path cannot be shortened. For this reason, we only consider the change which reduces the finish time of consequent data transfer. It can easy be seen that checking if the data transfer time can be improved is much shorter than computing the runtime table for the whole workflow.

With two comments and other remaining procedures similar to the standard Tabu search, we build the overall improvement procedure as presented in Fig. 14.12.

```
Let C is the set of sub-jobs in the critical path
Put last sub-job into C
next_subjob=last sub-job
do{
    prev_subjob is determined as the sub-job having
    latest finished data output transfer to  next_subjob
    Put prev_subjob into C
    next_sj=prev_subjob
} until prev_sj= first sub-job
```

Fig. 14.10 Determining critical path algorithm

Fig. 14.11 Sample critical path of the workflow in Fig. 14.1

```
while (num_loop<max_loop){
    Determine critical path
    For each sub-job in the critical path {
        For each RMS in the candidate set {
            If can improve the finished time of the
            sequence data transfer {
                Compute timetable for new solution
                Store tuple (sub-job, RMS, makespan) to
                candidate list
    }}}
    Pick the solution having smaller makespan
    or not affect tabu rule
    Assign tabu_number for the selected RMS
    If smaller makespan then store the solution
    num_loop++
}
```

Fig. 14.12 Configuration improvement algorithm in w-Tabu

14.4.2   H-Map Algorithm

The H-Map algorithm maps heavy workflow to the Grid RMSs. As the data to be transferred among sub-jobs in the workflow are huge, to ensure the deadline of the workflow, it is necessary to reserve bandwidth. In this case, the time to do a data transmission task becomes unpredictable as it depends on the bandwidth and the reservation profile of the link, which varies from link to link. The variety in the completion time of the data transmission task makes the total runtime of the work-flow also flexible. The goal of the H-Map algorithm is to find out a solution which ensures Criteria 1–5, and is as inexpensive as possible. The overall H-Map algorithm is presented in Fig. 14.13 and has proven to be better than the application of standard metaheuristics such as Tabu Search, Simulated Annealing, Iterated Local Search, Guided Local Search, Genetic Algorithm, Estimation of Distribution Algorithm to the problem as described in Quan [14].

Similar to the w-Tabu algorithm, firstly, a set of initial configurations C_o is created as starting points in the search space. The configurations in C_o should be distributed widely over the search space and must satisfy Criterion 1. If $C_o = \emptyset$, we can deduce that there is little resource free on the Grid and the w-Tabu algorithm is invoked. If w-Tabu cannot also find a feasible solution, the algorithm stops. If $C_o \neq \emptyset$, the set will gradually be refined to have better quality solutions. The refining process stops when the solutions in the set cannot be improved more and we have the final set C^*. The best solution in C^* will be output as the result of the algorithm. The following sections will describe in detail each procedure in the algorithm.

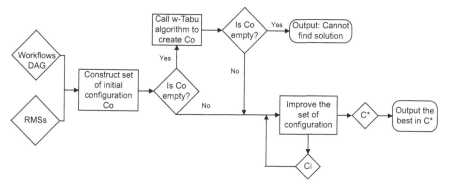

Fig. 14.13 H-Map algorithm overview

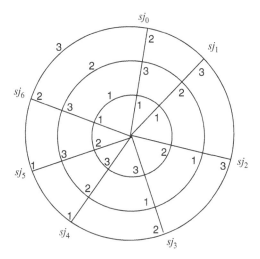

Fig. 14.14 The configuration space according to cost distribution

14.4.2.1 Constructing the Set of Initial Configurations

The purpose of this algorithm is to create a set of initial configurations which will be distributed widely over the search space.

Step 0: With each sub-job s_i, we sort the RMSs in the candidate set K_i according to the cost they need to run s_i, computed according to Formula 14.3. The configuration space of the sample now can be presented in Fig. 14.14 and Table 14.4. In Fig. 14.14, the RMSs lying along the axis of each sub-job have a cost increasing in the direction from inside out. The line connecting each point in every sub-job axis will form a configuration. Figure 14.14 presents three configurations with an increasing index in the direction from inside to outside. Figure 14.14 also presents the cost distribution of the configuration space according to Formula 14.3.

Table 14.4 RMSs candidate
for each sub-job in cost order

Sj_ID	RMS	RMS	RMS
sj0	R1	R3	R2
sj1	R1	R2	R3
sj2	R2	R1	R3
sj3	R3	R1	R2
sj4	R3	R2	R1
sj5	R2	R3	R1
sj6	R1	R3	R2

Fig. 14.15 The first
selection configuration
of the sample

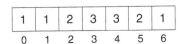

Fig. 14.16 Procedure to
create the set of initial
configurations

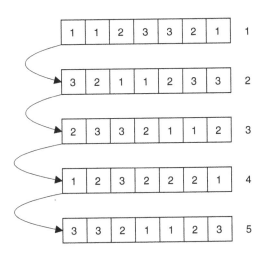

The configuration in the outer layers has a greater cost than those of the inner layers. The cost of the configuration lying between two layers is greater than the cost of the inner layer and smaller than the cost of the outer layer.

Step 1: We pick the first configuration as the first layer in the configuration space. The determined configuration can be presented as a vector. The index of the vector represents the sub-job, and the value of the element represents the RMS. The first configuration in our example is presented in Fig. 14.15. Although this has minimal cost according to Formula 14.3, we cannot be sure that it is the optimal solution. The real cost of a configuration must consider the neglected cost of data transmission when two sequential sub-jobs are in the same RMS.

Step 2: We construct the other configurations by following a process similar to the one described in Fig. 14.16. The second solution is the second layer of the configuration space. Then we create a solution having a cost located between layer 1 and layer 2 by combining the first and second configurations. To do this, we take the p first elements from the first vector configuration and then the p second elements from the second vector configuration and repeat until we have n elements to form the third one. Thus, we get ($n/2$) elements from the first vector configuration and ($n/2$) other elements from the second one. Combining in this way will ensure the target configuration of having a greater difference in cost according to Formula 14.3 compared to the source configurations. This process continues until the final layer is reached. Thus, we have in total $2*(m-1)$ configurations and we can ensure that the set of initial configurations is distributed over the search space according to cost criteria.

Step 3: We check Criteria 4 and 5 of all $2*m-1$ configurations. To verify Criteria 4 and 5, we have to determine the timetable for all sub-jobs of the workflow. The procedure to determine the timetable of the workflow is similar to the one described in Fig. 14.9. If some of them do not satisfy the Criteria 4 and 5 requirement, we construct more so as to have enough $2*m-1$ configurations. To do the construction, we change the value of p parameter in the range from 1 to ($n/2$) in step 2 to create the new configuration.

After this phase, we have set C_o including maximum ($2m-1$) valid configurations.

14.4.2.2 Improving Solution Quality Algorithm

To improve the quality of the solutions, we use the neighborhood structure as described in Sect. 14.4.1 and Fig. 14.7. Call A the set of neighborhood of a configuration. The procedure to find the highest quality solution includes the following steps.

Step 1: $\forall\ a \subset A$, calculate cost(a) and timetable(a), pick $a*$ with the smallest cost($a*$) and satisfy Criterion 2, put $a*$ to set C_1. The detailed technique of this step is described in Fig. 14.17.

```
For each subjob in the workflow {
    For each RMS in the candidate list {
        If cheaper then put (sjid, RMS id, improve_value)
        to a list }}
    Sort the list according to improve_value
    From the begin of the list{
        Compute time table to get the finished time
        If finished time < limit
            break
    }
    Store the result
```

Fig. 14.17 Algorithm to improve the solution quality

We consider only the configuration having a smaller cost than the present configuration. Therefore, instead of computing the cost and the timetable of all configurations in the neighborhood set, we compute only the cost of them. All the cheaper configurations are stored in a sorted list. And then we compute the timetable of cheaper configurations along the list to find the first feasible configuration. This technique helps decrease much of the algorithm's runtime.

Step 2: Repeat step 1 with all $a \subset C_o$ to form C_1.

Step 3: Repeat step 1 to 2 until $C_t = C_{t-1}$.

Step 4: $C_t \equiv C^*$. Pick the best configuration of C^*.

14.4.3   L-Map Algorithm

The key difference between the light workflow and the heavy workflow is the communication. HPCCs are usually interconnected by a broadband link greater than 100 Mbps. The length of one time slot in our system is between 2 and 5 min. Thus, the amount of data transferred through a link within one time slot can range from 1.2 to 3 GB. Since we assume less than 10 MB of data transfer between sub-jobs (workflows with light communications), the data transfer can easily be performed within one time slot (right after the sub-job had finished its calculation) without affecting any other communication between two RMSs. As the number of data to be transferred between sub-jobs in the workflow is very small, we can omit the cost of data transfer. Thus, the cost C of a Grid workflow is defined in Formula 14.3 which is the sum of the charge of using: (1) the CPU, (2) the storage, and (3) the expert knowledge.

The light communication can help us ignore the complexities in time and cost caused by data transfer. Thus, we could apply a specific technique to improve the speed and the quality of the mapping algorithm. In this section, we present an algorithm called L-Map to map light communication workflows onto the Grid RMSs (L – stands for light). The goal of the L-Map algorithm is to find a solution which satisfies Criterion 1–5 and is as inexpensive as possible. The overall L-Map algorithm to map DAG to resources is presented in Fig. 14.18. The main idea of the algorithm is to find out a high-quality and feasible solution. Starting from this solution, we limit the solution space and use local search to find intensively in this space the best feasible solution. This algorithm has proven to be better than the application of H-map, DBC, Genetic Algorithm to the problem as described in Quan and Altmann [15].

The following sections will describe in detail each procedure in the algorithm.

14.4.3.1   Creating the Initial Feasible Solution

The sequence of steps in the procedure of creating the initial feasible solution is presented in Fig. 14.19.

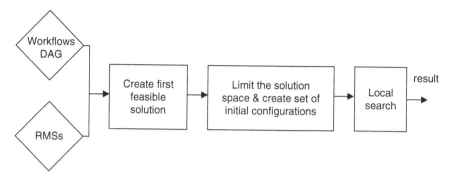

Fig. 14.18 Framework of the L-Map algorithm

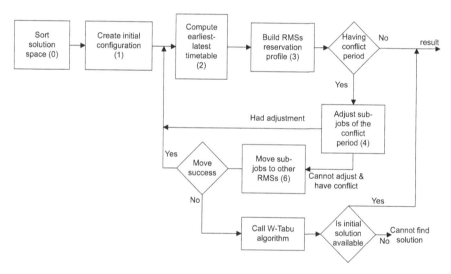

Fig. 14.19 Procedure to create the initial solution

Step 0: With each sub-job s_i, we sort the RMSs in the candidate set K_i according to the cost of running s_i computed according to Formula 14.3 but neglecting the cost of data transfer. The RMS having the lower cost to run the sub-job is located at the lower position. The solution space of the sample is presented in Fig. 14.20. Each box RMS-Rt represents the RMS and the runtime of the sub-job in this RMS.

Step 1: We form the first configuration by assigning each sub-job to the RMS having the lowest cost in the candidate list. The determined configuration can be presented as a vector with the index of the vector representing the sub-job and the value of the element representing the RMS. The first configuration in our example is presented in Fig. 14.21.

Step 2: As the runtime of each sub-job in the determined RMS was defined and the time to do data transfer is fixed, we can compute the earliest start time and the latest

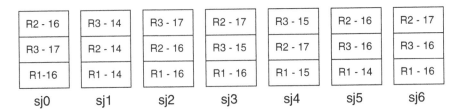

R2 - 16	R3 - 14	R3 - 17	R2 - 17	R3 - 15	R2 - 16	R2 - 17
R3 - 17	R2 - 14	R2 - 16	R3 - 15	R2 - 17	R3 - 16	R3 - 16
R1-16	R1 - 14	R1 - 16	R1 - 16	R1 - 15	R1 - 14	R1 - 16
sj0	sj1	sj2	sj3	sj4	sj5	sj6

Fig. 14.20 The solution space in cost order

Fig. 14.21 The first
selection configuration
of the example

1	1	1	1	1	1	1
0	1	2	3	4	5	6

Table 14.5 A sample valid
start time for sub-jobs of
workflow in Fig. 14.1

Sub-job	Earliest start	Latest start
0	10	37
1	26	69
2	26	41
3	42	69
4	26	69
5	26	69
6	58	85

stop time of each sub-job using the conventional graph algorithm. In the case of our example, assume that the user wants the workflow to be started at time slot 10 and stopped at time slot 85, the earliest-latest timetable is presented in Table 14.5.

Step 3: From the data of the earliest-latest timetable, with each RMS appearing in the configuration and each type of reserved resource in the RMS, we build the resource reservation profile. In this step, the runtime of the sub-job is computed from the earliest start time to the latest stop time. The built profiles could have many conflict periods in which the number of required resource is greater than the available resource. If we do not resolve those periods, we will not have a feasible solution. In this algorithm, CPUs, storage, and experts are considered in the same way. Each resource has its own reservation profile. The characters of each profile are very similar to each other. In order to have a feasible solution, we have to resolve the conflict in three profiles. As they are very similar to each other, in this chapter, we only present the CPU profile to demonstrate the idea. In our example, only RMS1 appears in the configuration. The CPU reservation profile of the RMS 1 is presented in Fig. 14.22.

Step 4: There are many sub-jobs joining the conflict period. If we move sub-jobs out of it, the conflict rate will be reduced. This movement is performed by adjusting the earliest start time or the latest stop time of the sub-jobs and thus, the sub-jobs

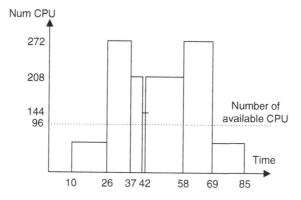

Fig. 14.22 Reservation profile of RMS 1

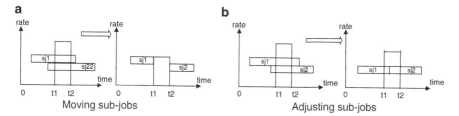

Fig. 14.23 Resolving the conflict period

are moved out of the conflict period. One possible solution is shown in Fig. 14.23a, where either the latest stop time of sub-job1 is set to $t1$ or the earliest start time of sub-job2 is set to $t2$. The second way is to adjust two sub-jobs simultaneously as depicted in Fig. 14.23b. A necessary prerequisite here is that, after adjustment, the latest stop time minus the earliest start time of the sub-job is greater than its runtime.

Step 5: We adjust the earliest start time and latest stop time of the sub-jobs relating with the moved sub-jobs to ensure the integrity of the workflow. Then we repeat steps 3 and 4 until we cannot adjust the sub-jobs further. In our example, after this phase, the CPU reservation profile of RMS 1 is presented in Fig. 14.24.

Step 6: If after the adjusting phase, there are still some conflict periods, we have to move some sub-jobs contributing to the conflict to other RMSs. The resources in the RMS having the conflict period should be allocated as much as possible so that the cost for using resources will be kept to a minimum. This is a knapsack problem, which is known to be NP-hard. Therefore, we use an algorithm as presented in Fig. 14.25. This algorithm ensures that the remaining free resources after the filling phase are always smaller than the smallest sub-job. If a sub-job cannot be moved to another RMS, we can deduce that the Grid resource is busy and thus w-Tabu

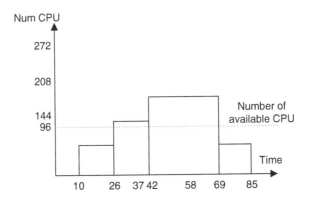

Fig. 14.24 Reservation profile of RMS 1 after adjusting

> *Select the most serious conflict period*
>
> *Determine all sub-jobs contributing to the period*
>
> *Sort those sub-jobs according to cost in descend order*
>
> *For each sub-job in the list {*
>
>   *If the resource free greater than the resource required by the sub-job*
>
>   *Let the sub-job stay in the RMS*
>
>   *Update the number of resource free of the period*
>
>   *Else*
>
>   *Assign the sub-job to the next RMS in its sorted candidate list*
>
> *}*

Fig. 14.25 Moving sub-jobs algorithm

algorithm is invoked. If the w-Tabu cannot find an initial feasible solution, the algorithm will stop.

In our example, the most serious conflict period is 42–69 with the contribution of sub-job 3, 5, and 4 sorting in descending order according to the cost. We can fill the period with sub-job 3, sub-job 4 is moved to RMS 2 and sub-job 5 is moved to RMS 3. After this step, we have a new configuration as presented in Fig. 14.26.

Step 7: As we have a new configuration, the process from step 3 to step 6 is repeated until there is no conflict period. After this phase, we have a feasible candidate solution as depicted in Fig. 14.27.

14.4.3.2 Limiting the Solution Space

Suppose that each sub-job has m candidate RMSs. Suppose that in the feasible solution, the RMS has the highest ranking at k. Thus, with each sub-job,

Fig. 14.26 The new configuration of the example

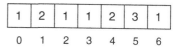

Fig. 14.27 The first feasible
solution of the example

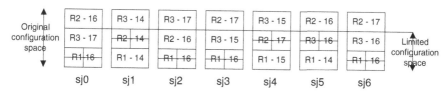

Fig. 14.28 The limited solution space

we remove all its candidate RMSs having rank greater than k. The process applied
to our example is presented in Fig. 14.28. We limit the solution space in this way
for two reasons.

- The lower area of the solution space contains inexpensive solutions for sub-jobs.
  Therefore, the ability to have high-quality solutions in this area is extremely
  likely and should be considered intensively. In contrast, the higher area of the
  solution space contains expensive solutions for sub-jobs and thus, the ability to
  have a high-quality solution in this area is very unlikely. For that reason, to save
  the computation time, we can bypass this area.
- The selected solution space contains at least one feasible solution. Thus, we can
  be sure that with this new solution space, we can always uncover an equal or
  better solution than the previously found one.

14.4.3.3 Creating the Set of Initial Configurations

The set of initial configurations should be distributed over the solution space as
widely as possible. Therefore, we create the new configuration by shifting onward
the first feasible solution. Suppose each sub-job has k candidate RMSs, then we
will shift $(k-1)$ times to create $(k-1)$ configurations. Thus, there are k configurations in the initial set including the found feasible solution. For our example, the
procedure is expressed in Fig. 14.29. It is noted that in this step, a configuration can
be either feasible or unfeasible.

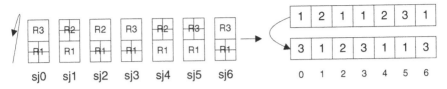

Fig. 14.29 Creating the set of initial configurations

```
Compute cost c of the configuration a
while (1) {
    For each neighbor in the neighborhood set of a{
        if a is feasible
            compute cost c' of the neighbor
            if c'<c put to the list of candidate
        else
            compute finished time p' of the neighbor
            if p'< deadline
                compute cost c' of the neighbor
                put to the list of candidate
    }
    if the list empty -> stop local search
    Sort the list
    If a is not feasible
        Replace a by the first solution in the list
    else
        for each candidate a' in the list
            compute finished time p'
            if p'< deadline    replace a by a' and break out the loop
}
```

Fig. 14.30 The local search procedure

14.4.3.4 Local Search

A local search procedure is used to find a feasible solution and to improve the quality of the solution as far as possible starting from a configuration in the initial set. The overall local search procedure is presented in Fig. 14.30.

If the initial configuration is not feasible, we search in the neighborhood of the candidate configuration for feasible solutions satisfying Criteria 4 and 5. Then, we replace the initial one by the best-quality solution found. In this case, we have to compute the timetable and check the deadline of all configuration in the neighborhood.

If the initial configuration is feasible, we then consider only configurations having less cost than the present solution. Therefore, instead of computing the cost and the timetable of all configurations in the neighborhood set at the same time, we only compute the cost of each configuration individually. All the configurations are stored in a sorted list. We then compute the timetable of the less expensive configurations along the list to find the first feasible configuration. This technique helps reduce the algorithm's runtime significantly as the computation timetable procedure takes a significant time to be completed. The computation timetable procedure is the one in Fig. 14.9.

The time to perform the local search procedure varies depending on the number of invoking module computing timetable. If this number is small, the computing time will be short and vice versa.

14.5 Performance Experiment

The performance experiment is done by simulation to check for the quality of the mapping algorithms. The hardware and software used in the experiments is rather standard and simple (Pentium 4 2,8 GHz, 2 GB RAM, Linux Redhat 9.0, MySQL). The whole simulation program is implemented in C/C++. We generated several scenarios with different workflow configurations and different RMS configurations to be compatible with the ability of the comparing algorithms. The goal of the experiment is to measure the feasibility, the quality of the solution, and the time needed for the computation.

14.5.1 w-Tabu Algorithm Performance

We employed all the ideas in the recently appearing literature related to mapping workflow to Grid resource with the same destination to minimize the finished time and adapted them to our problem. Those algorithms include w-DCP, Grasp, min-min, max-min, and suffer [14]. To compare the quality of all the described algorithms above, we generated 18 different workflows which:

- Have different topologies.
- Have a different number of sub-jobs. The number of sub-jobs is in the range 7–32.
- Have different sub-job specifications.
- Have different amounts of data transfer. The amount of data transfer is in the range from several 100 MB to several GB.

In the algorithms, the number of the sub-job is the most important factor to the execution time of the algorithm. We also stop at 32 sub-jobs for a workflow because as far as we know, with our model of parallel task sub-job, most existing Grid-based workflows include only 10–20 sub-jobs. Thus, we believe that our workload configuration can simulate accurately the requirement of real problems. Those workflows

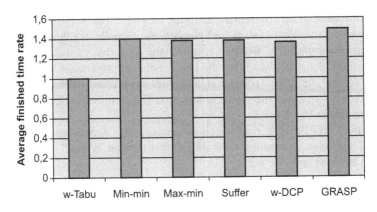

Fig. 14.31 Overall quality comparison of w-Tabu and other algorithms

will be mapped to 20 RMSs with different resource configurations and different resource reservation contexts. The workflows are mapped by 6 algorithms w-Tabu, w-DCP, Grasp, min-min, max-min, and suffer. The finished time and the runtime of solutions generated by each algorithm correlative with each workflow are recorded.

The experimental data shows that all algorithms need few seconds to find out the solutions. The overall quality comparison among algorithms is depicted in Fig. 14.31. The graph presents the average relative values of the solution's finished time created by different algorithms. From Fig. 14.31, it can be seen that our algorithm outperforms all other algorithms.

14.5.2 H-Map Algorithm Performance

In this experiment, the workload and the resource configurations are similar to those in the above experiment. The only difference is that the amount of data transfer among sub-jobs of the workflows is in the range 1–6 GB. The workflows are mapped with 7 algorithms H-Map, TS, SA, GLS, ILS, GA, and EDA. The cost and the runtime of solutions generated by each algorithm correlative with each workflow are recorded. The overall results are presented in Figs. 14.32 and 14.33.

The experiment results show that the H-Map algorithm finds out equal or higher-quality solutions within a much shorter runtime than other algorithms in most cases. With small-scale problems, some metaheuristics using local search such as ILS, GLS, and EDA find out equal results with the H-Map and better than the SA or GA. But with large-scale problems, they have an exponential runtime with unsatisfactory results.

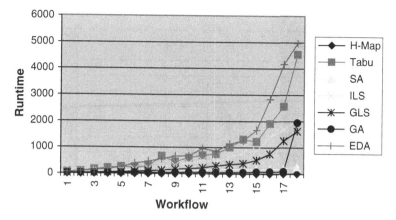

Fig. 14.32 Overall runtime comparison of H-Map and other algorithms

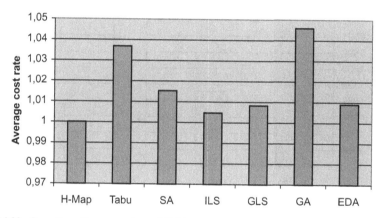

Fig. 14.33 Overall quality comparison of H-Map and other algorithms

14.5.3   L-Map Algorithm Performance

In this experiment, the resource configurations are similar to those in the above experiment. The workload includes 20 workflows. They are different in topologies, sub-jobs configuration. The number of sub-jobs is from 21 to 32. The amount of data transfer among sub-jobs of the workflows is in the range 1–10 MB. The workflows are mapped to resources with four algorithms L-Map, H-Map, DBC, and GA. The cost and the runtime of solutions generated by each algorithm correlative with each workflow are recorded. The overall results are presented in Figs. 14.34 and 14.35.

From the results, we can see that the L-Map algorithm created higher-quality solutions than all comparing algorithms. Compared to H-Map and GS algorithms,

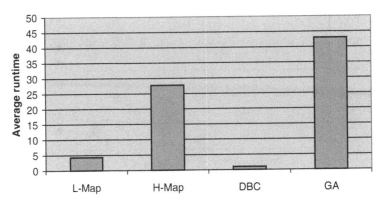

Fig. 14.34 Overall runtime comparison of L-Map and other algorithms

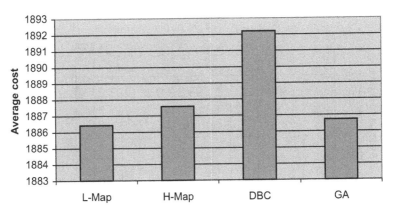

Fig. 14.35 Overall quanlity comparison of L-Map and other algorithms

the quality of L-Map algorithm is slightly better but the runtime is significantly smaller. The cost difference between solutions found by the L-Map algorithm and the DBC algorithm is small in absolute value. However, when we examine the difference within a business context and a business model, it will have significant meaning. From the business point of view, the broker does the mapping and the income is more important than the total cost of running the workflow. Assuming that the workflow execution service counts for 5% of the total running cost, the broker using the L-map algorithm will have the income 6% higher than the broker using the DBC algorithm. Moreover, experimenting the negotiation period of the SLA workflow with Web service technology, each negotiation round took a minute or more, mainly for user checking the differences in SLA content. Thus, in our opinion, the runtime of the L-Map algorithm is well acceptable in practical applications with just few seconds.

14.6 Conclusion

This chapter has presented concepts and algorithms of mapping Grid-based workflow to Grid resources within the Service Level Agreement context. The Grid-based workflow under Directed Acyclic Graph format includes many dependent sub-jobs which can be either a sequential or parallel application. The Service Level Agreement context implies a business Grid with many providers which are High-Performance Computing Centers. Each High-Performance Computing Center supports resource reservation and bandwidth reservation. The business Grid leads to the mapping with the cost optimization problem. To solve the problem, with each workflow characteristic and Grid resource state, a different specific algorithm is used. If there are a lot of Grid resources free, L-Map or H-Map algorithm is called on to find the cost-optimal solution. If there are few Grid resources free, w-Tabu is called on to find a feasible solution. The set of those algorithms could be employed as the heart of the system supporting Service Level Agreement for the Grid-based workflow.

References

1. Deelman, E., Blythe, J., Gil, Y., Kesselman, C., Mehta, G., Patil, S., Su, M., Vahi, K. and Livny, M. Pegasus: Mapping Scientific Workflows onto the Grid. In *The 2nd European Across Grids Conference*, Nicosia, Cyprus, LNCS Springer Press, (2004), pp. 11–20.
2. Georgakopoulos, D., Hornick, M., and Sheth, A. An Overview of workflow management: From Process Modeling to Workflow Automation Infrastructure, *Distributed and Parallel Databases*, 3, 2 (1995), 119–153.
3. Fischer, L. *Workflow Handbook 2004*, Future Strategies Inc., Lighthouse Point, FL, USA.
4. Singh, M. P. and Vouk, M. A. Scientific Workflows: Scientific Computing Meets Transactional Workflows. 1997 (available at http://www.csc.ncsu.edu/faculty/mpsingh/papers/databases/workflows/sciworkflows.html, accessed on March, 9, 2008)
5. Ludtke, S., Baldwin, P. and Chiu, W. EMAN: Semiautomated Software for High-Resolution Single-Particle Reconstruction. *Journal of Structure Biology*, 128, (1999), 146–157.
6. Berriman, G. B., Good, J. C., Laity, A. C. (2003) Montage: a Grid Enabled Image Mosaic Service for the National Virtual Observatory. *ADASS*, 13, (2003), 145–1 167.
7. Lovas, R., Dzsa, G., Kacsuk, P., Podhorszki, N., Drtos, D. Workflow Support for Complex Grid Applications: Integrated and Portal Solutions. In *The 2nd European Across Grids Conference*, Nicosia, Cyprus, LNCS Springer Press, (2004), pp.129–138.
8. Spooner, D. P., Jarvis, S. A., Cao, J., Saini, S. and Nudd, G. R. Local Grid Scheduling Techniques Using Performance Prediction. *IEEE Proceedings – Computers and Digital Techniques*, 150, 2 (2003), pp. 87–96.
9. Hovestadt, M. Scheduling in HPC Resource Management Systems: Queuing vs. Planning, In *the 9th Workshop on JSSPP at GGF8*, Washington, USA, LNCS Springer Press, (2003), pp. 1–20.
10. Wolski, R. Experiences with Predicting Resource Performance On-line in Computational Grid Settings. *ACM SIGMETRICS Performance Evaluation Review*, 30, 4 (2003), 41–49.
11. McGough, S., Afzal, A., Darlington, J., Furmento, N., Mayer, A. and Young, L. Making the Grid Predictable through Reservations and Performance Modelling. *The Computer Journal*, 48, 3 (2005), 358–368.

12. Zeng, L., Benatallah, B., Ngu, A., Dumas, M., Kalagnanam, J., Chang, H. QoS-Aware Middleware for Web Services Composition. *IEEE Transactions on Software Engineering*, 30, 2004.
13. Brandic, I., Benkner, S., Engelbrecht, G. and Schmidt, R. QoS Support for Time-Critical Grid Workflow Applications. In *The first International Conference on e-Science and Grid Computing 2005*, Melbourne, Australia, IEEE Computer Society Press, (2005), pp. 108–115.
14. Quan, D.M. *A Framework for SLA-aware execution of Grid-based workflows*, PhD thesis - University of Paderborn, Germany, 2006.
15. Quan, D.M., Altmann, J. Mapping of SLA-based workflows with light communication onto Grid resources. In *The 4th International Conference on Grid Service Engineering and Management – GSEM 2007*, Leipzig, Germany, LNI GI Press, (2007), pp. 135–145.

Chapter 15
Orchestrating e-Science with the Workflow Paradigm: Task-Based Scientific Workflow Modeling and Executing

Xiping Liu, Wanchun Dou, and Jinjun Chen

Abstract e-Science usually involves a great number of data sets, computing resources, and large teams managed and developed by research laboratories, universities, or governments. Science processes, if deployed in the workflow forms, can be managed more effectively and executed more automatically. Scientific workflows have therefore emerged and been adopted as a paradigm to organize and orchestrate activities in e-Science processes. Differing with workflows applied in the business world, however, scientific workflows need to take account of specific characteristics of science processes and make corresponding changes to accommodate those specific characteristics. A task-based scientific workflow modeling and executing approach is therefore proposed in this chapter for orchestrating e-Science with the workflow paradigm. Besides, this chapter also discusses some related work in the scientific workflow field.

15.1 Introduction

With the fast development of computer technologies, very large-scale complex science processes which could not be deployed in the past can now be explored. In e-Science, science processes refer to those computationally intensive solving

X. Liu (✉)
College of Computer, Institute of Computer Technology, Nanjing University of Posts and Telecommunications, Nanjing 210003, China
e-mail: liuxp@njupt.edu.cn

W. Dou
State Key Laboratory for Novel Software Technology, Department of Computer Science and Technology, Nanjing University, Nanjing 210009, China
e-mail: douwc@nju.edu.cn

J. Chen
Faculty of Information and Communication Technology, Swinburne University of Technology, Melbourne, Australia
e-mail: jinjun.chen@gmail.com

Xiaoyu Yang et al. (eds.), *Guide to e-Science: Next Generation Scientific Research and Discovery*, Computer Communications and Networks, DOI 10.1007/978-0-85729-439-5_15, © Springer-Verlag London Limited 2011

processes of scientific problems, usually with goals such as knowledge discovery, knowledge innovation, and so on. Science processes need to handle very complicated logic in scientific problems. Besides, in many cases, such processes involve a great number of scientists from different domains as well as distributed resources. To some extent, deploying such science processes involves extensive engineering, which requires automatic and reasonable management of the whole process. Fortunately, workflow technologies [1] provide useful ideas and paradigms for the automation of science processes.

Workflow originally emerged for the automation of a business process in whole or part, where a business process means a kind of process in the domain of business organizational structure and policy. The definition of a workflow consists of a coordinated set of activities that are connected in order to achieve a common goal. These activities can be organized in various routing forms such as sequential, parallel, and so on. Many workflow instances may be created and executed based on a workflow definition, and this process is deployed automatically under the control of workflow engines [2].

Many ideas and concepts from workflow technologies can be adapted to science processes, such as the idea of organizing a process as a workflow; the idea of using conditions to control automatic transitions between activities; the concept of building blocks, e.g., and-join, or-split, used for the representation of activity routings; and so on. More specifically, a science process can be modeled as a workflow before it is deployed. Such a workflow definition organizes the whole complex science process as a coordinated set of activities with data relationships and control relationships. The workflow should be verified according to certain rules or strategies. After the workflow is defined and verified at the modeling phase, the workflow engine can control the deployment of the science process automatically based on the verified workflow at the executing phase. In this way, the science process can be deployed effectively and efficiently in the form of a workflow. Consequently, the scientific workflow is proposed to represent science processes as workflows, which can facilitate the automatic and effective execution of science processes.

Though the scientific workflow has its roots in the traditional workflow, i.e., workflow for automation of business processes, it is unsuitable to apply workflow models designed for business processes to the definitions of scientific workflows directly. This is because compared with business processes, science processes have many characteristics that cannot be satisfied by current workflow models. Science processes differ greatly from business processes, because a science process is a tentative solving process without foregone stable solving schemes while a business process is a comparatively fixed procedure with a specific behavior description for each logical step. The detailed differences between business processes and science processes are analyzed as follows.

First, science processes are more data-centric and knowledge-intensive [3], and require more powerful computing ability and mental thinking behaviors. In contrast, business processes pay more attention to control specifications than data specifications. Most activities seem like fixed mechanical operations.

Second, control relationships in science processes are more complex and flexible. Except the common control relationships in business processes which are used to represent kinds of temporal order relationships among activities, more control relationships are required to represent the specific control logic semantic in science processes.

Third, science processes are often highly indeterminate, innovative, and dynamic. The predefined scientific workflow definitions are often significantly modified at run-time execution stage, while business processes are comparatively stable.

Fourth, participants of a science process, i.e., scientists, play an important role in the whole science process and may be the key factor to decide whether a scientific problem can be solved successfully. On the contrary, participants in business processes have comparatively simple interactive behaviors.

Due to essential characteristics of science processes analyzed above, science processes are hardly organized directly in traditional workflow forms, such as Petri Nets–based models [4–7], unified modeling language (UML)–based models [8–10], and so on. Therefore, it is necessary to design a reasonable model to define science processes as workflows at the modeling phase. Moreover, as the execution of an activity is probably influenced by changed scientists' locations, varied computing devices, data acquisition in different environments, etc., it requires extra contexts on workflow definition to provide corresponding directions. Sequentially, execution principles related to a reasonable workflow definition with extra contexts are also necessary for management and control behaviors of workflow engines.

In this chapter, a task-based scientific workflow modeling and executing approach is proposed for orchestrating e-Science with the workflow paradigm [11, 12]. The remainder of this chapter is organized as follows. Section 15.2 discusses some issues at the modeling phase. A task-based scientific workflow model (TBSWF) is put forward based on the analysis of data and control relationships in science processes. Context specifications appended to the workflow definition are also described to provide execution information. Moreover, the verification of TBSWF is discussed based on the presented soundness definition. Section 15.3 explores the workflow execution principles based on the TBSWF definition with context specifications. Primitives and specific rules to dynamically modify the predefined scientific workflow during execution are also presented in this section. Finally, evaluation and related work are discussed in Sects. 15.4 and 15.5 concludes the chapter.

15.2   Modeling Task-Based Scientific Workflow (TBSWF) Appended with Context Specifications

By introducing workflow to e-Science, scientists can focus more efforts on exploring methods of solving problems without elaborate considerations about data and resource management or other processing details which can be executed by computers. In a traditional workflow model, activities, i.e., basic modeling elements, are specified through their concrete behavioral descriptions, while the same descriptions are hardly applied to scientific workflow models. As a science process usually solves a problem with a few mature solving schemes through exploration, it is almost impossible to sketch a complete solving procedure, i.e., a set of logical steps with concrete behavior descriptions. For most scientific problems which have no comparative mature solving methods or schemes, what scientists can define before the execution of science processes is perhaps only the problem description, but not how to solve the problem, i.e., concrete behavior descriptions. Accordingly, one feasible method to model scientific workflow is to divide the problem into a set of minute well-defined tasks and describe the basic element as an abstract activity that can solve a certain task, i.e., a certain task, rather than a concrete behavior.

In science processes, tasks to solve subproblems decomposed from a scientific problem have more or less logical relationships with each other. The logical relationships have two dimensions: the data association and the control association. Connecting tasks through data and control relationships will generate a structured model. Such a model represents the definition of a scientific workflow model, where each task represents an activity to solve a certain subproblem. Consequently, executing a whole scientific workflow means accomplishing these tasks. In this way, science processes can be simulated in a structured model through the task-based modeling approach and be executed in a more automatic and effective way. In this section, logical relationships among tasks are first analyzed from both data and control perspectives, after which a formalized task-based scientific workflow definition is proposed to model science processes. Moreover, a related method to append execution contexts on a workflow definition is provided to adapt to the varied execution environments. The verification of a TBSWF is also discussed based on the given soundness definition.

15.2.1 Analysis on Data Relationships and Control Relationships

15.2.1.1 Data-Specific Analysis

It generally concerns input and output data to describe the task of solving certain subproblem decomposed from a complex scientific problem. Input data mean objects to be processed and output data mean expected results. Both of them are called application data. The input data can be classified into two categories according to the data source: the original data and the online data. Original data denote data which already exist at the workflow modeling phase and can be directly accessed from data resources once the workflow execution is commenced. On the contrary, online data do not exist at the modeling phase and are generated only after other relevant tasks are accomplished. In other words, output data of some tasks will be considered as input data of certain other tasks. Besides, the output data of a task can be classified into temporary results and permanent results. Temporary results are not final results and need further processing as inputs of other tasks. On the contrary, permanent results mean stable results which can be considered as partial results of the whole science process. Both categories of outputs might be transferred as inputs of relevant tasks.

During a science process that is solving a certain complex scientific problem, however, much more information needs to be transferred between tasks in addition to the above-mentioned application data which are called annotation data. Generally, annotation data include comments and suggestions on tasks from scientists, specifications about problem solving, meta-data of processed data, data provenance, etc. Annotation data are neither workflow relevant data nor workflow control data, both of which are used by a workflow management system or a workflow engine to coordinate the execution of a workflow. Annotation data are not directly used for executing a task but they provide relevant necessary information for task execution.

Annotation data concerning a certain task have two categories just like application data: annotation data to the task and annotation data from the task. The former implies the information employed by this task and it is from other tasks; and the latter implies the information provided by this task and it will be sent to other tasks.

Accordingly, based on the above analysis, two kinds of data relationships can be defined as follows.

Definition 15.1 (*Application data relationship, annotation data relationship*) The application data relationship implies that application data should be transferred between connected tasks. The annotation data relationship implies that annotation data used to direct or assist task execution should be transferred between connected tasks.

The concept of annotation data relationship is not referred in the traditional workflows. Since the procedure of a business process is comparatively stable and the annotation data relevant to activity execution is generally determined, nearly all instances of a business workflow will share the same or similar annotation data. Consequently, it is unnecessary to explicitly represent the annotation data in a workflow, where the annotation data are regarded as the default logic. However, considering the indeterminate and dynamic characteristics of science processes, the annotation data are instance-specific and will be uniquely generated during the execution, which results in the necessity to model annotation data relationships between tasks. Therefore, we argue that annotation data relationships should be seriously considered and handled for modeling science processes.

Here, annotation data relationships differ from application data relationships in the method of use of transferred objects. The application data will be processed during the task execution whereas the annotation data will not be processed but must be available during the task execution. Moreover, the annotation data can be generated while executing a task, whereas the application data can be achieved only after the task execution is accomplished.

It is not necessary that there should always be application data relationships between any two tasks as solving activities of some subproblems will require only original data as input and provide only permanent results. Moreover, annotation data relationships for any two tasks are also optional but not compulsory. In any case, all data relationships among tasks are determined according to the logic of the scientific problem to be solved.

15.2.1.2 Control-Specific Analysis

To automate a certain process consisting of many activities, issues about control relationships are very important and have attracted many research efforts. Here, the control relationship mainly implies the temporal order between activities. Transition conditions might be added to control relationships so that the relevant activity can decide which branch to take by matching real situations to predefined transition conditions. The control routing usually has forms like sequence, parallel, choice, iteration. As for science processes consisting of many tasks, we argue that two new control relationships should be included, which are defined as follows.

Definition 15.2 (*Force_end control relationship*) It means that one task can force the connected task to end the execution according to certain conditions.

Definition 15.3 (*Binding control relationship*) It means that one task should be executed along with the connected task in a loose-concurrent way and achieve reciprocity from the connected one's execution.

Force_end control relationships and binding control relationships are different from general control relationships, in that these two kinds of relationships are not used to represent temporal order between the task executions. In general traditional workflow models, since a business process is a comparatively rigid procedure consisting of ordered steps with concrete behavior descriptions, the control-specific research has mainly focused on modeling the temporal order of activities, while few efforts have been focused on the control logic, which is not relevant to the execution order. Nevertheless, as far as the science process modeling is concerned, it is important and necessary to represent certain control logic without order semantics, such as the force_end control relationship and the binding control relationship.

As far as the force_end control relationship is concerned, the workflow definition is tentative and not very determinate at the modeling phase, of a science process, so some tasks will perhaps become unnecessary or be already executed through a similar method at run time. At this point, such tasks had better stop the execution to avoid meaningless costs. Force_end control relationships are presented with the aim of dealing with such situations. In force_end control relationships, the forcibly terminated tasks had better provide intermediate results or rich annotation data for further considerations or references. Note that a task cannot force itself to end the execution; namely, the force_end control relationship is non-reflexive.

As far as the binding control relationship is concerned, it is possible to confuse this relationship with general parallel routings in traditional workflows. But, in fact, they are different. The parallel routing has stricter temporal semantics, in that the execution of activities should be enabled in parallel and the execution of activities subsequent to the parallel routing should wait until the completion of all paralleled activities. On the contrary, binding control relationships have much richer and more flexible control semantics. The tasks with binding control relationships can be executed in many ways, e.g., they can start and end at the same time, or one can start after the other and end after the other, or the execution period of one is included in the other. In other words, what the binding control relationships require is to ensure that connected tasks can exchange useful information with each other during a common executing time span. Usually, binding control relationships are accompanied by tight annotation data relationships and used for tasks with high relevancy such as similarity and interplay.

In summary, for a science process with more complex control semantics, we argue that both the force_end control relationship and the binding control relationship should be provided along with the general control relationships for modeling scientific workflows.

15.2.2   Formalized Definition and Modeling of TBSWF Based on Data Relationships and Control Relationships Analysis

As analyzed earlier, the scientific workflow definition about a scientific problem solving process is given based on the tasks corresponding to the solving activity of a subproblem decomposed from the complex scientific problem, where each task represents an abstract solving activity and connects with other tasks through data or control relationships.

Usually, control relationships can be implemented through certain building blocks such as sequence, or-split, and-join, and so on. However, certain complex control relationships between tasks need to combine two or more general building blocks. To achieve the compactness and the completeness of the building block set, virtual tasks are introduced to simplify the representation of complex control relationships. Virtual tasks do not imply any problem-solving activities and are only used to represent a control point in routings.

The formalized definition of TBSWF can be presented as follows.

Definition 15.4 (*TBSWF*) A task-based scientific workflow could be represented as TBSWF=$<S, \Omega, E, TC, F>$:

- S represents a coordinated set of tasks and is denoted as $S=S_1 \cup S_2$ ($|S|=m_1+m_2=m$), where $S_1=\{s_i|\ i=1,..,\ m_1\}$ represents the set of actual tasks which are relevant to solving activities of subproblems decomposed from a complex scientific problem, and $S_2=\{s_i|\ i=m_1+1,\ ...,m_1+m_2\}$ represents the set of virtual tasks which are control points between two tasks with combined control relationships. Each actual task can relate to a specification file that comprises requirement descriptions on resources and scientists. Such a file can provide necessary information for the workflow engine to manage the allocation and the scheduling in a science process.
- Ω represents the relationship types between tasks and is denoted as $\Omega=<\Psi, \Xi>$, where Ψ represents data relationships and Ξ represents control relationships.

The detailed definition is listed in Table 15.1. Note that control relationships ξ_2, ξ_3, ξ_4, and ξ_5 imply branches, i.e., at least two such relationships should connect with a same task, e.g., if $\xi_2(s_i, s_j)$ then there must be at least one (or more) task s_k satisfying $\xi_2(s_i, s_k)$.

- E represents existing relationships between tasks, $E \subseteq S \times S \times \Omega$, e.g., $e_1 = (s_1, s_2, \xi_1)$ means there is a control relationship ξ_1 between s_1 and s_2.
- TC represents the transition condition set appended on control relationships and is denoted as $TC = \{tc_i | i = 1, .., n\}$. A transition condition is used to decide whether the next task can start being executed according to current execution situations.
- F represents the relationship on which a specific transition condition should be appended, $F: TC \rightarrow E$.

In a TBSWF, tasks in S are connected through control arcs (maybe with transition conditions) and data arcs, which represent the execution semantic visually, where only one kind of control arc can exist between the same task pair. To model a scientific workflow as in Definition 15.4, detailed primitives had better be provided for scientists. Primitives should implement operations including creating tasks, building kinds of relationships between tasks, and also appending specific transition conditions on certain relationships. All the modeling primitives and corresponding graphical modeling elements are presented as in Fig. 15.1, where applying primitives on original workflow segments will form corresponding renewed workflow segments. The primitive $create(s_i, fn)$ will add an actual task s_i to the workflow, and the

Table 15.1 Specifications of relationship types between tasks

Items	Specifications
$\psi_1(s_i, s_j)$	Represents an application data relationship. Output of s_i should be transferred as input data of s_j
$\psi_2(s_i, s_j)$	Represents an annotation data relationship. s_i should provide annotation data for s_j
$\xi_1(s_i, s_j)$	Represents a sequence control relationship. s_j can start to be executed after the execution of s_i is completed
$\xi_2(s_i, s_j)$	Represents an and-split control relationship. Completion of the execution of s_i can cause the commencement of the execution of s_j and other one or more tasks connected with s_i
$\xi_3(s_i, s_j)$	Represents an and-joint control relationship. Completion of the execution of s_i and other one or more tasks connected with s_j can cause the commencement of the execution of s_j
$\xi_4(s_i, s_j)$	Represents an or-split control relationship. Completion of the execution of s_i can cause the commencement of the execution of s_j or another task connected with s_i
$\xi_5(s_i, s_j)$	Represents an or-joint control relationship. Completion of the execution of s_i or another task connected with s_j can cause the commencement of the execution of s_j
$\Xi_6(s_i, s_j)$	Represents a force_end control relationship which is non-reflexive. s_i can terminate the execution of s_j according to specific conditions
$\Xi_7(s_i, s_j)$	Represents a binding control relationship which is symmetric. s_i and s_j should be executed in a loose-concurrent way

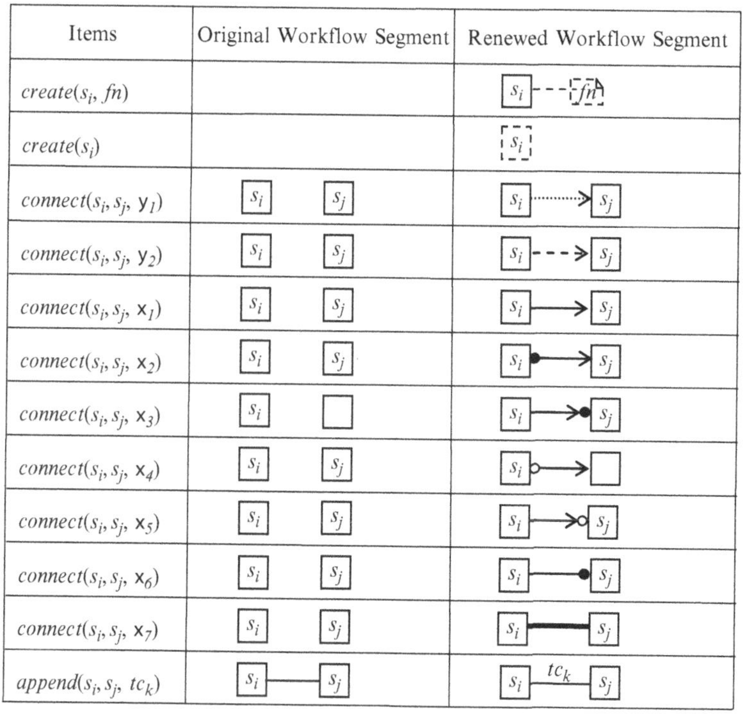

Items	Original Workflow Segment	Renewed Workflow Segment
$create(s_i, fn)$		s_i - - - fn
$create(s_i)$		s_i
$connect(s_i, s_j, y_1)$	s_i s_j	s_i ·······> s_j
$connect(s_i, s_j, y_2)$	s_i s_j	s_i - - -> s_j
$connect(s_i, s_j, x_1)$	s_i s_j	s_i ——> s_j
$connect(s_i, s_j, x_2)$	s_i s_j	s_i •——> s_j
$connect(s_i, s_j, x_3)$	s_i	s_i ——>• s_j
$connect(s_i, s_j, x_4)$	s_i s_j	s_i ○——>
$connect(s_i, s_j, x_5)$	s_i s_j	s_i ——>○ s_j
$connect(s_i, s_j, x_6)$	s_i s_j	s_i ——• s_j
$connect(s_i, s_j, x_7)$	s_i s_j	s_i —— s_j
$append(s_i, s_j, tc_k)$	s_i —— s_j	s_i tc_k s_j

Fig. 15.1 Primitives for modeling a TBSWF

specifications related to s_i can be found in the file named *fn*. The primitive *create*(s_i) will add a virtual task s_i to the workflow. The primitive *connect*(s_i, s_j, ψ_k) will build a data relationship ψ_k between s_i and s_j, and the primitive *connect*(s_i, s_j, ξ_k) will build a control relationship ξ_k between s_i and s_j. The primitive *append*(s_i, s_j, tc_k) will append a certain transition condition tc_k on the specific control relationship which exists between s_i and s_j. Here, the non-overstriking line without end marks is used to represent any kind of control relationships.

With the primitives presented above, scientists can define a science process as a TBSWF in a straightforward and understanding way. Moreover, the files with detailed specifications about tasks can be provided to engines to facilitate the automatic execution of the workflow. Figure 15.2 illustrates an example of a task-based scientific workflow corresponding to the science process of the short-term climate prediction, which could be modeled by applying above primitives.

To predict the short-term climate, the model simulation and the statistic analysis are two main promising solving methods. Unfortunately, neither is mature and perfect enough to predict the short-term climate correctively and exactly, which means that the whole science process is tentative and concerns more complex execution semantics. Specifically, the simulation method predicts the climate by simulating influences of certain factors on the climate. Since simulation concerns

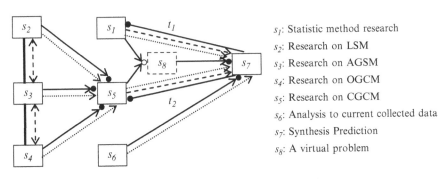

s₁: Statistic method research

s₂: Research on LSM

s₃: Research on AGSM

s₄: Research on OGCM

s₅: Research on CGCM

s₆: Analysis to current collected data

s₇: Synthesis Prediction

s₈: A virtual problem

Fig. 15.2 A simplified TBSWF about the short-term climate prediction

too many factors, meteorologists usually divide it into land surface model (LSM), atmospheric general circulation model (AGSM), and oceanic general circulation model (OGCM), each of which simulates a model in a specific domain. These models will then be integrated into a whole complete model, called comprehensive general circulation model (CGCM). In the TPSWF of the short-term climate prediction, research on the simulation of each specific model is viewed as a task. As shown in Fig. 15.2, the workflow definition of the short-term climate prediction concerns seven actual tasks and one virtual task. Each actual task is related to detailed specifications of requirements on resources and scientists, which can be accessed by the workflow engine and used for automatic scheduling.

The TBSWF shown in Fig. 15.2 is only a rough and simplified model which tries to define the science process of the short-term climate prediction. In fact, the actual prediction process is much more complex and could be divided into a large set of subtasks in much less granularity which are connected with much more complicated relationships, which could also be organized as TBSWF. Some more discussions about the meaning of new proposed relationships are presented as follows:

1. *Binding control relationships.* s_2 should be bound with s_3 so that these two tasks can learn much from each other during a certain common execution time span, and the same stands for s_3 and s_4. Note that this relationship is not transitive, so the binding relationship does not exist between s_2 and s_4.
2. *Annotation data relationships.* Driven by annotation data relationships shown in Fig. 15.2, s_1 and s_5 should provide annotation data, i.e., the evaluation report of a prediction method, to s_7, so that s_7 learns clearly about relevant execution behaviors, which can facilitate the decision making on the final prediction scheme.
3. *Force_end control relationships.* If s_7 is triggered by the completion of the execution of s_1, whether s_5 should be terminated will be decided based on the transition condition t_2 and the real execution situation. More specifically, if t_2 is satisfied, i.e., the evaluation report from s_1 shows the execution result of s_1 is perfectly right for the climate prediction according to the criteria in t_2, then s_7 will terminate the execution of s_5. On the contrary, if the execution of s_5 is completed earlier, the same control behavior might be deployed on the execution of s_1.

15.2.3 Appending Context Specifications on TBSWF

With the fast development of several kinds of computing terminals, data acquisition devices, and communication networks, science processes are not limited in fixed laboratories any more. To execute science processes in varied environments, it is necessary to append extra information on workflow definitions to provide some directions on methods of execution. Usually, two kinds of context, i.e., task context and relationship context, are necessary to provide information for the execution of scientific workflow in varied scenarios. The task context is used to determine the way in which the task of a workflow is executed. The relationship context is used to determine the time and method of the data transfer or the transition triggering. During the execution of workflows, the workflow engine should capture both the task context and the relationship context, and make correct responses to the corresponding context.

Definition 15.5 (*Task context*) The task context means the context information used to determine the way in which the task is executed, i.e., who or which device is relevant to the task execution, where the execution happens, which way the data collection adopts during the execution, etc.

Though task context is also used to provide information for the execution of a certain task, it is different from the annotation data for a task. The annotation data are relevant to the execution behavior itself and processed by scientists, while the task context is mostly relevant to the execution environment and processed by workflow engines.

Definition 15.6 (*Relationship context*) The relationship context means the context information used to control the progress of the workflow execution, i.e., when and how the data are transferred or transitions are triggered, etc.

Context usually includes specifications of information, such as location, time, device equipment, temperature, kinds of application-specified information, and so on. In essence, the representation method of both kinds of context is similar, while the main difference between them is how the context is used to control and mange the execution of workflows. Besides, context is often concerned with a certain entity, such as a person. Therefore, we represent the atomic context through a triple with three elements, i.e., the entity, the attribute, and the value. The atomic context could be connected through logic operations, such as AND, OR, NOT, to compose more complicated context. The following definitions give more precise descriptions.

Definition 15.7 (*Ontology library*) It provides the information of basic elements in the atomic context and is denoted as $O = <E, A, V>$, where $E = \{e_i \mid e_i$ represents a certain entity about which certain information needs to be sensed during the workflow execution$\}$, $A = \{a_j \mid a_j$ represents a certain information type about certain $e_i\}$, $V = \{v_k \mid v_k$ represents the certain value of certain $a_j\}$.

Definition 15.8 (*Atomic context*) It represents a certain situation in execution environments through a single triple. The set of atomic context relevant to a workflow is denoted as $SimC = \{sim\_c_p = <e_i, a_j, v_k> \mid e_i \in E, a_j \in A, v_k \in V\}$.

Definition 15.9 (*Composite context*) It represents a complex situation through a logic expression with one or more atomic context triples. The set of composite context relevant to a workflow is denoted as $ComC=\{com\_c_q::=NOT\ <com\_c_q>\ |\ <com\_c_q> \ AND\ <com\_c_q>\ |\ <com\_c_q>\ OR\ <com\_c_q>\ |\ sim\_c_p$, where $sim\_c_p \in SimC\ \}$.

Definition 15.10 (*Task context set and relationship context set*) The task context set represents the set of task context relevant to a workflow and is denoted as $TaskC=\{task\_C_i\ |\ task\_C_i$, which includes all task context relevant to the ith task in a workflow and $task\_C_i \subseteq SimC \cup ComC\}$. The relationship context set represents the set of relationship context relevant to a workflow and is denoted as $RelC=\{rel\_C_i\ |\ rel\_C_i$, which includes all relationship context relevant to the ith relationship in a workflow and $rel\_C_i \subseteq SimC \cup ComC\}$.

To execute a workflow in varied possible environments, the workflow definition should be appended with specifications on the relevant context. Both task context and relationship context could be specified through the form of atomic context or composite context. Each presented atomic context is supposed to be reasonable, that is, e_i, a_j, and v_k in an atomic context triple is supposed to be correct in semantic logic. Besides identifying a certain situation through atomic context or composite context, corresponding response actions should also be provided, which could be represented as reaction rules defined as follows.

Definition 15.11 (*Reaction rule*) It provides a context-based execution rule of a workflow in varied environments and the set of reaction rules is denoted as $R=\{<c_i$, $action_j|c_i$, which represents certain context and $c_i \in TaskC \cup RelC$. $action_j$ represents the concrete action description corresponding to a certain context, including the participant, the allocation, the executing pattern relevant to a task, the triggering of a control relationship, and so on}.

Similar to modeling TBSWF through primitives, the context specification could be also appended on workflow definition through primitives, which are presented in Fig. 15.3. Moreover, Fig. 15.4 illustrates a workflow definition segment with appended context specifications. Note that a task or a relationship might concern multiple rules. As rules with similar type of actions might be redundant or inconsistent, it would be necessary to predefine a preference order of those rules. The ontology library presents detailed information about numbered entities, attributions, and values for references. The real content of the ontology library is application-specific and could be constructed based on lots of researches relevant to ontology technology.

Items	Original	Renewed		
$append(s_i, c_j, action_k)$	s_i	s_i - - - c_j - - - - $<c_j, action_k>$		
$append(s_i, s_j, c_k, action_l)$	s_i —— s_j	s_i	s_j	c_k - - - $<c_k, action_l>$

Fig. 15.3 Primitives for appending context on a TBSWF

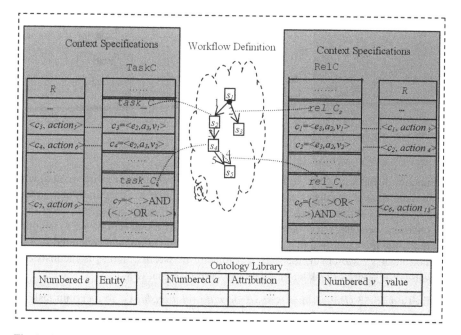

Fig. 15.4 The example of a workflow definition segment appended with context specifications

15.2.4   Verification of TBSWF

Besides the formalized definition, the graphical modeling method, and the context specifications, another important issue for scientific workflow modeling is to verify the soundness so as to prevent the incorrectness of a defined model from being propagated during the execution. Here, the verification of TBSWF is mainly discussed from the perspective of model structure, i.e., the structural soundness of data and control relationships among tasks, excluding the correction of appended execution context, transition conditions, and so on.

Definition 15.12 (*Soundness*) A TBSWF is sound if and only if it satisfies the following properties:

- Terminability: the workflow can finish in finite steps.
- Compactness: there are no redundant tasks, i.e., each task in the workflow has the probability of being executed.
- Consistency: there are no conflicting relationships, i.e., both data relationships and control relationships are consistent.

Figure 15.5 illustrates several examples of unsound TBSWF. As shown in Fig. 15.5, the cycle s_2–s_3–s_4 in Fig. 15.5a cannot be terminated and therefore the workflow will run for ever. The part surrounded by the dashed line in Fig. 15.5b cannot be executed since no activity will trigger its execution. So s_3 and s_4 are

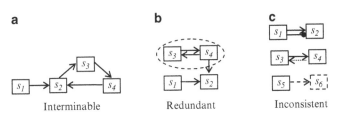

Fig. 15.5 Examples for the unsoundness of TBSWF

redundant in the workflow. In Fig. 15.5c, the control relationships between s_1 and s_2 are inconsistent because s_1 cannot enable and terminate the execution of s_2 at the same time. The data relationship and the control relationship between s_3 and s_4 are inconsistent because s_4 can start to be executed until the execution of s_3 is completed while the execution of s_3 is waiting for the application data generated by the execution of s_4. Moreover, the data relationship between s_5 and s_6 is inconsistent because s_6 is a virtual task and no data can be transferred to s_6.

Definition 15.13 (*Pre-set and post-set on data relationships*) To a certain task s_i, the pre-set and post-set on application data relationships are represented as $D_{i,1}^+ = \{s_j \mid (s_j, s_i, \psi_1) \in E\}$ and $D_{i,1}^- = \{s_j \mid (s_i, s_j, \psi_1) \in E\}$ respectively. Similarly, the pre-set and post-set on annotation data relationships are $D_{i,2}^+ = \{s_j \mid (s_j, s_i, \psi_2) \in E\}$ and $D_{i,2}^- = \{s_j \mid (s_i, s_j, \psi_2) \in E\}$. Besides, $D_i^+ = D_{i,1}^+ \cup D_{i,2}^+$ and $D_i^- = D_{i,1}^- \cup D_{i,2}^-$ are used to represent the pre-set and post-set on data relationships respectively.

Definition 15.14 (*Pre-set and post-set on control relationships*) To a certain task s_i, the pre-set on a specific control relationship is $C_{i,k}^+ = \{s_j \mid (s_j, s_i, \xi_k) \in E\}$, $k = 1, 2, \ldots,$ 7; and the post-set on a specific control relationship is $C_{i,k}^- = \{s_j \mid (s_i, s_j, \xi_k) \in E\}$, $k = 1, 2, \ldots,$ 7. To represent the temporal ordered routing, $C_i^+ = \bigcup_{k=1}^{5} C_{i,k}^+$ and $C_i^- = \bigcup_{k=1}^{5} C_{i,k}^-$ are used to present the pre-set and post-set on corresponding control relationships, respectively.

Definition 15.15 (*Source node, sink node, intermediate node*) s_i is a source node if $C_i^+ = \varphi$; s_i is a sink node if $C_i^- = \varphi$. Tasks which are neither source nodes nor sink nodes are called intermediate nodes.

Definition 15.16 (*Directed path, reachable*) if an integer sequence $M = v_1 v_2 \ldots v_t$ satisfies the following conditions: (i) if $i \neq j$, then $v_i \neq v_j$; (ii) $s_{v_i} \in S$, $i = 1, 2, \ldots, t$; (iii) $s_{v_{i+1}} \in C_{v_i}^-$, $i = 1, 2, \ldots, t-1$, then M is a directed path from s_{v_1} to s_{v_t}. If there is a directed path from s_i to s_j, then s_j is reachable from s_i, denoted as $s_i \rightarrow s_j$.

Definition 15.17 (*Cycle, in-node, in-edge, out-node, out-edge*) If the start point and end point of a directed path are the same task, then such a path is called as a cycle. Concerning a certain node s_i on this cycle, if there is s_j which is not on this cycle and satisfying $s_j \in C_i^+$, then s_j is an in-node of this cycle, and the corresponding control relationship incident with s_j and s_i is an in-edge. Similarly, concerning a certain node s_i on this cycle, if there is s_j which is not on this cycle and satisfying $s_j \in C_i^-$, then s_i is an out-node of this cycle, and the corresponding control relationship incident with s_i and s_j is an out-edge.

Based on these definitions, several theorems can be provided to verify the soundness of a TBSWF. Here, verification on soundness is mainly deployed from the syntax and structure perspectives but not from the semantics perspective.

Theorem 15.1 *A TBSWF satisfies terminability if and only if: (i) there is at least one source node and at least one sink node; (ii) $\forall$ task $s_i \in S$ (s_i is not a sink node), $\exists$ sink node $s_j \in S$ satisfying $s_i \to s_j$.*

Proof. If (i) and (ii) are satisfied, then the workflow can always be terminated through directed paths from source nodes to sink nodes in finite steps. Accordingly the TBSWF is terminable. On the contrary, assume that a TBSWF is terminable but (i) and (ii) are not satisfied. In this case, as there is no source node, the science process cannot start since each task in the TBSWF is waiting for the execution of certain other tasks in the corresponding pre-set. Similarly, as there is no sink node, the science process cannot end since any task should be followed by other tasks. Moreover, if there is a source node or an intermediate node which cannot reach any sink node, then the terminability cannot be satisfied once the corresponding task starts to be executed. That is to say, if a cycle without out-edge starts to be executed, then such a cycle will be running forever and the whole science process cannot be terminated. Sequentially, the TBSWF is not terminable if (i) and (ii) are not satisfied. It is not possible that a TBSWF is terminable and not terminable at the same time. Hence, if the TBSWF is terminable then (i) and (ii) are satisfied. □

Theorem 15.2 *A TBSWF satisfies compactness if and only if: $\forall$ task $s_i \in S$ (s_i is not a source node), $\exists$ source node $s_j \in S$ satisfying $s_j \to s_i$.*

Proof. The science process is a process that deploys along certain paths from source nodes to sink nodes. If each task s_i in a TBSWF is reachable from a certain source node, then s_i is always possible to be executed, i.e., the TBSWF is compact. On the contrary, assume that a TBSWF is compact and there is a certain task which cannot be reachable from a source node, then such a task will never be executed and is redundant to the TBSWF. Consequently, the TBSWF is not compact. It is not possible that a TBSWF is compact and not compact at the same time. Hence, if a TBSWF is compact, then it satisfies the above condition. □

Theorem 15.3 *A TBSWF satisfies data consistency if and only if: (i) if $(s_i, s_j, \psi_1) \in E$, then $s_i \to s_j$. (ii) if $(s_i, s_j, \psi_2) \in E$, then either $s_j \nrightarrow s_i$ is satisfied or both $s_i \to s_j$ and $s_j \to s_i$ are satisfied. (iii) if $s_i \in S_2$, then $D_i^+ = \varphi$ and $D_i^- = \varphi$.*

Proof. Concerning condition (i), if $(s_i, s_j, \psi_1) \in E$, i.e., s_i should transfer application data to s_j, as application data can be produced only after the execution of s_i is completed, so it is necessary to ensure that s_j should be executed after s_i. Concerning condition (ii), as annotation data can be generated during executing a task, the constraint relevant to annotation data relationships is weaker than that relevant to application data relationships. In detail, when $(s_i, s_j, \psi_2) \in E$, if $s_j \nrightarrow s_i$ then s_i can provide annotation data to s_j. Moreover, if s_i and s_j are in the same cycle, they can provide annotation data for each other as tasks are executed repeatedly, where $s_j \nrightarrow s_i$ is not satisfied but both $s_i \rightarrow s_j$ and $s_j \rightarrow s_i$ should be satisfied. Consequently, when annotation data relationships are concerned, condition (ii) should be satisfied to maintain the consistency. Concerning condition (iii), since virtual tasks have no actual execution behavior, the connected data relationships will put the workflow in confusion and bring inconsistency. Hence, condition (iii) should be satisfied. □

Theorem 15.4 *A TBSWF satisfies control consistency if and only if: (i) if $(s_i, s_j, \xi_k) \in E$, then $(s_i, s_j, \xi_{k'}) \notin E$, where $k' \neq k$. (ii) if $s_i \rightarrow s_j$, then $C_{i,4}^- = \varphi$ or $C_{j,3}^+ = \varphi$. (iii) if $(s_i, s_j, \xi_6) \in E$, then $s_i \nrightarrow s_j$. (iv) if $(s_i, s_j, \xi_7) \in E$, then $s_i \nrightarrow s_j$ and $s_j \nrightarrow s_i$.*

Proof. Concerning condition (i), it requires that exclusive relationships cannot appear between two tasks. Otherwise, the inconsistency will emerge. Each control relationship in TBSWF has different and exclusive semantics, e.g., if $(s_i, s_j, \xi_2) \in E$, i.e., s_j will be enabled to be executed after s_i is executed, then $(s_i, s_j, \xi_4) \in E$ will probably bring the inconsistency since it is possible that s_j is not enabled to be executed after s_i is executed according to the control semantics of ξ_4. Concerning condition (ii), if $s_i \rightarrow s_j$, while $C_{i,4}^- \neq \varphi$ and $C_{j,3}^+ \neq \varphi$, then as analyzed in [13], the inconsistency will emerge, whereas tasks in the pre-set on control relationships of s_j can never be all executed since they are in different chosen routing. Concerning condition (iii), if $(s_i, s_j, \xi_6) \in E$, then s_i will force s_j to end the execution according to certain conditions. However, $s_i \rightarrow s_j$ will disable this control semantic since s_i is already completed before the execution of s_j starts and a completed activity cannot terminate any activity. Therefore $s_i \nrightarrow s_j$ must be satisfied in the case of $(s_i, s_j, \xi_6) \in E$. Concerning condition (iv), if $(s_i, s_j, \xi_7) \in E$, then s_i and s_j should have a period of common execution time to exchange information, which means that the execution behavior of one cannot be completed before the other. Otherwise the inconsistency with the semantics of binding control relationships will emerge. Therefore, both $s_i \nrightarrow s_j$ and $s_j \nrightarrow s_i$ should be satisfied. □

Specific algorithms can be designed and implemented to verify a given TBSWF according to the theorems presented above. As far as the example in Fig. 15.2 is concerned, it could be proven easily that this definition is sound as it is satisfied with all above theorems. The verified workflow definition can be executed under the control of workflow engines. At the beginning of the execution, source nodes are executed at first. After that, according to specific semantics of control relationships incident with the nodes in the pre-set, the execution of intermediate nodes will be triggered by the completion of the execution of the previous nodes. If there are transition conditions on certain control relationships, the succeeding execution behavior can start only when the current execution situation satisfies the corresponding conditions. Besides, engines can also manage and coordinate the transfer of both application data and annotation data according to predefined data relationships in the TBSWF. Based on the predefined workflow definition, the execution of all tasks can be controlled automatically and effectively. When all sink nodes are executed completely, the execution of a TBSWF is completed and the corresponding science process is finished.

15.3   Executing TBSWF Appended with Context Specifications

15.3.1   Execution Principles of TBSWF Appended with Context Specifications

Based on a sound workflow definition with context specifications, the workflow engine can automatically control and manage the execution of workflows according to the real execution situation. Figure 15.6 shows our proposed workflow execution framework of TBSWF appended with context specifications. As the context specification module of Fig. 15.6 indicates, two kinds of context relevant to the workflow execution should be specified at the workflow modeling phase, along with the reaction rules corresponding to certain contexts, where the concrete method is described in the last section. After the workflow execution is commenced, the context capturing module would check the task context specifications on the tasks of source nodes to determine what kind of context information should be captured proactively. The captured context will be transferred to the context mapping module to find out matching context specifications. Then, the context response module will execute proper actions according to the reaction rules in which the matched context specifications are located. When the task execution is accomplished, similar operations will take place with the relationship context appending on the edge adjacent to that task. Such a dual context–based execution behavior will continue until the tasks of sink nodes are executed. Further details are presented as follows.

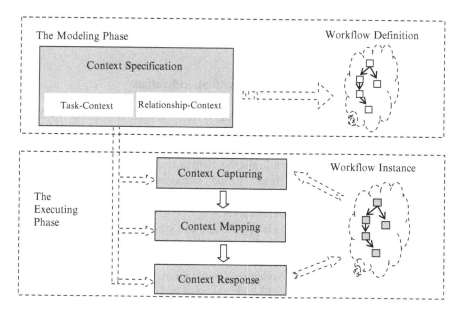

Fig. 15.6 The workflow execution framework of TBSWF appended with context specifications

15.3.1.1 Capturing Relevant Context Based on Specifications

As both task context and relationship context could be atomic context or composite context, we discuss the context capture mechanism without considering whether it is task context or relationship context.

To capture the relevant context is a key step of the context-based execution. Here, the relevant context is determined by both the progress of workflow instances and predefined context specifications, as shown in the framework in Fig. 15.6. More specifically, when the workflow is executed at a certain point of a task or a relationship, the workflow engine will check the corresponding context specifications on the task or the relationship, i.e., certain $task\_C_i$ or rel_C_i, to decide which context needs to be captured. Note that not every task or relationship has relevant context specifications. If a certain $task\_C_i$ or rel_C_i is Φ, the corresponding reaction rules could be formalized as $<null, null>$. At this time, the workflow engine does just what it usually does and pays little attention to the context-aware and response procedure during the task execution or relationship switch.

As far as the atomic context is concerned, e_i and a_j in a certain atomic context triple provide the relevant object and the type of context information, which are determinate and toned not be captured during the execution. However, what this kind of context about this object looks like is indeterminate, and this is the value v_k that the context capturing module should find out. As far as the composite context is concerned, it is a logic combination of multiple atomic context triples. Therefore, the content to be captured during the execution is the values of all atomic context triples in the composite context expression. In other words, in a context specification (either atomic context or composite context), to capture relevant context information means to capture the value v_k in one or more atomic context triples $<e_i, a_j, v_k>$. This process could be implemented with the assistances of wireless sensor network technology, mobile devices technology, and so on, but these details are not emphasized in this chapter.

15.3.1.2 Mapping Captured Context with Specifications

After the actual context information is captured from the execution scene, it will be sent to the context mapping module to search matched atomic context or composite context specifications. The captured actual context information is associated with a certain task or relationship, which limits the context specifications to be compared. Moreover, e_i and a_j in a certain triple of actual context information are determinate. Therefore, the comparison operation mainly focuses on values in actual context information and in limitative specifications.

The actual context information is represented as a single atomic context triple or the conjunction of multiple triples. There might be multiple matched context specifications (either atomic context or composite context) corresponding to the actual context information. All of these matched specifications can be found out based on the algorithm described in Fig. 15.7. If the matched context specifications are

```
Algorithm: Context mapping.
Input: a set of captured context triples relevant to the ith task or relationship, denoted as T
= {t_1, ..., t_m}.
Output: the set of matched context specifications in task_C_i or rel_C, denoted as MC
1  //find matched atomic context
2  for each atomic context triple sim_c_i in task_C_i or rel_C_i
3    do for each t_j in T
4        do if sim_c_i=t_j
5            then add sim_c_i in MC
6                break
7  //find matched composite context
8  for each composite context com_c_i in task_C_i or rel_C_i
9    do matched←FALSE
10       matched←MAP(com_c_i)
11       if matched=TRUE
12          then add com_c_i in MC
13 MAP(com_c_i)
14 if com_c_i is a single atomic context triple
15   then for each t_j in T
16       do if com_c_i=t_j
17            then return TRUE
18       return FALSE
19   else represent com_c_i as a binary tree
20     switch the root
21         case 'NOT': return not MAP(left-subtree);        //left subtree must be sim_c_i
22         case 'AND': return MAP(lef- subtree) and MAP(right-subtree)
24         case 'OR': return map(left-subtree)or MAP(right-subtree)
```

Fig. 15.7 Context mapping algorithm description

found, they will be transferred to the context response module to make proper actions according to the corresponding predefined reaction rules.

If no context specifications are matched with captured actual context information after running the context mapping algorithm, the engine will periodically repeat the procedure of catching and mapping until matched context specifications are found or the given time has elapsed. In case the matched context specifications cannot be found in the given time, the engine can present the abnormal execution information and organize the corresponding decision-making actions, such as dynamically modifying the workflow definition, aborting the execution of this instance, and so on.

15.3.1.3 Making Proper Actions According to Matched Context

As mentioned earlier, both task context and relationship context could be atomic context or composite context, which makes the capture and mapping methods similar. However, the response actions corresponding to task context and relationship context differ to some extent.

As far as task context is concerned, it affects the way in which a task of a workflow is executed. Multiple reaction rules might be provided to specify different execution actions corresponding to different context situations. The context response module should arrange participants of a certain task to execute it under the directions of those matched specifications.

As far as relationship context is concerned, it affects the progress of the workflow execution. After the execution of a task is completed, the data and control relationships adjacent to this task can be executed according to matched context specifications. Sometimes, there are relationships without special transition conditions. Such relationship switches may happen naturally without considering context capture and handling.

Sometimes, there might be more than one matched context specification for a task or a relationship, which means that more than one reaction rule will be applied. At this point, if actions in the rules corresponding to the matched context specifications are unrelated with each other, i.e., they are not of the same type, then all of them could be carried out. For example, the reaction rule which determines the person who will execute a certain task and the reaction rule which determines the relevant place could both be applied. However, if those actions are of the same type, they might be redundant or even conflicting. At this stage, the context response module can deal with the situation according to the preference order predefined at the modeling phase.

15.3.2 Dynamic Modification of TBSWF During the Execution

Because of the essential characteristics of science processes such as indeterminate, dynamic, and highly intelligent, the predefined scientific workflow definitions will generally be modified during the execution. Such modifications are deployed only for the unexecuted part of workflows. Possible modifications might include adding new inspired tasks and relationships, and altering or deleting existing tasks and relationships. Such modifications on predefined workflow definitions are called dynamic modifications, which take place during the execution. When scientists make decisions about dynamic modifications, the execution is interrupted and all tasks being executed are recorded. After the new workflow is remodeled based on the scientists' decisions, the interrupted execution should be continued according to the new workflow definition.

Many issues should be addressed for realizing dynamic modification on the predefined workflow. Preserving the execution situation completely is an important issue, which needs to record the execution state of each task and relevant audit data. It is also important to make a strategy about how scientists respond to the modification request and arrive at a decision regarding the modification scheme. Besides, other issues should also be addressed, such as propagating the changed workflow definition to instances being executed. In this chapter, we mainly focus on two issues: one is implementation of modification operations after scientists give a modification scheme; the other is verification of the modified part to ensure the soundness of the changed workflow.

15.3.2.1 Implementation of Dynamic Modifications on TBSWF

The predefined workflow might be dynamically modified frequently during the execution. Accordingly, after the execution of a TBSWF is completed, the corresponding final process trail may differ significantly from the predefined one. However, it does not mean that the predefined workflow is less significant. In fact, such a workflow definition implies the maximum cognition which can be achieved by scientists at that time. It will direct the deployment of a science process to a great extent in that the whole process will be more disordered if such a workflow definition does not exist. Moreover, scientists can learn a lot from comparing the final workflow after the execution with the predefined workflow before the execution, so as to deal with other similar science processes in a more automatic and effective way.

When implementation of modifications is referred, it means to transfer the thought into the graphical workflow definition after scientists make a decision regarding the scheme of modifications. Possible modification operations include creation, alteration, and deletion, all of which can be applied on three kinds of objects in a TBSWF, i.e., the task, the relationship, and the transition condition. The creation of new elements can be implemented by primitives presented in Fig. 15.1 and the remaining necessary primitives for modifications are presented in Fig. 15.8. In Fig. 15.8, the line without any end marks represents the general relationship, i.e., any kind of relationship. All these primitives assist scientists to remodel the existent TBSWF in an intuitive way.

Some modification operations will probably bring further modifications to the renewed workflow so as to maintain the soundness. Namely, when a certain task is

Items	Original Workflow Segment	Renewed Workflow Segment
$alt(s_i, f_n')$	s_i --- $\square$	s_i --- f_n
$alt(s_i, s_j, tck')$	s_i —tc_k— s_j	s_i —tc_k'— s_j
$del(s_i, f_n)$	$\square$ --- f_n	
$del(s_i)$	s_i	
$del(s_i, s_j, e_k\|y_k)$	s_i —— s_j	s_i s_j
$del(s_i, s_j, tc_k)$	s_i —tc_k— s_j	s_i —— s_j

Fig. 15.8 Primitives for dynamic modification of TBSWF

deleted, related relationships should be adjusted correspondingly. Otherwise the E in TBSWF will be incomplete and incorrect.

Usually, scientists only provide the most direct modification operations and hope the computer will automatically execute the indirect modifications caused by the direct modifications. To some extent, direct modifications determined by scientists are active modifications; and indirect modifications inferred by computers according to specific rules can be viewed as passive modifications, which are generally deployed from the structure perspective because the intelligence of computers cannot handle complex semantics inferring as yet.

In fact, passive modifications are usually caused by the deletion of a task or a concrete control relationship, while other primitive operations will not automatically generate modifications to the whole workflow definition through simple inferring.

Passive Modifications Caused by the Deletion of Tasks

The deletion of a task will be accompanied by many modifications on the relevant context and the corresponding incident relationships. The context relevant to this task will be deleted directly, and the modification details relevant to the corresponding relationships are listed as follows:

1. Data relationships: all incident data relationships of the deleted problem should be deleted since the initial vertexes or end vertexes of these relationships have already disappeared. Moreover, the context appended on those relationships should also be deleted. Such deletions will probably bring an inconsistency, which will be discussed in Sect. 15.3.2.2 in more detail.
2. Control relationships: all incident control relationships of the deleted task should be adjusted according to the specific situation. They can be deleted or merged according to the type of the deleted task, where types include the source node, the sink node, and the intermediate node. If the deleted task is a source node or a sink node, then all incident relationships should be deleted directly. If the deleted task is an intermediate node, then all incident relationships of the deleted task should be merged according to following specific rules (where s_i is the deleted task, and $s_j \in C_{i,l}{}^+$, $s_k \in C_{i,l}{}^-$, $l = 1, 2, ..., 7$). Besides, the context appended on old incident control relationships should be re-specified correspondingly.

   (i) $(s_j, s_i, \xi_t) + (s_i, s_k, \xi_t) \rightarrow (s_j, s_k, \xi_t)$, $t = 1, 2, ...,5$. If (s_j, s_i, ξ_t) and (s_i, s_k, ξ_t) exist in the old workflow, then they are merged into one control relationship (s_j, s_k, ξ_t) after s_i is deleted.
   (ii) $(s_j, s_i, \xi_1) + (s_i, s_k, \xi_t) \rightarrow (s_j, s_k, \xi_t)$, $t = 2, 3, 4, 5$. According to the control semantics of these relationships, the merging between ξ_1 and another relationship ξ_t will result in ξ_t.
   (iii) $(s_j, s_i, \xi_t) + (s_i, s_k, \xi_1) \rightarrow (s_j, s_k, \xi_t)$, $t = 2, 3, 4, 5$. Same as (ii).

(iv) $(s_j, s_i, \xi_t) + (s_i, s_k, \xi_{t'}) \to \varphi$, $t \in \{2, 4\}$ and $t' \in \{3, 5\}$. As ξ_t and $\xi_{t'}$ are exclusive of each other, they cannot be merged into one control relationship between the task pair (s_j, s_k) and are therefore are deleted.

(v) $(s_j, s_i, \xi_3) + (s_i, s_k, \xi_t) \to (s_j, s_{m+1}, \xi_3) + (s_{m+1}, s_k, \xi_t)$, $t = 2, 4, 5$. The merging is complex because the deleted task plays a role of a control point connecting combined control relationships in the old workflow. Therefore, a virtual task should be created to substitute the control point and the corresponding task number m should be replaced by $m+1$.

(vi) $(s_j, s_i, \xi_5) + (s_i, s_k, \xi_t) \to (s_j, s_{m+1}, \xi_5) + (s_{m+1}, s_k, \xi_t)$, $t = 2, 3, 4$. Same as (v).

(vii) $(s_j, s_i, \xi_2) + (s_i, s_k, \xi_4) \to (s_j, s_{m+1}, \xi_2) + (s_{m+1}, s_k, \xi_4)$. Same as (v).

(viii) $(s_j, s_i, \xi_4) + (s_i, s_k, \xi_2) \to (s_j, s_{m+1}, \xi_4) + (s_{m+1}, s_k, \xi_2)$. Same as (v).

(ix) $(s_j, s_i, \xi_t) \to \phi$, $t = 6, 7$. Both ξ_6 and ξ_7 are not control relationships on the temporal order and not transitive. Therefore, the deletion of s_i will result in the disappearance of corresponding control semantics of ξ_6 or ξ_7. Moreover, the deletion of the incident control relationship ξ_6 or ξ_7 will not affect the left part of the original workflow. Therefore, such control relationships will be deleted directly.

(x) $(s_i, s_k, \xi_t) \to \phi$, t = 6, 7. Same as (ix).

Passive Modifications Caused by the Deletion of Control Relationships

Not all deletion operations on control relationships will cause passive modifications. Generally, the deletion of $\xi_2, \xi_3, \xi_4, \xi_5$ may bring changes to workflows, which can be specified as the following rules, where the deleted relationship is denoted as (s_i, s_j, ξ_k).

(xi) In the case of $k = 2, 4$: if $|C_{i,k}^-| = 2$, then another control relationship incident with s_i, i.e., (s_i, s_j', ξ_1), should be substituted by (s_i, s_j', ξ_1). In this case, the task incident with the deleted control relationship, i.e., s_i, has only two branches. After (s_i, s_j, ξ_k) is deleted, only one branch is incident with s_i. At this point, the control semantics of ξ_2 or ξ_4, i.e., enabling the execution of all succeeding tasks or enabling the execution of only one chosen succeeding task, will disappear and become a simple sequential control relationship.

(xii) In the case of $k = 3, 5$: if $|C_{j,k}^+| = 2$, then another control relationship incident with s_j, i.e., (s_i', s_j, ξ_k), should be substituted by (s_i', s_j, ξ_1). Similar to the analysis in (xi), the deletion of such a control relationship will result in another incident control relationship (s_i', s_j, ξ_k) becoming a sequential control relationship.

15.3.2.2 Verification of Dynamic Modifications on TBSWF

After implementing all active and passive modifications, the soundness of the remodeled workflow should be checked to ensure that the redefined science process can be executed successfully. Some modifications will not affect the soundness, while others will probably bring dead cycles, redundancy, or inconsistency, and consequently make the remodeled workflow unsound. The cases where modifications might affect the soundness are analyzed as follows.

1. Deletion of tasks. If the deleted task is the unique source node or the unique sink node in the original workflow, and no intermediate nodes in the original workflow can substitute it to be a new source node or new sink node in the remodeled workflow, then terminability and compactness of the workflow cannot be satisfied.
2. Deletion of data relationships. If the deletion of the data relationship is a passive modification caused by the deletion of the corresponding initial vertex, then the corresponding end vertex of the deleted relationship cannot obtain data as expected. Accordingly, inconsistency of the workflow will emerge.
3. Creation of data relationships. If the new created data relationship dissatisfies the conditions in Theorem 15.3, then such a modification will cause data inconsistency in the workflow.
4. Deletion of control relationships. If the deleted relationship is the unique out-edge of a certain cycle, then the terminability of workflows will not be satisfied. Similarly, if it is the unique in-edge of a certain cycle, then the compactness of workflows will not be satisfied. Moreover, if the deleted control relationships dissatisfy condition (i) or (ii) in Theorem 15.3, then the corresponding data consistency will be broken.
5. Creation of control relationships. If one or more new cycles emerge after the appendance of a certain new relationship, and there are no out-edges in new generated cycles, then the terminability will not be satisfied. Similarly, if there are no in-edges in new cycles, then the compactness will not be satisfied. Moreover, if new relationships dissatisfy conditions in Theorems 15.3 or 15.4, then the consistency cannot be satisfied.

If the remodeled TBSWF is in the cases listed above, then the corresponding warning information about specific unsoundness should be presented to scientists. In this way, scientists can reconsider the modification decision of workflow based on those factors and provide a sound TBSWF.

15.4 Related Work and Evaluation

The special characteristics of science processes, such as the indeterminate, the dynamic, the creative, the highly intelligent, and so on, bring many challenges to the workflow employment in e-Science. The task-based scientific workflow modeling and executing approaches proposed in this chapter are a trial toward orchestrating e-Science with the workflow paradigm. In this section, the evaluation of our work is analyzed from four aspects. Moreover, other relevant work on scientific workflows is also discussed.

15.4.1 Comparison Analysis and Evaluation

Roughly speaking, four aspects to deploy e-Science processes with workflows are explored in this chapter, i.e., the representation pattern to represent the object to be modeled as a workflow; the verification theory to verify the soundness of the modeled workflow; the execution principles to direct the execution of a reasonable workflow; the modification method to modify the predefined workflow during the execution. Relevant comparison analysis and evaluation are presented as follows.

15.4.1.1 On the Representation Pattern

There are several representation methods for workflow modeling, such as Petri Nets–based models [4–7], UML-based models [8–10], and directed graph-based models [14–16].

Petri Nets–based models are most popular workflow patterns. Different types of Petri Nets–based workflow modeling methods have been presented, such as time PN [6, 7] and colored PN [5]. The common modeling idea of these models is to use the "transition" to represent an activity and the "place" for the condition of execution. Usually, research on Petri Nets–based models mainly focuses on the control-specific domain while few efforts are directed on the data-specific domain. Since Petri Nets–based models present strict and exact descriptions for workflows, they are generally used for rigid workflow definitions, i.e., for the modeling of fixable and determinate processes with clear control order.

UML-based models are also very common for the workflow definition. UML is a comparatively mature modeling language with wide application fields. Because of rich standard specifications and flexible extension mechanisms, UML activity diagrams provide a deep theory foundation for workflow modeling. In an activity diagram, the "activity" of a certain object represents the basic element of a work-flow; moreover, all building blocks recommended by WFMC, such as and-split, or-join, and so on, have corresponding representation constructs. UML-based models can be transformed into the workflow process definition language (WPDL) easily, which promotes the feasibility and the interoperability of models. Nevertheless, UML-based models have not yet focused much effort on rich and explicit representation of data logic in a process.

Directed graph-based models provide another flexible modeling way for the workflow definition. The basic idea of these methods is to take activities as nodes and represent building blocks through edges. However, different models extend the directed graph from varied perspectives. Bowers and Ludäscher [14] have proposed a method to model scientific workflows based on the actor-oriented design, where the actor represents components or tasks which can be a nested sub-workflow. Each actor has an associated set of data ports and is connected with other actors via data ports. Such "data flow connections" and "actors" constitute an actor-oriented work-flow model. The workflow model ADEPT introduces several new kinds of edges for specific control semantics, i.e., loop edges, failure edges, soft synchronization edges, and strict synchronization edges; moreover, the flow of data is represented explicitly through data links which connect task and service parameters with data elements [15]. Sadiq et al. classify nodes in a workflow into two types, i.e., activity nodes and coordinator nodes, and give a flexible workflow pattern by introducing the special build activity, which consists of workflow fragments and constraints [16].

To some extent, TBSWF proposed in this chapter is a certain directed graph-based model. The meaning of nodes in TBSWF is different from other models. In most workflow models, the activity is described as specific behaviors or detail tasks. However, the node in a TBSWF is an abstract task relevant to the solving activity of certain subproblems decomposed from the whole scientific problem to be solved.

The relationships among tasks in TBSWF vary a lot from those among activities in general workflow models. What current workflow models often deal with are application data relationships and control relationships with forms like sequence, parallel, and choice. However, TBSWF recommends three more relationships to represent the specific logic semantics between tasks in a science process, i.e., the annotation data relationship, the force_end control relationship, and the binding control relationship. The proposal of those new relationships is driven by special requirements of science processes with inherent characteristics like indeterminate and highly intelligent. Those relationships are necessary to represent special semantics for the science process definition, while such relationships can hardly be represented in general workflow models. The specific significance of these relationships is analyzed in detail as follows.

The annotation data relationship represents the transfer of the annotation information used to direct or assist executing tasks. The annotation information in the science process is often instance-specific and generated during the execution. To execute a task, it is very important to learn relevant annotation provided by execution behaviors of certain other tasks. Therefore, it is necessary to represent annotation data relationships explicitly for modeling a science process. However, such relationships are ignored in traditional workflow models. It is because the information is generally stable and not execution-related and is regarded as the default information without explicit expressions.

The force_end control relationship is proposed to represent that one task can force the connected task to end the execution according to certain conditions. In a science process, the execution of a certain task should be terminated when such a task is proved unnecessary or already accomplished through another method at the running time. At the workflow modeling phase, it can be anticipated that such a situation is likely to happen. This possible termination had better be modeled so as to keep workflow execution successfully when it really happens at the running time. Consequently, the force_end control relationship emerges. However, general workflow models do not involve such a relationship since it is often determinate that such a possible termination rarely exists.

The binding control relationship provides a loosely concurrent execution method for two tasks which can obtain useful information from each other when the connected task is being executed. Sometimes tasks in the science process do not have a strict temporal order requirement whereas they require a common executing period to learn necessary information from opponents' execution. Most workflow models do not support such special control semantics, while binding control relationship can work for this situation.

To model a science process, TBSWF proposed in this chapter is more suitable compared with other models. One important reason is that those models do not model the three necessary relationships with special semantics listed above which have important significance for modeling scientific workflows. Besides, those models have aspects that do not conform to the characteristics of science processes. Specifically, Petri Nets–based models [4–7] are used to model strict and exact control logic which is not possessed by science processes. Moreover, science processes are more data-centric and knowledge-intensive [3], while few Petri Nets–based models provide enough support for such characteristics, and so do UML-based models [8–10]. Though the directed graph provides good theoretical basis for workflow modeling and wide spaces for varied model extension, current directed graph-based models cannot fully satisfy the specific requirements of science processes, especially for the requirements on modeling context data relationships and two new proposed control relationships. With actor-oriented modeling [14], utmost concentration is put on the management to the dataflow within science processes, while few issues about control-specific logic in scientific problems are taken account of. The ADEPT model [15] requires that data links relevant to certain data elements are definite at the modeling phase. However, to a science process still without a specific mature scheme or procedure, it is very hard to determine such data links since data elements are indefinite in all probability. Furthermore, the flexible workflow modeling method put forward by Sadiq [16] pays utmost attention to control-specific research while little efforts are concentrated on data-centric characteristics.

15.4.1.2 On the Verification Theory

Verifying a workflow model is an important step before executing such a model through concrete instances. Such an issue has attracted a great deal of research. The basic idea of verification in the research is to ensure the represented model is sound, where the concept of the soundness usually implies terminability, compactness, consistency, and so on. However, the specific concept definition of the soundness and concrete verification theory varies with different representation methods.

Aalst puts forward the definition of soundness based on the Petri Nets–based workflow model [17]. The definition presents three conditions to ensure the correctness of workflows from the perspective of control-specific structure. Moreover, a verification tool is developed to verify defined soundness of workflows based on the specific theory analysis. Those three conditions are similar to our sound requirements on terminability and compactness. But the data-specific consistency relevant issues are not mentioned in that chapter.

Sadiq and Orlowska present a visual verification approach based on a set of graph reduction rules [13]. They concentrate only on verification of certain structural conflicts, i.e., "deadlock" caused by joining exclusive choice paths with a synchronizer and "lack of synchronization" caused by joining fork concurrent paths with a merged structure. Verification is implemented by removing definitely correct structures from the workflow model according to specific reduction rules, where a correct workflow can be reduced to an empty graph.

In the science process with the data-centric characteristic, verification will face many more challenges. Verification methods generally focus on the correctness of control-specific structures as Aalst and Sadiq do [13, 17, 18]. However, it had better take the data-specific verification into consideration for scientific workflows. The soundness definition in this chapter specifies requirements on both the data domain and the control domain. Moreover, four theorems are proposed to verify the soundness with synthetic considerations of the data and the control. Theorems 15.1 and 15.2 provide verification warranty for the terminability and the compactness, respectively. Theorems 15.3 and 15.4 provide verification warranty for the data consistency and control consistency, respectively, where the data consistency requires relevant control relationships to satisfy certain conditions. The concrete verification algorithms are beyond the scope of this chapter while they can be explored and implemented under the direction of research in this chapter.

15.4.1.3 On the Execution Principles

To adapt to possible varied execution environments, the execution of scientific workflow requires both task context and relationship context to provide necessary information for the execution of tasks, data relationship, and control relationships.

An increasing number of researchers have worked on the context-aware workflow execution. Montagut et al. propose an adaptive transactional protocol to support the execution of workflow in a pervasive setting [19]. Han et al. propose a language uWDL to specify the context information on transition constraints to support the execution of adaptive service in workflows [20]. Yu et al. propose a generic framework EkSarva to support people's generic collaboration in heterogeneous computing environments [21].

However, few existing researches focus efforts on both kinds of context, which affects the workflow execution in changeable environments. The dynamic partner assignment presented by Montagut and Molva [19] focuses on the partial task context; uWDL presented by Han et al. [20] mainly handles the relationship context; and Yu [21] pays little attention to the context relevant to transitions between activities.

Execution principles presented in this chapter provide specifications of both task context and relationship context appended on the workflow definition, through which relevant important information about possible execution environments could be represented formally so as to direct the actual execution behavior of certain workflow instances. Here, task context processed by workflow engines is different with annotation data in scientific workflow definition, which is relevant to problem logic and processed by workflow participants. Based on context specifications appended on workflow definitions, the corresponding context capture, mapping, and response progress are described. All of these could facilitate the automatic and effective execution of the e-Science process in varied execution environments.

15.4.1.4 On the Modification Method

Not much attention has been paid to the method for modifying the predefined workflow during the execution as most research on the dynamic modification is relevant to the dynamic change bug [22]. Such a dynamic change problem is originally proposed by Ellis [23]. While executing instances of a certain workflow model, the predefined workflow will possibly change. Consequently, those instances that are in progress should migrate from the old definition to the new one to adapt to the new workflow model, which creates plenty of research issues and attracts much effort [24].

However, the issues of dynamic modifications in scientific workflow models do not relate much with the general dynamic change problem. In traditional workflows, the deployment of modifications on the process definition is generally separated from the execution of instances. After the process definition is modified, the in-progress instances in the old definition will be migrated to the new one. On the contrary, in TBSWF, a process definition usually generates only one instance and modifications are usually inspired during the execution of this instance. Therefore, modifications on the TBSWF are deployed dynamically along with the execution of a certain instance. Specifically, when certain scientists propose that it is necessary to modify the workflow model, the execution will be suspended to wait for the generation of the remodeled workflow. Accordingly, no other in-progress instances need to adapt to the new definition and no dynamic change issues should be addressed.

Due to essential characteristics of science processes, the predefined workflow might be modified significantly during the execution. Consequently, it is important and necessary for a science process to provide automatic and intuitive modification methods so as to realize the numerous modification requests. Nevertheless, few researches have been done for such an issue since modifications involved in traditional workflows are not so frequent.

Reichert and Dadam [15] have handled the automatic implementation of dynamic modifications through a complete and minimal set of change operations (ADEPTflex). ADEPTflex comprises operations for inserting tasks as well as whole task blocks into a workflow, for deleting them, for serializing tasks that were previously allowed to run in parallel (and vice versa), etc. Moreover, correctness and consistency issues are also taken into consideration for the deployment of change operations. With the ADEPT, the data flow description based on data elements should be very clear and exact, and this is hardly satisfied by a science process with tentative execution. Accordingly, the corresponding change operations (ADEPTflex) are not suitable to be used for the dynamic modifications of scientific workflows.

In this chapter, a set of modification primitives are proposed for scientists to implement the decisions of dynamic modifications on the unexecuted part of a workflow. These primitives are proposed based on TBSWF, which is designed specially for the modeling of science processes with specific characteristics. Accordingly, these primitives provide special supports for modifications of scientific workflows. Moreover, besides the active modification provided by scientists, passive modifications inferred from other modifications can be automatically implemented by workflow engines based on suggested inferring rules. All of these assist scientists to implement modifications in an efficient way. The inferring rules are provided according to the varied logic semantics of involved relationships. With these rules, workflow engines can set scientists free from mass mechanical modification operations. Furthermore, the influence of modifications on the soundness is analyzed carefully, which can facilitate scientists to present a sound remodeled workflow definition.

15.4.2 Other Related Work

An increasing number of researchers have realized the significance of applying workflow technologies to the deployment of e-Science. Many researches on scientific workflows [25–31] have explored the application of service-oriented architecture. With the SOA paradigm, scientific workflow could compose distributed autonomic services in a loose coupling way, which could facilitate more flexible and effective execution and provide the reusability of a certain kind of service in different e-Science applications. Besides, Grid middleware tools have attracted much effort too [26, 28, 29, 31, 32] for they provide strong resource sharing ability. The ease of use is another important issue that most scientific workflow management systems (SWFMSs) take into account [26–31] as their users are often scientists in varied science fields who are perhaps not familiar with computer technologies. It is usual for SWFMSs to provide the complete graphical user interface for workflow modeling and executing or provide simple modeling languages and corresponding visualized windows. Moreover, the researches on reference architectures for SWFMSs [27], on scientific workflow patterns from formal methodology perspective [33] or on application context spectrums [34] are also worth paying attention to. Further details about related work are listed as follows.

Kepler [28] is an extension of the Ptolemy II system for scientific workflows, where the underlying Ptolemy II system aims at modeling and designing heterogeneous, concurrent systems. Differing from the design goal of Ptolemy II, Kepler is designed for supporting workflows oriented toward varied e-Science applications, such as workflows on data handling in plumbing and workflows on analytical knowledge discovery and applications. To adapt to different scientific workflows with various control structures, Kepler uses a director to explicitly represent the computational model of connection relationships among actors. To some extent, actors in Kepler [14] are similar with activities specified by WfMC [1] which are about the description of a piece of work that forms one logical step within a process. Actors have parameters to configure and customize their behaviors as well as interfaces called ports to communicate with other actors. Communications between actors are deployed via channels which connect output ports of an actor with input ports of another. Thus, they are independent components, i.e., actors could be composed into a workflow through communication of ports to represent data relationships and kinds of directors to represent control relationships. Moreover, sub-workflows could be abstracted into actors and sequentially arbitrarily nested. Kepler provides many directors (PN, SDF, DE, CT, CSP, etc.) to define how actors are executed and how they communicate with one another, e.g., PN director for concurrently executing actors and deploying communication by sending tokens through unidirectional channels.

Taverna [30] is an open-source family of tools developed by the myGrid team for designing and executing workflows. The family consists of the Taverna Engine, the Taverna Workbench as desktop clients, and Taverna Server as remote workflow execution servers that sit on top of the engine. It was originally developed for biologists and bioinformaticians to deploy e-Science more effectively and is now applied in multiple areas including astronomy, chemistry, genome and gene expression, etc. Through the Taverna Workbench, scientific users could create and run workflows written in the simplified conceptual workflow language (Scufl), which uses XML syntax, where the enactment capability is supported by Freefluo workflow engine. Feta component could provide semantic-based service discovery to complement the basic service panel in the workbench. Moreover, Taverna provides three levels of extensibility through a plug-in framework to add a new graphical user interface (GUI), processor types, and external components. Recently, Taverna was applied to build and execute workflows in caGrid [31], a project about cancer research based on the Globus Toolkit. Compared with BPEL-based tools, Taverna provides better support as a tool suite during the lifecycle of service discovery, service composition, workflow execution, and workflow result analysis, especially for data flow modeling.

Triana [29] is an open-source problem-solving environment developed at Cardiff University that combines an intuitive visual interface with powerful data analysis tools. Triana uses the GAP interface to transparently access various underlying middleware architectures. GAP has three middleware bindings implemented: JXTA, P2PS, and Web Service binding (WServe). WServe provides the key functionality to integrate Web services with Triana, including service discovery through querying a UDDI server, service composition through BPEL4WS integration, service invocation through WS Gateway, and composite service publishing through a GUI-based wizard. In this way, users could define and execute scientific workflows based on Web services in Triana.

GridNexus [26] is a graphical system for creating and executing scientific workflows in Grid environments. It is also based on Ptolemy II and has a similar GUI; however, it separates the GUI from the execution of workflows. More specifically, workflows could be created through JXPL, a kind of XML-based scripting language, while the execution of workflows could be executed locally and shown in the GUI through the JXPL processor, or be handled by a processor running as a persistent Grid service.

Pegasus [32] is different from the above systems as it does not offer complete support for the workflow modeling and execution. It can map complex workflows onto the Grid, i.e., transfer abstract workflow definitions to concrete workflows executed via appropriate data and Grid resources. In this process, varied planning strategies could be applied for execution optimization.

In addition to the above systems related to scientific workflows, there are some researches that focus on certain issues from specific perspectives. A reference architecture for SWFMSs is proposed to provide a guidance for the architectural design of SWFMSs in various scientific domains [27]. This reference architecture consists of four logical layers, seven major functional subsystems, and six interfaces. A service-oriented architecture for V_{IEW} is also presented to validate the feasibility of this reference architecture. Other than a guideline on the architecture of SWFMSs, an initial set of scientific workflow patterns combining control and data dependencies is proposed from the formal methodology perspective [33] which aims to provide the appropriate guidelines and abstract constructs for the development of workflow models. Moreover, a context- and role-driven scientific workflow development pattern is put forward to explicitly represent an application context [34], which could provide necessary information for an engine to assign definite subjects to suitable objects and provide a personalized context and role view for each participant to execute corresponding tasks in a more effective way.

15.5 Conclusions

In this chapter, some issues on orchestrating e-Science with the workflow paradigm are discussed. A new perspective for modeling science processes in the workflow form, i.e., modeling scientific workflows by taking tasks as basic elements, is proposed. In TBSWF, in addition to general data and control relationships, three new relationships, i.e., the annotation data relationship, the binding control relationship, and the force_end relationship, are proposed to represent special logic semantics in scientific problems. Based on control relationships and data relationships, a scientific workflow is organized as a structured model consisting of logically connected tasks which are relevant to abstract solving activities of subproblems decomposed from a complex scientific problem. The corresponding soundness of TBSWF is defined and four theorems are provided for verification. To adapt to varied possible execution environments, task context and relationship context specifications are provided to append necessary information on workflow definition. Consequently, the corresponding context-based execution principles are described for an engine to automatically control and manage the workflow execution according to the definitions. To realize the modification requirements during the execution, both active and passive modifications can be deployed on the predefined workflow through primitives and rules proposed in this chapter. Finally, comparison analysis and evaluation about our work is presented. Moreover, other related work about scientific workflow is also discussed.

Acknowledgments This chapter is partly supported by the Program for New Century Excellent Talents in University under Grant NCET-06-0440, Foundation of Jiangsu Educational Committee under Grant No. 08KJD520024, and Foundation of NJUPT under Grant No. NY207138. Part of this chapter is also cited from our previous research work.

References

1. Workflow Management Coalition (1999) Terminology and glossary, Technical report [WFMC-TC-1011], Issue 3.0.
2. Hollingsworth D (1995) The workflow reference model, Technical report [WFMC-TC-1003], Issue 1.1, Workflow Management Coalition.
3. Ludäscher B, Goble C (2005) Guest editors' introduction to the special section on scientific workflows. ACM SIGMOD Record, 34 (3): 3–4.
4. Aalst V WMP (1998) The application of Petri Nets to workflow management. Journal of Circuits Systems and Computers, 8 (1): 21–66.
5. Choi I, Park C, and Lee C (2002) Task net: Transactional workflow model based on colored Petri Net. European Journal of Operational Research, 136 (2): 383–402.
6. Li JQ, Fan YS, Zhou MC (2003) Timing constraint workflow nets for workflow analysis. IEEE Transactions on Systems, Man, and Cybernetics—Part A: Systems and Humans, 33 (2): 179–193.
7. Ling S, Schmidt H (2000) Time Petri Nets for workflow modeling and analysis, In: Proc. of the IEEE International Conference on Systems, Man, and Cybernetics: 3039–3044.
8. Bastos R, Dubugras D, Ruiz A (2002) Extending UML activity diagram for workflow modeling in production systems. In: Proc. of the 35th Hawaii International Conference on System Sciences: 3786–3795.
9. Chang E, Gautama E, Dillon TS (2001) Extended activity diagrams for adaptive workflow modeling. In: Proc. IEEE Fourth International Symposium on Object-Oriented Real-Time Distributed Computing: 413–419.
10. Dumas M, Hofstede AHM (2001) UML activity diagrams as a workflow specification language, In: M. Gogolla and C. Kobryn (Ed) UML 2001, Lecture Notes in Computer Science, 2185: 76–90.
11. Liu XP, Dou WC, Chen JJ et al (2007) On design, verification, and dynamic modification of the task-based scientific workflow model. Simulation Modeling Practice and Theory, 15(9): 1068–1088.
12. Liu XP, Dou WC, Chen JX (2009) The dual-context based workflow performance in pervasive environments. Communications in Computer and Information Science, 62: 60–67.
13. Sadiq W, Orlowska ME (2000) Analyzing process models using graph reduction techniques. Information Systems, 25(2): 117–134.
14. Bowers S, Ludäscher B (2005) Actor-oriented design of scientific workflows. In: L. Delcambre et al (ed) Proc. of ER 2005, Lecture Notes in Computer Science, 3716: 369–384.
15. Reichert M, Dadam P (1998) ADEPTflex—supporting dynamic changed of workflows without losing control. Journal of Intelligent Information Systems, 10 (2): 93–129.
16. Sadiq SW, Orlowska ME, Sadiq W (2005) Specification and validation of process constraints for flexible workflows. Information Systems, 30 (5): 349–378.
17. Aalst V WMP, Hofstede AHM (2000) Verification of workflow task structures: A Petri-Net-based approach. Information Systems, 25 (1): 43–69.
18. Hofstede AHM, Orlowska ME, Rajapakse J (1998) Verification problems in conceptual workflow specifications. Data & Knowledge Engineering, 24 (3): 239–256.
19. Montagut F, Molva R (2008) The pervasive workflow: a decentralized workflow system supporting long-running transactions. In: IEEE Transactions on Systems, Man, and Cybernetic-Part C: Applications and Reviews, 38(3): 319–332.

20. Han J, Cho YY, Choi J (2005) Context-aware workflow language based on Web services for ubiquitous computing. O. Gervasi et al (ed) ICCSA, Lecture Notes in Computer Science, 3481: 1008–1017.
21. Yu J, Reddy YVR, Selliah S, Bharadwaj V et al (2005) The design of a workflow-centric, context-aware framework to support heterogeneous computing environments in collaboration. In: Y. Luo (ed) CDVE, Lecture Notes in Computer Science, 3675: 22–29.
22. Aalst V WMP (2001) Exterminating the dynamic change bug: A concrete approach to support workflow change. Information Systems Frontiers, 3 (3): 297–317.
23. Ellis C, Keddara K, Rozenberg G (1995) Dynamic change within workflow systems. In: N. Comstock and C. Ellis (ed) Conf. on Organizational Computing Systems, ACMSIGOIS: 10 – 21.
24. Rinderle S, Reichert M, Dadam P (2003) Evaluation of correctness criteria for dynamic workflow changes. Lecture Notes in Computer Science, 2678: 41–57.
25. Barker A, Hemert JV (2008) Scientific workflow: a survey and research directions. In: Proc. of Parallel Processing and Applied Mathematics: 746–753.
26. Brown JL, Ferner CS, Hudson TC et al (2005) GridNexus: A Grid services scientific workflow system. International Journal of Computer and Information Science, 6 (2): 72–82.
27. Lin C, Lu SY, Lai ZQ et al (2008) Service-oriented architecture for VIEW: a visual scientific workflow management system. In: proc. of IEEE International Conferences on Services Computing 2008. doi:10.1109/SCC.2008.118.
28. Ludäscher B, Altintas I, Berkley C et al (2006) Scientific workflow management and the Kepler system. Concurrency and Computation: Practice and Experience, 18(10): 1039–1065.
29. Majithia S, Shields M, Taylor I et al (2004) Triana: a graphical web service composition and execution toolkit. In: proc. of ICWS: 514–524.
30. Oinn T, Greenwood M, Addis M et al (2006) Taverna: lessons in creating a workflow environment for the life sciences. Concurrency and Computation: Practice and Experience, 18(10):1067–1100.
31. Tan W, Missier P, Madduri R et al (2009) Building scientific workflow with Taverna and BPEL: a comparative study in caGrid. In: Feuerlicht G and Lamersdorf W (ed) ICSOC 2008, Lecture Notes in Computer Science, 5472: 118–129.
32. Deelman E, Blythe J, Gil Y et al (2004) Pegasus: mapping scientific workflows onto the Grid. In: AxGrids2004, Lecture Notes in Computer Science, 3165: 11–20.
33. Yidiz U, Guabtni A, Ngu AHH (2009) Towards scientific workflow patterns. In Proc. of the 4th Workshop on Workflows in Support of Large-Scale Science: 1–10.
34. Dou WC, Chen JJ, Fan SK et al (2008) A context- and role-driven scientific workflow development pattern. Concurrency and Computation: Practice and Experience, 20(15): 1741–1757.

Part V
e-Science, Easy Science

Chapter 16
Face Recognition Using Global and Local Salient Features

Dakshina Ranjan Kisku, Phalguni Gupta, Jamuna Kanta Sing, and Massimo Tistarelli

Abstract This chapter presents a robust face recognition technique which is based on the extraction of Scale Invariant Feature Transform (SIFT) features from the face areas. It uses both a global and local matching strategy. The local strategy is based on matching individual salient facial SIFT features as connected to facial landmarks such as the eyes and the mouth. As for the global matching strategy, all SIFT features are combined together to form a single feature. The Dempster–Shafer decision theory is applied to fuse the two matching strategies. The proposed technique has been evaluated with the Indian Institute of Technology Kanpur (IITK), Olivetti Research Laboratory (ORL) (formerly known as AT&T face database), and the Yale face databases. The experimental results demonstrate the effectiveness and potential of the proposed face recognition technique also in cases of partially occluded faces or with missing information. Besides this, some state-of-the-art face recognition techniques have been presented and the current face-matching technique is compared with those techniques while all the matching techniques use SIFT descriptors as local features.

D.R. Kisku (✉)
Department of Computer Science and Engineering, Dr. B. C. Roy Engineering College,
Durgapur 713206, India
e-mail: drkisku@ieee.org

P. Gupta
Department of Computer Science and Engineering, Indian Institute of Technology Kanpur,
Kanpur 208016, India
e-mail: pg@iitk.ac.in

J.K. Sing
Department of Computer Science and Engineering, Jadavpur University, Kolkata 700032, India
e-mail: jksing@ieee.org

M. Tistarelli
Computer Vision Lab, DAP, University of Sassari, Alghero, Sassari 07140, Italy
e-mail: tista@uniss.it

Xiaoyu Yang et al. (eds.), *Guide to e-Science: Next Generation Scientific Research and Discovery*, Computer Communications and Networks,
DOI 10.1007/978-0-85729-439-5_16, © Springer-Verlag London Limited 2011

16.1 Introduction

In this information age, security is one of the main concerns for individuals as well as for vulnerable things which would be susceptible to attack, and security threats often come from malicious users, criminals, and cross-border terrorists. Therefore, it is necessary to protect an individual's identity and all valuable things from these malicious users. As a result, biometric technology has emerged as a secure means of authentication and identification of individuals, which uses physiological and behavioral characteristics for measuring the individuality as an authentication. There exist several biometric characteristics such as fingerprint, face, iris, palm print, hand geometry, signature, ear, retina, DNA, gait, etc., to authenticate a person successfully. To date, many identification and authentication systems have been developed by using these biometric characteristics. However, face recognition is one of the most challenging areas in the field of machine vision and biometrics [1, 2]. The variability in the appearance of face images, either due to intrinsic or extrinsic factors, makes the identification problem ill-posed and difficult to solve. Moreover, additional complexities like the data dimensionality and the motion of face parts may cause major changes in appearance. In order to make the problem well posed, vision researchers have adapted and applied an abundance of algorithms for pattern classification, recognition, and learning. To cope with the data dimensionality, several appearance-based techniques have been successfully used, such as the Principal Component Analysis (PCA) [1], Linear Discriminant Analysis (LDA) [1], Fisher Discriminant Analysis (FDA) [1], and Independent Component Analysis (ICA) [1]. Other well-known methods are based on the extraction of salient facial features by means of cascaded scale-space filtering [3–6]. Very often, one missing part is the link between the features extracted from the face images and the geometry of the face itself.

16.1.1 E-Infrastructure and Face Recognition

Face recognition is a process through which a person can be recognized at a distance by using digital face images obtained from video sequences. Since the face system is a noninvasive process where a subject's face is photographed without the knowledge of the subject and the captured face is then converted into digital code for verification. Face recognition technologies can encounter enormous performance problems stemming from several factors such as noncooperative behavior of users, lighting conditions, facial expressions, occlusions, illuminations, clutters, and variability in poses. Hence, these factors have made face recognition a challenging task in computer vision. Therefore, it is necessary to provide such an infrastructure where the associated accessories can make the recognition process smooth by reducing the complexity of the surrounding environment of the face recognition system. Figure 16.1 shows a block diagram of e-Infrastructure for face recognition in an ATM machine. The complete system is divided into three parts: configuration,

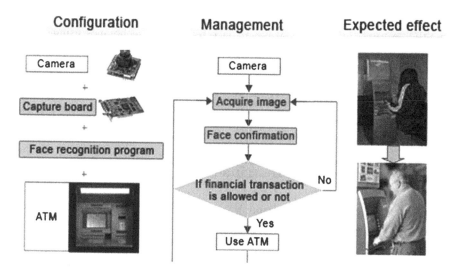

Fig. 16.1 E-infrastructure for face recognition system associated with ATM machine

management, and expected effect. The configuration part consists of camera, capture board, face simulation, and ATM machine. The management segment consists of the logic for face recognition which is embedded in the face recognition program. The third part, i.e., expected effect, consists of a setup where a person's face is photographed by the camera placed in a suitable position in the environment.

Faces are highly deformable objects, which may easily change their appearance over time. Not all face areas are subject to the same variability. Therefore, decoupling the information from independent areas of the face is of paramount importance to improve the robustness of any face recognition technique. The aim of this chapter is to demonstrate how to perform a robust and cost-effective face recognition [7] using Scale Invariant Feature Transform (SIFT) features [7–10] extracted from face images but also directly related to the face geometry. In this regard, two face-matching techniques, based on local and global information and their fusion, are proposed. In the local matching strategy, key SIFT features are extracted from face images in the areas corresponding to facial landmarks, such as the eyes, nose, and mouth. Facial landmarks are automatically located by means of a standard facial landmark detection algorithm [11, 12]. Then matching of a pair of feature vectors is performed by a minimum Euclidean distance metric. Matching scores produced from each pair of salient features are fused together using the sum rule [13]. In the global matching strategy, the SIFT features extracted from the facial landmarks are fused together by concatenation. Also in this case, matching is performed by means of a minimum Euclidean distance metric. The matching scores obtained from the local and global strategies are fused together using the Dempster–Shafer decision theory. The proposed techniques are evaluated with three face databases: IITK, ORL (formerly known as AT&T) [14, 15], and Yale [16, 17].

The chapter is organized as follows. Section 16.2 briefly describes the extraction of SIFT features. A few state-of-the-art face recognition techniques using SIFT features are presented in the next section. Local and global matching strategies are discussed in Sect. 16.4. The next section describes the fusion of local and global matching scores using the Dempster–Shafer theory. The experimental results are presented and discussed in Sect. 16.6, and concluding remarks are drawn in the last section.

16.2 Overview of SIFT Descriptor

This section presents a face recognition system which uses SIFT features [8, 9] extracted from face images. To recognize and classify objects efficiently, feature points from objects can be extracted to make a robust feature descriptor or representation of the objects. SIFT features are invariant to scale, rotation, partial illumination, and 3D projective transform, and they are shown to provide robust matching across a substantial range of affine distortions, change in 3D viewpoint, addition of noise, and change in illumination. These features provide a set of features of an object that are not affected by occlusion, clutter, and unwanted "noise" in the image. In addition, these features are highly distinctive in nature and have accomplished correct matching on several pairs of feature points with high probability between a large database and a test sample. Following are the four major filtering stages of computation used to generate the set of image features based on SIFT.

16.2.1 Scale-Space Extrema Detection

This filtering approach [8, 9] attempts to identify image locations and scales that are identifiable from different views. Scale space and difference of Gaussian (DoG) functions are used to detect stable key points. DoG is used for identifying key points in scale space and locating scale-space extrema by taking difference between two images, one scaled by some constant time of the other. To detect the local maxima and minima, each feature point is compared with its eight neighbors at the same scale and in accordance with its nine neighbors up and down by one scale. If this value is the minimum or maximum of all these points, then this point is an extrema.

16.2.2 Localization of Key Points

To localize key points [8, 9], a few points after the detection of stable key point locations that have low contrast or are poorly localized on an edge are eliminated.

This can be achieved by calculating the Laplacian space. After computing the location of the extremum value, if the value of DoG pyramids is less than a threshold value, the point is excluded. If there is a case of large principle curvature across the edge but a small curvature in the perpendicular direction in the DoG function, the poor extrema is localized and eliminated.

16.2.3 Assign Orientations

This step aims to assign consistent orientation [8, 9] to the key points based on local image characteristics. From the gradient orientations of sample points, an orientation histogram is formed within a region around the key point. Orientation assignment is followed by a key point descriptor which can be represented relative to this orientation. A 16×16 window is chosen to generate a histogram. The orientation histogram has 36 bins covering a 360° range of orientations. The gradient magnitude and the orientation are precomputed using pixel differences. Each sample is weighted by its gradient magnitude and by a Gaussian-weighted circular window.

16.2.4 Generation of Key Point Descriptors

In the last step, the feature descriptors [8, 9] which represent local shape distortions and illumination changes are computed. After candidate locations have been found, a detailed fitting is performed to the nearby data for the location, edge response, and peak magnitude. To achieve invariance to image rotation, a consistent orientation is assigned to each feature point based on local image properties. The histogram of orientations is computed from the gradient orientation at all sample points within a circular window of a feature point. Peaks in this histogram correspond to the dominant directions of each feature point. For illumination invariance, eight orientation planes are defined. Finally, the gradient magnitude and the orientation are smoothened by applying a Gaussian filter and are then sampled over a 4×4 grid with eight orientation planes.

Each feature point is composed of four types of information [8, 9] – spatial location (x, y), scale (S), orientation (θ), and key point descriptor (K). For the sake of the experimental evaluation, only the key point descriptor [6, 9, 10] has been taken into account. This descriptor consists of a vector of 128 elements representing the orientations within a local neighborhood. In Fig. 16.2, the SIFT features extracted from a pair of face images are shown.

More formally, local image gradients are measured at the selected scale in the region around each key point. The measured gradient information is then transformed into a vector representation that contains a vector of 128 elements for each

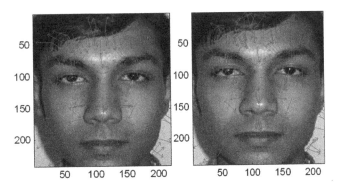

Fig. 16.2 Extracted SIFT features on a pair of face images

key point calculated over the extracted key points. These key point descriptor vectors represent local shape distortions and illumination changes.

16.3   State-of-the-Art Techniques in Face Recognition

This section presents some state-of-the-art face recognition techniques that use SIFT descriptors as local features [8, 9]. These features are highly distinctive in nature has and have accomplished correct matching on several pairs of feature points with high probability between a large database and a test sample. Following are the four major filtering stages of computation used to generate the set of image features based on SIFT.

16.3.1   Face Recognition by SIFT-Based Complete Graph Topology

In this subsection, three face-matching constraints [18, 19] are presented which are implemented using graph taxonomy: gallery image–based match constraint (GIbMC), reduced point–based match constraint (RPbMC), and regular grid–based match constraint (RGbMC). These techniques can be applied to find the corresponding subgraph in the probe face image for a given complete graph in the gallery image. The correspondence graph problem is to find a match between two structural descriptions, i.e., a mapping function between elements of two sets of feature points which preserve the maximum matching proximity between feature relations of face images. Detail definitions of the directional correspondence between two feature points is given by Kisku et al. [18, 19], and based on these two definitions these graph-matching constraints have been developed. This face recognition system uses the SIFT operator for feature extraction and each feature point composed of four different types of information such as spatial location, key point descriptor, scale, and orientation.

16.3.1.1 Gallery Image–Based Match Constraint

GIbMC [18] is based on the assumption that matching points can be found around similar positions, i.e., fiducial points on the face image. While establishing correspondence between two feature sets extracted from two face images, more than one feature point on the gallery face may correspond to a single point on the probe face and vice versa. To eliminate false matches and to consider only minimum pair distance from a set of pair distances for making a correspondence, it verifies the number of feature points that are extracted from the gallery and probe faces. When the number of feature points on the gallery face is smaller than that of the probe face, many points of interest from the probe face will be discarded. If it is the other case, i.e., if the number of points of interest on the gallery face is larger than that of the probe face, then a single interest point on the probe face may act as a match point for many points of interest of the gallery face. Moreover, many points of interest on the gallery face may have correspondence to a single point of interest on the probe face. In both cases, a single point of interest on the probe face may correspond to many points on the gallery face. After computing all distances between points of interest of gallery and probe faces that have made correspondences, two points with the minimum distance are paired. The Euclidean distance metric is used to compute distances and dissimilarity scores are computed between all pairs of vertices of two face images after constructing complete graphs on the interest points.

16.3.1.2 Reduced Point–Based Match Constraint

Multiple assignments determined in GIbMC are removed and the technique is extended in RPbMC [18]. It has been observed that in the GIbMC there can be some false matches. Usually, these false matches are obtained due to multiple assignments while more than one point is assigned to a single point on another face or due to the existence of one-way assignments. The false matches due to multiple assignments are eliminated by pairing the points with the minimum distance while those due to one-way assignments are eliminated by removing the correspondence links that do not have any corresponding assignment from the other face. The graph on the gallery face and the corresponding graph on the probe face have been shown in Fig. 16.3. All matches computed from left face to right face are shown in Fig. 16.3a while resulting graphs with few false matches are shown in Fig. 16.3b.

These false matches can be eliminated with the application of another constraint, namely, the RPbMC, which guarantees that each assignment from an image to another image would have a corresponding assignment from the second image to the first image. With this consideration, the false matches due to multiple assignments are eliminated by choosing the match pair with the minimum distance.

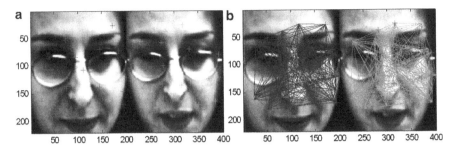

Fig. 16.3 An example of RPbMC for face matching

The false matches due to one-way assignments are eliminated by removing the
links that do not have any corresponding assignment from the other side. Examples
showing the matches before and after applying the RPbMC are given in Fig. 16.3.

False matches, due to multiple assignments, are removed by choosing the match
with the minimum distance between two face images. The dissimilarity scores on
reduced points between two face images for nodes and edges are computed in the
same way as for the GIbMC. Finally, the weighted average score is computed by
using the Gaussian empirical rule. This graph-matching technique is found to be
more efficient than the GIbMC since the matching is done for a very small number
of feature points with very few floating feature points.

16.3.1.3 Regular Grid–Based Match Constraint

The graph-matching technique [19] presented in this subsection has been developed
with the idea of matching corresponding subgraphs for a pair of face images. Face
image is divided into sub-images, using a regular grid with overlapping regions.
The matching between a pair of face images is performed by comparing sub-images
and by computing distances between all pairs of corresponding sub-image graphs
in a pair of face images and finally by averaging the dissimilarity scores for a pair
of sub-images. The final matching score is computed as a weighted score. Weight
assignment is performed by using the Gaussian empirical rule. From an experimental evaluation, it is found that sub-images with dimensions 1/5 of width and 1/5 of
height represent a good compromise between localization accuracy and robustness
to registration errors on a face image. The overlapping between regular grids has
been set to 30%.

16.3.2 Face Recognition Using SIFT Features

This section discusses four different face-matching techniques, namely, minimum
pair distance [20], matching mouth and eyes [20], matching on a regular grid [20],

and distinctive SIFT features for matching [21]. These matching techniques are computed with two sets of features on the testing and on the template face images.

The method of minimum pair distance [20] computes distance between all pairs of key point descriptors which are corresponding to a pair of faces and the final matching score provides the minimum distance obtained from all pairs. This matching constraint tries to find out a matching point on the face image which is a distinctive feature of the subject.

The second method [20] makes use of the feature points which are found to be around the eyes and the mouth positions. Initially these landmark positions are localized and a matching strategy is applied to the SIFT features belonging to the landmarks by ignoring irrelevant and less informative points.

The third matching strategy [20] initially subdivides the face image into a number of sub-images using a regular grid with overlapping and matching between a pair of faces performed by computing distances between all pairs of corresponding sub-images. Finally, the matching score is computed by taking the mean of all matched pair distances.

A robust face recognition technique has been proposed by Majumdar and Ward [21] in which discriminative ranking of SIFT features has been used. SIFT features make use of pruning the number of SIFT features for face recognition. This method also verifies the number of irrelevant feature points to be ignored and the reduced number of matched points to be taken for matching which eventually reduce the verification complexity. It also increases the overall recognition accuracy.

16.3.3 Person-Specific SIFT Features for Face Recognition

In this section a face recognition system [22] is presented which uses person-specific SIFT features and a nonstatistical matching technique with local and global similarity on key point clusters. Since the number and positions of the points selected by the SIFT descriptor are found to be different for each face image, the feature points are person-specific. Identical numbers of subregions are constructed in each face by comparing the matched pair points with a pair of gallery and probe faces and computing the similarity between each pair of subregions. Finally, the scores are matched as similarity values are computed. The subregions are constructed by using the K-means clustering approach, which is based on the locations of feature points in the gallery samples. Figure 16.4 shows the subregion construction and similarity matching scheme.

16.4 Local and Global Face Matching by Decoupling Process

In this section, we discuss two matching strategies [23], namely the local, based on parts, and the global face matching. In addition, we also introduce a classifier fusion technique, where the local and global matching techniques are fused together

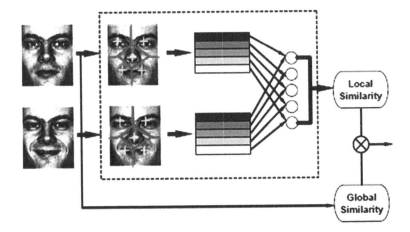

Fig. 16.4 Subregion construction and similarity matching scheme [22]

in terms of matching scores obtained from individual classifiers by a decoupling process. The decoupling process assesses the information, which is available from independent parts of the face and then local and global matching is applied on these salient facial features to fuse the information with the SIFT features.

16.4.1 Local Matching

Faces are deformable objects which are generally difficult to characterize with a rigid representation. Different facial regions not only convey different information on the subject's identity, but also suffer from different time variability, which is either due to motion or illumination changes. A typical example is the case of a talking face. While the eyes can be almost still and invariant over time, the mouth moves changing its appearance over time. As a consequence, the features extracted from the mouth area cannot be directly matched with the corresponding features from a static template. Moreover, single facial features may be occluded making the corresponding image area unusable for identification. For these reasons, to improve the robustness of the identification process, it is mandatory to decouple the image information corresponding to different face areas.

The aim of the local matching technique [23] is to correlate the extracted SIFT features with independent facial landmarks. The SIFT descriptors are extracted and grouped together at locations corresponding to static (eyes, nose) and dynamic (mouth) facial positions. Examples of the concept of independent matching facial features from local areas are shown in Figs. 16.5 and 16.6. The eyes and mouth positions are automatically located by applying the technique proposed in Refs. [11, 12]. The position of nostrils is automatically located by applying the technique proposed in [12]. A circular region of interest (ROI), centered at each extracted

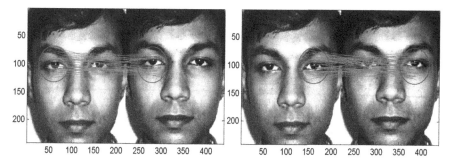

Fig. 16.5 Example of matching of static facial features [23]

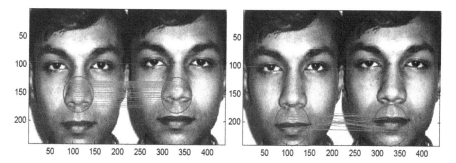

Fig. 16.6 Example of independent matching of static and dynamic facial features [23]

facial landmark location, is defined to determine the SIFT features to be considered for each face area.

Given a face image I, four independent ROIs are extracted. Two ROIs, $I_{left-eye}$ and $I_{right-eye}$, refer to the left and the right eyes respectively. The remaining two ROIs, I_{nose} and I_{mouth}, are the nose and the mouth locations. The SIFT feature points are then extracted from these four regions and gathered together into four groups. From these groups, pair-wise matching of salient features is computed. Finally, these matching scores are fused together by the sum rule and the fused score is compared against a threshold. More explicitly, the distance between a pair of left eyes $D^{Left-eye}(I^{gallery}, I^{gallery})$ can be defined as follows:

$$D^{Left-eye}(I^{test}, I^{gallery}) = \sqrt{\sum_{i \in m, j \in n} (I_j^{test}(k_{left-eye}) - I_i^{gallery}(k_{left-eye}))^2} \leq \Psi_{left-eye}^k \qquad (16.1)$$

where m and n are the dimensions of concatenated feature points for a pair of gallery and test samples and k refers to the key point descriptor.

Ψ^k is the threshold, which is computed a priori from a training set of face images. This face set is disjointed from the image sets used for testing and validation.

In the same fashion, the distances for a pair of right eyes, for a pair of noses, and for a pair of mouths can be determined as follows:

$$D^{Right-eye}(I^{test}, I^{gallery}) = \sqrt{\sum_{i \in m, j \in n} (I_j^{test}(k_{right-eye}) - I_i^{gallery}(k_{right-eye}))^2}$$
$$\leq \Psi_{right-eye}^k \tag{16.2}$$

$$D^{nose}(I^{test}, I^{gallery}) = \sqrt{\sum_{i \in m, j \in n} (I_j^{test}(k_{nose}) - I_i^{gallery}(k_{nose}))^2} \leq \Psi_{nose}^k \tag{16.3}$$

$$D^{mouth}(I^{test}, I^{gallery}) = \sqrt{\sum_{i \in m, j \in n} (I_j^{test}(k_{mouth}) - I_i^{gallery}(k_{mouth}))^2} \leq \Psi_{mouth}^k \tag{16.4}$$

Finally, the fused matching score, $FD(I^{test}, I^{gallery})$, is computed by combining these four individual matching scores together using the sum rule [13]:

$$FD_{LOCAL}(I^{test}, I^{gallery}) = sum(D^{Left-eye}(I^{test}, I^{gallery}), D^{Right-eye}(I^{test}, I^{gallery}),...$$
$$D^{nose}(I^{test}, I^{gallery}), D^{mouth}(I^{test}, I^{gallery})) \tag{16.5}$$

16.4.2 Global Matching with Major Facial Components

While in local matching each face area is handled independently, in global matching [23] all SIFT features are grouped together. In particular, the SIFT features extracted from the image areas corresponding to the four located facial landmarks are concatenated to form an augmented vector. The actual matching is performed by comparing the global feature vectors for a pair of face images. Before performing the face matching, a one to one correspondence is established for each pair of facial landmarks, as discussed in Sect. 16.4.1.

In order to compute the matching distance/score between gallery and probe samples by computing the distance between a pair of concatenated feature sets, let us consider $I^{Left-eye}(k), I^{Right-eye}(k), I^{nose}(k), I^{mouth}(k)$, which are the four facial features computed from both the gallery and probe face images. Two concatenated key point sets can be computed as

$$I_{gallery}^{Left-eye}(k_i) = \left\{I_{gallery}^{Left-eye}(k_1), I_{gallery}^{Left-eye}(k_2),..., I_{gallery}^{Left-eye}(k_m)\right\} \because i \in m;$$

$$I_{gallery}^{Right-eye}(k_i) = \left\{I_{gallery}^{Right-eye}(k_1), I_{gallery}^{Right-eye}(k_2),..., I_{gallery}^{Right-eye}(k_n)\right\} \because i \in n;$$

$$I_{gallery}^{nose}(k_i) = \left\{I_{gallery}^{nose}(k_1), I_{gallery}^{nose}(k_2),..., I_{gallery}^{nose}(k_p)\right\} \because i \in p;$$

$$I_{gallery}^{mouth}(k_i) = \left\{I_{gallery}^{mouth}(k_1), I_{gallery}^{mouth}(k_2),..., I_{gallery}^{mouth}(k_q)\right\} \because i \in q; \tag{16.6}$$

where m, n, p, and q are the dimensions of the extracted key point feature sets computed from the left eye, right eye, nose, and mouth, respectively. In order to obtain a fused feature set for a gallery sample face, we concatenate the key points of four components together, one by one, as

$$I^{gallery}(k) = \left\{ I_{gallery}^{Left-eye}(k_m) \cup I_{gallery}^{Right-eye}(k_n) \cup I_{gallery}^{nose}(k_p) \cup I_{gallery}^{mouth}(k_q) \right\}; \quad (16.7)$$

Similarly, the concatenated feature set for a probe sample is obtained by the equation

$$I^{probe}(k) = \left\{ I_{probe}^{Left-eye}(k_{m'}) \cup I_{probe}^{Right-eye}(k_{n'}) \cup I_{probe}^{nose}(k_{p'}) \cup I_{probe}^{mouth}(k_{q'}) \right\}; \quad (16.8)$$

The final matching score $FD_{GLOBAL}(I^{probe}, I^{gallery})$ is computed by determining all the minimum pair distances and then by computing a mean score of all the minimum pair distances as

$$FD_{GLOBAL}(I^{probe}, I^{gallery}) = \sqrt{\sum_{i \in M} \min \left\{ \min_{j \in N} \left\{ I^{gallery}(k_i), I^{probe}(k_j) \right\} \right\}} \quad (16.9)$$

In Eq. 16.9, the final distance is determined by the Hausdorff distance metric and the distance is compared against a threshold, which is computed heuristically from a training set of face images. As for the local matching threshold, this face set is disjointed from the image sets used for testing and validation.

16.5   Fusion of Global and Local Matching Scores Using Dempster–Shafer Theory

In the proposed classifier fusion, the Dempster–Shafer decision theory [23] is applied to combine the outcome of local and global matching for improving the overall results. The Dempster–Shafer theory is used to combine the evidence obtained from different sources of the system to compute the probability of an event. Generally, it is based on the idea of obtaining degrees of belief for one question from subjective probabilities for a related query and the rule for fusing such degrees of belief while they depend on independent items of information or evidence. This is obtained by combining three elements: the basic probability assignment function (*bpa*), the belief function (*bf*), and the plausibility function (*pf*).

The *bpa* maps the power set to the interval [0,1]. The *bpa* function of the empty set is 0 and the *bpa*s of all the subsets of the power set is 1. Let *m* denote the *bpa* function and *m(A)* represent the *bpa* for a particular set *A*. An element of a universal set *X* belongs to the set *A*, but to no particular subset of *A*, while *m(A)* represents the proportion of all the relevant evidence and claims the association of the element to the set *A*. The value of *m(A)* pertains only to the set *A* and makes no association to any subset of *A*. If we consider *m(B)* is the *bpa* for another set *B* and $B \subset A$, then we can say that any further evidence occurs in the subsets of A. Formally, the *bpa* function can be represented by the following equations:

$$m : P(X) \rightarrow [0,1] \tag{16.10}$$

$$m(\phi) = 0 \tag{16.11}$$

$$\sum_{A \in P(X)} m(A) = 1, \tag{16.12}$$

where $P(X)$ is the power set of A, $\emptyset$ is the empty set, and A is a set in the power set.$A \in P(X)$.

From the *bpa*, the upper and lower bounds of an interval are bounded by two nonadditive continuous measures called *Belief* and *Plausibility*. The lower bound *Belief* for a set A is defined as the sum of all the basic probability assignments of the proper subsets (B) of the set of interest (A) $(B \subset A)$. The upper bound *Plausibility* is the sum of all the basic probability assignments of the sets (B) that intersect (A) $((B \cap A) \neq \emptyset)$. For all the sets A that are elements of the power set $(A \in P(X))$.

$$Bel(A) = \sum_{B|B \subseteq A} m(B) \tag{16.13}$$

$$Pl(A) = \sum_{B|B \cap A \neq \emptyset} m(B) \tag{16.14}$$

Both Belief and Plausibility measures are nonadditive. It is not required for the sum of all the Belief measures and Plausibility measures to be 1.

An inverse function with the Belief measures can be used to obtain the *bpa*:

$$m(A) = \sum_{B|B \subseteq A} (-1)^{\gamma} Bel(B) \quad \because \gamma = |A - B| \tag{16.15}$$

where $|A - B|$ is the difference of the cardinality between the two sets A and B. It is possible to derive these two measures, namely Belief and Plausibility, from each other. If Plausibility can be derived from Belief measures, then the following equation can be established:

$$Pl(A) = 1 - Bel(\overline{A}), \tag{16.16}$$

where $\overline{A}$ is the classical complement of A. In addition, the Belief measures can be written as

$$Bel(\overline{A}) = \sum_{B|B \subseteq A} m(B) = \sum_{B|B \cap A = \emptyset} m(B) \tag{16.17}$$

and

$$\sum_{B|B \cap A \neq \emptyset} m(B) = 1 - \sum_{B|B \cap A = \emptyset} m(B) = Pl(A) \tag{16.18}$$

In the proposed approach, the two sets of matching scores, which are obtained from the local and global matching processes, can be fused together by using the Dempster–Shafer decision theory. Let Γ^{Local} and Γ^{Global} be two sets of matching scores computed from the two different matching processes. Also, let, $m(\Gamma^{Local})$ and $m(\Gamma^{Global})$ be the *bpa* functions for the Belief measures $Bel(\Gamma^{Local})$ and $Bel(\Gamma^{Global})$ for the two classifiers, respectively. Then, the *bpa*, $m(\Gamma^{Local})$ and $m(\Gamma^{Global})$, can be combined together to obtain a Belief committed to a matching score set $C \in \Theta$ according to the following combination rule or orthogonal sum rule:

$$m(C) = m(\Gamma^{Local}) \oplus m(\Gamma^{Global}) = \frac{\displaystyle\sum_{\Gamma^{Local} \cap \Gamma^{Global} = C} m(\Gamma^{Local})m(\Gamma^{Global})}{1 - \displaystyle\sum_{\Gamma^{Local} \cap \Gamma^{Global} = \varnothing} m(\Gamma^{Local})m(\Gamma^{Global})}, C \neq \varnothing. \quad (16.19)$$

The denominator in Eq. 16.19 is a normalizing factor which denotes that the amounts of the *bpa*, $m(\Gamma^{Local})$, and $m(\Gamma^{Global})$, are conflicting. Since two different classifiers are used, there is enough possibility for the Belief probability assignments to be conflicting, and this conflicting state is captured by the two bpa functions. Let $m(Local)$ and $m(Global)$ be the two matching score sets obtained from local and global matching strategies and these scores can be fused recursively as follows:

$$m(final) = m(Local) \oplus m(Global), \quad (16.20)$$

where $\oplus$ denotes the Dempster combination rule. The final decision of user acceptance and rejection can be established by the following equation and by applying a threshold Ψ to $m(final)$:

$$decision\ result = \begin{cases} accept, & if\ m(final) \geq \Psi \\ reject, & otherwise. \end{cases} \quad (16.21)$$

16.6 Performance Evaluation

To investigate the effectiveness of the proposed local and global face-matching strategies and their fusion, we have carried out extensive experiments [23] on the three databases, the IITK face database, the ORL face database [14, 15], and the Yale face database [16, 17]. The face dataset containing the face images varies in facial expressions, lightning conditions, illuminations, pose changes, age variations, etc. Prior to SIFT feature extraction, histogram equalization is performed on the captured face images. Two matching strategies as well as with their fusion are studied for face recognition. In the local face-matching strategy, SIFT key point features are extracted from the four salient facial landmarks. Then a pair-wise components matching is performed and a matching score from each local component matching is obtained. Finally, the matching scores obtained are fused using the sum rule [13] for further large-scale classifier fusion.

On the other hand, global face matching is performed with the concatenated feature set which contains SIFT key points extracted from each facial component. These key point features extracted from salient features are then concatenated into an augmented group. The final matching is performed between a pair of concatenated sets. The matching scores obtained from the proposed techniques (local and global matching) are fused with the help of the Dempster–Shafer decision theory for robust performance.

16.6.1 Evaluation with IITK Face Database

The proposed SIFT-based local and global face-matching strategies are tested on the IITK face database. The IITK face database consists of 800 face images with four images per person (200×4) which have captured, under a controlled environment $\pm 20°$, changes of head pose with almost uniform lighting and illumination conditions, keeping the facial expressions consistent with some ignorable changes. These face images have been acquired in different sessions. On the use of four face images for each individual, one face is used for training purpose as a gallery sample and the remaining three images are used for matching as probe samples. For face matching, all probe images are matched against all target images, yielding 800×3 genuine scores (images from identical subject) and $800 \times 799 \times 3$ imposter scores (images from different subjects).

On the use of the IITK face database, different performance metrics are determined as false accept rate (FAR), false reject rate (FRR), equal error rate (EER), and recognition rate from the receiver operating characteristics (ROC) curves. Evaluation results available from the IITK dataset exhibit robust performance. From the ROC curve in Fig. 16.7 and Table 16.1, it has been noted that pair-wise local matching of the facial feature components with the sum fusion rule reflects one of the best performances for individual verification while it is compared with the global matching strategy. For local face matching 96.76% recognition rate has been found with 1.21% FRR. On the other hand, global face matching exhibits 94.21% recognition rate with 1.4% FRR. Initially, for local matching, pair-wise matching of facial features is accomplished and then the matching scores devised from each pair component matching are fused rather than using self-facial component feature fusion in global matching.

16.6.2 Evaluation of ORL Face Database

The next experiment is performed on the ORL face database (formerly known as AT&T face database) [14, 15] with the following proposed face-matching

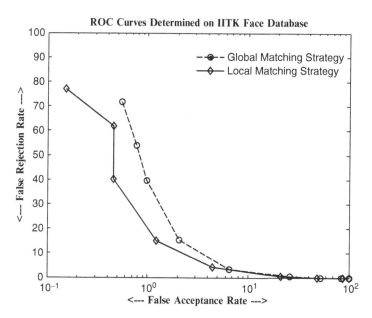

Fig. 16.7 ROC curves on the IITK face database for local and global matching strategies

Table 16.1 Various performance measures for local and global face matching

Matching strategy	FRR (%)	FAR (%)	EER (%)	Recognition rate (%)
Local matching	6.29	2.19	4.24	95.76
Global matching	9.87	3.61	6.79	93.21

techniques. The database consists of 400 images taken from 40 persons. Out of these images, we have used 200 face images for experimentation, in which orientation changes between ±20° and ±30° have been considered. The face images show variations of pose and facial expression (smiling/not smiling, open/closed eyes). The background of face images is uniformly dark. The original resolution of the face image is 92×112 pixels for each. However, for our experiment, we set the resolution as 140×100 pixels in line with other databases. To determine the usefulness and effectiveness of the two proposed matching techniques on the ORL database, one face is used for training and the remaining four images are used for verification. More explicitly, 200×4 genuine scores and 200×4×199 imposter scores are generated for the all the individuals. The same experimental setup is used for the ORL dataset as for the IITK database (Table 16.2). The identical set of performance parameters such as false reject, false accept, equal error rate, and recognition rate are determined from the ORL face dataset. Sample face images are shown in Fig. 16.8.

The experiments show best results when the local and global matching strategies are used. However, the local matching strategy outperforms the global matching

Table 16.2 Error rates and recognition rates for local and global matching

Matching strategy	FRR (%)	FAR (%)	EER (%)	Recognition rate (%)
Local matching	3.77	1.45	2.61	97.39
Global matching	5.86	2.48	4.17	95.83

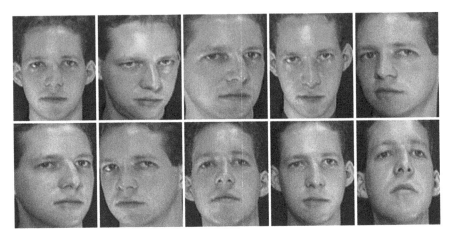

Fig. 16.8 Sample face images from the ORL face database

strategy in terms of recognition rates and FAR, which is identical to the IITK face database. Therefore, due to smaller ORL database size, overall recognition rates are increased both for local and global matching strategies. Local matching produces 97.39% recognition rate with 1.01% FAR and 1.35% EER, whereas global matching strategy produces 95.83% recognition rate with 1.26% FAR and 2.85% EER, as shown in Fig. 16.9.

16.6.3 Evaluation on Yale Face Database

The final experiment for local and global face matching is performed on the Yale face database [16, 17]. The database consists of face images of 15 subjects and each subject consists of 11 face images. In order to evaluate the performance of local matching and global matching strategies, 165 face images with various facial expressions are used. Some face images are shown in Fig. 16.10. The database consists of gray-level images. The training and the probe datasets are created using the face database with various facial expressions and occlusions, namely normal, smiling, and angry, with glasses or without glasses, and happy, sad, or winding. The face images show variations in the light source direction, such as light source applied on the center of the frontal view face, on the right profile of the face, or on

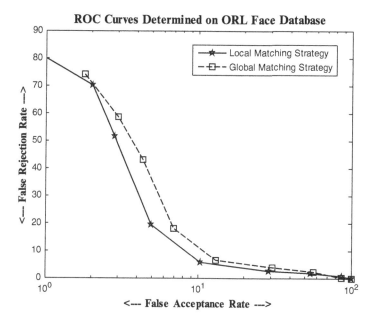

Fig. 16.9 ROC curves on the ORL face database for local and global matching strategies

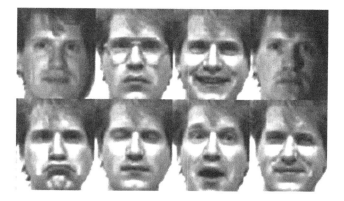

Fig. 16.10 Sample face images from the Yale face database

the left profile of the face image. To determine local and global matching with the Yale face database, we generate 15×10 genuine scores and $15 \times 10 \times 14$ imposter matching scores. Due to the frontal view face images with various facial expressions, each face image is evaluated with a certain degree of association to the database face image. Conversely, we can say that the degree of uniformity for the probe face images changes rapidly when testing is done with the proposed techniques. However, the overall accuracy determined on the Yale face dataset remained almost in line with the accuracy performed on the previous two databases.

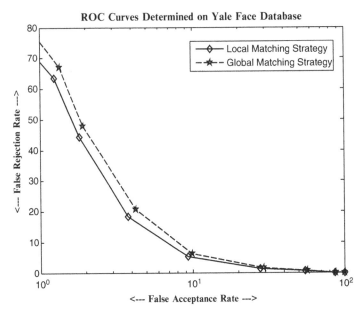

Fig. 16.11 ROC curves on the Yale face database for local and global matching

Table 16.3 Various error rates and recognition rates for both local and global matching

Matching strategy	FRR (%)	FAR (%)	EER (%)	Recognition rate (%)
Local matching	3.9	3.28	3.59	96.41
Global matching	8.81	5.25	7.03	92.97

The experimental results on the database with the proposed local matching technique again outperform the results of the global matching technique. Since the database size is small, with 15 subjects and various facial expressions, the experiment is challenging. In terms of recognition rate, EER, and FAR, the local matching strategy shows an increase in recognition rate and EER whereas a decrease in FAR. Local matching achieves 96.41% recognition rate with 3.59% EER and global matching achieves 92.97% accuracy with 7.03% EER, as shown in Fig. 16.11. For the matching techniques, low FARs are achieved while FRRs are higher in comparison (Table 16.3).

16.6.4 Experimental Results of Fusion of Global and Local Strategies

In order to determine robustness and effectiveness of score level fusion of local and global face matching, we use the Dempster–Shafer decision theory for fusion.

Matching scores are devised from two techniques, namely local matching and global matching. In local matching, matching scores are generated from the pairwise matching of the major facial components (eyes, nose, and mouth) for a pair of face images and then the matching scores of each component pair are fused by the sum rule to get a fused matching score.

On the other hand, global matching proposes a technique by which a vector is created by gathering the SIFT key point features of the major facial features using concatenation. Then face matching is performed between a pair of face images using corresponding feature vectors. Finally, when matching is completed, a fused score is generated from each pair of face images. This fused score is further used for local and global fusion.

Before score level fusion can be accomplished with two different matching techniques, data normalization of the matching scores is done with the well-known "min–max" technique. The Dempster–Shafer decision theory is applied to integrate the normalized scores devised from local and global methodologies. The fusion operation is performed using Eqs. 16.19 and 16.20 and the final acceptance and rejection notification can be established by Eq. 16.21.

The proposed fusion performance is evaluated with the three databases separately and it is found that the test performed on the ORL face database outperforms the others. Next, higher accuracy is obtained from the Yale face dataset and, subsequently, accuracy obtained from the IITK face dataset shows poor performance while it compares with the ORL and the Yale face datasets. In Fig. 16.12, the ROC curve shows the recognition rate of the proposed local and global fusion approach

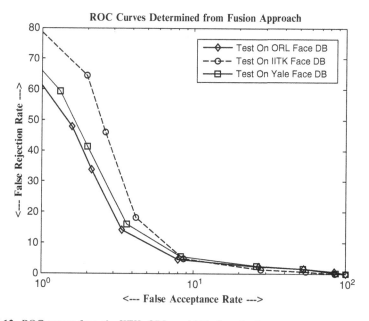

Fig. 16.12 ROC curves from the IITK, ORL, and Yale face databases

obtained from the ORL face database which is 98.93%. On the contrary, the tests performed on the Yale face database and the IITK face dataset achieve 98.19% and 96.29% accuracies, respectively.

Both the face-matching techniques have considered the SIFT features at some specific facial feature locations, such as at both eye positions and their surrounding area, the nostril and its surrounding area, and the mouth area. We do not consider feature points that do not belong to the specified regions for experiments. Since the minimum pair distance computed by two key points could not be obtained from the same face position, it would not be a practical approach to consider all face parts for experiments. We extend this less realistic phenomenon of matching to be accomplished with the whole face; we may consider the detected key points that are being extracted only from the pair of eyes, from the nose, and from the mouth positions. Extracted key points from these facial regions are further used for matching with all other faces. It can be assumed that the features localized on the mouth area of one face could be matched with the invariant features detected on the mouth area of another face. In addition, it has been seen that the key points that are located largely at the major facial components are more realistic for use in matching. Therefore, if the face image is not well registered, then major facial component matching might be better for overall performance. Due to the invariant nature of SIFT features, it is less sensitive to image enhancement and further processing rather than changes of feature points in counting.

16.7 Comparisons with Other Face-Matching Techniques

The face recognition techniques with SIFT features discussed in this chapter exhibit optimum performance in terms of recognition rates. These techniques use static and dynamic salient features of faces for local and global face matching as well as for the decoupling-based fusion approach. In this section, we compare our local, global, and fusion techniques with the available SIFT-based face recognition techniques. Mian et al. [24] discuss three face recognition techniques with local features devised from locally defined coordinate biases. The face-matching techniques have used a SIFT descriptor for invariant feature extraction and they have been evaluated with FRGC v2.0 face database. The 2D and 3D local feature methods have achieved 76% and 94% recognition rates with 24% and 6% EERs, respectively. However, fusion of the 2D and 3D local features with SIFT achieves 98.5% recognition rate with 1.5% EER. The local and global fusion approach which is based on the Dempster–Shafer decision theory achieves 98.93% recognition rate, which is determined on the ORL face database. The recognition rate determined on the Yale database also exhibits encouraging results with 98.19% recognition rate (Table 16.4).

Due to decoupling the local and global information with the Dempster–Shafer decision theory-based fusion, the results have successfully overcome the limitations mentioned by Mian et al., Wang and Miao, and Bicego et al. [20, 24, 25]. The method of Wang and Miao [25] has been tested on the ORL and the Yale face datasets

Table 16.4 Comparison between SIFT-based techniques

Algorithm	Database used	EER (%)	Recognition rate (%)
2D local features (SIFT) [24]	FRGC v2.0	24.0	76.0
3D local features (SIFT) [24]	FRGC v2.0	6.0	94.0
Fusion of 2D + 3D local (SIFT) [24]	FRGC v2.0	1.5	98.5
Scale invariant_PSM [25] (Train = 5)	ORL	19.5	80.5
Scale invariant_PSM [25] (Train = 5)	Yale	23.3	76.7
MPD (Prior EER on G2) [20]	BANCA	8.69	91.31
EM (Prior EER on G2) [20]	BANCA	6.38	93.62
RG (Prior EER on G2) [20]	BANCA	3.85	96.15
MPD (On G2) [20]	BANCA	7.4 (WER)	92.6
EM (On G2) [20]	BANCA	4.2 (WER)	95.8
RG (On G2) [20]	BANCA	3.04 (WER)	96.96
Proposed fusion method	ORL	1.07	98.93
Proposed fusion method	Yale	1.87	98.19
Proposed fusion method	IITK	3.71	96.29

and has achieved 80.5% and 76.7% recognition rates, respectively. The face-matching techniques discussed in this chapter have shown a robust performance compared with the methods presented in Wang and Miao [25]. Other SIFT-based face recognition techniques by Bicego et al. [20] also suppress recognition rates in contrast to higher accuracy while they are compared with the proposed techniques.

16.8   Conclusion

In this chapter, we have investigated a robust and integrated classifiers paradigm for face recognition with local and global face-matching strategy. Performances of individual matching techniques have been evaluated with three face databases, namely IITK, ORL, and Yale. It has been observed that the fusion of local and global face-matching strategies that is based on the Dempster–Shafer decision theory, which has been tested on the ORL face database, exhibits best accuracy with 98.93% recognition rate, whereas tests performed on the IITK and Yale face datasets show 96.29% and 98.19% recognition rates, respectively. It shows a 2.64% increase in the relative performance while the recognition rates which are computed on the ORL and IITK face databases have been compared with each other. On the contrary, while the overall accuracies have been determined from the ORL and the Yale face databases, 0.74% relative accuracy has been determined. The proposed fusion strategy has also been compared with the techniques discussed in Refs. [20, 24, 25]. It outperforms other face-matching techniques which are based on locally and globally collected SIFT features from salient facial parts.

The study on three techniques including local and global matching approaches, and their fusion, shows an increase in performance in terms of accuracies while the use of SIFT features accelerates the whole matching process. Therefore, it is expected that if the face image is not well registered, then major facial component matching might be better for overall performance. Due to the invariant nature of SIFT features, it is less sensitive to image enhancement and further processing rather than changes of feature points in counting.

References

1. Shakhnarovich, G., Moghaddam, B.: Face recognition in subspaces. In Li, S., Jain, A. (eds), Handbook of Face Recognition, pp. 141–168, Springer Verlag (2004).
2. Shakhnarovich, G., Fisher, J.W., Darrell, T.: Face recognition from long-term observations. IEEE European Conference on Computer Vision, 851–865 (2002).
3. Wiskott, L., Fellous, J., Kruger, N., Malsburg, C.: Face recognition by elastic bunch graph matching. IEEE Transactions on Pattern Analysis and Machine Intelligence, 775–779 (1997).
4. Bigun, J.: Retinal vision applied to facial features detection and face authentication. Pattern Recognition Letters, 23(4), 463–475 (1997).
5. Zhang, G., Huang, X., Li, S., Wang, Y., Wu, X.: Boosting local binary pattern (lbp)-based face recognition, SINOBIOMETRICS, 179–186 (2004).
6. Heusch, G., Rodriguez, Y., Marcel, S.: Local binary patterns as an image preprocessing for face authentication. IDIAP-RR 76, IDIAP (2005).
7. Kisku, D.R., Rattani, A., Grosso, E., Tistarelli, M.: Face identification by SIFT-based complete graph topology. IEEE Workshop AutoId, 63–68 (2007).
8. Lowe, D.: Object recognition from local scale-invariant features. International Conference on Computer Vision, 1150–1157 (1999).
9. Lowe, D.: Distinctive image features from scale-invariant keypoints. International Journal of Computer Vision, 60(2), 91–110 (2004).
10. Park, U., Pankanti, S., Jain, A.K.: Fingerprint verification using SIFT features. SPIE, Security and Defense.6944, 69440K-69440K-9 (2008).
11. Smeraldi, F., Capdevielle, N., Bigün, J.: Facial features detection by saccadic exploration of the Gabor decomposition and Support Vector Machines. 11th Scandinavian Conference on Image Analysis 1, 39–44 (1999).
12. Gourier, N., James, D.H., Crowley, L.: Estimating face orientation from robust detection of salient facial structures. FG Net Workshop on Visual Observation of Deictic Gestures (2004).
13. Snelick, R., Uludag, U., Mink, A., Indovina, M., Jain, A.: Large scale evaluation of multi-modal biometric authentication using state-of-the-art systems. IEEE Transactions on Pattern Analysis and Machine Intelligence, 27(3), 450–455 (2005).
14. Samaria, F., Harter, A.: Parameterization of a stochastic model for human face iden tification. IEEE Workshop on Applications of Computer Vision (1994).
15. http://www.cl.cam.ac.uk/research/dtg/attarchive/facedatabase.html
16. Tan, K., Chen, S.: Adaptively weighted sub-pattern PCA for face recognition. Neurocomputing 64, 505–511 (2005).
17. Yale face database. http://cvc.yale.edu
18. Kisku, D.R., Rattani, A., Grosso, E., Tistarelli, M.: Face Identification by SIFT-based Complete Graph Topology. 5th IEEE International Workshop on Automatic Identification Advanced Technologies, 63–68 (2007).
19. Kisku, D.R., Rattani, A., Tistarelli, M., Gupta, P.: Graph Application on Face for Personal Authentication and Recognition. 10th IEEE International Conference on Control, Automation, Robotics and Vision (ICARCV), 1150–1155 (2008).

20. Bicego, M., Lagorio, A., Grosso, E., Tistarelli, M.: On the use of SIFT features for face authentication. IEEE International Workshop on Biometrics, in association with CVPR (2006).
21. Majumdar, A., Ward, R.K.: Discriminative SIFT features for face recognition. IEEE Canadian Conference on Electrical and Computer Engineering, 27–30 (2009).
22. Luo, J., Ma, Y., Takikawa, E., Lao, S., Kawade, M., Lu, B.-L.: Person-specific sift features for face recognition. IEEE Conference on Acoustics, Speech and Signal Processing, 593–596 (2007)
23. Kisku, D. R., Tistarelli, M., Sing, J.K., Gupta, P.: Face Recognition by Fusion of Local and Global Matching Scores using DS Theory: An Evaluation with Uni-classifier and Multi-classifier Paradigm. 3rd IEEE Computer Vision and Pattern Recognition Workshop on Biometrics (CVPR), 60–65 (2009).
24. Mian, A., Bennamoun, M., Owens, R.: Face recognition using 2D and 3D multimodal local features. International Symposium on Computer Vision, 860–870 (2006).
25. Wang, Z., Miao, Z.: Scale invariant face recognition using probabilistic similarity measure, International Conference on Pattern Recognition, 1–4 (2008).

Chapter 17
OGSA-Based SOA for Collaborative Cancer Research: System Modeling and Generation

Tianyi Zang, Radu Calinescu, and Marta Kwiatkowska

Abstract The CancerGrid consortium is developing open-standards cancer informatics to address the challenges posed by modern cancer clinical trials. This chapter presents a framework for the metamodel-driven development of Open Grid Services Architecture (OGSA)-based Service-Oriented Architecture (SOA) for collaborative cancer research. We extend the existing Z model and the generation technology to support OGSA in a distributed collaborative environment. A generic SOA model is built based on a combination of the semantics of a standard domain metamodel and metadata, and the Web Services Resource Framework (WSRF) standards. This model is then employed to automate the generation of the trial management systems used in cancer clinical trials. The integration of the Web services standards with the standard domain metamodel enables the generated systems to support syntactic, semantic, and computational interoperability that is essential for collaborative cancer research. Automating the model-driven system generation not only speeds up its development, but also enforces its conformance to these standards. The SOA model and generated system are currently being evaluated for use in early-phase clinical trials. Our approach is also applicable to other research areas.

T. Zang (✉)
School of Computer Science and Technology, Harbin Institute of Technology,
Harbin 150001, China
e-mail: tianyi.zang@gmail.com

R. Calinescu
Aston University, Birmingham B4 7ET, UK

M. Kwiatkowska
Computing Laboratory, Oxford University, Oxford, UK

Xiaoyu Yang et al. (eds.), *Guide to e-Science: Next Generation Scientific Research and Discovery*, Computer Communications and Networks,
DOI 10.1007/978-0-85729-439-5_17, © Springer-Verlag London Limited 2011

17.1 Introduction

Cancer clinical trials pose significant challenges to the e-Science community [1, 2], as they increasingly take the form of large-scale translational studies, combining the latest laboratory techniques and bioinformatics with traditional statistical analysis based on detailed descriptions of clinical outcomes. Their costly-to-build information systems are often composed of incompatible variants of the same modules, and record data in ways that prevent any meaningful result analysis across similar projects. The information technology required to enable this kind of large-scale, collaborative science will need to support easy and rapid development and deployment of reliable and flexible software systems that enable syntactic, semantic, and computational interoperability.

CancerGrid [3], an e-Science consortium funded by the UK Medical Research Council, and involving five UK universities, is addressing these challenges through the development of model-driven, service-oriented technology for cancer informatics [4, 5]. The CancerGrid systems are based on a comprehensive metamodel of cancer clinical trials [6], and use controlled vocabulary services and reusable, curated metadata elements to enable automatic software generation, interoperability, and data sharing.

In the USA, the National Cancer Institute's Center for Bioinformatics (NCICB) has taken a similar approach, although looking at the whole range of cancer informatics requirements. Its cancer Biomedical Informatics Grid (caBIG) initiative is assembling data sets and tools for the creation of a global cancer research infrastructure [7, 8]. The CancerGrid systems interoperate with the existing caBIG architecture, and allow for data and metadata integration across clinical trial operations, demonstrated through a recent collaboration with the Veterans Administration Cooperative Studies Program [9]. However, in current information systems for trial-based cancer clinical research, there is a lack of a standard software paradigm for modeling and managing the clinical trial data.

The Open Grid Services Architecture (OGSA) standards represent an evolution toward a grid system architecture based on Web services concepts and technologies [10–12]. It describes an architecture for a service-oriented grid-computing environment for business and scientific application, developed within the Open Grid Forum (OGF) [13]. OGSA standards define a set of core capabilities and behaviors that address key concerns in grid systems. These concerns include execution management, data resource management, security, self-management, and information management.

The Web Services Resource Framework (WSRF) [14, 15] is an open framework for modeling and accessing persistent resources using Web services. WSRF is a set of Web service specifications being developed by the OASIS organization. These specifications describe how to implement OGSA capabilities using Web services. They build on existing Web services standards to address the limitation of statelessness inherent to plain Web services through the concept of WS-Resources [16], and also by defining conventions for the management of a state. The WSRF specifications define how WS-Resources can be represented, accessed, managed, and collected [17–21].

OGSA and WSRF are adopted in our SOA model for the following reasons:

- OGSA helps addressing major key concerns in collaborative cancer research in a distributed environment, such as execution management, data sharing and management, security, and so on. So we can focus on the business logics of trial management of collaborative cancer research.
- WSRF enables the use of Web services to model and access clinical trial data resources (databases and files) across organizational and administrative domains in a standard and interoperable way for collaborative cancer research.
- WSRF supports the grouping and management of related trial WSRs together. This facilitates the implementation of role-based access control enforced in the trial metamodel.

OGSA allows the developed clinical trial SOA to interoperate seamlessly across administrative domains as well as with the cancer research ecosystem linked by OGSA-compliant caBIG [7].

The Z formal specification language [22] is selected to define the clinical trial metamodel semantics and the OGSA-based SOA model, based on our prior experience with using Z in software engineering projects. The availability of a concise and unambiguous specification is essential for a joint project involving multidisciplinary teams located at several research institutions across the UK. The resulting Z specification has been of great help in gaining and conveying a good understanding of the system model, and in guiding the actual system design and development.

The efforts presented in this chapter are built on previous work in the CancerGrid project: developing the metamodel [6], constructing the generation technology, and specifying the latter in Z [4]. The key contribution of this work is in extending and adapting the previous work to target OGSA-based grid services for collaborative cancer research. We use the same domain metamodel as before. The generation technology and its Z specification are modified and extended to address the new target. The major contributions are outlined as follows:

- The framework for the development of OGSA-based SOA for collaborative cancer research is based on a standard domain metamodel and metadata developed in CancerGrid, and the WSRF Web services standards.
- The generic SOA model for the trial management system is built based on a combination of the standard domain metamodel and metadata and the WSRF standards, and defined formally using Z notation. This SOA model enables syntactic, semantic, and computational interoperability that is essential for collaborative cancer research.
- Based on the OGSA-based SOA model and on concrete *clinical trial protocols* that are instances of the domain metamodel, the OGSA-based clinical trial management systems are generated automatically using model-driven technology. This not only speeds up the development of trial management systems and

improves their reliability, but also enforces their conformance to relevant standards – the prerequisite for the system interoperability.

• Since the OGSA-based SOA model is constructed by binding the WSRF Web services standards to standard, high-level domain specifications (i.e., the domain metamodel and metadata), our approach can be extended easily to other application scenarios and domains for which a similar metamodel and similar metadata are available.

17.2 Metamodel-Based Development Framework

Our overall approach to the development of cancer information management system is depicted in Fig. 17.1. The clinical trial metamodel [6] underlying the architecture is built as an embodiment of the Consolidating Standards of Reporting Trials (CONSORT) statement [23], the de facto set of guidance rules for the reporting and execution of clinical trials. This use of a common metamodel for the design of different clinical trials enables the model-driven development of reusable software components for cancer research.

The cancer metadata are sets of well-defined common data elements (CDEs) (i.e., cancer domain- and clinical trial-specific community data standards). The metamodel enables data sharing between clinical trials by matching all data collected during their execution to CDEs. Well-defined CDEs are basic units composing the clinical trial data, and provide sufficient information to enable syntactic and semantic interoperability at the CDE level. The interoperability denotes the

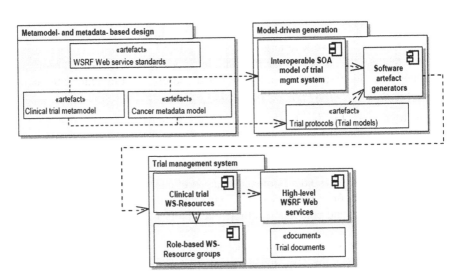

Fig. 17.1 Metamodel- and metadata-based development of cancer information management systems

ability of a system to access and use the parts of another system. The consistent use of CDEs is key to sharing data for collaborative cancer research.

By binding the WSRF Web services standards to the cancer metamodel and metadata, we build a generic OGSA-based SOA model for clinical trial information management systems. Cancer clinical trial protocols are XML-encoded instances of the metamodel. They are generated by means of a trial design tool that applies the rules specified in the trial metamodel and uses the cancer trial CDEs. Based on the combination of OGSA-based SOA model and concrete clinical trial protocol, an assembly of software artifact generators builds the complete code for the trial Web services composing a trial management system. The details of the SOA model and how to automate the system generation are described in the following sections.

17.3 Trial Metamodel and Its Implied Semantics

There is lack of semantics of location, personnel, patients, and their relationship in the trial model in [4]. These semantics are essential for cancer research collaboration across research sites, especially for geographically distributed resources sharing between diverse organizations. We enhanced the trial and authorization-aware trial semantics by introducing a Settings and Locations section in the CancerGrid trial metamodel [6]. The enhanced trial semantics first underpin the new OGSA-based trial model and then the trial management system generation described in Sects. 17.4 and 17.5 respectively.

17.3.1 Clinical Trial Metamodel

The clinical trial metamodel is built as a CONSORT embodiment. The CONSORT statement provides a checklist of items that need to be used in writing, reviewing, and assessing clinical trial reports, and a flow diagram of the progress through the phases of a clinical trial. The CancerGrid philosophy is that the best way to ensure the availability of all this information for inclusion in clinical trial reports is to specify it explicitly during the design phase of trials.

The CancerGrid clinical trial metamodel [6] reflects this philosophy as shown in Fig. 17.2:

- The general section of a trial design groups together overall data required or recommended by CONSORT, such as the name and a summary of the trial, its registry numbers, sources of funding, and contact details.
- The items in the methods section of the CONSORT checklist are captured in the methods and randomization sections of the model. This includes the interventions (i.e., treatments) for each patient group, the eligibility criteria for patients, the settings and locations for data collection, and a specification of the techniques used in the random allocation of interventions.

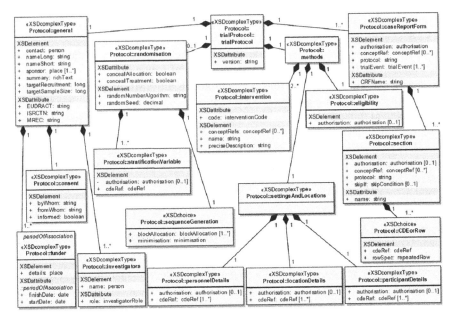

Fig. 17.2 High-level class diagram of the CancerGrid clinical trial metamodel

- The caseReportForm section of the model defines the case report forms (CRFs) required to support the patient workflow through each stage of a clinical trial. Recruitment, adverse events, and other items from the results CONSORT checklist section are provided for by these CRFs.
- The metamodel enables data sharing between clinical trials by matching all data collected during their execution to well-defined CDEs, i.e., controlled sets of cancer concepts and measurements.

Although UML class diagrams are a powerful design tool, the clinical trial metamodel covers only part of what is required for modeling the clinical trial data. Therefore, the design and development of the clinical trial system also rely on implicit knowledge about cancer clinical trial semantics.

17.3.2 Common Data Element

The consistent use of a controlled vocabulary (i.e., a set of domain-specific terms managed by a vocabulary registration authority) is key to sharing data between projects in any field of research. This is particularly relevant to cancer research, where tremendous human and financial resources are employed for the generation of small amounts of data [1]. The CancerGrid project is addressing this important requirement by basing its clinical trial model on the use of thesauri (i.e., collections of controlled vocabulary terms and their relationships) and CDEs. A CDE is defined in terms of several basic types:

- CdeID, the set of CDE identifiers used to refer uniquely to specific CDEs.
- CdeType, the set of types that CDE values may have. This supports the syntactic interoperability that allows for data to be moved between different information systems.
- CdeInfo, the metadata that fully define the semantics of the CDE. This supports the semantic interoperability that allows for different data sets to be compared to identify overlapping or related content.

These basic types are summarized below using Z notation [22]:

[*CdeID, CdeType, CdeInfo*]

and the CDE type can be specified as:

```
___Cde_____
 id: CdeID
 valueDomain: CdeType
 info: CdeInfo

```

CDEs used to model data in a specific research field are maintained in a CDE (or metadata) repository for that area of research:

```
___CdeRepository_____
 cdeSet: ℙ Cde
_____
 ∀ x, y: cdeSet • x.id = y.id ⇒ x = y

```

17.3.3 Case Report Forms

Clinical trial data are generated during the execution of a trial as a result of a number of trial events, each of which corresponds to a stage in the execution of the clinical trial. For instance, clinical and personal patient data are collected during the registration stage, treatments are allocated in the randomization stage, and periodical follow-up data collection is performed to assess response to treatment. The complete set of trial events in the CancerGrid trial model is given below:

TrialEvent ::= registration | eligibility |
  randomization | onStudy | treatment | offStudy |
  response | followUp | adverseEvent

Clinicians gather the data corresponding to the trial events by filling in CRFs that comprise CDEs drawn from the cancer CDE repository,

  | *cancerCdeRep: CdeRepository*

A CRF is fully defined by the sequence of trial events corresponding to its sections:

```
__CaseReportForm____
 events: seq TrialEvent
```

17.3.4 Settings and Locations

As indicated in [23], the settings and locations where the data were collected affect the external validity of a trial study. All the related information that could influence the observed results should be reported so that readers can assess external validity.

The settings and locations component of the metamodel specifies the data collected about the trial locations (i.e., hospitals or clinical trial units), personnel, and patients. These are all a combination of CDEs drawn from our metadata repository:

```
__SettingsAndLocations_____
 locationCdeSet: P cancerCdeRep.cdeSet
 personnelCdeSet: P cancerCdeRep.cdeSet
 patientCdeSet: P cancerCdeRep.cdeSet
```

17.3.5 Trial Design

For the purpose of our WSRF-based trial system development, a clinical trial is composed of the *SettingsAndLocations* definition, CRFs of all patients, and the CDEs corresponding to all locations, personnel, patients, and events of each of these patient forms:

```
__TrialDesign_____
 forms: P CaseReportForm
 eventCdeSet: TrialEvent ↠ P cancerCdeRep.cdeSet
 SettingsAndLocations
 _____
 dom eventCdeSet = ∪ {f: forms • (ran f.events)}
 ∀ f₁, f₂: forms • f₁≠f₂⇒ranf₁.events ∩ ranf₂.even=∅
```

The location, personnel, and patient instances specific to a clinical trial are defined as:

```
__LocationInstance _____
 id: N
 locationDetails: P (Cde × CdeType)
```

$$\begin{array}{|l}
\underline{\quad PersonnelInstance\quad\quad\quad\quad\quad} \\
id: \mathbb{N} \\
locationIds: \mathbb{P}\,\mathbb{N} \\
personnelDetails: \mathbb{P}\,(Cde \times CdeType) \\
\hline
\end{array}$$

$$\begin{array}{|l}
\underline{\quad PatientInstance\quad\quad\quad\quad\quad} \\
id: \mathbb{N} \\
locationId: \mathbb{N} \\
patientDetails: \mathbb{P}\,(Cde \times CdeType) \\
\hline
\end{array}$$

The relationships between the location, personnel, and patient instances in a clinical trial are specified as:

$$\begin{array}{|l}
trialLocations: TrialDesign \rightarrow \mathbb{P}\ LocationInstance \\
trialPersonnel: TrialDesign \rightarrow \mathbb{P}\ PersonnelInstance \\
trialPatients: TrialDesign \rightarrow \mathbb{P}\ PatientInstance \\
trialPatientCrfs: TrialDesign \times PatientInstance \rightarrow \\
\qquad\qquad\qquad \mathbb{P}\ CaseReportForm \\
\hline
\forall\ t:\ TrialDesign\ ;\ c:\ Cde\ ;\ v:\ CdeType\ ; \\
\quad l:\ trialLocations\ t\ ;\ p:\ trialPersonnel\ t\ ; \\
\quad pt:\ trialPatients\ t\ ;\ l_1,\ l_2:\ trialLocations\ t\ \bullet \\
\quad ((c,\ v) \in l.locationDetails \Rightarrow c \in t.locationCdeSet)\ \wedge \\
\quad ((c,\ v) \in p.personnelDetails \Rightarrow c \in t.personnelCdeSet) \\
\quad \wedge ((c,\ v) \in pt.patientDetails \Rightarrow c \in t.patientCdeSet) \\
\quad \wedge (l_1.id = l_2.id \Rightarrow l_1 = l_2) \wedge p.locationIds \subseteq \{l.id\} \\
\quad \wedge pt.locationId \in \{l.id\} \wedge trialPatientCrfs\ (t,\ pt) \subseteq t.forms
\end{array}$$

The location is used to group together patients and personnel from the same clinical trial unit or hospital, which is essential when the access to certain data and/or operations is confined to users from the same location. The same patient is not allowed to make multiple registrations at several locations. Personnel are not limited to one location. A patient can be treated by several personnel members, and a personnel member can treat several patients.

The trial data belonging to the patients are gathered using several CRFs. The subset of CDEs that are used to map CRFs to specific patients is specified explicitly in the settings and locations section of the model. The patients for which the forms were completed, the trial personnel that filled them in, and the locations of both classes of people are always stated explicitly in the forms for the trial.

17.3.6 Authorization

One of the main objectives in CancerGrid's development of open standards cancer informatics is the enforcement of strict confidentiality constraints associated with cancer clinical trials [1]. This objective is achieved by building the data and operation access policies on top of a role-based access control system [24]. The role-based access control is enforced by the CancerGrid clinical trial model through the inclusion of an *authorization* element within each part of the model that specifies the sensitive clinical trial data. For instance, the authorization component associated with a CRF is mandatory, while those of individual CRF parts are optional. The location is used to group together patients and personnel from the same clinical trial unit or hospital so that access to certain data and/or operations is confined to users from the same location.

The set of roles that trial personnel and patients can play is:

Role ::= patient | coordinator | clinician |research_nurse | statistician

And the set of possible operations available to a specific role is:

AccessType ::= creation | modification | querying |retrieval

An authorization-aware trial design defines the rules that specify the CDEs on which each role can perform the allowed operations:

$$
\begin{array}{|l}
\underline{\text{AuthorizedTrialDesign}}\underline{}\\[2pt]
\textit{trial: TrialDesign}\\
\textit{accessRules: Role} \times \textit{AccessType} \twoheadrightarrow \mathbb{P}\ \textit{Cde}\\[4pt]
\hline
\forall\ \textit{roleCdeSet: } \mathrm{ran}\ \textit{accessRules} \cdot \textit{roleCdeSet}\\
\quad \subseteq \cup\ \{(\cup\{\ e:\ TrialEvent \cdot (trial.eventCdeSet\ e)\}),\\
\quad (\cup\{trial.locationCdeSet\}),\ (\cup\{trial.patientCdeSet\}),\\
\quad (\cup\{trial.personnelCdeSet\})\}
\end{array}
$$

17.4 OGSA-Based SOA Model

17.4.1 Layered Architecture

Based on the clinical trial semantics described Sect. 17.4.1, we propose an OGSA-based SOA model for a cancer research virtual organization (VO) to conduct a clinical trial study. As depicted in Fig. 17.3, the layered architecture naturally maps into a collaborative cancer research VO.

From bottom to top there are the CancerGrid data resource layer (resource layer), the WS-Resource modeling layer (site layer), and the high-level cancer research logic layer (VO layer). Cancer research features diverse crucial data resources stored and managed at different institutions under different contractual and

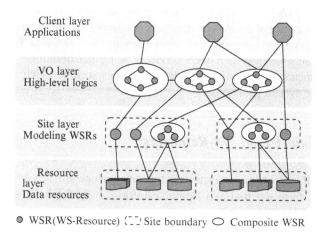

Client layer
Applications

VO layer
High-level logics

Site layer
Modeling WSRs

Resource
layer
Data resources

◉ WSR(WS-Resource) ⌐⌐¦ Site boundary ◯ Composite WSR

Fig. 17.3 Layered architecture SOA

regulatory environments. The resource layer consists of numerous crucial clinical and tissue-based data sources involved in cancer research, such as CancerGrid clinical trial CDE repository, clinical trial and trial data model repositories, databases storing the confidential information pertaining to the clinical trial and the associated staff and patients, etc.

The WS-Resource modeling layer comprises single and composite CancerGrid WS-Resources on each site. The CancerGrid WS-Resources model the states of the underlying data resources and provide a standard interface to interact with them. Generally, these modeling WS-Resources are deployed on each site to manage and manipulate the site-specific information and data. The site-specific WS-Resources are behind the firewall and protected within the site domain. Each site and its available WS-Resources need to register with the VO registry. The instantiation and termination of the site WS-Resources can be managed by the services on the VO layer. Especially, in order to support secure access to the underlying resources, the WS-Resource-based access control mechanisms are provided on this layer. The entire modeling WS-Resources on this layer form a virtual clinical trial resource level, and serve as the fundamental WS-Resource infrastructure with access control mechanisms for building cancer research business logics.

Based on the modeling WS-Resources infrastructure, the VO layer constructs the high-level business logics for collaborative cancer research by means of Web service composition and choreography technologies. In addition, besides managing and maintaining the memberships according to the VO rules, the VO layer implements the security policies for cancer study by exploiting the WS-Resource-based access control mechanisms. The more business logic implemented on the VO layer, the less is the workload left at the client layer.

A generic OGSA-based SOA model is built on the combination of the trial meta-model and metadata and the WSRF standards to describe key properties of the trial management system comprising sets of trial resources, role-based WS-Resource groups, and high-level WSRF Web services. A formal definition in Z of the platform-independent SOA model is defined in this section which is crucial to automating the system generation.

17.4.2   Clinical Trial WS-Resources

The trial WS-Resources provide standard fundamental operations to manipulate the trial data and form the trial WS-Resource infrastructure for building high-level cancer research business logics.

In theory, any piece of trial data can be a trial resource. For the trial management system, there are the following trial resources composing a trial protocol (i.e., trial model):

TrialResource ::= patient | personnel | location | event | crf | trialInfo

Their semantics are described in the previous section. As basic units composing clinical trial data, the trial CDEs are used to define the resource properties describing the states of each trial resource. The resource properties are combined together to form an XML *resource properties document* for describing the whole resource. They are specified in Z as follows:

[*ResourceProperties, ResourcePropertiesDocument*]
| *resourcePropertiesDefinition:* ℙ *Cde* → *ResourceProperties*

| *resourcePropertiesDocumentDefinition:*
    ℙ *ResourceProperties* → *ResourcePropertiesDocument*

In tAnGo, a cancer clinical trial described in [25], for example, the patient data are specified by a well-defined set of CDEs describing the patient's date of birth, the number of the hospital where the patient is treated, and the patient's name initials:

Patient = { DoB, HospNo, Initials }

So, the resource properties of a patient in tAnGo can be defined as:

PatientResourceProperties = { DoB → "20/12/1968",
    HospNo → "1234", Initials → "XYZ" }

The standard XML schematic definitions for the resource properties can be derived from the trial protocol and its semantics. Due to CDEs supporting syntactic and semantic interoperability on the CDE level, the (meta)model-compliant CancerGrid resource properties, together with the resource properties document, support syntactic and semantic interoperability on the data resource level.

Clinical trial WS-Resources are created by wrapping the resource properties with standard Web service interfaces specified in the WS-ResourceProperties specification [18]:

[*WsrpPortType*]

```
__TrialWsr_____
  trialWsrPortTypes: ResourceProperties → P WsrpPortType
```

The clinical trial WS-Resource enables computational interoperability as well as syntactic and semantic interoperability on both the CDE and the resource levels.

The six portTypes defined in WS-ResourceProperties specification allow us to dynamically get (retrieve), put (replace), query, update, insert, and delete the resource properties of a WS-Resource at runtime. These can meet the operation requirements for accessing trial data specified by AccessType in the trial metamodel.

In order to support resource sharing, in terms of the access type, these portTypes can be split into two kinds:

WriteWsrpPortType ::= *updateResourceProperty*
  | *insertResourceProperty* | *deleteResourceProperty*
  | *putResourcePropertyDocument*

ReadWsrpPortType ::= *getResourcePropertyDocument*
  | *getResourceProperty* | *getMultipleResourceProperties*
  | *queryResourceProperties*

They provide the operations with read and write permissions respectively.

Accordingly, the two kinds of WS-Resource for a trial resource, *read-only WS-Resources* for a Web service only implementing read portTypes and *read-write WS-Resources* for a Web service implementing both kinds of portTypes, are respectively defined:

```
__ReadOnlyTrialWsr _____
  readTrialWsrPortTypes: ResourceProperties →
                      P ReadWsrpPortType
```

```
__ReadWriteTrialWsr_____
  readTrialWsrPortTypes: ResourceProperties →
                      P ReadWsrpPortType
  writeTrialWsrPortTypes: ResourceProperties →
                      P WriteWsrpPortType
  _____
  dom readTrialWsrPortTypes = dom writeTrialWsrPortTypes
```

17.4.3 Role-Based WS-Resource Groups

Cancer research is the collaboration of different roles in highly regulated and complex security environments. For the development of a service-oriented system to support conducting a clinical trial study, the following challenges come into focus:

- Each role deals with different kinds of confidential information about the clinical trial. How to effectively limit and control the role's access to the corresponding resources?
- The various resources for a role to process are usually tightly coupled, and due to this interdependency, all of the corresponding WS-Resources must coexist before the role may interact with them successfully. How to effectively organize and manage the interdependent WS-Resources?
- In order to handle resource states, a role must identify which WS-Resources it should use. How to effectively discover and manage the set of WS-Resources a role is able to use?

On the basis of the WS-ServiceGroup specification [20], a role-based WS-Resources group is designed to implement role-based access control semantics specified by the trial metamodel and handle the problems mentioned above.

$$
\begin{array}{l}
\underline{\quad RoleBasedServiceGroup\underline{\qquad\qquad\qquad\qquad\qquad}} \\
readOnlyServiceSet:\ TrialDesign \times Role \rightarrow \\
\qquad \mathbb{P}\ ReadOnlyTrialWsr \\
readWriteServiceSet:\ TrialDesign \times Role \rightarrow \\
\qquad \mathbb{P}\ ReadWriteTrialWsr \\
\hline
\forall\ t:\ TrialDesign;\ r:\ Role;\ cdes1,\ cdes2:\ \mathbb{P}\ Cde;\ rows: \\
ReadOnlyTrialWsr;\ rwws:\ ReadWriteTrialWsr \\
\bullet\ \exists\ at:\ AuthorizedTrialDesign\ |\ at.trial = t \\
\quad \bullet\ \mathrm{dom}\ readOnlyServiceSet = \mathrm{dom}\ readWriteServiceSet \\
\quad \wedge\ (\mathrm{dom}\ rows.readTrialWsrPortTypes \\
\qquad = \{resourcePropertiesDefinition\ cdes1\} \\
\qquad \wedge\ rows \in readOnlyServiceSet\ (t,\ r)) \\
\qquad \Rightarrow cdes1 \subseteq roleReadCdeSet\ (at,\ r) \\
\quad \wedge\ (\mathrm{dom}\ rwws.writeTrialWsrPortTypes \\
\qquad = \{resourcePropertiesDefinition\ cdes2\} \\
\qquad \wedge\ rwws \in readWriteServiceSet\ (t,\ r)) \\
\qquad \Rightarrow cdes2 \subseteq roleWriteCdeSet\ (at,\ r)
\end{array}
$$

A role-based WS-Resources group is the collection of WS-Resources whose resource property (i.e., CDE) access permissions (read-only or read-write) are authorized to the role. The TrialDesign Z schema specifies CDEs to describe the components (i.e., trial resources) of a trial protocol conforming to the trial metamodel.

The AuthorizedTrialDesign Z schema defines the rules that specify the CDEs on which each role can perform the allowed operations.

In tAnGo, for instance, a trial coordinator is allowed to read the trial data about patients, CRFs, personnel, etc., while the clinician is allowed to read and write his/her patient data. Therefore, the coordinator group is:

$$CoordinatorGroup = \{\ ReadOnlyPatientWsr,\ ReadOnlyCrfWsr,$$
$$ReadOnlyStaffWsr,\ ...\},$$

and the clinician group is:

$$ClinicianGroup = \{\ ReadWritePatientWsr,\ ReadWriteCrfWsr\ \}$$

The role-based WS-Resource group is implemented as a WS-Resource that groups together end-point references (EPRs) of other WS-Resources meeting the membership rule criteria. The WS-Resource EPRs are generated dynamically, and can be discovered and inspected dynamically. The membership is restricted to allow only the WS-Resources whose access permissions (read-only or read-write) are authorized to the role to join the group.

The role-based WS-Resource group is not only a fundamental security mechanism to effectively support role-based access control, but also a self-organized classification mechanism to simplify the discovery and management of sets of WS-Resources for a role to interact with trial resources.

17.4.4   High-Level Trial Web Services

Based on the trial WS-resource infrastructure, we can build high-level interoperable Web services, including event services, case reporting services, analysis services, etc., to deal with corresponding activities specified in the trial metamodel.

The event service is dedicated to handling individual trial events, such as registration, randomization, etc., and their associated CDEs by invoking the read and write operations of corresponding event WS-Resources. Event services are called when the submission of a CRF is handled.

$$eventWsrfWs:\ TrialDesign \times TrialEvent \rightarrow ReadWriteTrialWsr$$

$\forall\ t:\ TrialDesign;\ e:\ TrialEvent$
  • $\mathrm{dom}\ (eventWsrfWs\ (t,\ e)).readTrialWsrPortTypes$
    $= \mathrm{dom}\ (eventWsrfWs\ (t,\ e)).writeTrialWsrPortTypes$
    $\subseteq \{resourcePropertiesDefinition\ (t.eventCdeSet\ e)\}$

The case reporting service handles the submission of a CRF in the trial by means of the read and write operations on the CRF resource properties, and calls the event-specific services for all form of events.

> *caseReportingWsrfWs: TrialDesign × CaseReportForm →*
> *ReadWriteTrialWsr*
>
> ---
>
> ∀ *t: TrialDesign; f: CaseReportForm* ·
> dom (*caseReportingWsrfWs* (*t, f*)).*readTrialWsrPortTypes*
> = dom (*caseReportingWsrfWs* (*t, f*)).
> *writeTrialWsrPortTypes* ⊆ {*resourcePropertiesDefinition*
> { *c:* ∪ { *ef:* ran *f.events* · (*t.eventCdeSet ef*)}}}

The validation of the submitted form against the schema and logging the form and its validation result are supported by the service.

The analysis service is built based on the trial and/or cross-trial CDE query. The cancer researchers need to analyze data pertinent to patients with similar characteristics at the same stage of their treatment. This requires the analysis service to identify CDEs that are associated with the same trial event in all clinical trials involved in the query. The query functionality is implemented by means of the standard operation queryResourceProperties provided by read-only trial WS-Resources, which allows us to use some kind of query dialect, such as XPath, XQuery, etc.

> *analysisWsrfWs: ResourceProperties → ReadOnlyTrialWsr*
>
> ---
>
> ∀ *rps: ResourceProperties* · *queryResourceProperties* ∈
> (*analysisWsrfWs rps*).*readTrialWsrPortTypes rps*

For instance, let us analyze NEAT [26] and tAnGo trials by cross-trial query. The two trials have some common events. Let us for simplicity say:

{ *registration, randomization* }

In terms of CDE set, the two events in NEAT and tAnGo trial protocols are defined respectively as:

> *Neat.registration* = { *QualityOfLifeSubstudyConsent,*
> *OestrogenReceptorStatus, TumorSize, TumorGrade,*
> *ECOGStatus, CyclophospamidePlan,*
> *MenopausalStatus, TamoxifenPlan* }
>
> *Neat.randomisation* = { *NodalStatus, RadiotheraphyTiming* }

and

> *tAnGo.registration* = { *TissueSubstudyConsent,*
> *QualityOfLifeSubstudyConsent,*
> *ProgesteroneReceptorStatus, OestrogenReceptorStatus* }
>
> *tAnGo.randomisation* = { *NodalStatus, Her2Level,*
> *AdjuvantRadiotherapy, ECOGStatus* }

Using the query operation exposed in the event WS-Resources, the analysis service can output the result of an event-based query across the tAnGo trial and the NEAT trial as below:

$NEAT.registration \cap tAnGo.registration = \{$
$QualityOfLifeSubstudyConsent, OestrogenReceptorStatus \};$

$NEAT. randomisation \cap tAnGo. randomisation = \{$
$NodalStatus \}$

17.4.5   OGSA-Based Trial Management System

With the OGSA-based SOA defined as a combination of read-only and read–write WS-Resources,

$$
\begin{array}{|l}
\_WsrfSoa_____ \\
readOnlyWsrfWSs: \mathbb{P}\ ReadOnlyTrialWsr \\
readWriteWsrfWSs: \mathbb{P}\ ReadWriteTrialWsr \\
\end{array}
$$

The OGSA-based trial management system can be generated as given below:

$$
\begin{array}{|l}
trialManagementSystem: \mathbb{P}\ TrialDesign \rightarrow WsrfSoa \\
\hline
\forall\ T: \mathbb{P}\ TrialDesign \\
\quad \cdot (trialManagementSystem\ T).readOnlyWsrfWSs \\
\quad = \cup \{ rbsg: RoleBasedServiceGroup;\ t: T;\ r: Role \\
\qquad \cdot (rbsg.readOnlyServiceSet\ (t, r))\ \} \\
\qquad \cup \{\ rps: ResourceProperties \cdot analysisWsrfWs\ rps\ \} \\
\qquad \cup \{analysisWsrfWs\ (resourcePropertiesDefinition\ (\cup \{ \\
\qquad\quad t: T;\ at: AuthorizedTrialDesign \mid at.trial = t \\
\qquad\quad \cdot (roleReadCdeSet\ (at, statistician))\}))\} \\
\quad \wedge (trialManagementSystem\ T).readWriteWsrfWSs \\
\quad = \cup \{\ rbsg: RoleBasedServiceGroup;\ t: T;\ r: Role \\
\qquad \cdot (rbsg.readWriteServiceSet\ (t, r))\ \} \\
\qquad \cup \{ t: T;\ e: TrialEvent \cdot \cup eventWsrfWs\ (t, e)\ \} \cup \\
\qquad \{ t: T;\ f: CaseReportForm \cdot caseReportingWsrfWs\ (t, f)\}. \\
\end{array}
$$

As a result, the trial management system is built based on WS-Resources and comprises the trial WS-Resources; the role-based trial WS-Resource service groups; and high-level services including per-trial case reporting service instances, all the event-specific services, and the data analysis service for the considered set of trials used by trial statisticians.

17.5   OGSA-Based SOA Generation

Our OGSA-based SOA model as described in Sect. 17.3 is platform- and programming language–independent. It can be implemented on any OGSA platform. Globus Toolkit 4 (GT4) [27], the de facto grid middleware, was chosen as our implementation

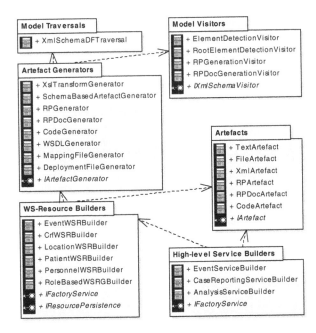

Fig. 17.4 SOA generation framework

platform, as it can benefit us with OGSA capabilities implemented in GT4, such as Globus Security Infrastructure Data Management Services, as well as development toolkits.

Our previous work [4] is for the generation of plain Web services. All the generated artifacts are based on .net platform. They are not used in the OGSA-based GT4 platform. So we have to redesign each part to automate the generation of the OGSA-based SOA for collaborative cancer research.

As depicted in Fig. 17.4, the CancerGrid OGSA-based SOA generation framework consists of several parts. The *WS-Resource Builders* and *High-level Service Builders* produce the *Artifacts* that compose the clinical trial SOA modules by employing a number of *Artifact Generators*. In turn, the generators use *Model Traversals* to apply specialized *Model Visitors* to fragments of the trial protocol (i.e., trial model), as described in detail below.

17.5.1 OGSA-Based SOA Components and Artifacts

As specified in Sect. 17.4, the clinical trial OGSA-based SOA comprises sets of fundamental WS-Resources, which form the trial resource infrastructure with role-based access control mechanisms, and high-level WSRF Web services constructed on the infrastructure for collaborative cancer research. Several classes of artifacts are used to build these components:

- *TextArtifact*, a simple, runtime-generated string, such as namespace, etc.
- *FileArtifact*, a file on the local file system, e.g., the template configuration and deployment files that a generator will include in the components it creates. Typically, file artifacts are independent of the trial for which they are used.
- *XmlArtifact*, an XML document, typically WSDL, and trial-specific files produced at runtime by a generator.
- *RPArtifact*, an XML document describing trial resource properties, generated by *RPGenerator*.
- *RPDocArtifact*, an XML document representing the collection of the resource properties for a trial resource, produced by *RPDocGenerator*.
- *CodeArtifact*, a generated code module.

Common to all these artifacts is their implementation of an *IArtifact* interface, whose single method permits artifacts to be saved to an output stream.

17.5.2   Model Traversals and Visitors

The model traversal class library provides the model traversal support required during artifact generation. In the current version of the system, its only component is a depth-first (DF) traversal of XML schemas represented as Document Object Model (DOM) trees. Potential candidates for new versions of the generation toolset include traversal of XMI-encoded UML models.

The DF schema traversal provides simple methods for the traversal of schemas, schema sets, and specific elements within schemas. Each such method uses a visitor that does the actual work of generating artifacts from the model.

The implementation of visitor classes adopts the hierarchical visitor design pattern [28] to build resource properties and resource properties documents based on XML schemas derived from a trial protocol. Each type of visitor generates an artifact or contributes a part to the generation of an artifact:

- *RootElementDetectionVisitor* identifies the single root element of a simple XML schema.
- *ElementDetectionVisitor* finds a prespecified element from an XML schema.
- *RPGenerationVisitor* and *RPDocGenerationVisitor* are used to generate the schema fragments of resource properties and resource properties documents for a trial resource respectively.

Visitors implement the IXmlSchemaVisitor interface, which specifies the operations that visitors must support. This includes methods to be employed when entering and exiting each type of non-leaf node encountered during the traversal of a schema object (i.e., VisitEnter and VisitExit), and simple Visit methods that are used when a leaf node in the schema is reached. The Boolean value returned by each of these methods indicates the direction in which the traversal should continue after the method returns.

17.5.3 Artifact Generators

This module comprises elements that generate individual artifacts from a trial protocol fragment.

- *XslTransformGenerator* produces XSL transformations that are used to filter the trial protocol.
- *SchemaBasedArtifactGenerator* contributes to the generation of the schemas of XML documents.
- Resource property schema artifacts are generated by an *RPGenerator* by means of the trial protocol filters. Various kinds of trial protocol filter extract the CDE sets associated with individual trial resources. These filters represent a combination of the mappings from trial resources to CDE sets, and the *resourcePropertiesDefinition* conversion of CDE sets to resource properties (XML schematic definition), as described in the Z specification in Sect. 17.3.1.
- The resource properties document schema generated by an *RPDocGenerator* conforms to the WS-Resource property specification and is referenced by the WSDL files of WSRF-compliant Web services.
- *WSDLGenerator* generates WSDL files for a WSRF Web service and its factory service which define the resource properties and interfaces (i.e., portTypes) exposed on them. Generated WSDL files have features that are specific to the Globus implementation of WSRF we are using.
- *MappingFileGenerator* creates a Globus-specific mapping file, which maps WSDL namespaces to Java packages of Web service stub classes.
- *CodeGenerator* generates service-specific codes and Globus-specific codes for the Web services.
- *DeploymentFileGenerator* creates two Globus-specific deployment and configuration files: a Web Service Deployment Descriptor (WSDD) file including information about the Web service, and a Java Naming and Directory Interface (JNDI) file containing information about the resource management.

17.5.4 Trial WS-Resource Builders

Trial WS-Resources builders exploit Globus-supplied Web service development tools and WSRF portType operation providers to build the WS-Resource gar files [27] for the trial resources. These builders base their implementation on the specifications defined by *ReadOnlyTrialWsr* and *ReadWriteTrialWsr* Z schemas in Sect. 17.4.2.

The *IFactoryService* interface generates the *Factory Service* for each WS-resource to support the factory/instance pattern recommended by the WSRF specifications. Factory Services are in charge of creating the instances of WS-Resources and enabling the implementation of WS-ResourceLifetime portType.

Obviously there are persistent semantics in WS-Resources for trial-based clinical research. WSRF does not specify a paradigm to store resource properties persistently. To handle this kind of issue, our WS-Resources implement *load()* and *store()* operations specified in the *IResourcePersistence* interface. They enable resource properties to be loaded from and persisted to permanent storage. Invoking the two methods on demand, we can make sure the value of a resource property in memory is synchronized with that on disk.

The role-based WS-Resource group conforms to the WS-ServiceGroup specification [20]. It is created by *RoleBasedWSRGBuilder* and implemented as a WS-Resource that groups together EPRs of other WS-Resources meeting the membership rule criteria. The WS-Resource EPRs are generated dynamically by Factory Services, and can be discovered and inspected dynamically.

17.5.5 High-Level Trial Web Service Builders

The high-level trial Web services (i.e., the gar files) are built based on various kinds of trial WS-Resource, and artifacts generated from trial protocols. Each high-level services builder uses Globus-supplied development tools and bases its operation on the WS-ResourceProperty interfaces of related trial WS-resources and trial protocol–specific information by filtering the trial protocol by means of a set of XSL transforms.

EventServiceBuilder implements the *eventWsrfWs* transform (Sect. 17.4.4) to generate the WSRF Web services for handling specific trial events such as registration, eligibility, randomization, etc.

For instance, the patient randomization services are built based on standard operations exposed by the randomization WS-Resource, and the trial information about the way in which the value domains of the stratification CDEs are partitioned into sub-domains for the purpose of treatment allocation. This kind of information is used to generate the code for the Web service method that decides the treatment allocations for the trial.

CaseReportingServiceBuilder is responsible for generating the case reporting WSRF Web service required in a clinical trial based on the CRF WS-Resources. The *caseReportingWsrfWs* transform (Sect. 17.4.4) is used for the generation. The generated services take care of the validation of a submitted form against the schema and logging the form and its validation result.

AnalysisWsrfWs implements the *eventWsrfWs* transform (Sect. 17.4.4) to generate the WSRF Web services for data analysis across multiple trials based on the interfaces of trial WS-Resources. In the current implementation, it is supported to search for and compare the CDE sets that are part of the set of all trial events appearing in analyzed trials.

17.6   Case Study

By applying the development framework presented in this chapter, three prototype implementations of the clinical trial information management systems are generated for NEAT, tAnGo, and Neo-tAnGo [29] clinical trials, respectively. They are used to evaluate the effectiveness of our approach.

NEAT, tAnGo, and Neo-tAnGo are real cancer clinical trials. They have completed their data acquisition and are currently in the analysis stage. This enables us to conduct simulated executions of the trials based on made-up but realistic patient data. The experimental results are then used to improve the specification of OGSA-based SOA model, and the general usefulness of the trial management system generated based on it.

The NEAT, tAnGo, and Neo-tAnGo trial protocols, which are instances of the clinical trial metamodel, were used as main input for the trial information management system generators described in the previous section. For each of the three trials, the generated trial management system includes various kinds of WS-Resource with different Web service interfaces, WS-Resource groups, high-level trial Web services, as well as JSF Web pages.

The generation of trial management WS-Resources is depicted in Fig. 17.5. Beside trail-specific WS-Resrouces and data types, trial-independent WS-Resources components, some XML schemas, and configuration files and certificates for deployment are contained in the trail management WS-Resources package. The generated Web services were then deployed on GT4.

JavaServer Faces [30] technology was adopted for the end-user interface to collect trial data together with generated trial WS-Resources. Figure 17.6 shows the generated

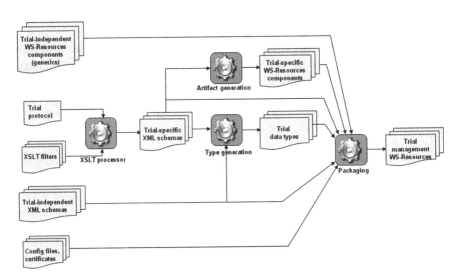

Fig. 17.5 Trial management WS-Resources generation

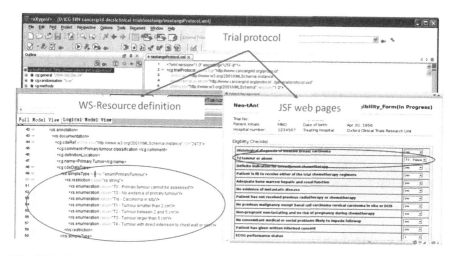

Fig. 17.6 Trial resource definition and its JSF Web pages

Neo-tAnGo trial WS-resource schematic definition and corresponding JSF Web pages.

As a result of the simulated execution of the prototype systems, valuable comments and suggestions for improvement have been obtained from these intended users. The ability to speed up the trial information management system development, and syntactic, semantic, and computational interoperability enabled by the enforced usage of trial metamodel and controlled cancer metadata were consistently deemed as the key advantages of our approach. The role-based WS-Resource groups and data analysis services were also perceived as effective and powerful tools for manipulating and analyzing cancer research data both within and across clinical trial boundaries. Patient workflow monitoring and management services were reported as insufficiently supported in the current implementation, and we are in the process of adding these to the Z specification in the first instance.

17.7   Related Work

Introduce [31] is intended to address a need that arose in caBIG [7], whose goal is to implement a US-wide cancer research network in order to significantly enhance basic and clinical research on all types of cancer disease. Introduce can reduce the service development and deployment effort by hiding low-level details of GT4, and to facilitate the implementation of strongly typed services which enable data-level syntactic interoperability. Our approach features automatic generation of OGSA-based SOA for clinical trial management systems based on binding the WSRF standards to the trial (meta)model and metadata, and enables semantic and computational interoperability as well as syntactic interoperability.

Like CancerGrid, the importance of a model-driven development approach to generating grid service-oriented architectures is also demonstrated in [32]. This uses Java annotations to generate grid services for GT4. The separation of the business logic of a service from the grid service implementation is quite relevant to the design philosophies exposed by our approach. In our method, the clinical trial metamodel and metadata underlie the whole system architecture. The Platform Independent Model of clinical trial information management systems is derived from the combination of the WSRF standards and clinical trial metamodel and metadata as described in Sect. 17.3. This allows us to automate the generation of clinical trial information systems supporting syntactic, semantic, and computational interoperability.

17.8   Lessons Learned

Using the metamodel- and metadata-driven development approach proposed in the chapter, we have generated OGSA-based trial management systems for a couple of clinical trials for the cancer research e-science community. What we have learned is summarized as the following aspects.

High-level domain specifications, including metamodel and metadata and Web services technological standards, are very important in the e-science community. A generic metamodel- and metadata-based SOA model is fundamental and crucial for the development of the e-science application systems. A high-level SOA model allows the developed system to support syntactic, semantic, and computational interoperability, and avoids producing more and more "silo" systems in the e-science community.

A formal system specification is essential to the design and development of the applications in the e-science community. The system specification should be platform-independent, and can be used for the verification of the developed system, such as Z notation. By means of a formal system specification, the VO members in an e-science community can understand and communicate the system in a concise and unambiguous manner.

The idea about automating the metamodel-driven generation of e-science applications should be encouraged in the e-science community. Automating the system generation can enforce the compliance of generated systems with the standard and high-level specification, as well as improve the quality of generated codes and lower the coding effort.

17.9   Conclusions

The chapter presented a framework for the metamodel-driven development of cancer informatics for collaborative cancer research. The successful generation of a fully operational OGSA-based trial management system for a couple of clinical trials starting from their trial protocols demonstrates the feasibility and effectiveness of our approach.

Based on the combination of the semantics of standard trial metamodel and metadata and the WSRF Web services standards, we formally defined a generic, OGSA-based SOA model of clinical trial management systems that underpins our generation of these systems. The Z specification used for this purpose is platform-independent and expresses key properties of the OGSA-based SOA. In addition to being used for the verification of the generators and builders in our framework, this specification is helpful in improving our understanding of the system and in describing it to other members of the project and to intended users. The use of a formal system specification was essential to the design and development of our trial management system in a concise and unambiguous manner.

The combination and enforced consistent usage of standard high-level domain specifications and the Web services standards during the system design and generation enables the generated system to support syntactic, semantic, and computational interoperability, which is essential to collaborative cancer research. The role-based WS-Resource groups effectively support security-aware data sharing both within and across clinical trial boundaries.

Automating the model-driven generation of OGSA-based trial management systems not only speeds up the development of the trial management system and improves the quality of the generated system, but also ensures that the generated system complies with the standard trial metamodel and metadata, and the Web services standards.

Some extensions to our current framework are being investigated, including the generation of more complicated data queries for trial data analysis, and workflow management services to support the patient workflow associated with clinical trials. Although primarily targeted at cancer research, our approach can be readily applied to other e-science applications for which a CDE-based information model is available. Moreover, the techniques used in our approach and the experiments to generate Web services are directly applicable to other service-oriented systems for other e-science communities.

Acknowledgment This work was supported by the UK Medical Research Council under grant G0300648.

References

1. Brenton J, Caldas C, Davies J, Harris S, and Maccallum P (2005) CancerGrid: developing open standards for clinical cancer informatics, in Proc. UK eScience All Hands Meeting, Nottingham, UK, pp. 678–681
2. Begent RHJ.; Brady JM et al (2005) Challenges of ultra large scale integration of biomedical computing systems in *Proc. 18th IEEE Symposium on Computer-based Medical Systems*, Dublin, Ireland, pp.64–69.
3. CancerGrid project. http://www.cancergrid.org. Accessed June 2009.

4. Calinescu R, Harris S, Gibbons J, Davies J et al (2007) Model-driven architecture for cancer research, in *Proc. 5th IEEE Int. Conf. on Software Engineering and Formal Methods*, London, pp. 59–68.

5. Zang T, Calinescu R, Harris S, Tsui A, Kwiatkowska M, Gibbons J, Davies J, Maccallum P and Caldas C (2008) WSRF-based modeling of clinical trial information for collaborative cancer research, in *Proc. 8th IEEE Int. Symp. on Cluster Computing and the Grid*, Lyon, France, May 2008, pp. 73–81.

6. Harris S and Calinescu R (2006) CancerGrid clinical trials model 1.1, Oxford University Computing Laboratory, Oxford, UK, CancerGrid Tech. Rep. MRC/1.4.1.3. http://www.cancergrid.org/public/documents/2006/mrc/ Report MRC-1.4.1.3 Clinical trials model 1.1.pdf

7. caBIG project. https://cabig.nci.nih.gov. Accessed Jan. 2009

8. US National Cancer Institute. (2007). The caCORE Software Development Kit. http://ncicb.nci.nih.gov/infrastructure/cacoresdk

9. Veterans Administration Cooperative Studies Program. http://www.vacsp.gov. Accessed Jan. 2009

10. The Open Grid Services Architecuture, http://forge.gridforum.org/sf/docman/do/ downloadDocument/projects.ogsa-wg/docman.root.published_documents.ogsa_1_5/ doc13553/11. Accessed Jan. 2009

11. Foster, I, Kesselman, C, Nick, J et al (2002) The Physiology of the Grid: An Open Grid Services Architecture for Distributed Systems Integration. Globus Project. http://www.globus.org/alliance/publications/papers/ogsa.pdf. Accessed Jan. 2009

12. Foster I, Kesselman C, and Tuecke S (2001) The anatomy of the grid: Enabling scalable virtual organizations, International Journal of High Performance Computing Applications, vol. 15, no. 3, pp. 200–222

13. GGF OGSA work group, http://www.ogf.org/gf/group_info/ view.php?group=ogsa-wg. Accessed Jan. 2009

14. Web Services Resource Framework–Primer v1.2. http://docs.oasis-open.org/wsrf/wsrf-primer -1.2-primer-cd-02.pdf. Accessed Jan. 2009

15. Globus Alliance. Web Service Resource Framework. http://www.globus.org/wsrf. Accessed Jan. 2009

16. Web Services Resource 1.2. http://docs.oasis-open.org/wsrf/wsrf-ws_resource-1.2-spec-os.pdf

17. WS-Addressing 1.0. Available: http://www.w3.org/TR/ ws-addr-core. Accessed Jan. 2009

18. Web Services Resource Properties 1.2. http://docs.oasis-open.org/wsrf/wsrf-ws_resource_properties-1.2-spec-os.pdf. Accessed Jan. 2009

19. Web Services Resource Lifetime 1.2. http://docs.oasis-open.org/wsrf/wsrf-ws_ resource_lifetime-1.2-spec-os.pdf. Accessed Jan. 2009

20. Web Services Service Group 1.2. http://docs.oasis-open.org/wsrf/wsrf-ws_service_group-1.2-spec-os.pdf. Accessed Jan. 2009

21. Web Services Base Faults 1.2. http://docs.oasis-open.org/wsrf/wsrf-ws_base_ faults-1.2-spec-os.pdf. Accessed Jan. 2009

22. Woodcock J and Davies J (1996) Using Z Specification, Refinement and Proof. Prentice Hall

23. Altman DG, Schulz KF, Moher D et al (2001) The revised CONSORT statement for reporting randomized trials: explanation and elaboration, Annals of Internal Medicine, vol. 134, no. 8, pp. 663–694, 2001

24. Ferraiolo DF, Sandhu R, Gavrila S et al (2001) Proposed NIST standard for role-based access control, *ACM Transactions on Information and System Security*, Aug. 2001, vol. 4, no. 3, pp. 224–274

25. Poole C, Howard H, and Dunn J (2003) tAnGo: A phase III randomized trial of gemcitabine in paclitaxel-containing, epirubicin based adjuvant chemotherapy for women with early stage breast cancer. http://www.isdscotland.org/isd/ files/tAnGo protocol version 2.0 July 2003.pdf. Accessed Jan. 2009

26. Poole C and Earl H (2003) NEAT: National breast cancer study of epirubicin plus CMF versus classical CMF adjuvant therapy. http://www.ncrn.org.uk/portfolio/dbase.asp. Accessed Jan. 2009
27. Globus Toolkit. http://www.globus.org/toolkit. Accessed Jan. 2009
28. Gamma E, Helm R, Johnson R et al (1995) Design patterns: elements of reusable object-oriented software, Addison Wesley
29. Earl H (2004) Neo-tAnGo A neoadjuvant study of sequential epirubicin + cyclophosphamide and paclitaxel +/- gemcitabine in the treatment of high risk early breast cancer with molecular profiling, proteomics and candidate gene analysis, http://www.ncrn.org.uk/portfolio/dbase. asp, accessed 9 May 2006
30. JavaServer Faces. http://java.sun.com/javaee/javaserver faces. Accessed Feb. 2009
31. Hastings S, Oster S, Langella S, et al (2007) Introduce: An Open Source Toolkit for Rapid Development of Strongly Typed Grid Services, Journal of Grid Computing, vol. 5, no. 4, pp. 407–427
32. Smith M, Friese T, and Freisleben B (2006) Model driven development of service oriented Grid applications, in Proc. Int. Conf. on Internet and Web Applications and Services, Guadeloupe, pp. 139–146

Chapter 18
e-Science, the Way Leading to Modernization of Sciences and Technologies: e-Science Practice and Thought in Chinese Academy of Sciences

Baoping Yan, Wenzhuang Gui, Ze Luo, Gang Qin, Jian Li, Kai Nan, Zhonghua Lu, and Yuanchun Zhou

Abstract This chapter mainly introduces our understanding and practice of e-Science in the Chinese Academy of Sciences. We present the current situation of the information infrastructure from five aspects including digital network and communication infrastructure, high performance computing environment, scientific data environment, digital library, and virtual laboratory. In terms of e-Science applications, we focus on an e-Science application conducted in Qinghai Lake region to show how various information and communication technologies can be employed to facilitate the scientific research, providing an infrastructure for protecting wildlife and ecological environment and decision-making. We have realized that e-Science is the way leading to the next-generation scientific research, and we have been promoting e-Science practice and application systematically. By e-Science, to easy Science.

18.1 Introduction

As the leading academic institutions in science and technology, the national comprehensive research and development center in natural science and high technology, the Chinese Academy of Sciences (CAS) always considers building e-Science infrastructure as one of its important tasks. CAS launched the Tenth 5-Year Informatization Program in 2000. In the research of informatization strategic planning, CAS proposed that the long-term development goal of informatization is to create a digital CAS [1], and its informatization strategy is mainly composed of

B. Yan, Z. Luo (✉), G. Qin, J. Li, K. Nan, Z. Lu, and Y. Zhou
Computer Network Information Center, Chinese Academy of Sciences, Beijing, China
e-mail: luoze@cnic.cn

W. Gui
Bureau of High-Tech Research and Development, Chinese Academy of Sciences, Beijing, China

Xiaoyu Yang et al. (eds.), *Guide to e-Science: Next Generation Scientific Research and Discovery*, Computer Communications and Networks,
DOI 10.1007/978-0-85729-439-5_18, © Springer-Verlag London Limited 2011

two parts: one is Academia Resources Planning (ARP), which borrows the idea and concept from Enterprise Resources Planning (ERP) to implement the e-Management for CAS; the other is informatization of research activities, known as e-Science.

Professor Baoping Yan in 2002 proposed that "CAS should advance the development, practice and application of e-Science systematically" when she was the director of the Informatization Office of CAS and the general director of the Computer Network Information Center (CNIC) of CAS. She realized that the traditional ways to conduct scientific research were experiencing changes which are based on the inclusion of modern cyberinfrastructure as part of the science, or an experiment environment which includes not only the already ubiquitous high-end computers, storage, and network infrastructure, but also emerging Web technologies.

This chapter introduces our understanding to e-Science, and describes the e-Science-supporting infrastructure we built. A case study of typical e-Science practice involving multidisciplinary, cross-domain collaboration and a large amount of scientific data is presented. Lessons we learned, our experiences, and our thoughts in e-Science are also discussed.

18.2   e-Science: Our Understanding

In our words, e-Science is the informatization of scientific research, which highlights the novel scientific research environment and activities in information age. The connotation of e-Science includes not only the new generation of information infrastructure underlain by many advanced information and communication technologies, but also the scientific application supported by these infrastructures and technologies, and research activities carried out in such an unprecedented environment. The realization of e-Science will provide an information-oriented research environment for scientists, change the way they conduct research, and can even make a direct impact on the development of a number of disciplines and domains.

e-Science is the core of the CAS informatization and has two aspects in our opinion. One is information infrastructure, known as e-Infrastructure in the United Kingdom and the European Union, and cyberinfrastructure in the United States. It includes: (1) network infrastructure, high performance computing infrastructure, mass data and mass storage, digital library, digital herbarium, etc., which provides fundamental information infrastructure to serve the research; (2) digitalized research instruments, devices, various kinds of digitalized sensors, and associated networks, which provide fundamental tools to acquire scientific data or produce massive data; (3) application software, middleware, tools, and services based on these facilities and digitalized equipments, especially the collaborative work environment, as well as the grid and cloud computing environment, which enable research to be conducted across domains, collaboration across agencies to realize resource sharing, and the creation of a virtual organization; (4) the soft environment of e-Science, such as standards, policies, mechanisms, regulations, and laws introduced to tackle problems caused by resource sharing, virtual organization, information security, operation services, and human resource training, etc.

The other side of e-Science is the informatization of research activities. Research activities usually involve multiple disciplines, where the requirements, work patterns, and disciplines are obviously different. Because of these reasons the informatization of research activities can be very complicated. This complication determines that the informatization of research activities should start with specific disciplines and certain domains, to build digitalized facilities, tools, systems, and research environment to meet the requirements.

18.2.1   e-Science Model of CAS

An e-Science model was proposed by CAS in the research of informatization strategic planning of the Eleventh 5-Year Informatization Program [2]. The model is composed of five interrelated, bottom-up layers, which are: (1) information infrastructure, (2) resource integration, (3) digitalized research facilities, (4) application supporting environment, and (5) e-Science application. The model is illustrated as shown in Fig. 18.1.

1. Based on high-speed network, information infrastructure mainly consists of high performance computing, mass storage, large-scale scientific databases, and digital library. They are the common information infrastructure and provide services to support research and innovation in all disciplines, innovation centers, and institutes of CAS.

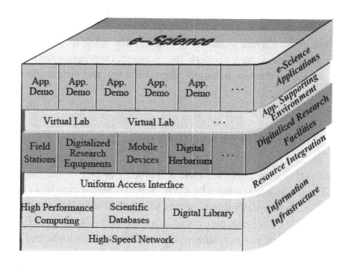

Fig. 18.1 e-Science model of CAS

2. The resource integration platform organizes and integrates common information infrastructure, and provides uniform access interface to upper-level research facilities and e-Science applications.

3. Digitalized research facilities include network-connected field stations, digitalized devices, large digitalized research equipments, digital herbarium, digital library of natural resources, etc. These facilities provide basic research tools for scientists to conduct research.

4. The application supporting environment is a user environment directly supporting e-Science applications, which is a collaborative research environment that takes the virtual laboratory as an organization model to integrate information resource and research facilities. The virtual laboratory will be research-oriented, user-friendly, customizable, and a scalable virtual research environment providing an interactive interface to scientists.

5. e-Science applications take advantage of novel tools, methods, and means provided by information infrastructure and technologies to conduct research activities under the support of a networked collaborative research environment. Through an interdisciplinary, interorganizational, and global collaborative research, e-Science can improve research efficiency and promote the development of science and technology.

Generally speaking, e-Science is an environment that applies information infrastructure and technology to every aspect of research activities, to support, serve, and facilitate scientists with better research, and results in a novel research pattern compared with traditional methods. Next, we will introduce the e-Science progress in CAS from two aspects: information infrastructure and e-Science applications.

18.3 Information Infrastructure

We will introduce the current situation of information infrastructure of CAS from five aspects, which are research network environment, high performance computing environment, scientific data environment, digital library, and virtual laboratory [3].

18.3.1 Research Network Environment

China Science and Technology Network (CSTNET) is one of the major research networks in China, which is operated by CNIC. Up to now, the core layer of CSTNET has 10 Gbps switching capacity and connects 12 regional subcenters such as Beijing, Shanghai, Guangzhou, Xinjiang, etc., interconnected by WAN. CSTNET has covered more than 30 provinces, municipalities, and autonomous regions, and linked 139 institutes and organizations, large scientific facilities, and field stations of CAS. The backbone topology of CSTNET is shown in Fig. 18.2. CSTNET interconnects major

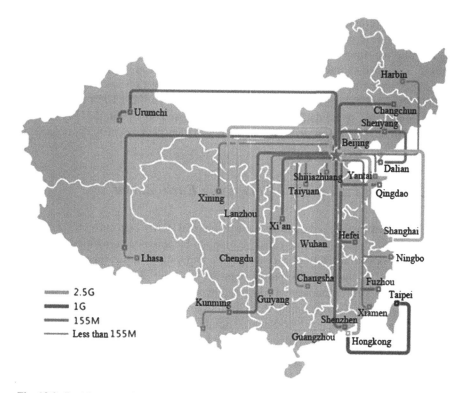

Fig. 18.2 Backbone topology of CSTNET

Chinese ISPs with high-speed links and has several international outbound links connecting with the United States, Russia, Korea, Japan, etc.

CSTNET joined the China Next Generation Internet (CNGI), which is a nationwide IPv6-based Internet. CSTNET built seven backbone nodes within CNGI, including Beijing, Shanghai, Guangzhou, Shenyang, Changchun, Chengdu, and Lanzhou. We have completed the construction of 103 customer premise networks of CNGI deployed in research institutes of China. These achievements have paved the way to support research on Next-Generation Internet (NGI) technology and science applications.

As for the cooperation with international research networks, CSTNET is one of the sponsor members of the Global Ring Network for Advanced Application Development (GLORIAD), which is a research network infrastructure surrounding the north hemisphere with backbone bandwidth over 2.5 Gbps. CSTNET has built the Hong Kong Open Exchange Point (HKOEP), which has become the rendezvous point of Asia-Pacific Internet and the exchange center of international Internet connecting with research networks in Japan, Korea, Hong Kong China, Taiwan China, and other places.

CSTNET has directly supported a number of science applications by providing data transmission service for scientific resources such as large volume of data, computing facilities, and field stations. For example, we support the e-Very Long

Baseline Interferometry (e-VLBI) application in the field of astronomy, providing dedicated optical paths for international observations, and long distance, high-bandwidth, real-time massive data transmission service. We provide technical support for reliable data transmission between Daya Bay Nuclear Power Plant neutrino laboratory of the Institute of High Energy Physics (IHEP) of CAS, and National Energy Research Scientific Computing Center (NERSC) of the United States. An international high-speed data platform for the Chinese participant of ITER project was built to provide integrated services such as data access, security, storage, and network acceleration.

18.3.2   High Performance Computing Environment

The high performance computing environment of CAS can currently provide totally 4.2 Petaflops computing capacity supplied by common computing facilities (common process unit, CPU) and dedicated computing facilities (graphic process unit, GPU). The common computing capacity is about 200 Teraflops, which is organized in a 3-layer hierarchy constituted by one Head Supercomputing Center, ten regional subcenters, and more than 20 campus centers, as shown in Fig. 18.3.

The Lenovo DeepComp 7000 Supercomputer, as shown in Fig. 18.4, was developed by the project "High Productivity Computer and Grid Service Environment" under the support of the High-Tech Research and Development Programme of China. This supercomputer is currently deployed in the Supercomputing Center of CAS (SCCAS) located in CNIC with a peak value of 146 Teraflops, and was ranked No. 19 on the TOP500 list of supercomputers of the world in November 2008.

Resources of the Head Supercomputing Center, Regional Subcenters, and Campus Centers are aggregated together by grid middleware, which provides unified operation, management, and services support.

In April 2009, collaborating with domestic enterprises, the research team of academician Li Jinghai from the Institute of Process Engineering (IPE) of CAS successfully developed a GPU-based supercomputer, which is the first one in China with a peak value more than 1 Petaflop. This supercomputing system has been applied to not only pseudo-particle modeling simulation computing in process

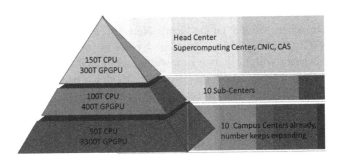

Fig. 18.3   Three-layer hierarchy of high performance computing environment of CAS

Fig. 18.4 The Lenovo DeepComp 7000 supercomputer

engineering design, but also many other fields. Up to now, GPU computing capacity of CAS has exceeded 4 Petaflops, and is located in several institutes, which will, as Campus Center, be joined into the three-layer hierarchy of the high performance computing environment of CAS.

18.3.3   Scientific Data Environment

CAS has realized very early about the importance of development and application of scientific data resource, and has launched a project called "Scientific Database and information System" in the early 1980s. By the end of the Tenth 5-Year Plan (2005), 45 institutes of CAS had been involved in this project, and 503 domain-specific scientific databases were built with a data volume of more than 16 TB, and a distributed networked data services system was established. Scientific Database has become the most comprehensive scientific data repository in China with advanced supporting infrastructure and intensive data covering multiple disciplines.

By the end of Eleventh 5-Year Plan, the Scientific Data Center of CAS (SDCCAS) will establish 37 open, research-oriented scientific databases in domains such as ecology, ocean, geology, biology, new materials, new energy, etc. The SDCCAS will work closely with research institutes and provide technical database support for scientists. We have integrated data resources in geoscience, biology, chemistry, material science, space science, and astronomy, and have constructed eight subject databases including man–land systems, microbes and viruses, animals, chemistry, materials, space science, astronomy, and resource environment remote sensing. These databases can provide large amounts of data to support research in the associated disciplines. Reference databases such as plant species in China and structures of compounds are primarily completed. We will build four thematic databases focused on directions of research on the ecological environment of western China, regional ecological planning, fusion research, and comprehensive studies of Qinghai Lake region. Currently, the total shared data are about 140 TB. A data grid environment was developed to provide unified data access and integration, and support the application of these scientific data resources.

The mass storage environment of SDCCAS currently has a 6 PB physical storage capacity of disks and tapes in which 200 TB are high-end online storage, 800 TB are middle-end nearline storage, and 5 PB are tape library for data archive. Automatic migration of data among high-end disk array, middle-end disk array, and tape library is executed by hierarchical storage software. There has been more than 1,000 CPUs (over 150 Teraflops) capability for data-intensive applications in the environment. The structure of this massive storage system is shown in Fig. 18.5.

Based on the scientific data resource inside and outside of CAS, SDCCAS has developed data mining, analysis, and visualization tools according to the requirements of specific research and direction to achieve integration of data, model, computation, and visualization. SDCCAS has provided a domain-oriented and integrated application environment to serve scientists directly. The architecture of scientific data environment of CAS is illustrated in Fig. 18.6.

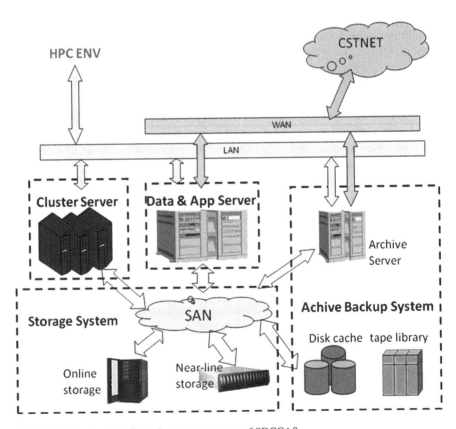

Fig. 18.5 The structure of massive storage system of SDCCAS

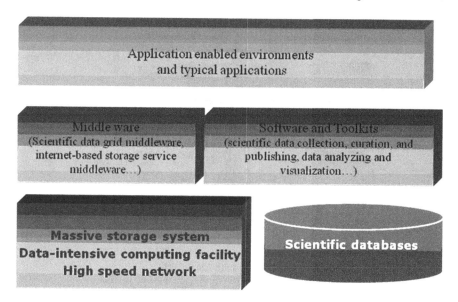

Fig. 18.6 The architecture of scientific data environment of CAS

18.3.4 Digital Library

The CAS has also built the science and technology digital library in 2001. This digital library is open to the public and user-centered, providing openURL-based open linking framework and offering services such as discipline information portal, cross-database retrieval, integrated browsing, and Online Union Catalog.

18.3.5 Virtual Laboratory

Virtual laboratory is an integrated collaborative working environment, which integrates resources like hardware, software, data, information, and instruments. Virtual lab supports interdisciplinary, cross-organization collaboration, and provides a convenient and flexible way to create a virtual organization according to the requirements of research activities and tasks. It aims to promote resource sharing and help scientists organize academic activities. Virtual lab will support pervasive research, which means that scientists can access research resource at anytime and from anywhere, for example, office, home, field stations, or on the road, and can timely access interesting information. One of the most distinguished characteristics of virtual lab is the integration of multi-scientific resources. Virtual lab will integrate high performance computing resource, large-scale scientific data resources, digital library, and digitalized scientific instruments into a research-oriented, user-friendly, scalable, and flexible virtual research environment, and provide customizable and personalized services. Virtual lab will help scientists focus on research, rather than on complex application environments.

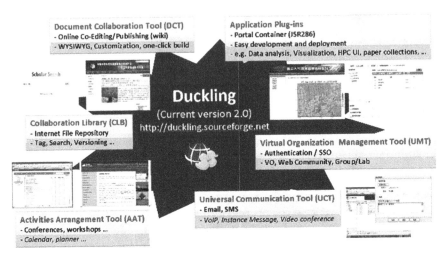

Fig. 18.7 Collaboration environment software suite (Duckling)

The Collaboration Environment Research Center (CERC) of CNIC has developed a software suite to provide functions like document-based collaboration, organizing of academic events, and management of virtual organization. It supports customized plug-ins development for different scientific domains. CERC provides software and services to support networked collaborative research for scientists, as shown in Fig. 18.7.

18.4 e-Science Applications

CAS started e-Science practice and applications from 2000. In the Tenth 5-Year period (2000–2005), under the CAS Scientific Databases Program and the China National Grid program, the following e-Science applications were supported:

- Integrated Information Platform and Early Warning System for Diseases like Avian Influenza
- International Cosmic Ray Data Preprocessing System
- Development and Application of Dynamic Monitoring and Evaluation System for Resource Environment
- China Virtual Observatory

In the Eleventh 5-Year (2006–2010) informatization program, CAS has strengthened the efforts to support e-Science practice and application. We have started 12 e-Science applications involving areas of high energy physics, geology, biology, energy, ecology, wildlife protection and monitoring, space science, etc. Some of them are listed as follows:

- e-Science Application of Research on Resources, Disease Monitoring, and Risk Assessment of Important Wild Birds in Qinghai Lake Region

- North-East Asia Joint Field Investigation and Collaboration Research Platform
- Data-Intensive Grid Platform and Applications
- e-Coast Science Platform for Coastal Environment and Ecological Process Monitoring
- e-Science Environment Supporting Ecosystem and Hydrological Models Integrated Research on Heihe River Basin
- e-Science Environment and Applications for China Flux Integrated Research
- e-Science Application for Space Weather
- e-Science Application of Research on New Generation of Microbial Community Genomics

Most of the e-Science applications involve international collaboration. For example, The "International Cosmic Ray Data Preprocessing System" of high-energy physics was a collaborative research with Italy and Japan. Based on high-speed network, the massive cosmic ray observation data were transferred from Yang Bajing Cosmic ray observatory in Tibet to Beijing. The massive data are preprocessed by high performance computing facilities at the Institute of High-Energy Physics, Chinese Academy of Sciences (IHEP, CAS) and CNIC scheduled by grid middleware, and the results are transmitted to partners in Italy and Japan. The "Data-Intensive Grid Platform and Applications" took part in the research and deployment of the Large Hydron Collider (LHC) Computing Grid (LCG) as a tier 2 site based on EGEE to provide grid computing support for high-energy physics.

The China Virtual Observatory (ChinaVO) is a member of the International Virtual Observatory Alliance. Under the grant of project "High Performance Computer and Its Core Software" from the National High-Technology Research and Development Program of China, and the research program "Research on Network-based Science Activities Environment" from the National Natural Science Foundation of China, ChinaVO has successfully supported several scientific research activities which include: (1) research on abundances gradients of galaxy chemical substances in grid environment, (2) research on the galactic spiral arm structure by searching OB stellar association based on TwoMass star catalog, and (3) research on the galactic structure by using SDSS DR5 photometric data to find galactic substructure with VO-DAS. Furthermore, ChinaVO has designed and developed some networked tools and services, accumulating a wealth of experience in data management, analysis, and data mining.

18.4.1 e-Science Practice in Qinghai Lake Region for Disease Monitoring and Environmental Risk Assessment

We will briefly describe our e-Science practice in disease monitoring and environmental risk assessment of wild birds in the Qinghai Lake region. This is a continuation of the project "Integrated Information Platform and Early Warning System for Diseases like Avian Influenza" in the Tenth 5-Year period to facilitate multidisciplinary and cross-organization research collaboration in the Qinghai Lake region. There are five CAS research institutes involved in this project, which are: (1) CNIC, (2) Institute of Zoology, (3) Wuhan Institute of Virology, (4) Institute of Microbiology, (5) Institute of Remote Sensing Application, and Cold and Arid Regions Environmental and Engineering Research Institute. This project aims to address issues of bird species identification, discovering bird spatial distribution pattern, disease monitoring, and environmental risk assessment of wild birds in the Qinghai Lake region. The project has employed various information and communication technologies (e.g., wireless network and communication, high performance computing, large-scale data management) to facilitate cross-disciplinary, cross-organization, and internationally collaborative research.

18.4.1.1 Qinghai Lake Region and Associated Environmental Issues

Qinghai Lake is located in the eastern part of the Tibetan plateau, at a latitude of 36°32′N–37°15′N and a longitude of 99°36′E–100°47′E. It is the largest inland saline lake in China with a surface area of more than 4,300 km². The map and scene of Qinghai Lake is shown in Fig. 18.8.

The altitude of the Qinghai Lake is 3,200 m. The terrain around the Qinghai Lake is complex and varies with distinctly different altitudes. The climate of this region is a typical plateau continental climate with characteristics like aridness, cold, and windiness. The alpine vegetation is the richest and has the widest distribution around the region. The main types are alpine scrub, high-cold meadow, high-cold steppe, high-cold desert, and sparse vegetation on alpine flowstone slope and alpine cushion vegetation [4].

At the same time, the Qinghai Lake is a wetland of international importance. The basin is rich in wildlife resources and is an important habitat of wildlife in the Tibetan plateau. There are 37 kinds of wildlife under first- or second-class state protection. Some species are unique to the Qinghai Lake, like the *Procapra przewalskii* (see Fig. 18.9), which is an endangered species whose total number in the world is less than 500, and the *Gymnocypris przewalskii*. There are a total of 189

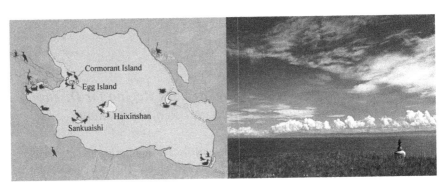

Fig. 18.8 Map of Qinghai Lake region and scene of Qinghai Lake

Fig. 18.9 *Procapra przewalskii* and bar-headed goose

kinds of birds breeding and wintering around the Qinghai Lake because it is an intermediate point on one of the global migration routes of migratory birds connecting Asia and Europe. The main species of birds include the bar-headed goose (*Anser indicus*) (see Fig. 18.9), the brown-headed gull (*Larus brunnicephalus*), the Pallas's gull (*Larus ichthyaetus*), cormorants, tern, black-necked crane (*Grus nigricollis*), swans (*Cygnus cygnus*), and ruddy shelduck (*Tadorna ferruginea*) [5]. Because of its biodiversity, the Qinghai Lake region is called the "plateau's biological gene bank."

The Qinghai Lake plays an important role in maintaining the ecological balance of the Tibetan plateau and preventing the eastward spread of desertification. It is not only an important place for biodiversity protection, but also a unique alpine ecosystem consisting mainly of aquatic organisms, pisces, avifauna, and grassland.

Since the 1960s, influenced by natural changes like global warming and human activities like overgrazing and reclaiming turf, the ecological environment of the Qinghai Lake region has been worsening. The water level of the Qinghai Lake keeps dropping and wetlands keep shrinking. The water level of the Qinghai Lake declined totally by 3.37 m from 1957 to 2000. As the result of water level decline and surface area shrinkage, the water mineralization degree rose from 1.249% in 1962 to 1.6% in 2001. The uprising of the water mineralization degree had serious influences on aquatic food organisms, and on the growing development of *Gymnocypris przewalskii* as well as the pisces–avifauna symbiotic ecosystem [6]. Desertification and degradation of grassland vegetation are severe. Research results showed that desertification of land around the Qinghai Lake increased at an average of 18.07 km^2 annually from 1956 to 2000 [7]. Alpine ecosystems were destroyed, causing rare and endangered wildlife to face the threat of extinction. Currently, about 15–20% of the species resource of wildlife is on the verge of extinction. In 2005, more than 6,000 waterfowls were killed by H5N1 avian influenza virus on Bird Island of the Qinghai Lake [8]. Avian influenza became a great threat to wildlife protection and livestock breeding around this area.

In 1997, the Qinghai Lake National Nature Reserve (QLNNR) was established and became one of the eight major national nature reserves for wild birds in China.

Its main functions include protection of nature resource, protection of ecological environment, and protection of biodiversity. QLNNR gradually realized that the protection and research must be based on a cyberinfrastructure to support effective acquisition of complete, accurate data and information about ecological system and biodiversity, to support the evaluation of the situation, to support making conservation policy and decision-making, while the cyberinfrastructure ensures that the protection and research will not destroy ecological environment and disturb the wildlife.

18.4.1.2 Summary of Research Discoveries

Scientists have carried out comprehensive research in the Qinghai Lake region. We conducted a study of highly pathogenic H5N1 influenza virus infection in migratory birds. They reported the outbreak among migratory birds on the Qinghai Lake, China, in May and June 2005, in which more than a thousand birds were affected. Pancreatic necrosis and abnormal neurological symptoms were the major clinical features. Sequencing of the complete genomes of four H5N1 AIV strains revealed them to be reassortants related to a peregrine falcon isolate from Hong Kong with highly pathogenic characteristics. Experimental animal infections reproduced typical highly pathogenic avian influenza virus infection symptoms and pathology (Fig. 18.10).

A study of avian influenza virus on migratory birds in Qinghai was conducted in April 2006. Three influenza viruses were isolated from three species of migratory birds and were identified as highly pathogenic H5N1 influenza viruses. In experimental infection, all three viruses were pathogenic to chicken and mice. Nucleotide sequence and phylogenetic analysis revealed that the three Qinghai

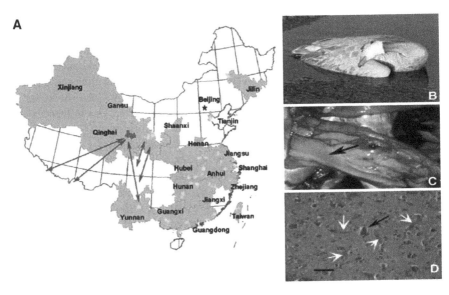

Fig. 18.10 Highly pathogenic H5N1 Influenza virus infection in migratory birds

viruses were very similar to each other and were closest to isolates obtained from Qinghai and Siberia in 2005, but distinct from other poultry viruses found in Southeast Asia. Additionally, the data demonstrate that viruses isolated from this region can spread to other regions via wild bird migration.

A study of endemic bird species in China and their distribution was conducted. The diversity and distribution patterns of endemic bird species in China were analyzed with GIS software using a database of specimen collections and published references. There are 100 endemic bird species in China, belonging to 53 genera, 16 families, and seven orders, accounting for 8% of China's avifauna. In terms of recognized zoogeographical subregions, 68 species are distributed in the "southwest mountainous subregion", 58 species in the "western mountainous plateau subregion," and 56 species in the "Qinghai–Zangnan subregion," with much fewer species in other subregions.

In recent decades, the understanding of bird migration has become very important to the conservation of migratory bird species. The cross-boundary nature of long-distance migration requires that international strategies be formulated to ensure protection of water bird species across their geographic ranges. Dr. John Y. Takekawa and Dr. Diann J. Prosser from the US Geological Survey (USGS), Dr. Scott H. Newman from FAO, QLNNR, and CAS team, studied together the seasonal movements and migration of Pallas's gull from the Qinghai Lake to assess migratory routes and stopover areas. Each individual bird was captured and equipped with an 18 g solar-powered platform transmitter terminal to track its movements from September 2007 to May 2008. They observed that some individuals that overwintered in coastal Bangladesh arrived much later than the outbreak of high pathogenic avian influenza in poultry in 2007. This disparity in timing would tentatively suggest that this species was not involved in long-distance movements of the virus. Instead, the converse may be true: previous work demonstrates the potential for virus spillover from poultry to gulls and other wild bird species upon arrival into locations with widespread HPAI H5N1 outbreaks and environmental contaminations (Fig. 18.11).

In order to explore the impact of climate change and human activity on the ecological environment, combined with GIS technology and remote sensing technology, we conducted a study on the dynamic change patterns of ecological environment factors such as plantation, sandy desertification land, and water area of the Qinghai Lake region to provide scientific guidance for the sustainable development of resources and environment around the Qinghai Lake region.

Currently, more than 50 research papers are published in important international journals and magazines. These achievements demonstrate that the cyberinfrastructure approach for e-Science activities in the QLNNR can promote multidisciplinary integration and cross-disciplinary collaboration, change the way scientists carry out research, and enhance research efficiency significantly.

In the next few sections, we will focus on how we investigated the bird migration route via an e-research approach, including data acquisition, knowledge discovery, knowledge representation, and a virtual organization created for research collaboration.

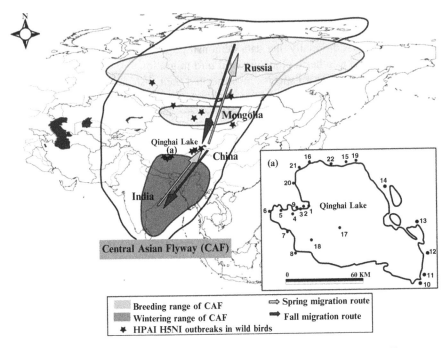

Fig. 18.11 Location map of Qinghai Lake, including the range of the Central Asian Flyway

18.4.1.3 Data Acquisition

We have employed a combination of various approaches/technologies to acquire the required data: (1) networked video monitoring system, (2) field investigation using GPS-enabled device, (3) satellite tracking system, (4) remote-sensing observation system, and (5) sensor-based monitoring.

We started to deploy networked video monitoring systems in the Qinghai Lake region from 2006. By the end of 2009, 19 sets of networked video monitoring systems were deployed, and two of them are devices supporting infrared observations which could be used for behavioral surveillance of birds at night. Figure 18.12 shows a networked video monitoring facility deployed on the SanKuaiShi Island. Currently, these digital cameras can cover most of five core protection areas with harsh environment. The communication link is a combination of wired and wireless networks, and all digital video data are converged and stored in the office locally.

More than 50 GB video data are produced by these cameras. A software tool was developed to import the video data directly into local database, and provide support for data query, search, and classification. The networked video monitoring system has played a significant role in the monitoring and protection of migratory birds, and the detection of an epidemic situation. In 2006, a highly pathogenic avian influenza struck the Qinghai Lake region again, and more than 900 migratory birds were killed. The networked video monitoring system helped researchers with the

Fig. 18.12 Networked video monitoring systems deployed in the core protection area of reserve

early discovery of an abnormal situation of wintering birds and contributed to the prevention of an avian influenza epidemic.

Networked video monitoring system provides scientists with a method to conduct behavioral observation remotely, and many behavior patterns which cannot be identified in traditional ways have been discovered from the video data. For example, scientists got new research discovery on the territorial behavior of the male bar-headed goose in early breeding season, as well as the behavior pattern of the female bar-headed goose before and after egg-laying in early breeding season.

Furthermore, in order to support researchers to conduct behavior analysis and epidemic surveillance, we have primarily developed a software tool which can analyze the motion patterns of birds with help of image-based motion detection and object tracking technology. The motion detection technology can extract information such as the number of birds, location, and direction of movements from video images. Based on statistic analysis and data mining on the information acquired from long-term (for example, 1 month) video data, we can figure out the motion patterns of birds in an observed area. When one bird is infected by avian influenza or another disease, it is possible that this disease will spread quickly and vicinal birds could be infected. This will result in motion patterns changing dramatically in a short time, such as a sharp decline in the level of activities of movement. Compared with motion patterns of birds in an observed area, we can judge whether there is anything wrong with the birds' activities, and can further notify the staff to focus on that area to determine whether there is an epidemic situation.

Field investigation is one important method to acquire scientific data. Field investigation around the Qinghai Lake mainly involves survey of vegetation and sample plot, survey of endangered species, survey of avifauna, etc., and produces a lot of valuable scientific data and information. We found that traditionally scientists had to carry various forms and tables on paper in advance, and fill up the forms and record all the information on their field trip. Scientists then had to re-input all data collected during field investigation into a computer after they return to the laboratory. This traditional data collection approach is error-prone and inefficient, and the paper forms are defacement-prone and difficult to preserve in the field trip. In order to address this issue, we developed a field data collection system based on a personal digital assistant (PDA), which can help scientists to flexibly customize the schema and the structure of the data and generate the associated data entry interface automatically, as shown in Fig. 18.13.

Furthermore, according to the demand of scientists, this system can integrate the functions provided by the PDA, such as GPS and digital camera, to record the accurate location information of sampling, such as pictures of samples, and associate all relative data together. All data acquired on the field trip are stored in an embedded database preserved in a storage card equipped for a PDA such as a secure digital memory card. After return to the laboratory, the data collected in the field research can be directly imported into the database system. The survey route, data, and information about the sample, pictures, and videos can be visualized and displayed via GIS.

Institutes of CAS have been collaborating with USGS since 2007 to investigate the migration route of migratory birds in the Qinghai Lake. The research method adopted is using a satellite tracking system to track and monitor the migration route of the main migratory birds of the Qinghai Lake, such as the bar-headed goose and the Ruddy Shelduck goose.

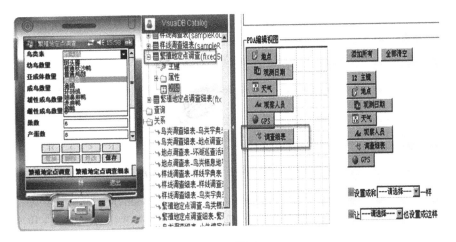

Fig. 18.13 Field data collection system based on PDA

The satellite tracking system applied in this research is the Argos system. USGS provided the platform transmitter terminal (PTT), which is a tiny device that can be banded on a bird, and is in charge of collecting the concerned data such as temperature and location. Most of the PTTs banded on the birds of the Qinghai Lake are equipped with a GPS receiver that can record the exact location of the birds. The transmitter on the PTT is programmed to send signals to satellites at periodic intervals. Polar orbiting satellites flying at an orbit of 850 km above the earth pick up the signals and store them on board and relay them in real time back to the earth. Receiving stations relay data received from satellites to processing centers. The processing centers then collect all incoming data, process them, and distribute them to users.

Compared with the traditional bird tracking method (e.g., banding tracking), satellite tracking technology has distinguished advantages such as wider tracking scope, and more accurate time and location information of tracking objects, which could provide almost real-time location and associated information about tracking objects. Up to now, 57 birds have been equipped with satellite tracking devices, and by the end of 2009, more than one million readings of location information have been collected, and 150,000 records were produced after data preprocessing (details can be found in later sections). Scientists cannot analyze these data in conventional ways. Specialized software and tools are required to face the challenge of this data deluge.

The investigation on bird spatial distribution and migration routes of migratory birds depends on data and information about ground ecological environment and ecological process of breeding place, wintering place, and stopover on the migration route. Remote-sensing earth observation system has the advantages of wild detection range, with few limitations on ground conditions. Our researches require multi-source remote-sensing background information expressed as ecological remote-sensing response factors that reflect regional characteristics and patterns. This basic characteristic information is extracted from remote-sensing images based on computer recognition and classification. Combined with observation and tracking information of wildlife, this information will help scientists conduct research on interrelation between habitat selections, migration patterns, and ecological background, revealing the correlative relationship between behaviors of wildlife and elements of ecological environment. It can also investigate the research of dynamic relationship between the spread of disease and spatial distribution of wildlife.

18.4.1.4   Data Analysis and Process

We have collaborated with USGS Western Ecological Research Center and USGS Patuxent Wildlife Research Center to conduct research on the investigation of migratory routes and spatial distribution patterns of migratory birds based on satellite tracking technology since 2007. With the continuous accumulation of bird tracking data, scientists want to acquire knowledge about the range of migration, territory, and habitat utilization of birds. Due to the huge amount of data, conventional analysis methods for migratory birds, for example, plotting points in GIS or manual calculation of spatial statistics to discover the habitats and migratory routes, cannot be used in the analysis and process of mass tracking data.

We applied data mining technologies into analysis and process of birds' satellite tracking data. The first step is the preprocessing, which includes clean-up and normalization, and the storage of classified data into different tables of relational databases according to different populations or different sensor types. Data mining technologies based on cluster algorithms were chosen and habitat information produced regarding where birds stay for a relative long time. Clustering results are used to define the range of stopover and habitat on the migratory routes by way of Convex Hull Algorithm and Polygon Area Algorithm, and these areas are directly visualized on the WEB GIS platform.

For the convenience of application and development, we developed a data preprocessing tool to transform the data presented in DIAG format of Argos satellite into a data format that could be stored in relational databases, as shown in Fig. 18.14. Some additional works are also included in the preprocess procedure such as removing duplicated records and some other kinds of data transformation. For example, all the time in the data records are converted to the time zone of China. Preprocessing is a necessary step to support subsequent analysis and processing.

One of the important questions in the research of migration and spatial distribution patterns of birds is to discover the habitat information along the migratory routes. In the habitat, the activities of birds are relatively more frequent. More tracking data are recorded than in other places, and form a relatively denser range of activities. Birds' tracking data mainly include longitude, latitude, precision of geographic coordinates, and time when the geographic coordinates are recorded. The activity area of birds is irregular, and there are a lot of isolated points on the migratory route where birds pass by or stay for a very short time. Based on the

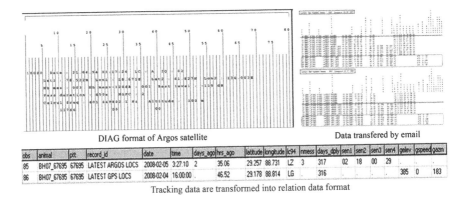

obs	animal	ptt	record_id	date	time	days_ago	hrs_ago	latitude	longitude	lc94	nmess	days_dply	sen1	sen2	sen3	sen4	gelev	gspeed	gazm
85	BH07_67695	67695	LATEST ARGOS LOCS	2008-02-05	3:27:10	2		35.06	29.257	88.731	LZ	3	317	02	18	00	29			
86	BH07_67695	67695	LATEST GPS LOCS	2008-02-04	16:00:00			46.52	29.178	88.814	LG		316					385	0	183

Tracking data are transformed into relation data format

Fig. 18.14 Preprocessing of tracking data

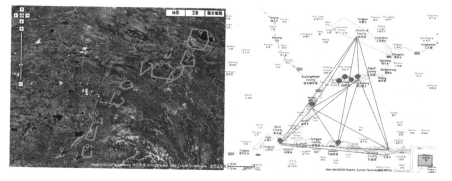

Fig. 18.15 Habitat discovery based on data mining

above consideration, we improved the density-based cluster algorithm which is less affected by isolated point data, and applied the algorithm to the research application system. We used algorithms like Minimum Area Algorithm and Convex Hull Algorithm to identify the border and region of birds' activity areas according to the cluster information from data mining [9]. The border and region information are presented on WEB GIS system, as shown in Fig. 18.15.

One ongoing task is to extract ecological factors from remote-sensing images according to birds' positions, to further analyze the habitat niche along the migratory routes. This information is used to evaluate the habitat and stopover, and support scientists in conducting research on habitat analysis and migration strategy.

Another example of data analysis and process is from research on bird disease monitoring and risk assessment. The differences in molecular sequences between birds and human influenza virus, and cross-host transmission ability of avian influenza virus are scientific issues in which scientists are interested. A-type avian influenza virus can step across different hosts, and directly infect humans and other higher mammals. Although for the time being this kind of virus cannot spread within human populations, it has preliminarily adapted to mammals like human beings, and it is possible that the virus could spread within humans in the future. In order to tackle this problem, we have developed a classifier to detect the cross-host transmission ability of different kinds of avian influenza viruses [10]. The classifier transforms the genome sequence of avian influenza viruses isolated by the user into a series of signals and extracts energy features by way of wavelet decomposition method. We use k-nearest neighbor (KNN) algorithm to compute the Euclidean distance between the virus pattern and cross-host transmission phenotype patterns that we have already known to predict whether the virus strain can cross-host transmit or not. The whole process is illustrated in Fig. 18.16. The software tool can classify accurately and efficiently new virus strains submitted by the user, and indicate cross-host transmission ability of the virus.

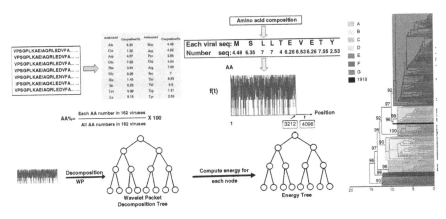

Fig. 18.16 Research on cross-host transmission ability of avian influenza virus

18.4.1.5 Data Presentation and Visualization

In order to provide intuitive information to scientists, we developed an integrated data analysis and visualization tool based on GIS. Data visualization on WEB GIS platform has been applied in several research application systems. This visualization solution takes the geographical location as a reference, helps scientists to access multidisciplinary data related to the same location, and visualizes evolving processes of ecological factors and the distribution of biodiversity in the Qinghai Lake region. We are still working on the interactive research application platform based on GIS, which hides interrelated mass data and geographical location information (e.g., data of remote sensing, ecology, climate, hydrology, migratory route of birds) at the back-end, but provides end users with an interactive, WEB GIS-based interface to facilitate the use, management, and presentation of data and experimental results.

18.4.1.6 Joint Research Center of CAS and Qinghai Lake Reserve

The Joint Research Center (JRC) of the CAS and the QLNNR was established in 2007. The JRC is a nonprofit and self-regulatory organization, which is a long-term, stable, open research environment built by all participating organizations. It provides a platform promoting interdisciplinary cooperation and e-Science applications. The JRC will integrate different resources, share complementary advantages, and apply advanced sciences, technologies, and research achievements into QLNNR to facilitate the protection and management. This virtual research organization creates an innovative research collaboration pattern. This pattern integrates information technology with science research, combines theory with practice, and promotes interdisciplinary research activities.

The JRC consists of research institutes and universities following the instructions from the Research Council. Besides the charter, we have stipulated the administrative measures for intellectual property and data-sharing policy. All these regulations provide a standardized mechanism to coordinate the interests among the members of the JRC.

The JRC allows scientists to carry out research conveniently. At the same time, the openness of the JRC also promotes the interdiscipline and across-region collaboration. Our cooperation with USGS is a typical example. Academic exchanges are common and frequent under this kind of cooperation. Workshops for specific subjects such as avian influenza and e-Science are held regularly. Besides USGS, there are other international partners that have joined us such as the Food and Agriculture Organization (FAO) and the Wildlife Conservation Society (WCS).

The JRC is a virtual organization conducting comprehensive research in the Qinghai Lake region. At the same time, the JRC becomes a workforce development environment in which engineers of information technology work closely with scientists and carry out joint research activities. Postgraduates can acquire multidisciplinary knowledge, as a research team generally consists of scientists from different domains.

This e-Science application is the first one applied in the national nature reserve in China and is also the first attempt in China to construct a cyberinfrastructure to support protection and research in the plateau area. This e-Science application is driven by the demands of wildlife and ecology protection of reserve. The research results and achievements will help the management and decision-making of reserve protection. Instead of providing an answer of a specific question to scientists, which is traditionally the way how science is driven and conducted, the e-Science application should also provide a solution to meet the social needs. Such requirements determine that the cross-disciplinary collaboration and open research should be the nature of e-Science applications.

18.5 e-Science Philosophy, Our Thinking

The relationship between information technology and scientific research could be considered as an interesting spiral. Information technology itself is the achievement of science and technology, and it further promotes the development of almost all aspects of human society including science and technology. e-Science is the presentation that information technology infiltrates into the procedure of science and research. e-Science enables a kind of brand-new research pattern with distinct features such as cross-disciplinary, data-intensive, terascale computing, resource sharing, and collaboration beyond the barriers of time, space, and organization.

e-Science is an inevitable outcome as a result of science and technology development. The driving force comes from three different levels. Firstly, e-Science is driven by the advance of information technologies. The rapid development of computing, storage, network, and software has provided a substantial foundation to e-Science. Secondly, requirements and challenges from science and engineering with growing complexities, scope, and scale require appropriate IT facilities.

Although IT infrastructure is necessary for e-Science, it is just the first step. The analysis challenges posed by data deluge are new challenges raised by scientific research, and these kinds of challenges cannot be handled with traditional research methods. Thirdly, at the highest level, the driving force comes from the sustainable development of mankind itself. New science applications should focus more on providing solutions to meet the social needs. For example, in the research on the global climate change, achievements in physics or biology regarding the continental or global aspects influenced by climate change are not enough; overall solutions that can coordinate global climate change and the sustainable development of ecology, economy, and society are also essential. Requirements at this level inevitably ask for open, collaborative, and resource-sharing research patterns.

e-Science is not information technology plus science (IT+Science), but the amalgamation of information technology and research activities. This kind of amalgamation can be described from the following aspects: first of all it is a combination with research philosophy, which means a good match between scientific requirements and IT facilities; secondly, it is the integration of science applications and technologies, which means technical solutions are decided by the actual scientific requirements, rather than the other way around. Actually, failures of many e-Science applications lie in adopting technology-oriented strategies, which tend to emphasize on the technologies employed but ignore the real scientific needs of scientists. This has resulted in the development of software and application systems that are not friendly to scientists. From this point of view we can say that e-Science is a long process of amalgamating technology and philosophy, which complement each other simultaneously. In the future, when scientists can concentrate on solving scientific issues, no longer confused on how to acquire, access, analyze, and process data, and feel comfortable when they face mass data, we can say yes we have made it. From this perspective, we believe that e-Science is actually easy Science.

We also believe that information technology and capability for innovation will be enhanced when supporting e-Science. The requirements of science applications are often more complicated than business applications. For example, in the networked video monitoring system, we found that surveillances products and systems could not always meet the actual observation requirements of scientists, such as customizable observation task setting, automatic performance of observation task like unattended automatic observation at night, and powerful video data statistics and analysis tools. The personalized and complicated requirements of science applications pose great challenges to IT facilities.

e-Science will have a profound influence on the mechanism and system of scientific research. In general, the current research system is organized by disciplines. Scientists produce publications like papers, monographs, and other achievements by research activities, and research institutes and universities provide scientists academic tenure and promotion as their reward. This system promotes scientists to constantly seek new ideas and new funding, and has achieved great success in the development of science and technology. But this mechanism, including the peer review system, can have negative aspects, for example, granted projects are of inherent interest to the scientific community, but may not be necessarily required or have practical value in real society. There is the growing disconnection between the supply of scientific knowledge and the demand for that knowledge from social and government sectors. New research mechanisms and systems should be considered to promote cross-disciplinary, collaborative, open, and resource-sharing research patterns, and to provide solution to meet social needs. This is also the essential requirement of e-Science.

18.6 Conclusions

e-Science will systematically employ advanced information technologies in research activities, and develop new research methods, patterns, and environments, and will change the way science research is conducted today. The basic methods of modern research activities include theoretical studies, experimental observation, and scientific computation (numerical simulation and analysis), with the addition of more comprehensive academic exchanges and collaboration. Scientific literature, digital library, laboratory instruments and scientific equipments, various types of sensors and their network, specimens and samples, and computing resources for data analysis, are all resources supporting research activities. e-Science is branched out into all of these sections.

This chapter introduces e-Science progress of CAS mainly from the two aspects of information infrastructure and e-Science applications, and introduces our understanding and thinking about e-Science. In general, e-Science of CAS is still in its primary stage, and we also realize that e-Science is the way leading to the modernization of science and technology. CAS will advance the development of e-Science systematically. By e-Science, to easy Science.

Acknowledgments Funding was provided by the Fund of President of CAS, Fund of Director of CNIC, and Special Project of Informatization of Chinese Academy of Sciences in "the Eleventh 5-Year Plan", e-Science Application of Research on Resources, Disease Monitoring and Risk Assessment of Important Wild Birds in the Qinghai Lake Region under Grant No. INFO-115-D02, Special Project of Informatization of Chinese Academy of Sciences in "the Eleventh 5-Year Plan," Basic Databases of Joint Research Center of Chinese Academy of Sciences and Qinghai Lake National Nature Reserve under Grant No. INFO-115-C01-SDB2-02 and the National Science Foundation of China under Grant No. 90912006. We extend our gratitude to the staff of the Qinghai Lake National Nature Reserve and Professor Lei Fumin, Professor Li Tianxian, Professor Ma Juncai, Professor Guo Shan, Professor Zhang Yaonan, and all other members of research groups that participated in research activities in the Qinghai Lake region. We thank Dr. John Y. Takekawa and Dr. Diann J. Prosser of USGS, and Scott Newman of FAO for supporting research in the Qinghai Lake region. We thank Dr. Yang Xiaoyu of University of Southampton, UK for providing constructive suggestions to the manuscript.

Any use of trade, product, or firm names in this publication is for descriptive purpose only and does not imply endorsement by the P. R. China government.

References

1. The Tenth Five-Year informatization Strategic Planning of Chinese Academy of Sciences
2. The Eleventh Five-Year informatization Strategic Planning of Chinese Academy of Sciences
3. *"Annual Report of Computer Network Information Center, Chinese Academy of Sciences"*, 2009
4. X. Chen, J. Li, *"Vegetation Coverage and Its Relation with Climate Change in Qinghai Lake Area"*, Journal of Desert Research, Vol. 27 No. 5 Sep. 2007
5. Y. Hou, F. Lei, *"Distribution and Diversity of Waterfowl Population in Qinghai Lake National Nature Reserve"*, Acta Zootaxonomica Sinica, 34 (1) : 184–187, Jan, 2009
6. R. Liu, Y. Liu, "Area changes of Lake Qinghai in the latest 20 years based on remote sensing study", J. Lake Sci., 2008, 20(1): 135–138
7. F. Li, L. Li, F. Shen, *"Evolution of Lakeshore of Qinghai Lake and its Causes"*, Resource Science, Vol.26, No. 1, Jan., 2004
8. G., Zhang, D. Liu, *"The Current Status of Waterbirds after Avian Influenza Outbreak at Qinghai Lake, China"*, Chinese Journal of Zoology 2008, 43(2): 51–56
9. M. Tang, Y. Zhou, P. Cui, W. Wang, H. Zhang, L. Hu, Y. Hou, B. Yan, " *Discovery of migration habitat and routes of wild bird species via data mining"*. ICCS, 2009.
10. Z. Kou, F. Lei, S. Wang, Y. Zhou and T. Li, *"Molecular patterns of avian influenza A viruses"*, Chinese Science Bulletin, Volume 53, Number 13, 2008.

Index